THE PUBLIC PAPERS OF
THE GOVERNORS OF KENTUCKY

Melba Porter Hay and
Thomas H. Appleton Jr.
General Editors

SPONSORED BY THE
Kentucky Historical Society

THE PUBLIC PAPERS OF

GOVERNOR BRERETON C. JONES

1991–1995

Penny M. Miller, *Editor*

THE UNIVERSITY PRESS OF KENTUCKY

Scholarly publisher for the Commonwealth,
serving Bellarmine University, Berea College, Centre
College of Kentucky, Eastern Kentucky University,
The Filson Club Historical Society, Georgetown College,
Kentucky Historical Society, Kentucky State University,
Morehead State University, Murray State University,
Northern Kentucky University, Transylvania University,
University of Kentucky, University of Louisville,
and Western Kentucky University.

Editorial and Sales Offices: The University Press of Kentucky
663 South Limestone Street, Lexington, Kentucky 40508-4008

05 04 03 02 01 5 4 3 2 1

Frontispiece: Gov. Brereton C. Jones

Library of Congress Cataloging-in-Publication Data

Jones, Brereton.
The public papers of Governor Brereton C. Jones, 1991-1995 / edited by Penny M. Miller.
p. cm. — (The public papers of the governors of Kentucky)
Includes bibliographical references and index.
ISBN 0-8131-2196-5 (acid-free paper)
1. Kentucky—Politics and government—1951- I. Miller, Penny M., 1943- II. Kentucky. Governor (1991-1995 : Jones) III. Title. IV. Series.

J87.K4 A15 2001
352.23'8'0976909049—dc21 00-012375

This book is printed on acid-free recycled paper meeting the requirements of the American National Standard for Permanence of Paper for Printed Library Materials.

Manufactured in the United States of America

CONTENTS

HEALTH CARE

EDUCATION

ECONOMIC DEVELOPMENT

APPALACHIA

ENVIRONMENT

AGRICULTURE

HEALTH, WELFARE, AND PUBLIC SAFETY

CORRECTIONS, CRIME, AND THE LAW

STATE GOVERNMENT

TOURISM AND RECREATION

GENERAL EDITORS' PREFACE

THREE decades ago the Kentucky Advisory Commission on Public Documents, which had been created by executive order, recommended the publication of the Public Papers of the Governors of Kentucky. Dr. Robert Sexton served as the first general editor of the series, which was designed to preserve and disseminate the official record of the Commonwealth's chief executives. In 1988 the Kentucky Historical Society publications manager assumed the role of general editor.

To date, the public papers of seven governors—Edward T. Breathitt Jr., Bert T. Combs, Wendell H. Ford, Keen Johnson, Louie B. Nunn, Lawrence W. Wetherby, and Simeon Willis—have been published. The eighth volume in this series, the papers of Governor Brereton C. Jones, records the thoughts and actions of the Jones administration (1991–95) through the public speeches of the governor. We hope this volume will prove useful to a variety of audiences, from scholars, journalists, and public servants to the general public.

Melba Porter Hay
Thomas H. Appleton Jr.
General Editors

EDITOR'S PREFACE

THIS volume contains 203 public statements made by Governor Brereton C. Jones between December 10, 1991, and December 11, 1995. For the most part, the statements are speeches; however, when appropriate to the organizational arrangement and topical content of the papers, press conferences and statements issued from the governor's office have been included. The precedent established in preceding volumes of this series of excluding veto messages and executive orders has been followed here. Governor Jones vetoed one Senate Bill and six House Bills, and applied four line-item vetoes on two separate House Bills. Those veto statements are published in the respective journals of the two houses of the General Assembly; and official copies of the governor's veto messages are housed, along with executive orders, in the office of the Secretary of State.

This volume is a carefully selected cross section of the public papers of Governor Jones and therefore contains no correspondence or other private papers. The emphasis upon speeches and press releases is not solely the result of their availability. Two factors make these kinds of public, but not easily accessible, papers uniquely valuable. First, nowhere else has the full text of these speeches and press releases been printed, and speech texts have not always been preserved intact after the close of a gubernatorial administration. Second and more important, together these speeches and press releases are the publicly pronounced policies of Governor Jones. They are the articulated public policy of the executive branch of Kentucky state government for a period of four years.

Unlike most past administrations, the Jones administration preserved carefully every public paper; I was provided as editor an abundance of riches—copies of each document in chronological order by the Kentucky Department for Libraries and Archives. Thus, my primary task was first to peruse the mass of material and analyze the content of each item to avoid later duplication and to assure that all significant subjects would be covered in the published form.

The papers in this volume are organized by topic, with chronological arrangement under each heading. The topics—health care, education, economic development, Appalachia, environment, tourism and recreation, agriculture, state government, and so on—reflect the principal issues with which his administration was concerned. To be sure, the arrangement fails to provide absolute topical demarcation because Governor Jones saw significant interrelationships between many of the challenges of his administration. Thus, economic development was dependent upon the expansion of educational opportunity, and improved highway and park systems were dependent upon the passage of the bond issue. Yet, despite his tendency to reflect these interrelationships in his addresses, the topical ordering retains its integrity.

The speeches were originally prepared for public delivery rather than publication. Many were printed in speech-size type, with paragraphing designed for oral delivery; others contained penned-in notes, typographical errors, and awkward lists. Governor Jones often departed from the written text; and this editor was given copies of the speeches as delivered, which versions were used in each case. Editorial attention was limited to corrections necessary for publication. Generally, editorial changes in regard to capitalization, punctuation, and similar grammatical matters have been done without comment. When I have intervened to provide other changes, it has been noted. Any omitted material is so cited by ellipses. In no case has the meaning of Governor Jones's statements been disturbed. Notes have been included identifying individuals the first time they are mentioned. Other notes, either explanatory or citing a source of information, have been included when appropriate. Where materials have been omitted to avoid unnecessary repetition this is noted, and a reference to duplicate material is given.

A timeline of "Some Important Events of the Brereton Jones Administration" is found in Appendix One. A complete listing of the speeches and releases in chronological order (both of items included and of items omitted) appears in Appendix Two. The Index will assist readers in locating materials which transcend the topical divisions.

A number of people have provided invaluable assistance to the preparation of these papers. Christine Gilgore, a former graduate student in the Martin School of Public Administration, catalogued each of the speeches chronologically and topically. A special debt is owed to Chuck Ellis, a former graduate student in the Martin School of Public Administration, who is now the deputy director of parks for the Lexington-Fayette Urban County Government. Chuck helped select the enclosed papers, having read and critiqued every speech and press release. Several undergraduate political science students at the University of Kentucky have labored tirelessly in researching and writing the original drafts of many of the notes: Amanda Cooper, Brooke Johnson, Erin Logsdon, Josh Mahan, Brian Patten, Colleen Reid, Bryan Sunderland, Miranda Vance, Angie Van Berkel, and Russ Woodward. Special thanks are owed Jason Glass, a doctoral student in political science; Jason wrote the first drafts of the biography of Governor Jones and the description of the Jones administration. I have also made use of the advice from two colleagues, Phillip Roeder and Ernie Yanarella. The Kentucky Historical Society provided limited funds for research assistance. Melba Porter Hay of the Kentucky Historical Society and Thomas H. Appleton Jr. of Eastern Kentucky University provided valuable editorial advice and moral support. Governor Jones was invariably helpful in providing information when it was requested. My husband, Bob, has long been a patient and supportive reader as well as a good editor.

As chair of the Kentucky Commission on Women and a member of the Kentucky Long-Term Policy Research Center Board during the Jones administration, I was able to view firsthand the workings of state government in Frankfort. Though there was a risk of becoming too much of a participant, these roles gave me the opportunity to talk on an informal basis with many legislators, administrators, lobbyists, judicial officers, journalists, and participants in the political process at every level.

In the preparation of these papers and in the writing of the biographical sketch and the description of the administration, I have attempted to avoid critical judgments of Governor Jones and his administration. That task belongs to the student who will at some future date write a definitive evaluation of this important period in Kentucky history. I hope these papers will encourage someone to undertake that project.

P.M.M.

BIOGRAPHICAL SKETCH OF BRERETON C. JONES

BRERETON CHANDLER JONES, born June 27, 1939, grew up on a prosperous dairy farm in the small West Virginia river community of Point Pleasant, which lies at the convergence of the Ohio and Kanawha Rivers. The second son of Nedra Wilhelm Jones and E. Bartow Jones II, both from families with roots in Virginia's Shenandoah Valley, Brereton acquired from his father a work ethic and business sense and more. The elder Jones, a two-term state senator and successful businessman, a passionate, moralistic Christian, born and raised a Democrat, ran the local Republican Party in Mason County from the mid-1930s into the 1970s, and in 1952 briefly considered a run for governor of West Virginia. Throughout his adult life, Bartow Jones engaged in a variety of occupations, including contractor, car dealer, bank board chairman, farmer, and stockyard owner, eventually becoming the largest stockholder in Point Pleasant's chief bank. He was also widely known for his general disdain for dishonest politics and politicians, all the while a prominent citizen-politician himself.

Born in the nearby town of Gallipolis, Ohio, Brereton Jones was raised in an elegant home built in the 1830s, the Maples. Five days before Jones's birth, his two-and-one-half-year-old elder brother had been killed in an automobile accident. The future Kentucky governor's mother attended the funeral for her elder son while pregnant with Brereton. The expectations for the new Jones son were high. "They looked on me like two sons rolled into one," said Jones of his early childhood.[1] One of six children, Jones recalls his first experience managing money—buying candy bars for three cents each and selling them for a nickel. In Point Pleasant, too, Jones learned the rural values of community and family and developed the strong Christian beliefs which lay on or near the surface of his public voice.

Jones was educated in the small public school system of Point Pleasant. He developed a love for horses through the 4-H program, riding and showing in local and state contests. In school, he was a standout football player and graduated valedictorian of his high-school class. A dedicated member of the Episcopal Church, Jones often offered prayers before Point Pleasant High's football games. For a time, he considered attending the seminary and earned the sobriquet "little minister." He was offered numerous football scholarships and in 1957 settled on the University of Virginia, the academic choice of some of his forebears. He enjoyed playing offensive and defensive end in college, even though the Virginia Cavalier teams lost a record twenty-eight consecutive games in 1958–60. Like his paternal grandfather, Jones was a member of the Honor Committee at Virginia, the body which enforces the university's honor code. A gregarious student, Jones was an active member of the Beta Theta Pi fraternity. He was popular with his peers and elected president of the School of Commerce; he graduated in 1961 with a bachelor's degree in commerce and public finance. Knee and foot injuries disqualified Jones from military service; and after college he tried Virginia Law School, attending one semester to take property and contracts courses in an effort to prepare for the real estate business.

Jones's summers in high school and college were spent working in construction, and after graduation he returned to West Virginia and built a successful real estate and home construction business. He quickly realized that business success in West Virginia was closely linked to politics and in 1964 became the county chairman for Barry Goldwater's presidential campaign. He developed an ambivalent attitude toward the relationship of politics and finance, which has endured. Jones ran the only successful Republican campaign in his county in 1964 and was elected to the West Virginia legislature, where to some he was a "dilettante" and to others a "moralist." At twenty-five, he was the youngest person ever elected to that legislative body. While Jones, the son of a converted Republican, naturally became a Republican, he has commented that John F. Kennedy's "idealism" and "call to sacrifice" played a strong role in his motivation to enter politics. As one of only nine Republicans in the West Virginia legislature, Jones was frustrated with the small degree of influence wielded by this minority and decided not to run again. Republican Party leaders urged him to reconsider—offering to make him minority leader of the legislature—and he changed his mind. He ran again and won, and, as leader of the thirty-seven Republicans elected with him to the legislature, he tasted the greater influence of being the spokesman for a substantial vocal minority. Former West Virginia Governor Gaston Caperton, a Democrat and close friend of Jones, said of him, "I think Brerry's always been very sensitive about people. But he's also a very fiscally responsible person who understands you have to balance the budget. Those are the two strongest principles guiding Brerry."[2]

Jones's opportunity to impact the Democratic-controlled West Virginia legislature remained limited. In his second term he had unseated the House minority leader, a follower of Arch Moore, who was elected governor in 1968. Moore, the most successful Republican in West Virginia in recent times, had himself defeated a Jones family ally in the Republican gubernatorial primary in 1968.[3] Jones considered Moore, who later served time in a federal penitentiary, to be a dishonest man and was not prepared to deal with him as Republican minority leader—and vice versa. Moore's victory, the perceived corruption of West Virginia state government, and Richard Nixon's presidency all contributed to Jones's disenchantment with Republican politics. Speaking of this period of his life, Jones has said, "I probably had the best potential political future of any person in his 20s in the country at that time, in terms of being a possible governor or congressman or senator or something. I really made a hard decision (to quit politics). But I made the decision based on my ethical standards, and I decided I wasn't going to compromise my ethical standards. And so I walked away from it."[4] Jones had lost his taste for politics, was uncomfortable with the direction of his party, and decided against becoming a professional politician. The role of a citizen-politician became unacceptable. He quit politics in 1968 to concentrate on his Huntington real estate development business. This decision came as a shock to many involved in West Virginia politics, where rumors were already surfacing that he might have his sights on the governorship itself. His business, however, made him wealthy, building on real estate ventures which included subdivisions in a time of great growth.[5]

Jones also established a small horse farm at the outer edge of Huntington that was a small opening to what was to be a large part of his future. His family had often taken vacations to central Kentucky, where he developed the dream of owning a Kentucky horse farm. "I thought Kentucky was paradise," he has said of his excursions to the Bluegrass State.[6] During a trip to Keeneland racetrack in 1967, he met Elizabeth ("Libby") Lloyd, his future wife, the daughter of a prominent, political Kentucky father and of a Kentucky mother whose family owned a historic farm (part of a land grant in the late 1700s) on Old Frankfort Pike. Mutual friends introduced Brereton and Libby, who were on dates with others, and soon they began to date each other. They married three years later in 1970.

Jones began another career in 1972, when he came to Kentucky with his wife to her childhood home, Airdrie Farm, a tobacco and cattle farm in Woodford County. He leased a portion of the farm from his father-in-law, former Adj. General A.Y. Lloyd, and began to work with horses there. Airdrie Stud, now a large and successful thoroughbred operation, has grown to 2,700 acres and almost 300 horses, including the winners of European and American classic races. Jones's business sense has driven Airdrie to the top in the horse world. His timing was perfect; a convergence of national and international events in the late 1970s and early 1980s brought enormous levels of investment to the horse business. His yearlings were much sought after in the escalating thoroughbred market of the early 1980s. Now he was rooted on a farm, the proper setting for Jefferson's image of the citizen-politician.

On December 31, 1975, Jones registered as a Democrat. In response to criticisms during his 1987 lieutenant gubernatorial campaign that he was a former Republican and not a native Kentuckian, Jones had a light but controlled reply: "I was and am very fond of my mama, and I wanted to be close to her when I was born. She just happened to be in West Virginia, but I got here as quickly as I could."[7] Even though Jones was nominally out of politics, he continued to be involved in public issues. He was appointed by Governor John Y. Brown Jr. to the University of Kentucky Board of Trustees and the University of Kentucky Chandler Medical Center Board. His interest in health-care reform grew from his exposure to the Medical Center, when, he believed, the board improperly discouraged UK doctors from providing free indigent care. The policy of turning people away or sending them to other hospitals disturbed Jones. He said, "It's not like you have a sick cow and don't want to spend the money to help her so you just let her die. These are human beings."[8] This treatment of poor but sick and injured people, which would require a better system for health care in Kentucky, would be an enduring issue for Jones and one he would revisit once he became governor.

Before initiating his political career in Kentucky, Jones worked as fund-raising chairman for the McDowell Cancer Research Foundation and chaired Governor Martha Layne Collins's task force on the state Medicaid program, along with his university positions. His highest profile of public activity was as head in the mid-1980s of the Kentucky Health Care Access Foundation. Overcoming an initial resistance from the medical community, the foundation soon had enlisted many doctors, dentists, pharmacists, and other practitioners to provide free health care for tens of thousands of Kentuckians below the poverty level, who were not quite poor enough to qualify for Medicaid. The Kentucky Health Care Access Foundation was initially launched by a considerable personal donation from Jones and his wife. It continues to operate and now assists over five thousand indigent Kentuckians annually.

Jones's involvement with this issue (and then his entrance into politics in Kentucky) was spurred by his involvement in fund-raising for a cancer center at UK. He and his wife hosted a fund-raising party, "Twist and Bid," which was held at a Lexington hotel, and Jones asked Lucille Markey of Calumet Farm to match any dollar raised at the event. Partygoers paid to hear Chubby Checker, the Crystals, and the Drifters, and to attend an auction of breeding rights to such stallions as Alydar, Affirmed, and Seattle Slew. The event raised over $1.6 million, which was in fact matched by Mrs. Markey, and a total of $3.2 million was a meaningful step in the creation of the Markey Cancer Center. Jones's success at raising money was, not incidentally, the demonstration of an important requirement for late-twentieth-century politicians.

Jones entered politics with a race for lieutenant governor in October 1986, a dozen years after his change of party affiliation and twenty years after his retirement from West Virginia politics. He made his decision on a Florida vacation, in some part because of a chance meeting with William H. May of Frankfort, one of Kentucky's classic power brokers. Until May died the next year, he was an acknowledged expert on the politics of highway and political finance. May was so impressed with Jones's incredible success in getting Kentucky doctors to give free medical care that he urged Jones to run for governor—but first for lieutenant governor. Jones's other godfather in Kentucky politics, the late Edward Prichard Jr., had encouraged him to run for office as well. Jones also received support from his wife, an ardent environmentalist and preservationist, and from former Kentucky Governors Bert T. Combs and Edward T. "Ned" Breathitt. Secure in his private life, Jones was ready to become a citizen-politician again, at a new level and in a new place.

When Jones announced for lieutenant governor at age forty-seven, he had already been building his organization, raising funds, and campaigning across the state for many months, with the open admission that he would use the largely ceremonial office as a springboard to the governorship. Jones ran for lieutenant governor on his record of achievement in business and his leadership skills from his diverse charitable endeavors. His good looks, impeccable manners, and philanthropic image attracted many young and old voters across the Commonwealth.

Jones's large personal financial resources made him a credible candidate overnight. He spent just over $2.2 million in the lieutenant gubernatorial primary; almost three-quarters of this—$1.7 million—came from a personal loan. That loan both launched and dogged his Kentucky political career. Each of the five candidates in the Democratic primary brought significant political strengths to the campaign, most in the accustomed ways. David Armstrong, Alice McDonald, and David Boswell were all completing four years in high office—as attorney general, superintendent of public instruction, and commissioner of agriculture, respectively. Another opponent, Paul Patton, who was later to become Jones's lieutenant governor and then his successor as governor, was already a former state chair of the Democratic Party under Governor Brown and was completing a second term as Pike County judge-executive. Jones was the only candidate who had never held or sought political office in Kentucky.[9]

In many ways, this race was typical of recent gubernatorial campaigns. There was a large field of candidates; there were major shifts in voter sentiment during the campaign; and television advertising had a significant effect on the outcome. Moreover, in the 1987 lieutenant gubernatorial race, the election was won by a wealthy political amateur who could afford extensive television advertising and who used it effectively.

Jones won the May 1987 Democratic lieutenant gubernatorial primary with 33 percent of the vote; he finished seven percentage points and forty thousand votes ahead of Armstrong, his nearest competitor. Three weeks earlier, the *Louisville Courier-Journal*'s Bluegrass State Poll had shown him trailing Armstrong by nine points, with 39 percent of the likely voters still undecided. Another Bluegrass State Poll in early March had shown Jones running last, with only 3 percent of the vote.

Jones and Patton raised the financial stakes in Kentucky lieutenant gubernatorial politics. The total cost of the record-breaking, exorbitantly expensive campaign was over $5 million, with Jones spending $2.2 million and Patton almost $1.6 million. The Jones organization relied on a wide variety of community leaders, some but not all of whom had been active in politics. In a campaign dominated by personalities rather than issues, Jones worked harder, spent more, and assembled a more attractive, saleable media package. In the November general election, Democratic gubernatorial nominee Wallace Wilkinson (another wealthy businessman-turned-politician) and Jones faced token opposition and easily won by a margin of 65 to 35 percent.

Jones experienced his tenure as lieutenant governor as frustrating. The post had little power on its own; and Jones's relationship with Wilkinson was, in Jones's word, "terrible."[10] The final break between the two came during a teachers' demonstration in Frankfort. Jones was sympathetic to the teachers' demands for more money for education than Wilkinson then supported, and he wanted to address the very large crowd that had gathered at the Capitol. Wilkinson told Jones, while the two were in the governor's office, that if he spoke to the crowd he need never "step foot in this office again."[11] Jones spoke and never in fact visited Wilkinson's office again.

As lieutenant governor, Jones was praised for his efforts to attain a "Made in Kentucky" label for homegrown produce; he was a strong advocate for the preservation of family farms. He worked closely with the Prichard Committee for Academic Excellence, a strong promoter for school reform and tax-hike legislation. While serving as lieutenant governor, Jones illustrated his "fiscal restraint" by reducing the budget allotted to his office by living at Airdrie. He also donated his salary to an exchange program for high-school students.

At this time the lieutenant governor was still the president of the state senate. In that role, Jones developed a collegial relationship with legislators—in contrast to Wilkinson's combative relations with many members of the General Assembly. He "worked hand-in-glove with the General Assembly during its battles with the governor."[12] He was able to demonstrate his ability to negotiate and to act out his campaign theme that "we can work together." His style and political savvy attracted many of the "young progressives" in the Kentucky Democratic Party; and he also surrounded himself with several old associates of former Governors Julian Carroll, John Y. Brown Jr., and Martha Layne Collins.

After his experience and exposure as lieutenant governor, Jones was poised to make his run for the governor's office in 1991.[13] The front runner from start to finish, he faced personal negative campaigning from Martha Wilkinson, the incumbent governor's wife (who ran for office but who then withdrew eighteen days before election day), Scotty Baesler (the three-term mayor of Lexington and future U.S. Sixth District congressman), and Dr. Floyd Poore (a former transportation secretary and fund-raiser for Governors Collins and Wilkinson). Lexingtonian Gatewood Galbraith (later to run in 1999 as a Reform Party nominee), a maverick pro-marijuana attorney, also ran. Running against taxes and spending over $2.6 million, Poore worked tirelessly, but he spent so much money early in the campaign that he did not have enough at the end to match the late media blitzes of Jones and Baesler. Tobacco farmer Baesler spent nearly $2 million and positioned himself as the "outsider" in the race, promising reform and a new concern for ethics. Martha Wilkinson's unexpected exit (after spending over $3 million), and then her transparent behind-the-scenes financial and organizational assistance to Baesler's underfinanced and understaffed campaign, undermined Baesler's carefully crafted image. Martha Wilkinson's harsh attacks on Jones, hammering at his failure to release his income tax returns (he had released a ten-year summary), were replaced by Baesler's direct attacks. Jones tied Baesler to Wilkinson—charging Baesler with following "the Wilkinson campaign in resorting to the negative politics of the past."

Garnering 38 percent of the vote and spending $4 million, Jones conducted on the whole a positive campaign that emphasized ethics and campaign-finance reform—contrasting himself with the Wilkinson image of dishonesty, and the grand jury problems of some people who did business with the Wilkinson administration. He put together an efficient fund-raising team and a smooth-running grassroots organization. Using sophisticated television and radio spots and direct mailings, he contested every county in the state, often with locally tailored messages, and he had precinct captains in all 120 counties. The Jones organization pressed labor and teacher groups harder than the usual candidate. The teachers helped in most counties and labor in some key ones. Jones received ten daily newspaper endorsements, including the *Louisville Courier-Journal*, the *Paducah Sun*, and the *Kentucky Post*, and those of several county weeklies. Serious journalists credited Jones's charm and personal charisma for many votes: he "titillated table-full after table-full of older ladies."[14]

The general election was expected to be the Republicans' best chance for the state's highest office since Louie Nunn's victory in 1967. Seven-term Sixth District Congressman Larry Hopkins had squeaked by with 50.7 percent of the vote in the Republican gubernatorial primary, defeating Lexington attorney Larry Forgy. In the markedly issueless general election campaign, Jones outspent Hopkins two to one and was elected with a surprising, record margin—of nearly two to one.[15] There was much personal mudslinging and numerous gaffes by the Republican. Hopkins focused on Jones's finances, a theme continued by the state's leading newspapers throughout Jones's tenure as governor. Jones would not commit to refrain from raising money to pay off the 1987 lieutenant gubernatorial race debt, and there were vague assertions about his personal finances, because he would not open his tax returns to the public. Because of his emphasis on Jones's finances, Hopkins was hurt badly by revelations of thirty-two overdrafts in the U.S. House bank. Hopkins carried only thirteen small counties, losing every county in his own Sixth Congressional District. Only 31.8 percent of the voting-age population voted, and over $19 million (a new record) was spent in the quest for the governorship. All statewide Democratic candidates were victorious; it was a crushing defeat for the minority, fragmented (but recently resurging) Republican Party.

Jones inherited a difficult financial situation when he took office as Kentucky's fifty-fourth governor in December 1991. State government faced an almost $400 million budget deficit that the governor and the legislature were forced to confront immediately. By the end of Governor Jones's term, Kentucky boasted a $300 million surplus.

As one would expect from his upbringing and early life, Jones came to the governor's office pledging to put an end to politics for personal gain. The governor fought for and won dramatic ethics reforms that made Kentucky's laws on the subject some of the most progressive in the nation. Reforms were made in both the executive and legislative branches, adopting more restrictive campaign finance laws, enacting tougher state contract laws, prohibitions on the use of public office for career-building, and limitations on lobbying—among other reforms.

On August 7, 1992, a state Sikorsky helicopter carrying Jones and five others crashed onto a steep hillside near the Franklin-Shelby County line. All passengers miraculously survived, but the governor sustained back injuries and a bruised kidney. Jones looks back on his survival of the helicopter accident as a message from God not to fret about criticism from the media and to maximize his rare opportunity to help people. "It sounds strange, but I think the crash was the turning point of my administration. The crash focused me on doing what I thought was right and the push to do it."[16] He said the life-threatening experience allowed him to ignore media criticism and focus his energy on health-care reform and his other goals. In fact, the airplane crash seems to have recast the balance between Jones's religious bent and his political instincts, a tension always evident in his public life.

After the crash, Jones concentrated on health-care reform, a deeply felt issue that he carried forward from his days on the UK Chandler Medical Center Board. While he did much in the fields of education and economic development, along with many other issues, the uniqueness of his administration came from his health-care initiatives. Jones believed that the people of the state needed, and the government could provide, universal health care for all its citizens. He crossed swords with members of the General Assembly over the issue many times in the course of his tenure and finally won a limited embodiment of his plan in 1994. While falling short of his goal of providing universal health care for all Kentuckians, the 1994 legislation was a solid beginning for future governors and legislatures to build on.

When Jones ended his term in 1995, he became again a full-time Kentucky horseman. He left as the most popular governor in recent memory—61 percent approval rating.[17] Although the governor never paid for an opinion poll during his tenure, he was very conscious of his popularity among the citizens, as opposed to the press, which was never satisfied by his persistent unwillingness to expose the details of his private business to their scrutiny. He opened up the governor's office to the public on regular occasions during his tenure ("Open Door After Four"[18]), but he refused to allow any invasion of his personal life, either as to his religious convictions or his financial affairs—at the risk of persistent innuendo in the press that he was hiding some conflict of interest from their view.

After his term, Jones returned to the appropriate setting for Jefferson's yeoman/statesman—growing crops and tending to the breeding, foaling, and boarding of thoroughbreds at Airdrie. His focus now allowed him to know every stallion and every mare on his farm. His usual ten-hour daily schedule was no longer involved with budgets and policies, but included walking the barns, meeting owners, negotiating deals, and promoting Airdrie. The beautiful Midway farm prospered, in yet another thoroughbred boom, as an international business firm involved in acquiring top stallions for breeding, marketing horses all over America and in Europe and Asia, and continued to grow and sell cattle, tobacco, and other crops. He also started Commonwealth Broadcasting, a radio broadcasting company, in which he and his partners purchased numerous stations in Kentucky and Tennessee.[19] He was also involved in land development in northern Kentucky.

Jones was now, as he had always been, a family man. He and his wife were involved in the renovation of the century-old brick southern colonial home on their farm. Also, they planned to refurbish the childhood home of antiliquor crusader Carrie Nation, which stands on their land. In the years after his governorship, he mentioned with pride his daughter Lucy, an undergraduate at Emory University, and his son Bret, a graduate from Lexington's Sayre Academy.

While Jones moved his focus from the spotlight of the governor's office to his farm, he continued to be involved with issues he considered important to the state. The duty of a former governor was, he believed, to continue to lead by example and by publicly voicing his concerns. Thus, he has been outspoken on the legislature's changing of campaign finance laws and health care. More recently, he became involved in the debate over casino gambling in the state through editorializing in several papers statewide—criticizing casinos as being rigged, as detrimental to the horse industry, and as attracting unwanted elements to Kentucky. An effort to post the Ten Commandments in public schools, an issue which surfaced late in his gubernatorial administration, is another cause he supported after leaving office. Rumors surfaced of his seeking the governor's office again—talk which he gleefully toyed with and then denied.

---

1. Some of the information for this biographical sketch is drawn from personal interviews with the former governor on January 24, 1996, February 12, 1997, June 23, 1999, and March 27, 2000.

2. Robert T. Garrett, "Brereton Jones," *Louisville Courier-Journal*, April 28, 1991:D4.

3. Arch Moore was a Republican congressman from West Virginia who defeated Cecil Underwood, a previous governor, in the Republican primary.

4. *Louisville Courier-Journal*, April 28, 1991:D4.

5. Ibid., April 6, 1987:B1,B3.

6. Personal interview, June 23, 1999.

7. *Lexington Herald-Leader*, March 2, 1987:C12.

8. Personal interview, June 23, 1999.

9. For an in-depth analysis of the 1987 lieutenant gubernatorial contest, see Penny M. Miller and Malcolm E. Jewell, *Political Parties and Primaries in Kentucky* (Lexington: University Press of Kentucky, 1990), 96–124.

10. Personal interview, June 23, 1999.

11. Ibid.

12. *Louisville Courier-Journal*, April 28, 1991:D4.

13. For an analysis of the 1991 Democratic gubernatorial primary, see Penny M. Miller, *Kentucky Politics and Government: Do We Stand United?* (Lincoln: University of Nebraska Press, 1994), 200–202.

14. *Louisville Courier-Journal*, April 28, 1991:D4.

15. For an analysis of the 1991 gubernatorial general election, see Miller, *Kentucky Politics and Government*, 212–13.

16. *Lexington Herald-Leader*, December 10, 1995:A16.

17. *Louisville Courier-Journal*, December 10, 1995:A1.

18. On December 4, 1993, Jones opened his door to the public-at-large with his first monthly "Open Door After Four," an opportunity for people

to come see him without missing work. More than eighty individuals and groups met with him during the first "Open Door," discussing topics ranging from road construction to child sexual abuse.

19. In May 2000, Jones began a weekly radio commentary called *Common Sense for the Commonwealth* on stations he co-owned in Kentucky. The sixty-second radio show became a forum for Jones to express his views on a variety of issues. *Lexington Herald-Leader,* May 2, 2000:B1.

THE BRERETON C. JONES ADMINISTRATION

December 10, 1991, to December 11, 1995

IN 1991 voters elected Brereton Chandler Jones as Kentucky's fifty-fourth governor by a record-setting margin of victory—almost two to one over his opponent, Republican Congressman Larry Hopkins.[1] The new governor came to Frankfort with the promise of a spirit of reconciliation and renewed cooperation between the governor's office and the General Assembly, and between the governor and the media, at a time when public faith badly needed restoration.[2] The voters looked to the new governor for integrity and progress in Kentucky government and hoped he would provide clear leadership after two scandal-plagued administrations and the apparent breakdown of collegiality between the chief executive and the General Assembly. "The clash between the legislative and executive branches ha[d] become almost a staple of Frankfort's political life in the era of the independent General Assembly."[3]

In his inaugural address on December 10, 1991, Jones said, ". . . this is a new and different day in Kentucky. This administration is committed to having the most positive, progressive, exciting four years in our state's history. When our term is finished, things will never be the same in this Commonwealth." Jones had emphasized reform: reform in government finances, ethics, and organization, and reform of health care. Four years later, when Jones left Frankfort to return to his Woodford County thoroughbred farm, Airdrie Stud, there was a budget surplus of more than $300 million, some improvement in executive-legislative relations, the passage of an array of government reform legislation, and a scandal-free but sometimes controversial record for Jones's supporters to applaud. Jones fell short of achieving his most ambitious goal—health-insurance coverage for all Kentuckians—but he left office with the voters' admiration. In the *Louisville Courier-Journal*'s Bluegrass State Poll, conducted in September 1995, Jones received a 61 percent approval rating for his gubernatorial efforts—considerably higher than his two immediate predecessors at the end of their terms.[4]

RESTORING PUBLIC FAITH

WHAT most marked Governor Jones's promise to the people of Kentucky was the citizen-politician's commitment to restoring the faith of the people in their state government.

STATE EXECUTIVE GOVERNMENT REFORMS

UPON becoming governor, Jones went to work in the executive branch to ensure high ethical standards. Within sixty seconds of his inauguration, he issued an executive order barring the use of public office for personal gain—forbidding top executive officials from taking positions with companies that do business with the state until six months after they leave government work. In 1992, at Jones's request, an executive ethics code was passed into law by the legislature, prohibiting state employees from becoming lobbyists for one year after leaving government. The code also barred employees from using their positions or influence in matters in which they have a conflict of interest. The law also established an Executive Branch Ethics Commission to review and investigate complaints on ethical matters. Several other government-improvement bills were passed by the 1992 General Assembly. Legislation was enacted regulating "build-to-suit" leases and creating a selection committee to recommend developers to the administration. A similar procedure was established for selecting architects and engineers for personal service contracts.[5]

Throughout his administration, Jones received much personal criticism from the press and his political adversaries because the state's new executive ethics code did not require him to identify names of his business partners or associates at Airdrie Stud, which he continued to direct. Jones said that contracts with his farm included clauses requiring his partners and customers to attest that they were not seeking any gain from state government and were not trying to obtain no-bid contracts, but the media was never satisfied, and Jones, persistently the citizen-politician, insisted that there be boundaries. He refused to expose the details of his private life and business to press scrutiny. Jones was not accused of favoring any business associate—or of any corrupt act—but the press never forgave his insistence on privacy.

Jones was also criticized for his plan to set up off-track betting parlors and use some of the profits to fund rewards for persons who breed successful thoroughbreds in Kentucky, programs which are widely used in other states to encourage the development of quality home-breds. The program was passed by the 1992 legislature, and the governor has profited from it, although he used the money he had won to give bonuses to farm employees. Jones also argued that his participation in the awards program was not a conflict of interest because he had no advantage over any other breeder. Livingston Taylor, a former newspaperman and then the chair of the Executive Branch Ethics Commission, an innovation which Jones had sought and appointed, disapproved of Jones's action: "My feeling is that, by the governor having pushed for creation of these awards, and for him now to financially benefit himself, it just looks bad."[6] It seems fair to credit Jones for creating a public process for questioning the behavior of executive branch employees—including, not incidentally, himself. Richard Beliles, chairman of Common Cause of Kentucky, compared the ethics of the Jones administration favorably with its predecessors—"In Kentucky, he didn't have too many shining examples."[7]

CAMPAIGN REFORMS AND GUBERNATORIAL SUCCESSION AMENDMENT

JONES championed the cause of campaign finance reform for state legislative races and Kentucky's future gubernatorial races, hoping to remove the perceived "for sale" sign from the governor's mansion. The $20 million spent by gubernatorial candidates in 1991 confirmed popular doubts about the process. Campaign spending limits, coupled with partial public campaign funding, and a gubernatorial succession amendment to the constitution were enacted in 1992, significantly due to Jones's effort. The sweeping legislation of April 1992 provided that in return for accepting public money, slates of candidates must agree not to spend more than $1.8 million in an election and to participate in televised debates. After receiving $600,000, each team of governor and lieutenant governor would receive a two-to-one match from the state treasury. Moreover, the maximum amount an individual or political action committee (PAC) could give a candidate for governor or the legislature was slashed from $4,000 to $500, the lowest in the nation.[8] The influence of PACs was further limited by a provision prohibiting slates for governor and lieutenant governor from receiving more than 25 percent of their money from PACs. An additional campaign reform was the reduction of the number of elections, making one year out of every four election-free.

On November 3, 1992, Kentuckians made the most dramatic change in state government and politics in decades, adopting the succession amendment, which permits a governor and other state constitutional officers to run for second terms. Incumbents who have earned the trust and support of the voters would have a better opportunity to promote an extensive, comprehensive policy agenda over an eight-year period. No longer would a new governor always have to prepare a budget in a month, and then become a lame duck after his or her first legislative session. The succession amendment passed, largely because Jones was willing to exempt himself from the amendment's provisions, removing the major obstacle that had defeated previous attempts by Governors John Y. Brown Jr., Wallace Wilkinson, and others to accomplish that reform.

Jones was praised by the media for his support of gubernatorial succession, but he was attacked for being "hypocritical on campaign finance reform." Repeatedly, Jones was criticized for raising money to recover the $1.7 million loan he made to his 1987 campaign for lieutenant governor. He was collecting contributions of up to $8,000, while advocating, as part of the campaign finance reform bill, a sharp reduction in the limit on individual giving—$500. It was reported that on the evening before his inaugural address, about six hundred people attended a Lexington fund-raiser, the suggested donation being $1,000 a couple, to help him pay off the 1987 debt. The event was sponsored by former Governor "Ned" Breathitt and fifteen heads of newspapers and broadcasting companies. At the time, Jones said that Jack Hall, his chief fund-raiser during the campaign, would continue raising money to pay off the debt.[9] Newspaper editorials subsequently attacked Jones's appointments of Hall, first as head of a commission to oversee the removal of underground gas tanks and later as chair of the powerful Kentucky Health Policy Board. The press persisted in its distrust of Hall despite the absence of any accusation of wrongdoing of any sort.

The Jones administration was scandal-free, but the lingering doubts of the media may have reflected (and surely in some part caused) a lingering doubt among the citizenry that any politician is free from improper motives and actions. Jones's goal of "restoring public faith in elected officials" was not completely fulfilled.

APPOINTMENTS AND PERSONNEL

GOVERNOR Jones's cabinet-level appointments reflected a search for new people to direct state government—not predominantly campaign stalwarts. Jones also recognized the need for more women and minorities at the highest levels. Some of his trusted campaign notables were given top positions—Joe Prather as secretary of finance and administration, Billy Wellman as secretary of justice, and Carol Palmore as secretary of labor. But Jones also enlisted the support of well-respected former administrators, such as Kevin Hable (Wilkinson's first budget chief) to become secretary of the cabinet. Newcomers to state politics included an African American woman, Kim Burse, as secretary of revenue. Other noteworthy appointees included Mary Helen Miller as legislative liaison and chief executive officer for administration, Phillip Shepherd as secretary of natural resources, Crit Luallen as tourism and finance secretary, Ed Holmes as public protection secretary, and Masten Childers II as secretary of the Cabinet for Human Resources. The absence of scandal in the Jones administration was very much the result of the high caliber of men and women he appointed to serve.

Building on a tradition of Kentucky governors' support for civil rights, Jones also sought diversity in his appointments and generally in state hiring practices. By the end of his administration, he had exceeded the long-established goal of 7.4 percent minority representation in the state work force; he appointed the first woman to the Kentucky Supreme Court; and he appointed three times the number of African Americans and far more women than the previous administration.[10]

In early 1992, Jones moved to fulfill a campaign pledge to remove politics from the appointment of trustees and regents for state university governing boards. One of Governor Wilkinson's last actions as chief executive was to appoint himself to the University of Kentucky Board of Trustees, an affront to the academic world. During his administration, Wilkinson had struggled openly with the university community—influencing the resignation of President David Roselle and appointing his high-school teacher and friend, Charles Wethington, to the presidency of UK. Legislation passed by the 1992 General Assembly—Jones's "trustees bill"—dissolved all state university boards and the Council on Higher Education as of July 1, 1992. Appointments to reconstituted university boards (formerly perceived as simple political pay-offs) were mandated first to be reviewed by an independent panel that then recommended to the governor three applicants for each position. Wilkinson was not selected by Jones under the new appointment system, nor were most other Wilkinson supporters.

COOPERATION AND CONFRONTATION WITH THE LEGISLATURE

JONES assumed office after a period of strife between the legislative and executive branches of Kentucky government. The General Assembly over the course of three decades had matured and assumed its constitutional role in Kentucky state government, relatively free of any governor's control. And the legislature had clashed openly and bitterly with Wilkinson. It was hoped that Jones would reconcile the personalized rift that had grown between these two branches, that he might heal the scars of the past while providing a model of cooperation for the future. "Jones eased into office as the leader of what he seemed to believe was a happy crusade—with the legislature and news media at his side—to expunge the political excesses of the Wilkinson administration."[11]

There was a noticeable thaw in legislative-gubernatorial relations during Jones's first year in office. In an atmosphere of cooperation and support, significant legislation was passed—including campaign finance and other election reforms, executive-branch ethics and state contract reform, and the creation of the Kentucky Economic Development Partnership. Jones's "honeymoon" relationship with the General Assembly deteriorated during the closing days of the 1992 legislative session when the FBI made public its BOPTROT investigation, an event not related to Jones at all.[12] The eighteen-month-long undercover probe of the General Assembly and the Wilkinson administration led to the conviction of fifteen current or former state legislators, including Speaker of the House Don Blandford, and Governor Wilkinson's nephew, Bruce Wilkinson, who had coordinated appointments to state boards and commissions. While Jones's administration was not implicated in any way, either in the scandal or the investigation, statements made by the governor to the press would irreparably damage his relations with the untarnished legislative leaders. Jones called BOPTROT "a cleansing process,"[13] while stressing that most legislators were honest and hard working. Legislators were infuriated by Jones's comment, sensing that he was taking "the high ground"—above them. The governor would later say that his apparently neutral statements, which were not taken as neutral, "created dramatic problems" for him in trying to deal with the General Assembly.[14]

The power vacuum created in the wake of BOPTROT required new leadership in the legislature, and Governor Jones's relationship with a body that felt under a cloud was tenuous. In February 1993, promptly after BOPTROT, the legislature passed a legislative ethics code in a special session called by Jones. As one of the toughest legislative ethics laws in the nation, its provisions included limiting the amount lobbyists could spend on food and drink for legislators; forbidding gifts from lobbyists; requiring lobbyists to register and file expense accounts; limiting campaign contributions to legislative candidates; restricting former legislators from becoming lobbyists until two years after they had left office; and establishing the Legislative Ethics Commission to investigate complaints and issue rulings. But the General Assembly was not cooperating with the governor; it was reacting as it had to—to pressures from the public and the press . . . and Jones.

Jones's relations with legislators never recovered. His "relationship with the legislature bottomed out on the infamous final day for passing bills during the '94 session. Jones seized KET's airwaves to bash some legislative leaders for cowering before special interests while the health-care bill and the budget bill were hanging fire."[15] The last day of the session he used public television to promote his health-care bill and his budget. He said that lobbyists influenced some legislative leaders to oppose him. A budget was passed, but it pointedly eliminated many of Jones's priorities. The governor responded dramatically. He vetoed the legislative budget, attacking the legislators on state parks spending, a popular cause, saying that the General Assembly had "cut out every single project and every single dollar for parks revitalization, no matter how meritorious, how urgently needed, or how basic."[16] The senate, by refusing to approve his proposed tax increase, forced the house to eliminate popular construction projects, enabling Jones to apply still more public pressure. The 1994 regular session ended without a budget for Kentucky, and, after a brief cooling-off period, Jones called a special session two months later, which restored $70 million for state park repairs but not most of his other construction projects—an uneasy, unhappy compromise.

The special session became a Jones staple. He called a record nine special legislative sessions during his tenure. A January 1995 special session allowed him to cut the income tax on private pensions and to reduce the state inheritance tax. Three of his priority construction projects were also passed—the Kentucky History Center in Frankfort, the Northern Kentucky Convention Center in Covington, and the expansion of the Commonwealth Convention Center in Louisville. In the summer of 1995, he called a special session to augment the state's "rainy day" account of $100 million and to spend $50 million on rural roads. The General Assembly also adopted a redistricting plan in place of one that had been declared unconstitutional—which new plan Jones vetoed.

Although the relationship between Jones and the legislature and its leaders was regularly hostile and the initial hope for collegiality became an impossibility, the governor and the legislature were able to cooperate to some degree and pass some highly important and highly controversial legislation, notably health-care reform. Often very critical public exchanges took place between the governor and the legislative leadership—especially between Jones and his chief nemesis, Senate President John "Eck" Rose, who emerged as the most powerful legislator. Later Rose challenged Jones's claims to many of the accomplishments of his tenure. Rose credited the legislators' endeavors to hold spending in check in the 1994–96 budget, and he credited favorable national economic conditions for lowering Kentucky unemployment and raising state revenues.[17] In contrast to Rose, Senate Majority Leader David Karem gave Jones higher marks. Karem traced the antipathy of the two branches to Jones's personal beliefs and style, suggesting that he "reacts from emotion, and very strong emotional commitments at a far, far more intense level than I originally understood. Over the last two years I finally began to realize he wasn't mean-spirited, he just really believes a lot more emotionally in things than I ever understood."[18]

BULLY PULPIT

SENATOR Karem was correct in noting Jones's "very strong emotional commitments," and Karem was like most of those in Frankfort, including in the press, who underestimated the "intense level" at which the governor considered policy. This underestimation was due in some part to the fact that Jones did not openly express the personal nature of his beliefs. These beliefs were to be seen in the annual prayer breakfasts he instituted; and his religious enthusiasms surfaced at the end of his administration when he spoke passionately of his wish to place the Ten Commandments in public school classrooms. On the whole, however, he demonstrated publicly less fervor than might have been expected of a man who once considered the seminary and the pulpit. That being said, Jones's speeches are to be read with Senator Karem's understanding of the emotion that underlay them.

Though not a brimstone orator, Jones skillfully used his legislative messages as a platform for his agenda and as a means of capturing the state's attention. Many addresses were scheduled for prime-time television, the best place for the "bully pulpit." Jones periodically held press conferences and gave interviews to the Frankfort press corps to build public confidence and support for programs. He also participated in several bus tours to tout his policy initiatives around the Commonwealth. His statewide bus tour to obtain funding support for a massive renovation of Kentucky's park system was characteristically dubbed by one newspaper editorial as a "tour to nowhere." The monthly "Open Door After Four" to his office, while principally explained as a means of obtaining feedback from the citizens, served, too, as a channel for his views.

One of Jones's most memorable speeches was the KET speech on April 1, 1994, which attacked the legislators, an attempt to try to get his health-care bill and budget passed. Some critics claimed that he failed to make full use of his bully pulpit later, as in 1995 when he was still trying to win public acceptance of his health-care reform initiatives. That criticism can only fairly apply to his inability to achieve more media coverage of his speeches, since the twenty-nine health-care speeches appearing in his public papers are merely a sampling of over fifty that he gave (he mentioned health care in at least a hundred more)—all across the state, and all through his four years in office. It is impossible to know the degree to which Jones's speeches, their frequency, and their intensity, mobilized public opinion to achieve the results that were accomplished. What is clear is that without his advocacy, there would have been no material reform of health care in Kentucky in the mid-1990s.

If health care was promoted by fifty speeches, economic development was advanced by hundreds of speeches. In Jones's travels, he raised the subject of a modern Kentucky economy, localizing his standard stump address to fit the topic and place of that day's speech. He focused on the difference he saw, which he wanted his audience to understand and apply, between expenditures and investments. In this way, Jones the entrepreneur and Jones the politician preached the same message to the public.

Each of the subjects of Jones's policy concerns found a place in his speeches, from specific government reforms to general calls for fiscal responsibility, from specific education programs to general calls for family and community values—from specific unpopular causes (the Brady Bill) to general, even vague, popular causes (the diversification of Kentucky agriculture). Some of his specifically favored projects were not achieved—for example, his concern for the environment was often focused on the unrealized need for the government to acquire even more acreage in Blanton Forest in

Harlan County. Some of his generalized concerns could not be judged except by increments—for example, this former West Virginian, the states' co-chair of the Appalachian Regional Commission, frequently emphasized the unique needs of eastern Kentucky, even while discussing broader matters such as education, economic development, health care, and housing.

Since a governor of late twentieth-century Kentucky does not control massive patronage resources, does not direct a party machine that dictates nominations and elections, and does not have a monopoly on expertise and political skills, the chief executive must apply pressure and persuasion through his ability to motivate the legislature's constituents to share and express his/her views to individual legislators. Jones understood this, and his speeches reflect that understanding. They may not often express the "strong emotions" that motivate them, but they were an integral part of the Jones administration. The Jones speeches were an important factor in his administration's successes, including in the dominant subject areas which are discussed below.

FISCAL PROGRESS

JONES inherited a state in bleak financial straits and quickly moved to correct its course. Kentucky labored under a $400 million revenue imbalance when he took office and had not been able to return state income tax refunds on time for two years because of revenue shortfalls. He undertook a plan to cut public waste and simultaneously stir private growth. In 1992 the governor created the fifty-three-member Quality and Efficiency Commission to find ways to streamline state government and then acted on the commission's recommendations, a move that was estimated to save the state $234 million over a five-year period.[19] State bonds were refinanced at lower rates, saving millions of dollars. Through attrition for the most part, rather than lay-offs, Jones cut the size of state government by some two thousand workers, from about 36,200 to 34,200 full-time, permanent state employees—a move that saved the state some $50 million per year. Jones reversed the trend of overestimating revenues, which inevitably resulted in a reduction in the budget of state agencies. He reduced state travel expenses by $3 million and eliminated 1,000 state vehicles, which were sold at auction. By the end of his term, Jones left the largest budget surplus in Kentucky history, some $300 million for the next administration.

EDUCATION

DESPITE his emphasis on trimming the state budget, Jones supported the continuation of education reform in his "bully pulpit" and in his budgets. The governor enabled the Kentucky Education Reform Act (KERA) to progress during his administration, making sure KERA was fully funded, even in times of budget shortfalls. Jones reflected the tension between downsizing and reform, denying the notion that "we could do more than we did." He claimed that short-term bureaucratic belt-tightening would create more money for education in the future; and public education was a priority in his tight first budget. The governor also promoted reform in a series of widely publicized school visits. Robert Sexton, executive director of the Prichard Committee for Academic Excellence, endorsed Jones's approach—"keeping the focus on the need to reform schools and implement KERA." But, Sexton said, the revolution in education while Wilkinson was governor made it certain that "there was almost nothing Jones could have done to become an 'education governor.'"[20] Some education advocates criticized him, labeling his education record only "adequate." Jones himself believes that he maintained the integrity and "nurtured the Kentucky Education Reform Act of 1990."[21]

In the last two years of his administration, Jones was able to do more in education. He shifted more than $74 million into local school-building programs and pupil transportation; for the first time since those programs were established, they were fully funded. His second budget also made Kentucky the first state to link all its districts together and to the world through the Internet. Teachers and students in 176 Kentucky public school districts in all corners of the state had access to the World Wide Web by the end of the Jones administration—an accomplishment that appears in most education speeches of his successor.

ECONOMIC DEVELOPMENT

DURING the 1992 General Assembly, the governor and legislators reorganized and depoliticized the state's economic-development apparatus. All economic-development functions previously controlled by the governor were transferred to a twelve-member board, the Kentucky Economic Development Partnership, composed largely of business leaders. This public-private partnership approach provided continuity in long-range planning of the state's economic initiatives and added professionalism to efforts to help business firms and attract new jobs. Governor Jones also proposed and won approval in 1992 for tax incentives to attract new jobs and save existing ones through the new Kentucky Jobs Development Authority and the new Kentucky Industrialization Authority.

The modern era of economic development had begun in Kentucky with Governor Martha Layne Collins's massive initiative to attract Toyota Motor Manufacturing Company to Georgetown in 1985. Governor Wilkinson expanded that approach to attract small companies, including many which supplied Toyota and the other automobile companies that located near Kentucky on the I-75 corridor. Thus, Jones's innovations were more structural than substantive. By December 1995, 200,000 more Kentuckians were employed than when Jones took office. With the wooing of more national and international firms to Kentucky during his tenure, more than 300,000 people were working in manufacturing-based jobs in 1995—another record high for the state. Economists will debate all the causes, but the facts are that at the end of the Jones term, Kentucky had the lowest unemployment rate in two decades; welfare rolls were reduced by fifty thousand people; sixty-five thousand new jobs were created; taxes for those with private pensions and major inheritance were reduced. The national economy was on an upturn as well, but Kentucky's per capita income was increasing faster than that of forty other states.[22]

HEALTH CARE

THE centerpiece of the Jones administration was the battle the governor waged to ensure affordable health care for all Kentuckians. As a member of the University of Kentucky Chandler Medical Center board, and as founder of the Kentucky Health Care Access Foundation, and in countless other places, Jones had seen that many Kentuckians were not receiving the health care they needed or deserved. Once governor, he made controlling health-care costs and making quality health care available to all Kentuckians his top priority. Since KERA would guide Kentucky education for decades and the Toyota deal would exemplify economic development in Kentucky for the foreseeable future, it would be difficult for Jones to become "the education governor" or the "economic development governor" of his generation. If he was to dominate a policy area, it would be health care, where he was an expert and an advocate; and that is what he undertook to do.

Jones started by appointing a forty-five-member Task Force on Health Care Access and Affordability and a smaller commission, the Task Force on Health Care Reform, to study ideas on health-care reform with the goal of coming up with a plan to cover and provide Kentuckians with care. In May 1993, he called a special session of the General Assembly to consider legislation to provide health care for all Kentuckians. All the forces which were arrayed against President Bill Clinton's national plan appeared in Frankfort—providers and insurers were present in full force. Although this special session ended fruitlessly for the governor (the legislative leaders claimed the state could not afford the comprehensive plan the governor advanced), there was an agreement to work with the governor on crafting an acceptable health-care bill for the next session.

Health care became the priority in the 1994 session as Jones, legislators, and lobbyists battled to shape House Bill 250, the omnibus state health-care reform bill. House Bill 250 was amended, compromised, and attacked; and it was pronounced dead many times on its rocky road to passage. It was approved in a weakened form by the senate on April 1, the last regular day of the legislative session, but seemed doomed when the house would not go along. Jones, who had championed reform for years, added to the strange April Fools' Day ending by suddenly lobbying house members to kill the bill. Later, he said he was not sure what was in the hastily drawn eleventh-hour compromise. He even discovered that there was a page missing from his copy of the bill; and he preferred to allow the legislators to pass it in the house during the veto session.[23] Another volatile moment came the night of April 1 when he went on Kentucky Educational Television to denounce legislators for not adopting his broader reform plan. The KET speech "created long-term animosity with the legislature," he later said. "It offended them but I would do the same thing again."[24] Then, "on April 15, 1994, Jones signed into law the same bill he tried to kill two weeks earlier, saying 'the people of Kentucky have won a great victory.'"[25]

In the end, after a tumultuous battle, Jones was successful in getting some health-care reform passed. The legislature passed, and Jones signed, a health-care bill that included insurance reforms but not Jones's priority of universal coverage. The law assured that no Kentuckian could be denied health insurance because of pre-existing health conditions and that no Kentuckian would lose health insurance merely by changing jobs ("portability"). The legislation created a mechanism to make the policies of all companies uniform (and thus understandable and subject to competition); and it created the statewide Health Purchasing Alliance, which was designed to keep costs low and make services available in all areas of the Commonwealth. The law established a Health Policy Board to oversee Kentucky's $10 billion health-care system and regulate rate increases. It included consumer education and mandated posting of rates by health-care providers. The commissioner of insurance was given the authority to review insurance rates and reject unreasonable increases.

Reaction was predictably varied. Activist Roy Gividen called the bill a significant improvement, while conservative Rep. Bob Heleringer, R-Louisville, labeled the bill "a government takeover" of health care and warned his colleagues that "we'll be back here in two years to undo our mistake."[26] Several insurance companies filed lawsuits, challenging the law. Anne Joseph of the Kentucky Task Force on Hunger saw the fight as a successful test of Jones's character: "There is a side to him that is compassionate and thoughtful and willing to listen." But Lowell Reese, publisher of *Kentucky Roll Call*, a political newsletter in Frankfort, said it exemplified a personal trait of a different sort: "With his political background, you would have thought he would not build political expectations with the public that a realist could see would not occur."[27] Neither of these views is necessarily wrong. The citizen-politician may combine a "political background" with "compassion and thoughtfulness"—and occasionally lose (or modestly win) a landmark political fight.

The adoption of health-care reform put Kentucky at the forefront of a national movement. Governor Jones had notably succeeded where President Clinton would later fail, foreshadowing the national administration's later technique of accepting gradual steps toward universal coverage for all citizens. The adoption of this health-care bill was not a completion of the reform Jones envisioned, but it was a stepping stone which could be built on. Nonetheless, "Jones today says his biggest disappointment was the lack of substantial progress toward 'universal coverage'—providing insurance for the roughly 400,000 uninsured Kentuckians."[28] Although universal coverage was defeated, Jones's initiative was one of the few health-care bills passed in the country.[29]

PARTY LEADER

As titular head of the Democratic Party, Jones was not challenged when he selected as party chair Grady Stumbo, perhaps the most popular Democrat in eastern Kentucky and a former gubernatorial candidate himself. Jones also was not challenged when he tried to set priorities for the state party organization. Unlike Wilkinson, whose supporters had targeted some hostile legislative leaders, Jones did not intervene in legislative primaries, but he did utilize the party organization somewhat effectively to help legislators in general elections. Jones was committed to a revitalization of the state party. Stumbo and vice-chair Gayle Rogers were charged to reinstitute former party activities which had languished under the prior governor—grassroots mobilization for campaigns, voter registration drives, polling and campaign advertising assistance, workshops for aspiring candidates and their key campaign workers. Under Stumbo and Rogers, a new Minority Issues Program was implemented in order to attract more African Americans into party activities. Another large undertaking was an attempt to establish a state party platform, apparently the first ever for Kentucky's Democratic Party.[30]

As noted above, during the Jones administration, especially post-BOPTROT, interaction between the state party and the party's legislative leaders was limited and at times hostile. The Democrat-dominated legislature was flexing its muscles, and its leaders often did not want to be associated with the state party, which they perceived as the governor's vehicle. During the last three years of the Jones administration, although the state party spent about $200,000 on legislative races, legislators raised less than $5,000 for the financially drained state party. Still, the state party, sometimes with legislators' assistance, tried to recruit viable legislative candidates and targeted certain legislative races.

JONES'S OWN APPRAISAL

IN an interview on Kentucky Educational Television at the end of his administration, Jones joked that if he had said, "I want us to have the lowest unemployment rate that the state has had in two decades, I want us to reduce the welfare rolls by 50,000 people, I want us to have our per capita personal income increasing faster than it is in 40 other states, I want to have 2,000 fewer state employees, and I want to have 200,000 more [private sector] jobs statewide, and by the way, I want to pass on a $300 million surplus, and would also like to make certain we have changed the way campaigns are run and gotten gubernatorial succession . . . you would have looked at me and said, 'This guy's in Never Never Land.' But this is what happened."[31]

Brereton C. Jones, the citizen-politician, spent his last days in office touring the state in a leased bus, announcing various projects and receiving thank-yous from supporters. In the final days of his administration, he said "his biggest surprise is that he was able to accomplish so much—reducing the size of government and cutting taxes; establishing new ethics laws and electoral reforms to restore public confidence in government; winning passage of a health reform law; presiding over declining welfare rolls and a healthy state economy that reflects the success of his economic-development policy and has helped produce a growing surplus in state revenue."[32]

---

1. Jones defeated Hopkins 540,468 votes to 294,452 votes in the general election of 1991. For an analysis of the 1991 gubernatorial general election, see Penny M. Miller, *Kentucky Politics and Government: Do We Stand United?* (Lincoln: University of Nebraska Press, 1994), 212–13.

2. Some of the information for this description of the Jones administration is drawn from personal interviews with the former governor on January 24, 1996, February 12, 1997, June 23, 1999, and March 27, 2000.

3. Tom Loftus, "The Jones Administration: An Appraisal," *Louisville Courier-Journal*, December 10, 1995:D1.

4. *Louisville Courier-Journal*, December 10, 1995:A1.

5. A selection committee (including career merit employees) now recommends three finalists based on their qualifications, an attempt to remove political considerations from the contract process, which was an inevitable perception when the finance secretary could award engineering contracts at will—and frequently (if not usually) awarded them to large political contributors.

6. Jack Brammer, Chad Carlton, and Jamie Lucke, "Ethics Code, Health-Care Reform Cornerstones of Jones Years," *Lexington Herald-Leader*, December 10, 1995:A16. Jones received bonuses of more than $16,000 in 1994 and more than $18,000 in 1995.

7. *Lexington Herald-Leader*, December 10, 1995:A16.

8. In 1996 the General Assembly modified campaign finance legislation that was passed during the Jones administration. Changes included raising the maximum amount an individual or PAC can give from $500 to $1,000.

9. Bob Geiger, "600 Attend Fund-Raiser for '87 Debt," *Lexington Herald-Leader*, December 10, 1991:A1, A6.

10. See *The Administration of Governor Brereton C. Jones: 1991–1995*, a state publication cataloging Governor Jones's accomplishments.

11. *Louisville Courier-Journal*, December 10, 1995:D1.

12. The BOPTROT (an acronym coming from the legislature's Business Organizations and Professions committees and trotting-horse-racing legislation) probe was centered around allegations of bribery, extortion, and racketeering in the passage of banking and horse-industry legislation dating back to 1984.

13. Al Cross, Tom Loftus, and Mike Brown, "Jones Calls Probe 'Cleansing Process,'" *Louisville Courier-Journal*, April 3, 1992:A12.

14. *Louisville Courier-Journal*, December 10, 1995:D4.

15. Ibid.

16. Ibid., D1.

17. Senator Rose summarized his feelings as Jones left office by quoting the title of a country music song by Roy Clark: "Thank God and Greyhound." According to Rose, "The last two governors have not understood the separation of powers—that the legislative branch has its own constitutional responsibilities, too. And when these governors didn't get things done, they took it personally." Ibid.

18. Ibid., D4.

19. See *The Administration of Governor Brereton C. Jones.*

20. *Louisville Courier-Journal*, December 10, 1995:D4.

21. Ibid.

22. See *The Administration of Governor Brereton C. Jones.*

23. According to Jones, the press never seemed to understand his actions in lobbying house members to kill the health-care bill. Jones said that it would have been totally irresponsible to encourage legislators to pass a compromise bill which was hastily drafted, without complete knowledge of its contents. Interview with Jones, March 27, 2000.

24. *Lexington Herald-Leader*, December 10, 1995:A16.

25. Ibid.

26. Ibid.

27. Ibid.

28. *Louisville Courier-Journal*, December 10, 1995:D1.

29. Legislators revised Jones's health-care reform legislation in 1996 and 1998. Some provisions of the 1996 act included Health Policy Board abolished, functions given to Cabinet for Health Services; Health Purchasing Alliance retained, with membership voluntary for all state employees and retired teachers; size of companies allowed to join alliance cut from one hundred workers to fifty; exclusion on coverage of pre-existing conditions extended from six to twelve months; modified community rating to be phased in over three years; and those with old pre-reform health policies may keep them a year. Some aspects of the 1994 and 1996 acts that were repealed or amended by the 1998 act included only one offering required of standard benefit plans; abolition of the Health Purchasing Alliance by July 1, 1999; reintroduction of a limited degree of experience rating; the establishment of a high-risk pool to which insurers could gradually move non-group-insured persons with specified diagnoses; and individual market guaranteed issue limited to federally eligible persons, although others could be guaranteed issue within the high-risk pool.

30. In 1993, some tensions began to surface in the Democratic Party over the creation of the first state party platform, discussed in a series of seventeen town forums. Several Louisville party activists and other Clinton/Gore supporters were concerned that Stumbo, a born-again evangelical and

mountain populist, might push for a conservative agenda in order to deny Republicans a free raid on the allegiances of deeply religious Democrats. See *Courier-Journal*, January 17, 1993:D1. According to Pat Goins, executive assistant to Stumbo, the primary issues on the minds of Democrats (emanating from the town forums) were jobs, health care, ethics in government, support for education, and the environment; abortion and gay rights were not even discussed. Interview with Goins, Frankfort, March 2, 1993.

31. *Louisville Courier-Journal*, December 10, 1995:D1; interview with Jones, March 27, 2000.

32. *Louisville Courier-Journal*, December 10, 1995:D1

INAUGURAL ADDRESS

Frankfort / December 10, 1991

LET there be no doubt from the very beginning. Thanks to you, this is a new and different day in Kentucky. This administration is committed to having the most positive, progressive, exciting four years in our state's history. When our term is finished, things will never again be the same in this Commonwealth.

Recognizing that in 1992 we commemorate Kentucky's two-hundredth year of history with our bicentennial celebration,[1] I cannot help but think of all those fifty-three inaugural addresses that have preceded this one. Every new governor has certainly been filled with enthusiasm, probably convinced that his or her remarks were unique and that their wisdom would be acclaimed throughout the ages. Governors have a tendency to think that way. But when all is said and done, that which is said is most often forgotten and the real focus is on that which is actually done.

Bert Combs[2] was a doer—a real doer. History will record that this honorable, dedicated, Kentucky statesman set many standards by which future leaders will be judged. God has taken Bert Combs from this life, but He has also given us something very special in return. He has given us a challenge: a challenge for each of us to rise to a higher level of commitment and understanding, a challenge for politicians to become statesmen, a challenge to substitute common sense and fairness for boastfulness and self-interest.

As the fifty-fourth governor of this Commonwealth,[3] I accept the challenge of this office. I do not boastfully say that I can match the awesome footprints left by Bert Combs, but I do say that I have the courage to try, and I ask for your help. I ask for God's help and I ask for the continued help of Bert Combs.

No one can succeed alone. We must all work together, and the common-sense way to get people to work together is through fair and equal treatment for all of our people in every section of this great Commonwealth.

Over the next four years, I pledge to never forget that the people of Kentucky did not conduct a popularity contest in this year's election; instead we conducted a referendum on a philosophy . . . a philosophy that all Kentuckians are equal in the eyes of our maker, that every section of our state[4] deserves fair and equal treatment, that the purpose of government is to help people to help themselves, that we must unite our people, not divide them, and that there is absolutely no limit to what we can accomplish if we all work together.

We begin on this first day to build our team by saying something to the members of the General Assembly. You have officially come of age. You are equal partners with the judicial and the executive branches of government, and I will work closely with you in a spirit of cooperation. Cooperation and mutual respect will give us a fighting chance to take a national leadership role in providing quality health care for all people. Cooperation and mutual respect will allow us to make the promise of education reform a reality for all Kentucky children. Cooperation and mutual respect will allow us a chance to provide good jobs with good wages for our people. Such logical behavior will surely lead us to agree to change our election laws and dramatically reduce the amount of money that is spent on our elections, to make certain that the merit system[5] is doing what it was intended to do and to give a clear focus to the governance of higher education.

Our administration has already begun to speak in terms of action, not words. Already we have begun to make history. We have appointed more women and more African Americans to cabinet-level positions than any administration in history.[6] Such selections should not be unusual or worthy of special praise, but must be expected of all who might aspire to be governor.

There are so many things that I want to say, but I cannot take the time to say them all today. More importantly, there are so many things that we need to do and we have only four short years in which to do them. So we had best not waste any more time with words. Let us get on with the business at hand. Let us join together to unite this great Commonwealth. Let us set the standards by which all future generations will be judged. There is no limit to what we can accomplish. As a wise man once said, "If the mind can conceive it and the heart can believe it, we can achieve it."

---

1. Kentucky became the Union's fifteenth state on June 1, 1792.

2. Bert T. Combs (1911–91), city attorney, Prestonsburg, 1950; judge, Kentucky Court of Appeals, 1951–55; Democratic gubernatorial candidate, 1955, 1959, 1971; governor of Kentucky, 1959–63; judge, United States Court of Appeals, 6th Circuit, 1967–70; practicing attorney, Louisville and

Lexington, 1970–91. *Who's Who in America, 1974–75* (Chicago, 1975),1:620. Combs filed a lawsuit in 1985 which led to the landmark state supreme court decision declaring the entire state school system unconstitutional.

3. Jones referred to his mentor Combs in many of his later speeches.

4. While Kentucky describes itself as the Bluegrass State, it varies greatly by region. Western Kentucky is primarily rolling hills used for tobacco farming and some strip mining. Central Kentucky, the actual Bluegrass region, consists of soft, grassy fields used for horse farms and tobacco farming. Eastern Kentucky is primarily mountainous and is considered the center of coal mining in Kentucky.

5. Legislation enacting the merit system was drafted and guided through the legislature in 1960 by Commissioner of Personnel Edward Breathitt under the direction of then-Governor Bert T. Combs.

6. During Jones's first year in office, he named four women to head cabinets (one-third of his top-level appointments), putting the female representation in his cabinet in the top fifteen in the United States. Moreover, two of his cabinet appointments were African Americans.

LEGISLATIVE MESSAGES AND STATEMENTS

STATE OF THE COMMONWEALTH ADDRESS
Frankfort / January 13, 1992

I AM honored and proud to be with you on this historic evening to review the state of our Commonwealth and to share with you our blueprint for action in the coming years. As governor, it is my constitutional duty to appear before you from time to time to discuss our problems and to propose solutions.

But this is much more than a duty to me. It is an occasion that marks the beginning of a relationship that I believe will set a new standard for mutual respect and cooperation between the executive and legislative branches.[1] And I think it is only fitting that this new relationship is forged in the year when we are celebrating the two-hundredth anniversary of our statehood. What better tribute could we pay to those courageous men and women who gave us our beginning than to take this important step together?

Although I have been governor for only a short time, I have given considerable thought to the challenges we face. Tonight, I would like to share with you some of our proposals that I believe will help us to meet these challenges together. Everyone in this chamber realizes that we are in a recession.[2] Every one of us has friends, family members, or constituents who are suffering from the tightening bands of economic uncertainty. This national recession is taking a very human toll in the day-to-day struggle it is imposing on our people. It is also taking its toll on our state finances.

More than forty states have cut their budgets in the last year. Many of them have slashed spending for vital programs such as health and human services, education reform, and higher education. Kentucky is not immune to those realities. Never before in our modern history have we faced a financial challenge of the magnitude of the one now before us. We have already taken steps to start reducing the size of government.[3] But we will have to make some very tough choices in the days ahead—choices that in better times we would never consider. We are making those decisions now and in two weeks' time I will come before you again with the result of that process—a balanced budget that reflects my commitment to working our way through these problems.

The key to long-term success for any venture is quality people, and state government is no exception. I am proud to report to the taxpayers of Kentucky that your state government has some of the hardest-working, most qualified people I have ever seen. These employees deserve our thanks and our strong support. I will work with our cabinet secretaries to develop a bonus system that will set rewards for those who reach certain standards. We must also recognize that, like most large enterprises, there are some employees who are not willing to put in a good day's work for a good day's pay and we will change these attitudes or remove these people from the payroll. This is the only way we can fairly deal with the budget crisis that confronts us.

Faced with our painful fiscal circumstances, it would be easy for us to take refuge in the numbers and do nothing. It would be easy for us to be mere caretakers. But I didn't run for governor to do the popular thing or the expedient thing. I ran for governor to do the right thing, to make the tough decisions. We might be broke, but we are not broken. We might have a revenue shortfall,[4] but there is no shortfall of leadership ability in this chamber tonight. We might have a budget deficit, but there is no deficit of courage or spirit here.

We will solve our problems, but not with the same old solutions. Ours will be a different style, and there will be some who will not understand at first. But I have a reasonable request. If your intent is fairness and you want to help solve problems, then join us and judge us on the results. If you have other motives, then do not be offended if we drive on without you. We have so much to do and so little time in which to do it.

I cannot and I will not allow a temporary budget problem to deter us from achieving our goals of making education reform a reality, of giving every child across this Commonwealth a fair start in life, of guaranteeing adequate and affordable health care to every Kentuckian, of establishing a foundation for job creation in every community, of improving the quality of our land, air, and water, and of returning government, honest, ethical government, to the people.

It is time to act and we are prepared to act to work toward our goals. I will soon submit for your consideration proposals that will focus on preserving and creating jobs across our Commonwealth. Our priority will be support for our existing jobs. But we will also seek new business investments for our state.[5] We will recommend enactment of the Kentucky Jobs Development Act[6] to create jobs in technology, communications, and service industries, and to attract corporate headquarters and regional offices. We will locate economic-development offices in east Kentucky and west Kentucky where experts will be charged with developing a plan to preserve and create jobs at the county level. They will also help our county governments make the most of their assets and enhance their development efforts.

I believe we must give even greater attention to an industry that has long been a mainstay of our economy, the coal industry.[7] We will have two experts working full-time in our Economic Development Cabinet to market Kentucky coal throughout the United States and the world.

Officially our statewide unemployment rate is 7.1 percent, but we need to understand that in reality our jobless rate is greater than that. In eastern Kentucky alone, a recent University of Kentucky study determined that actual unemployment was approximately 30 percent, with unemployment in some counties exceeding 50 percent. It is imperative that we act now to alleviate this situation. We must realize that when we help one part of our Commonwealth, we help the entire Commonwealth.

To that end, I am committed to returning 50 percent of the coal severance tax revenues to coal counties.[8] Our budget for the second year of the next biennium will reflect that commitment by starting the process of phasing in the increased return with an objective of reaching the full 50 percent by the end of my term. I believe this additional revenue must be dedicated to helping our coal counties prepare for a future economy when the coal is gone.

As part of our economic-development initiatives, I will also propose a restructuring of our Economic Development Cabinet[9] to establish a governing board that will, for the first time, set statewide goals and keep us on track to achieve them. This board will assure the continuity of our economic-development efforts and take the politics out. I also intend to propose in my budget package an ambitious capital construction program of up to $100 million to revitalize our state parks and re-establish Kentucky as the home of the nation's finest park system. And I want to make it clear that I intend for this money to be spent on Kentucky companies which employ Kentucky workers who will be paid the prevailing wage.

I will continue the efforts I began as lieutenant governor to improve the marketing of Kentucky agricultural products. Agriculture is still our number-one competitive advantage in trade. I intend to work closely with Agriculture Commissioner Ed Logsdon[10] and our agricultural experts at the University of Kentucky on projects to expand and diversify our farm economy and to enhance our marketing efforts of Kentucky agricultural products worldwide. We cannot, however, retain our competitive advantage in agriculture without a major commitment and a long-term investment in research. During my term, we will develop with UK a major new animal research center at Pin Oak Farm.

There is another area of agriculture that is of special interest to me, the horse industry. When I became lieutenant governor four years ago, I could find no documentation on just what the horse industry means to our state. Since then, the University of Kentucky has conducted an economic impact study that concluded that the equine industry in Kentucky accounts for 79,820 jobs in our state. I know that as members of this General Assembly you realize what 79,820 jobs mean to Kentucky. Can you imagine what we would do to encourage 79,000 jobs to come to our state? I believe we should commit ourselves to preserving and protecting this industry with the same zeal we would employ to attract such a prospect. I will offer for your consideration during this session several proposals that will strengthen our thoroughbred industry. I fully recognize that some may say I am interested in this area because of my involvement in the horse industry. To them I would say: any governor who would not do everything in his power to save the jobs of 79,000 Kentuckians ought to be impeached. I am going to do everything I can to preserve and protect those jobs while strengthening a Kentucky industry that is much more than a business. It is very much a part of our heritage and culture. And it will be part of our legacy.

We will, and should, be measured by that legacy. Speaking of legacies, there is nothing that will tell future generations more about us than the decisions we make in education. Kentucky's education reform[11] is an epic saga with thousands of heroes. There are none greater, however, than those of you in this chamber who two years ago had the collective courage to craft the boldest reform effort in this country and to find the revenue to fund its beginning stages.

We cannot allow that courage to leave us unattended now as we move ahead with the next stage of education reform. We cannot and we will not allow tight budgetary times to deter us from fulfilling the covenant that we have with the children of Kentucky. We must strive to maintain in the next fiscal year the essential elements of reform, even if it is at the expense of other worthy programs in government. Then in the following year, we must act with vigor to advance education reform the next step.

Working together we can make education reform a reality. We can effect a social revolution in this state that will guarantee that a child's future is no longer determined by an accident of geography or economic circumstance. The children of farmers and factory workers will have the very same opportunities as the children of the rich and privileged. All children will have open before them, as Ed Prichard[12] said, "the path to a larger life."

To make education reform complete, we must also focus our attention on higher education. We must adopt the same principles in higher education that made our primary and secondary education reform effort the model for the nation. I want to work with you and with the higher education community to devise specific goals for our colleges in instruction, research, and public service. We need to agree on a system of assessing the progress of each institution toward those goals. And those colleges that succeed should ultimately be rewarded through our funding system.

Let there be no misunderstanding; I am not proposing a simplistic testing mechanism, but a thorough assessment of each part of a university's mission to determine progress toward their goals. To be successful, our higher education system must be free of the taint of petty politics. I intend to propose in this session the creation of a nominating commission to select qualified nominees to be recommended to the governor for appointment to university boards and the Council on Higher Education.[13]

This process will remove political considerations from these very important decisions—and I believe it is a change that will have a very positive, lasting effect on higher education in Kentucky. Improvements do not always require more money. Now is the time to demand this action. Because I believe it is so important, I am unwilling to wait for this change or to phase it in gradually. That is why as part of my package I will be asking you for the authority to reorganize immediately every board of trustees and board of regents in our state. Then every seat in every board will be subject to the non-political nominating process I have outlined.

With this reorganization in place, we will have eliminated almost immediately the influence of politics on our university boards. Then we can direct our attention to effecting meaningful change for the improvement of higher education. All the spending we can muster on education reform, and all of our efforts in higher education, will ultimately be for naught unless all of our children have a fair start on life.

Fully one-fourth of our children are born into and live in poverty.[14] Every day of their lives they know first-hand the pain and despair of poverty. Many of the parents of these children have known nothing but that same debilitating poverty throughout their own lives. For these children to have a fair start, we must not only help them but provide encouragement and assistance to their parents. I am committed to our early childhood education program adopted as part of our historic reform package. I will also put my best efforts to work to see to it that sufficient funds are made available for our new family resource centers.[15]

I am also committed to the parents[16] of these children. We must give them a stake in society to enable them to pass along to their children the proper attitudes and values. That is why I will make every effort to avoid, even in next year's difficult budget, any cuts in our state and federal welfare reform programs. These programs are providing educational training and job opportunities and are concrete examples of my belief that government should help people to help themselves.

We must also recognize our responsibility to senior citizens. The newly formed Association of Older Kentuckians—AOK[17]—will have the full support of this administration. And we will work during our four years to put programs in place that will help all Kentuckians lead vital, independent lives as they grow older. Too many Kentuckians—especially women and children—awaken every day to lives that are darkened by the threat of violence in their own homes. We must act immediately on their behalf and our administration will lead the effort to strengthen our laws against domestic violence.

There is no area more clearly in need of government action than health care. We must begin now to reach a consensus for solving the long-term problems of providing affordable, quality care for all our citizens. While we must take care of immediate, acute-care needs, our focus should be on improving the general health of our citizens over the long run. The humane approach is a coordinated primary preventive health-care system linked with comprehensive school health education. I anticipate a coordinated system that uses the best of private medicine and public health and integrates private competitive insurance with governmental support. It is imperative that we gain control of health-care costs. There are some things we can do today to more aggressively pursue our goals of improved care for our citizens. A recent report of the Cabinet for Human Resources, "Healthy Kentuckians 2000," contains numerous recommendations to improve our health status. I am directing the secretary for Human Resources to place major emphasis on the following goals:

To reduce the infant mortality rate;
To reduce the fetal death rate;
To reduce the maternal mortality rate;
To reduce low birth weight;
To reduce deaths from uterine and cervical cancer;
To promote the immunization of every child.

We will accomplish these goals by putting our major focus on preventive health care.

You know by now that I believe in consensus building to solve problems. I believe that this is the kind of process we need to find a way to make health care available and affordable to all our citizens. Looking for villains and pointing fingers at each other will not solve the problem. Bringing everyone to the table—consumers, providers, business, labor, government—talking it out and building a consensus is the way to solve any problem.

Our administration will provide leadership to the consensus-building process. We have a unique opportunity in Kentucky to show the nation what can be done to reform our health-care system. Kentucky's population is small enough to allow us to plan efficiently and effectively. Our geographic area is small enough to ensure that people in one part of the state can communicate with people in the other parts. I will appoint a special task force for comprehensive health-care reform. This task force will be charged with developing reform recommendations this year because this issue requires action as soon as possible. I will then ask you to consider those recommendations in a special legislative session.[18]

In the area of environmental protection,[19] our mandate from the people is clear and compelling. We will enforce the law without fear and without favor. To all who will commit themselves to seeking solutions to our common problems, we extend an open invitation to join us in the search for new ideas that work. With this invitation, we expect all parties to bring to the table only an open mind and a willingness to become part of the solution. To skeptics who argue that this new approach will not work, we submit a challenge: judge us by our actions.

The recent resolution of the Lake Cumberland[20] controversy teaches us that new solutions to environmental problems are not only possible, they are attainable. We rejoice in the hope that this achievement inspires. And we pledge to be patient in the difficulties that will come as we seek to extend the boundaries of possibility into other areas of environmental conflict. We have a leadership in the Cabinet for Natural Resources and Environmental Protection that has the capacity and the commitment to set the standards for future generations.

This epic of conservation and stewardship is not an option or a luxury, it is a necessity. Our disposable society must change if our children and grandchildren are to have access to the clean air, land, and water necessary for life. Disposable values, like disposable bottles, merely shift the costs of the cleanup effort to the next generation. And we will come before you in this session with our proposals—including a bottle bill—that will reflect our recognition that the time to act is now.

I have saved for last the discussion of an issue that is very important to me—governmental reform.[21] Thirty-two years ago in his inaugural address, Gov. Bert Combs identified as one of his chief goals the "Elevation of the moral and political tone of government." His goal must be our goal as well. We must give back government to the people. We must re-establish our government as being dedicated to the high ideals of public service rather than the low-down deals of petty politics.

We must take immediate action on campaign finance and election reform.[22] I will propose in this session a tough campaign finance bill that will lower the maximum campaign contribution to $100, and attempt to lower the total amount of money that is spent by providing for a system of public financing for gubernatorial and lieutenant governor elections. And we will propose that a runoff primary be instituted for those two offices.

I favor gubernatorial succession[23] and will enthusiastically support a constitutional amendment on succession that will not apply to me as the sitting governor. I will also support a constitutional amendment[24] that would reduce the number of elected statewide offices to four: the governor, lieutenant governor, auditor of public accounts, and attorney general. As I have said in the past, I favor granting to the lieutenant governor the duties of the current offices of treasurer and secretary of state. I have already issued, by executive order, a code of ethics[25] for executive branch officials. I will present a bill in this session to establish that code as a permanent part of state law.

And I believe we must reduce the number of elections[26] we have in Kentucky—moving all of our elections to even-numbered years. I feel very strongly about each and every one of these reform measures. I believe they are necessary to restore the public's confidence in government and its elected and appointed officials.

Restoring the public's confidence must be our objective, and to do that we must leave for our successors a government that is more efficient and effective than the one we inherited. Our administration will institute a comprehensive review of the structure, organization, and function of government. I will ask Auditor Ben Chandler[27] to assist in this effort to streamline government and make it responsive to the needs of Kentuckians.

As we enter our third century, we must demand more of ourselves and of each other. We must willingly embrace new ideas and make these marble halls echo with a new spirit. But I caution you, do not confuse compassion for another human being with approval of that person's actions. Do not confuse a desire to be fair and build a consensus with a lack of leadership. The leadership from the governor's office will be real. It will be fair.

And it will be successful. Together, we can create a progressive government, a caring society, and a robust economy that will be the envy of the nation. Thank you.

---

1. The relationship between the executive and the legislature had eroded over the course of the previous three administrations: John Y. Brown Jr. (1979–83), Martha Layne Collins (1983–87), and Wallace Wilkinson (1987–91).

2. The U.S. economy was in a recession from 1989 through 1992.

3. For the ten years preceding the Jones administration, the number of permanent, full-time employees in state government increased at an average rate of 450 per year. Jones stopped this upward trend and reversed it. During his administration, the number of permanent, full-time employees was trimmed primarily through attrition by over 2,000.

4. A revenue shortfall of more than $155 million resulted from the national economic recession, the allocation of the 1990 $1.3 billion tax increase, the commitment of one-time windfalls from the lottery, and the sluggish state economy. The shortfall was covered through cuts in higher education, construction projects, and some state agency budgets.

5. Governor Jones proposed and won approval in 1992 for tax incentives to attract new jobs and save existing ones, through the new Kentucky Jobs

Development Authority and the new Kentucky Industrial Revitalization Authority. At the end of the Jones administration there were 200,000 more Kentuckians working than on Jones's inauguration day. During the Jones administration, Kentucky's per capita income grew faster than the national average and the unemployment rate was the lowest in two decades.

6. Legislation proposed during the 1992 General Assembly resulted in the Kentucky Jobs Development Act. This program became one of the most innovative and comprehensive job-creation programs in the nation.

7. The U.S. market for Kentucky coal declined after federal acid rain legislation, a part of the Clean Air Act of 1990, mandated that sulfur dioxide emissions be reduced by 20 percent. This reduction was to be accomplished through the use of low-sulfur coal or the installation of expensive pollution control equipment, called "scrubbers." Because Kentucky coal has a high sulfur content, many users opted for the lower-sulfur-content coal of Wyoming, instead of installing expensive scrubbers necessary for use with Kentucky coal.

8. During the 1992 General Assembly, despite severe budget shortfalls, the legislature approved a larger, phased-in return of coal severance tax money to coal counties. Twelve percent of the coal severance tax was being returned to coal counties in 1992, in 1993 the level was increased to fifteen percent, and in 1994 the level was increased to 21 percent.

9. During the 1992 General Assembly, Governor Jones and legislators, led by State Representative Bill Lear, reorganized the state's economic-development apparatus. All economic-development functions previously controlled by the governor were transferred to a twelve-member board, the Kentucky Economic Development Partnership, led by the governor as chair. Remaining positions are filled by the secretary of the Economic Development Cabinet, appointed by the governor from a list of people recommended by the board, two members selected from the governor's cabinet, and eight members chosen from the private sector, at least one from each of the state's six congressional districts.

10. Ed Logsdon (1947–), Edmonson County judge-executive (Democrat); director of shows and fairs for the agriculture department in 1985; employee of the state transportation department, 1988–91; commissioner of agriculture, 1992–95; commissioner of the vehicle regulation department, 1996– ; farmer.

11. A 1989 Kentucky Supreme Court decision found the Kentucky primary and secondary educational system unconstitutional and forced the legislature to redesign the entire system. In response to this mandate, the Kentucky Education Reform Act (KERA) was adopted by the 1990 General Assembly.

12. Edward Fretwell Prichard Jr. (1915–84), law clerk to U.S. Supreme Court Justice Felix Frankfurter; Immigration Service in the Justice Department; assistant to the U.S. attorney general, the War Production Board legal counsel, and adviser to President Roosevelt, 1942; appointed by Governor Breathitt to the Council on Higher Education, 1966; Prichard Committee for Academic Excellence named in his honor.

13. Jones succeeded in removing politics from the process by which trustees and regents are appointed to state university boards. Under his leadership, the General Assembly approved a new system in which an independent panel of respected citizens selects nominees based on their ability to improve higher education. The governor then makes the final appointments by selecting from the list of qualified nominees.

14. As of the 1990 U.S. Census, Kentucky ranked 10th in the percentage of people receiving public aid, fourth in food stamps, and forty-second in per capita income. *Lexington Herald-Leader*, March 1, 1992. Following a measured decline in poverty from 1969 to 1979, Kentucky's poverty rate rose from 17.6 percent in 1979 to 19 percent in 1989. In 1994 the General Assembly passed Senate Concurrent Resolution 74, creating the Commission on Poverty, a panel of citizens and legislators responsible for recommending changes in state programs to improve responsiveness to the poor.

15. Family resource centers are a provision of the Kentucky Education Reform Act (KERA).

16. Kentucky became the first state to elevate adult education services to a department level when the Department of Adult Education and Literacy was created. Jones supported a 50 percent increase in funding for adult education programs.

17. AOK was established in 1989 with the help of then-Lt. Gov. Brereton Jones, his staffers, and individuals from the private and public sectors. A helpline for senior citizens was created, and a radio show hosted by Al Smith featured topics that assisted the elderly.

18. Jones called nine special legislative sessions, a record for any single-term Kentucky governor. The 1993 special session on health care failed to enact a reform bill; however, the bill was passed after the 1994 session of the General Assembly and signed into law on April 15, 1994.

19. Governor Jones actively supported several bills that passed during the 1994 session of the General Assembly that strengthened the stewardship of Kentucky's natural resources. Legislation addressed improvements to the Commonwealth's drinking water, soil erosion, and the preservation of Kentucky's rapidly disappearing farmland.

20. The Lake Cumberland controversy revolved around the town of Jamestown's request in 1988 to use a seven-mile pipeline to pump treated sewage directly into Lake Cumberland. Fears of damage to the lake and the tourism industry were pitted against concerns that Fruit of the Loom (the area's largest employer, with 3,100 workers), which sent 1.7 million gallons of waste a day to the Jamestown treatment plant, would have to close or cut back without the pipeline. A compromise was reached between the two interests, and Jones was given much of the credit for defusing the controversy. *Lexington Herald-Leader,* February 4, 1993, A:1, 8.

21. Most legislation on government ethics failed in the 1992 General Assembly. An FBI probe, code-named BOPTROT (an acronym coming from the legislature's *B*usiness *O*rganizations and *P*rofessions committees and

*trot*ting-horse-racing legislation), became public in the closing days of the 1992 session. The probe centered on allegations of bribery, extortion, and racketeering in the passage of banking and horse-industry legislation dating back to 1984. The investigation led to the conviction of fifteen current or former state legislators. In February 1993, in the aftermath of BOPTROT, a special session of the General Assembly was called by Governor Jones to reconsider the 1992 ethics legislation. Legislators passed a sweeping reform package which, among other things, limits each lawmaker to receiving $100 in food and drink a year from each lobbyist, limits the amount of PAC money that a legislative candidate can receive to $5,000 or 35 percent of the candidate's total contributions, whichever is greater, and prohibits former lawmakers from becoming lobbyists until two years after they leave the General Assembly. These provisions gave Kentucky some of the nation's toughest laws on legislative ethics and campaign finance. Although some changes were made to the ethics code in the 1996 General Assembly, Kentucky's code is still considered one of the toughest in the United States. Only Hawaii, Tennessee, and West Virginia rank as high in terms of overall strength. Most states, including Kentucky, prohibit contingent fee lobbying, have conflict of interest statutes, and restrict the use of public resources for private gain. Most states prohibit campaign contributions by lobbyists only during legislative sessions. Only Kentucky and South Carolina prohibit campaign contributions by lobbyists at any time. Thirty-six states, along with Kentucky, have independent ethics commissions. Only twenty state ethics bodies, including Kentucky's, have the power to initiate an investigation against a legislator without a complaint being filed.

22. During the 1992 legislative session, Jones pushed through a campaign finance reform law. The law reduced the maximum individual contribution received by any state or local official from $4,000 to $500 and required candidates for governor and lieutenant governor to run together. In addition, the law established public financing of campaigns, providing $1.2 million in state funds for candidates who raise $600,000, and established a total spending limit per candidate of $1.8 million.

23. As of December 1991 Kentucky governors could not serve consecutive terms. In 1992, a constitutional amendment was adopted that allowed governors to serve a maximum of two consecutive four-year terms. Previous governors failed at getting this amendment passed largely because they intended to use it as a means to run for office after their first term as governor. Jones structured the amendment so as to exclude himself from the benefits of succession.

24. The amendment which was adopted eliminated only one statewide elected office, that of the superintendent of public instruction. Kentucky currently has seven statewide elected offices.

25. The ethics code guarantees that those in positions of authority will not make personal profits from their public service. The ethics code was

subsequently passed into law by the 1992 General Assembly to apply to future administrations.

26. A modified version of this bill was adopted in 1992. The campaign finance reform law that was passed restructured Kentucky's election schedule by designating one "election-free" year out of every four.

27. Albert Benjamin "Ben" Chandler III (1960–), B.A. and J.D. (1986), University of Kentucky; grandson of former Kentucky governor A.B "Happy" Chandler; associate in law firm of Brown, Todd & Heyburn, Lexington, Kentucky, and Reeves & Graddy, Versailles, Kentucky; elected Kentucky state auditor, 1991–95; elected Kentucky attorney general, 1995–99; re-elected, 1999–2003; Democrat. *Who's Who in America 2000*, 54th ed. (New Providence, N.J., 1999).

EXECUTIVE BUDGET MESSAGE TO THE GENERAL ASSEMBLY

Frankfort / February 6, 1992

THREE weeks ago I stood before you in this chamber to share the vision I have for our Commonwealth in the coming years. I spoke then of a new spirit that, together, we must generate to move our great state into the 21st century with pride, prosperity, and a renewed dedication to public service. This spirit will be borne of cooperation between our branches of government. It will require much of us as we jointly strive to make the right decisions on behalf of the women, men, and children whose interests we are here to serve.

None of these decisions will be more important than the ones we make on our spending priorities for the next two years.[1] Tonight, I want to share with you our administration's budget recommendations for the 1992–94 biennium. These recommendations come at a time when our resources have been severely limited by the national recession. They reflect the reality of revenue projections that show we will have approximately the same amount of money available to spend in the next fiscal year that we are spending this year.

And while our resources remain flat, our obligations continue to grow. Federal and state mandates in education, the environment, and health care require hundreds of millions of new dollars that we simply do not have available. As a result, we have many difficult choices to make. We could choose to cut the budgets of all state agencies and tell the children and parents of this state that education reform will have to wait. To balance this budget, we could slash programs for the poor and the needy. We could do just enough to get by and hope for better times. But we are not adopting that approach. The people of Kentucky have elected us to lead, to move forward to a truly progressive society and a robust economy. If we use hard economic times as an excuse to avoid hard policy decisions, we will have defaulted on our obligation to lead. And that's just not going to happen. The budget I am presenting tonight reflects our best efforts to redirect the spending and the policies of state government. It also reflects and furthers those areas of highest priority for our government: fulfilling the promise of education reform; giving every child a fair start on life; improving access to affordable, quality health care for every Kentuckian; and providing a foundation for economic development in every Kentucky community.

OUR plan is predicated on three major principles:

First, there will be no tax increase proposed. We must deal with our problems within our existing tax base.

Second, we will take appropriate, necessary actions to control the cost of government. Our major task lies in balancing the budget in the first year of the biennium. We will use a combination of selective rollbacks of salaries, a reduction in the number of employees, and shifts in spending away from the central office in Frankfort and into the field and the direct delivery of services. Massive layoffs will be avoided. But selective cutbacks will be necessary.

Third, we will position our state to take advantage of a better year in 1994—a year that will get us on track again to provide the services, programs, infrastructure, and economic opportunity that Kentuckians expect and deserve from their state government.

While we expect 1994 to be a better year, we recognize that the strength of Kentucky's economy will reflect the condition of the national economy. We are committed to working our way through this fiscal challenge. But our task will be easier or harder depending on the actions of the federal government. We're doing what needs to be done in Kentucky. Our budget—while tight—is balanced. And I strongly believe that a change in policy in Washington—a change that will result in a balanced federal budget—is what Kentucky and all states need to ensure long-term prosperity.

We will recommend some bold initiatives in the second year of the biennium. At least two of these will start taking shape tonight but will await full implementation until an extraordinary session of this General Assembly is convened later in the year. These two are a complete restructuring of our health-care system and a revitalization of Kentucky's parks system.[2]

As I mentioned earlier, we have had to make several tough choices to obtain the funds necessary to address the highest priorities of government. We have recommended cuts in most areas of government. We have tried in every case to do this thoughtfully and with due regard for the mission of each agency. I believe that these cuts are manageable. They will, however, challenge every cabinet secretary and program manager in government. I ask, therefore, that you provide each policymaker with the flexibility necessary to administer a lean, smaller budget. The cabinet officers and other top administrators will face major challenges in the next two years. They will need to have your support in managing the workforce in the most effective way and in using the funds you provide most productively. We have structured the draft Appropriations Bill for the Executive Branch to reflect the need for both austerity and flexibility.

Unfortunately, we have been forced to suspend some statutory obligations, such as the 5 percent mandate for state employee salary raises. We have also used every other fund source in government to augment the General Fund—including $29 million in each year of the biennium from road funds to finance part of the State Police budget and to step up efforts by the Revenue Cabinet to collect road fund taxes. We will also recommend that surplus funds generated by certain fees and charges be transferred into the General Fund. In a number of cases, we have incorporated recommendations for organizational realignment in the budget in the expectation that cost savings will result. These actions, in concert, have enabled us to redirect state spending into our highest-priority areas. They have also given us the ability to manage our budget better than many of the states suffering similar fiscal and economic difficulties.

As you have heard me say many times, education is my highest priority. We must find the means to move ahead with education reform, even in the midst of this recession. Historic opportunities do not always pick the most convenient times to present themselves. We must act now because the opportunity is before us now. We will not, we cannot, break our covenant on education reform with the children of Kentucky.

Our budget plan has enhanced the most important elements of education reform. There will be no reduction in the basic per-pupil grant to local school districts in the SEEK program[3] in 1993. We will provide sufficient funding in fiscal 1994 for a 3 percent increase in the SEEK base funding. Moreover, we have proposed full funding for the Tier I equalization program[4] at a level of nearly $160 million over the next biennium, an increase of more than $100 million above the current biennium. As you know, the Tier I program provides state funds to those local school districts that raise additional local revenues to enhance their educational offerings.

These state funds are weighted to provide the greatest assistance to the least-affluent school districts. Tier 1, as much as any other program, promotes the dual goals of excellence and equity embodied in our education reform effort.

Our pre-kindergarten program[5] is vital to the long-term success of education reform. If funded and administered properly, this program can give many Kentucky children a fair start on life. With the $33 million provided in fiscal 1993 and the $37 million recommended for 1994, we will be able to serve approximately 80 percent of the eligible at-risk children in the first year of the biennium and 90 percent in the second year.

To increase the availability of social services and health services to those schoolchildren most in need, we have provided for $48.3 million over the biennium for the family and youth services centers.[6] Our plan will allow us to maintain the other important elements of the education reform package. Not every program has been funded at the requested levels, but every program has been preserved. This has been done at a time when other states are cutting their education efforts. Three examples warrant mentioning: the technology program, the student assessment program, and the school rewards fund.[7]

Currently, $48 million is available for the design and implementation of a long-range technology plan for elementary and secondary education. Our budget will preserve that funding and increase it by $15 million over the next biennium to provide a $63 million fund for the technology plan. While this amount of new funding is below the requested level, it evidences a significant commitment to a program with tremendous long-term potential.

Our budget allows for full funding of the biennial request for the student assessment program. Accurately measuring how well our children are learning is vital to continued educational progress. Under our plan, $11.7 million will be directed toward that effort in the next biennium. The current funding of $30 million for the school rewards program will be preserved. Moreover, we propose adding $15 million to that trust fund during the next biennium. The other state programs in elementary and secondary education have been maintained. While all do not reflect the requested levels, sufficient funds will be available to ensure continued progress.

We have also preserved the funding levels for vocational education.[8] Additional funding of $5 million for staffing and operations in fiscal year 1994 will allow us to take full advantage of the eight new or expanded advanced technical and vocational schools you authorized in the 1990 session.

Our education reform efforts will not be complete if we ignore the critical role libraries play in supporting our teachers and students. Indeed, one of the major goals of reform is to make students more independent in their learning and to prepare them for a lifetime of self-sufficiency and individual productivity. To this end, I am increasing state aid to our public libraries 12.5 percent in 1993 and an additional 11 percent in 1994. For the first time since this body adopted the state aid reform bill in 1986, the Executive Budget will meet the fifty-three cents per capita funding formula established by statute.

We have also recommended full funding of the state contribution to the teachers' retirement fund and full funding of the supplemental contribution required by statute. We have asked that a portion of that supplemental contribution be used to provide necessary funding for the medical insurance program for retired teachers.

Our commitment to education and education reform must not diminish. Our recommendations will enable us to move to the next step in education reform. And they will ensure that Kentucky's education system remains a model for the nation.

To enable us to fund our education reform efforts in elementary and secondary education, we have had to recommend that the budgets of our four-year institutions be reduced by 5 percent in fiscal year 1993. This decision is personally painful to me because of my involvement, interest, and commitment in higher education. It is, however, the right decision under the circumstances. And I will do everything in my power to more than make up for this cut in the second biennium of our administration.

Our four-year institutions received increases in their state funding of 22.1 percent during the 1990–92 biennium. Even after budget cutbacks in the prior administration, state funding for these institutions increased by 15.2 percent during this biennium. While I know it will not be easy, I also know that the four-year schools have management flexibility and other sources of funds that should help them through the next fiscal year. Our budget plan recommends a restoration of a portion of those reductions through a 3 percent across-the-board spending increase in fiscal 1994.

Despite the limited money available for higher education, we must press ahead with our accountability and assessment efforts. Funding of $2.4 million has been provided to the Council on Higher Education[9] for this effort during the next biennium. This must be a cooperative effort with the higher education community. For this reason, a significant portion of this funding will be provided to the individual campuses in the form of grants to implement a system of assessing each institution's progress in establishing and meeting their goals in instruction, research, and public service.

Our budget plan sets forth a recommendation that community-college funding be preserved intact in fiscal year 1993 and increased by 3 percent in fiscal 1994. Our community-college system[10] has experienced a remarkable 109 percent growth in enrollment during the last ten years. Many of those new students have been "non-traditional" students who were seeking additional education to help them find or keep jobs. The community colleges also prepare thousands of students annually to continue their education at one of our four-year universities. They are truly the people's colleges and are doing a great job of making educational opportunities available across our Commonwealth.

We cannot have a truly progressive society unless government helps those who are least able to help themselves. We cannot say that we are providing true economic opportunity for all unless government assists those who want to work their way out of poverty. That is why we have devoted special attention to the budget for the Cabinet for Human Resources. The General Fund budget of the cabinet will, according to our budget plan, increase by 20.9 percent over the biennium.

Other states experiencing our national economic turmoil have reduced their budget deficits or balanced their budgets by slashing spending on health and human service programs. Such thinking is, as we know, insensitive and shortsighted. Many programs and services in this cabinet are preventive in nature and actually save us money in the long run. That is why it is in our best interests to preserve and protect them.

To obtain sufficient resources for health and human service programs, we have cut budgets for administration and related services within the Cabinet for Human Resources. We have eliminated positions in central offices to enable us to add more funding for beneficial programs and to hire more people in the field to provide needed assistance.

A task force I will announce soon will study our health-care system and make recommendations to me that will form the basis of legislation to be proposed to you in an extraordinary session. Health-care access and preventive health-care measures will be two important issues for that group. Our budget plan for health services focuses on those issues.

Medical experts tell us that preventive health care is perhaps the most effective way to promote good health at the lowest cost. We have recommended that $3 million in new funds over the biennium be devoted to preventive care. That new money will enable our local health departments to expand their programs for preconceptional care, well-child care, nutrition services, family planning, immunization, breast and cervical cancer, and other maternal- and child-health programs.

I have already restored $2.1 million of budget cuts imposed by the previous administration in the area of health services, and I want to thank Rep. Tom Burch[11] for bringing to my attention the impact of those cuts. With that funding restored, assistance can be preserved for AIDS patients; immunization programs can be preserved fully; grants can be maintained for local emergency medical services; newborn intensive-care programs at UK and U of L can be preserved as well as the indigent prenatal program and the children and youth program at U of L; and the high-risk infant program can stay intact.

The medical card is the passport for the poorest Kentuckians to secure entry into the health-care system. It is estimated by the end of the biennium that approximately half a million people will be enrolled in the Medicaid program.[12] Medicaid will require a commitment of more than $915 million in state funds to maintain services at these current levels over the next two years. Although it was difficult, with our present revenue picture, to find these dollars, I could not turn my back on those Kentuckians who rely on their state government for medical care. I found the dollars and can assure all recipients that we will continue to provide the full array of Medicaid services to those eligible for medical assistance. In addition, for the first time all medically necessary services identified in preventive health checkups will be covered by the Medicaid plan.

We have recommended that payments to hospitals under our disproportionate share provider assessment program be reduced to enable us to have sufficient resources to preserve our Medicaid program intact. Without these additional funds our Medicaid program could not be continued without reducing benefits, which I just could not tolerate.

I am also going to ask that those hospitals receiving additional Medicaid payments through the disproportionate share plan provide outpatient services as well as the inpatient services they currently provide free of charge for those Kentuckians who do not qualify for Medicaid, whose incomes are 100 percent of poverty or below. This should assure that indigent Kentuckians will be afforded the full array of services provided through hospitals.

The mentally ill have all too often been the most neglected patient population in the health-care system. Programs serving these patients generally lag behind the rest of health care in the good times and are the most vulnerable to cuts when dollars are scarce. We have restored $2.8 million of current-year budget cuts in the mental-health system.

State funding for mental health and mental retardation will increase from $104 million to $124 million over the next biennium. Of that amount, $2 million in both years of the biennium will be devoted to expansion of the contracts with our fourteen regional community health comprehensive care centers. One million dollars from the general fund will be devoted to staff expansion at our residential facilities. Our rape crisis center program will be expanded to every region of our Commonwealth through an additional $676,000 in funding over the biennium. We will provide $5.1 million in fiscal year 1993 and $10.2 million of general funds the following year to enable new group homes and other new facilities to be opened and maintained during the next biennium.

We intend to provide strong support for those who are seeking to work their way out of poverty. Our educational and job training and placement efforts under the auspices of the Federal Family Support Act will be expanded from thirty-two to ninety-two counties. We will not cut AFDC benefits in this time of economic trouble. Moreover, we have recommended increased funding to provide for continuation of our state welfare reform effort that allows those welfare recipients who gain employment to retain medical coverage and income supplementation while they move toward self-sufficiency.

Domestic stress increases with economic difficulties. Thus, expansion of programs that deal with and prevent that stress deserve special attention now. Our budget plan calls for an expansion of $500,000 in fiscal year 1993 and $750,000 in fiscal year 1994 for spouse abuse centers. We have recommended that our Family Preservation program be expanded by $2.6 million over the biennium. Under our plan, Intensive Family Based Services programs would be expanded by $500,000 in each year of the biennium. We have also asked for new spending in the amount of $1,259,000 to expand the protective service social worker complement by fifty. This will increase greatly our ability to respond promptly to reported child abuse.

If we are to have enough money over the long term to operate government and create a society in which all have true economic opportunity, we must spare no effort to create jobs. We cannot wait on Washington to act. We must help ourselves now. I am proposing a $100 million bond issue for your consideration for the second year of the next biennium. The proceeds of this issue will be devoted to major capital construction improvements at our state parks and recreation areas. Our first task is to study our tourism and recreation needs in every area of the Commonwealth. Based on that study, I will then recommend specific appropriations for particular projects later this year in an extraordinary session.

It is important that any new parks, lodges, and other attractions considered for addition to the state parks system be solid investments that have a clear chance to be successful and profitable. We cannot afford to waste this opportunity. There is no sense in spending our resources on projects that will simply require a perpetual public subsidy. In addition, we must take advantage of this opportunity to address the need to upgrade and renovate existing park facilities which have deteriorated over the past thirty years. This is not a time for massive expansion—but a time to return to the highest standards of quality.

These funds will enable us once again to have the finest state park and recreation system in the United States. More important, these funds will be used to create jobs—good-paying construction jobs to be followed by permanent positions at our parks and recreation areas. Of course, more important are the off-site economic benefits that a fine state park can anchor. This bond issue will enable us to build projects like the golf course at Jenny Wiley State Park, the campground and boating facilities at Yatesville Lake, the lodge at Kincaid Lake State Park, the beach at Paintsville Lake, and the improvements at Ben Hawes State Park.[13]

There are many Kentucky communities that do not have the advantage of being the home of a state park or a large factory. Those communities need to build a foundation for economic development. And they need money to develop infrastructure and site locations to attract and keep businesses. Nowhere is this need greater than in our coal counties. These counties are facing the immediate challenge to diversify their economic base. They need assistance, and they need it now—not years from now. That is why I am committed to doing everything possible to return 50 percent of the severance tax revenues to coal counties to be used for infrastructure needs. And that is why I want to begin the process right now. Our budget plan proposes increasing from 12 percent to 15 percent the amount of coal severance tax funds set aside for coal counties in the first year of the biennium. And we are calling for an increase to 18 percent the following year. This amounts to more than $15 million in new revenues for the coal counties in the next biennium.

It is important that we get started on this program now—even under our current financial conditions. We cannot afford to wait to begin. For many years, our coal-producing counties have experienced far worse conditions than we now face as a Commonwealth. The true unemployment in our Appalachian counties averages in excess of 30 percent, with some of those counties having a true unemployment rate in excess of 50 percent. And our western Kentucky coal counties are just as deserving—and hurting just as much. We must understand the plight of a young person in a coal county who must leave home and look elsewhere for a good job and a bright future. We must act now to create a new economy for our coal counties. This means more than simply providing additional funding under the existing formula for coal tax distribution. The additional funds must be targeted to infrastructure and economic development. I will support legislation you are considering to do just that. I am proud to recommend this very important step.

Communities throughout our Commonwealth also need help in creating that foundation for economic development. Government is an essential partner with the private sector and with local communities in making strategic investments in people, institutions, and infrastructure to create and maintain jobs.

I am recommending $30 million in new bonding authority for the Kentucky Infrastructure Authority to enable it to provide the necessary financial assistance to communities interested in laying this foundation for creating and preserving jobs. This will match over $100 million in federal funds and allow us to extend vital water, sewer, and other fundamentals of economic development into more communities. We all recognize how important transportation is to economic development. Our budget proposes that an additional $150 million of bonds be sold in year 1993 to continue the progress on high-priority road projects initiated during the 1990 session. You and I have made a commitment to the people of Kentucky to build these roads and, together, we will honor it.

We will also take full advantage of the new Federal Highway Act and the additional funds Kentucky can attract. We will minimize these funds and continue to match every federal dollar that we can reasonably get. We will continue an ambitious resurfacing and maintenance program to take care of our existing network of highways and bridges. We will, however, cut back on unnecessary mowing to allow more money to be spent directly on maintenance and reconstruction.

Because of our fiscal situation, we must be judicious in the use of bond funding for capital projects. Our budget plan sets forth reasonable capital construction recommendations. These recommendations are directed toward maintenance of our current physical plant and construction of new facilities that have already been partially funded or that have significant local and private support. We are recommending funding in fiscal 1994 for the next phase of the expansion of the south wing of the Kentucky Fair and Exposition Center at a cost of approximately $25 million.[14] We also recommend an expenditure of $8 million in addition to the $10 million already authorized for the regional events center at Murray.

In addition, we have requested that $12.5 million be appropriated for waterfront development in Louisville. The availability of these funds is contingent upon our receiving commitments of at least $12.5 million in private contributions toward the effort. Because of strong fiscal financial commitments, we have recommended that $1 million be appropriated in fiscal 1994 for design work for the Northern Kentucky Convention Center.[15]

This is not the time for a large number of new building projects in higher education. We have recommended authorization for three new projects only. We request that the University of Kentucky be authorized to spend approximately $12 million of privately raised funds in this biennium to begin the Commonwealth Library project at the Lexington campus. The library will be truly a statewide asset and the impressive amount of private funds already raised by the University of Kentucky shows significant support for this project. I recognize that there are many other worthy projects, such as the Sanders-Brown Center on Aging, that need and deserve our support. Unfortunately, we will not be able to move ahead on those until some later time.

We have recommended that design funds be made available in fiscal 1994 for a new building at the Hazard Community College and for a new classroom building at Ashland Community College. We have also recommended that $30 million worth of borrowing authority be granted to the School Facilities Construction Commission during the biennium.

One of the fastest-growing areas of the state budget for more than a decade has been corrections. Over the next biennium it is estimated that we will have approximately a 16 percent increase in our prison population. This translates into 1,680 additional felons for whom the Commonwealth will be responsible. The budget I have proposed will provide for this projected growth. We will use a combination of methods to house felons involving existing institutions, greater reliance on county jails that have available space and meet proper standards, and private contract facilities. We will design Phase II of the Muhlenberg County Prison and plan to open Phase I near the end of the biennium.

As you know, I am recommending the consolidation of the Corrections Cabinet into the Justice Cabinet. I believe this will save administrative costs and provide better direction for our criminal justice efforts. In doing so, I intend to preserve our commitment to the Kentucky State Police. Despite the fiscal situation, we will not reduce the ranks of the State Police officers at all. In fact, the budget cut in fiscal year 1993 for State Police will be held to just 2.5 percent. I am confident that the service level provided by the State Police and the entire Justice Cabinet will continue in its present excellent fashion.

We also cannot diminish our level of support for the environment. This budget funds and supports the continuation of the ambitious Environmental Management Plan begun in 1990. It maintains our support for surface mining reclamation and enforcement consistent with the national Wildlife Federation Settlement Agreement. The budget also begins implementation of our efforts to meet the Clean Air Act mandates required by federal law. To do so, we will propose the enactment of a fee structure to allow proper phasing-in of the increased costs to both the Commonwealth and private industry. As you know, we must be in full compliance by 1995.

As I noted in my State of the Commonwealth address, one of my main priorities is governmental reform. The most important step we can take in this session to further the cause of good government is to adopt a campaign finance law that will provide for public funding for governor and lieutenant governor campaigns.

I expect a tough new campaign finance bill, with public financing, to be introduced within a few days. I intend to work on behalf of that bill wholeheartedly. I am confident that, with your support, we can enact that bill this session. Our budget plan includes an appropriation of $3 million in fiscal 1994 to begin that system of public financing, recognizing that the need could vary depending on the content of the legislation and the number of candidates who participate.

Certainly one of the most important areas of the budget for our government is our personnel policy. We have worked as hard as we could during our brief time in office to effect savings in government. Have we been perfect? Of course not. I don't need to remind anyone in this chamber of a well-publicized incident.[16] But I do want to let you know that we have corrected this misstep. And I want to share with you some examples of success. We are cutting the no-merit overhead across the board. In the Finance Cabinet, we have cut the number of upper-level, non-merit jobs by almost 16 percent compared to a year ago. And we are down in Tourism overhead by almost 17 percent. And the reduction in the Human Resources Cabinet is 15 percent. Our approach is saving Kentucky taxpayers millions in dollars. And we are just beginning.

It is our goal that, by the end of the current fiscal year, we will reduce the number of non-merit principal assistants in our agencies by 50 percent. I believe this is appropriate and very much in keeping with our commitment to redirecting the priorities and resources of state government to programs that serve the citizens of this Commonwealth.

As I mentioned earlier, additional selective cutbacks will in all probability be necessary because of our financial circumstances. Wherever possible, we will achieve these reductions through attrition. But it is very important that our cabinet secretaries be given the flexibility to identify and eliminate positions that are unnecessary to the missions of their agencies. This flexibility will also help them direct our resources to the areas of greatest need. I ask for your assistance in giving our managers the tools they need to do the best possible for our taxpayers.

We have chosen a different approach to our pay policy for the next biennium. Regrettably, the salaries of those employees making more than $50,000 will be cut by 2 percent in the fiscal year beginning July 1, 1992. I am also inviting participation in this aspect of our salary policy by other officials in state agencies not directly covered by our central state personnel system. Sacrifices are necessary, and I believe that those who make the most are best able to bear the burden. Every member of my cabinet has already agreed to take the 2 percent pay cut in fiscal 1993. And, of course, I will also take the cut next year. Full-time state workers who currently are paid less than $20,000 will receive a 2 percent raise in fiscal 1993. These employees and all others will receive a 3 percent raise the following year under our plan. We will continue to provide support for the health insurance benefit package for state employees and school system personnel. We are recommending continuation of the current employee contribution rate to the state employees retirement system.

I recognize that all of us would prefer to be serving our state in times of greater economic prosperity. I predict that we will have that opportunity in the next few years. But the reality of the present makes our cooperative relationship even more important. We can—and we must—work together, Democrats and Republicans, to bring our Commonwealth through these challenging times. I know that we will do just that because—despite our lack of dollars—we do not suffer from a poverty of leadership in Kentucky. I know that we have the shared will and commitment to get the job done right.

---

1. Kentucky has operated on a biennial budget since 1966, proposing budgets for two years as opposed to annually.

2. Governor Jones called special sessions of the General Assembly on health care in May 1993, and on the Kentucky parks system in May 1994.

3. The Support Education Excellence in Kentucky Fund (SEEK) was established to set standards in education spending through state and local support. SEEK also sets standards on special program funding and teacher salaries.

4. Tier I is a provision permitting a school board to increase revenue by up to 15 percent of the revenue guaranteed by the SEEK program by levying additional taxes.

5. Any child with a disability who is three or four years of age or who turns five after October 1 is eligible for free and appropriate preschool education and related services.

6. Family and youth resource centers provide programs and make referrals to service agencies to assist students and families in need. The purpose is to enhance a student's ability to succeed in school. In 2000, there were more than 650 centers serving 1,000 schools.

7. The use of technology in public education is a critical component of education reform. The Council on Education Technology developed a master plan outlining activities to purchase, develop, and use technology. The state board developed a primarily performance-based student assessment program to determine school success. Successful schools receive monetary rewards from the state; unsuccessful schools are required to develop plans for improvement.

8. Vocational education was a priority in Governor Jones's education plan. He spoke on many occasions about "creating a workforce for the future" and the importance of technical training for future companies to invest in Kentucky. The Kentucky Labor Cabinet participated with the Workforce Development Cabinet in a program that involved business, labor, education, and government to help students make a successful transition from school to the workplace.

9. The Council on Higher Education was created by the legislature in 1934. The council provided statewide planning, set guidelines, and regulated higher education until it was supplanted by the Council on Postsecondary Education.

10. The Community College System comprises fourteen community colleges located throughout the state. The General Assembly has charged the Community College System with three specific functions: 1) to offer career-oriented programs that prepare students for immediate employment upon graduation; 2) to offer the first two years of a baccalaureate degree; and 3) to offer general educational opportunities for citizens in the areas served by the colleges. Until 1997, the Community College System was under control of the board of trustees of the University of Kentucky.

11. Thomas J. "Tom" Burch (1931–), B.A., Bellarmine College; Democratic representative from Jefferson County, district 30, elected, 1971, re-elected, 1973–2000; chair of Health/Welfare; retired, General Electric, Louisville. *Who's What in Kentucky Government 1999–2000* (Frankfort, 1999).

12. The Medicaid program provides health care to the poor and disabled and long-term care for the elderly. Medicaid is a supplement support income to the Medicare program. In 1990 Kentucky faced a Medicaid deficit of $27 million, primarily the result of new mandates and requirements from the federal government.

13. To boost tourism and create jobs in Kentucky, bond issues were established for Jenny Wiley State Park in Floyd County, Yatesville Lake in Lawrence County, Kincaid Lake State Park in Pendleton County, Paintsville Lake in Johnson and Morgan Counties, and Ben Hawes State Park in Daviess County.

14. The expansion of the south wing of the Kentucky Fair and Exposition Center (KFEC) was approved through a special session of the legislature called by Governor Jones in January 1995. The KFEC now has one million square feet of exhibit space under one roof.

15. The Northern Kentucky Convention Center in Covington was approved in the January 1995 special session of the legislature.

16. The well-publicized incident concerned a proposal by Kevin Hable, secretary of the cabinet. Hable had proposed doing away with the merit system in certain areas. Some state employees became very upset. After Governor Jones read about Hable's proposal in the newspaper, he quickly corrected the misstep.

BILL SIGNINGS FOR HOUSE BILLS 157 AND 239
Frankfort / March 10, 1992

HB 157 establishes committees to assess and recommend the awarding of state architectural and engineering contracts on the basis of merit rather than politics. There are three committees in all—two in Finance (architectural services and engineering services) and one in Transportation (engineering only). Each committee is composed of six members, five of whom are state merit employees in the applicable cabinet. The architectural committee is composed of two architects/merit employees; two merit employees from the agency hiring the service; one merit employee from the state auditor's office to monitor selection process; and one selected by the finance secretary from three selected by the governor from a pool of nine recommended by Kentucky Society of Architects. (Other committees are similar except members are engineers and one is a member from Kentucky Society of Engineers.) There is a conflict of interest clause: For a period of one year after a person ends his service on a selection committee, the Commonwealth shall not consider a firm for an architectural or engineering services contract if that person, his spouse, either of his parents, or any of his children is employed by a firm or has a financial interest in a firm which was awarded a contract by a selection committee on which he served. The bill provides for committee interviews of bidders on architectural services with a fee exceeding $50,000 and on engineering services with fees exceeding $100,000.

HB 239 establishes a competitive process for the awarding of build-to-suit leases. It establishes a defined committee that evaluates proposals based on weighted evaluation factors such as project cost, design, and quality of materials through a request for proposal and advertisement process. The committee is composed of three merit employees appointed by the finance secretary, two merit employees of the agency seeking the project, one merit employee from the state auditor's office, and two private-sector members appointed by the finance secretary.

STATEMENT ABOUT CAMPAIGN FINANCE BILL AND GUBERNATORIAL SUCCESSION AMENDMENT

Frankfort / March 20, 1992

THESE are exciting times in Frankfort, made even more so by the potential for Kentucky's General Assembly to enact meaningful, progressive election reform for our Commonwealth. Our administration is strongly supporting initiatives that I believe represent a major step forward for Kentucky. These initiatives take two forms: a campaign finance bill and a constitutional amendment that would provide for gubernatorial succession.

I welcomed the opportunity during my campaign for governor to talk with many of you about the challenges facing our state and the very real need to restore Kentuckians' confidence in state government. As I listened to your concerns, one theme emerged very clearly—we must act decisively to eliminate as much as possible the influence of money and wealthy special interests on the operation of our state government. We must make our government truly representative of all Kentuckians.

Addressing those concerns is the focus of our campaign finance bill. This measure dramatically reduces the maximum allowable contribution by an individual to a candidate. It puts in place stringent enforcement provisions to guard against abuses. It limits the amount of PAC contributions to any candidate and requires a primary runoff when no candidate for governor receives at least 40 percent of his or her party's vote. The bill also calls for partial public financing for races for governor and lieutenant governor.

I'm confident that you have heard some of the debate on public financing. There are those who decry the proposal as being nothing more than "welfare for politicians." While I respect differing views on any issue, I believe strongly that to dismiss public financing with such a cliché is to fail to consider the big picture.

First, the courts in our country have ruled that public financing is the only way we may legally limit campaign spending. If we are sincere in our desire to eliminate the political influence of big money, public financing is our only solution.

Second—and perhaps of greater significance—public financing is not a "give-away" program. It is a very necessary investment in good, honest government.

No Kentuckian with even a passing interest in state government needs to be reminded of the countless news accounts we have seen in the past revealing that a big campaign contributor received a big state contract. Were these occurrences the result of coincidence, as some would maintain? Maybe. But too often they have raised questions about the appearance of a conflict of interest or bestowing favors—paid for with your tax dollars—on someone's political friends.

Limiting campaign spending would offer relief in another area: it would mean that candidates would have less money to spend on the thirty- and sixty-second television ads that have become the primary means of communicating with voters. You and I both know that neither candidates nor voters are well served by this growing reliance on TV spots to frame the themes of a race for the state's highest offices. Campaigns cannot hope to convey—and voters cannot hope to learn—what a candidate believes or what he or she proposes to accomplish in a message that is limited to a few seconds.

The campaign finance bill now under consideration would require candidates who receive public money to participate in a series of forums, produced by Kentucky Educational Television, to discuss in detail their plans for the future of our Commonwealth. These forums—coupled with other appearances candidates would be well advised to make before the public—will help give Kentuckians a more realistic view of the candidates seeking their votes.

Campaign finance is, as you know, one part of the reform package we are supporting. The second is a long-needed amendment to our state constitution to permit gubernatorial succession for one additional term. There is one major difference between this amendment and similar measures Kentuckians have considered in the past—it does not apply to the current governor.

I spoke often of my support for gubernatorial succession during my campaign for governor. And I always tried to make it clear that I would not want the measure to apply to me as the sitting governor. My views and commitment have not changed. I believe the question of whether Kentucky will permit gubernatorial succession should be decided on the merits of the issue—not on the basis of the current governor's popularity.

Gubernatorial succession, in my opinion, is important if we are to have a government that provides for continuity. Our current system of changing direction every four years denies Kentuckians the opportunity to benefit from longer-range programs a particular governor may undertake. Succession will give us the chance to decide whether we want a governor to continue in office four more years or whether it is time for a change in leadership. I also believe that succession should only be permitted if a primary run-off is in place. As I mentioned earlier, a run-off provision is included in the campaign finance bill.

Our support for the run-off stems from the belief that it is an important safeguard against possible abuses by a governor who is seeking a second term. Our government structure bestows a great deal of power and influence on the office of governor. As a result, it would not be difficult for a sitting governor to garner a simple majority of primary votes in a crowded field. I believe, however, that a governor and any candidate for governor should have the primary support of at least 40 percent of his or her party's voters to ensure nomination. If no candidate receives 40 percent of the primary vote, a run-off between the top two finishing candidates should be held.

As we work for the passage of these and other proposals before the General Assembly, it is sometimes easy to consider only the matters immediately at hand. Anyone who has witnessed or been part of a legislative session can appreciate the sense of urgency that attends virtually every action.

But I do have an opportunity from time to time to welcome groups of schoolchildren to my office for a brief visit. It is in this interaction with the children of our state that strengthens my commitment to doing everything I can to bring about meaningful reform for our government and our elections. The government these children inherit from us must be one that is open, honest, and truly representative of the people of Kentucky. It must be one in which they have confidence. I strongly believe that the campaign finance and constitutional reforms now being considered will go far in helping us meet our responsibility to our future leaders.

AMERICANS WITH DISABILITIES PRESS CONFERENCE AND SENATE BILL 210 SIGNING

Frankfort / April 8, 1992

TODAY, we are signing a very important piece of legislation passed by the 1992 General Assembly and announcing a major administrative initiative. Senate Bill 210, sponsored by Sen. Joe Meyer,[1] affords

Kentuckians with disabilities full civil rights and protections under the law of the Commonwealth, thereby recognizing that Kentucky values all of her citizens and believes in first-class citizenship for all Kentuckians.

Also today, I want to talk about an exciting opportunity we have in Kentucky and what we are going to do to make the most of it. As we mark our bicentennial as a state, it is appropriate to focus on the abundant resources with which we have been blessed.

There is one resource, however, that we have not developed to its full potential. That resource is found in the thousands of Kentuckians with disabilities who have not been afforded equal opportunities. With the congressional enactment of the Americans with Disabilities Act [A.D.A.]—and Kentucky's response to that legislation—we have a chance to change that reality for the benefit of our entire Commonwealth.

The Americans with Disabilities Act provides a national mandate to eliminate discrimination against people with disabilities. Discrimination is prohibited in the areas of employment, public accommodation, transportation, communications, and activities of state and local government.

Our administration is firmly committed to implementing the provisions of this act. To ensure state government compliance, I am appointing a task force to plan and oversee the steps necessary to comply with the A.D.A. The task force will involve representatives from all state government agencies. To ensure that individuals with disabilities have an active role in this process, I am also appointing representatives from several consumer and advocate groups, including the Kentucky Coalition for Persons with Disabilities; Commission on Human Rights; Protection and Advocacy Advisory Board; and the Protection and Advocacy Advisory Council.

This task force will recommend a comprehensive plan to ensure that all state government programs, services, and facilities are accessible to persons with disabilities. Technical assistance will be available to Kentucky cities, counties, industries, and businesses through various state agencies. The A.D.A. task force will ensure that persons with disabilities are included as active participants in the self-evaluation and transition plan processes.

. . . As a further commitment to the full implementation of this act, I am appointing Sharon Fields, currently the director of client assistance for the Workforce Development Cabinet, as the chief of staff for the task force. Sharon will oversee the day-to-day planning and implementing of A.D.A.

All Kentuckians regardless of disability, ethnic background, religion, national origin, sex, and age should enjoy the same opportunities for personal advancement. To ensure that state agencies afford equal employment opportunity to the approximately 350,000 working individuals with disabilities, I am asking the task force to develop a plan to implement Project Workable, which will be a comprehensive approach to employment for persons with disabilities. Project Workable is intended to identify jobs in state government which can be accomplished by persons with disabilities.

We want to tap the resources of our Commonwealth that have been concealed by our tendency to focus on disability instead of ability. We will move ahead to remove architectural, communication, and attitudinal barriers which prevent qualified, able individuals from participating in the mainstream of society.

Let us continue our tradition of excellence and celebrate two hundred years of progress by uniting to erase discrimination against persons with disabilities.

I sign Senate Bill 210 and challenge all other states and challenge the business community . . .

---

1. Joe Meyer (1948–), A.B., Bellarmine College; M.A., St. Louis University; J.D., Chase College of Law; Democrat; member of Kentucky house, 1982–88; elected to Kentucky senate (district 23), 1989; re-elected, 1990–94; general counsel, Kentucky Association of Counties, 1998– . *1994 Kentucky General Assembly Directory.*

HOUSE BILL 28 SIGNING
Frankfort / April 13, 1992

WE are all aware of the effects of the recession on our state and the brutal effects it has had on the homeless and the very poor. Today, I am pleased to sign House Bill 28, which establishes the state's first Affordable Housing Trust Fund to provide housing for very low-income Kentuckians. The fund will be administered by the Kentucky Housing Corporation [KHC].

On Thursday and Friday I signed two other bills that will enhance this overall effort—Senate Bill 3 and House Bill 7—which strengthen the Corporation and allow KHC to continue to issue housing revenue bonds to further its house ownership programs as it pays off current debt.

The heart of this new effort—House Bill 28—requires KHC to provide $100,000 in start-up funds. I am very pleased to announce today that additional funds of up to $100,000 will be made available to support affordable housing for the very low income from savings we will realize from this year's Derby Breakfast.

First, let me say very quickly that we do not intend in any way to change the history or spirit of the Derby Breakfast. As you all know, the Governor's Derby Breakfast has, through the years, become one of the most colorful and popular Kentucky traditions surrounding the Derby. I'm told that Governor Chandler actually began this tradition over fifty years ago when, on Derby Day 1936, he asked a few of his friends to stop and have breakfast at the Mansion on their way to Louisville for the Derby.

We all know that since Governor Chandler's day, the guest list has increased dramatically—and so have the costs associated with this event. In these tough economic times, and with the state budget as tight as it is, Libby and I took a long, hard look at this event, just as we did with the inauguration. With the inauguration, we decided from the outset that we wanted to have an event that was dignified and special—and that included all the people of Kentucky. We also decided we wanted to spend less than what had been spent previously. We were successful with the inauguration, and I believe we will be successful with the Derby Breakfast as well.

Therefore, I am very pleased to announce the following changes in the Governor's Derby Breakfast: This year no invitations will be sent; rather, everyone is invited to come to the Capitol on Derby morning, beginning at 8:00 a.m., and to bring their families. There will be no large breakfast tent and no sit-down meal offered, thus eliminating the long line that people have had to stand in, sometimes as long as three and four hours in order to get into the breakfast tent. Rather, there will be six small tents located throughout the Capitol grounds that will offer coffee, juice, Danish, and country ham and biscuits. The Department of Parks will, as they have in the past, cater this event; but the food costs alone will be less than half the cost of previous years ($2.20 instead of $5.30). Also, any food left over will be taken to local soup kitchens for distribution to the needy and the homeless.

Everything else that has become associated with the Derby Breakfast will all be maintained and will be happening throughout the morning until 12 noon—the crafts tents (thirteen, with a total of fifty-two craftsmen and women); the hot air balloons; the entertainment (on three different staging areas); and tours of the Capitol and the Governor's Mansion.

With the changes we are announcing today in this event, we are estimating that we will save the state $100,000, which will go to support the trust for the homeless. The Affordable Housing Trust Fund will put Kentucky in a position to qualify for federal matching money to finance programs for our very low-income citizens. The match requirements vary depending on whether we use the money for housing rehabilitation, new construction, or rental assistance.

Many people have devoted many hours and much energy to this initiative. The contributions of the Homeless and Housing Coalition of Kentucky have been unmeasurable. . . .

ADDRESS TO JOINT SESSION OF THE GENERAL ASSEMBLY

Frankfort / May 10, 1993

LIEUTENANT Governor Patton,[1] constitutional officers, Senator Rose,[2] Speaker Clarke,[3] honorable members of the General Assembly, members of the Executive Cabinet, ladies and gentlemen.

We gather tonight to continue our history-making journey together in this 201st year of our Commonwealth. There is always a special feeling to these reunions of men and women who work tirelessly on behalf of our extended family of Kentuckians. But the atmosphere tonight has a certain electricity, one that is sparked not only by the magnitude of the challenge before us but also by the realization that we have a tremendous opportunity to do for our Kentucky family what no other state has done—contain costs and provide affordable, quality health care for each and every citizen.

We've been on this journey for a while now. The "few more weeks" and "few more days" have all finally passed in bringing us to this point. And we're not here because this is easy or enjoyable. We're here because we are unwilling to shirk the responsibility that our election to public office has assigned to us. That responsibility directs us to do the right thing for the good of all Kentuckians. *All*

Kentuckians—not just those we know or those whose voices we hear through special-interest groups. But all Kentuckians—and especially the thousands whose names and faces are unfamiliar to us and whose voices have been muffled by fear, isolation, or poverty.

We have not only the opportunity, but the obligation, to ease the burdens that have been imposed on our people by the skyrocketing costs of a health-care system that inadequately meets their needs. Fulfilling this obligation will require sacrifices that must be shared by all of us. And those who have profited the most from this dollar-driven system must now, in fairness, be asked to give the most. Not more than they can afford, but a fair share. We need parity, not punishment, for all—individual Kentuckians, businesses, providers, government. At the same time, we must not destroy the desire of our brightest young people to become health-care providers.

You have before you the details of our reform proposal. I am confident that your review of the legislation will be thorough and complete. There have been countless questions and suggestions, and undoubtedly there will be many more. As we have throughout this process, we stand ready to respond and to listen. We are open to better ideas because we know that the strength of many minds will only serve to bolster our efforts.

As you begin your deliberations, I ask that *you also* stand ready to respond and to listen. This has not been and will not be a painless process. But it is necessary that we give it the time and attention it deserves. We cannot hope to resolve problems that took decades to create in a matter of a few legislative days. And, yes, each of those days costs $37,000. But, based on the unchecked increases in what we are spending on health care, it costs us $250,000 a day to do nothing. If we invest $37,000 a day to save $250,000 a day, we have made an excellent investment for our Commonwealth. We simply cannot afford to wait, and I believe the people of Kentucky want us to stay here until the job is done.

There is a reason that these gatherings are called extraordinary sessions—they were designed to address extraordinary issues. And I can think of none that better fits into that category than health-care reform. Every member of the house and senate—not just those who serve on certain committees—deserves to have access to all the information necessary to make a decision based on the facts. Gaining that level of knowledge won't happen overnight, and I want you to know that we will put at your disposal the actuaries and economists and other experts who advised us in this process. We, too, had a lot of issues to resolve. Because of the complexity and the need for genuine understanding on the part of all members of the General Assembly, I was pleased to hear that the House Health and Welfare Committee will meet tomorrow in the House Chamber, where all of your members will have room to participate in this process. I ask that you consider continuing this practice throughout the session to ensure that every representative and every senator has access to all the information that is shared as questions are asked and issues are debated.

As I said before, the strength of many minds will bolster our reform efforts. On a subject as complex as health care, there are many areas where we must all be willing to compromise; however, I cannot in good faith compromise on the two goals that provide the foundation of our health-care reform initiative. We must control health-care costs and restrict increases to the cost of living. We must provide universal coverage for all Kentuckians without exclusions for pre-existing conditions. And we must do it now because we cannot afford to wait.

There are those who would describe these goals as unrealistic, unworkable, too much too soon. There are those who would remind us that politics is the art of the possible—and say that this is impossible. In response, I say that, not only are these goals realistic and workable, it is long past time that we met them. Our people are waiting—nearly 450,000 without insurance, thousands more just one illness or accident away from an economic catastrophe, the rest of us paying too much and picking up the tab for the uninsured. And we are picking up the tab—every time we pay an insurance premium or go to the doctor or check into a hospital.

A popular phrase for this is cost shifting. And it means simply this. When my son gets a sore throat, I take him to the family doctor's office in Woodford County and the office visit costs $34. When the child of an uninsured parent gets a sore throat, they take him to the hospital emergency room, where the cost is $114. That $114 has to come from somewhere, and it comes from the higher rates those of us with insurance have to pay for health care and coverage. Kentuckians—both those with insurance and those without—are waiting for us to lead the way out of this perverse system. It is wrong to force those who pay for health insurance to also pay the hidden tax that comes from cost shifting. We cannot get control of health-care costs until we stop the cost shifting, and we cannot stop the cost shifting until we get coverage for every Kentuckian.

A majority of those 450,000 Kentuckians who have no coverage are children and working individuals—people who go to work every day trying to make ends meet but who cannot pay the rapidly escalating cost of health coverage.

There are undoubtedly many ways to reach our goals of universal coverage and cost controls, and we must all be willing to keep our minds open to compromise on how we get there. But we must get there.

Big numbers can get our attention, but I feel that it is often the individual story that truly helps us appreciate the reality of a situation. A mother from Wallins, Kentucky, recently shared the story of her son with me in a letter that I want to share with you in part.

> Dear Governor Jones:
>
> I am a mother of a four-year-old boy who needs an operation and can't get it because we have no insurance. My husband works in a small coal mine making $9 an hour, but the mines carry no insurance for the families. I took my son to the doctor and he told me that David needed his tonsils and adenoids taken out. He has gone from 58 pounds down to 42 1/2 pounds because he can't eat much; it won't go through his neck because his tonsils are so enlarged and growing. He can't breathe at night and can't play too hard because of smothering so bad. They informed me that I would have to have $400 to $800 for the hospital and $250 for the doctor's fee before they would even consider it. . . . We don't have that kind of money, so they said to save it up and come back when I have it. . . . My son's condition is not life threatening right now, but it is very hard on him and us to hear him gasp for breath. It scares us to death and kills us because we can't help him.

Another Kentuckian, a man from Harrodsburg, wrote that he earns about $30,000 a year and pays a family coverage premium of $5,660 annually. His wife has Hodgkin's disease which, thankfully, is in remission. But his fear is that his employer's insurance company won't renew its coverage when the contract expires in December or that the premiums will be raised again. And they have increased over 100 percent in just three years. To quote from his letter, "The pre-existence of my wife's disease will make her uninsurable with any other company. Taxes and insurance take nearly 45 percent of my weekly pay. It's no wonder the American dream is gone for so many middle-class, working families."

It is an unfortunate reality that there are hundreds of thousands of Kentuckians who share these experiences every single day. These are hardworking, tax-paying Kentuckians who are not looking for a handout. They are looking for fairness and equity and relief from this unfair burden they must bear. And our reform initiative is not a welfare program to make people more dependent on government. It is just the opposite of that. It provides a solution to a long-standing problem within our welfare system—when a single mother can't afford to take a low-paying job with no benefits because it will mean losing the medical card that guarantees care for her children. Our program is structured to change that—to encourage that single parent to get a job because she will have insurance—not only for her children but for herself as well.

I hope that there isn't a single man or woman in this chamber who would not be moved to act out of compassion. But I also recognize that the reality of our state's financial condition makes it impossible to solve all the problems we would like to solve because we know in our hearts that the need exists. Ours is not a wealthy state, where meeting a challenge by writing a check on the state's bank account is a readily available solution. But in this case, we have a situation that is rare in our history: our humanitarian needs and our economic needs coincide. We will benefit financially from doing the right thing.

If we do not act, and act now, to control health-care costs, they will bankrupt us as a state, as individuals, as businesses, as communities. If we do not act, your Appropriations and Revenue Committees will find budgeting the vast majority of our new resources a relatively simple task—the money will go to health care. What little is left will be woefully inadequate to continue our progress in education reform, protect our environment, sufficiently compensate state employees, guard our citizens against crime, help create new jobs, or perform the many other services for which state government exists.

Here, the big numbers speak for themselves. Health-care costs have increased an average of nearly 15 percent a year in recent years. State government will spend more than $900 million this year on health care. Medicaid expenditures have increased 300 percent over the past decade, with no end in sight. By fiscal year 1997, it is estimated that half of all new general fund money will be used to fund health care. And this uncontrolled spiral isn't limited to the government's expenses. It is attacking every business and every individual in this Commonwealth. Our correspondent from Harrodsburg that I spoke of earlier wrote of a 100 percent premium increase in the last three years alone. That isn't the exception. It's the rule. We can't let this go on forever. We cannot—and we must not—let this go on any longer. We're talking plain dollars and cents and we simply cannot afford it. More importantly, our people cannot afford it.

This is a call to action that we cannot ignore, and I am convinced that the courage we have seen exhibited time and again in the Kentucky General Assembly will come to the fore in meeting this challenge. I am also convinced that the plan we have presented to you will meet our goals of controlling costs and providing universal coverage. In addition, it will provide long-term reform in placing a strong emphasis on training more primary-care physicians and on locating these physicians in the underserved areas of our state. As I mentioned earlier, the details of our proposal are numerous, and we could spend hours discussing each of them. In fact, I expect that hours will be devoted to discussing and debating each of them. But tonight I want to offer a closer look at the effect of our plan on individuals and employers because I know that you and the Kentuckians you represent have concerns in these areas.

We do not want to ask more of anyone than they can afford in reforming health care. But we will ask a fair share from everyone. And we will require that all Kentuckians have health insurance by next year. With that requirement, however, will come assistance for low-income individuals and families. To give you an example of how this assistance will work, I want to talk again about the young mother from eastern Kentucky whose son needed an operation the family could not afford.

Her husband's $9-an-hour salary translates into an annual income of $18,700, an amount that is 130 percent of the federal poverty level for a family of four. This family would receive coverage for the little boy's care—and that of his nine-year-old sister—at no cost to them because our plan will cover all children up to 200 percent of poverty under the Medicaid program. The parents would each be eligible for the low-cost minimum benefit coverage we have proposed at a per-person cost of $85 a month. But since their income level is under 200 percent of poverty—at 130 percent of that level—they would receive assistance amounting to 70 percent of their premium costs. That means that both parents would receive coverage for a total of $51 a month. All of their preventive care would be free. There would be no deductibles on their plan, and they would be expected to make reasonable co-payments, such as $7 for a physician's visit or for a prescription.

What about Kentuckians who are already receiving coverage through their employers? This group represents the majority of Kentuckians, and I think it is imperative that I clearly outline what they can expect from reform. First of all, if they keep their current insurance, they will see a lowering of premium cost increases.

Secondly, if they choose, they can opt for a comprehensive benefit package at a lower cost for family coverage through the state megapool. And this will be something they can count on, no matter what kind of medical catastrophe they or their family members experience. They cannot be denied coverage because they suffer from a pre-existing illness such as cancer, heart disease, or diabetes. And there will be no maximum lifetime benefits imposed on them. There will be no more experiences like the one a teacher told us about recently where, while both he and his son receive treatments for cancer, his insurance company sends him regular reports detailing how close he is coming to his $1 million lifetime maximum on coverage. Kentuckians can expect security, reasonable rates, and lifetime protection under our reform proposal.

Protecting the businesses that provide jobs for Kentuckians has always been a focus of our administration. That was especially true when we were looking at a number of options in health-care reform. We knew that the vast majority of Kentucky employers—72 percent—already provide insurance for their workers. We also knew that the cost of that insurance has been escalating unchecked every year, that one employee with a serious illness could break the bank for group coverage, and that more and more business owners were finding themselves struggling to obtain coverage at any cost. And we knew that those providing insurance were paying a hidden tax because they were paying twice—once for their own employees' insurance and once to cover the uninsured. We haven't heard much discussion of this hidden tax, but it is very real and very expensive for our Kentucky employers. One other reality also confronted us: dramatic increases in workers' compensation insurance rates threatened the viability of many employers, and by dramatic increases I'm talking about 54 percent in the past two years.

Our approach here, as with individuals, focused on savings and security. Our plan will give Kentucky business owners the option of reducing their insurance costs by joining the state megapool. These costs will be controlled, and the employers won't find themselves facing the prospect of being denied group coverage—or offered inordinately expensive group coverage—because one of their employees has suffered a catastrophic illness or accident. Workers' comp rates will be reduced by 5 percent across the board and then frozen for two years. This will be a savings of $193 million for Kentucky businesses by 1996. And we can save even more. We must be creative in our thinking and explore the possibilities offered by twenty-four-hour coverage and by merging automobile insurance with health-care coverage.

Yes, we will impose a 3.75 percent payroll tax. But credits will be given to businesses for the money they spend on health care for their employees. And that means the vast majority of Kentucky businesses will pay no more in taxes and will actually save money when workers' comp rates are reduced and they no longer have to pay that hidden tax I mentioned earlier. In short, we are easing the tax burden on nearly three-fourths of Kentucky employers with the passage of this legislation, and we will ease it even further as health-care costs are controlled in the future. And that will send a signal to the entire country that Kentucky is the place to create jobs because we have had the courage to confront this problem and overcome it.

If businesses spend nothing on health care, they won't receive a tax credit. But it is important to remember that the business owner's insurance, or that of his or her family members who work for the business, can be claimed as a credit against the payroll tax.

Some opponents have expressed the belief that those employers who cover their workers now will drop their insurance and pay the 3.75 percent payroll tax instead. This is illogical for two reasons:

(1) The employers have already voluntarily chosen to cover their employees because they think it is the proper business decision.

(2) Only those employees whose income is at 200 percent of the poverty level or less will automatically qualify for the standard $85 plan.

I had a chance recently, during a meeting with one of you, to respond directly to one of your constituents' concerns. This woman has a welding company with only three employees, plus her husband, herself, and her son. When I called her, I said, "I understand you've got some problems with my health-care plan." And she said, "You better believe I've got some problems with it. It would drive me out of business."

But then we began talking details and she expressed the fear that either the employer mandate, which we had considered earlier, or the payroll tax would be more than she could afford. She told me that she is currently paying half her employees' health-insurance costs and that her husband had a heart attack five years ago and the cost of his insurance is three times hers.

She was good enough to share some of her numbers with me and, when she did, we found out that the credit she will receive will mean that she will have no additional taxes to pay. I also pointed out that our plan makes it illegal to discriminate against a person because of a pre-existing condition and that her husband could not be charged more for his insurance than she paid for her own. "Well, Governor," she said, "I didn't realize that. I've been getting all the wrong information. I've been confused about all this. This is the best thing that could ever happen to me."

It is important to us to protect our people and our businesses. It is also important to us to protect and preserve the community hospitals that serve so many of our citizens. The Kentucky Hospital Association told us recently that, if we do nothing, between twelve and eighteen hospitals may be forced to close in the next twelve to thirty-six months. We want to do everything we can to save those hospitals, and that is why our reforms are designed to help them develop a new niche in the marketplace—not to close them down. We cannot, and we will not, turn our backs on this very important part of our health-care delivery system.

Through the work of the Health Care Authority,[4] we will develop a master plan of health services for the entire state. Every hospital cannot compete with every other hospital for open-heart surgery or organ transplants. But each hospital must find its niche in the market and also provide certain emergency services for the people in its community. Woodford Memorial Hospital in Versailles is a classic example of the type of hospital that can be saved with our reform legislation.

What we accomplish in the coming days and weeks will tell not only our Kentucky family but the rest of the nation that, in this Commonwealth, we are prepared to meet the most pressing problems head-on and solve them. Kentucky is not the first state to address health care, but every other state has failed to adequately control costs because it has succumbed to the special interests and reached a political solution rather than a real solution. The vast majority of Kentuckians are not represented by the so-called special interests, but their interests are the most special of all. The nearly 450,000 of our family members without insurance and the thousands of others who are literally on the brink of economic collapse have no powerful lobbyists to bring their message to Frankfort. But I want everyone to know that I will be their lobbyist. And I predict that a majority of the Kentucky General Assembly will join me in working on their behalf.

Normal political posturing will give us the same result as every other state has had, and our people deserve more than that. We cannot afford to fail. And we cannot afford $250,000 a day to wait on

Washington. We must chart our own course to ensure that Kentuckians do what is best for Kentuckians. We will not relinquish this right—or this responsibility.

We have never faced a greater challenge as a state government. And I have never faced a tougher fight in my life. But I have also never been more committed to anything than I am to this effort. Those who speak of politics as the art of the possible are talking about politics as usual. In this case, politics must be the art of expanding our horizons and embracing new solutions so that what once seemed impossible becomes a reality. There comes a time when we must renew the pioneering spirit that established Kentucky, break the stranglehold of the special interests, and take a leadership role in solving the most complex and difficult problem facing our state and nation today. And that time is now.

---

1. Paul E. Patton (1937–), born in Lawrence County; active in many aspects of the coal business; judge-executive of Pike County; chair of Kentucky Democratic Party, 1981–82; secretary of Cabinet for Economic Development; lieutenant governor, 1991–95; elected governor of Kentucky, 1995–99; re-elected, 1999–2003. *Who's Who in America, 2000,* 59th ed. (New Providence, N.J., 1999).

2. John A. "Eck" Rose (1940–), Eastern Kentucky University, B.S.; Democratic legislator, elected to the Kentucky senate, district 28, in 1977; re-elected, 1981–98; president pro tem of senate, 1987–92; president of senate, 1993–96; unsuccessful gubernatorial candidate, 1995; unsuccessful congressional candidate in 6th district, 1998; real estate broker, auctioneer, farmer from Winchester. *Who's Who in the South and Southwest, 1999–2000,* 26th ed.

3. Joe Clarke (1933–), Notre Dame University, B.S.; Georgetown University, J.D.; Democratic legislator, elected to Kentucky House of Representatives, district 54, 1969; re-elected, 1971–98; served as chair of House Appropriations and Revenue Committee (1970–92); speaker of the house (1993–94); attorney. *Who's What in Kentucky Government, 1997–98* (Frankfort, 1997).

4. The Health Care Authority, later called the Kentucky Health Policy Board, was established per provisions of House Bill 250 and was created as an independent agency of the state government. The board consisted of five full-time members appointed by Governor Jones in August 1993. The Kentucky Health Policy Board was established to concentrate primarily on the collection of data from health-care providers, health insurers, auto insurance health benefits, and preparation of reports on health-care costs; the development of standard and supplemental health benefit plans; oversight of the Health Purchase Alliance created by HB 250; authorization of

pilot projects for twenty-four-hour coverage; review and approval of certificate of need applications; and authority to establish a purchasing cooperative for the purchase of medical supplies, equipment, and medications. The Kentucky Health Policy Board was later abolished by legislation enacted by the 1996 Kentucky General Assembly.

STATE OF THE COMMONWEALTH AND BUDGET ADDRESS COMBINED

Frankfort / January 24, 1994

INTRODUCTION

LIEUTENANT Governor Patton, President of the Senate Rose, Speaker Clarke, distinguished members of the General Assembly, Mr. Chief Justice Stephens,[1] members of the Supreme Court, honored guests, ladies and gentlemen:

Sunday night a week ago, a record snowfall blanketed our state. From Boyd County to Ballard County, the Commonwealth was covered with cold, sleet, and snow. Like many of you, we have spent most of our waking hours in the last week making sure that our families and our neighbors were warm and safe. As I reflected on that snow and the incredible difficulties it brought to many families, I was struck once again with a sense of community—a sense of how connected we all really are—how much we need each other.

That snowstorm reminded me again that all of us are one community, bound together, with common needs. As thousands of Kentuckians from National Guardsmen to state troopers, from transportation employees to volunteers in trucks and jeeps, worked tirelessly to unblock our highways and see that food, fuel, and provisions were able to reach our neighbors, it became clear to me that our job here tonight in this great chamber is very similar. Our job is to move Kentucky ahead, to keep Kentucky moving, to open up, if you will, highways of learning and economic opportunity that have too long remained frozen and blocked for too many of our citizens.

We must be one united community. However, this community of Kentuckians can only be built on a foundation made of equal parts of *opportunity* and *responsibility*. The politics of the past will not work anymore! Rhetoric and good intentions alone will not solve our problems or create the future that our people deserve. We must band together as a team. We must use our united strengths to overcome our individual weaknesses. You and I must stand united for *all* of Kentucky!

The need to work together has never been greater than it is now that the mistakes of a few individuals have cast a shadow over all of us in public life. In years to come, however, the mistakes of a few will be but a footnote to the four years we will have spent working together. *Our* efforts will be remembered as years of progress and reform in lean and trying times! Look at what we have already accomplished *together*: We have reduced the maximum campaign contribution from $4,000 to $500[2] and dramatically reduced the amount of money that will be spent in future elections. We have saved millions of dollars and greatly reduced public stress by eliminating one year of elections out of every four and have given the people the opportunity to have eight years of continuity in the executive branch if a governor is doing a good job.

We have changed the way state contracts are awarded to architects and engineers. We award bond transactions and contracts based on merit—not politics. Through legislation we have changed the focus from politics to qualifications. We have changed the way trustees are chosen for our universities and have made it nearly impossible to get a bad board. We have changed our approach to economic development and have created over twice as many new jobs in the last two years as were created in the preceding two years.[3] We have appointed more African Americans and women to boards, commissions, judgeships, and cabinet posts than any administration in history.[4] We have changed the operations of the state racing commissions by combining them into one commission and saving the taxpayers over $400,000. The record shows that we have had eight consecutive years of parimutuel increases for thoroughbreds and have increased live racing dates for standardbreds by 62 percent and their purses by 80 percent. Absolutely no other state in America has done as much for the standardbred industry.

We have changed the way lobbyists, legislators, and members of the executive branch of government interact with each other and the general public because of strong ethics legislation that you passed.

In tight budget times, you and I have kept education reform alive by funding our reform efforts. We have received a waiver from the federal government that will allow us to obtain health-care coverage for an additional 201,000 Kentuckians without any increase in taxes. We have built more roads and laid more blacktop in the first two years of this administration than the first two years of any administration in history. And we did it with fewer employees in Transportation than they have had in the last two decades. We established a Quality and Efficiency Commission[5] that has identified innumerable ways to save the taxpayers dollars. This is in addition to the more than fourteen hundred permanent, full-time jobs we have eliminated through attrition.

Today we have a state government that is *leaner, smarter, more efficient, more progressive,* and *less political* than anytime in modern history. You and I and a host of talented dedicated people, *working together,* have made this possible. We have accomplished much these last two years, and we can do even more in the next two!

So where do we go from here? Let me suggest a road map and outline our proposed budget for the coming biennium.

HEALTH CARE

LET me begin by saying that there is no greater impediment to our ability to manage our budget than our lack of control of health-care costs. If we do not control runaway health-care costs, we will not have the necessary money for other needs. This fact still exists and very few would dispute it. I am confident that we will pass meaningful health-care reforms in this session of the legislature.

Some say that it would be unfair for a qualified board to have the power to keep our citizens from being charged *unreasonable* health-insurance premiums. I totally disagree! If our health-care reform bill does not protect all Kentuckians from *unreasonable* charges, then we will have failed. I ask you to stand with me on this point! A centerpiece to the health-care financing issue and to the state budget is, of course, the retention of the provider tax.[6] We must collect this amount of money, have it more than tripled in Washington, and give it to providers to pay for the health care of thousands of Kentuckians.

MEDICAID WAIVER EXPANSIONS

WE announced last month that the federal government granted Kentucky's request to expand Medicaid coverage to all Kentuckians below the poverty line, effective July 1, 1994. More than 201,000 Kentuckians will stand to benefit from this initiative. This program will allow the working poor to have access to health-care services in a cost-efficient manner that saves lives and money. Actions have been taken and will continue over the upcoming biennium that will crack down on fraud and abuse and change the way the program is managed. Aggressive managed care and preventive services also will be made part of the Medicaid program to contain costs and assure quality services.

EDUCATION

ALONG with health care, one of our top priorities in this budget continues to be our commitment to education reform and the children of Kentucky. We must be leaders rather than followers, winners rather than losers, in our educational reform efforts. The proposed recommendation in this budget, when coupled with the General Fund appropriation approved in the 1992 session, will result in an increase of total General Fund appropriations to the Department of Education during our administration of nearly $300 million. General Fund support for the SEEK and Tier I programs has increased by $150 million during this administration. Perhaps most important, both the 1992 budget and the proposed budget recommend full funding of the Tier I component of SEEK. General Funds appropriated for Tier I have increased from $25 million in fiscal year 1992 to $78.2 million in fiscal year 1994, a threefold increase. If the proposed budget is adopted, Tier I appropriations will increase another 18 percent during the 1994–96 biennium.

There is no way to build a good school without paying special attention—and that means money—to the most important part of our educational system: the teachers. Teaching today is a very high-stress occupation. Teachers in many instances must teach children who are ill prepared to learn, who come from broken homes with difficult economic circumstances. Teachers today are not allowed to exert proper discipline in the class, are not given sufficient support and encouragement to excel. We must do better! The proposed budget includes a substantial increase in state support for professional development and training—from the current $10 million to $14.5 million by the end of the 1994–96 biennium. *Additionally, I ask every school board across this state to make teacher pay raises a top priority in every local district*!

Recognizing the importance of meaningful training for both practicing and prospective teachers, we appointed a Task Force on Teacher Preparation that issued its report last month. Among its recommendations is the development—by the Educational Professional Standards Board—of results expected of teachers, administrators, and other certified school personnel. These results are modeled after the already approved "new teacher outcomes." These outcomes will establish various levels of proficiency for new and experienced teachers alike. To this end, our budget includes funding for transformation of the current certification system to an outcomes-based model and the development of expectations and standards that are realistic, equitable, and in the end hold our teachers accountable.

One of the most important programs is the Family Resource and Youth Service Centers. This program was born from the real-life notion that in order for our children to have an opportunity to learn, they cannot be inhibited by social, health, and other problems they bring to school with them. The proposed budget includes a $10 million increase in General Fund support in fiscal year 1995 and a $20 million increase in fiscal year 1996 to complete this program. This will provide for a total of 673 centers by the end of the new biennium compared to the current number of 373. If the proposed funding is approved, all currently eligible schools, approximately 1,100 statewide, will be served by a center.

No discussion regarding educational reform is complete without the state's commitment to the funding of public libraries. In the 1992 session, we were able to provide our libraries with the 53 cents per capita funding formula for the first time since that standard was adopted in 1986. Because libraries are essential for independent, individual learning over a lifetime, I am proposing that the state aid base grant to public libraries be doubled in this budget. It has been over forty years since this base grant formula has received budgetary attention. Ignorance is slavery and knowledge is freedom. Our public libraries are essential to our democratic way of life. We must ensure that they flourish.

HIGHER EDUCATION

TO compete in the 21st century, our universities, as well as all of state government, likewise must be held accountable. Today, we are too often satisfied with too much duplication and too much mediocrity. There is too much hand wringing and too little forceful leadership; too much blaming, finger pointing, and too little positive action. Part of the problem, of course, is that we have eight public universities and fourteen community colleges in a state with fewer than four million people. There is no central governing body, no one body or person to be held accountable to see that efficient and effective uses of our higher education resources exist. That is why I created a commission earlier this year with each college president being a member to devise a plan to put our $700 million annual investment in higher education to better use.

I had hoped the presidents, as members of that committee, along with university board chairmen and administration and legislative representatives, would make significant progress toward eliminating duplication in our higher education system and creating a system that emphasizes excellence. They jointly eliminated over two hundred programs, but I believe they can do more! The commission made *major* progress in devising a plan for financially rewarding universities in the future for measurable results and progress toward agreed-upon goals in the area of instruction, public service, and research. While this concept of funding based on results and progress toward goals of excellence will take years to *fully* implement, it will eliminate inefficiency and wastefulness and provide proper incentives for excellence.

For the new biennium, the higher education budget will provide a 2 percent net operating increase in the first year and a 3 percent increase in fiscal year 1996, with all of the second-year funding to be earned solely through the new performance-based process. If additional money is needed, further reductions of duplication can be achieved by the university presidents.

Few areas in higher education are as critical as engineering. In recognition of this, the proposed budget fully funds the Council on Higher Education's budget request for the engineering education enhancement program.

Engineering education also will be enhanced in the Paducah area. One million dollars over the biennium is being added to the University of Kentucky budget for course offerings or other programming in the field of engineering at Paducah Community College. The University of Kentucky will be required to identify $1,000,000 to be spread equally between the two fiscal years, from its internal sources, to match these additional state funds and enhance engineering offerings. Moreover, should local governments in the Paducah area or private fund raising be able to raise up to $2,000,000 per year beyond these amounts for engineering enhancement, I am recommending that these local funds also be matched with up to $2,000,000 each year from the General Fund surplus account, on a contingent basis. This will provide a potential of up to $10,000,000 for the new biennium in new, targeted funding available for the Paducah and

Purchase areas for engineering enhancements. At the University of Kentucky in Lexington, the budget will provide for construction of a new Mechanical Engineering Facility to meet a critical need. Already some $2 million in private funds have been raised, with $4 million as a goal.

Although not currently listed in the proposed budget, we must help the University of Louisville build the badly needed Health Research Facility. In addition to the authorization to spend up to $9 million in private or university funds, if the University of Louisville will commit to raise an additional $5 million in private or university funds, I will propose that the capital budget be amended to allow the expenditure of an additional $14 million in state funds.

Additionally, I propose amending the budget to authorize Northern Kentucky University in this biennium to spend as much as $2 million in private or university funds to begin the design of the Sciences Classroom Building, a teaching facility at Northern.

The community college system will receive a 3 percent increase in funding each year of the biennium. Too often in recent years, our higher education administrators have postponed tough management decisions by increasing tuition charges to our students. That is wrong. Our proposed budget will prohibit any further tuition increases in the next biennium at our universities.

WORKFORCE DEVELOPMENT

According to the 1990 U.S. Census, the Commonwealth of Kentucky ranks forty-ninth in the number of adults who have completed high school. Among Kentucky's adult population, 36 percent do not possess a high-school diploma and, of those, 18 percent did not complete the eighth grade. This intolerable level of illiteracy and lack of preparation for the workforce must stop. Seventy-five percent of our labor force for the year 2010 is already on the job. If our businesses are to achieve and maintain success in a global economy, a workforce of skilled, well-educated adults must be created. Thus, our budget recommendation includes a commitment to the State of Kentucky Investment in Lifelong Learning (called SKILL) Initiative and increases the total Workforce Development budget by 21 percent.

STATE WORKERS

OUR budget also recognizes and rewards one of our greatest resources—our state workers. Most state workers are honest, hard-working people who work for considerably less than their counterparts in the private sector. Instead of constantly bashing these people, we need to join with them as partners, encourage them to economize the expenditures of state money, and challenge them to accomplish even more for all Kentuckians. The Coalition of State Employees, represented by Jack Sharp, Sarah Hurst, and Marvin Terry, did a fabulous job with the Governor's Quality and Efficiency Commission and greatly impressed the other members from the private sector.

Because of the great strides we have made toward a leaner, more efficient government, I am very proud that I can announce that our budget gives state employees a 5 percent raise in each year of the biennium. I want to mention two categories of dedicated state employees to whom we have given special adjustments in pay. We are raising the entry-level salary of correction officers at our prisons and patient aides at state mental retardation facilities by an additional 15 percent. We have been grossly unfair to these people for far too long.

HUMAN RESOURCES

FOR Kentucky to compete in the next century, we must demand accountability and a timely and meaningful transition from welfare to the workplace. To provide the health and human services we need, we must reinvent welfare and the government that delivers the programs. We must cut the budgets for central administration and related services within the Cabinet for Human Resources. Many of you in this chamber and countless Kentuckians across this state have shared my concern that too much money is wasted in programs and in a bureaucracy too often administered by technocrats that is too large, too unaccountable, and too wasteful. We have already made significant changes in this area, and we are prepared to make many more.

CHR's original mission was to provide for the health and human service needs of all Kentuckians. Over the past decade, the CHR workforce, however, has grown by 22 percent. This is because when policymakers asked them to assume new responsibilities, they did not require the agency to evaluate the need to continue to provide existing services. As a consequence, CHR simply added more personnel, rather than retraining and redeploying workers. Over the past twenty years, CHR has evolved into a large, multi-layered bureaucracy that frustrates not only the citizens it was created to serve, but the dedicated public servants who struggle to work within it. Our budget recommends a complete redesign of the entire CHR organizational structure to create a leaner, more productive agency that delivers higher value to Kentucky taxpayers. This will be accomplished through attrition.

Our budget recommends more than $600,000 in each year of the 1995–96 biennium for community services for the mentally ill. These funds will provide a full range of support services including medicines which prevent rehospitalization. New dollars have also been included to provide individual and group therapy for mentally ill and mentally retarded nursing home residents and to expand community-based services to emotionally disturbed children through the Kentucky Impact Program. Three million dollars over the new biennium is recommended for the Supported Living Program, which provides a full array of services to help integrate persons with disabilities into the community. More than $6 million in the upcoming biennium will be used to keep mentally ill persons undergoing incompetency hearings out of our jails.

WELFARE REFORM

MANY Kentuckians agree that the current system of public assistance—welfare—has failed both the people it was intended to serve and the taxpayers who support it. Although Aid to Families with Dependent Children provides for the basic subsistence needs of its beneficiaries and attempts to move recipients into the workforce through the JOBS program, too few parents are successful in making the transition to work. This is unacceptable. Job training is not coordinated and comprehensive; transitional support services are limited; child support payments are sporadic or non-existent; goals are loosely defined and poorly communicated; and sanctions for recipients who refuse to participate in the JOBS program are weak and ineffective.

I strongly believe that it is government's responsibility to help those citizens who are *unable* to help themselves. However, it is not government's responsibility to help those who are *unwilling* to help themselves. If we are to be serious about welfare reform we must develop a program that provides adequate AFDC benefits, child care, transportation, housing, health care, and education. In return, we must require participation and employment.

I believe that with the proper federal waiver we can create such a program with the welfare legislation we now have. I want to work with Rep. Tom Burch, Sen. Benny Ray Bailey,[7] and all others who are genuinely interested in this subject. At the present time, we are not being fair to the welfare recipient, and we are also not being fair to the Kentucky taxpayer.

PARKS

TWO years ago I proposed that we revitalize the Kentucky state park system and once again make it the nation's finest. I recommended, and you approved, the issuance of $100 million in state revenue bonds to maintain, renovate, and upgrade our parks system. You endorsed that package of timely improvements and admonished those of us who were to compile the list of individual projects for your final consideration to stress basic infrastructure over new construction; roofs and renovations over frills and extras; the existing parks system over additions to that system. I am proud to say that Tourism Secretary Luallen[8] has met your charge with a list of some seventy-one projects, made public some six weeks ago.

You have seen "the list." It is lengthy and well considered. It will not have on it all of the park projects you and I might want. I hoped to go farther and to establish some new lodges, but the funds and the priorities simply would not permit this. Thus, with the $100 million investment, we will focus on the basics. However, I will ask the Privatization Commission to explore the feasibility of privatization options for needs not contained on "the list." This investment to reclaim our parks will be a great economic boost to our entire commonwealth as our bid specifications will require the use of Kentucky products and materials and the payment of the prevailing wage.

COAL SEVERANCE

OUR coal-producing region must increase its efforts to diversify its economic base. We cannot wait until the coal runs out—the foundation for a diversified economy must be completed now. That's why, as a candidate for governor, I advocated the return of more coal severance tax dollars to eastern Kentucky as well as to the coal counties in western Kentucky. We increased this amount by 6 percent in our first budget and increase it by an additional 7 percent in this budget.

ROADS

THERE is another promise that must be kept that does much for the economies of rural and urban areas throughout the state. The Economic Development Road Bond program you first authorized in the 1990 session for $600 million of new bond authority on eight major road systems statewide must be continued. This budget proposes that the next phase of road construction move forward on schedule with $150 million of bonds to be sold in fiscal year 1995. I realize this is a significant investment. We must understand, however, that there remain many unmet road and bridge needs.

Another program of statewide importance, with strong economic development and environmental implications, is the Kentucky Infrastructure Authority wastewater treatment program. Our budget will include $15 million in new state funding that will attract $75 million in federal funds for statewide wastewater treatment plant improvements.

AGRICULTURE

IN the last few months, I have engaged in a vigorous debate and candidly taken some heat from several quarters because of plain talk about the future of Kentucky's farmers. We must fight to maintain the viability of the family farm. It is a way of life and living for thousands of Kentuckians and unless we openly and honestly debate its future and find new solutions, it will only continue to decline and diminish. In addition to the debate I called for at the federal level regarding the plowback of a portion of the tobacco tax to help Kentucky farmers, this budget calls for an array of new programs that will help make Kentucky farmers a more viable economic force.

We will authorize the University of Kentucky to develop the Pin Oak Farm property you purchased as a replacement for Coldstream Farm. Progress has been slow to date, and while Coldstream has seen some significant economic activity, there has been no corresponding activity at the old Pin Oak Farm. This budget authorizes and encourages the University of Kentucky to move forward with the Agricultural Economic Development Initiative and the first phase of the development of the Animal Science Research Center to be located at the former Pin Oak #1 Farm. Although the university requested state General Fund support for these projects, the budget provides authority from university funds. It is intended that these funds be generated from the revenues realized by the university from the development of the Coldstream Research Park. It is important to recall that Coldstream Farm was provided to the university specifically for use in the development of the agriculture program. Therefore, it is only appropriate that the university use this impressive resource to replace the agriculture facilities that are being converted to other uses and to further the interests of agriculture. To allow time for a planned transition, it is not intended that the university use the revenues generated by the Coldstream Research Park solely for agricultural purposes.

The budget also includes authorization to create a major farmers' market development to be located in northern Kentucky, in partnership with the federal government, which will provide substantial matching funds. The total development could approach $8 million, including $3 million in state bond support.

ECONOMIC DEVELOPMENT

In the 1992 session, House Bill 89 created the Economic Development Partnership Board, which for the first time required the creation of a comprehensive strategic plan for economic development for the entire state. This plan will be finished next month. It will only be as good as its execution and implementation. It will be up to all of us, together with Economic Development Secretary Strong,[9] to demand and require accountability in this process as we begin the difficult task of implementing this plan. One of the primary catalysts in this plan will be the funding we propose to create flexible manufacturing and agriculture networks that will encourage Kentucky businesses to share information, technology, and marketing strategies and promote a cooperative environment as we restructure certain of our economic-development programs.

We have continued the proven economic development bond program and the significant tax credit programs you authorized in the 1992 General Assembly. In the first two years of this administration we have announced nearly thirty thousand new jobs—jobs like the Fidelity Investment in northern Kentucky and Dana Corporation in Elizabethtown. These programs work. Instead of cash giveaway programs, these programs require a company to earn its way by creating the jobs first.

To create the strong economy we need, we must deal with the workers' compensation problem. I support the concept of the compromise reached by labor, business, Secretary Palmore,[10] and others. This legislation is currently being drafted, and I invite your comments. Our present patchwork tax code is a deterrent to job creation in this Commonwealth. While we have more than enough on our plate for this session, I ask that you give serious thought to addressing comprehensive tax reform study as soon as this session is completed. With the proper commitment, we could be ready to deal with tax reform immediately after the November elections.

ENVIRONMENTAL PROTECTION

COMPLEMENTING these economic-development efforts, our Natural Resources and Environmental Protection Cabinet will continue its efforts to enforce environmental regulations, including full implementation of the Clean Air Act amendments. Natural Resources forestry experts plan to begin a reorientation of the Division of Forestry so that the wood products industry, and modern forestry management practices supporting sustained growth, can be melded with sound environmental stewardship.

Modeled on the President's National Service Corps, Natural Resources Secretary Phillip Shepherd[11] has requested, and I support in the proposed budget, the creation of a new Kentucky Environmental Service Corps for citizens of all ages beginning in fiscal year 1996. This Service Corps will enlist the time, talent, and energy of Kentuckians who want to be of service in the cause of environmental protection. Initially, forty positions will be created and the corps will respond to projects proposed by local governments, businesses, and environmental groups. We will also expand the Nature Preserves Commission staff to oversee the Commonwealth's resources and unique assets for which they are stewards, and we provide funding to acquire unique areas, such as old-growth forests.

REVENUE COLLECTION

WE intend to support the Revenue Cabinet and Secretary Burse[12] in her efforts to collect the taxes already on the books. In the interests of fairness, equity, and accountability, we must collect what is already due to the state treasury under the current tax laws. Truthfully, we are not doing the best job of that now. Consequently, I am recommending approval of the budget request from the Revenue Cabinet to increase the collections staff, the audit staff, the field audit program, criminal enforcement activity, and administration of the delinquent tax fund. We will also provide funds for a new infusion of technology that will lead to long-term modernization of our revenue collection activity. The effort will require an additional 118 workers above the levels you approved in the 1992 session. Nonetheless, conservative estimates provided by the Revenue Cabinet are that we can reliably expect to collect over $33 million of new General Fund revenue over the biennium from existing tax levies simply with proper collection efforts.

BOND PROJECTS

During the 1992 legislative session, I proposed to you a limited capital project agenda to be financed with state revenue bonds. You authorized that proposal in the amount of $439 million in new bonded indebtedness to support the parks bonds, and a previous installment of the road bonds, as well as basic infrastructure and a few new projects.

While our economy has improved and our financial position also has improved, now is not a time for extensive borrowing. Therefore, I will again present a limited and carefully selected capital projects agenda. The new projects recommended total $474 million for the biennium, and this is the third-lowest total new debt amount approved in any budget in the past fourteen years. This level of new debt when coupled with the lowest interest rates in thirty years makes this debt package a prudent and sound investment in Kentucky's future.

None of us should embark upon new debt lightly. Neither should we shrink from the responsibility we have to provide public facilities that meet standards of health, safety, and public access. We have sobering responsibilities with respect to criminal justice that must be met, and we have a long-term commitment to the development of Kentucky's economy through jobs creation projects and education enhancements.

Among the projects we will be proposing are the following:

- The Commonwealth Library at the University of Kentucky
- The Muhlenberg County Prison, Phase II
- The Northern Kentucky Convention Center in Covington
- The Commonwealth Convention Center in Louisville
- The Kentucky History Center in Frankfort
- Hazard Community College Student Performing Arts/Convention Center
- Hopkinsville Regional Tech Training Center
- Danville Kentucky Tech Facility

- Morehead State University—Lappin Hall, Phase II for a new science facility
- Ashland Community College Classroom Building
- Phase I of a new office building for state government in Frankfort
- A $7 million share of the new University of Louisville football stadium

BUDGET SUMMARY

LET me conclude this budget outline with two observations about the budget process.

BUDGET RESERVE

FIRST, when we took office we inherited a budget that was dramatically out of balance, with a rainy day account of approximately $23 million. That problem was only compounded by the impossible task any new governor faces under the current constitutional requirement of an early January legislative session, only three to four weeks after inauguration. Today I propose a truly balanced budget with $130 million in the rainy day account, *the largest budget reserve in history*! This has been accomplished without any increase in taxes.

REVENUE FORECAST

SECOND, no budget can be built without a responsible revenue forecast. We have endured budget cuts twelve times in the last fourteen years in this state. There's no way we can work under these conditions. We have this year for the first time joined forces—legislative and executive branch together—to develop a consensus revenue forecast. It is my belief that this new partnership together with a responsible level of spending will allow us to end the cycle of budget cuts our state too often endures. Because of the court's findings in the *ARMCO Steel* and the *Peabody Coal* cases, we are proposing technical, corrective legislation to the tax code. It is our judgment that the rationale and interpretation of the courts in these two lawsuits does not comport with original legislative intent, and, thus, this $69 million mistake must be corrected, and I intend to take the lead on this issue.

As I said, we are proposing a Budget Reserve Trust Fund of $130 million, *over five times the size of the rainy day fund we inherited when we took office. This rainy day fund is the biggest in the state's history and is approximately 2 1/2 percent of the annual General Fund.* Now, there are three additional initiatives that are critical to accomplish during the next two years: crime prevention, improvement of the personnel system, and improved utilization of communications technology.

CRIME PREVENTION

ALL of our efforts to create jobs and economic opportunity for the people of Kentucky mean nothing if our families cannot live in homes and neighborhoods that are free from violence and the fear of violence. A few days ago, I announced my support for significant crime-fighting measures that will be introduced in this legislative session. These measures limit the access of juveniles to unsupervised weapons, including depriving juveniles of their ability to obtain assault rifles.

Crime-control measures need not involve increased costs. Some, in fact, can decrease our costs. Currently, we are unnecessarily incarcerating people better dealt with in other settings, such as community settings. This practice must cease. Some measures do cost money, and I am prepared to recommend additional funding. The budget includes over $6 million in construction funds to support the development of a secure juvenile detention facility in eastern Kentucky and northern Kentucky, and to design a similar facility for western Kentucky should that need develop.

We will authorize the Kentucky State Police to attain a trooper strength of one thousand, equaling its highest authorized level ever, an addition of thirty sworn officers. We will also strongly support Attorney General Chris Gorman's[13] Task Force on Child Sexual Abuse. A full-time Victims Advocate will be authorized for each of the fifty-six commonwealth attorneys' offices to assist people who are victims of crime. Both the State Police Crime Lab and the Cabinet for Human Resources will also receive additional funding in support of the child sexual offense initiative.

The budget also contemplates strong support for an often-neglected aspect of the criminal justice system. Ever since the Office of Public Advocacy was established in 1972, it has survived from "hand to mouth." In my judgment, this was attributable not only to their often-unpopular job of defending poor people charged with crimes, but also to a lack of imagination with respect to seeking financial support.

Under the leadership of Public Protection Secretary Holmes,[14] the Task Force on the Delivery and Funding of Public Defender Services recently concluded its work with a recommendation that the public advocate receive significant additional funding from non-traditional sources. These include an increase in the DUI service fee of $50 and a $40 user fee for those criminal defendants who have the money to help pay for the legal services they receive. These two non-General Fund fees will enable the public advocate substantially to expand services and properly discharge their responsibilities.

PERSONNEL SYSTEM IMPROVEMENTS

ALL of these programs are no better than the ability of our state employees to work in a state government that is accountable to the customer, the taxpayers of Kentucky. Recognizing this need, we established earlier last year the Governor's Commission on Quality and Efficiency to review state government operations and chart a new course for Kentucky. The fifty-five members of that commission, drawn from merit employees and private sector citizens alike, delivered to me approximately six weeks ago the first report of this commission, a "Wake Up Call for Kentucky." The conclusion of the work of that commission is that Kentucky has all of the resources we need to transform government services and meet people's needs. The only question is whether we have the political will to make the tough decisions necessary to prepare for the twenty-first century. If we do, Kentucky can be a leader in the nation. If we fail in this task, our ability to compete in the next century will be sorely diminished.

The one refrain that this commission heard over and over again was the crying need to empower our state employees to do their jobs. Our state employees are demanding a career service system that secures their employment free from political whim; provides competitive wages, benefits, and incentives; creates meaningful training and development opportunities; gives them freedom to make decisions and flexibility to manage; and defines measures that recognize success and correct failures. State government is the largest employer in Kentucky. If we are to retain our best and brightest people, we absolutely must follow the model of American business and change our personnel management system to support productive employees. To that end we have created the Career Service System Task Force that will propose during this General Assembly the creation of pilot programs across this government to begin the process of transforming our personnel system. We can no longer run a government with five different personnel systems and over sixteen hundred job classifications. That stifles efficiency and creativity.

TECHNOLOGY

NO discussion of our vision for Kentucky in the next century would be complete without addressing the issue of technology, what Vice President Gore[15] calls the information superhighway that is coming closer to reality every day. The applications of technology in today's world are only limited by our imagination. Our children will receive much of their education, health care, and the delivery of innumerable essential services on electronic networks of which we can barely conceive. Our proposed budget continues the implementation of this network. Some months ago, I instructed the Finance Cabinet to develop a plan to build and construct an information network to handle all of state government's information needs into the next century and to be accessible to private sector users across the state as well. I have directed that this process be competitively bid and involve as much private sector capital investment as possible. That process is on track and Kentucky will be one of the first states in the nation to begin this exciting and vital effort.

CONCLUSION

THE hour is late and I thank you for your patience. I hope in some measure I have been able to share with you our dream, our vision for Kentucky—a community where each and every Kentuckian has a chance to be educated, to work, to own a home, to raise a family, and to be secure and safe in their old age. It is a community built on a commitment to opportunity for every Kentuckian and the responsibility of every Kentuckian to carry their own weight. The problems are numerous, but the solutions are available. President Kennedy once said, "Our task is not to fix the blame for the past, but to fix the course for the future." You and I must fix the course. We asked for the job . . . So let's get on with it!

---

1. Robert F. Stephens (1927–), born in Covington, Kentucky; assistant Fayette County attorney, 1964–69; Fayette County judge, 1969–75; Kentucky attorney general, 1976–79; justice, Kentucky Supreme Court, 1979–82; chief justice, Kentucky Supreme Court, 1982–98; Kentucky secre-

tary of justice 1999– ; Democrat. *Who's Who in America, 1999–2000,* 54th ed. (New Providence, N.J., 1999).

2. The 1996 General Assembly changed again the maximum contribution by an individual to $1,000.

3. Legislation enacted by the 1992 General Assembly established the Kentucky Economic Development Partnership to govern the Cabinet for Economic Development. With the governor serving as chairman and eight of the eleven members from the private sector, the partnership gave the private sector its first formal involvement in the planning and implementation of the cabinet's mission. Building on the 1992 legislation which enhanced Kentucky's ability to retain existing jobs and attract new ones, the Commonwealth saw a net gain of 14,522 new jobs in 1992 and 15,418 in 1993, bringing the total number of new jobs created under the Jones administration to a record 29,940, more than double the number of new jobs created in the previous two years by the previous administration.

4. In his first two years, Governor Jones appointed 147 African Americans to boards and commissions, nearly twice the number of people the previous administration appointed in four years. In the same two years, Jones appointed 563 women to state boards and commissions, over 75 percent more than the previous administration's two-year total.

5. The Quality and Efficiency Commission was established by the Jones administration to determine how services could be more efficiently delivered to the people of Kentucky. The fifty-three-member commission was composed of both public- and private-sector leaders. The commission's final report, presented to Governor Jones in 1993, included 270 recommendations to streamline government. Jones acted upon the commission's recommendations with a variety of executive orders that, among other things, took steps to modernize the thirty-year-old state personnel system and established the first state government-wide strategic-planning procedures.

6. As of May 1993, Kentucky had 513,000 people on Medicaid. The provider tax was passed during the 1993 special session with moderate opposition. Despite protests from physicians, hospitals, and pharmacists, lawmakers enacted a new tax on all Medicaid providers in order to meet federal mandates. The state had been taxing hospitals, doctors, and other providers, but they were guaranteed to get back the tax, plus additional reimbursements. New federal rules removed the guarantee and required that the tax be paid by all members in each provider group. With federal matching funds added in, the new provider tax is estimated to raise approximately $713 million, or about one-third of the state's Medicaid budget. Jones later vetoed a section obtained by hospitals automatically returning $120 million to them.

7. Benny Ray Bailey (1944–), Alice Lloyd College, A.A.; Pikeville College, B.A.; Indiana State University, M.S.; Ohio University, Ph.D; Democratic legislator, elected in 1979 to the 29th district Kentucky senate seat; re-elected, 1983–2000; co-leader of senate coup, 1997; Appropriations/ Revenue Committee chair, 1997–99; Education Committee, State and Local

Government Committee; health-care administrator. *Who's What in Kentucky Government 1999–2000* (Frankfort, 1999).

8. Eugenia Crittenden Blackburn "Crit" Luallen (1952–), born in Frankfort; B.A., Centre College, 1974; public relations and marketing consultant, 1977–82; media coordinator, Collins for Governor Campaign, 1982–83; special assistant to the governor, 1983–84; commissioner, Kentucky Department of the Arts, 1984–88; senior public affairs manager, Humana, 1988; president, Greater Louisville Economic Development Partnership, 1991–92; secretary, Kentucky Tourism Cabinet, 1992–94; secretary, Kentucky Finance and Administration Cabinet, 1994–95; deputy secretary, Kentucky Governor's Executive Cabinet, 1995–96; Kentucky Budget Director, 1998–99; secretary, Kentucky Governor's Executive Cabinet, since 1996; *Who's Who in America, 1999–2000*, 54th ed. (New Providence, N.J., 1999).

9. Marvin E. "Gene" Strong (1953–), born in Jackson, Kentucky; B.S., Eastern Kentucky University, 1974; director of fiscal affairs, Kentucky State Police, 1976–81; executive vice-president of leasing, The Webb Companies, Lexington, 1981–91; deputy secretary, Kentucky Cabinet for Economic Development and special advisor to governor, 1991–93; secretary, Kentucky Cabinet for Economic Development, 1993–present.

10. Carol Palmore (1949–), B.S., Murray State University; J.D., University of Kentucky, 1977; secretary of labor, 1983–94; deputy secretary of personnel under Governor Paul Patton, 1995–98; secretary of personnel under Patton, 1998– ; Owensboro native and attorney. *Who's Who in America, 1999–2000*, 54th ed. (New Providence, N.J., 1999).

11. Phillip J. Shepherd (1955–), A.B., Asbury College, 1977; J.D., University of Kentucky College of Law, 1980; attorney, Shepherd and Childers, 1984–91; Natural Resources and Environmental Protection Cabinet secretary during the Jones administration, 1991–95; member of Prichard Committee for Academic Excellence, 1996– ; unsuccessful candidate for Kentucky Supreme Court, 1999; Frankfort attorney, frequently represents environmental causes.

12. Kim Burse (1954–), served as secretary of Revenue Cabinet during Jones administration, 1991–95; former assistant state treasurer, assistant director of Kentucky Development Finance Authority, and treasurer of the Commonwealth Small Business Development Corporation; Prospect, Kentucky, native and certified public accountant and cash manager.

13. Chris Gorman (1943–), graduate of University of Kentucky and University of Kentucky law school; former Jefferson County commissioner; Kentucky attorney general, 1992–96; unsuccessful congressional candidate in 3rd district Kentucky, 1998. *Who's Who in America, 1999–2000*, 54th ed. (New Providence, N.J., 1999).

14. Edward J. Holmes (1952–), former director of planning and housing for the Bluegrass Development District, 1978–91; secretary of Public Protection and Regulations, 1991–95; former project planner for Howard K. Bell Engineers, and city planner for Beloit, Wisconsin; chair of Kentucky Public Service Commission, 1996– .

15. Albert Gore Jr. (1948–), son of U.S. Senator Albert Gore and Pauline Gore; B.A. cum laude, Harvard, 1969; Grad. Sch. of Religion, 1971–72; law school, 1974–76, Vanderbilt; U.S. Army, 1969–71, Vietnam; investigative reporter, editorial writer for the *Nashville Tennessean*, 1971–76; homebuilder and land developer, Tanglewood Home Builders Co., 1971–76; livestock and tobacco farmer, from 1973; member 95th–98th Congresses from Tenn., 1977–85; U.S. senator from Tenn., 1985–93; author, *Earth in the Balance: Ecology and the Human Spirit* (1992); vice-president of the U.S., 1993–2001; presidential candidate, 2000. *Who's Who in America, 2000,* 54th ed. (New Providence, N.J., 1999).

AUDIT BILL—HOUSE BILL 443
Frankfort / February 1, 1994

I'D ALSO like to announce my support for the passage of House Bill 443, sponsored by Jim Wayne of Louisville.[1] His bill requires, among other things, that each sheriff's office, county clerk, and fiscal court be audited by the state auditor's office at least once every four years. Passing this bill into law is not only another step toward ensuring ethical behavior, but also a method of guaranteeing the Kentucky taxpayer gets the most money at the local level, as well as the state level.

I commend Representative Wayne for his foresight on this bill, and I urge the members of the General Assembly to pass it into law.

---

1. Jim Wayne (1948–), B.A., Maryknoll College; M.A., Maryknoll School of Theology; M.S.W., Smith College; Democrat; elected to Kentucky 35th house district, 1990; re-elected, 1992–2000; president, Wayne Corp. *Who's What in Kentucky Government 1999–2000* (Frankfort, 1999).

BILL SIGNING OF HOUSE BILL 238 ON LOCAL GOVERNMENT ETHICS

Frankfort / February 22, 1994

As I sign this legislation, it's important for us to recognize where it will take local government. House Bill 238 sets minimum standards for ethics. It should be viewed as an opportunity for cities and counties to write their own standards—their own rules of conduct—rules that will be given the harshest review not only by the state, but through the ballot box. Elected officials will be expected to administer their offices honorably and will be expected to answer to the people who put them into office if they don't.

The new law says that each local code of ethics must include, at the very least, standards of conduct, requirements for financial disclosure, a policy on nepotism, and the designation of a person or group to enforce the code of ethics.

While House Bill 238 provides the opportunity for local governments to establish honorable rules of conduct, it must be viewed as a starting point only. We must all pay attention to how well this law is implemented, and we must all be ready to act further, if it is not implemented as was intended for it to be.

I commend the bill's sponsors who join me here today for beginning the process of asking cities and counties to rewrite their rules for better government and for better public service.

BILL SIGNING—HOUSE BILL 359

Frankfort / March 7, 1994

. . . To the sponsors of House Bill 359, to all of you standing with us today, you have helped create a better tomorrow for all generations. I thank you for taking a stand against the proliferation of guns among young people, and say to them, guns are present in society so that they can be used responsibly. Guns are a responsibility, as well as a right.

House Bill 359 will help ensure that kids don't get their hands on handguns for the purpose of committing a violent act. House Bill

359 will help ensure that parents know when their children have guns, and that their children have guns for the right reasons. And the penalties imposed by this legislation—penalties for handgun possession and for unlawfully providing handguns to juveniles—will help ensure that the law is obeyed.

. . . This legislation would not be possible without Attorney General Chris Gorman, Greg Stumbo,[1] and all the senators and representatives you see here today.

. . . Now, let's sign into law House Bill 359.

---

1. Gregory D. "Greg" Stumbo (1951–), B.A., University of Kentucky; J.D., University of Louisville; past vice-president, Floyd County Young Democrats; assistant Floyd County attorney, 1977; trial commissioner to district court, 1978; city attorney, Martin, 1978–80; elected to the 95th district of the Kentucky House of Representatives, 1979; re-elected, 1981–2000; Democratic floor leader, 1985– ; Prestonsburg attorney. *Who's What in Kentucky Government 1999 2000* (Frankfort, 1999).

BILL SIGNING—HOUSE BILL 215
Frankfort / March 9, 1994

IT'S not often that a governor can literally save lives, just with the stroke of a pen. But that's what we will do today. By requiring people in Kentucky to "buckle up," we can finally "buckle down" and work toward decreasing the number of traffic fatalities in Kentucky.

Here's why this piece of legislation is so important. In the latest edition of *Kentucky Traffic Facts,* published by the Kentucky State Police, there were more than eight hundred people killed in motor vehicle crashes in a year; 83 percent of the people who were killed were not wearing a seat belt. And 73 percent of the people in crashes [who] suffered an incapacitating injury were not wearing a safety belt.

State and national statistics show that by correctly and consistently using a safety belt, you can cut by half your chances of being killed or seriously hurt in a crash. That's an amazing fact. But even if this law saved only one life, wouldn't it be worth it?

Current information shows that even after years of public information and education, only four in ten people buckle up in

Kentucky. If you're still part of the majority who do not use your safety belt, think of it this way: Don't do it for yourself. Do it for your family—your children, your spouse, your loved ones. Do it for them. Buckle up so they won't have to bear the pain and suffering and grief of losing you. That should make your decision a little easier.

My thanks to the sponsors of this legislation. . . .

Now, I'll sign this bill into law.

BILL SIGNING—HOUSE BILL 368

Frankfort / March 30, 1994

House Bill 368 is a very important piece of legislation. It amends the Kentucky Heritage Land Conservation Act. It will provide money to buy and maintain land for wildlife management areas, recreation areas, state forests, nature preserves, and wetlands.

Libby[1] and I supported House Bill 368 because we feel it is important to preserve the natural heritage of this Commonwealth. Already, we are recognizing rare and endangered plant and animal species that should be protected. We find fewer and fewer natural areas that exemplify the forests and grasslands and abundant wildlife that sustained Native Americans in Kentucky thousands of years ago. Our remaining high-quality streams and rivers need to be protected. And we must save a generous portion of that "rich land beyond the mountains" that enticed settlers through the Cumberland Gap.

The 1990 General Assembly enacted the Kentucky Heritage Land Conservation Act to provide for land acquisitions that would preserve natural areas, as well as provide critical wildlife habitat and outdoor recreation areas. Now, with this legislation, land can be purchased on a willing seller/willing buyer basis and be managed by the Department of Fish and Wildlife Resources, the Division of Forestry, the Department of Parks, the Kentucky State Nature Preserves Commission and the Wild Rivers Program.

Money will be available to local governments, colleges, and universities to purchase and maintain heritage land. Part of the proceeds from environmental fines will be allocated to the Environmental Council to develop and implement a sustained statewide educational program to protect the environment and natural resources of the Commonwealth. Also, money will be set aside to promote coal-related issues.

This legislation will benefit all of us. It will protect land and water for present and future generations. It also will contribute to the state's economy by providing even more outdoor recreational areas that Kentuckians and our visitors can enjoy.

As I sign this legislation, I'd like to take this opportunity to thank Representative Brown[2] and Sen. Ed Ford,[3] and all of the bill's co-sponsors for their support and work. It is just another example of how this administration and the legislature can work together to make strong decisions for the good of Kentucky.

---

1. Elizabeth Lloyd "Libby" Jones (1943–), B.A., Finch College, 1965; co-owner, Airdrie Farm; director, Kentucky Opera; vice-chair, Bluegrass Conservancy; President's Council, American Farmland Trust; member, Henry Clay Memorial Foundation; director, Land and Nature Trust of the Bluegrass; trustee, Midway College; director, Thomas D. Clark Foundation; executive committee, Kentucky Historical Society; Advisory Committee on Natural Resources and Environmental Protection, Bluegrass A.D.D.; director, Lexington-Frankfort Scenic Corridor Committee; director, Kentucky Agriculture and Environment in the Classroom; steering council for Women Build, Habitat for Humanity International.

2. Mark S. Brown (1951–), attended Western Kentucky University; board of directors, Doe Run Employees Federal Credit Union; member, United Assn. of the Plumbing and Pipefitting Industry, Local 522; Democratic Kentucky state representative, 27th district, 1984–98; pipefitter, mechanical technician.

3. Edward Ford (1930–), D.V.M., Auburn University; Harrison County Board of Education, 1971–77 (chairman, 1973–77); Democratic Kentucky state senator, 30th district, 1978–95; veterinarian; deputy secretary, Executive Cabinet under Governor Patton.

BILL SIGNING—HOUSE BILL 250

Frankfort / April 15, 1994

LADIES and gentlemen, thank you for coming this afternoon for this extraordinary moment in the 200+ year history of our great Commonwealth. The enactment into law of House Bill 250, this Health Care Reform Bill, will bring security and peace of mind to all who call Kentucky home.

Please let me begin by expressing deep, sincere gratitude to the Kentucky house and senate leadership and both chambers' members-at-large. Their dedication to all Kentuckians will become more and more evident in the coming months as we implement the landmark legislation we are signing into law on this, the last day of Kentucky's 1994 General Assembly.

We are also indebted to the Kentuckians for Health Care Reform this great day. This diverse organization, comprised of more than two hundred citizen-oriented interest groups, has worked relentlessly against all odds and obstacles placed in their path since they came together as a force following our special session nearly a year ago. Finally, our gratitude is extended to those visionaries among the provider community, businesses, labor, and major association groups across Kentucky who have helped us reach the signing of health-care reform legislation.

Allow me to take a moment to outline the many good features HB 250 brings to businesses, labor, providers, and citizens in every region of the Commonwealth:

- This legislation will ensure that we do not repeat the cost increases over the past twenty years, when health care rose nearly six times faster than family income and other essentials of life such as utilities.
- Businesses which to a great extent provide benefits to Kentucky employees will now see a leveling off of their insurance premiums, bringing more stability to their cost of doing business in Kentucky.
- Individuals will no longer have to fear accepting a job change for more opportunity, or higher pay, or both, because of the health of a family member. They will now be assured of continuous health insurance when making a job change.
- High-risk individuals will see significant changes in the availability and cost of insurance benefits.
- Family bankruptcy due to a large health claim will no longer cast a shadow over Kentucky's individuals or families.
- In the past, none of us was able to truly know just what we were paying and the product we received in health care. Now, with enactment of HB 250, all of us will be better informed about insurance through reporting of data on cost and quality of health care in Kentucky.
- Providers who now come under the heavy gun of the rising cost of malpractice insurance will have more information to

defend their decisions, with practice guidelines in place as legal standards of care. While this is an issue we had hoped would bring a greater level of reform, this will be a strong step forward in dealing with malpractice and costly defensive medicine.

- Preservation of the rights of insurance companies to compete fairly, in the same free-enterprise manner to which they are accustomed, will bring new responsibility, which will accrue to the benefit of all Kentuckians. An approval process will be required, in open, public view, with all insurers able to compete on a level playing field.
- Small community hospitals, now the first line-of-life to many Kentucky families suffering a health crisis, will benefit in that their performance and their costs will show Frankfort as well as local folks who may now be heading elsewhere for care that the care they need can be of the highest quality—right there in their own community.
- A Health Policy Board will be implemented and will serve as the referee in the $10 billion health industry in Kentucky. Just as we appreciate a well-officiated basketball game, when we almost forget that the referees are even out on the court doing their job, we envision this board quietly carrying out its task, doing the people's business on an on-going basis—stepping in only when flagrant fouls against the principles of health reform are committed.

As we move forward over the next several months, we share the belief of many members of the house and senate who have made enactment of HB 250 possible. While this may not be the perfect solution to all the problems in our health-care system, it is a very good foundation stone of stateside health-care reform, one which will serve us well as we learn more through its implementation and operation. It will be a wise Kentuckian who gives his or her attention to the work of this assembly gathered here today in support of health-care reform. And it can truly be said that the people of Kentucky have been well represented in the process of passing this landmark legislation.

Thank you, and God bless you all for your dedication, commitment, and your helping hands in making today a reality.

STATE OF THE COMMONWEALTH ADDRESS
Frankfort / January 17, 1995

PRESIDENT of Senate Rose, Speaker of the House Richards,[1] distinguished members of the General Assembly, Mr. Chief Justice Stephens, members of the Supreme Court, Kentucky Historian Laureate Dr. Tom Clark,[2] honored guests, ladies and gentlemen: I don't want you to think that Ross Perot[3] is going to speak here today because we have these charts, but they tell a story that I think is important to tell. I want you to know that I've got as fine a staff as has ever been assembled in the governor's office. And we jointly have spent many, many hours putting together a speech that I think is exceptionally good. I thought of this as I walked up here today, as to whether or not I should give my last State of the Commonwealth Address from the prepared text looking into the TelePrompTer so that it looks to the people out there as if the governor is the brightest person that ever was and never has to look down for a note.

I'm going to put this speech aside and ask you to turn off the TelePrompTer, if you will. There's not a person in here who knew I was going to do that. But I want to talk to you today from my heart, not that there's anything wrong with these words, and every one of these words are words that I mean, or they wouldn't be in that speech. They're things that I feel strongly about or they would not be in that speech. But somehow it seems more appropriate for me to look out into the eyes of each one of you and talk to you about some things that I'm excited about.

Time really flies when you're having fun. Three short years ago I stood here, Mike Bowling,[4] as a newly elected governor to give the Commonwealth Address and it was a very, very interesting moment for me, to say the least. We talked about the things that we needed to do, the members of the General Assembly and the executive branch of government, things that we'd talked about in the campaign that allowed us to get elected to this high office, and in doing so I'm awfully pleased to look back now three years later and see what you and I have accomplished.

When I ran for governor, if you were not a millionaire, or if you did not have some good friends who were millionaires, your chances of getting elected governor were slim and none. And as Happy Chandler[5] used to say, "Slim just left town." But you and I changed all that because we knew it was wrong, and we reduced campaign contributions from $4,000 to $500. And boy was that a step in the right direction. And we've cut out a lot of the money, a lot of the lobbyist involvement, not that there's anything wrong with most of the lobbyists; most of them are good people, just as good as you or I or anybody else in this chamber. But the whole system had gotten out of control, and the legislature had the courage to do something about that, and for that all of Kentucky will be deeply indebted.

We focused not only on campaign finance reform, but we focused on how we were going to change the way economic development was done, how we were going to create more jobs. We got legislation passed, you and I did, to change that permanently. And now the record speaks for itself about what we have done in the way of creating jobs.

If you look at this chart on my right you will see that we have downsized state government every year since we took office, because as a candidate for governor, I heard the people of Kentucky say to me that government was too big and too wasteful, and they asked me if I would do something about it. And I'm indebted to the people of Kentucky for many things, but particularly I'm indebted to the people of Kentucky because what they said to me three years ago allowed us to get a head start on what the rest of the country just heard in this past November elections.

So we've cut out over sixteen hundred permanent, full-time jobs in state government. And we've done it I think, Paul,[6] the right way, because we didn't go in and just fire somebody and not care about how he or she was going to make a living for their family. Instead of that, I told all the cabinet secretaries that whenever somebody leaves in your cabinet for any reason whatsoever, you cannot automatically replace that job. What you've got to do is to see if you can get by without replacing that job. Talk to the people in that department and see if they won't roll up their sleeves and do a little more and make up the difference. And let me tell you, we've got some of the greatest state employees of any place in America, and they have rolled up their sleeves. And we've got over sixteen hundred fewer jobs in state government for a savings of over $40 million, and they deserve a round of applause for that.

And at the same time that we have done that, we have created jobs in the private sector because of the economic-development legislation that you passed. We've now got an economic-development team that's made up of folks from all across Kentucky, from every walk of life. We didn't leave out western Kentucky or eastern Kentucky or northern Kentucky. Everybody is part of it, and we have started creating jobs.

Now, you and I both know that if you do anything you get criticized. There's not a thing that a member of this General Assembly can do that somebody is not going to find a reason to criticize it. But when all is said and done, Hubie,[7] we just have to look at the record, look at the bottom line to see whether it worked or whether it didn't work.

Ten years ago we were so far out of control in Kentucky that our unemployment rate was 2.3 percent above the national average. That zero line, the red line in the middle, running right across into the blue line, that is the national unemployment rate. Ten years ago we were 2.3 above that. And now ten years later, we've been a full percentage point below that. What that means is we've got more people working. The unemployment rate for the month of December is the lowest that it has been in more than two decades, 4.4 percent.

We're not just talking about low-wage jobs, we're talking about good jobs. Because if you will look at the statistics that are available for the last two years of available comparisons of all states in America, our per capita personal income is increasing faster than forty other states. We have the tenth-highest per capita personal income increase. So don't let anybody ever tell you that what you passed, the legislation that you put on my desk and allowed me to sign, is not being successful. Because it is being tremendously successful. And you deserve credit for that; we all deserve credit for that; because it was a team effort.

As I walked over here this evening, I couldn't help but think about what a difference just a year makes. This time last year we had twenty inches of snow and it was twenty degrees below zero. And my relationship with the legislature was probably colder than that. And today I walk over, and the sun is shining, and I feel good, and I do not believe it is a false sense of security. I think I feel good because you and I are working together now. And I've given you a call, and I'm here today to ask you once again to give me an affirmative answer on this call. Because I think it needs to happen.

Let's look at it item by item. First of all we have some dubious distinction right now because, today as I speak to you, we have, without question, the highest inheritance tax rate of any state in America. And by the time this legislative session is over I want to be able to walk out of this statehouse and go to the people of Kentucky and say, "Now you are at the bottom of that terrible list, because there is no state in America that has a lower tax than we have." We need to get to the bottom of that list, and I ask you in this call to help us to do that and to eliminate the inheritance tax completely.

How many people have you talked to that are getting to the senior citizen part of their life, and when they say, "I would like to retire in Kentucky, I would like to stay here because this is my home, but when I've got the highest inheritance tax and then you tax my pension on top of that, then I just can't do it." How many of you have talked to a farmer that has said "We're going to have to sell part of the family farm when I die in order to pay the inheritance tax?" And Billy Ray,[8] you've heard that time and time again. So what we've got to do is address that issue because it's an issue of fairness.

Secondly, let's look at the pension tax. I think I probably have heard more about that in the last three years than any single tax. The people of the Commonwealth of Kentucky have said that if you're not going to tax government pensions, then you ought not to tax my pension. Because that is unfair. Now we've looked at this issue, and there were a number of people that said, "Let's put a tax on all of the pensions and let's put it at a fair rate." And that sounded sensible at the beginning, until we got into it. And let me tell you why that is not sensible to me.

For the simple reason that as I have asked state employees to do more work and have fewer people to help them do that work, I cannot then look them in the eye and say, "By the way now, your reward for that is that I'm going to put a tax on your pension if you get beyond $15,000 or $18,000 or $20,000." There are a lot of good state employees who will retire this year who fortunately will be beyond that. There will be those who will retire in five years or ten years, many of whom will be beyond that. If we tax those pensions beyond $25,000, I would be asking you to increase taxes on thirteen thousand Kentuckians. And I don't believe there are very many people in here who would vote to increase taxes on thirteen thousand Kentuckians. And so this, again, is an issue of fairness. If there is no tax on the government pensions, there ought not to be any tax on the private pensions.

Now let me tell you something that I didn't even know until yesterday. This may come as a surprise to you. We are the only state in America that exempts government pensions and taxes private pensions. No other state in America does that. So we can't go back to our people and say, "Oh, we thought it was okay to go ahead and tax your pensions. We thought it was okay to give you the highest inheritance tax rate in the country." Because if we do, they're going to grade our paper in a very negative way. And you know that and I know that. So I want to ask you to give us support on that issue as well.

Now let's talk about some projects. I think everybody knows my position on a number of projects. I gave you a budget a year ago, and immediately there were some who said, "Well, these numbers don't make sense. We don't have enough money to do these projects." And if you will recall, I argued and argued and fought and fought. But we were unable to get these projects.

You know a person shouldn't have to be kicked by a mule very many times until they begin to get the message. And the message was that, regardless of how good these projects were individually, there was a limit beyond which I could not reasonably expect the legislature to go. So we worked with legislative leadership in both the senate and in the house and we came up with three projects. And these three projects together, as a package, will create twenty-six hundred jobs and will give us a net surplus of nearly three-quarters of a million dollars.

Those are projects that we have to vote for, and I'm asking you to give us the support. Let's look at them individually. First of all it's the convention center expansion in Louisville. Thank you, David Karem.[9] This by itself will create more jobs and more actual surplus dollars, surplus dollars in excess of $1.2 million and total jobs of about sixteen hundred. But we know what companies will come, what groups will come to this Convention Center if we build it. We've already been in contact with those people. We're not guessing about what those numbers are going to be.

Secondly, it is of extreme importance that we build the convention center in northern Kentucky. The people of northern Kentucky have already taken it upon themselves to be willing to build a parking garage to go with it. They're going to build a couple of hotels to go with it. This is going to create jobs and opportunity for the people of northern Kentucky. This is an economic-development project that must be done.

The third project is a fabulous project, because this is a project that will allow us to take the history of this great Commonwealth and put it on display, so that all people will be able to see it. We think that is of significant importance. Right now 90 percent of the artifacts that we have, the historical treasures that this state has, are stored in basements, are stored in warehouses in ways that they will be damaged and that we will be creating grave problems for the future. If we do not preserve our heritage for our children and our children's children, to show them who they are and where they came from, then we have done a terrible thing. In 1990 the legislature agreed to put $2 million into the budget for this history center.

Over a million dollars of that, about $1.2 million, has already been spent, because it has been designed, some property has been bought. And the time has come now for us to go on with this history center. The time has come for us to go ahead and to give this opportunity to our children. And if I have not convinced you, Dr. Thomas Clark is here today, and before you leave this chamber, I hope you will talk with him, because he knows it, and he understands it, and it is of extreme importance that we recognize this.

Now as we look at these three projects, I'm very, very much aware that these three projects are in the golden triangle. I'm very much aware that they're not in the mountains of eastern Kentucky. They're not in western Kentucky, but I ask you please not to get bogged down in regionalism. We must get up on a little higher level and get the big picture of all of Kentucky, because when you help one person in this state, you help the entire state.

Some of you remember when I was a candidate for governor and I won Louisville. It was nearly a full year before the election, and I was very fortunate that fifty elected officials stood up that day and endorsed my candidacy for governor. You were there, Larry Clark.[10] You remember that. And do you remember what I started talking about in downtown Louisville with all the media there? I started talking about the need to give more of the coal severance tax money back to the coal-producing counties. And I could see people begin to look at each other and start whispering. And I read the lips of one lady who said, "Where does he think he is? Did somebody give him the wrong speech?" And they really began to sort of giggle about it. And I said, "I know what you're thinking. Please hear me out. Because if we have a person on welfare in eastern Kentucky or Louisville or western Kentucky, wherever they are, that is a drain to the economy of this entire Commonwealth. So what we had better do is get serious about helping one another. If we are truly a family, we ought to be a family, and we ought to recognize that when we create opportunities in one part of the state it does good for the entire state."

The people of Jefferson County said, "We agree with that." And I went over to western Kentucky and started talking about doing something for Louisville. And as I went around the state, I found out, and I'm here to say without fear of contradiction, that the people of Kentucky are tired of petty politics. They want us to get the big picture. They want us to be a family. They want us to help each other. They want us to look at how we're going to make this family of Kentucky really function together.

So, please, I ask you, don't look at these as projects in one part of the state. Remember when I vetoed the budget, and we came back, and we had to fight to get more money for the state parks? We put over $30 million in the parks in eastern Kentucky. We put over $30 million in the parks in western Kentucky. There aren't any parks in Louisville. There aren't any parks in Covington. And they stood up and they were willing, most of them, to go along with us in that. They didn't ask that question. Most of them were willing to help us.

This is what it's all about. This is the way we're going to make things happen. This is the way we're going to get to a higher level. This is the way we're going to get a bigger picture. And this is the way we are going to build a better Kentucky. Because we can do it. And now that we've got all this other stuff behind us, let's really focus on it. Let's please pass the legislation that will be presented to you.

And let me tell you something else, too. The first year I was governor, I probably hated the job about as much as anybody ever hated anything in the Commonwealth of Kentucky for ten thousand different reasons, and I won't bore you with all those now. The next year I began to tolerate it. Last year I started to like it, and this year I love it. And I'm never running again for anything, I want you to understand that. And Libby's not going to announce for anything.

Now that we've got things working, these last eleven months will be *the* most productive last year in the history of any administration in this Commonwealth, and I ask you to help me do that because the people of Kentucky deserve it. Thank you, and may God continue to bless the great Commonwealth of Kentucky.

---

1. Jody Richards (1938–), A.B., Kentucky Wesleyan College; M.A., University of Missouri; Indiana University; Army Reserve; past president, Bowling Green-Warren County Jaycees; past president and vice-president, Kentucky Young Democrats; past national director and past state secretary, Kentucky Jaycees; past president board of directors, Southern Kentucky Fair Board; girls' club of Bowling Green Jaycee representative; Bowling Green-Warren County Chamber of Commerce; board of directors, United Way, 1983; Outstanding Young Men of America, 1972; JCI Senate; Governor's Task Force on Education Steering Committee; Southern Region Education Board; Legislative Advisory Committee; elected to Kentucky House of Representatives, 1975, re-elected, 1977–2000; Democratic caucus chairman, 1987–97; speaker of the house, 1997– ; owner, Superior Books. *Who's What in Kentucky Government, 1999–2000* (Frankfort, 1999).

2. Thomas Dionysius Clark (1903–), graduated from the University of Mississippi in 1928; M.A., University of Kentucky, 1929; Ph.D., Duke

University, 1932; teaching career began at Memphis State University in 1930; began teaching at the University of Kentucky, 1931; chairman UK history department, 1942–65; started UK special collections; helped found University Press of Kentucky and Kentucky Department for Libraries and Archives; popular lecturer, historian. *The Kentucky Encyclopedia* (Lexington, 1992).

3. H. Ross Perot (1930–), U.S. Naval Academy; served with USN, 1953–57; data-processing salesman, IBM, 1957–62; founder, Electronic Data Systems Corp., 1962–84, chairman, CEO, director, to 1986; chairman Hillwood Development Corp., 1984– ; founder Perot Systems Corp., Washington, 1988– ; independent candidate for president of U.S., 1992, 1996; author: *Not For Sale at Any Price* (1993). *Who's Who in American Politics, 1999–2000,* vol. 2 (New Providence, N.J., 1999).

4. Michael D. "Mike" Bowling (1956–), Middlesboro; University of Kentucky, B.A.; Chase College of Law, J.D.; Democrat; elected in 1990 to the 87th district seat of the Kentucky House of Representatives; re-elected, 1992–98; chair of Judiciary Committee; businessman/attorney; owner of retail food stores. *Who's What in Kentucky Government 1997–1998* (Frankfort, 1997).

5. Albert Benjamin "Happy" Chandler (1898–1991), born near Corydon, Kentucky; L.L.B., University of Kentucky, 1924; Democrat; elected to Kentucky senate, 1929; lieutenant governor of Kentucky, 1931–35; governor, 1935–39, 1955–59; U.S. senator, 1939–45; commissioner of baseball, 1945–51; candidate for governor, 1963, 1967, 1971. *Who's Who in America, 1978–1979,* 40th ed. (Chicago, 1978); *The Kentucky Encyclopedia* (Lexington, 1992).

6. Paul Mason (1935–99), Whitesburg; Alice Lloyd College, A.A.; University of Louisville; Pikeville College; Democrat; elected to the 91st district seat of the Kentucky House of Representatives in 1986; re-elected, 1988–98; automobile dealer. *Who's What in Kentucky Government 1997–1998* (Frankfort, 1997).

7. Hubert "Hubie" Collins (1936–), Morehead State University, B.A., M.A.; Democrat; elected to the 97th district seat of the Kentucky House of Representatives in 1990; re-elected, 1992–2000; chair of Transportation Committee; teacher; auto dealer; real estate broker; auctioneer. *Who's What in Kentucky Government 1999–2000* (Frankfort, 1999).

8. Billy Ray Smith (1944–), Western Kentucky University, B.S.; Democrat; elected to the 21st district seat of the Kentucky House of Representatives in 1981; re-elected, 1984–95; Kentucky secretary of agriculture, 1995–99; re-elected, 1999–2003; co-owner and EVP, Pan American Mills Inc.; farmer and cattle-breeder. *Who's What in Kentucky Government 1999–2000* (Frankfort, 1999).

9. David Karem (1943–), University of Cincinnati, B.S.; University of Louisville, J.D.; Democrat; elected to the 35th district seat of the Kentucky House of Representatives in 1971; re-elected, 1973–74; elected to the senate, 1975– ; majority floor leader of senate, 1992–2000; executive director/pres-

ident of Louisville Waterfront Development Corp.; attorney. *Who's What in Kentucky Government 1999–2000* (Frankfort, 1999).

10. Larry Clark (1945–), Louisville Democrat; elected to the 46th district seat of the Kentucky House of Representatives in 1984; re-elected, 1986–2000; speaker pro tem of the Kentucky House of Representatives, 1995– ; electrician, United Electric. *Who's What in Kentucky Government 1999–2000* (Frankfort, 1999).

SPECIAL SESSION BILL SIGNING
Frankfort / January 27, 1995

We have in the last two weeks taken several very significant progressive steps:

(1) We have taken a major step away from regionalism. We have begun to get the big picture. We have by our actions declared that when we help one part of Kentucky we help all of Kentucky. This attitude will yield great dividends in the future.

(2) We have taken a major step toward fairness for our retired citizens. All pensions will be treated the same, regardless of whether the person worked for the government or private enterprise.

(3) We have taken a major step to encourage Kentuckians not to leave their home state when they retire. When this session started we had the highest inheritance tax in America. As legislators return to their homes, they can take pride in the fact that we now are tied for the lowest inheritance tax in America for children, grandchildren, and brothers and sisters.

(4) Finally, we have taken a major step in restoring the public's confidence in our government. We are economizing our government, and we are passing the savings back to the people who pay the bills—the taxpayers of Kentucky. At the same time, it must be clearly understood that we are not jeopardizing education, or health care, or other needed services of government.

We will pass on to the next administration a financial house that is in the best order in modern history. We will pass on the biggest surplus in the history of Kentucky government. This is a great day for the Commonwealth of Kentucky.

HEALTH CARE

NEWS CONFERENCE ON HEALTH CARE
Frankfort / March 11, 1992

TODAY we are formally beginning the process that will bring meaningful health-care reform to our Commonwealth. Our goal is simply stated, to provide quality, affordable health care for every Kentuckian. We all recognize that a health-care system does not exist to provide economic or professional opportunities for some of our people. It exists to serve the very real and necessary needs of all our people. While our goal is simply stated, it will not be easily reached. This effort will require many hours of dedicated work by Kentuckians who have both vision and courage. I am fully confident that the Kentuckians who are joining in this endeavor have that vision and courage.

Several weeks ago, I asked Human Resources Secretary Len Heller[1] to convene a small group of advisors to recommend the appropriate approach to meeting our goal. I want to outline the initiative that we will undertake in the coming months. As I have said previously, I plan to call a special session of the Legislature in November to put our new health-care system in place. We believe that the magnitude of the task before us requires a coordinated, two-pronged approach. Enacting meaningful health-care reform will require the support of both the legislative and executive branches of government.

For that reason, today I am creating by executive order the Commission on Health Care Reform. This commission will include representatives of both branches of government. It is the recommendation of Senator Rose and Speaker Blandford[2] that the legislative representatives include the leadership from both chambers as well as the chairmen of the house and senate Health and Welfare and Appropriations and Revenue Committees. We will also ask the Republican leadership of each chamber to designate a member, bringing to sixteen the total number of legislative members on the commission. In addition to Secretary Heller, who will chair the commission, the executive branch representatives include the secretaries of the [Executive] Cabinet and the Finance and Administration Cabinet, the commissioner of insurance, the executive director of the Kentucky Commission on Women, and the governor's deputy general counsel. We also felt it was important to include one representative each from the University of Kentucky and University of Louisville medical schools and two representatives from the Kentucky Health Care Access Foundation. This twenty-six-member commission, which Speaker Blandford and Senator Rose will co-chair, will be responsible for drafting and submitting our reform package to the General Assembly.

Another essential element in effecting health-care reform is involving and informing the public and the many entities that are involved in providing care. Hearing what providers and consumers say about health care and making sure those views are shared with the reforms commission will be the responsibility of the task force on Health Care Access and Affordability. The membership of this task force will include the current Health Care Access Foundation Board and several other members representing consumers and provider groups. You have been provided a list of these individuals, and I have asked Jim Newberry[3] of Lexington to chair this group.

The task force will hold a series of public meetings in our area development districts to inform Kentuckians about health-care issues and to listen to Kentuckians' concerns and suggestions about those issues. After these hearings are complete, the task force will present recommendations to the commission for its consideration in drafting the reform package. When the commission comes forward with its proposals, the task force will return to the public for additional comments. The coordinated effort of the commission and the task force will help ensure that our efforts and energies are focused on making Kentucky a national leader in health-care reform. I extend my sincere thanks to all of the men and women who have agreed to help our state move forward in this vital area.[4]

---

1. Leonard E. Heller (1946–), B.S. and graduate degree in education from the University of Kansas; former teacher and administrator at Baylor Uni-

versity and the University of Michigan; former administrator and professor at the U.K. College of Medicine; former vice chancellor for academic affairs at the Albert B. Chandler Medical Center, 1983–86; partner in Illinois Diverstech; president and chief officer of WTT in Lexington; served as human resources secretary, 1991–93. *Louisville Courier-Journal*, January 6, 1992.

2. Donald J. Blandford (1938–), farmer; elected from the 14th district to the Kentucky House of Representatives, 1968; re-elected, 1970–92; speaker pro tem, 1983–84; speaker, 1985–92. *1992 Kentucky General Assembly Directory* (Frankfort, 1992). Longest-serving speaker in Kentucky's history; convicted in BOPTROT FBI sting, sent to federal prison, 1993.

3. James H. "Jim" Newberry Jr. (1957–), B.A., University of Kentucky, 1978; University of Kentucky College of Law, 1981; counsel, Jones's Airdrie Stud horse farm, 1984–87; executive officer in Lt. Gov. Brereton Jones's office, 1987–89; Newberry, Hargrove & Rambicure law offices, 1990–99; acting secretary of the Natural Resources and Environmental Protection Cabinet under Governor Jones for about four weeks, 1991; unsuccessful congressional candidate, 6th congressional district, 1998; Lexington attorney. *Kentucky Gazette*, May 1997.

4. On January 1, 1992, Jones spoke to the Kentucky League of Cities. The speech discussed "rebuilding Kentucky during hard times." Jones named health-care reform first in a list of state problems.

ADDRESS TO HEALTH CARE TASK FORCE AND COMMISSION
Frankfort / March 26, 1992

I WANT to welcome you to this first meeting of the task force on health-care access and affordability and the commission for health-care reform. I am delighted you are here as this is a special day in the life of our Commonwealth. This is the day that we begin the process of solving the persistent problems of access and affordability of quality health care for all Kentuckians. Each of you is important to this opportunity. Our ultimate goal is for Kentucky to be a place where its citizens are healthy, educated, and productive.

The key to this goal is to achieve and maintain good health for the total population. Healthier children are better able to achieve a stronger education. Healthier workers contribute more productively to our economy. Healthier mothers have healthier babies. Healthier elders are more likely to remain self-sufficient. Our humanitarian motive is wrapped in economic wisdom and common sense. Maximizing our potential begins with and is dependent upon having a healthy society. Every citizen in the Commonwealth benefits.

While everyone may agree on our general goals for society, we must recognize the reality of the health-care situation as it is today. The quality of medical care remains generally high, but cost for both private and government insurers is out of control. Overall, the situation continues to deteriorate as increasing numbers of Kentucky businessmen and individuals find themselves unable to afford health insurance, while government has been unable to find the means and innovative ideas that would provide coverage for all who are uninsured and uninsurable. While the crisis of affordability is real, we must not lose sight of the fact that we have dedicated providers who are providing quality care and are truly interested in a total society solution.

Many Kentucky physicians, hospitals, dentists, nurses, pharmacists, and other providers have joined together through the Kentucky Health Care Access Foundation to voluntarily serve those Kentuckians whose income is below the poverty level. This demonstrates that Kentucky is fortunate to have responsible providers. But our ultimate solution requires a more coordinated approach. Kentucky is, of course, a part of the national health-care environment and of the national economy. As HHS Secretary Louis Sullivan recently stated, clearly, costs are growing at an unsustainable rate.

The U.S. Commerce Department reports health-care costs are expected to reach 14 percent of the U.S. Gross National Product in 1992—and anticipates average annual increases of 12 to 13 percent over the next five years. This is about two and a half times faster than the GNP. In Kentucky, the growing crisis is evidenced by the following:

1. Per capita health spending has risen from $806 for each individual in 1980 to $1,875 in 1990. It is projected to be $4,266 by the year 2000.
2. In 1991, the average health payment by families was $3,206. When the $1,329 paid by business is added, the total cost per family rises to $4,535.
3. The estimated number of uninsured persons in Kentucky rose from 328,638 in 1980, or 9 percent of the population, to 485,000 people, or 13 percent of the total population in 1990. This includes an estimated 248,388 people with income below the federal poverty level.

4. In addition to this, 1990 figures show 524,000 Kentuckians were eligible for Medicare and this year 480,000 for Medicaid. Together they represent 25 percent of our population. Medicaid is projected to reach 551,000 persons by FY 94.
5. The percentage of Kentuckians who have private insurance coverage decreased from 69 percent in 1980 to 61 percent in 1990.

WHAT is needed is vision, leadership, and the courage of our convictions to deal realistically and prudently with the situation. I accept that challenge. Please visualize what I believe Kentucky should have and can achieve. Kentucky needs a coordinated system that will:

1. Improve and maintain the general good health of our people.
2. Provide universal access to medically necessary care.
3. Define and maintain high standards of quality care.
4. Manage costs relevant to the general economy.
5. Provide a system of health professions education which emphasizes primary care, health promotion, and disease prevention.
6. Establish priorities for expenditures of available health-care dollars.

WE must look at reality with an open mind and work together to structure a system that maintains quality but has control of costs. This is imperative. To reach a consensus on long-term solutions that will accomplish our goals, I have instituted the following plan: The first step is to secure a clear mandate from the people of Kentucky of what Kentucky's health policy and goals should be. To accomplish this, I have appointed this task force on health-care access and affordability, composed of the members of the boards of the Kentucky Health Care Access Foundation, and a selection of qualified people who represent broadly diversified experience, knowledge, and points of view. I am pleased that Jim Newberry has agreed to chair the task force.

The task force will allow people to express themselves and participate in the process. The task force will educate Kentuckians and listen to their concerns, holding town forums in each area development district. I am calling on the area development districts to make sure that people attending the forums will represent the public we need to serve. The task force will present their findings to the Commission for Health Care Reform in June when the commission will draft its proposals for changing our health-care system. The commission includes both legislative and executive branch leadership. It will develop a specific detailed plan to accomplish the basic goals of healthy people, universal access, affordability, quality, and appropriate health professions education and to set priorities for the expenditure of available health-care dollars.

The commission will develop a comprehensive set of recommendations to be crafted into legislation for the special session. We are fortunate that Human Resources Secretary Leonard Heller will chair the commission with the Senate President Pro-Tem John "Eck" Rose and House Speaker Donald Blandford serving as co-chairs. Legislative Research Commission and Cabinet for Human Resources staff will be assigned to provide support to the commission. The task force will then hold a second round of town forums to provide the commission with a public response to the detailed plan. This will occur in September. For reforms requiring legislative action, the plan will be submitted to the General Assembly at a special session which I plan to call in November of this year. This is without question one of the greatest challenges ever to face our Commonwealth. But I know that we are up to the task. I know that we will do what needs to be done to give all Kentuckians access to quality, affordable health care.

MORATORIUM

LET me conclude with one final measure that will reflect my confidence in your ability to provide a reform. Today I am signing an executive order placing a moratorium on certificates of need and a suspension of the State Health Plan. The moratorium on certificates of need is broad-based, including various types of beds, equipment, and services. The moratorium will be in effect until the reform package is approved by the legislature. There are provisions in the moratorium for the secretary for the Cabinet for Human Resources to act on emergency situations. Further, the entities having received CON [Certificate of Need] approval prior to this date can continue to pursue licensing. The suspension of the State Health Plan and the CON Moratorium are warranted because it is highly likely that the reform plan will have a major impact in areas such as services supported by the state, alternatives to traditional types of care, and reimbursement rates for health-care providers. Consequently, the business plans that have been developed may change. The revised 1990–93 State Health Plan, although improved, will be changed based on the outcome of the reform. Even though I approved the revision of the existing plan, it is time to begin with a new three-year plan which will be created as a result of the reform. With this action, you now have the time to pursue reform without concern about existing plans in place. We will rewrite the health plan and improve new facilities and services all based on the reform. There is no panacea. There are no overnight cures for the ills of our health-care system. Today, however, we begin the treatment.

HEALTH-CARE REFORM TOWN FORUM VIDEO
Frankfort / April 1992

GOOD evening, and welcome to this town forum on health-care reform for Kentucky. Throughout this month, Kentuckians are gathering at these town forums to discuss what must be done to meet the challenge of providing access to affordable, quality health care for all Kentuckians. Reaching this goal will require a strong commitment from all of us. For this is not only a challenge, it is an opportunity for Kentuckians to once again lead the nation in an area of vital importance to *every* citizen. We are beginning a process that promises to put Kentucky in the national spotlight, to let Kentuckians exert the kind of leadership our country must have if we are to solve our health-care problems.

Health care is *the issue* that inescapably touches the lives of each person in this room tonight. Whether you came to this meeting because you're a young parent or the caretaker of a senior citizen, whether or not you have insurance, whether you're a medical provider, an educator, a regulator, or an elected representative, we all are consumers of a system of health-care services. And we all share the costs of those services.

Reforming our health-care system is an investment in our people and our society. Healthier mothers have healthier babies. Healthier children are able to achieve a stronger education. Healthier workers contribute more productively to our economy. Healthier elders are more able to remain self-sufficient. As a first step toward meeting this challenge, the forty-eight volunteer members of my task force on health-care access and affordability need to hear from you. They need your thoughts on some of the choices that will help make

Kentucky a place where its citizens are healthy, educated, and productive. I want to emphasize that *your* participation is *the* most important element of this process. The information you offer at tonight's town forum will go into a report to the Commission on Health Care Reform. That panel of citizens, lawmakers, and policymakers will draft a comprehensive plan to change Kentucky's health-care system. That plan will then be presented for implementation at a special session of the legislature. From this and fourteen other town forums across the state, the leadership of the General Assembly and I are looking to you for a clear mandate of what Kentucky's health policies and goals should be.

The task we have undertaken poses what is without a doubt one of the greatest challenges ever to face our Commonwealth. You and I know there are no overnight cures for the ills of our health-care system. Yet, tonight, by your attendance and your participation, together we are beginning the treatment.

KENTUCKY COMMISSION ON HEALTH-CARE REFORM
Frankfort / July 10, 1992

THERE is no greater problem facing America today than the cost of health care. If we continue on the road that we are now traveling, the health-care system will bankrupt this nation. The federal government is either unable or unwilling to solve this problem. Therefore, we must show the necessary leadership. Kentucky must lead the rest of America. The health-care reforms we envision will not be a minor tinkering with our current system, trying to stretch the tentacles of government this way and that to temporarily plug a hole or patch a crack. Reform means finding a new way. It will require a bold and dramatic restructuring of our health-care system to control costs and assure access and quality for all—all—of our citizens. When we established this commission in March, I outlined our goals of establishing a coordinated system that will:

1. Assure universal access to medically necessary care;
2. Make certain our people receive quality care; and
3. Control costs.

I fully recognize that these are ambitious goals. But we must provide access to quality health care for every Kentuckian. Any effort that falls short of this goal will be unacceptable to me. We will keep working until we get there, however long it takes, however difficult and wrenching the process, whatever obstructionist attitudes we may encounter. We will get there. I know what is required: leadership from the governor's office and an unwavering commitment. I proudly and willingly accept that challenge because there is nothing that is more important to me as governor than reaching our goals for health-care reform.

We have no other choice, if we are to fulfill our obligation to the people of Kentucky who put us here. Our people know, as we all do, that our health-care system, the old way, is failing us. More than four thousand Kentuckians attended the Health Care Task Force forums to tell us that directly. I commend the task force for responding aggressively to our challenge to heighten public interest in and awareness of our reform efforts and for giving the people of Kentucky an opportunity to be heard. The problems of our system are clearly defined: escalating health-care costs that will literally bankrupt our state and nation if they are not controlled; Medicaid expenditures that have risen 300 percent in less than ten years; an estimated 500,000 Kentuckians with no health-insurance coverage and another 500,000 who are eligible for Medicaid.

On a more personal level is the fear that has gripped Kentuckians who know they could lose most everything they have worked for to a catastrophic illness. This fear is very real—even for working Kentuckians with health-insurance coverage. We cannot, and we will not, let this plague upon the homes and families of Kentucky continue.

I have first-hand knowledge of the cooperative base upon which we can build our reforms. Since the formation of the Kentucky Health Care Access Foundation in the mid-1980s, more than 45,000 Kentuckians have received free care from physicians, hospitals, pharmacists, and dentists who have proven that their desire to serve comes from the heart—and not from the pocketbook.

As governor, I am appreciative on behalf of our entire Commonwealth for these vital services and the public spiritedness they represent. Now it is time to ensure that all Kentuckians receive the care they need in a system that includes much more than volunteerism.

The problems of our health-care system don't lend themselves to quick or simple fixes. And they don't have politically painless cures. Under our reforms, it will not be possible to be on the playing field and not have the new rules affect you. That will be true for businesses, physicians, hospitals and other providers, working Kentuckians, the uninsured, the unemployed, and those who receive government assistance. There will be an array of proposals for us to consider as we craft a package for a special legislative session in November. No doubt all of them will entail a change in the rules to some degree.

Today, I have some proposals to share with you that I ask you to consider. Let me be absolutely clear, these do not represent a program that we have etched in stone. Rather, they are ideas that I believe have merit and warrant your attention and review. After you've had the opportunity to consider them, I want to know what you think, and we will work together to determine their feasibility. I have strong views on this subject but I am open to innovative suggestions.

First, in the area of cost control, as we all know, the unrestrained growth of health-care costs is eating away our future. To control that growth I ask that you look at establishing a state regulatory commission that would have broad powers in rate-setting for health-care services and authority in determining which services should be available in which parts of the state.

Another idea in the area of cost control is a new approach to malpractice awards, one that might include outright limits on damages, alternative dispute-resolution procedures, or establishing practice standards for physicians with legally enforced liability limits for those who comply.

Equity in sharing the burden for the cost of health care is imperative in the restructuring of our system. Too many working Kentuckians are denied health-care coverage because they work in part-time jobs or for employers who do not offer the coverage as a benefit. I ask that you consider this question of equity by looking at requiring businesses whose employees collectively work a certain number of hours a week to provide insurance for those employees. The fast-food industry provides a good example of what I am addressing here. In any particular restaurant, there might be a number of people working but many of them are part-time employees without insurance benefits. Rather than looking at the person-by-person hours worked, let's consider the total numbers of hours all of them work collectively as a possible basis for determining when coverage should be required. This, of course, is a proposal addressing access to care. Also along those lines is my next suggestion.

Our state could be in a very strong position to demand the lowest possible insurance rates with the creation of a huge pool of Kentuckians who need the coverage. This pool could include state and local government employees, teachers, retirees, businesses that choose to participate, and, importantly, those hundreds of thousands of Kentuckians who currently have no insurance. Our pool could bid its very attractive policy through the private sector, ensuring lower rates. While benefits would continue for those Kentuckians who already have coverage, we could expand our system to include the currently uninsured, giving them a basic coverage policy.

I do not want this to be viewed as a give-away program, however. We would have to look at residency requirements, making the coverage available only to uninsured Kentuckians who have lived here for a certain length of time. And I strongly feel we should require something in return for the coverage we provide the uninsured—especially those who are able to perform public service work or enroll in educational or training programs. Sharing the responsibility should be a requirement of all of our able-bodied citizens.

My final proposal to you today addresses Kentucky's chronic problem of physician shortages. More than forty of our counties are classified as physician-shortage areas. We cannot hope to deliver adequate health care to all of our citizens if this condition persists. Let's look at offering full medical scholarships to our best and brightest students in return for their agreement to spend a certain number of years in an underserved area. Let's consider programs that start early in the educational process to encourage a long-term commitment from those students. And let us continue to change medical education to get more students to enter primary-care residencies. Primary and preventive care must be our priorities. Every Kentuckian must have an annual physical checkup. If it makes sense for the corporate executive, it makes equal sense for the Kentucky worker. But we cannot give primary and preventive care the proper emphasis unless our medical schools produce more physicians who deliver such care. We need to change what young doctors do and where they do it.

As I mentioned earlier, these are some of my ideas that I put forward for your consideration. I can assure you there will be others as we tackle the challenge of paying for this new system and redirecting our focus in other areas. I know all of us recognize that Kentucky's financial condition means there will not be substantial amounts of new public money available for our reforms. We must look first to redirecting our existing resources to stretch every dollar toward the attainment of our goal. We must also be innovative—

generating ideas that deliver more for less cost. Some of these ideas may require waivers from the federal government or statutory or constitutional changes. But my objective is for all of them to move us closer to our goal.

Much will be required of all of us in this process. And we must be ever mindful of the three elements that some could try to use against us—power, profits, and politics. It is a safe bet that none of us will face a greater challenge during our public service. But this day marks a new beginning for Kentucky. We cannot, we must not, we will not lose our resolve.

We must work together with a spirit of cooperation. We must not waste time by pointing fingers at each other but will spend our time making the hard decisions that must be made. We will not be sidetracked from achieving our goal of providing health-insurance coverage and the access to quality care it guarantees for every Kentuckian.

We must reach this goal in the November special session. If we do not, we will reach it in December. If need be, we will be in session on Christmas Day. I cannot think of a better Christmas gift for the people of Kentucky.

KENTUCKY PRIMARY-CARE ASSOCIATION
Lexington / October 16, 1992

FROM the moment I involved myself in the issue of health-care reform, I have been convinced of one undeniable fact: more primary and preventive care means less sickness and waste, both in human and in financial terms. It just makes so much common sense that it almost appears to be too easy. When people get regular checkups, physicians can catch conditions earlier. When they do, they often can initiate less-costly treatment to correct the ailment with much less trauma to the patient. Preventive care should be our first line of defense for good health, but it is often ignored.

We know we can improve the health and productivity of our people and save lives. We know we can redirect misused health-care dollars. Yet, society has failed to find a meaningful way to put this knowledge to use. I don't propose to stand before you today and suggest that all of society's failures are answered in the plan currently under study by the Commission on Health Care Reform. Those of you who have read the outline have questions and I want you to know that I have questions, too. But I do believe we have a solid foundation on which to rebuild our health-care system, and the cornerstone of that new structure is preventive and primary care.

Most of you here today know far better than I the plight facing the medically underserved citizens of our Commonwealth. Indigent patients make up from one-third to more than one-half of the clients of the primary-care centers in urban Louisville and Jefferson County. The numbers are comparable in the centers in Bowling Green, Lexington, and northern Kentucky, and even higher in the rural centers in eastern Kentucky. These Kentuckians are the target of our plan to assure health insurance, and thus access to care, for all residents of this state.

We know there are as many as a half-million Kentuckians without insurance today. Many of these are hardworking, taxpaying citizens laboring in minimum- or near-minimum-wage jobs that provide paychecks that may put food on the table or repair the car, or patch the winter coat, but in no way enable the family to handle the cost of even a short-term stay in the hospital or an ambulance trip to the emergency room in a true crisis.

If we are able to provide health insurance to these Kentuckians, the role of the primary-care center will become even more vital in this state than it is today, and it already is a critical partner in our existing system of health-care services. Your teaming of doctors with physician assistants, nurse practitioners, nutritionists, social workers, and other professionals can address the complicated problems most Kentucky families face in health-care needs.

You provide the health education, health promotion, wellness programs, and emphasis on prevention that it will take to get the message home to your clients, and that message is this: just having access to health insurance isn't enough. You have to learn the importance of getting those physicals. You have to learn about diet and nutrition and heart disease and diabetes and smoking and exercise and all the other elements that combine for a healthy lifestyle. You have to learn that failure in these areas drives up the cost of health care and drives down your own chances for survival when illness strikes.

Those of you already committed to the profession of primary care are going to need help. You're going to need help because we're already a state virtually starving for a sufficient number of primary-care providers to meet the current demand, much less the higher demand once we get people actually realizing their own personal stake in health care for all. That's why I have said from the day this plan was proposed that the focus of Kentucky's new health-care-delivery system must be on primary care. We're working with our two medical schools to bring new urgency to new residencies in primary and preventive medicine. We're proposing higher compensation for primary-care givers, especially those who set up practice in currently underserved areas of the state. We need to change the laws to increase the abilities of physician assistants and nurse practitioners to provide care such as writing prescriptions. Kentucky needs a more regionalist, less localized health-care-delivery system.

The thousands of empty hospital beds this very day stand testament to the fact that every community can no longer sustain a hospital with the newest medical technology and the most advanced programs. We can supplement regional full-service hospitals with limited-service community hospitals to handle trauma care or other routine care. Then, we need more primary-care clinics to join with our local health departments and the individual practitioners to form the entry point to this new health-delivery system. You already have an example of this type of networking and cooperation developing among the primary-care centers in Louisville. They share patient data, follow common eligibility guidelines, and regularly fax medical consultations and other data back and forth. We can do the same thing between clinics and health departments and community hospitals and regional medical centers, and we can cut our costs and improve the care provided to patients through this type of networking.

I am convinced that working together we can solve these problems facing our health-care system in Kentucky. And when we do, we can all be proud that Kentucky has taken the lead in what I believe is the greatest single problem facing the entire nation: providing quality, affordable health care for every one of our citizens.[1]

---

1. On October 13, 1992, in a health-care press release, Jones announced Kentucky's home health agency's participation in the Kentucky Health Care Access Foundation Program.

KENTUCKY PEOPLE WITH AIDS SERVICE
Louisville / December 1, 1992

AIDS. The term itself strikes fear and causes a deep emotional reaction. It is a disease, a tragic attack on the body's defense system. But in addition, AIDS victims suffer greatly beyond the disease itself. They are often victims of fear and ignorance. All this must change. We must find a cure. We must find understanding and compassion for the victims and their families who suffer so greatly.

AIDS has forever altered the lives of 857 people in Kentucky alone, 123 of those diagnosed this year. Six hundred and five have died. Through education and research we can cure AIDS and end the fear and prejudice that so often compound the pain.

Mankind may measure itself in lofty achievements or monuments built, but I firmly believe we will be judged by our compassion, what we do for those who cannot help themselves. Our greatest achievements will be in what we do to alleviate the suffering of our fellow human beings. On that rests our legacy and this evening we must join in a grand cause to make compassion our hallmark, and we must dedicate ourselves to finding a cure for this disease and an end to the misunderstanding.

KENTUCKY FARM BUREAU
Louisville / December 11, 1992

I APPRECIATE the opportunity to be here today as part of one of Kentucky's most significant annual events. In thinking about what to say to you, I couldn't help but reflect upon the great history of the Kentucky Farm Bureau and what it has meant to our state. For seventy-three years, the Farm Bureau has been a powerful voice for Kentucky's farmers. Over the years your organization has helped farmers pull through economic depressions, natural disasters, and a host of other crises that are all too common to our volatile agriculture industry.

In Frankfort, the Farm Bureau has long been highly regarded as a strong voice in public-policy debates. On the national level, the

Farm Bureau played a key role in developing agricultural policy that brought us out of a tragic farm recession in the past decade. At the same time, the Kentucky Farm Bureau was instrumental in preserving the tobacco program that is so crucial to our farm economy. Today, you are 340,000 members strong and growing. And your voice continues to shape public policy that improves the quality of life for all Kentuckians, not just farmers.

I think you know that I come from the farming community and have an understanding of the nature of farming. I think you know that I would not do anything as governor to harm the farming industry. I know there are concerns about my health-care reform and the smoking policy we are developing for state buildings, and I want to talk about both of these issues today. Let me first address health-care reform.

The health of our business is essential to the economic health of our Commonwealth. As a businessman and farmer for most of my adult life, and having had to make a payroll for about thirty years, I understand and appreciate the challenges that farmers, as businessmen and women, face every day. And from my involvement in the health-care community for much of my public life, I also know that the health-care crises in the nation and our Commonwealth, if ignored, will bankrupt us all. So we have a dilemma, and you have concerns that our efforts to reform health care could be harmful to your economic health.

I am here to address those concerns because I believe sincerely that we can have comprehensive health-care reform and protect the viability of our farms and small businesses. I do not want to solve one problem and create another. I pledge to you now that in our reform package we will help economically sensitive businesses—and farms are businesses—adapt, adjust, and accommodate to our health-care reform efforts. I am asking you to join our team to see that this happens to the benefit of us all.

Now let me explain the philosophy of our health-care reform package. Our plan will focus on cost containment, affordability, and competition. Government should let free-market forces promote competition, and government should regulate only as a last resort. These two business concepts underlie and drive our health-care reform plan. The whole plan is geared toward controlling health-care costs and promoting competition. There is no question that health-care costs are out of control. It is also beyond question that the escalation in health-care costs directly affects every taxpayer in the state. If nothing is done to control and contain costs, the taxpayers of Kentucky, each and every one of us, will foot the bill and pay dearly.

As you study our plan, you will see that every component will control costs in some way—some more dramatically than others. I want to review three major cost-containment provisions in our plan. With a megapool of up to two million Kentuckians, we hope to keep monthly premiums to a minimum. With a health-care authority, we will regulate those health-care providers where prices exceed the rate of inflation by more than a determined percentage. Also, we will stress universal access and preventive care to make sure everyone can get high-quality, affordable health care. We hope to head off or adjust many of the lifestyle problems that lead to much of our health-care costs. All three of these control costs, and we believe that all three are necessary if we are to meet our goals in this area.

How will we pay for the plan? First of all, our administration is convinced that new taxes will not be necessary to fund the plan. Financing will be achieved through cost savings plus a redistribution of resources in the system. In addition, everyone will have to pay their share to solve the problem. The current tax on providers will be expanded. Employers will be required to pay for single coverage for the employees, and I know this is a sensitive area for small businesses and farmers.

To address the financing more specifically, individuals will be required to purchase coverage for their dependents and the state will be required to cover the indigent. Obviously, businesses and citizens won't be able to afford these coverages unless costs are brought under control. Once they are, then coverage will be a more manageable cost. With vulnerable businesses, we will have a system of softening the impact with state assistance, depending on a number of factors, but you will not have to shoulder it alone. Our administration is currently working to determine how best to assist small- and medium-sized businesses and farms which simply won't be able to afford the required coverage. Our initial calculations include $140 million set aside for the first two years to provide subsidies for this purpose.

Obviously, we cannot create an economic-development problem to solve the health-care crisis. I want to emphasize one point that tends to get lost in many discussions about health-care reform. Controlled health-care costs will give Kentucky an economic-development tool unmatched by any other state. When we can assure our existing businesses and prospective employers alike that these costs are controlled in Kentucky, I have no doubt that we will see significant economic growth. When the plan is complete, it will be presented to a special session of the legislature which, at this time, looks like it will be early next year.

In the meantime, I ask for your help, your comments, and your good-faith efforts to be a part of the solution. For too long we've wrung our hands over this problem and said it's too big to solve or let Washington solve it. That approach has gotten us farther into the hole and with a much greater number of people in desperate need of our help. Now, I for one don't want to wait for Washington to tell Kentucky how to solve this problem. I want Kentuckians to tell Kentucky how to solve this problem. I want Kentuckians meeting this challenge, and I sincerely want our state to lead the way. Your cooperation and support in this endeavor, which is of such critical importance to so many, is greatly appreciated.

Now to address another area that I know is of concern to you—the smoking policy we are developing for state-owned buildings. It is estimated that tobacco will mean about $800 million to the state's economy this year. I grow a lot of tobacco on my farm in Woodford County, and I understand personally the importance of this crop to Kentucky. But, I feel we must look at both sides of this health-related and farm-economy issue. It is simply a matter of fairness. We are currently receiving information from all state agencies to form our smoking policy. I want it to be fair to both smokers and non-smokers. We must take into consideration the concerns of the many who do not want to breathe the smoke of others. We will have our policy formed around the first of the year. I have already met with Bill Sprague[1] and other farm group representatives to discuss your concerns, and I assure you they are being taken into consideration.

We know the successes of our farming industry, and tobacco has been and is a cornerstone of this state's economy. Health concerns are rising, and our state workers want a fair and equitable policy that protects them. We are answering those concerns. . . .[2]

---

1. William R. "Bill" Sprague (1938–), B.S. in agricultural engineering from University of Kentucky, 1961; vice-president of the Kentucky Farm Bureau Federation, 1977–91; president of Kentucky Farm Bureau Federation, 1991–98; president of Kentucky Farm Bureau Mutual Insurance Company and other Farm Bureau affiliate companies, 1991–99; American Farm Bureau Board of Directors, 1994– ; member of the Kentucky Economic Development Partnership Board; a principal in Ag Project 2000; represents

AFBF on the National Cattlemen's Beef Association Board of Directors and the U.S. Meat Export Federation Board.

2. The second part of this speech to the Kentucky Farm Bureau dealt with farming problems; this portion can be found in the section on agriculture issues.

CHAMBER OF COMMERCE
Frankfort / February 11, 1993

THANK you very much for this opportunity to speak at your winter gathering. Creating economic vitality is a cornerstone of this administration. The health of our businesses is essential to the economic health of our Commonwealth. But our administration, just as President Clinton's incoming administration has said, is convinced that we cannot unlock the problems of our economy without addressing the rising cost of health care and bringing health-care coverage to the thousands of Kentuckians who have none.

As a businessman and farmer for most of my adult life, and having had to make a payroll for about thirty years, I understand and appreciate the challenges small businesses face every day. I also know that about 80 percent of the job growth in any state comes from cultivating existing businesses, and our administration considers that to be of paramount importance. And from my involvement in the health-care community for much of my public life, I also know that the health-care crisis in this nation and our Commonwealth, if unaddressed, will bankrupt us all.

The humanity involved is staggering, with about 430,000 Kentuckians having no health-insurance protection at all, keeping them on the edge of financial disaster with any medical emergency. So, we have a dilemma, and your businesses and companies may have concerns that our efforts to reform health care could be harmful to your economic health. I am here to address those concerns because I believe sincerely that we can have comprehensive health-care reform and protect the viability of our small businesses. I do not want to solve one problem and create another. I do want you to know that our reform package will help economically sensitive businesses adapt, adjust, and accommodate to our health-care reform efforts, and I am asking you to join our team to see that this happens to the benefit of all of us.

Now I'd like to explain the philosophy of our health-care reform package. Our plan focuses on cost containment, affordability, and competition. There is no question that health-care costs are out of control. Health-care costs equal 13 percent of our gross national product. Health-care insurance premiums have been going up 10, 15, 20 percent every year for the past several years. Most people's earning power has not kept pace with inflation, let alone with these types of health-care cost increases. It is also beyond question that the escalation in health-care costs directly affects every taxpayer in the state; $600 million from the general fund is spent each year on health care. Three cents of every six cents of the sales tax goes to health care. Medicaid budget expenditures have increased over 300 percent in the last ten years. If nothing is done to control and contain costs, the taxpayers of Kentucky, each and every one of us, will foot the bill and pay dearly. Health-care reform is nothing more than controlling costs. This is something business people do every day or they do not stay alive in the business world.

As you study our plan, you will see that every component will control costs in some way, some more dramatically than others. I want to review three major cost-containment provisions in our plan. With a megapool of up to two million Kentuckians, we hope to keep monthly premiums to a minimum. With a health-care authority, we will regulate those health-care businesses where prices exceed the rate of inflation by more than a determined percentage. And, we plan to regulate those businesses from the start, as soon as we can get the authority together and gather the necessary data. And we will stress universal access and preventive care to make sure everyone can get high-quality, affordable health care and head off or adjust many of the lifestyle problems that lead to much of our health-care costs. All three of these elements control costs, and we believe that all three are necessary if we are to meet our goals in this area.

Let me go into each of these areas in a little more detail. With the megapool of about two million Kentuckians grouped together, the state can negotiate with providers and insurance companies to get the best possible rates for services and coverage. The megapool is the ultimate in cost containment. Most of us know from our experience that the smaller the pool covered and the higher the rates, the more dramatic the effect that even a single catastrophic illness will have on the rates for everyone in the pool. The larger the pool, the more the risk is spread, and, therefore, the lower the rates. The inclusion of the megapool concept in the plan also signifies the plan's preference for competition, not regulation. Our administration did not opt for a single-payer plan where the state essentially becomes the only health insurer or claims administrator in the state. We opted for competition between providers and insurance companies to generate the lowest possible health-care costs for Kentuckians.

The health-care authority will have extensive duties and responsibilities. The most important duty is to set health-care rates to be certain that increases are controlled. The third cost-containment feature of our plan is actually a combination of two separate elements. First, the plan will implement a tremendous focus on preventive care. Too many Kentuckians enter the system at a stage of illness or disease that is too advanced. If we can get to those people earlier, we can relieve a huge cost pressure on the system. Second, the plan calls for universal access to health care. As I mentioned, our administration believes that access to health care for the nearly one-half-million Kentuckians who do not have it is a fundamental right and a moral imperative.

However, universal access also has two important cost-containment side benefits. They are: once all Kentuckians have access to health care, the emphasis on preventive care is doubly beneficial. We can then start to prevent disease among those not covered who currently aren't even in the system. Universal access also has actuarial benefits that would bring down costs. Currently, many younger, healthier people don't have insurance because they feel like they don't need it and don't want to pay for it. If they are in the system with all other Kentuckians, the rates for everyone will be lower.

Finally, the bottom line: financing. How will we pay for the plan? First of all, our administration is convinced that new taxes will not be necessary to fund the plan. Financing will be achieved through cost savings plus a redistribution of resources in the system. In addition, everyone will have to pay their share to solve the problem. The current tax on providers will be expanded. Employers will be required to pay for single coverage on their employees, and I know this is a sensitive area for small businesses, and I plan to address that in just a moment. Individuals will be required to purchase coverage for their dependents, and the state will be required to cover the indigent. Obviously, businesses and citizens won't be able to afford these coverages unless costs are brought under control. Once they are, then coverage will be a more manageable cost. With vulnerable businesses, we will have a system of softening the impact on economically sensitive companies with state assistance, depending on a number of factors, but you will not have to shoulder it alone and at the expense of your company's existence. Our plan would provide assistance to those businesses with a payroll of less than $200,000 per year and a net profit of less than $50,000 a year.

I'd also like to emphasize a point that I feel tends to get lost in the debate over health-care reforms and economic development. I strongly feel that health-care reform will become one of our most effective economic-development tools, giving Kentucky a significant advantage over other states in attracting businesses. Just think how much of a benefit it will be for companies which are considering locating in Kentucky to know that their health-care costs will not rise each year above a specific rate. Our initial calculations include $140 million set aside for the first two years to provide subsidies to these vulnerable businesses.

Criticism that our plan will cost the state jobs is erroneous, irresponsible, and off base. I also want to point out that, under our plan, we'll be able to reduce workers' compensation rates by 5 percent and hold that reduction for two years. Workers' compensation rates, excluding coal, have been rising at a rate of about 20 percent a year recently, so a guaranteed 5 percent reduction for two years would be a tremendous savings. Obviously, we can't solve the health-care problem by putting businesses out of business on a wholesale basis. We cannot create an economic-development problem to solve the health-care crisis, and we will do our best to see that they not only survive but thrive to help our entire commonwealth. Seventy-three percent of our businesses and industries already cover their employees, and many may find that our plan will be more economical for them. The only ones that may have to pay a penalty are those who can afford to pay for coverage but refuse to purchase it. And that will be a very small portion of the population.

Recently, we unveiled our plan to the legislature, and the public will see the full plan very soon. As you know, we plan to have a special session on health-care reform in the near future. I ask for your help, your comments, your good-faith efforts to be a part of the solution. For too long we've wrung our hands over this problem and said it's too big to solve, or let Washington solve it. That approach has gotten us farther into the hole, and with a much greater number of people in desperate need of our help now. I for one don't want to wait for Washington to tell Kentucky how to solve this problem. I want Kentuckians meeting this challenge, and I sincerely want our administration to lead the way. I ask you to join our efforts to reach a solution, be part of this monumental task that will help so many. Your cooperation and support in this endeavor, which is of such critical importance to so many, is greatly appreciated. And, if I or anyone in my administration can help you, your company, or your community better understand our efforts, just call.[1]

---

1. Similar speeches were given on March 16 to business leaders at the Henderson Chamber of Commerce; March 17 to business leaders in Paducah who belonged to Lions, Rotary, and Kiwanis Clubs; on March 26 to labor supporters at the AFL-CIO Health Care Forum in Frankfort; on March 26 to Cabinet for Human Resources employees in Frankfort; on April 8 to business executives of the Kentucky Chamber of Commerce at Eastern Kentucky University; and on April 15 to participants at the Governor's Safety and Health Conference in Louisville.

KENTUCKY HEALTH CARE REFORM COMMISSION
Frankfort / March 1, 1993

I KNOW that you have read and heard about many of the components of our health-care reform plan, and I want to address the key elements of that plan today. But, first, I want to take some time to emphasize the human side of this plan, how it will meet the human needs, not only of the thousands of Kentuckians who have no health insurance, but also of Kentuckians who currently have coverage but are threatened by reduced benefits and sky-rocketing costs, costs that, if unchecked, could lead to financial disaster for our citizens, our state, and our nation.

The fact is, we can honestly say that health care can be a matter of life and death, either physically, economically, or both. Does that statement seem overly dramatic? Not when you consider that many of the almost 430,000 Kentuckians who have no health insurance all too often cannot afford to seek medical care until it is too late. Not when you consider that thousands of Kentuckians with life-threatening illnesses are denied medical insurance because of pre-existing conditions. Not when you consider that medical care currently represents 13 percent of our gross national product and is costing Kentuckians $9 billion a year.

Statistics are revealing and valuable resources, but they don't always clearly reflect the human side of the health-care problem. Perhaps the urgent need for health-care reform can best be demonstrated by the appeals for help heard during last year's regional town forums. For example, a mother in Somerset said she didn't get a regular Pap smear because, without insurance, she would have no way of paying for treatment or caring for her children if the test revealed a problem. An Ashland man, who said access to affordable care is a critical issue, told us he was forced to take bankruptcy after his wife's illness cost $200,000. A woman from Louisville told us she and her husband were paying $300 a month for health insurance until he needed a life-saving kidney transplant. Now their health insurance has quadrupled to $1,200 a month. A Hazard man with four children, who worked in the coal mines but now is a college student, said he and his wife, who is employed in a minimum-wage job, cannot afford insurance for their family. A married couple in Mayfield are using their savings to pay a $724 monthly health-insurance premium, the least expensive coverage they could find. A small business owner in Cave City said business people cannot afford to continue providing employee health insurance because of the tremendous increase in premiums.

These are just a few examples. Consider that there are 430,000 similar stories that could be told, and you get an idea of the magnitude of the medical-care crisis facing Kentucky, 430,000 without health insurance. That's almost as many people as the populations of Louisville and Lexington combined. Think of the worry that these people must feel, knowing that if they or some member of their family becomes seriously ill, they don't know how they're going to pay the bills.

Doing what is right to help people who need help is simply what government is all about. And it would be a mistake to think that those who currently have good health insurance are immune to this problem. When people are unable to obtain health insurance because of pre-existing conditions, everyone pays. The costs from unpaid bills are shifted to those who do pay, driving up the price of premiums for everyone and resulting in even more people who can't afford coverage. According to one national publication, cost shifting accounts for about one-third of the increase in insurance premiums, which are rising at the rate of 15 percent a year. The cost of medical care, which is increasing two to three times faster than the rate of inflation, is responsible for the rest. And those of us lucky enough to have insurance through our employers know that we're still not safe from those skyrocketing costs. Chances are that our insurers are responding to the rapidly rising cost of health care by providing less coverage for more money. As a result, many employers will require their employees to pay a larger share of health-insurance premiums, which means substantially less take-home pay.

So, either physically, economically, or both, health-care reform is a matter of life and death for our people. Health-care reform is not an option or something that can be postponed. It must be addressed, and it must be addressed now. All of you are very familiar with my feelings on this point. I have spoken with you individually on several occasions about my goals for this process, but I want to reiterate them today.

We must control the escalating costs of health care. And we must ensure that every Kentuckian has coverage regardless of any pre-existing condition. These goals are interrelated, and I do not believe we can accomplish one without the other. Each element of the plan you have before you is designed to help us reach those goals. And there is one thing that I want to make very clear today. As I have always been, I remain open to suggestions about ways to improve our reform plan, refinements, alterations, new ideas that will give us a better program. But all of these things must, must, reach our goals of controlling costs and universal coverage. I am unwilling to accept anything else.

Now, I would like to review the major elements of our plan. Later in the meeting, you'll hear from experts who will provide more specific details. Our plan will control costs through a health-care authority, a mega-purchasing pool, workers' compensation reform, a system of standardized claim forms and insurance cards, and medical liability reform. The mission of the health-care authority will be to control costs while assuring quality health services. It will have the power to set rates to control the cost of health-insurance premiums and payments made to health-care providers. It will ensure that health-care costs do not exceed a predetermined target tied to the cost of living. The importance of the cost control is evident when you consider that, if we allow health-care costs to continue to rise at the present rate, about one dollar of every five spent in our nation by the year 2000 will be for health care. That will be more than 20 percent of our gross domestic product. The health-care authority also will establish service-delivery regions. It will work with local communities and health-care providers to create networks which ensure that all Kentuckians have access to medical services. The authority also will assess community health needs. The authority will consist of four members appointed by the governor and confirmed by the senate with the secretary of human resources serving as chair. The appointed members will serve six-year terms.

The megapool will consist of more than one million Kentuckians, enabling the state to negotiate with health-care providers from a position of financial strength. This will give the state the leverage needed to eliminate unnecessary services, increase efficiency, control duplication of services, and secure discounts from providers. The megapool will include the following groups: public employees, Medicaid recipients, currently uninsured/unemployed persons, employees of businesses choosing to participate, and individuals or families choosing to participate. The individual benefit packages offered under the megapool will vary. For example, state employees will have coverage very similar to their present plan. Businesses or individuals will be able to purchase the health insurance basic plan for $116 per month for a single plan. Medicaid will be incorporated into the megapool to improve its negotiating position. Services provided to Medicaid recipients will not be changed, but steps will be taken to control costs. The workers' compensation system will be modified. It will require health-care services for industrial injuries and occupational diseases to be provided under managed-care plans. This will be accompanied by a 5 percent reduction in workers' compensation premiums, and that rate will be frozen for twenty-four months. This revised workers' compensation system will also allow twenty-four-hour health-care coverage through pilot projects. Under these pilots, a single administrator will manage both general health care and workers' compensation medical care. Studies confirm that a savings of 5 to 35 percent can be achieved in workers' compensation health-care costs with implementation of the reform package. Other savings will result from the use of standardized insurance forms and cards and setting up a system of arbitration for malpractice disputes.

I'd like to turn now to universal coverage. All Kentuckians will have at least the basic health-insurance protection identified in the plan. Employers will be required to purchase a basic plan for each full-time employee at the megapool rate of $116 per employee per month. The premiums of eligible small businesses will be subsidized by the state. Employers will be required to pay a pro-rata share for part-time employees, based on a forty-hour week. State assistance will be provided on a sliding scale to assist part-time workers with their share of health-insurance costs. Employers will be required to offer a family plan, but the additional cost of family coverage will be the responsibility of employees. Eligible employees identified in the plan will receive state subsidies to help pay premiums. Unemployed adults will be assisted by state government in the purchase of health insurance, and those with household incomes below 100 percent of poverty will be fully subsidized. Each person covered under the megapool will receive one free health examination and appropriate lab tests each year. Immunizations and well-baby care will also be covered. These procedures can detect or prevent many health problems at their early stages, when they can be more easily and effectively treated at a lower cost. Employers will find that reform will reduce future health-insurance costs and create a healthier, more productive workforce.

Kentucky's economic-development efforts will be helped significantly by health-care reform. In fact, our economic-development team is already using Kentucky's draft plan for health-care reform as an industry-recruiting tool. Health-care delivery reforms are also addressed by the plan. Delivery and system reforms will take into consideration transportation factors and the health-care needs that may be unique to certain sections of the state. The curriculum in our state medical schools will be rewritten to emphasize primary-care practice and prevention. The University of Kentucky will expand nurse midwifery, nurse practitioner and physician assistant programs, services which can reduce costs. The University of Louisville will implement programs in at least two of these areas.

Quality assurance is a key part of the plan. Quality guidelines will be implemented for all medical professionals by the health-care authority. Provider profiles will enable consumers and insurers to determine which providers consistently deliver effective and cost-efficient services. And there are still other reforms in the plan. Seat belt use will be mandated. Health education will be provided to all Kentucky children, and consumer education programs will inform adults about health resources, healthy lifestyle choices, and disease-prevention methods.

Now let's discuss plan financing, where the dollars will come from. Former United States Surgeon General C. Everett Koop[1] and others with health-care expertise agree that 25 to 30 percent of what we spend on health care is for medically unnecessary procedures. Much of these costs result from defensive medicine as providers work under the constant fear of malpractice lawsuits. For example, the University of Kentucky medical school dean, Emery Wilson,[2] says that it is becoming normal emergency-room procedure to perform an MRI on a child who has fallen out of bed. The physician knows that he or she should just tell the family to wake the child every two or three hours to make sure everything is normal. But because of the fear of lawsuits, highly expensive MRIs have become standard procedure. Defensive medicine is expensive medicine.

Another example of unnecessary cost is paperwork resulting from billing, bureaucracy, and marketing in the health-care industry. It is becoming increasingly apparent to everyone that we spend huge amounts of money processing paperwork to get the providers paid, or perhaps to keep them from getting paid. The only people who benefit from this nightmare of paperwork are the ones employed to pass the documents back and forth. These are just examples of the 25 to 30 percent of health-care costs wasted on unnecessary procedures and processing. If we agree that a minimum of 25 percent of the $9 billion Kentuckians spend on health-care costs each year is unnecessary, that means $2.25 billion already in the system can be redirected toward primary care and prevention. Dollars needed to fund the plan will also come from savings generated by state government through implementation of the reform. For example, Kentucky allocates millions of dollars each year to underwrite the cost of medical care for indigent citizens. These patients will have insurance through the reform plan, freeing funds to expand Medicaid or to purchase health-insurance coverage for the uninsured, or to do both.

Also consider the medical services provided by county health departments for those who cannot pay. Based on current expenditures, $10 million annually could be redirected if these persons were to obtain health-insurance coverage through the reform plan. Although coverage for state employees will remain virtually the same, premium costs will be controlled since state workers will be part of the megapool. State payments to hospitals which serve a large number of indigent patients will be reduced, since this population will be covered. The health-care provider tax program will be restructured, and a portion of the Medicaid expansion will be financed by these provider taxes. Other savings which will be used to fund health-care reform have been identified and are listed in the plan you have received.

To summarize, health-care reform is imperative, and it is an issue that must be addressed now. Controlling health-care costs is critical to both those who currently have health-insurance coverage and to those who do not. Kentucky's health-care reform can be largely financed by dollars already in the system, with the megapool, the health-care authority, an emphasis on prevention, and other initiatives controlling costs. Business owners have far more to fear from uncontrolled health-care costs than they do from mandatory health insurance for their employees, and those eligible for premium subsidies will be assisted by the state. Health-care reform will be an economic boost for all Kentuckians. Universal coverage and control of health-care costs will encourage the expansion of existing businesses and industries while attracting new companies to our state. As I said earlier, the plan is not written in stone. We're open to suggestions and new ideas. However, please remember our goals. We must control costs, and we must provide coverage for all Kentuckians, regardless of pre-existing conditions. I ask for your support as we work to implement this reform. But, more importantly, your support is needed by that mother in Somerset, the young family in Hazard, the small business owner in Cave City, and that Mayfield couple who are losing their life savings to medical expenses. To them, health-care reform is long overdue. We can, we must, work together to meet this challenge for them and for all Kentuckians.[3]

---

1. Charles Everett Koop (1916–), surgeon, educator; A.B., Dartmouth College, 1937; M.D., Cornell University, 1941; surgeon general of the U.S., 1981–89. *Who's Who in America, 1997,* 51st ed. (New Providence, N.J., 1996).
2. Emery A. Wilson (1942–), dean and vice chancellor for clinical services, University of Kentucky College of Medicine; B.A., Emory University, 1964; M.D., UK College of Medicine, 1968.
3. On March 10, Jones gave a similar speech to the Louisville Chamber of Commerce/ Alliant Health Care System at the Kentucky Center for the Arts. He discussed the "human side of costs," the importance of a megapool, controlling costs, and general support for reform. On May 12, the governor made similar remarks at a talk to the Frankfort Rotary Club; he praised Kentucky for leading the nation in health-care reform. On May 13, at the National Federation of Independent Business Gold Anniversary, Jones gave a similar speech; he congratulated the group but told them he was disappointed that they did not agree on health-care issues. In a talk to the Lexington Chamber of Commerce on May 17, he spoke about the good of health-care reform in the current bill.

HENDERSON CHAMBER OF COMMERCE
Henderson / March 26, 1993

I WANT to thank the Henderson Chamber of Commerce for the invitation to join you today and for the opportunity to share with you details of our goals for restructuring Kentucky's health-care system.

You represent a segment of Kentucky that is justifiably concerned about escalating health-care costs: Kentucky's business leaders. That concern was well expressed by one of your colleagues in testimony at a health-care reform town forum last spring in Cave City. He said that there was no way his business could continue to provide medical insurance for his employees if the cost of that coverage continued to grow as it has for the past several years.

Many of you in the room today no doubt share those sentiments. So do I. I was a businessman before becoming governor, I remain a businessman today, and in three years I'll be back full time with responsibilities that each of you faces daily, meeting payrolls, trying to hold onto quality employees, facing the challenges of competitors, and balancing customer demand with what your company is able to supply. If there's one thing I hope you will remember from this meeting today, it is this: when we talk about health-care reform, first, last, and always, there are really two principal goals: controlling the runaway spiral of health-care costs and ensuring that all Kentuckians have affordable medical insurance. Our approach revolves around one very simple premise: health-care reform is nothing more than controlling costs—something business people do every day, or they don't stay alive in the business world.

Today in the United States, health-care costs equal 13 percent of our gross national product. In Kentucky last year that equated to an estimated $9.5 billion, and yes, that is *billion* with a capital "B." Three cents out of every six cents of Kentucky's state sales tax pays for health-care bills. Think about that for a moment: half of the tax on every sale your business makes today is spent on health care. That means the cost of educating our children, maintaining our roads, cleaning up the environment, providing police protection, operating our court system, and all the other government services are fighting it out for those other three cents.

Insurance premiums in America are escalating between 10 and 20 percent every year. In pocketbook terms that means the cost of providing health-care insurance to your employees is rising roughly four times faster than you can provide raises in your employees' paychecks. Health-care costs represent a fiscal condition which threatens the public and the private sectors alike with bankruptcy if it continues unchecked.

And yet, while the dollar cost of the health care we're paying for is staggering, the humanity of our health-care crisis is even more stunning. Today, there are an estimated 430,000 Kentuckians with no medical insurance. Don't confuse those folks with the half-million

Kentuckians covered by Medicaid. These other 430,000 people, many of whom are working part time or even full time in minimum-wage jobs, often either make too much to qualify for Medicaid but too little to buy their own insurance or they have a pre-existing medical condition that is blocking them from getting a policy.

Who are these Kentuckians without medical insurance? If you attended any of the fifteen health-care-reform town forums last spring, you heard them identify themselves. The mother in Somerset who said she didn't get a Pap smear because, not having insurance, she couldn't afford the cost of treatment and taking care of her children if the test found a problem. The husband who spoke in Ashland of going bankrupt paying his wife's $200,000 in medical bills, and who now can't take a job paying more than $600 a month or his wife will lose her medical card. The senior citizen in Highland Heights who paid for health insurance for forty years—forty years—but whose current medical condition cost him his coverage and prevents him from getting another insurance policy. The former coal miner in Hazard who is studying to become a nurse while his wife works in a minimum-wage job, and cares for their two children, and prays that they don't get sick because they can't afford insurance.

Four hundred thirty thousand Kentuckians with no medical coverage. Let me put that into perspective. If you took every man, woman, and child in this community and in every county surrounding this one and, in fact, the total population of every county in this entire area development district and added them together and took away their medical insurance, you still wouldn't even come close to the number of Kentuckians who go to bed at night living on the edge of financial disaster with any medical emergency.

That, in a nutshell, is the snowballing dilemma that demands reform of our existing health-care system. The bill being paid now is mushrooming, while the humanity still unprotected is overpowering. And remember this, insuring the uninsured is not simply a lofty humanitarian goal. It is a cold, hard financial necessity. We must set aside any idea that controlling health-care costs can be separated from universal access to medical insurance.

Why? Because people without medical insurance still get sick. Uninsured people don't have access to a primary-care physician. They don't get annual checkups. They don't get prenatal care or well-baby care. When they get sick, people without insurance end up in the hospital emergency room with conditions requiring medical care far more expensive than the preventive care they might have had if they had insurance. When people without insurance get sick and can't pay their medical bills, who do you think pays? You and I pay. We pay because the hospitals, the doctors, the ambulance services, and others raise their charges to those who can pay to cover the expenses for those who cannot. Then, we pay because insurance companies raise their premiums to pay the higher fees charged by the providers. Then, we pay because businessmen and women like yourselves have to raise your own prices to pay the higher medical insurance premiums. Cost control and universal access to medical insurance are health-care reform's version of Siamese twins, inseparably joined, now and forever.

Our health-care reform plan has other very important features that I'm certain you've read about or heard about: a five-member health-care authority charged with enforcing cost controls and assuring quality health services, mandatory fee or charge reporting, and developing performance outcome measurements for health-care providers; establishment of a megapool to purchase insurance using the buying clout of at least one million Kentuckians, including those covered by Medicaid, working in our schools and state agencies, and state retirees, and those unemployed and uninsured; standardized insurance forms to simplify the process and reduce the time-consuming, expensive paper pushing required of medical providers; medical liability reform using arbitration panels as a first, less costly step to settle claims without depriving anyone of their due-process rights; producing more primary-care physicians through re-emphasis of this career choice at our medical schools and financial incentives for this discipline; more professionals in medically underserved areas, through aggressive physician recruitment and a heightened service use of nurse practitioners; educating us to the critical importance of living healthy by lifestyle choices we make such as diet, exercise, smoking, and wearing seat belts.

There is one more element of our plan that you have all heard something about, right or wrong, and which will affect, on the average, about one in three of you in this room: mandatory employer-paid insurance for businesses not already providing such and state subsidies for economically sensitive companies. At this point, I think it is paramount to assure every person in this room that I have no intention of solving one problem and creating another damage to the economic health of your business. We certainly don't want to reverse the economic improvements you have recorded in Henderson over the past year. According to the latest figures, Henderson County's unemployment rate is down from 8.2 percent last January to an even 7 percent this January, and that's below the statewide jobless rates. Compared to a year ago, there are more than eight hundred additional full- and part-time jobs filled in this community.

And yet, each of us must accept, as an indisputable fact, that to do nothing or to take a halfway stab at health-care reform simply leaves in place the causes of the unbridled medical cost corkscrew that is now, has for years, and will continue to do that very same economic harm to your company that many fear will result from the idea of required employer-paid coverage. We have proposed that employers purchase a minimum health-insurance benefit policy for all full-time workers by January 1, 1994. Part-time employees and their employers would cover the cost of insurance on a pro-rata share based on a forty-hour work week. Businesses which are financially able to insure their workers but fail to do so would be subject to a 16 percent payroll tax.

Kentuckians and their businesses can afford these coverages if two things happen. First, costs now being paid by the 73 percent of Kentucky businesses and industries who already insure their employees must be controlled. And second, the coverage available for employers to purchase must be affordable. To address those issues, we have proposed to allow any business wishing to do so to join the insurance megapool. A solid actuarial study by one of the nation's top health-care financial-analysis firms indicates that the buying power of the megapool can achieve coverage at a cost of $116 per employee a month.

At the same time, we will reduce workers' compensation rates by 5 percent and freeze those rates for a period of two years. Workers' compensation rates, excluding the coal industry, have been rising at a rate of about 20 percent a year, so a 5 percent reduction and a two-year freeze will produce a tremendous savings. Additionally, under the plan, the state would provide assistance to cover those costs to businesses with a payroll of less than $200,000 per year and a net profit of less than $50,000 annually. The subsidies are targeted to businesses whose workers are most likely to lose their jobs as a result of the mandate—for example, workers earning less than $230 a week. The state and the qualifying employer will split the cost of the insurance premium using a sliding scale based upon each worker's earnings. The initial calculation places the cost of these subsidies to vulnerable businesses for the first two years at $140 million.

Finally, let me go over what you, more than most, understand is the bottom line: financing the plan. We have not proposed new or increased broad-based taxes to fund health-care reform in Kentucky. Financing will be achieved through three elements: cost savings from current expenditures, redistribution of resources already being expended, and a broadening of the current tax on many of this state's health-care providers. Savings will be achieved because, once everyone has insurance, tens of millions will no longer be spent annually on medical care for indigent Kentuckians.

Insurance reforms will cut costly red tape. Malpractice arbitration, cost containment in the Medicaid program, and employment of managed-care principles in a single health-care policy for state employees also will produce significant savings. With all Kentuckians insured, some funds currently expended for indigent care through hospitals, local health departments, and community mental-health centers can be redirected to the cost of subsidies for eligible businesses and individuals. And the provider tax paid by hospitals, physicians, nursing homes, pharmacies, home health agencies, and others will be brought into compliance with new federal regulations that mandate that these taxes be broad-based in nature, touching all providers in a class. This expansion will produce additional revenue that will be put back into a more cost-effective system of health-care delivery.

In conclusion, permit me a brief redundancy by returning to those twins of health-care reform that are our primary goals: health-care cost containment and health-care coverage for all with no pre-existing condition exclusions. I don't know of anyone who doesn't agree with those broad goals, and most folks who have examined the health-care crisis we face, see them as necessities rather than just goals. I have said numerous times that this plan is not written in stone and also that the plan represents only one way to achieve those goals almost everyone agrees on. This administration and the legislators who will turn health-care reform plans into Kentucky law will be working to achieve those goals, whether by following this plan or by finding alternatives to reach the same end. There is much to our plan. It has been called by experts in the field outside Kentucky as the most comprehensive attempt at health-care reform proposed by any state administration in this nation.

In short, there's a lot there, a lot to like and a lot to disagree with. I cannot urge you too strongly to take the time to read the plan yourself, and ask questions yourself. Don't rely simply on the analysis you may read in the newspaper or on someone else's opinion of what the plan does and what it doesn't do. And once you've studied this plan for health-care reform, let your state representative and your state senator know what you think. But I implore you to let them know just as vocally what you like about the plan as what concerns you or what you absolutely cannot support. It is just as important that they hear what you want done as it is to make them aware of elements of the plan that trouble you.

The concept of health-care reform in Kentucky has now been proposed in written form, but that is just part of the process. It is a process that won't be achieved alone in a special session of the legislature next month, or in the implementation and enforcement of new laws this year or next. And from this point on, there is no more important part of that process than your active, thoughtful participation. For this generation and the next, you and I can do no less.

GRANT COUNTY CHAMBER OF COMMERCE
Williamstown / April 2, 1993

I WANT to say how much I appreciate being here this evening to once again speak to the Grant County Chamber of Commerce. I believe this is the first time I have spoken to this group since I was here as lieutenant governor, and it is certainly good to sit with you and to learn about the changes taking place in Williamstown and Dry Ridge and throughout Grant County. As I tell people all the time, these are exciting times in Kentucky, and a lot of positive changes are taking place within your own community.

When we talk about progress in Kentucky, we are really talking about progress within our communities . . . because that is where it all must happen. State government is a catalyst for economic development, and state government can support and do many things that stimulate growth and development. But in the end it is our local communities that really determine whether growth takes place. Leadership is important, and I am always appreciative of the role chambers of commerce play throughout Kentucky, and I want to commend each of you for being a part of your local chamber. I commend you for all the things you are doing to move your community forward, especially projects like your amphitheater. With the purchase of the hundred-acre site, you are now in a position to move forward on developing this facility to become home to Kentucky's newest outdoor drama. You know that Kentucky has quite a reputation for its outdoor dramas, and I am confident that once underway, the drama you have planned for Williamstown, "Lincoln, Before the Memories," will not only be successful in drawing good crowds, but will help enhance our overall tourism industry. I am a strong believer in developing the specific resources of our individual communities and different areas of the state. The amphitheater you are developing is a fine example of that, and you accomplish these things by forming business associations and economic-development committees, as you have done in Williamstown and in Dry Ridge.

I think you will find that in no time in Kentucky's history has state government been more responsive to the needs of our local communities and in developing innovative programs for tourism, economic development, and things that will help communities grow and develop. We are going to invest one hundred million dollars in improvements in our state parks, already one of the best park systems in the country. We have regional economic-development offices with specialists assigned to work regularly with local communities to make the state's economic-development programs more accessible to them. Our incentive programs for new and expanding industries are the most innovative in the country. Kentucky is leading the nation in education reform. *Forbes* magazine, in its March 1 issue, said Kentucky's economy is one of the ten strongest in the nation. Last fall, *U.S. News and World Report* showed Kentucky ranking second in income growth. Our challenge is to continue to move forward by using our resources and new programs to the fullest extent, and to continue to be a leader in things that will meet the needs of Kentuckians.

But what I want to talk about tonight is how we must respond to a crisis that threatens to totally undermine our efforts because it will bankrupt us if we do nothing. I know that you have read and heard about many of the components of our health-care reform plan, and I want to address the key elements of that plan tonight. But first I want to take some time to emphasize the human side of this plan, how it will meet the human needs . . . of the thousands of Kentuckians who have no health insurance. . . . The fact is, we can honestly say that health care can be a matter of life and death, either physically, economically, or both.

Does that statement seem overly dramatic? Not when you consider that many of the almost 430,000 Kentuckians who have no health insurance all too often cannot afford to seek medical care until it is too late. Not when you consider that thousands of Kentuckians with life-threatening illnesses are denied medical insurance because of pre-existing conditions. Not when you consider that medical care currently represents 13 percent of our gross national product and is costing Kentuckians $9 billion a year. Statistics are revealing and valuable resources, but they don't always clearly reflect the human side of the health-care problem.

Perhaps the urgent need for health-care reform can best be demonstrated by the appeals for help heard during last year's regional town forums. For example, a mother in Somerset said she didn't get a regular Pap smear because, without insurance, she would have no way of paying for treatment or caring for her children if the test revealed a problem. An Ashland man, who said access to affordable medical care is a critical issue, told us he was forced to take bankruptcy after his wife's illness cost $200,000. A woman from Louisville told us she and her husband were paying $300 a month for health insurance until he needed a life-saving kidney transplant. Now their health insurance has quadrupled to $1,200 a month. A Hazard man with four children, who worked in the coal mines but now is a college student, said he and his wife, who is employed in a minimum-wage job, cannot afford insurance for their family. A married couple in Mayfield are using their savings to pay a $724 monthly health-insurance premium, the least expensive coverage they could find. A small business owner in Cave City said business people cannot afford to continue providing employee health insurance because of the tremendous increase in premiums.

These are just a few examples. Consider that there are 430,000 similar stories that could be told, and you get an idea of the magnitude of the medical-care crisis facing Kentucky, 430,000 without health insurance. That's almost as many people as the populations of Louisville and Lexington combined. Think of the worry that these people must feel, knowing that if they or some member of their family becomes seriously ill, they don't know how they're going to pay the bills. Doing what is right to help people who need help is simply what government is all about, and it would be a mistake to think that those who currently have good health insurance are immune to this problem. When people are unable to obtain health insurance because of pre-existing conditions, everyone pays.

The costs from unpaid bills are shifted to those who do pay, driving up the price of premiums for everyone and resulting in even more people who can't afford coverage. According to one national publication, cost shifting accounts for about one-third of the increase in insurance premiums, which are rising at the rate of 15 percent a year. The cost of medical care, which is increasing two to three times faster than the rate of inflation, is responsible for the rest. Those of us lucky enough to have insurance through our employers know that we're still not safe from those skyrocketing costs. Chances are that our insurers are responding to the rapidly rising cost of health care by providing less coverage for more money.

As a result, many employers will require their employees to pay a larger share of health-insurance premiums, which means substantially less take-home pay. So, either physically, economically, or both, health-care reform is a matter of life and death for our people. Health-care reform is not an option or something that can be postponed. It must be addressed, and it must be addressed now. All of you are very familiar with my feelings on this point. I have spoken on several occasions about my goals for this process. But I want to reiterate them today: We must control the escalating costs of health care, and we must ensure that every Kentuckian has coverage regardless of any pre-existing condition.

These goals are interrelated, and I do not believe we can accomplish one without the other. Each element of the plan we have presented is designed to help us reach those goals, and there is one thing that I want to make very clear today. As I have always been, I remain open to suggestions about ways to improve our reform plan, refinements, alterations, new ideas that will give us a better program. But all of these things must—must—reach our goals of controlling costs and universal coverage. I am unwilling to accept anything else.

Now, I would like to review the major elements of our plan. Our plan will control costs through a health-care authority, a mega-purchasing pool, workers' compensation reform,[1] a system of standardized claim forms and insurance cards, and medical liability reform. The mission of the health-care authority will be to control costs while assuring quality health services. It will have the power to set rates to control the cost of health-insurance premiums and payments made to health-care providers. It will ensure that health-care costs do not exceed a predetermined target to the cost of living.

The importance of cost control is evident when you consider that, if we allow health-care costs to continue to rise at the present rate, about one dollar of every five spent in our nation by the year 2000 will be for health care. That will be more than 20 percent of our gross domestic product. The health-care authority also will establish service-delivery regions. It will work with local communities and health-care providers to create networks which ensure that all Kentuckians have access to medical services. The authority also will assess community health needs. The authority will consist of four members appointed by the governor and confirmed by the senate with the secretary of human resources serving as chair. The appointed members will serve six-year terms. The megapool will consist of more than one million Kentuckians, enabling the state to negotiate with health-care providers from a position of financial strength. This will give the state the leverage needed to eliminate unnecessary services, increase efficiency, control duplication of services, and secure discounts from providers. The megapool will include the following groups: public employees, Medicaid recipients, currently uninsured/unemployed persons, employees of businesses choosing to participate, and individuals or families choosing to participate.

The individual benefit packages offered under the megapool will vary. For example, state employees will have coverage very similar to their present plan. Businesses or individuals will be able to purchase the health insurance basic plan for $116 per month for a single plan. Medicaid will be incorporated into the megapool to improve its negotiating position. Services provided to Medicaid recipients will not be changed, but steps will be taken to control costs. The workers' compensation system will be modified. It will require health-care services for industrial injuries and occupational diseases to be provided under managed-care plans. This will be accompanied by a 5 percent reduction in workers' compensation premiums, and that rate will be frozen for 24 months.

This revised workers' compensation system will also allow twenty-four-hour health-care coverage through pilot projects. Under these pilots, a single administrator will manage both general health care and workers' compensation medical care. Studies confirm that a savings of 5 to 35 percent can be achieved in workers' compensation health-care costs with implementation of the reform package. Other savings will result from the use of standardized insurance forms and cards and setting up a system of arbitration for malpractice disputes.

I'd like to turn now to universal coverage. All Kentuckians will have at least the basic health-insurance protection identified in the plan. Employers will be required to purchase a basic plan for each full-time employee at the megapool rate of $116 per employee per month. The premiums of eligible small businesses will be subsidized by the state. Employers will be required to pay a pro-rata share for part-time employees, based on a forty-hour week. State assistance will be provided on a sliding scale to assist part-time workers with their share of health-insurance costs. Employers will be required to offer a family plan, but the additional cost of family coverage will be the responsibility of employees. Eligible employees identified in the plan will receive state subsidies to help pay premiums. Unemployed adults will be assisted by state government in the purchase of health insurance, and those with household incomes below 100 percent of poverty will be fully subsidized. Each person covered under the megapool will receive one free health examination and appropriate lab tests each year. Immunizations and well-baby care will also be covered. These procedures can detect or prevent many health problems at their early stages, when they can be more easily and effectively treated at a lower cost.

Employers will find that reform will reduce future health-insurance costs and create a healthier, more productive workforce. Kentucky's economic-development efforts will be helped significantly by health-care reform. In fact, our economic-development team is already using Kentucky's draft plan for health-care reform as an industry recruiting tool. Health-care delivery reforms are also addressed by the plan. Delivery and system reforms will take into consideration transportation factors and the health-care needs that may be unique to certain sections of the state.

The curriculum in our state medical schools will be rewritten to emphasize primary-care practice and prevention. The University of Kentucky will expand nurse midwifery, nurse practitioner, and physician assistant programs, services which can reduce costs. The University of Louisville will implement programs in at least two of these areas. Quality assurance is a key part of the plan. Quality guidelines will be implemented for all medical professionals by the health-care authority.

Provider profiles will enable consumers and insurers to determine which providers consistently deliver effective and cost-efficient services, and there are still other reforms in the plan. Seat belt use will be mandated. Health education will be provided to all Kentucky children, and consumer education programs will inform adults about health resources, healthy lifestyle choices, and disease-prevention methods.

Now let's discuss plan financing, where the dollars will come from. Former United States Surgeon General C. Everett Koop and others with health-care expertise agree that 25 to 30 percent of what we spend on health care is for medically unnecessary procedures. Much of these costs result from defensive medicine as providers work under the constant fear of malpractice lawsuits. For example, the University of Kentucky medical school dean, Emery Wilson, says that it is becoming normal emergency-room procedure to perform an MRI on a child who has fallen out of bed. The physician knows that he or she should just tell the family to wake the child every two or three hours to make sure everything is normal. But because of the fear of lawsuits, highly expensive MRIs have become standard procedure. Defensive medicine is expensive medicine.

Another example of unnecessary cost is paperwork resulting from billing, bureaucracy, and marketing in the health-care industry. It is becoming increasingly apparent to everyone that we spend huge amounts of money processing paperwork to get the providers paid, or perhaps to keep them from getting paid. The only people who benefit from this nightmare of paperwork are the ones employed to pass the documents back and forth. These are just examples of the 25 to 30 percent of health-care costs wasted on unnecessary procedures and processing. If we agree that a minimum of 25 percent of the $9 billion Kentuckians spend on health-care costs each year is unnecessary, that means $2.25 billion already in the system can be redirected toward primary care and prevention.

Dollars needed to fund the plan will also come from savings generated by state government through implementation of the reform. For example, Kentucky allocates millions of dollars each year to underwrite the cost of medical care for indigent citizens. These patients will have insurance through the reform plan, freeing funds to expand Medicaid or to purchase health-insurance coverage for the uninsured, or to do both. Also consider the medical services provided by county health departments for those who cannot pay. Based on current expenditures, $10 million annually could be redirected if these persons were to obtain health-insurance coverage through the reform plan.

Although coverage for state employees will remain virtually the same, premium costs will be controlled since state workers will be part of the megapool. State payments to hospitals which serve a large number of indigent patients will be reduced, since this population will be covered. The health-care provider tax program will be restructured, and a portion of the Medicaid expansion will be financed by these provider taxes.

To summarize, health-care reform is imperative, and it is an issue that must be addressed now. Controlling health-care costs is critical to both those who currently have health-insurance coverage and to those who do not. Kentucky's health-care reform can be largely financed by dollars already in the system with the megapool, the health-care authority, an emphasis on prevention, and other initiatives controlling costs. Business owners have far more to fear from uncontrolled health-care costs than they do from mandatory health insurance for their employees, and those eligible for premium subsidies will be assisted by the state. Health-care reform will be an economic boost for all Kentuckians. Universal coverage and control of health-care costs will encourage the expansion of existing businesses and industries while attracting new companies to our state.

As I said earlier, the plan is not written in stone. We're open to suggestions and new ideas; however, please remember our goals. We must control costs, and we must provide coverage for all Kentuckians, regardless of pre-existing conditions. I ask for your support as we work to implement this reform, but, more importantly, your support is needed by that mother in Somerset, the young family in Hazard, the small business owner in Cave City, and that Mayfield couple who are losing their life savings to medical expenses. To them, health-care reform is long overdue. We can, we must, work together to meet this challenge for them and for all Kentuckians.

---

1. The Workers' Compensation Reform Act passed by the 1994 General Assembly and supported by the Jones administration dramatically changed the system to expedite claims processing and provide an alternative dispute-resolution mechanism. The bill includes an ombudsman program and ensures that medical treatment is delivered in a cost-effective way which also speeds an employee's return to work. The bill caps attorney fees and reduces reimbursements to medical providers. It also creates a state employers' mutual insurance authority to grant employers access to affordable coverage.

KENTUCKY ASSOCIATION OF TRANSPORTATION ENGINEERS
Lexington / April 10, 1993

I WANT to thank you all for inviting me to speak today. As trained professionals who are keenly aware of the workings of state government, I feel certain that you are also aware of how constrained our finances are, and I'm sure most of you know that budget difficulties of the present are nothing compared to what we will face if we fail to address a growing crisis of unparalleled importance. As we face this crisis, I need your help and support. Like it or not, we'll either pay now or we will pay dearly later. Most of the time, when we think about reforming the health-care system, we think of it in terms of our own needs, our own experiences.

Perhaps many of us have experienced firsthand, personally or through a relative or close friend, the results of a serious illness or injury. First, there is the fear and misery. Then, if we are fortunate, there is the miracle and marvel of our medical care that is rivaled by none in the world. And then there is the experience of the cost. For the vast majority of us, we breathe a sigh of relief in knowing that our health insurance will pay most of it. But, we shudder at the amount we might have had to pay and wonder how we would have paid for it all.

For almost 450,000 Kentuckians that fear is very real, very near, and very constant. That is the human quotient that in part drives this engine of health-care reform. It is a moral imperative that we help all Kentuckians. But there is also a pragmatic catalyst in this effort. Either we all do something to get a handle on health-care costs, or they will crush us economically as individuals, as families, as companies and industries, as governments, and as a commonwealth and as a nation. We cannot reform health care without covering those who are not now covered, because we either provide them with coverage or bear the costs ourselves through cost shifting.

They enter the health-care system through its most expensive avenue, most often the emergency rooms of our hospitals. They pay three to four times as much as they would if they had a family physician, not to mention how much would have been saved in preventive care. And we pay the tab in increased medical costs to make up the difference and increased insurance premiums to offset increased costs of providing health care for the uninsured. It is a constant and critical cycle that has sent health-care costs spiraling at a rate of 15 percent per year for the past decade, two to three times faster than the rate of inflation and our paychecks, and it will not subside unless we address it head on.

According to one national publication, cost shifting accounts for about one-third of the increase in insurance premiums. And those of us lucky enough to have insurance through our employers know that we're still not safe from skyrocketing health-care costs. Chances are that our insurers are responding to the rapidly rising costs by providing less coverage for our money. Medical care currently represents 13 percent of our gross national product and is costing

Kentuckians $9 billion a year. I've been told by the budget experts in our administration that, eventually, paying for health care in this state will take half of all new revenue. All other programs will have to fight over the other half of the pie. And it doesn't take a mathematical genius to figure out what that will mean in terms of funding our schools, providing other services, or running state government. This is not a threat to any group, but the harsh face of reality. If we fail to act, health-care costs will bankrupt us, pure and simple.

On the human side again, there are also the thousands of Kentuckians who currently have coverage but are threatened by reduced benefits as costs spiral upward. And the thousands of others with life-threatening illnesses who might be able to afford *reasonable* health-care insurance but are denied coverage because of a pre-existing condition. Insurance that is available to them is cost-prohibitive. Denying anyone insurance because they've had cancer, a stroke, or a heart attack would be illegal under our health-care reform plan. Think of the tremendous burden lifted from these people and their families.

Recently, we revealed some modifications to our original proposal. We have listened to the concerns that have been expressed in recent weeks, as we said we would. As a result, we are now looking at requiring individuals to be responsible for their insurance rather than requiring the employers to cover their workers. We continue to hold to our two main goals of universal coverage and cost containment. State subsidies on a sliding scale would be available for individuals who earn between 100 percent and 200 percent of poverty. The unemployed and individuals who earn up to 100 percent of poverty will be provided coverage through the state. *All* children in families with incomes less than 200 percent of poverty will be covered by Medicaid. Through a megapool used as a bargaining tool with insurers, people above 200 percent of poverty could obtain a basic package of benefits which would cost $85 a month per adult. Coverage per child would be $55 a month. This plan has a co-payment of $10 per doctor's visit, $7 per prescription, and $250 per hospital visit. Mental-health coverage will be included and strongly improved from our previous plan. Details are being refined. Employers who don't provide health insurance would pay a 3 to 4 percent payroll tax to help fund reform. If an employee does not have health coverage, the employer will withhold from the employee's pay the amount needed for the basic package in the megapool.

For state employees, their benefits package will be better than in the previous plan. The other elements of our health-care reform packages remain unchanged. Our plan will control costs through a health-care authority, a mega-purchasing pool, workers' compensation reform, a system of standardized claim forms and insurance cards, and medical liability reform. The mission of the health-care authority will be to control costs while assuring quality health services. It will have the power to set rates to control the cost of health-insurance premiums and payments made to health-care providers. It will ensure that health-care costs do not exceed a predetermined target tied to the cost of living.

The importance of cost control is evident when you consider that, if we allow health-care costs to continue to rise at the present rate, about one dollar out of every five spent in our nation by the year 2000 will be for health care. That will be more than 20 percent of our gross domestic product. The health-care authority also will establish service-delivery regions. It will work with local communities and health-care providers to create networks which ensure that all Kentuckians have access to medical services. The authority also will assess community health needs. The authority will consist of five members appointed by the governor and confirmed by the senate. They will serve six-year terms. The megapool, with at least one million Kentuckians, will give the state the leverage needed to eliminate unnecessary services, increase efficiency, control duplication of services, and secure discounts from providers. The megapool will include the following groups: public employees, Medicaid recipients, currently uninsured/unemployed persons, employees of businesses choosing to participate, and individuals or families choosing to participate.

Medicaid will be incorporated into the megapool to improve its negotiating position. Services provided to Medicaid recipients will not be changed, but steps will be taken to control costs. The workers' compensation system will be modified. It will require health-care services for industrial injuries and occupational diseases to be provided under managed-care plans. This will be accompanied by a 5 percent reduction in workers' compensation premiums, and that rate will be frozen for twenty-four months. This revised workers' compensation system will also allow twenty-four-hour health-care coverage through pilot projects. Under these pilots, a single administrator will manage both general health care and workers' compensation medical care.

Studies confirm that a savings of 5 to 35 percent can be achieved in workers' compensation health-care costs with implementation of the reform package. Other savings will result from the use of standardized insurance forms on cards and setting up a system of arbitration for malpractice disputes. Each person covered under the megapool will receive one free health examination and appropriate lab tests each year. Immunizations and well-baby care will also be covered. These procedures can detect many health problems at their early stages, when they can be more easily and effectively treated at a lower cost.

Employers will find that reform will reduce future health-insurance costs and create a healthier, more productive workforce. Health-care delivery reforms are also addressed by the plan. Delivery and system reforms will take into consideration transportation factors and the health-care needs that may be unique to certain sections of the state.

The curriculum in our state will be rewritten to emphasize primary-care practice and prevention. The University of Kentucky will expand nurse midwifery, nurse practitioner and physician assistant programs, services which can reduce costs. The University of Louisville will implement programs in at least two of these areas. Quality assurance is a key part of the plan. Quality guidelines will be implemented for all medical professionals by the health-care authority. Provider profiles will enable consumers and insurers to determine which providers consistently deliver effective and cost-efficient services. And there are still other reforms in the plan. Seat belt use will be mandated. Health education will be provided to all Kentucky children, and consumer education programs will inform adults about health resources, healthy lifestyle choices, and disease-prevention methods.

Now let's discuss plan financing, where the dollars will come from. Former United States Surgeon General C. Everett Koop and others with health-care expertise agree that 25 to 30 percent of what we spend on health care is for medically unnecessary procedures. Many of these costs result from defensive medicine as providers work under the constant fear of malpractice lawsuits. Another example of unnecessary cost is paperwork resulting from billing, bureaucracy, and marketing in the health-care industry. It is becoming increasingly apparent to everyone that we spend huge amounts of money processing paperwork to get the providers paid, or perhaps to keep them from getting paid. The only people who benefit from this nightmare of paperwork are the ones employed to pass the documents back and forth. These are just examples of the 25 to 30 percent of health-care costs wasted on unnecessary procedures and processing. If we agree that a minimum of 25 percent of the $9 billion Kentuckians spend on health-care costs each year is unnecessary, that means $2.25 billion already in the system can be redirected toward primary care and prevention.

Dollars needed to fund the plan will also come from savings generated by state government through implementation of the reform. For example, Kentucky allocates millions of dollars each year to underwrite the cost of medical care for indigent citizens. These patients will have insurance through the reform plan, freeing funds to expand Medicaid or to purchase health-insurance coverage for the uninsured, or to do both. Also consider the medical services provided by county health departments for those who cannot pay. Based on current expenditures, $10 million annually could be redirected if these persons were to obtain health-insurance coverage through the reform plan.

Although coverage for state employees will remain virtually the same, premium costs will be controlled since state workers will be part of the megapool. State payments to hospitals which serve a large number of indigent patients will be reduced, since this population will be covered. The health-care provider tax program will be restructured, and a portion of Medicaid expansion will be financed by these provider taxes. We have had some positive reaction to this slight retooling of our efforts, while some are still concerned.

I know the bottom line is real. Having had to make a payroll for most of the past thirty years, I know the hardships involved in running a business. But we either bear the burden now or health-care costs will drive more and more companies out of business. Ford Motor Company estimates the cost of health care for their workers now represents a larger portion of the sticker price on their cars than the steel used to build them. If we get a handle on health-care costs now it can become an economic stimulus. Our state can become the first in the nation to control health-care costs and provide coverage for every one of its citizens. I have talked with many CEOs who have said a guarantee to keep health-care costs in line with the cost of living would be a major factor in their decisions to locate new plants or to expand existing industries.

In the short term, there will be some pain, but I am convinced, and have sufficient data from experts around this nation, that health-care reform will be, in the long run, an economic boon to Kentucky. Again, this is the pragmatic side. Will it work, how will it affect us individually? But again, there is the pressing side of human needs demonstrated by the appeals for help heard during last year's regional town forums. We heard from a mother in

Somerset who cannot afford a regular Pap smear out of fear that if it showed she had cancer, she would have no way of paying for treatment or for caring for her children. A Louisville woman said a life-saving kidney transplant for her husband drove their health-insurance premium from $300 to $1,200 a month. A man from Ashland was forced into bankruptcy when his wife's illness cost $200,000. A Hazard coal miner-turned-college student trying to find a better life for his wife and four children says his minimum-wage job makes health insurance a luxury he cannot afford. A married couple in Mayfield are using their life's savings to pay a monthly health-insurance premium of $724, the least expensive coverage they could find. And a small business owner in Cave City says increased insurance premiums will force him to drop coverage for his employees. This is where the pragmatic meets the human quotient and in essence becomes the bottom line. Business owners have far more to fear from uncontrolled health-care costs than they do from health-care reform.

The economic ruin of us all will be a reality if we are unwilling to share the burden and act now. We have a common goal, and we are beginning to merge into a common direction. Let us not waver in our efforts to bring about health-care reform in our state. There are many who would rather maintain the status quo; many of those stand to gain much if we do nothing. But they will be short-term gains at the expense of our humanity, ourselves, and our posterity.[1]

---

1. This health-care speech is very similar to previous speeches given on February 11 and March 1, 1993. Major points of Jones's reform plan are pointed out in most of the health-care speeches.

ASSOCIATION OF OLDER KENTUCKIANS LUNCHEON
Frankfort / May 4, 1993

ORGANIZATIONS such as Association of Older Kentuckians (AOK) have as their prime objective the interests of many of our older citizens who have special needs and concerns. AOK represents a lot of people trying to make life a little better for its members and the many others who share the same concerns. And hopefully, we all know that we are here to help each other and make the world a little better than it was before. That, we hope history will record, is the hallmark of our administration, to help many people in our Commonwealth who cannot help themselves. That is the driving force behind our efforts and the key to our health-care reform legislation.

As you have read by now, in just a few short days, the General Assembly of Kentucky will gather in Frankfort for what will prove to be a historic session, if conscience rules. This session more than any other will be the interests of the people versus the special interests, and I am here today to seek your assistance in helping us do what is right, provide health-care insurance coverage for all Kentuckians and control health-care costs before they bankrupt us all. When we released the bill form of our proposal in Frankfort recently, I restated then our dual goals of providing insurance for every Kentuckian without regard to any pre-existing condition and getting control of rising health-care costs. We are proposing the formation of a health-care authority that would have the power to tie future increases in health-care costs to the consumer price index. Our proposal, in bill form, is now before the General Assembly's interim Health and Welfare Committee, which began hearings on the measure a week ago today. Our bill would require all Kentuckians to have health insurance by January 1 of next year. The state would assist low-income citizens with the purchase of insurance. The health-care authority would have five members who would be confirmed by the senate and serve four-year terms. Two, but no more, would be former health-care providers. The authority would begin setting rates by January 1, 1994, for all insurance and medical-care providers. And the authority would have broad oversight and regulatory powers over the state's $9 billion health-care industry where right now no one is in charge. This authority would make it illegal to deny anyone insurance coverage because of age, illness, or past medical condition.

Presently, there are 450,000 Kentuckians who have no health insurance. Many, many others who are underinsured or working poor live in constant fear that even a moderate illness or injury will destroy their families. A catastrophic illness could take away their homes. You deal with these types of fears daily and know from your own experiences how family tragedies can be compounded by the crushing costs of health care. Under our proposal, all employers would pay a 3.75 percent payroll tax and would get a credit against the tax for their health-related expenditures on employees, including insurance. Doctors, hospitals, and other providers would be taxed a percentage of their revenues and would be prohibited from passing the tax on to consumers in higher charges. Providers would be required to submit detailed information to the authority, which would publish comparisons of prices and quality of care and would also develop practice guidelines for providers. The authority would also develop a minimum benefits plan to be offered by every health-insurance carrier in Kentucky. This plan would be available to individuals and groups in a new state "megapool." The pool, made up of public employees, Medicaid recipients, and others, would bargain for rates with health-care and insurance providers for services, regionally and statewide. A low-cost benefit plan would be available to low-income Kentuckians. The state would provide financial assistance to individuals whose household income is less than 200 percent of the federal poverty level. Our plan calls for no deductibles or co-payments for preventive care.

What we have attempted to do in our plan is not to ask anyone to do what they cannot financially afford to do, but we must ask people to jointly share in the responsibility to solve what I believe is the greatest problem facing society today. I have said from the beginning in forming our plan almost a year ago that we wanted to have everyone's suggestions but that I will not compromise on my goals of universal coverage and controlling health-care costs. I firmly believe that we cannot get control over rising costs without providing insurance coverage for everyone. Roughly a third of the rising costs of health-care coverage comes from cost shifting, where we pay for those who have little or no coverage.

Next Monday, legislators from around the Commonwealth will gather in Frankfort. The eyes of the state, and the nation, and I believe the collective conscience of us all will be focused on this effort. I have said, and continue to maintain, that I will go to the wall on this because to fail is to fail humanity and continue a cycle of spiraling costs that will consume government and individuals alike. Again, this session marks a historic test: the needs of the people versus the special interests. I am confident that with your help and prayers and the good-faith efforts of the many people who truly want to do what is right and make this world a little better than it was before, we can set an example for our nation as we care for the many who look to government to literally and figuratively save their lives.

GREATER LEXINGTON MINISTERIAL FELLOWSHIP LUNCHEON
Lexington / May 5, 1993

MINISTERS are by their very nature the embodiment of conscience and hope. People seek wisdom and guidance from them, and they seek wisdom and guidance in the words and deeds of a higher authority as best as can be understood. We make sense out of our lives each day with the help of the many good people who try to understand what it is we are supposed to do while we are here on earth. But we all know that we are here to help each other and make the world a little better than it was before. That, we hope history will record, is the hallmark of our administration: to help the many people in our Commonwealth who cannot help themselves. That is the driving force behind our efforts and the key to our health-care reform legislation.

As you have read by now, in just a few short days, the General Assembly of Kentucky will gather in Frankfort for what will prove to be a historic session if conscience rules. This session more than any other will be the interests of the people versus the special interests, and I am here today to seek your assistance in helping us do what is right: to provide health-care insurance coverage for all Kentuckians and control health-care costs before they bankrupt us all.

When we released the bill form of our proposal in Frankfort recently, I restated then our dual goals of providing insurance for every Kentuckian without regard to any pre-existing condition and getting control of rising health-care costs. We are proposing the formation of a health-care authority that would have the power to tie future increases in health-care costs to the consumer price index.

Our proposal, in bill form, is now before the General Assembly's interim Health and Welfare Committee, which began hearings on the measure a week ago today. Our bill would require all Kentuckians to have health insurance by January 1 of next year. The state would assist low-income citizens with the purchase of insurance. The Health Care Authority would have five members who would be confirmed by the senate and serve four-year terms. Two, but no more, would be former health-care providers. The authority would begin setting rates by January 1, 1994, for all insurance and medical-care providers. Also, the authority would have broad oversight and regulatory powers over the state's $9 billion health-care industry where right now no one is in charge. This authority would make it illegal to deny anyone insurance coverage because of age, illness, or past medical condition.

Presently there are 450,000 Kentuckians who have no health insurance. Many, many others who are underinsured or are the working poor live in constant fear that even a moderate illness or injury will destroy their families. A catastrophic illness could take away their homes. You deal with these types of fears daily and know from your own experience how family tragedies can be compounded by the crushing costs of health care. Under our proposal, all employers would pay a 3.75 percent payroll tax and would get a credit against the tax for their health-related expenditures on employees, including insurance. Doctors, hospitals, and other providers would be taxed a percentage of their revenues and would be prohibited from passing the tax on to consumers in higher charges.

Providers would be required to submit detailed information to the authority, which would publish comparisons of prices and quality of care and would also develop practice guidelines for providers. The authority would also develop a minimum benefits plan to be offered by every health-insurance carrier in Kentucky. This plan would be available to individuals and groups in a new state "megapool." The pool, made up of public employees, Medicaid recipients, and others, would bargain for rates with health-care and insurance providers for services, regionally and statewide.

A low-cost benefit plan would be available to low-income Kentuckians. The state would provide financial assistance to individuals whose household income is less than 200 percent of the federal poverty level. Our plan calls for no deductibles or co-payments for preventive care. What we have attempted to do in our plan is not to ask anyone to do what they cannot financially afford to do, but we must ask people to jointly share in the responsibility to solve what I believe is the greatest problem facing society today.

I have said from the beginning in forming our plan almost a year ago that we wanted to have everyone's suggestions but that I will not compromise on my goals of universal coverage and controlling health-care costs. I firmly believe that we cannot get control over rising costs without providing insurance coverage for everyone. Roughly a third of the rising costs of health-care coverage come from cost shifting, where we pay for those who have little or no coverage.

Next Monday, legislators from around the Commonwealth will gather in Frankfort. The eyes of the state, and the nation, and I believe the collective conscience of us all will be focused on this effort. I have said, and continue to maintain, that I will go to the wall on this because to fail is to fail humanity and continue a cycle of spiraling costs that will consume governments and individuals alike.

Again, this session marks a historic test, the needs of the people versus the wants of the special interests. I am confident that with your guidance and prayers and the good-faith efforts of the many people who truly want to do what is right and make this world a little better than it was before, we can set an example for our nation as we care for the many who look to government to literally and figuratively save their lives.[1]

---

1. This speech is a reflection of many of the previous health-care speeches given in 1993. See especially the health-care speeches given to the Chamber of Commerce (February 11), the Kentucky Health Care Reform Commission (March 1), and the Kentucky Association of Transportation Engineers (April 10).

KENTUCKY CHAMBER OF COMMERCE BOARD MEETING
Lexington / May 6, 1993

As you know, we are beginning a special session next week on an issue that touches the lives of every Kentuckian: health-care reform. The inadequacies and high costs of our health-care system present a challenge that is greater than any of us individually can combat. You deal with this challenge daily and know from your own businesses that if we don't do something soon, rising health-care costs will bankrupt us all—governments, businesses, and individuals alike. That much we all agree on, and we all agree that something has to be done soon. It is my heartfelt belief that we cannot accomplish this alone.

In order to truly get control of health-care costs, we must—must—get insurance coverage for everyone. That is a necessity that, quite candidly, will require some sacrifice now to stave off certain destruction in the future. And we cannot wait for Washington. We can fool ourselves into thinking that we have time or that we should let someone else at the national level take care of this problem, but these are all delays and baseless arguments that are the equivalent of sticking our heads in the sand or are fronts that hide real reasons for delaying a solution or denying the problem.

In addition to the economic need, there is also a compelling humanitarian argument. Simply put, providing health-care coverage for 450,000 people in this state who presently do not have insurance is a moral imperative that has the practical effect of helping us all. That, we hope history will record, is the hallmark of our administration: We want to help the many people in our Commonwealth who cannot help themselves. And we all benefit. That is the driving force behind our efforts and the key to our health-care reform legislation.

The special session that begins Monday, more than any other we have seen, will be the interests of the people versus the special interests, and I am here today to seek your assistance in helping us do what is right: provide health-care insurance coverage for all Kentuckians and get control of health-care costs before they bankrupt us all. When we released the bill form of our proposal in Frankfort recently, I restated then our dual goals of providing insurance for every Kentuckian without regard to any pre-existing condition and getting control of rising health-care costs.

We are proposing the formation of a health-care authority that would have the power to tie future increases in health-care costs to the consumer price index. Our bill would require all Kentuckians to have health insurance by January 1 of next year. The state would assist low-income citizens with the purchase of insurance. The Health Care Authority would have five members who would be appointed by the governor and confirmed by the senate and serve four-year terms. Two, but no more, would be former health-care providers.

The authority would begin setting rates by January 1, 1994, for all insurance and medical-care providers. And the authority would have broad oversight and regulatory powers over the state's $9 billion health-care industry, where right now no one is in charge. This authority would make it illegal to deny anyone insurance coverage because of age, illness, or past medical condition.

As I have mentioned, there are 450,000 Kentuckians who have no health insurance. Many, many others who are underinsured or the working poor live in constant fear that even a moderate illness or injury will destroy their families. A catastrophic illness could take away their homes. Under our proposal, all employers would pay a 3.75 percent payroll tax and would get a credit against the tax for their health-related expenditures on employees, including insurance. Doctors, hospitals, and other providers would be taxed a percentage of their revenues and would be prohibited from passing the tax on to consumers in higher charges. Providers would be required to submit detailed information to the authority, which would publish comparisons of prices and quality of care and would also develop practice guidelines for providers. The authority would also develop a minimum-benefits plan to be offered by every health-insurance carrier in Kentucky. This plan would be available to individuals and groups in a new state "megapool."

The pool, made up of public employees, Medicaid recipients, and others would bargain for rates with health-care and insurance providers for services, regionally and statewide. A low-cost benefit plan would be available to low-income Kentuckians. The state would provide financial assistance to individuals whose household income is less than 200 percent of the federal poverty level. Our plan calls for no deductibles or co-payments for preventive care. What we have attempted to do in our plan is not to ask anyone to do what they cannot financially afford to do, but we must ask people to jointly share in the responsibility to solve what I believe is the greatest problem facing society today. I have said from the beginning in forming our plan almost a year ago that we wanted to have everyone's suggestions but that I will not compromise on my goals of universal coverage and controlling health-care costs.

Again, I firmly believe that we cannot get control over rising costs without providing insurance coverage for everyone. Roughly a third of the rising costs of health-care coverage come from cost shifting, where we pay for those who have little or no coverage. Next Monday, legislators from around the Commonwealth will gather in Frankfort. The eyes of the state and the nation, and I believe the collective conscience of us all, will be focused on this effort. I have said, and continue to maintain, that I will go to the wall on this because to fail is to fail humanity and continue the cycle of spiraling costs that will consume governments and individuals alike. Again, this session marks a historic test—the needs of the people versus the wants of the special interests.

I am confident that with your help and cooperation and the good-faith efforts of the many people who truly want to do what is right, we can set an example for our nation and provide answers to a national dilemma as we care for the many who look to government to literally and figuratively save their lives.[1]

---

1. This speech is very similar to the speech given the previous day to the Greater Lexington Ministerial Fellowship Luncheon.

KENTUCKY CABLE TELEVISION ASSOCIATION ANNUAL CONVENTION
Lexington / May 11, 1993

BEING with you today allows me this opportunity to personally congratulate you on your *Capital Link* cable channel that KCTA has undertaken with KET to share the coverage of the health-care session with cable viewers in different regions of Kentucky. The *Capital Link* offers a window to everyone, from the most ardent political analyst to the most uninitiated observer, as we tackle health-care reform, unquestionably an issue that affects every single Kentuckian. Just as the new *Capital Link* will make the political processes of the state accessible to all Kentuckians, our administration's driving force has been to help all of our people. That is the key to our health-care reform legislation.

As you know by now, the General Assembly of Kentucky has gathered in Frankfort for what will prove to be a historic session, if conscience rules. This session, more than any other, will be the interests of the people versus the special interests, and I am here today to ask your support in helping us do what is right: provide health-care insurance coverage for all Kentuckians and control health-care costs before they bankrupt us all. When we released the bill form of our proposal in Frankfort recently, I restated then our dual goals of providing insurance for every Kentuckian without regard to any pre-existing conditions and getting control of rising health-care costs. We are proposing the formation of a health-care authority that would have the power to tie future increases in health-care costs to the consumer price index. Our bill would require all Kentuckians to have health insurance by January 1 of next year. The state would assist low-income citizens with the purchase of insurance. The health-care authority would have five members who would be confirmed by the senate and serve four-year terms. Two, but no more, would be former health-care providers. The authority would begin setting rates by January 1, 1994, for all insurance and medical-care providers, and the authority would have broad oversight and regulatory powers over the state's $9 billion health-care industry, where right now no one is in charge. This authority would make it illegal to deny anyone insurance coverage because of age, illness, or past medical condition. . . .

. . . Yesterday, legislators from around the Commonwealth gathered in Frankfort. The eyes of the state and the nation, and I believe the collective conscience of us all, will be focused on this effort, and thanks to *Capital Link*, Kentuckians can see how the process works. I continue to maintain that I am going to the wall on this because to fail is to fail humanity and continue a cycle of spiraling costs that will consume governments, our government in Kentucky, and individuals alike. This session marks a historic test, the needs of the people versus the special interests. I am confident that with your special connection with your communities you all know action is required now to do what is right.[1]

---

1. The above comments represent only a portion of Jones's talk; the omitted remarks are similar to those found in Jones's earlier speeches on his health-care reform initiatives (for example, speech presented on May 4, 1993).

KENTUCKY MEDICAL ASSOCIATION LEGISLATIVE SEMINAR
Lexington / May 19, 1993

I SUSPECT that probably almost every one of you in the audience has some criticism of the plan as you know it at this point. I would encourage you to keep an open mind and recognize that there are two things that we have to accomplish to have health-care reform. These are first, getting control of costs with future increases to be in line with the consumer price index, and second, providing everyone with coverage without regard to pre-existing conditions.

In whatever manner coverage is provided, we believe that it has to be for everyone in the state. We cannot afford to continue fueling health care with more and more money. We will be spending 20 percent of the gross domestic product on health care by the year 2000, if current trends continue. Health-care costs are growing at 15 percent or more every year. This is squeezing out everything else. If it takes 15 percent each year to pay for health insurance for state employees and the Medicaid population and to subsidize the uninsured the way we currently do it, with only 1 or 2 or 3 percent growth in the Kentucky economy, every year there will be less money in the total Kentucky economy for anything else. This signals continued budget cuts for all the rest of state government, including universities, elementary and secondary schools, roads, etc.

Some people who are involved in health care will say it doesn't matter how much we spend, we have the best health care in the world. That is true, but a lot of people do not get health care, care is not equally distributed, and some people get too much care. C. Everett Koop, the former surgeon general, says that 25–30 percent of all the money spent on health care in America is for medically unnecessary care. At least 25 percent and maybe a lot more of what we spend on health care does not need to be spent. As physicians, you know how much you do that you do not need to do because you are afraid of being sued or because your malpractice carrier tells you that you have to do it. Then there is the "bureaucracy" and the "red tape" involved in health care. Some of the things we have done in the past to try to control costs have just added expense. Competing health plans and complicated payment processing have created a bureaucratic nightmare for everyone in health care. This adds to the cost of health care but does not add anything to quality.

Many people believe that a lot of the things done at the "end of life" are not necessary and that the individual, if they had their faculties about them, would say, "This is enough, I don't want anything else done." But if they do not have living wills and they have not talked to their families and their doctors in advance about what they want and don't want, there is no way to stop the process. With all of these factors together, clearly in this country we are spending significant money on the wrong things. It is not being well spent. It is not adding any quality to anyone's life. So when you say that no matter how much we spend, it is worth it because we have good health, we are fooling ourselves or we are being fooled.

We can spend less and still have good health care. We are wasting a lot of money on health care. How much? We spent from all sources in 1992, over $9 billion on health care in Kentucky. Twenty-five percent of that was spent for things that did not need to be done. Twenty-five percent of nine billion is $2.25 billion. Over two and a quarter billion dollars was squandered on defensive medicine, unnecessary procedures, red tape, and marketing. All of this is eating up resources and taking money out of the economy that could be better used for other things. I believe that we need to fundamentally change how health care is delivered in this state and in this country and put much more emphasis on primary care and on preventive-health services. What we would like to do long term is redirect that 25 percent into primary care and prevention, to stop doing things we do not need to do and do what needs to be done, such as immunizing all of the children in the state. Half of the children in Kentucky under the age of two have not been immunized. Everyone does not get prenatal care. Many people do not get physicals; many people do not get early detection, thus running into a serious illness and ending up in the ER for treatment.

Some critics say government should not be involved, that would just make it worse. Well, government is already involved, and someone has to assume responsibility to get this thing under control. Medicare, Medicaid, and other public monies account for over half of the dollars going into health care in Kentucky. Without health-care reform, we will be spending more than $19 billion on health care in Kentucky by the year 2000. With reform it will be slightly over 15 billion. When people talk about where we are going to get the money to pay for health-care reform, our response is, "We are actually going to save money by doing this." Instead of America having a health-care system, what we have is a non-system. We work in counterproductive ways, what we call "gaming the system." You have employers who, in large measure, provide health insurance. You have the payer, which is the private insurance company or the government, who pays the bill. Then you have the provider. Each one is spinning around in a circle, frustrated in dealing with the others, trying to figure out how to make sense of the system, getting increasingly angry, each one at the other. They shout. They do not communicate. There is a tremendous amount of energy tied up in this process. If this energy were directed at solutions rather than at fussing at each other, we would find the solutions to these problems.

I understand the "hassle factor." Every time you leave the exam room after seeing a patient your employees are lined up, asking questions, or voicing something that you have to do in terms of paperwork and bureaucracy: a letter from Medicare saying you kept the patient in the hospital too long, another from Medicare saying you didn't keep another patient in the hospital long enough, a phone call to be returned to a third-party reviewer to make sure it is OK to do surgery or something. Between seeing patients, every doctor in America is faced with that kind of hassle constantly. It adds to the cost of medicine, it doesn't improve the quality, and it doesn't accomplish anything other than to increase the frustration factor. Our plan, if fully understood, is business smart. We can help many people who cannot help themselves and at the same time solve a situation that if left unchecked will bankrupt us all.

The goals of our health-care reform efforts have remained unchanged since we began forming our plan last summer. We want to hold down health-care cost increases and provide insurance coverage for the hundreds of thousands of people in our state who presently do not have insurance. Doing both has practical and humanitarian effects. We help those who cannot help themselves, and in the process we help ourselves by stopping cost shifting, which drives up costs for everyone. That, we hope history will record, is the hallmark of our administration, to help the many people in our Commonwealth who cannot help themselves. That is the driving force behind our efforts and the key to our health-care reform legislation.

The General Assembly of Kentucky has begun meeting in special session in Frankfort for what will prove to be a historic session, if conscience rules. I am here today to seek your understanding and assistance in helping us do what is right, to provide health-care insurance coverage for all Kentuckians and control health-care costs before they bankrupt us all. We are proposing the formation of a health-care authority that would have the power to tie future increases in health-care costs to the consumer price index. Our bill would require all Kentuckians to have health insurance by January 1 of next year. The state would assist low-income citizens with the purchase of insurance.

The health-care authority would have five members who would be confirmed by the senate and serve four-year terms. Two, but no more, would be former health-care providers. This authority would make it illegal to deny anyone insurance coverage because of age, illness, or past medical condition. The authority would also develop a minimum-benefits plan to be offered by every health-insurance carrier in Kentucky. This plan would be available to individuals and groups in a new state "megapool." The mega-purchasing pool will enable the authority to get enough money together in one pot to get the attention of the provider community and begin to bring about change. There are at least one million people, and possibly two million people, that the health-care authority would be buying care for. As of July 1, 1993, workers' compensation rates will be reduced 5 percent and frozen at that level for twenty-four months.

We are proposing a mediation system. We are also proposing that practice guidelines be developed. If a physician does things within a certain range, there is the presumption that they did the right thing and that gives them some legal standing in court. We think these things will be helpful to begin to do something about defensive medicine. We cannot address a cap on non-economic damage except in a regular session of the General Assembly. That takes a constitutional amendment and only a regular session can put a constitutional amendment on the ballot. I committed early on to leadership of KMA that if we passed the comprehensive reform legislation in the special session, I would support the constitutional amendment in the 1994 regular session.

There seems to be logic in asking the hospitals of an area to work together and to appropriately downsize. Most hospitals would stay in business but now everyone would have to do everything. Some small rural hospitals, without health-care reform, are in trouble and will not survive. With health-care reform, some of the small rural hospitals will have the opportunity to become something else, not just an acute-care hospital, [but] perhaps an ambulatory care center, perhaps a nursing home, or perhaps a primary-care center. Another part of delivery-system reform is that we need more primary-care physicians. We must change the medical schools. We must get to the point that we graduate a lot more family practitioners, general internists, general pediatricians and obstetricians, and not so many super specialists. Right now, about 30 percent of the graduates at both the University of Louisville and the University of Kentucky medical schools graduate and go into primary care. We've got to have more than 50 percent for primary care. We also need to have nurse practitioners, nurse midwives, and physician assistants to supplement for the lack of primary-care physicians in order to provide health care to everyone.

Presently there are 450,000 Kentuckians who have no health insurance. Many, many others who are underinsured or working poor live in constant fear that even a moderate illness or injury will destroy their families. A catastrophic illness could take away their homes. A low-cost benefit plan would be available to low-income Kentuckians. The state would provide financial assistance to individuals whose household income is less than 20 percent of the federal poverty level.

Our plan calls for no deductibles or co-payments for preventive care. What we have attempted to do in our plan is not to ask anyone to do what they cannot financially afford to do. But we must ask people to jointly share in the responsibility to solve what I believe is the greatest problem facing society today. I have said from the beginning in forming our plan almost a year ago that we wanted to have everyone's suggestions but that I will not compromise on my goals of universal coverage and controlling health-care costs. I firmly believe that we cannot get control over rising costs without providing insurance coverage for everyone. Roughly a third of the rising costs of health-care coverage come from cost shifting, where we pay for those who have little or no coverage.

The eyes of the state, and the nation, and I believe the collective conscience of us all, are focused on this effort. Again, this session marks a historic test. I am confident that with your understanding and cooperation and the good-faith efforts of the many people who truly want to do what is right and make the world a little better than it was before, we can set an example for our nation as we care for the many who look to government to literally and figuratively save their lives.

Our plan offers a number of positive results for Kentucky's physicians. First of all, every patient you see will be covered if our plan is enacted. There will no longer be indigent patients whom you will be asked to see without compensation. No longer will cost shifting have to occur, as all patient services will be paid for. Secondly, we are addressing the hassle factor. It is our intention to dramatically streamline the payment process by standardizing claims forms, pressing forward with electronic billing, and in other ways eliminating much of the hassle in your office. Finally, our plan addresses, to the extent possible, the issue of medical liability. As I indicated earlier, I believe the mediation process in our proposal will offer some relief. Additionally, we believe that the development of practice parameters will give you some standing in court, a presumption that you did the right thing if you were within the practice parameters; this will reduce the number of suits.

We have an opportunity as Kentuckians to lead the nation. We have a chance to participate in meaningful change before somebody, somewhere does it for and to us. The greatest burden is currently on those least able to provide for their care: the poor, the working poor, the unemployed, the disabled, children, and the frail elderly. We have an obligation to relieve this hardship for all Kentuckians.[1]

---

1. This speech is very similar to earlier health-care speeches given by Governor Jones; see talks given on February 11, and March 1, 1993. This speech contains a similar format with several other 1993 health-care speeches, such as the one given to the Kentucky Academy of Family Physicians on June 10, 1993.

KENTUCKY HEALTH CARE ACCESS FOUNDATION BOARD MEETING
Lexington / June 24, 1993

IT IS a real pleasure to be here today to speak to all of you who are members and guests of the Kentucky Health Care Access Foundation board. Obviously this is an organization for which I have deep feeling. This organization was created as a result of my desire to see health care become accessible to all of the citizens of Kentucky. Many of you have been members of this foundation board since its inception. Others have joined throughout the years.

Most of you served on the Task Force on Health Care Access and Affordability last year. I know that you and the other members of the task force worked very hard. I have always felt that the report was an outstanding document which addressed the issues of health-care reform in a very constructive way. I'm sure you recognize much of the plan which I submitted to the General Assembly was based on the task force report, and I thank all of you for your participation in that process.

But all of you came to this board because you share my commitment to having affordable, appropriate health-care services available to all of the people of this Commonwealth. You know that not only do we need to make health care available, we tried to make health insurance available so that everyone has the means to pay. You also understand that we must eliminate cost shifting so that those of you who are providers don't have to charge more to the people who can pay in order to make up for the people who cannot pay.

I believe that all of you also share a commitment that health-care cost increases at the rate of 15 percent a year are intolerable. This is eating up more and more of our economy each year. If we do not get control of health-care costs, health care will take 20 percent of our gross domestic product by the year 2000. In the meantime we will have cut elementary and secondary education, colleges, universities, roads, prisons, local jails, and the court system. Everything else that the government does will experience budget cuts year after year after year if we don't fix health care.

I believe most of you understood my plan, and I know that most of you were out there doing your best to help sell it to members of the General Assembly and within your own constituency groups. You know that our plan was good for the physicians in that all patients would have had insurance coverage if our plan had been enacted. No longer would cost shifting have to occur, because needed patient services would have been paid for. We were also addressing the hassle factor. It was our intention to simplify and streamline the payment process by standardizing claims forms, pressing forward with electronic billing, simplified insurance forms, and in other ways reducing the hassles for doctors.

Finally our plan addressed, to the extent possible under the Kentucky constitution, the issue of medical liability. By instituting practice guidelines we were giving the physician some protection in court and by establishing a mediation process we were trying to eliminate some suits from taking place. You also know that I committed to the Kentucky Medical Association, when we started the reform discussion nearly two years ago, that when comprehensive reform was enacted in a special session, I would support a constitutional amendment's being placed on the ballot in a regular session which would address the tort reform issues that the KMA wanted addressed.

I think that most of you know that the propaganda regarding the governor's plan to close thirty or fifty hospitals was totally unfounded. It was our plan to create regional delivery systems involving all of the hospitals, health departments, primary-care centers, and other providers. We intended to develop a coherent plan for services at the local level, but we did not intend to put anyone out of business.

I believe that if you go to most of the administrators of Kentucky's smaller hospitals and say, "Do you really think that you can survive into the next century as an acute-care hospital?" the answer would probably be, "No, we need to change our role to something else." Our plan created a mechanism for those changing roles and budgeted funds to assist in that transition. Clearly, without reform or without a continued substantial subsidy, many of Kentucky's small hospitals will close. It was not our plan that would have caused the closure; it was our plan that would have saved those hospitals.

I think that most of you know that our plan was also business smart. While we were asking employers in the first approach to provide health insurance to their employees and in the second approach to pay a payroll tax if they didn't provide health insurance, in all cases we could show employers that in a couple of years they would be better off. They would be better off because:

1. We were going to do something about the cost of workers' compensation by rolling back premiums 5 percent and holding them constant for two years so that instead of seeing another 54 percent increase in comp in the next two years as they saw in the past two years, people would actually see their comp rates go down a little and stay at that level.
2. Every small employer has to worry about their own health insurance and their family's health insurance. Small businesses with only a few employees, under our plan, could have purchased insurance for their families as well as their employees, cheaper than what they are currently paying for just themselves.
3. We were doing away with the lifetime limit on health benefits so that the self-employed person or small employer who might have kidney disease, heart disease, be in a catastrophic accident, or whatever, would not have to worry about their lifetime limit on their insurance.
4. Employers who provide health insurance would benefit by no longer having to subsidize the uninsured through higher premiums.
5. With comprehensive health-care reform, everyone who did business in Kentucky would have seen reductions in future cost increases for health care. This would have had a rippling effect on business. When a small business person buys something, they buy from a supplier who is absorbing a 15 percent per year increase in health-care costs. He or she passes that on. That goes through to the whole society. Once we get costs under control and stop that rapid escalation, that rippling effect will be diminished.

WE all know . . . Dr. Bosomworth[1] knows, that we have to change our medical schools; we have to graduate a lot more general physicians, particularly family practitioners, nurse midwives, and physician assistants. We have to teach our physicians to practice as part of teams. We have to create delivery systems, particularly in the rural areas, so that we are not just putting a doctor in a small county and expecting them to solve the problem. They have to be linked to regional systems, they have to have backup, they have to have weekend coverage, and they have to have people other than just physicians to help them.

We cannot get enough physicians to meet the total need, so we have to train people in other disciplines. Our medical schools understand this. Both medical schools have received significant grant funding from the Robert Wood Johnson Foundation in the areas of curriculum revision, the general physician initiative, and the sights initiative.

I know that all of you understood that everyone was being asked to give up something in our plan, but we hoped that no one was being singled out or treated unfairly. As you know, our plan was not enacted, but you know we must ultimately achieve meaningful reform. To fail to do so will destroy our economy and will jeopardize the financial stability of all Kentucky families no matter what health insurance plan they may have today.

All Kentuckians are trapped in a senseless cost-shifting spiral, paying hidden taxes to help the uninsured, most often at a level of care higher than they need. Without reform, we will maintain a predictable rate of double-digit health-care inflation and leave hundreds of thousands of uninsured Kentuckians to suffer and some to die rather than leave their families bankrupt.

I feel certain that the Health Care Reform Task Force, consisting of legislative leaders, myself, and other representatives of my administration, will develop a report and ultimately a plan. We will have a special session. We will have health-care reform. We will reach our goals of getting control of health-care costs and getting everyone covered. In whatever manner we provide that coverage, we recognize that it has to be for everyone in the state.

I know that I am preaching to the choir. I know that you are as committed to health-care reform as I am, but I want you to know that we have to keep fighting. We were not successful in the special session in getting reform, but we were successful in focusing attention on the issue. Clearly, many more members of the General Assembly now understand the issue. Most members are committed to reform. Most members are committed to learning about the problem, looking at alternatives, and coming up with a good Kentucky solution.

They need your support and encouragement. They need to know that there are people who want reform. Usually people who contact their legislators are against something rather than for something. It was much easier for the supporters of the status quo to muster telephone calls and letter-writing campaigns to legislators to be against Governor Jones's plan, to kill the governor's plan or to stop reform, than it was for us to generate that kind of campaign to be for reform, to be for getting control of costs, or to be for getting everyone coverage. If we are going to have reform, the people of the Commonwealth of Kentucky must recognize the need. We must make sure that all citizens understand the need and properly express their opinions to their legislators.

It is imperative that the Kentucky Health Care Access Foundation stays involved and stays active. I believe that the foundation will have a very legitimate role to serve as something like the Prichard Committee[2] for health care to observe, monitor, and advise the system as reform is implemented. Reform will come because we have logic and reason on our side, and we will never give up.[3]

---

1. Peter Bosomworth (1930–99), B.S., Kent State University, 1951; M.D., University of Cincinnati, 1955; director, anesthesiology research, Ohio State, 1958; Navy, chief of anesthesiology, Great Lakes, 1959–60; professor and chair of anesthesiology, UK Medical Center, 1962; vice-president of UK Medical Center, 1970–80; chancellor, UK Medical Center, 1980–94; Governor Brereton Jones's Commission on Health Care Reform, 1993; chancellor emeritus and professor of anesthesiology and health care administration, University of Kentucky Medical Center, 1995–99.

2. The Prichard Committee for Academic Excellence began in 1980 as the Committee on Higher Education in Kentucky's Future, when the Kentucky Council on Higher Education appointed thirty citizens to recommend future directions for public universities. Edward F. Prichard Jr., a well-known Frankfort attorney, was appointed chairman. Upon completion of the committee's 1981 report, the members renamed the group the Prichard Committee. In 1983 committee members, frustrated by the limited governmental response to their recommendations, formed a new organization, the Prichard Committee for Academic Excellence, an independent, privately funded citizen group. Prichard was the first chair of the new group, and Robert Sexton, who organized the original group for the Council on Higher Education, became the committee's executive director. In 1990 the committee began a multiyear program of monitoring results and stirring public support to ensure implementation of KERA. *The Kentucky Encyclopedia* (Lexington, 1992).

3. A similar speech was given on October 16 to the participants at the Health Care Access Foundation retreat in Jamestown.

SEVEN COUNTIES SERVICES
Louisville / July 14, 1993

IT IS a real pleasure to be here today to address such a large cross-section of mental-health professionals, business leaders, and governmental representatives. I am particularly pleased to recognize Ken Reinhardt, the current vice-chairman of the board of Seven Counties Services and chairman of the Strategic Planning Committee. Ken is a friend and longtime associate in the area of health-care access and reform. Ken has served on the Kentucky Health Care Access Foundation and has been extremely valuable over the years in helping the foundation develop visibility and credibility.

As you probably know, the foundation has created a number of programs to serve as interim steps to provide health care to Kentucky's indigent population. These include the Kentucky physicians care program, the hospital fair share program, the dental program, and the pharmacy program. Ken is also an articulate spokesman for the cause of mental-health and mental-retardation services. He wrote me one of the most thoughtful letters that I received during the entire health-care reform debate. Obviously you will not be surprised to know that Ken was expressing concern about the mental-health coverage in our basic benefit plan and the needs for comprehensive mental-health services to be available to everyone.

I want to thank Ken for his years of friendship and support, his dedication to the cause, and his commitment to what is right for people. Ken is one of the best examples I know of a citizen being involved for the good of the people and not for personal gain. I am very impressed with the strategic-planning process that Seven Counties Services has sponsored in the past six months to fulfill its obligation as the planning authority for mental-health/mental-retardation and chemical-dependency services in this region. I understand that you have involved a large number of people from numerous organizations and all parts of the community interested in these topics in developing this report. It is impressive that so many people put aside their differences and came together to achieve a common goal. I applaud your commitment to substantial and sustainable change and your focus on the three areas of health care, education, and housing.

As you know, health-care reform is the major goal of my administration. I wish that I could report to you that meaningful health-care reform had already taken place and that the dollars would be available to finance all of the needs you have identified, but you recognize that is not possible. In fact, I understand that as this report was developed, the availability of funding was not allowed to determine the recommendations.

However, funding must always be an issue as we go about setting priorities. I know that you have read the paper and you understand the current budget problems we are facing in the Commonwealth of Kentucky. We have an estimated shortfall in this new fiscal year of up to $300 million. My staff in Frankfort worked almost around the clock last week on budget issues, and we will be making determinations very quickly regarding how to reduce the budget. I want to spend some time talking about our previous effort at health-care reform, what we tried to do and why. The underlying issue for all of us must be the budget. The fact is we have a fairly flat economy with a continuing double-digit increase in health-care cost. I regret that our plan was not enacted but am confident that our legislators now agree that there is a problem and that we will ultimately achieve meaningful reform.

To fail to do so will:

1. jeopardize the financial stability of all Kentucky families no matter what health-insurance plan they may have today;
2. leave us in a senseless cost-shifting spiral, paying hidden taxes to help the uninsured, most often at a level of care higher than they need;
3. maintain a double-digit health-care inflation;
4. leave hundreds of thousands of uninsured Kentuckians to suffer and die, rather than leave their families bankrupt (presently there are 450,000 Kentuckians who have no health insurance);
5. and destroy our economy.

We cannot afford to continue fueling health care with more and more money. Health-care costs are growing at 15 percent or more every year. We will be spending 20 percent of the gross domestic product on health care by the year 2000, if current trends continue. We will lose half of any new growth in our state's economy, fifty cents of every new dollar, to pay increased costs in just seven years. Health-care costs are squeezing out everything else. This signals continued budget cuts for all the rest of state government, including the department for mental-health and mental-retardation services, the comprehensive care centers, universities, elementary and secondary schools, prisons, roads, etc.

Some people who are involved in health care have said it does not matter how much we spend, we have the best health care in the world. That is true, but a lot of people do not get health care, particularly mental-health and chemical-dependency services. The care is not equally distributed, and some people get too much care. C. Everett Koop, the former surgeon general, says that 25–30 percent of all the money spent on health care in America is for unnecessary care. Competing and difficult-to-understand health-insurance plans and complicated claims payment processing have created a bureaucratic nightmare for everyone in health care. This adds significantly to the cost of health care but does not add anything to quality.

Many people believe that a lot of the things done at the "end of life" are not necessary and that if individuals had their faculties about them, they would say "this is enough, I do not want anything else done." If they do not have living wills and they have not talked to their families and their doctors in advance about what they want and do not want, there is no way to stop the process. It is not adding any quality to anyone's life. So when we say that no matter how much we spend, it is worth it because we have good health care, we are fooling ourselves or we are being fooled. We can spend less and still have good health care. We are wasting a lot of money on health care.

How much? Kentuckians spent from all sources over $9.5 billion on health care in 1992. At least 25 percent of that was spent for things that did not need to be done. Twenty-five percent of $9.5 billion is $2.375 billion. More than two and one-third billion dollars were squandered on defensive medicine, unnecessary procedures, red tape, and marketing. All of this is eating up resources and taking money out of the economy that could be better used for other things. It is also taking money that could be better spent on mental-health, mental-retardation, and chemical-dependency services.

I believe that we need to fundamentally change how health care is delivered in this state and in this country and put much more emphasis on primary care, including mental-health service and on preventive-health services. What we would like to do in the long term is redirect that 25 percent into prevention and primary care, including mental health, to stop doing things we do not need to do and do what needs to be done. Far too many people, even with insurance, cannot get mental-health or chemical-dependency service. Many people are treated "medically" for a symptom when they really have an emotional problem. We are failing to act in preventive services, such as immunizing all of the children in the state. It is a travesty that half of the children in Kentucky under the age of two have not been properly immunized.

Everyone does not get prenatal care. Many people do not get physicals, many people do not get early detection and run into a serious illness and end up in the ER for treatment, and others choose not to get care because they simply cannot pay for it. Some critics say government should not be involved, that government would just make it worse. Well, government is already involved, and someone has to assume responsibility to get things under control. Medicare, Medicaid, and other public monies account for over half of the dollars going into health care in Kentucky. Unless we have a strong health-care authority to oversee and regulate health care, we will never achieve parity of funding between acute-care physical medicine and mental-health, mental-retardation, and chemical-dependency services.

Without health-care reform we will be spending over $19 billion on health care in Kentucky by the year 2000. Much of it is for acute medical care. With our reform it would have been only slightly over $15 billion. When people talk about where we were going to get the money to pay for health-care reform, our response is "we are actually going to save money by doing this." Let me address the issue of mental-health coverage in our plan. You were correct in pointing out that the mental-health coverage in our initial draft proposal was inadequate. We made substantial changes in it prior to legislation being drafted. If our plan had been enacted, every Kentuckian would have had insurance coverage by July 1, 1994.

While the mental-health benefit was not perfect, and we would not have achieved immediate parity, every Kentuckian would have had mental-health coverage. It would have been illegal to sell health insurance in Kentucky that did not cover mental health. As I have said before, health-care costs are increasing at 15 percent per year. Much of that cost is acute-care medicine—in hospital and physician services. A substantial part of that expense is not necessary, but because we have a non-system in which no one is in charge, it is not possible to stop much of the waste that occurs. It seemed rather basic to us that if we got health-care costs under control and held future health-cost increases in line with the consumer price index that we would be saving literally billions of dollars for Kentuckians within a very few years.

It was my commitment that as we saved money, we would

enhance the benefit package and reform the health-care delivery system. We particularly wanted to enhance coverage in the areas of mental health, mental retardation, and chemical dependency. I believe that mental-health, mental-retardation, and chemical-dependency needs of Kentuckians would have been better addressed in a reformed health-care delivery system than they will be in our current system. This is a chicken and egg issue.

Our approach was to ask you to help us get control of costs, get everyone covered with some sort of basic plan that addressed their immediate physical needs, and help us over time build a complete reform. We were also addressing the hassle factor in health care. It was our intention to simplify and streamline the payment process by standardizing claims forms, pressing forward with electronic billing, simplified insurance forms, and in other ways reducing the hassles for providers. As these savings occurred, mental-health, mental-retardation, and chemical-dependency services could have been increased. Our plan addressed medical liability by instituting practice guidelines which would have given the practitioner some protection in court.

We also proposed a mediation process to eliminate some suits from taking place. Practice guidelines would also help eliminate unnecessary medical procedures, and, I might add, practice guidelines should address the length of stays in some mental-health facilities. We need more mental-health professionals and we need them in underserved areas. We need them to work in collaboration with primary-care practitioners. We all know that we have to change our medical schools. We have to graduate a lot more generalist physicians. We have to develop new programs and expand our programs to train nurse practitioners, nurse midwives, and physician assistants. We have to teach our physicians to practice as part of teams.

It was our plan to create regional delivery systems involving all of the hospitals, health departments, comprehensive-care centers, primary-care centers, and other providers. We intended to develop a coherent plan for services at the local level. The strategic-planning process used by these Seven Counties Services could offer a guide for such a process throughout the Commonwealth. We were not successful in the special session in getting reform, but we were successful in focusing attention on the issue. Clearly, many more members of the General Assembly now understand the issue. Most members are committed to reform. Most members are committed to learning about the problem, looking at alternative solutions, and coming up with a good Kentucky solution. They need your support and encouragement. They need to know that there are people who want reform.

Usually, people who contact their legislators are against something rather than for something. It was much easier for the supporters of the status quo to muster telephone calls and letter-writing campaigns to legislators to be against Governor Jones's plan, to kill the governor's plan, or to stop reform, than it was for us to generate that kind of campaign to be for reform, to be for getting control of costs, or to be for getting everyone coverage. As with many of the "advocacy groups," the mental-health/mental-retardation and chemical-dependency community was not perceived to be in favor of reform.

What legislators heard from you was "it's not perfect, we do not have parity, we do not like the governor's plan." I hope you will re-examine this issue and instead of asking for a perfect plan immediately, ask your legislators to vote for health-care reform. Ask them to commit to health-care reform so that we can implement a plan which will save money and allow services to increase in the areas of mental health, mental retardation, and chemical dependency. I know that as advocates in the area of mental health, mental retardation, and chemical dependency, you were all interested in parity. Of course, I am in favor of parity. It is foolish to spend scarce dollars treating someone's symptom, medically or surgically, when they really need the care of a professional in the area of mental health or chemical dependence. It is, to use an old cliché, penny-wise and pound-foolish.

However, I hope you recognize that no matter how hard I try, and indeed I did try, to change health-care financing in Kentucky, I can not overcome the lobbying power of the large money interests in health care without wide support from citizens. We asked people to jointly share in the responsibility to solve what I believe is the greatest problem facing society today. I have said from the beginning in forming our plan almost a year ago that we wanted to have everyone's suggestions but that I would not compromise on my goals of universal coverage and controlling health-care costs. We asked everyone to give up something in our plan, but we hoped that no one was being singled out or treated unfairly. We must ultimately achieve meaningful reform.

I feel certain that the health-care reform task force, consisting of legislative leaders, myself, and other representatives of my administration, will develop a report and ultimately a plan. We will have a special session. We will have health-care reform. We will reach our goals of getting control of health-care costs and getting everyone covered. In whatever manner we provide that coverage, we recognize that it has to be for everyone in the state. To fail to do so will destroy our economy, will jeopardize the financial stability of all Kentucky families no matter what health-insurance plan they may have today.

In closing, let me return to the purpose of your luncheon today. The strategic plan you have before you is the product of many hours of work by many of you here today. I compliment all of you who took part in its development, and I endorse the strategies you have selected. As the rest of you hear more about its potential for substantial and sustainable change, I encourage you to commit your time and talents to seeing it implemented.[1]

---

1. This speech is very similar to the health-care talks given on February 11, March 1, May 19, and June 10, 1993.

WELCOME TO SECRETARY OF HEALTH AND HUMAN SERVICES DONNA SHALALA
Louisville / September 27, 1993

THANK you, Judge Armstrong.[1] I am delighted today to have this opportunity to welcome to Kentucky U.S. Secretary of Health and Human Services Donna Shalala.[2] We are a warm and caring people greatly concerned about the status of health care in this state and in this nation. The presence of all those in attendance today is proof of that concern. On Wednesday I was privileged to be in Washington as the president presented his health-care plan to Congress. For more than sixty years the leaders of this country have recognized the need for a national health plan. Now, at last, we have a president who actually has taken steps to ensure that all of our citizens will receive the medical care they need and deserve.

In Kentucky, we are well aware of the effort that goes into preparing a health-care plan that works. Health-care reform has been the most important goal of our administration. My goals, our goals, are cost containment and coverage for all Kentuckians. Neither will be an easy challenge. We stand on common ground with President Clinton in his effort to make certain that we join with the other leading nations of the world in providing health care for all our citizens.

The task and the challenge are tremendous, but for those who are committed to carrying out this reform and for the beneficiaries of their efforts, the rewards will be equally great. In Kentucky, some programs already under way show the commitment, the understanding of our needs. As we toured the Family Health Center on Portland Avenue this morning, the importance of services of this sort became clear. Primary health care and immunizations, both essential to all families, are provided at the center.

Another program working toward meeting the needs of families now unable to provide health care is the "Young Families at Risk" program. Their emphasis on prenatal care and immunization is basic to the maintenance of a healthy and happy young family. I commend Judge Armstrong for his vision in providing the leadership for "Young Families at Risk," and I congratulate the "Young Families at Risk" advisory group. Those representatives of more than thirty businesses and organizations have given their time to address the issue of childhood poverty by addressing the needs of these families.

No program, whether serving a community, a state, or a nation, can survive without the dedication and commitment, without the total support, of those who legislate and those who administer the program, or without the support of the people who stand to benefit from it. Health care is everybody's business, and each individual can make a difference as we move into the twenty-first century, a new age for health care in this state and nation. Secretary Shalala, we are grateful to you for the role you have played in developing the national plan, and we are also grateful for the role you are playing in taking the message of need to the Congress and to the people. We give you our thanks and most assuredly the thanks of the 470,000 Kentuckians without health insurance. And we give you our support as you carry this vital message across the land.

---

1. David Armstrong (1941–), B.S., Murray State University, 1961; University of Louisville, J.D., 1969; attorney general of Kentucky, 1983–87; Jefferson County judge-executive, 1989–98; Louisville mayor, 1998– . *Who's Who in American Politics, 1995–96*, 15th ed. (New Providence, N.J., 1995).

2. Donna Edna Shalala (1941–), A.B., Western College, 1962; M.S.S.C.,

Syracuse University, 1968, Ph.D., 1970; volunteer, Peace Corps, Iran, 1962–64; assistant to dean, Syracuse University, Maxwell Graduate School, 1969–70; assistant professor of political science, CUNY, 1970–72; associate professor of political science and education, Teachers College, Columbia University, 1972–79; assistant secretary for policy development and research, Housing and Urban Development, Washington, 1977–80; professor of political science, president of Hunter College, CUNY, 1980–88; professor of political science, chancellor, University of Wisconsin, 1988–93; secretary of Department of Health and Human Services, Washington, 1993–2001. *Who's Who in America 1997*, 51st ed. (New Providence, N.J., 1996).

DEMOCRATIC WOMEN'S CLUB
Frankfort / October 1, 1993

GOOD evening and welcome to Frankfort, your capital city and the place we'll soon gather to pass health-care reform. Please let me begin by thanking each of you for helping me reach the first of two related personal goals, just two short years ago. Because of you, the hopes of my being elected to Frankfort to serve as your governor became a reality. You may recall my telling you that you can give my opponents the courthouse crowd, but give me one Democratic woman in every county, and we'll win every time. Well, we did win. But we have another challenge that remains to be won: health-care reform. This goal is now before us.

Kentucky enjoyed some proud moments just one week ago when President Clinton unveiled his plan for reform of our nation's health-care system. Did you hear the close parallels in his words and concepts to last May, when we, in our special session, first talked about cost containment and coverage for all? President Clinton was not shy about citing specific examples of Americans cut out of our health-care system by exponential insurance cost increases. The cases he talked about could just as easily have come from Owensboro, Pikeville, Howardstown, Covington, or Russellville.

To ignore Clinton's reality is to ignore the fact that every day which passes without health-care reform, hundreds of Kentuckians who have worked all their lives, paid taxes, educated their children, and, like you, participated in making a difference for others, are forced to join the ranks of the uninsured. Please let me take a moment to talk about just one Kentuckian, who will soon be without insurance through no fault of her own if we do not act. A couple of weeks after the end of May's special session, I received a letter from a woman in Louisville. She expressed sorrow that we went home without reform. This woman, whom I'll call Mary, had left a full-time position several years ago, to come to the side of her terminally ill husband. After his death, she returned to the workforce to find few opportunities for a fifty-five-year-old woman. She now works two part-time jobs; neither provides health-insurance benefits. She has continued to pay for her own health coverage, even though insurance companies have found it convenient to rate by age, sex, and illness for the past decade or so. She wrote to tell me that she had just received a double-digit rate increase, not remarkable on its own, with health-care costs soaring. What was remarkable and intolerable was that a week later the same insurance company sent her still another double-digit increase. Why? Because she had just turned fifty-six years old and moved into the next high-cost age band!

In every courthouse, school, church, and other gathering place we've been in Kentucky, we are hearing the same story. This will not be tolerated. This will be against the law in Kentucky when we pass health-care reform. Don't believe for a minute that President and Mrs. Clinton[1] don't expect Kentucky to pass its own health-care plan. Not only do they expect this legislature to act, they want us to enact reforms on the state level. As you may know, I have been in close contact with Bill and Hillary Clinton and with their health-care advisor, Ira Magaziner,[2] for a number of months, working with them on a national plan that will enhance, not hurt, Kentucky's plan.

Your commitment, dedication, and untiring drive brought me into office. Now, we need you to apply your knowledge of democracy, your skills with people, and your extraordinary networks all across our great Commonwealth, on a mission for health-care reform. Recently, I was characterized as being obsessed with reform. If this is the case, I am grateful for the compliment. There is nothing more important to the security of each and every family in Kentucky and the nation than affordable health care and insurance!

As we leave this meeting later this evening, please go away with the name and telephone number of your state senator and representative. Plan to call them and, in your own words, ask for their health-care reform support. It is so very important that no one in this room deprive their legislator of your opinion on the need for immediate action, through a special session on reform by year's end. We are also making a fact sheet on health care available to you tonight, so that your house and senate members know that you fully understand the urgency of addressing the problem. Thank you for your commitment and your friendship. When we meet once again, let's all savor the joy that Kentucky has led the way in making our families and future generations secure against catastrophic loss from the cost of health care and insurance.

---

1. Hillary Rodham Clinton (1947–), B.A. with high honors, Wellesley College, 1969; J.D., Yale University, 1973; attorney for Children's Defense Fund, 1973–74; legal counsel, Carnegie Council on Children, 1973–74; counsel, impeachment inquiry staff, Judiciary Committee, U.S. House of Representatives, 1974; assistant professor of law, director of Legal Aid Clinic, University of Arkansas, Fayetteville, 1974–77; assistant professor of law, School of Law, Little Rock, 1979–80; partner, Rose Law Firm, Little Rock; headed Committee on Health Care Reform, 1993–94; First Lady of United States; elected to U.S. Senate from New York, 2000. *Who's Who in America 1997*, 51st ed. (New Providence, N.J., 1996).

2. Ira Magaziner (1937–), B.A., Brown University; Rhodes scholar, Oxford University; co-founder, Telesis, 1979–88; issues advisor, Clinton campaign, 1992; senior advisor, policy development, the White House, 1993–2001; chief architect Health Security Act, 1993. *Who's Who in America, 1997.*

BREAST CANCER AWARENESS MONTH RALLY
Frankfort / October 4, 1993

ACCORDING to American Cancer Society statistics, 2,600 women will be diagnosed with breast cancer in Kentucky in 1993, and 650 women will die as a result of the disease. This is why it is so important to recognize October as breast cancer awareness month in our state. We can save many Kentucky women through effective public and professional awareness campaigns, which emphasize the importance of self-breast exams, clinical breast exams, and mammograms. We've made much progress in fighting this disease in Kentucky.

First of all, physicians treating women with breast cancer are required to inform women of all options by giving them an informational booklet prepared by the Markey and Brown Cancer Centers and our Department for Health Services. Also, our Medicaid program now pays for screening mammograms for eligible women, and insurers who pay for surgery for breast cancer are required to cover the cost of mammograms. We now have a cancer registry at the Markey Cancer Center in Lexington. This provides us with important information about the number of cases of cancer and who is being stricken by this disease.

Last, but not least, we have a successful public screening program for low-income women who do not have insurance or qualify for Medicaid. This is operated through our local health departments in each of Kentucky's 120 counties. While these are significant accomplishments, there is still much to be done. Health-care reform proposals already submitted by this administration to the legislature would guarantee that all Kentucky women have access to screening mammograms. And I remain committed to assuring that all women have insurance coverage for this important early detection tool. By proclaiming October breast cancer awareness month in Kentucky, stressing the importance of breast cancer screening for every woman, I express my commitment to fight this disease that takes the lives of so many women each year, and I ask all Kentuckians to join me in this fight.

LEADERSHIP BLUEGRASS
Frankfort / January 13, 1994

THANK you for this opportunity to appear before you today. Perhaps you won't be too surprised to hear that my primary message will be about health-care reform. Our determination to implement cost containment and to bring health-care coverage to all Kentuckians continues to be the top priority of this administration. We will not stop until our goals are accomplished. Before bringing this message to you, please let me first pay tribute to your legislator, friend, and neighbor, an innovator and one of the great minds in the legislative process, Bill Lear.[1] Those who know Bill come quickly to the conclusion that he is to the fullest degree a leader.

Through his past efforts on such vital legislation as an improved DUI statute and his current work on a seat belt law, Representative Lear has gained statewide respect. Knowing that we will lose Bill from the house at the end of his current term, please join in showing appreciation for all he has done for Kentucky.

Leadership Bluegrass, along with your sister programs in communities across Kentucky, and the Leadership Kentucky Program, have brought together a tremendous number of outstanding people. The philosophy and leadership principles each of you bring to and carry away from this program will serve you well in your professional and personal lives. Your dedication and unselfish contributions to the Bluegrass are being mirrored by your colleagues in their respective cities and towns across the state.

In recognition of the importance of your leadership I now ask for your help with health-care reform. You will hear little argument against the statement that our nation's health care is second to none. Following the Truman administration in the late 1940s, we made a concerted effort to increase our emphasis on research and technology. In the 1950s, we opened up Hill-Burton Community Hospitals throughout the United States. In the 1960s, we implemented Medicare and Medicaid for our elderly and poor. But to date, we have not achieved a system which assures all Americans care and protection from financial ruin should they become ill.

Let me take a moment to set the stage for health-care reform, based on what we know about costs today. Our total expenditure for health care in Kentucky now exceeds $9.5 billion. We can gain back nearly $2.4 billion with reform. Without reform, costs will rise to $19 billion by the year 2000; with reform it will be $15 billion. And with Kentucky's annual economic growth rate at only 1 to 3 percent, by the year 2000, fifty cents of every new dollar we create will have to go toward rising health-care costs. This means that half of all economic growth for which you work so hard—half of your time and energy in building for the future—will be absorbed by rising health-care costs without reform. Think how wonderful it would be instead to use these new dollars to create jobs, improve education, and provide essential services to Kentuckians in need. This would help create the highest level of production economics rather than the consumption economics characteristic of our current system of health-care delivery.

We do have many very good reasons to be pleased with Kentucky's health-care delivery system. Let me touch on just a few. Our advancements in burn treatments, micro-surgery, and human organ transplants have distinguished Kentucky, both in Lexington and Louisville, as leading health-care centers in our nation. We can all be proud that Dr. Phillip Sharp,[2] a native son, won the 1993 Nobel Prize for medicine for his work in genetics. Also, we are working with leaders of the Columbia/HCA Hospital Corporation to convince them to make Kentucky the home of the world's largest chain of health-care facilities.

At the same time, we need to consider some of the shortcomings of our state's and nation's health system. In particular, we are one of only two major industrialized nations without a coordinated system of health care for all of our citizens. Our health costs have risen to a dangerous economic level. Look at our small businesses. They are the backbone of Kentucky's economy, and they face great problems buying and maintaining health coverage for their employees. In fact, three out of every four Kentucky businesses are subsidizing others, perhaps even their competition, if the others go without health insurance. Meanwhile, some 230,000 Kentuckians without coverage are either going without needed care, or seeking it late in an illness, so that it costs more than necessary. We all pay a high "hidden tax" for their inability to get care at the earliest possible moment.

There are other significant areas we must address in our health-care reform efforts. Too many people who have for years received health insurance through Kentucky employers are now losing their benefits due to changes in marketing and insurance underwriting. In speaking recently about the problems with insurance, one Republican house member angrily chided the insurance industry over a practice he appropriately termed "risk avoidance." Perhaps the most telling and vivid example of this comes from Lexington. You may know James Johns, the young man who came last year to testify in Frankfort. His story is almost beyond belief. After leading what he describes as the most healthful lifestyle among all of his friends and having been not only a licensed insurance agent but owner of a small brokerage firm, he fell ill and needed both a kidney transplant and a long-term, high-cost prescription regimen. Today, after many professional years with an upper-middle-class income, James Johns, a licensed insurance broker, has been turned down by all the insurance companies to which he has applied. "Risk avoidance" to this young Lexington resident is now a fact of his life. In his testimony he stated that health-care costs have risen to the point that we must all be concerned, as he now is, about the financial future of our families.

We must get back to basics in health-care delivery, through an emphasis on primary care. This means graduating a high percentage of family and general practice physicians, ob-gyns, and pediatricians. Currently, specialists outnumber primary-care physicians two-to-one. Along these same lines, we must now recognize the good economic and health sense of team medicine, utilizing the skills of nurses and physician assistants and others to the fullest. Reflecting again for a moment on Kentucky, inpatient care in Kentucky cost $80 a day in 1972, compared to $1,000 a day in 1992. All forms of care, taken collectively, are rising 15 percent per year.

Alternative forms of health-care delivery, while already underway, must be further emphasized. Malpractice litigation and defensive medicine contribute from 25 percent to 30 percent more than is needed to the cost of health care for everyone. During the 1994 General Assembly, we will pass legislation to mediate claims in a fair and reasonable manner. Another step to support this effort will be to implement standards of care and practice guidelines. In doing this, hospitals, physicians, and all health-care practitioners in Kentucky will have assurances that they will be protected if and when a case is litigated.

Further supporting this initiative, we will help consumers, the business community, and health-care providers gain a measure of cost and quality which has never before been available in Kentucky. Education and prevention, along with an increased emphasis on prenatal care and an immunization program statewide, will help round out health-care reform. We will put into place a health-care policy board with broad powers to implement these initiatives. Also, health-purchasing alliances will be established to increase the insurance access and purchasing power of individuals and groups and bring new ideas into our evolving health-care system. Savings from state health-care programs already in effect would be placed into a health-care trust to bring coverage to those 230,000 Kentuckians who have no care. In closing, I once again call on you as a group of Kentucky leaders. You can help make a difference. By joining forces with your legislators, you can help us reach the goals of cost containment and coverage for all.

---

1. William M. Lear Jr. (1950–), B.A., economics, Davidson College; J.D., University of Kentucky College of Law; Army Reserve; assistant, Fayette County Attorney, 1978–79; commissioner of law, Lexington-Fayette Urban County Government, 1979–80; board chairman, Lexington Urban Renewal

Commission, 1980–present; Democrat; elected to the Kentucky House of Representatives, 79th District Fayette County, 1985–94; chair, House Economic Development Committee; retired from House of Representatives, 1994. *1994 Kentucky General Assembly Directory* (Frankfort, 1994).

2. Dr. Phillip A. Sharp (1944–), B.S., Union College; 1993 Nobel Prize for medicine; Massachusetts Institute of Technology Center for Cancer Research.

LEAGUE OF WOMEN VOTERS
Frankfort / February 2, 1994

IT IS a pleasure for me to greet each of you and to welcome Kentucky's League of Women Voters here to our state's capital. In the nearly three-quarters of a century in which the league has existed, each of you, and those who came before you, have made this nation greater through your intensive research on the issues facing our society. The balance you bring to your analysis of the issues is critical to the issue most dear to my heart, that is the issue of health-care reform. This is not an issue of Democrats against Republicans, businesses versus labor unions, liberals fighting conservatives.

Health-care reform is something that will work to the benefit of all Kentuckians! Thankfully, the League of Women Voters understands that. You understand the critical need to change the course we are on, if people of all circumstances are to be assured their lives will not be turned upside down by a claim they are unable to pay. In the next few minutes, I will try to reflect on health care, its many great accomplishments, its availability and cost. I will also outline tremendous deficiencies, then bring you up to date on where we are in Kentucky's health-reform efforts.

Let me say from the beginning that we are constantly looking to you and all others for new ideas and answers to the complex questions we face as we try to bring health-care costs back in line with other goods and services. Considering the collective knowledge and expertise in this room today, it would be my hope that you *can* and *will* add greatly to our efforts to bring health-care reform to all Kentuckians.

Let me take you back to the early 1970s to look at Kentucky's health-care system. Our technology was still largely limited to such things as routine x-rays. We hadn't heard much about advanced procedures such as human organ transplants. The cost per day in hospitals throughout Kentucky was, on average, about $80 and cost per case was about $500. Very few of us could name anyone who had ever been involved in a malpractice case. Health-insurance contracts largely followed a simple principle of underwriting: "The dollars of the many, for the ills of the few."

But that was then. This is now. We've gone through *three* generations of CAT scanners, *two* litho-triptors, and now we're on our *second* MRI. Where many of us were in awe of those first successful kidney transplants, today, we consider them routine. It is likely that each of us in this room knows of at least one friend or family member who has had open-heart surgery. That hospital bed which cost $80 per day in 1972 now costs a thousand dollars a day in Kentucky.

The average case costs $7,000. Think of the effect this has on businesses. For example, Chrysler must pay nearly twice as much for health care for their workers as their foreign counterparts. It can devastate our small-business community, the backbone of Kentucky's economy. Whereas in the early 1970s, malpractice litigation was the exception, today, few hospitals or physicians will go through many years without at least the threat of being sued. Former Surgeon General C. Everett Koop says this has resulted in the cost of defensive medicine adding nearly 25 percent to our health costs. Insurance claims and insurance forms have become so complex that it costs a great deal just to sort through it all. One Burkesville family practice physician wanted me to know recently that his office must work through a private sector maze of 183 different claim forms now in use in Kentucky. One hundred and eighty-three different forms!

When health-insurance plans made a conscious, calculated effort to gain an advantage in a competitive marketplace, they lost an important focus, that the very purpose of health coverage is to bring together pools of people to insure the unfortunate few through the collective strength of many. It was called "community rating." But now, as one conservative Republican state lawmaker recently put it, "we no longer have health insurance in Kentucky; companies are selling risk-avoidance." This is a major factor to a growing number of Kentuckians. Perhaps they've enjoyed insurance coverage for years. But they may well be in danger of losing this security, through circumstances such as the loss of a job or a change in a job, a change of insurance companies, early retirement, catastrophic illness or injury, or many other factors which are now characteristic of insurance.

We simply must once again put health insurance within reach of all Kentuckians. The unfortunate result of not having done this in the past is that all of us in this room and in this state who are now covered pay a huge "hidden" tax to cover those who can't pay the high-cost insurance premiums. At the same time, those high costs are made even greater by the fact that, in many cases, people without coverage avoid going to the doctor until their problem becomes major and then more costly. Simply stated, community rating, at least in the modified sense currently stated in House Bill 250, is needed in all insurance contracts. Along with community rating, other insurance principles must be addressed, such as portability of coverage job-to-job, limits on pre-existing conditions and waiting-period clauses, uniformity of claim forms, and high-cost claims administration.

Those complex insurance forms have dramatically increased even the best insurance companies' administrative costs nearly threefold, and that adds to your costs. Let me revisit malpractice and tort reform for a few minutes. If we are to gain any ground on rising health-care costs, we must address the concerns expressed in the quote by Surgeon General Koop. Through tort reform, standards of practice can be established. These standards would then become accepted levels of care and would shield physicians and all health-team members from unfounded lawsuits.

In today's tort situation, the best example I can give comes from one of Kentucky's small community hospitals, which paid $68,000 to settle some out-of-court cases last year. Although their attorneys fully understood that these cases lacked merit, they settled rather than risk what's called the "sweepstakes psychology" of going to trial. Although we have a major section on tort reform in House Bill 250, we must continue in future years to address this problem.

One of the most important aspects of health-care reform is the inclusion of provisions on data reporting. Imagine with me for a moment being in any business or industry where you did not have access to the cost or quality of raw materials you needed for your daily operations. Essentially, this is all too true in Kentucky health care.

There is an interesting piece of history attached to this concept. Back in the late 1970s, an outstanding member of Kentucky's House of Representatives, Gerta Bendle,[1] had a vision for health care which included data release and reporting. Her progressive thinking was thwarted and her legislation failed, stifled at the hands of the special interests which since that time have gained from a lack of financial and outcome reporting.

Back during the May session, we passed a concept called a data commission. This little-known entity, envisioned all those years ago by Gerta Bendle, has been in place for several years in other states. These states are now able to publish very specific information on all health-care costs. Just as important, they merge the health-care-cost data with the data on quality. The very principles upon which all other goods and services are measured will now be put in place through House Bill 250.

Hopefully, my remarks today will help clarify some of the discussions we are having in Frankfort regarding health-care reform. This is a dynamic process, one which can be solved only through the collective input of Kentucky leaders, such as you who are here today, providers from throughout the health-care system, and all of us who are paying too high a price because of cost-shifting and costly delayed care for those without health-insurance benefits. We are moving ahead with these basic principles. Our success will come with your help and continuing input.

At the same time that we make progress in Kentucky, we are also coordinating our reform efforts with the Clinton administration in Washington. I just returned from there this morning. I'm sure that you have become aware that there is a move out of Washington to encourage states to move ahead with plans that best meet their needs. We want to capitalize on this and bring affordable health care and insurance to all Kentuckians as quickly as possible.

Harry S. Truman[2] tried to put something similar in place back some forty-five years ago when it cost less than $10 per day to stay in a hospital. The same arguments we hear today were used back then. But no one could foresee the amazing advancements and their amazing costs. Please help us to get others to understand that health care is becoming an "economy of consumption" rather than solely one of lifesaving production.

Here's one more interesting statistic to share with you before I go. Today, two-thirds of all physicians are specialists. This comes at a time when prevention and attention to one's lifestyle is the prescription for change which makes the most sense. And there are too few general practice physicians to go around. Health-care reform comes down to our willingness to act, to assure all Americans that they can have peace of mind, knowing that a single claim, catastrophic illness, or injury will not lead to personal financial ruin. . . .[3]

1. Gerta Bendle (1931–87), attended Pennsylvania College for Women, studied operatic singing; member of board of aldermen in Louisville, 1971–75; Kentucky House of Representatives, 34th district, 1976–87; first female chair of a standing committee, Health and Welfare; created Nursing Home Bill of Rights; strong advocate for women, elderly, handicapped, and children; drafted and pushed bill that raised marriage license fees to fund spouse-abuse centers. *1986 Kentucky General Assembly Directory* (Frankfort, 1986).

2. Harry S. Truman (1884–1972), Missouri judge, 1922–34; U.S. senator, 1935–45; vice-president of U.S., 1945; president of U.S., 1945–53. *Who Was Who in America . . . 1969–1973*, 5:732.

3. In a speech on February 8 to participants at the Kentucky Retail Federation's Legislation Seminar in Frankfort, Jones discussed the business side of health care and the economic need for insurance. The governor was very defensive about his health-care policy initiatives.

KENTUCKY EDUCATIONAL TELEVISION ADDRESS
Frankfort / April 1, 1994

FOR quite some time the people of this Commonwealth have been saddened by the action of a few members of the legislature. They have watched with dismay as they responded with arrogance and showed a great insensitivity to the people's needs. Today, I'm afraid we have reached *another* low point as it has become evident that the high-paid lobbyists have more control over some of the legislative leaders than do the average, hard-working people of this Commonwealth. It appears that the legislature is about to adjourn—and I certainly hope this is not the case, but they appear that they are about to adjourn without enacting a health-care reform bill or even enacting a budget as required by law. As I said, I hope this is not the case, but if they do, then I think that will be a mistake. I urge them to proceed with the people's business.

On January 24, I submitted to the legislature a balanced budget with the largest reserve fund in the history of the Commonwealth. I said in my address that day that this budget was dependent upon the legislature's reaffirming two positions they had already taken. First, that the provider tax would yield approximately $225 million as they had stated in the special session in May. Second, that they would close the tax loopholes that the court created with the Armco and Peabody cases. If the legislature would take this action, we would be able to fund true health-care reform and get control of runaway costs. We would be able to save our state parks and create many more jobs through tourism. We would be able to build the UK library and the Louisville and Northern Kentucky convention centers. And we would do this with the third-lowest bonded indebtedness in the last fourteen years.

The legislature chose not to do these things. The big insurance companies combined with the medical lobby, and they have great control over some legislators. Fortunately, there are many legislators who are willing to do the right thing. Reps. Greg Stumbo[1] and Larry Clark distinguished themselves on the floor of the house today. They have the big picture and are in a position to show courageous leadership.

You and I must unite with these and other legislators. We must never give up. We *can* enact a budget that is both progressive and fair to all Kentuckians. We *can* provide health care for all of our people and get control of runaway costs. I pledge to you that I will continue this fight until we win.

---

1. Gregory D. "Greg" Stumbo (1951–), B.A., University of Kentucky; J.D., University of Louisville; assistant Floyd County attorney, 1977; trial commissioner to District Court, 1978; city attorney, Martin, 1978–80; elected by the 95th district to the Kentucky House of Representatives, 1979; re-elected, 1981–2000; Democratic floor leader 1985– ; Prestonsburg; attorney. *Who's What in Kentucky Government 1999–2000* (Frankfort, 1999).

HEALTH CARE NEWS CONFERENCE
Frankfort / July 15, 1994

It gives me a great deal of pleasure this morning to tell you the names of the five people who will make up the Health-Policy Board. This board, as you know, was established by the Health-Care Reform Act I signed into law on April 15, and the people you see here with me who have agreed to serve have accepted the challenge of helping to implement this sweeping legislation. Please allow me to introduce them. Donald B. Clapp is the vice president for administration at the University of Kentucky. He is the former vice chancellor for administration at the University of Kentucky Medical Center. He has long served this administration as a key health-policy advisor, and Don Clapp will serve as the chairman of the Health-Policy Board. Dr. Beverly M. Gaines comes to us from her pediatric practice in downtown Louisville. Long an advocate for those in need and the disenfranchised, Dr. Gaines also assisted us as we worked to move the health-care reform effort along. We have long appreciated her unselfish interest and support, and we thank her for accepting a position on the board. Michael J. Hammons has been a part of health care for more than a decade. His service on the board of trustees at the St. Elizabeth Medical Center, a major provider of care to the indigent; his tenure as chairman of that board; his ongoing membership on the board of directors of the Kentucky Health Care Access Foundation; and his excellent work as director of boards and commission places him very high in the esteem of many. Mike says, "Serving on this board is like being in the All-Star Game for health care." Mike, we know you'll serve just as well as you play baseball. Thanks. Sister Michael Leo Mullaney's service to the public has been her vocation and avocation. Her wise counsel and her excellent administrative abilities have been a blessing to us as we tried to move health-care reform along to passage. Sister Michael Leo currently serves as the associate director of health affairs for the Catholic Conference of Kentucky. She is the former president of the Sisters of Charity of Nazareth Health Corporation, and the former president of St. Joseph Hospital in Lexington. Sister, we are grateful to you for your service in the past, and we are grateful to you for your service in the future. And Stephen R. Nunn, long a friend to health-care reform in the General Assembly, is a man with the desire to do right. He represented the people in the 23rd District with dignity and integrity. He served ably on the House Health and Welfare Committee, and he is committed to seeing the right application of law as regards House Bill 250, the reform act. We are very glad, Steve, that you have agreed to be such an integral part of the reform implementation. Thank you.

These five people will do a superb job because they each possess a unique and rare combination of the intellect to implement the Health-Care Reform Act and the compassion to see that it's implemented with fairness and vision. I think they deserve our applause. These people have a broad range of duties including establishing and supervising a health-purchasing alliance; instituting insurance reforms, such as defining up to five standard health-insurance benefit plans to be offered by companies doing business in Kentucky; collecting health data; collecting information on maximum provider charges for services and prescriptions and disseminating information; compiling and disseminating information on various aspects of health-care services, usage, costs, and quality; promoting integrated health-care delivery networks in rural areas; designating health-professional shortages by region and implementing regional physician-extender training programs and a physician-respite program; developing clinical-practice standards and outcome measures for health-care providers; and making certificate of need determination. . . .

COMMONWEALTH NEWS CONFERENCE
Frankfort / September 8, 1994

To Governor Jones.

Dear Sir:

I urge you to hasten the enactment of your medical health program. My husband retired in 1992, and my insurance coverage expired the end of July of this year. The conversion policy I was offered will cost me $1,518 per month, more than ten times the premium I paid previously. What's more, they require six months advance payment of $9,106. I am 63 years old and not eligible for Medicare yet. One insurance company refused me coverage because of my medical history. I had a small malignant breast tumor removed last year, but have now passed ensuing physical examinations. Please help me soon. The consequences of a heart attack, etc. would be financially draining. It is a dreadful way to exist.

Respectfully yours,
Ruth G. Cummins of Augusta, Kentucky.

RUTH, I'm happy to tell you, you won't have to exist that way much longer. Ruth is the first person who will get an insurance card through the state's new Commonwealth Program. Ruth was one of the first to send in a request for an application for insurance. Once the Health-Policy Board set the rates, the state was able to send out the application forms, along with the list of participating plans, and a rate sheet. That happened last Friday. Today, Ruth is turning in her application form. She has chosen Kentucky Kare Select. Instead of paying more than $1,500 a month for insurance, she will pay $250.89 a month. That figures out to a little over $3,000 a year, quite a bit less than the $18,000 figure she otherwise would have had to pay.

Ruth will now have a six-month waiting period for pre-existing conditions but otherwise will be covered as of October first. I think this is one of the first of many success stories of Kentucky's new Health-Care Reform Act. And I'm happy to have the members of the Health-Policy Board here with us today to see firsthand the good that they will be doing, taking a dreadful situation, and making it better.

KENTUCKY HEALTH-PURCHASING ALLIANCE PRESS CONFERENCE

Lexington / July 17, 1995

. . . TODAY'S launch of Plansource, Kentucky's new health-purchasing alliance, represents the successful result of a difficult health-care struggle in Kentucky. After years of debate we are finally seeing the result of our work, a real improvement in the health-care options available to the people of the Commonwealth. Plansource will provide Kentucky's small businesses with something they haven't had—affordable, high-quality health-insurance choices for themselves and their employees. This was one of my key goals for health-care reform in Kentucky. I'm very happy to see this goal realized. The new health-care reform which went into effect this past weekend will, quite simply, afford Kentuckians the best health-care coverage in America. Plansource and the alliance will provide the best private health-care solutions for small businesses and individuals. I want to commend the leading private health insurers and HMOs that are participating with Plansource. It's their insurance and health-care products that make this worthwhile; by participating in the alliance, these health insurers are working for a better future for health care. They're working with all of us to provide the best health care in the world to everyone who needs it, at a cost that won't bankrupt us all. Our task from today forward is to adequately explain health-care reform to every Kentuckian. They need to know that Plansource is not a government health-insurance provider. Rather, it is a purchasing pool enabling Kentuckians to buy quality health-care insurance coverage from America's leading health-insurance providers. It's a way to have quality health-care coverage at rates previously only available to large corporations or governments. And it's a way to "level the playing field" so all Kentuckians will be treated fairly. Our message today is that Kentuckians now have a choice, and Kentuckians do not have to be uninsured. Finally, I want to welcome Healthplan Services to Kentucky. The Health-Purchasing Alliance Board selected Healthplan Services to administer Plansource here in Kentucky. The company has extensive experience managing health-purchasing alliances. They're currently successfully administering Florida's small-business health-purchasing alliance. Healthplan Services understands how to make the alliance work for everyone—individuals, small businesses, and public employees. I appreciate their commitment and welcome Jack Murray and his company to the Commonwealth. And you know, one exciting by-product of health-care reform is the new jobs created as we move to reduce the number of uninsured Kentuckians. This new office for Plansource will have sixty new employees by the fall and dozens more as they continue to grow to meet everyone's insurance needs.

KENTUCKY HOSPITAL ASSOCIATION
Frankfort / October 26, 1995

FIRST of all, I want to say thank you to the Kentucky Hospital Association, its administrators, trustees, and staff for the support you've given this administration through recent years as we moved to reform health care in the face of tremendous pressures and changes locally and nationally. You have figured prominently in the many positive developments and initiatives of our administration, and I am certain the many people of Kentucky who depend on us for their health care join me in thanking you. The KHA and its leadership, and especially members like Joe Gross[1] . . . have been very helpful in our efforts.

Now, we are about to embark on a new venture in health-care delivery. As you have heard from news accounts, we have received approval from the federal government to amend our 1993 Section 1115 waiver to begin moving Kentucky's Medicaid program into managed care through the formation of "health-care partnerships." These partnerships will be made up of public and private providers, hospitals, doctors, and other provider groups along with local health departments who will deliver services through a risk-based and capitated payments system.

The partnerships will emphasize preventive and intervention services. This amendment to our waiver does not include long-term and mental-health services. The health-care partnerships allow a regionalist approach that will permit tailoring of services to meet unique local needs. They are designed to insure that all providers have an opportunity to participate, especially local health departments and the medical teaching universities.

We also believe that these partnerships will provide an opportunity for our smaller and often rural hospitals to be a viable and working force in the health-care delivery system for years to come. We *must* keep these hospitals open. They are the front line in our delivery system.

In a traditional HMO approach to managed care, the bottom line becomes the dominant theme, and we fear this approach would cause local health departments and the rural hospitals to fall to the wayside. Without the local hospitals, health care in rural areas would all but dry up and health-care reform would become a hollow shell for many of our most needy.

Through these "health-care partnerships," we expect to save the Commonwealth 3 to 5 percent annually when the program is fully operational. Based on current eligibility and expenditure levels, this would amount to almost $120 million into total medical savings and could be as high as $170 million annually.

The savings will be placed in a trust fund reserved for indigent health care. This will allow us to keep the promise we made Kentuckians to provide the best possible health care to the state's needy. Together, we can make significant savings and still keep patient care a top priority.

That is why the Kentucky Hospital Association and its members will be even more crucial in the future to reshape the delivery system in the face of expected enormous changes from Washington. If we do not act now, if we do not form this public-private bond, if we wait to see what is to come from the federal government, the impact on our system could be devastating. By forming these partnerships, we can bolster the system as we make it more effective and more efficient, so that it can adjust to whatever Washington proposes.

In the very near future we will be talking with your organization and its members to begin a dialogue on how to form these partnerships, what is expected, and how much it will cost. Our secretary of human resources, Masten Childers,[2] who has been a vital force in this reshaping process, will continue to be the point man as we move this concept from the drawing board to the doctors' offices, clinics, hospitals, emergency rooms, health departments, medical schools, and to the people who so desperately need our assistance.

For a decade and a half I have worked both privately and as a public official to improve health care in Kentucky. From my first experiences with bringing health care to the indigent of Kentucky through my tenure as lieutenant governor and now in the final months of my administration as governor we have striven to bring better health care to the state's needy.

You have been there and Kentucky is better for our cooperative efforts. I am excited and very optimistic that we will continue to expand and improve on health-care delivery in our Commonwealth. This will not be easy, but as I have said so many times, together we can accomplish anything if we but try using the resources, talent, minds, backs, and sheer fortitude of Kentuckians who truly want to do what is best, what is right.

---

1. Joseph W. Gross (1947–), health-care executive; B.S. in business administration, Creighton University, 1968; M.S. in health-service management, University of Missouri, 1971; vice-president operations, Wausau Hospitals, 1974–77; executive vice-president, Wausau Hospitals, Inc., 1977; president and CEO of Luther Health Care Corporation, Wisconsin, 1978–85; FACHE, Fellow of the American College of Health Care Executives, 1983; president and CEO of St. Elizabeth Health System, Northern Kentucky, 1986–present; regent, American College of Health Care Executives, 1997.

2. Masten Childers II (1950–) B.G.S, University of Kentucky, 1973; J.D., Salmon P. Chase College of Law, 1983; deputy commissioner, Kentucky Bureau of Public Properties, 1977; deputy secretary, Kentucky Department of Finance, 1977–79; chief executive assistant to the lieutenant governor, 1979; commissioner for the Department of Law of the Kentucky Cabinet for Human Resources, 1979–80; deputy secretary of the Kentucky Cabinet for Human Resources, 1992–93; commissioner of the Kentucky Department for Medicaid Services, 1993–94; secretary of the Kentucky Cabinet for Human Resources, 1993–95; attorney, Gary C. Johnson Attorneys at Law.

EDUCATION

PARTNERSHIP FOR KENTUCKY SCHOOL REFORM LUNCHEON
April 23, 1992

I'M HAPPY to be here this afternoon to speak to a special group of people who have made a commitment to the future of Kentucky. I'm honored to be here alongside visionary leaders such as "Oz" Nelson of UPS,[1] David Jones of Humana,[2] and John Hall of Ashland Oil.[3] I'm also pleased to be here today as the governor of a state which is currently leading the country in the breadth and scope of its educational-reform efforts.

As members of the Partnership for Kentucky School Reform, we have all made a ten-year commitment to the successful implementation of the Kentucky school reform act. Despite the fact that we are facing tough economic times in Kentucky, I believe in my heart that we were able to continue the momentum of restructuring and reform when we crafted our budget for the Commonwealth for the coming two years.

I want everyone here to understand that there is no higher goal in our administration than to see the vision of KERA totally fulfilled and fully implemented. I know that I am standing before a remarkable group of individuals who have made a personal commitment to change in Kentucky, and who understand the link between excellence in education, economic vitality, and a good quality of life for all Kentuckians.

I appreciate the efforts of each and every one of you, but you know and I know that there is much work to be done. Implementing education reform in Kentucky is going to demand hard work, not only from members of groups like the partnership and the Prichard Committee,[4] but also from individuals and groups from every local community in the Commonwealth.

I applaud and support the efforts of the Prichard Committee and the partnership to bring the vision and the reality of KERA to every county, town, and city in Kentucky. As you all know, Kentucky's new education reforms have moved responsibility for excellence and student achievement to the local level. If KERA is to be implemented successfully, we must focus on strategies and actions which will engage citizens, business leaders, professional organizations, civic groups, and parents in the work of transforming our schools into vibrant learning centers, where all children are expected to learn and where high achievement is the norm, rather than the exception.

So today, I am calling on all Kentuckians to make the same personal commitment that you, John, David, Oz, and the entire membership of the partnership have made, a personal commitment to our children and to the future of the Commonwealth of Kentucky. This means that we will need to change more than just schools. Schools cannot accomplish this monumental task alone. Our schools will need help from the entire community, and not just from those that have an obvious stake in the success of schools.

We must ask for and get the support of those citizens who do not have children in their households. Every citizen in the Commonwealth must come to understand that the quality of our schools, more than at any time in our history, will determine the quality of our lives.

We must give careful consideration to how we reach beyond the important, but normal, constituency of parents and teachers, to harvest the talent of every segment of our local communities. This is why the work of the Prichard Committee and the partnership is so vital. You are in the vanguard, spreading the word through a well-thought-out public information campaign and working at the grassroots level to establish local KERA support committees.

Not only must we reach out to those citizens who may have not been involved in our public schools before, but we must also redirect our focus to the parents of the Commonwealth. KERA invites parents to become part of the decision-making process at school council meetings. It also provides for assistance for parents and families through family resource centers. But new programs, approaches, and services are not enough. We must encourage every parent in our state to become actively involved in the education of his or her child.

We know that children succeed when their parents become actively engaged in the educational process, so we must encourage parents of preschool children to read to them every day and to instill a love of learning in their children. We must urge parents of primary-aged children to ask about their child's school day and to help that child prepare for the next. We must teach parents of elementary- and middle-school children to review assignments that are due and to check to see that homework is done. Finally, we should help parents of high-school students to talk to their children about college, careers, and training for work.

I also call on every local superintendent, every school board member, every principal, every counselor, and every teacher to open the school doors even wider to make room for the parents of your students. Let's make school an inviting place not only for children, but for families as well.

In addition to a new role for ordinary citizens and parents, the business community must be encouraged to examine the role it has traditionally played in supporting education. Today, I join the partnership in asking every business in Kentucky to join the fight for Kentucky's future. I hope all employers across the state will adopt the employee initiatives plan which the partnership has put together. In order to demonstrate our willingness to lead in this effort, I have signed into effect today an executive order which enlists the aid of every agency in state government to move this effort forward. Specifically, I have directed all state agencies:

1. to cooperate fully with efforts to promote the success of KERA;
2. to keep and display promotional materials pertaining to KERA;
3. to encourage state employees to participate in school conferences and meetings concerning their children, and to encourage all other employees to be actively engaged in their communities' schools;
4. and finally for all senior officials in state government to increase their efforts to provide assistance to students and teachers in achieving educational excellence.

Additionally, I have asked Secretary Jelsma[5] to develop a program in cooperation with the Kentucky Department of Education which will identify and recognize schools, communities, and organizations which have made significant progress in implementing the goals of KERA.

In closing, let me say that I know that this has been a difficult time for many who had hoped for more in the budget process. I wish with all my heart that this national recession had not visited Kentucky and driven revenues down. But, I believe we have survived this difficult time with KERA intact. I am now calling on all of us to roll up our sleeves and to tighten our belts a little bit further and continue the work of building a better Kentucky. It is my wish that we will all work together—school boards, professional educators, business people, community organizations, civic clubs, citizens, parents, and legislators—to make education reform a reality for our children.[6]

---

1. Kent C. "Oz" Nelson (1937–), B.S., Ball State University, 1959; UPS senior vice-president, 1983–85; UPS finance group manager and chief financial officer, 1984–87; UPS executive vice-president, 1986–88; vice-chairman of the board 1989; CEO of UPS, 1989–97; chairman of the board, 1997.

2. David A. Jones (1932–), born in Louisville; B.S., University of Louisville, 1954; CPA, 1954; Navy, 1955–57; J.D., Yale University Law School, 1960; co-founded Humana, 1961; CEO, Humana, 1961–97; founding chair of Peter F. Drucker Graduate Management Center's Board of Visitors; director of Abbott Laboratories; honorary doctorates from the Chicago Medical School, University of Louisville, Transylvania University, and Claremont Graduate School; chairman of the board of Humana, 1997– .

3. John R. Hall (1932–), B.S., Vanderbilt University; Ashland Inc., 1957–97; Banc One Corporation Board; Canada Life Assurance Co. Board; CSX Corporation Board; Humana Inc. Board; LaRoche Industries Board; Reynolds Metals Co. Board; UCAR International Inc. Board; Transylvania University Board; National Petroleum Council Board; chairman of the Commonwealth Endowment Fund for Kentucky Educational Television and Leadership Kentucky; honorary director of the American Petroleum Institute; retired chairman of the board and CEO of Ashland Inc., 1981–96; served as Kentucky state chairman for the U.S. Olympic Committee, 1991–96; inducted into the Marshall University Business Hall of Fame, 1995.

4. Prichard Committee for Academic Excellence, founded in 1980; non-profit, non-partisan organization of parents and volunteers; thirty-member citizen panel on future of higher education in Kentucky; published *In Pursuit of Excellence* recommending change in Kentucky's colleges and universities; reorganized in 1983 into independent organization; Dr. Robert Sexton, executive director.

5. Sherry Keith Jelsma (1938–), born in Louisville; B.A., Harvard-Radcliffe College, 1960; M.A., New York University, 1962; secondary schoolteacher, Jefferson County Public schools; elected member Jefferson County School Board, 1982–90; Kentucky secretary for Education, Arts and Humanities Cabinet, 1991–95; interim president, Kentucky Center for the Arts, 1997–98.

6. Jones gave some earlier speeches dealing with education issues. On February 28, he spoke at the Kentucky School Board Association meeting in Louisville; he discussed KERA's successes and his administration's contin-

ued commitment. He promised full funding of the Tier 1 component of SEEK, an increase of more than $100 million over the current biennium. At a press conference on March 13, Jones announced changes in the budget to add revenue to secondary vocational education.

KERA EVALUATION BOARD ANNOUNCEMENT
Louisville / November 30, 1992

TODAY I am signing an executive order that creates a KERA evaluation board. Many of the members of the board are here with us this morning. Lila Bellando of Berea, Judith Clabes of Covington, Judy Thomas of Ashland, John Hager of Owensboro, Doug Keulpman of Louisville, Joe Wright of Harned, and Bob Sexton of Lexington, I want to thank each of you for your willingness to answer the call to serve your Commonwealth. Additional board members who could not be with us today are David Grissom of Louisville, Ben Richardson of Louisville, and Gary Dodd of Georgetown. Our thanks to these fine people as well.

The KERA evaluation board is to be an independent and, as you can see, blue-ribbon panel of distinguished Kentuckians who will develop a mechanism to attract the best research possible on the results of the Kentucky Education Reform Act. I am also asking the board to issue an annual KERA progress report to the citizens of Kentucky, my office, the General Assembly, and the education community.

It is vitally important that the people of Kentucky receive an independent report on the results of KERA.

It is equally important to establish a long-term research agenda that will provide the information that is necessary to determine if KERA is accomplishing its original intent. The education research community around the world is eager to study the outcomes of Kentucky's education reforms, and we want to ensure that Kentucky has the benefit of the best research possible.

I have great confidence in these dedicated Kentuckians that I have asked to lead this effort. Each of them has demonstrated a deep commitment to educational progress in Kentucky and has a good understanding of the kind of evaluative information that Kentuckians need. I am also pleased to announce that initial funding for this effort will come from the Annie B. Casey Foundation, which has committed $400,000 to get this project started. The foundation has funded several activities aimed at supporting KERA over the past two years, and we appreciate their continued support.

You are also going to hear today from my good friends Don Swain[1] of the University of Louisville and Charles Wethington[2] of the University of Kentucky about a new educational policy research partnership between these two great universities. I don't want to steal too much of their thunder this morning, but let me say that I applaud this new collaboration between Kentucky's major research universities. This will go a long way toward ensuring that Kentucky institutions of higher learning play a competitive role in national research on educational policy. Both UK and U of L have made significant strides in developing valuable KERA research projects.

I anticipate that the KERA evaluation board will encourage research now under way and stimulate new involvement from *all* of our Kentucky colleges and universities. Finally, again, I want to thank the members of the new KERA evaluation board who are volunteering their time to set this research and evaluation process in motion. If there is any way that we can help you in your efforts, let us know. You have my unqualified support. Now, I know that Dr. Swain and Dr. Wethington have a very important related announcement, so let me turn the podium over to them.[3]

---

1. Donald Christie Swain (1931–), B.A., University of Dubuque, 1953; M.A., history, University of California, Berkeley, 1958, Ph.D., 1961; assistant research historian, University of California, Berkeley, 1961–63; faculty member, University of California, Davis, 1963–81; president, University of Louisville, 1981–95; professor of history, 1981–95; president emeritus, 1995; board of directors, LGE Energy. *Who's Who in America 2000,* 54th ed. (New Providence, N.J., 1999), vol. 2. For the announcement, see below, Speech to the Kentucky Association of School Superintendents, November 30, 1992.

2. Charles Turner Wethington Jr. (1936–), A.B., Eastern Kentucky University, 1956; M.A., University of Kentucky, 1962; Ph.D. in education, University of Kentucky, 1965; instructor in educational psychology, University of Kentucky, 1965–66; director, Maysville Community College, 1967–71; assistant vice-president for the Community College System, 1971–81; vice-president of the Community College System, 1981–82; chancellor for the Community College System, 1982–88; chancellor for the Community College System and University Relations, 1988–89; interim president of the University of Kentucky, 1989–90; president of the University of Kentucky, 1990–2001; member, Kentucky Coal Marketing and Export Council, 1990– ; member, Southern Growth Policies Board, 1990–96;

president, Southeastern Conference, 1993–95; chairman, Southeastern Universities Research Association Council of Presidents, 1995– ; member, board of directors, Lexington Chamber of Commerce, 1997– ; member, NCAA Division 1, board of directors and executive committee, 1997–2000.

3. On January 8, 1993, Jones gave a speech to the KERA evaluation board members concerning the board's organization.

KENTUCKY ASSOCIATION OF SCHOOL SUPERINTENDENTS
Louisville / November 30, 1992

. . . I'M particularly pleased to be here this morning to speak to Kentucky school administrators, Kentucky's front-line leaders in school reform. We know that the eyes of the entire nation are on Kentucky these days, and you are the vanguard of the national education reform effort.

Not only is education reform attracting the nation's attention, but a whole host of other recent developments has caused policymakers and national leaders to look toward Kentucky for answers to tough problems. It is hard to imagine a state that has embarked upon a more ambitious course of reform on such a variety of issues as Kentucky.

Education reform, a tough code of ethics for the executive branch, economic-development reform, the restructuring of higher education boards, campaign finance reform, passage of the gubernatorial succession and charitable gaming amendments, and reform of the bidding process for state engineering and architectural contracts are all important, positive changes in the way government and politics operate in Kentucky. We can all take great pride in these accomplishments which are bringing such positive attention to Kentucky.

As you know, there is one big change on the horizon that I am committed to and for which I ask your support. Sometime in the very near future, I want to walk into the office of the president of the United States and say, "Mr. President, every Kentuckian now has a guarantee of adequate health care at a reasonable cost. Here is a model for the rest of the country." We are going to need everyone's help on this, and I solicit your support and your ideas as we work together to solve the problem of access to and affordability of high-quality health care in Kentucky.

The message that I am bringing to you today is that these changes are necessary if we are to make progress in Kentucky. They are necessary if we are going to compete in the international economy. And they are necessary for the people of Kentucky to enjoy a decent standard of living and a high quality of life. The reason that I am bringing this message of the necessity of change to you this morning is because you, the school administrators of Kentucky, are among those Kentucky is calling on to be the agents of change. It is you that we are calling on to make sure that school reforms work.

To achieve positive results in our reform efforts calls for a renewed commitment to creative leadership in Kentucky, and you, the school administrators, are a vital part of that leadership effort. I am here today to express our administration's support for you and the positive changes that KERA is designed to bring about and to discuss with you some of the leadership issues involved with managing this historic process of educational and cultural change.

Now that we are well into the beginning stages of the implementation of KERA, we are feeling in our daily lives the impact of the KERA reforms. Last year, we started putting a new and, to many people, unfamiliar assessment and accountability system into place, the initial results of which were released this fall.

You, your staffs, and your teachers are not only faced with implementing this new system of assessment, but are also responsible for refocusing your instructional strategies, while at the same time explaining the results to parents, the press, and your local communities. This is a large and challenging task, and yet it is only one piece of a much larger and continually expanding picture. Many of you are now facing the challenge of implementing our new primary program; multi-age and multi-ability grouping; a new system of evaluating student progress; integrating kindergarten youngsters into the primary program; reaching the valued outcomes. These are big issues that you, your teachers, your parents, your school boards, and your community must deal with on a daily basis.

Successfully implementing the primary program takes a lot of time, extra attention, intensive training, and, of course, endless patience and persistence. To some degree, nearly all of you have been involved in planning for the installation of Kentucky's new system of educational technology. I share many of your concerns about the delays that you have experienced in the implementation of this revolutionary new tool for efficient school administration and student learning.

And as you are well aware, there are even more changes in store for us as we move toward creating world-class schools for Kentucky. There are the high-school restructuring task force recommendations to be considered; the model curriculum frameworks to be developed; school-to-work transition plans to be implemented; more school-based councils to be elected; and a host of other critical items to be added to your work plans as we move forward with the implementation of all the strands of KERA. Such massive change in so short a time is a challenge to all of us.

You have our support as you face the challenge of achieving success for today's students and creating a new tomorrow for generations of Kentuckians to come. I want you to know that our administration is right beside you as you grapple with the challenge of change. We are going to do everything we can to help you in your role as leaders of national education reform and educational improvement in your communities.

When I became governor, we faced a budget crisis of massive proportions. We were confronted with some very difficult choices in the very first days of our administration. One of the first decisions that I made as governor was that if we were going to have to make cuts in state government, it was not going to be at the expense of our children and schools in Kentucky. As you know, funding for KERA was held harmless from any budgetary cuts in our appropriations proposals in the last session of the General Assembly, and I will do everything in my power to maintain the level of funding that is necessary to fully implement historic education reforms.

As many of you know, implementing the Kentucky education technology system has been more difficult than many of us might have imagined. Many of you have expressed your concern to me and members of my staff about the slow pace of phasing in our educational technology plans. I have asked Secretary of Education, Arts and Humanities Sherry Jelsma and former Secretary of Finance Joe Prather[1] to give this issue their special attention and to work closely with the Department of Education and the General Assembly to move educational technology plans forward as quickly as possible.

We have met with the leadership of the General Assembly and Commissioner Boysen[2] on this issue, and I will be placing the issue of education technology on the call for a special session of the General Assembly in early 1993 to resolve the funding issues which are inhibiting our progress.

Immediately after our session here this morning, I will be meeting with the press to announce a new research-based effort to evaluate the results of KERA. By executive order I have created a KERA evaluation board, a blue-ribbon panel that will commission research and make an annual report to the citizens of Kentucky on the results of the implementation of KERA. This effort will be an ongoing source of information that will guide us in the process of educational improvement.

Simultaneously, the University of Kentucky and the University of Louisville will announce the formation of a joint center for the study of educational policy. The KERA evaluation board and the joint policy center will be parallel efforts which will attract educational research funds to Kentucky, add to Kentucky's knowledge base and expertise in educational reform, and allow us to build on the strong foundation that KERA provides.

When I was traveling throughout our Commonwealth in my campaign for governor, I said over and over again, "There is nothing that we cannot accomplish if we work together." Bill Clinton, when he came to Kentucky in his campaign for president, said over and over again, we can get America back on track again if American government, American institutions, American education, and the American people have "the courage to change." Well, what a model! What a proving ground! What an opportunity we have in Kentucky! We have shown that we have the courage to change and I *know* that we can work together.

Perhaps there is no group that this challenge of working together for positive change more directly affects than Kentucky's educational leaders. And make no mistake, change is uncomfortable; change requires us to swim in uncharted waters; change requires that we learn and adapt as we go. The change that is mandated by KERA requires us to develop new styles of leadership. KERA calls on us to become facilitators, team leaders, coaches, mentors, and role models rather than the sole source of authority and responsibility. KERA calls for us to assume new roles which we might feel ill prepared to take on. KERA calls for us to retool our administrative and instructional structures into dynamic, learning organizations. We also have the responsibility to help others understand the need for change.

Now that the changes mandated by KERA are being implemented, we need to help our parents understand why we have to restructure our schools. When I talk to business leaders that are considering relocating in Kentucky, among the first questions asked are: Will Kentucky have the well-educated workers that we are looking for? Are Kentucky schools teaching their students how to think for themselves? How to solve problems? How to work as a member of a team?

How to communicate effectively? Will they be able to make use of knowledge and information to make my business more productive?

These prospects know that right now we have a shrinking, aging workforce in Kentucky. And they want to know what Kentucky is doing to ensure that we are preparing every one of our children, every member of our future workforce, to be productive workers and productive citizens. You can imagine the pride that I feel when I tell them that Kentucky has made a lasting commitment and an expression of faith in every child in Kentucky by stating our belief that "all students can learn and all students can learn at high levels."

I am proud to show them Kentucky's goals and valued outcomes. They are impressed when I show them the commitment we have made to fund our reform. And finally, I am proud to look them in the eye when they ask me, "Do you think it will work?" And I say, "You bet it will work. We are all working together in Kentucky to make sure that it will work." And the key to "making it work" is our willingness to come together, recognizing that it takes a willingness on the part of everyone, beginning with us in this room, in cooperation with the Department of Education, and in partnership with school administrators, the General Assembly, school boards, teachers, parents, businesses, civic groups, and our local communities to communicate clearly and cooperate faithfully to make the vision of KERA become a reality.

Our children's future, Kentucky's future, depends on it. Our children have my commitment, and I know they have yours. We look forward to working with you in the months to come.[3]

---

1. Joe Prather (1939–), native of Vine Grove; elected Kentucky house, 1968–74; Democratic whip, 1970; elected Kentucky senate (10th District), 1974–86; senate president pro tem, 1976–86; chairman, State Democratic Party under Governor Collins; chairman of Jones's campaign for governor; finance secretary, 1991–93; chair of Farmers Deposit Bank in Brandenburg and of Hardin County Bank and Trust.

2. Thomas C. Boysen (1940–), B.A. in history, Stanford University, 1962; diploma in graduate education, Makerere University, Kampala, Uganda, Africa, 1964; Ed.D. in education administration, Harvard University, 1969; geography master, Kabaa High School, Thika, Kenya, Africa, 1964–66; director of administration, Bellevue Public Schools, Washington, 1968–70; superintendent of schools, Pasco School District, Washington, 1970–73; Pelham Public Schools, New York, 1973–77; Redlands Unified School District, California, 1977–80; Conejo Valley Unified School District,

Thousand Oaks, California, 1980–87; San Diego County Schools, 1987–90; Kentucky commissioner of education, 1991–95; senior vice-president of education, Milken Family Foundation, 1995– .

3. In October and November, Jones gave some other speeches dealing with education issues. On October 14, he spoke at a student rally for higher education in Frankfort. He discussed higher education cuts in the budget and pledged his continued support to Kentucky's colleges and universities. On November 12, he spoke at the Kentucky Tech-Central Campus dedication in Lexington, stressing the importance of a higher-skilled workforce in the next few years and saying that Kentucky would have an edge on surrounding states by working "harder and smarter." Also on November 12, he spoke at the Inter-Agency Commission on Educational and Job Training Coordination in Frankfort; he discussed the commission's responsibilities—flexibility for students to transfer credits, eliminating loss of credit, and cooperative job and education training. During October 1993, Jones announced the Kentucky Tech Scholarship Program, which allows high-school seniors to continue their technical education.

KERA EVALUATION CONFERENCE
Lexington / May 24, 1993

THANK you, Secretary Jelsma, for that very kind introduction. Chairman Kelly,[1] Commissioner Boysen, distinguished members of the General Assembly, and honored guests. Welcome to the National Conference on the Kentucky Education Reform Act. It gives me great pleasure to welcome you to the Commonwealth of Kentucky, a state filled with natural beauty and steeped in tradition, and one of our proudest traditions is the warm hospitality we offer our guests.

While you are here to share ideas, compare programs, and renew your commitment to education reform, I know you will find your Kentucky hosts to be among the friendliest anywhere. We extend to each of you an invitation to return to our Commonwealth in the years to come. You won't find a friendlier or more beautiful place to visit. We appreciate that so many of you have taken the time to be with us for the next few days.

You have come here to discuss one of the most crucial issues facing our nation today. Education reform: how to craft it, how to fund it, and how to sustain it, and I presume the question on everyone's lips these days is, "How is it going in Kentucky?"

School reform in Kentucky today is progressing. We have a statewide consensus among our citizens, our business and civic leadership, and our elected officials that the Kentucky Education Reform Act of 1990 was the right thing to do, at the right time, and for the right reasons. We are committed to staying the course, to seeing KERA through to full and complete implementation so that *all* Kentucky's children will have the educational opportunities they need.

The membership of the Kentucky General Assembly has put children first in Kentucky. Without their leadership Kentucky would not be where it is today in education reform. We have also had leadership support from Secretary Jelsma to Chairman Joe Kelly and the state school board; from Commissioner Boysen and his staff to the Kentucky Education Association; from our local school boards and administrators to our newly formed school councils; from our colleges of education to our professional education organizations; and finally, last but not least, we have unparalleled leadership from the Kentucky General Assembly.

We recognize that, with KERA in its third year of implementation, education reform in Kentucky is in its infancy. But we are committed to give it the time that it needs to work. We understand that the future of our children and grandchildren depends on our will to stay the course and continue the reforms that we have put in place.

In Kentucky we recognize the key to a brighter future for our children and our Commonwealth is education. In June of 1989, we received a mandate for change from our state supreme court that gave us the following charge: restructure the system of common schools in Kentucky so that it provides efficient, adequate, and equitable education for all Kentucky schoolchildren and ensures that all Kentucky students have equal opportunity to develop good communication skills, sufficient knowledge to make economic, social, and political choices, an understanding of governmental processes, self knowledge and other healthy living habits, a grounding in the arts sufficient to appreciate our culture and historical heritage, opportunities to choose and plan for a life of learning and work, and finally, the necessary skills to compete successfully with children from other states. It then became our responsibility to change and restructure our state system of elementary and secondary education, and I can truthfully say to you that Kentucky accepted this responsibility with hope and enthusiasm. We looked at our method of curriculum instruction and assessment. We debated different financing models, and we came to grips with the issues of governance and leadership. We took advantage of the best minds in

Kentucky and in the nation. From this input and available research, we molded KERA.

KERA establishes high standards of learning. It proclaims first and foremost that *all* children can learn and that our children can learn at a much higher level than in the past. It moves from that fundamental principle of faith in our children's abilities to establishing the mechanisms that will ensure achievement at dramatically higher levels. KERA is based on outcomes, not on input; it holds local schools and districts accountable for results. It provides a financing system that substantially equalizes educational funding across our Commonwealth and raises per pupil funding in most districts.

Furthermore, KERA coordinates health and social services through family resource centers. Kentucky has established high standards for students, teachers, and administrators, as well as elected officials. KERA is bringing an end to nepotism and cronyism that could rob our children of opportunities for quality education. At the same time, it is putting into the hands of teachers, administrators, and parents the tools that they need to create successful schools. KERA constructs a strong foundation for the future by offering a preschool program for at-risk youngsters. At this time 75 percent of all eligible four-year-olds are being provided with a developmentally appropriate preschool program.

We build on the preschool program with our new primary schools that are based on the principle of continuous progress for all children- and student-centered teaching. In this year alone 836 schools initiated the ungraded primary program. KERA empowers local schools through site-based councils to design the best instructional program possible for each student.

Today more than six hundred schools have made this transition. This year, two hundred new councils will go online. Newly developed curriculum frameworks will be available to all schools to tie our new system of performance-based assessment with instruction. In the very near future the state board of education will bring forward recommendations for the restructuring of Kentucky high schools.

Finally, we cannot talk about building schools for the twenty-first century without mentioning Kentucky's commitment to educational technology. In the past year we have developed a comprehensive, statewide master plan which calls for spending $420 million to put computers in every classroom and building a fully networked system which allows for quick reporting on everything from daily attendance to assessment results.

We recognize our challenge. We must maintain the momentum

that we have. Change, real change, is difficult. Kentucky teachers have been asked to take on new roles in the way they work as part of the school team. Administrators are being asked to apply new management styles. Parents are being asked to become more involved by making decisions that affect their schools. All of this is a change, a real change, from past practices. It will take all of us, working together, to build the kind of future that we want for our children.

I am proud to say that Kentuckians have responded to that call by the support of the Kentucky General Assembly, by our business and civic leaders, and by the people of the Commonwealth. So my message to you today is clear: Kentucky is staying the course! We believe that what we did in 1990, and what we are doing today for our children, is the right thing.

We are committed to giving Kentucky's reform efforts the time and resources that it will take for them to work. Our time line for full implementation extends to 1996. Only then, when new instructional methods are being practiced daily, when students get the help they need to succeed, when our schools have a system of educational technology, when all local schools are fully empowered, and when the vestiges of failed past practices are wiped away will we see the positive results of our efforts. We are confident that the results will be positive because in Kentucky we had the courage to change and the will to support those changes. Best wishes for a very successful conference. Enjoy your stay in Kentucky.[2]

---

1. Joseph W. Kelly (1949–), staff sergeant, U.S. Air Force, 1969–73; B.S., Campbellsville College, 1976; M.P.A., Kentucky State University, 1986; Governor's Commission on Corrections and Community Services, 1980–88; general manager of Kentucky Transportation Cabinet's District 4, 1981–84; director of the Kentucky Water Patrol, 1984–86; consultant, 1986–88; Economic Development and Governmental Affairs manager, 1988–90; president, Kentucky Industrial Development Council, 1990; director of Regulatory and Governmental Affairs, 1990–96; chair of Kentucky Board of Education, 1991–98; vice-president and general manager, Columbia Gas of Kentucky, 1996–present; recipient of Hellard Award, 1998.

2. On April 14, Jones spoke at a rally for a dropout-prevention program (Project Esteem); he emphasized the coordination of this program's goals with those of KERA.

PRICHARD COMMITTEE ANNUAL MEETING
Shakertown / July 12, 1993

WHAT a pleasure it is to be here with so many friends. My experiences as a member of the Prichard Committee are the basis of my commitment to equal and adequate educational opportunities for every child in Kentucky. As lieutenant governor, I worked for education reform. I spoke to the teachers when they marched to Frankfort. As president of the senate, I worked with legislators to ensure that H.B. 940 would be the reform that they envisioned and that Kentucky children needed. I am proud to stand before you as the governor of the state that has begun implementation of systematic reform in public education.

Now, we are working closely with President Clinton in taking the national reform agenda further by proposing Goals 2000, a plan to codify the national goals and encourage the states to follow in the footsteps of Kentucky. The president's education initiatives are designed to encourage other states to take the same bold steps that we have taken. And I can assure you, the eyes of the entire nation are on Kentucky. We are recognized as the leading state in education reform.

Our challenge is to accept the mantle of leadership and demonstrate to the citizens of Kentucky and to the rest of the nation that Kentucky can and will fully implement KERA. No matter what the obstacles, we can and we will meet the challenges of education reform.

I had my first lessons in education reform here with you at the Prichard Committee. Like so many of you I looked up to Ed Prichard. Prich was an intellectual giant, who saw clearly Kentucky's need for systematic reform. More than anyone else, it was Ed Prichard who inspired me and so many other Kentuckians to seek lifelong learning opportunities. The image of Ed Prichard that I will carry with me forever is one of an old and proud warrior, close to his final days, standing to address colleagues and adversaries alike to say, "As long as there is one breath left in this old body, I will fight for equal educational opportunities for all of Kentucky's children."

So today we are here to recommit ourselves to the great vision that Ed Prichard had for Kentucky. So what better place to talk about our vision for this administration than here with you, the members and the supporters of the Prichard Committee! Combined with the partnership for Kentucky school reform, the Prichard Committee has been the citizen voice in support of education in the Commonwealth.

Kentucky owes each of you in this audience a debt of gratitude and a promise of support. In 1990, we made a sacred pledge to the people in Kentucky and to future generations of Kentuckians. In 1990, we not only made a vow to seek educational excellence in Kentucky, but we proposed to make the public schools of Kentucky the best in the country. I am here today to say that we must and we will hold true to that promise.

This administration will take the opportunity to extend systematic change instituted by KERA into other areas of state government. We began the important effort to reform Kentucky's health-care system more than a year ago. Today I am pleased to say that we have developed with the General Assembly a process that will lead to a consensus on solving this complex problem. Many of you have heard me state that case for health-care reform before. It will be almost impossible to implement KERA without reforming health care as well.

Consider these numbers for a moment. Health-care costs are rising at a rate of 10 percent to 15 percent per year. If we do nothing to control the rise in health-care costs, next year and beyond we will be paying $100 million a year more for health care in Kentucky. There will be no end in sight. Let's do a little math here; you run the numbers. We are now spending around $1 billion a year on health care in Kentucky. That is increasing by about 10 percent a year, or about $100 million. What would $100 million a year in savings in health care mean to our family resource/youth service centers? How many dollars could we save for extended school-service programs? How many professional-development programs for our teachers? $100 million a year not spent on health care would mean more for the SEEK formula, for instructional materials, for teacher salaries, for technology in the classroom. $100 million a year in savings would pay for how many course offerings and other needed programs at our colleges and universities?

We need systematic reform, not only in education and in health care but throughout all of government. We have pledged during this administration to raise forever the expectations that Kentuckians have of their government. That is why we held the line on KERA in the 1992 session of the General Assembly, and that is why we are doing everything in our power to maintain our commitment to adequate funding for our education reform in the coming fiscal year.

Considering what we are facing, up to perhaps a $300 million shortfall for this fiscal year, I cannot promise that KERA will not be affected by our shortfall. I want to emphasize to all Kentuckians today that we are *all in this together,* and we will all meet this challenge *together*. I will promise you this: maintaining the maximum financial support possible for KERA is our first priority for this year's budget and for the budget we will propose for the coming biennium.

While KERA remains the most far-reaching education reform effort in the country, there is much that remains to be done. To guide our efforts, I am happy that we have talented and imaginative leaders such as all of you working together. As we move forward together in the coming months, we will continue to foster the same atmosphere of trust and cooperation that has been developed among the leaders of our education reform efforts.

One of the many challenges that we face is to fully engage Kentucky's colleges and universities in support of KERA. Another need is to bring a greater focus to our efforts to develop a world-class, high-performance corps of teaching professionals.

In my conversations with Kentucky's teachers, they tell me that they support KERA, and they are willing to go the extra mile to put in the extra hours necessary to meet the new mandates of KERA. But they also tell me that they and those who are currently in training at our colleges of education need more help and support in applying the new concepts in assessment, learning styles, interdisciplinary learning, multi-age grouping, and school-based decision making, just to name a few.

So to meet that need, I will soon be issuing an executive order establishing a task force on teacher preparation, which will work with the Department of Education, the Educational Professional Standards Board, the Council on Higher Education, and our Commonwealth's colleges and universities to further develop our system of teacher preparation. I also expect this new commission to help bridge whatever gap there may be between KERA and Kentucky's schools of education.

When I decided to run for lieutenant governor and then for governor, I was motivated by the belief that people should expect more from their government. Just as KERA raises the expectations we have of Kentucky's students, I believe that we should be raising expectations of Kentucky's government and Kentucky's public officials.

In 1990, we called for systematic reform of the way we educate our children. I am continuing the call from the beginning of this administration for systematic reform of the way we do business in state government. That is why in the first year of this administration we achieved the passage of campaign finance reform. It is why I eliminated myself from the process so we could have gubernatorial succession in Kentucky. It is why we implemented a tough new ethics code for the executive branch. It is why we changed to a more fair and honest way of awarding state contracts. It is why we have fundamentally reformed the selection process for university boards. It is why we have completely restructured our approach to economic development in Kentucky.

To follow up on the progress that we have already made, we have established the Governor's Commission on Quality and Efficiency. In the coming months we are going to be looking for ways for state government to be driven by a mission of quality service delivery, not bureaucracy. I will be looking to the commission to recommend ways of making state government more responsive to the needs of all Kentuckians. The hallmark of this effort will be an expectation for quality and for collaboration and teamwork.

Furthermore, I am going to ask every cabinet secretary to review the management structure of their cabinets. Where it makes sense to flatten the organizational pyramid, we will do it. Where we can involve the state's front-line workers in decisions to foster efficiency and improve quality, we should. Where there can be new linkages and networks across cabinet and agency lines, we will call for increased collaboration. Where we can develop new partnerships with the private sector, we will pursue them.

In short, even during this era of diminishing resources, we should be looking for new, more efficient ways to deliver essential services to our citizens with quality. The goal for all of us who provide services to the public—from universities to hospitals, from Head Start to health departments, from the justice system to social welfare agencies, from the Transportation Cabinet to where the buck finally stops in Kentucky, in the governor's office—is to meet the needs of citizens of this Commonwealth, and not only to meet those needs, but to raise the expectations of our citizens for quality in their government. We will be efficient and honest stewards of tax dollars, and we ask you to join us in building networks and partnerships to accomplish this goal. We need to reinvent our government, to reallocate existing resources, to keep the promise of KERA for the children of the Commonwealth, to provide a government that Kentuckians can trust. We need your help. For, after all, the Prichard Committee *is* Kentucky. Working together, there is no limit to what we can accomplish.[1]

---

1. On July 29, Jones spoke at a scholarship awards ceremony where he also stressed his commitment to education. On November 1, he visited a Shelby County school that housed a technology pilot project, a KERA initiative.

HIGHER EDUCATION REVIEW COMMISSION
September 21, 1993

THANK you for agreeing to spend time on a very important issue, the future of Kentucky higher education. The Commonwealth faces a number of challenges that affect our colleges and universities. Our colleges and universities must play a leadership role in helping solve these problems. A major challenge that I must address is to bring state government into balance. Your organizations must be a part of this effort. Revenues will not be adequate to support government in its current structure and size. Government is too big, too unwieldy, and too inefficient. Emphasis must be placed on making government more efficient and effective. Our focus must be quality. We must get back to basics, understand our fundamental mission, carry out these responsibilities, and evaluate the effectiveness of each activity. These same principles apply to higher education.

When I faced the most recent budget reduction, a number of difficult decisions had to be made. The easy way out was to cut programming across the board. We rejected that approach. Every effort was made to spare education, higher education as well as elementary and secondary education. Through sacrifice by others, higher education was spared further cuts in 1993–94. This reprieve from the latest budget cut must be seen as an opportunity. I know higher education has absorbed budget cuts amounting to 14 percent over the last two or three years. These more than $80 million in cuts have been damaging, and I want to avoid additional damage. I know you do, too.

The opportunity I allude to is the opportunity to address quality and efficiency issues; to find ways to cooperate; to get maximum mileage out of the resources you have. I realized that it would be very difficult for you to address these issues if you were dealing with yet another budget cut. You have dodged that bullet. This is your opportunity to remake higher education in Kentucky. When I met with the university presidents in August, they embraced this opportunity and suggested other issues to address. I appreciate their willingness to get personally involved. There is no doubt about the willingness of your board chairs, either. I considered your abilities and level of commitment in making your appointment.

Failure to seize this opportunity will have dire consequences. We see this system of colleges and universities straining to meet student, community, and economic-development needs. Over the years, constituents have asked you to take on more challenges, to meet more needs, and you have responded. New challenges have been accepted without adequate attention being given to eliminating programs and services in other areas.

Emphasis has been placed on access, and you have been successful. Students have enrolled in record numbers; citizen needs are addressed in a number of locations and program areas. As in other areas of state-related activities, attention must now be focused on quality and effectiveness. Economic realities tell us that expansion must be limited. We have to find ways to live within our means. The burden of paying for services, whether government or higher-education services, cannot be shifted continually to recipients of those services.

Your friends need our help in gaining more support for higher education. I noted Speaker Clarke's comments at the trusteeship conference when he pointed out that higher education has suffered because of its inability to effectively demonstrate its success and value to the Commonwealth. You and I know there are many positive aspects of higher education. I believe in what you do, but I also believe that major changes in the way you operate must occur. The focus must be on specialization, on quality, on performance, on cooperation, and on controlling expenditures.

As a believer in what you do, I have spent some time reviewing your efforts. Joe Prather, Kevin Hable, other staff members, and I have asked the Office for Policy and Management and the Council on Higher Education staffs for various types of information. My review tells me we have strengths to lean on in improving this system.

When I met with university presidents on August 10, I listed several areas that should be addressed. My review has reinforced that belief. The areas that I am asking you to review include:

MISSION REFINEMENT

KENTUCKY is a large, diverse state. Admittedly, we need some amount of duplication. However, the time of being all things to all people has passed. Your focus must be on issues of quality, performance, specialization, and cooperation. There are several issues I am asking that you address here.

Reduce program duplication. I asked to see a listing of academic programs by discipline and number of graduates. The information revealed that we have bachelor's programs duplicated at more than four universities. Many of these programs graduate less than ten students a year. I suggest that you work together to eliminate this type of duplication.

Community-college programs deserve the same scrutiny. The guiding principle must be, "What programs are absolutely necessary and have a track record of graduating sufficient numbers of students?" instead of doing what various groups want.

How many graduate programs do we need? Master's programs are offered across the state, especially in teacher education disciplines.

I encourage you to review the work of the task force on teacher preparation. That group is addressing several issues that may affect your work on program duplication and other issues.

You have my full support in dealing with the issue of professional education. Our goal here must be to produce an adequate number of doctors, dentists, lawyers, and engineers, not to provide access to everyone who wants to enroll. With the exception of law, these programs are expensive to operate. We must refine our commitment in these areas.

I urge you to give special attention to medical and engineering education. The health-care work we are doing tells us that much more attention must be given to training primary-care physicians and physicians who will practice in underserved areas of Kentucky. This is your chance to craft a plan by which this will be accomplished.

A healthy economy has quality, technology-based education at its core. Kentucky needs a top-notch engineering school, one that ranks among the nation's best. Areas of the state need better access to engineering education. You must find innovative ways to achieve these objectives without adding programs around the state.

Strengthen quality. All efforts must accrue to the improvement of quality. College classes cannot accentuate academic rigor if unprepared students are enrolled. Our universities must enroll only well-prepared students. I urge you to send this message to our high schools and their students: If you are unprepared, you cannot enroll at this university. Why would we enroll students at our universities who have not achieved at least a C+ average in high school and at least the statewide average ACT score?

Access can be maintained for interested high-school graduates through our community colleges and community-college programs. As I understand the situation, all universities have or can have community-college programs. These community-college programs plus our fourteen community colleges should provide access and remedy any student deficiencies. I suggest that students not meeting university admissions standards complete at least their first year in one of these community colleges or community-college programs. If successful after one year, their enrollment in university classes is the next step.

Making community colleges the major entry point into higher education places great pressure on you to make sure that students can transfer credits. The General Assembly is interested in this issue, and I know you are working on it. This must be achieved.

Measure student performance. KERA offers higher education good information on measuring student performance. Only qualified students, based on some agreeable standard, should be allowed to progress and graduate. Perhaps only students that have achieved an average score on each part of the ACT exam should be allowed to progress to the junior year. I defer to your expertise here, but student performance must be measured and the results must be used.

I have listed these ideas under mission refinement. If you make a series of changes like I have listed, your schools will be streamlined, committed to cooperation, and based on quality.

EFFICIENCY AND EFFECTIVENESS

EMPHASIS must be placed on improved management techniques, cooperation, and coordination. I will offer a few suggestions here:

Evaluate campus management [and] set efficiency goals. I know that each university has been active in this area. No doubt, the impulse of the presidents and board chairs is to say "we've done this." My response is: "That's a good start." In today's environment this is a continuous process. Institutions of higher education have been granted a substantial amount of autonomy and flexibility by the General Assembly. I agree with these actions; however, you must use this authority to make each institution a model of efficiency and effectiveness.

No division, duty, or individual should be exempt. The administration must be reviewed with the concepts of job restructuring being used. The way faculty uses its time must be reviewed. Goals must be established to reduce the size of administration and to set expectations for how faculty divides their time among teaching, research, and service, with teaching being emphasized.

Your management reviews should include an assessment of your effectiveness in caring for the buildings and equipment on campuses. We cannot allow these physical plants to deteriorate.

Resist expansion. Base necessary expansion on creation of resources internally. Citizen requests are difficult to resist. We have become the victim of being too eager to please, with a shallow revenue base. Maximize existing resources, find ways to cooperate, be innovative, and be cost conscious. I understand that in addition to eight universities and fourteen community-college campuses, there are a dozen or more extended-campus programs around the state. I applaud your effort to meet demand, but question the Commonwealth's ability to support such a system of campuses and programs.

We have more than twenty independent colleges in Kentucky. Let's find ways to use this resource. Making them affordable to our citizens will save taxpayer dollars, improve access, and strengthen organizations that provide jobs and aid communities.

Improve coordination. Virtually every suggestion that I will make today requires improved cooperation, the development of statewide strategies, and the application of innovative approaches. I have great confidence in our presidents and in our governing boards. However, I also realize that improved statewide leadership is necessary. Maintaining campus autonomy while strengthening the role of the Council on Higher Education is the best way to achieve this objective.

The council must be given a stronger leadership role in seeing that these reforms are carried out, in board member orientation, in providing statewide direction, in mediating institutional interests, and in assuring continued emphasis on quality and performance. Improved coordination can be achieved while recognizing the value of campus-based decision-making and management flexibility. Campuses must exercise autonomy within clearly defined statewide objectives and purpose.

FUNDING CHANGES

THE improvements that I have suggested can be achieved and sustained only if funding arrangements are supportive. I am asking you to make funding changes that recognize fiscal realities and support and promote the changes proposed. My ideas here include:

Protect existing funding levels. I realize the difficulties you have faced as a result of budget reductions. If we can make the changes I have outlined, I will recommend that, at a minimum, existing nominal dollar levels will be maintained for each institution in the upcoming biennium. Savings that you achieve will be yours to commit to enhanced efforts. Also, I will consider funding increases within fiscal realities to implement the decisions you make.

[Regarding] transition funding [in the] 1994–96 biennium, your responsibility here will be to advise me on how we make the transition to a new funding arrangement. For the 1994–96 biennium, I propose that funding increases be tied directly to restructuring of missions and quality improvement effort. Higher-education support for KERA also continues to be a major priority of mine. Funding emphasis will be placed on KERA initiatives as well as cooperative endeavors such as the implementation and utilization of telecommunications technology. Capital funding will emphasize the importance of protecting the state's investment in campus facilities and equipment.

[Regarding] funding changes [in the] 1994–95 interim, the restructured higher-education system you propose must be linked to a funding approach developed through a review of the higher education funding formula in the 1994–95 interim. Principles guiding that review must be developed by you. They must include an emphasis on performance and achievement of objectives included here. Funding enrollments should be de-emphasized, especially the enrollment of unprepared students. Occasional students should be funded in a public service category, with degree-seeking students receiving most attention.

The implementation of the accountability program included in Senator [Ed] Ford's bill will provide good information on which to base a performance-funding-oriented formula. Emphasis should be placed on funding basic mission-related responsibilities. Academic success of students is another important criterion to be included. In simple terms, the funding formula must promote the decisions you make; however, you run the risk of losing credibility and consideration of your basic needs if the formula generates an unrealistic statement of need or fails to carry out a reform agenda.

At this point, I will get out of your way so you can begin work. I know you cannot make all necessary changes in two months, but you can make basic decisions and deliver a plan to me that sets the appropriate direction. The ideas I put before you today aren't new. They don't require a lot of study and research. I like to say that this is a "fact-facing" rather than a "fact-finding" mission.

Make meaningful recommendations so that appropriate action may be taken. Legislation may be necessary in some areas. The appropriations process must include your recommendations. We have the legislative leadership on this commission to get that job done. I will make appropriate budgetary and legislative recommendations to carry out new ideas. . . .

COMMUNITY SERVICE COMMISSION
Frankfort / February 14, 1994

I'D LIKE to welcome you here this morning to your first meeting and thank you for agreeing to serve on the Kentucky Community Service Commission. As you may know, the word "service" means a great deal to me. It reminds me of a person who inspired me as a young man, John F. Kennedy. One phrase from his inaugural speech has stuck with me throughout my life: "Ask not what your country can do for you, ask what you can do for your country."

I think what is really unique about this commission is that it will give young people the opportunity to do something for their country, and, at the same time, the country will do something for them. As members of this commission, you have the opportunity to help further the education of a young person who otherwise might not be able to afford it. And you have the opportunity to provide needed help to a great many schools, groups, and nonprofit agencies which desperately need manpower.

Of course, the reason we're here in the first place is because of President Clinton's National and Community Service Trust Act of 1993. Under his national service initiative, a student could become eligible for more than $4,600 in educational help, plus a minimum-wage salary, in exchange for a year of full-time community service.

Under a formula that's been set up, Kentucky stands to receive nearly $750,000 to help those young people who want to help themselves. But if this commission is successful in the competitive application process, Kentucky could receive as much as $2,000,000. And, of course, I expect you to be extremely competitive and extremely successful.

But it's up to you to get the state's mechanism into place. I know you have a lot to cover today. So I'll leave you with this one last thought. Consider yourselves "the Commission of Opportunity." You have the opportunity to make the leaders of tomorrow. If you can create the opportunity for young people to see firsthand how they can make a difference in the lives of others in this world, and give those young people the opportunity to help themselves at the same time, you could be creating a whole new generation of young people who will dedicate themselves to public service. And then you will be able to see how much difference you've been able to make. And that should make you very proud.[1]

---

1. On November 2, 1993, Jones encouraged students at Bellarmine College to become involved in public service.

UNIVERSITY OF KENTUCKY KING LIBRARY NEWS CONFERENCE
Lexington / May 23, 1994

AS YOU all know, Frankfort is the capital of Kentucky. But the University of Kentucky Library is the "intellectual capital" of this Commonwealth. The library is the source of wealth for the people of Kentucky, perhaps the richest resource we have, because students who walk through these doors, walk out richer in intelligence and ability. They walk out empowered to improve life in Kentucky, in our country, and, yes, in the world. If knowledge is power, the UK library is the power center of this Commonwealth. Just think of the thousands of people who have used this library over the years, and the contributions they have been able to make to society.

But the time has now come to invest in our future; to improve the intellectual capital of our people; and to properly nurture future leaders. We must build a new library for the University of Kentucky. We must provide more room for students to study and learn. We must put this university in a more competitive position to attract more outstanding students and faculty members. We must take advantage of current technology and position ourselves for the twenty-first century to pave the way for the information highway to run right through this Commonwealth.

We must meet the needs of the hundreds of thousands of people throughout Kentucky who use the information and the growing database that the UK library has to offer: physicians in rural areas; public libraries throughout the state; businesses; agricultural extension agents and 4-H agents; and public and private educational institutions, including the UK community colleges.

Some people will tell you we cannot afford it right now. I say, how can we not afford it? How can we not afford to make a solid investment in the intellectual capital of our young people? How can we not afford to continue the progress of the Kentucky Education Reform Act, at a time when we are starting to see real progress being made in our students' thinking and writing skills? How can we not afford to position ourselves right now, with interest rates as low as they are, to take advantage of the technology of the future?

The people who say we cannot afford to do this are wrong! Thousands of Kentuckians are voting for this project with their pocketbooks. An incredible 80 percent of UK faculty and staff, more than ten thousand people, have given their own money to make this library become a reality. Also, UK students have been investing money in their own future by raising money through their own "pack the stacks" campaign. And thousands of people throughout the state have given money, from a few cents to $5,000,000, to the library campaign.

Many of those people are here today, again to show how important this is for the future of Kentucky. Together, you have contributed more than $20,000,000 to the library campaign, including $12,000,000 for this project, and $8,000,000 for book endowments! That is phenomenal! And we cannot, and will not, let you down!

Our new budget proposal allocates just over $2.3 million in cash in this next fiscal year; and then, in fiscal year '96, $4.6 million per year over a twenty-year bond issue. In addition, we have included in our proposal the construction of a new UK mechanical engineering building. It's critical to the enhancement of the engineering program here at the University of Kentucky; in fact, a crucial final piece in the puzzle that will allow us to provide the best engineering program possible. It's not possible to operate quality programs without a quality foundation, and this new mechanical engineering building will provide that foundation. Quality education leads to quality, high-paying jobs. And quality, high-paying jobs improve our economic base. This is another project in which people—especially our employers—are showing their support through their donations. The employers know how important it is to have highly trained workers who will be able to compete with the finest minds in the world. And many of those employers have donated money to show that they are investing in their future workforce.

This mechanical engineering building will help empower Kentucky students to be able to compete with the best. As part of our plan, we will achieve this goal by committing $738,000 a year over a twenty-year bond issue, starting in fiscal year '96. Again it's an investment in our students that will pay back great dividends in the future.

One other project that I'd like to bring to your attention is also critically important to the people of Kentucky because it will help educate and train Kentuckians to land well-paying jobs. And that is the Danville, Kentucky, tech building. As you may know, I'm going to Japan tomorrow to seek out new businesses to move to Kentucky. And the last time I went to Japan, I asked a company executive how Kentucky workers measured up. And this company executive told me, Kentucky workers are *the best*.

This new Kentucky tech building in Danville will ensure that we continue to train our people to be the best. That way, we can keep attracting new businesses to Kentucky, and we can keep providing our existing businesses with top-quality employees. We are prepared to commit $682,000 a year over a twenty-year bond issue for this project, beginning in fiscal year '96.

These projects that I have mentioned to you today are all sound investments in our future. And with interest rates still low, we have a golden opportunity to position Kentucky for the twenty-first century. I ask you to contact your legislator and other legislators throughout the state and let them know how crucial these programs are for our future.

It's important for you to know that we are not raising taxes, and we are not mortgaging our future. We are paying for all three projects with money that the economists say will be there from year to year. It's also important for you to know that these projects are not pork. They're vital nourishment for Kentucky, and they will ensure a more intelligent, more prepared, and more vital Kentucky workforce for years to come. Please help us get these projects passed.

STARS SCHOOL GRANT PRESS CONFERENCE
Frankfort / August 24, 1994

It is my pleasure to announce that Kentucky has been chosen to receive a $3.6 million grant from the U.S. Department of Education Star Schools Program to expand our Kentucky tele-linking network. The impact of this grant will be far greater because we are going to match each federal dollar with state and local funds to create a total pool of $7.3 million.

Officials of the U.S. Department of Education had only one multi-million-dollar grant to award for the development of a statewide educational network, and they made the right choice. They chose Kentucky. Through this grant the Commonwealth is also eligible to receive an additional $4 million for the Kentucky tele-linking network next year. This is a great honor and certainly a tribute to the strides we are making to reform education in Kentucky.

The receipt of this grant is also a testament to the hard work of our strong collaborative efforts with our partners in state government. When I took office, I pledged to make state government more efficient and more effective. Collaboration is required to achieve that goal. If government is to serve the citizens of our Commonwealth more effectively, we have to break down the traditional barriers of bureaucracy and get our agencies and employees to talk to each other and work together. The success of this grant is the result of that kind of collaboration and cooperation.

Representatives from the Education, Arts and Humanities Cabinet, the Finance and Administration Cabinet, the Council on Higher Education, the Kentucky Department of Education, and our universities and local schools are here today, because they all played an important role in the development of this project. Together, these partners crafted a grant proposal and submitted it to the U.S. Department of Education in April. In a total statewide effort, Kentucky's congressional leaders gave this proposal their full support.

Last week Senator Ford[1] received a call from U.S. Secretary of Education Richard Riley,[2] notifying us that we had become the big winner in the Star Schools Competition. Rather than give a technical explanation of this exciting, cutting-edge technology and how it will be used by our schools, we thought it would be more effective to provide a demonstration. We have invited students from Fulton County High School to join us today, via tele-link. Fulton County

High was the first public school in the state to be connected to one of our eight regional universities, Murray State University, on the Kentucky tele-linking network. . . .

---

1. Wendell Hampton Ford (1924–), born in Daviess County; attended University of Kentucky; U.S. Army; Maryland School of Insurance; Democratic Kentucky state senator, 1965–67; lieutenant governor of Kentucky, 1967–71; governor of Kentucky, 1971–74; U.S. senator, 1974–99.

2. Richard W. Riley (1933–), B.A. *cum laude,* Furman University, 1954; J.D., University of South Carolina, 1959; U.S. Naval officer; Democratic state representative and senator, South Carolina, 1963–77; governor of South Carolina, 1979–87; U.S. secretary of education (1993–2001).

SCHOOL-TO-WORK CONFERENCE
Louisville / September 20, 1994

I'VE HAD the opportunity to speak at several conferences, but this is one of the most important. It's important because Kentucky *must* have a highly trained and productive workforce to be successful in an increasingly competitive global economy, and you, as key players in our state's school-to-work initiatives, are helping develop that workforce.

Although we are focused on our own state's school-to-work transition, we should recognize that this is a nationwide concern. Most American workers do not have skills equal to the skills of workers in Western Europe and the Pacific Rim, our nation's major competitors. Eleven percent of all Americans ages sixteen to twenty-four have not completed high school. Also, according to a Harris poll, employers turned down five of every six young people who applied for a job in the early 1990s because they lacked the required skills.

With passage of the School-to-Work Opportunities Act of 1994, the federal government made a commitment to enhance the skills of Americans by building on what Kentucky and other states already had accomplished in school reform and workforce development. Kentucky is recognized as a leader in education and job-training initiatives and, as you are aware, was one of just eight states to receive an initial school-to-work implementation grant.

Those who put our state's proposal together did an excellent job and certainly deserve our compliments and thanks. It's important to emphasize that Kentucky's school-to-work initiatives have been a team effort. In the past, society has usually looked to single institutions to solve problems, but we're now living in a "shared power" world where complex issues can go beyond the capacity and jurisdiction of a single organization and need to be addressed by several groups that must share the power and resources to get things done.

The strength of Kentucky's school-to-work proposal—and the reason we believe it was among the first to be funded—is its level of collaboration and its shared vision. We have a public/private partnership among large and small businesses, labor, education, and government in school-to-work, and it's obvious we have a winning team. It's also important to note that people who live and work in the various labor market areas are the folks deciding how *local* school-to-work transition programs will work. This makes good management sense, because local residents know best what meets local needs.

School-to-work is a system that will provide maximum opportunities to all students and will be a key component of Kentucky's focus on lifelong learning. It will lower school dropout rates and help our young people participate effectively in society. School-to-work is vital to the preparation of our emerging workforce and therefore to Kentucky's economic vitality.

Kentuckians have always been recognized for their strong work ethic, but just working harder isn't enough anymore. We've got to work smarter as well. With school-to-work and other Kentucky initiatives being implemented, our state can soon boast of its world-class workforce. We can announce that:

1. If you want workers who construct the best buildings, manufacture the best products, and provide the most efficient services, come to Kentucky;
2. If you want workers who lead the world in quality, craftsmanship, and dedication, come to Kentucky;
3. If you want workers who have vision, determination, and a work ethic second to none, come to Kentucky;
4. And if you want workers who are highly skilled, quality focused, and performance driven, come to Kentucky. . . .

WORKFORCE PARTNERSHIP COUNCIL
Frankfort / November 28, 1994

TODAY I have the pleasant task of presenting checks to local labor market areas, checks that will help fund school-to-work efforts across our state. The awards being distributed today total $2.8 million and represent part of the $24 million Kentucky is expected to receive during the next five years as part of its school-to-work federal grant. These awards typify the positive workforce initiatives which have recently occurred in Kentucky. Let me give you some examples:

1. Kentucky was one of only eight states to receive an initial school-to-work implementation grant, and we were the only southern state on that list;
2. We were the first to hold a statewide school-to-work conference;
3. We recently received a $200,000 planning grant for a one-stop career center;
4. We expanded our school-to-work partnership council by forming what's known as the Kentucky Workforce Partnership Council and establishing an entity that can address such issues as school-to-work and one-stop career center.

These awards also demonstrate what can be accomplished when we all work together. In the past, we've depended on a single institution to solve problems. But we now live in a "shared power" world, where complex issues can exceed the capacity of a single organization, and where these issues need to be addressed by several groups that share the responsibility and resources needed to get things done.

Those of you receiving grants today are examples of what can be accomplished by this type of teamwork. You've involved business and industry, government, labor, and education in your local school-to-work efforts, and your willingness to collaborate has resulted in your success. It is very important to the economic vitality of your community and our state that you continue to be successful as you implement a school-to-work program. It's important because the availability of a skilled workforce is a top priority when companies decide where to build new plants and what existing plants to expand. It's important that Kentucky have a highly trained and productive workforce to be successful in an increasingly competitive global economy. It's important because most future new jobs will require the types of technical skills that an effective school-to-work initiative will provide. And perhaps most important of all, your success will have an extremely positive effect on Kentucky's young people.

As school-to-work is fully implemented, the school dropout rate will dramatically decrease, education and skill levels will significantly increase, and thousands more students will have the opportunity to pursue personally satisfying and financially rewarding careers. Kentucky's future lies with its young people. Through your foresight, dedication, and commitment, you are helping our young people prepare for the years to come. Thank you for your part in ensuring that Kentucky's future is in skilled hands.

"COME SEE FOR YOURSELF" SCHOOL VISIT
Sandy Hook / December 6, 1994

THANK you, Secretary Jelsma, for that gracious introduction. We're here today because your support for education is key to the success of all our children. With your involvement, as parents, grandparents, business and community leaders, teachers, neighbors, and volunteers, we will be able to reach our educational goals for Kentucky children. With your support, our children will experience academic success and attain the basic skills needed to ensure that they will become productive members of this community. Because there is nothing more important than community involvement in public education, I want you to have the opportunity to see the progress we are making in our community schools.

As public facilities, our schools are always open to you, and I hope that you will never hesitate to walk across a campus, observe a classroom, or stop in to say hello to a student, teacher, or principal. Today, I want to take this special opportunity to join with some of the vital members of this community, the bank manager, the grocer, your hairdresser, the county extension agent, and parents, so that together we can see for ourselves the progress we are making in our schools. Once we see what's going on, we can challenge ourselves to become more involved.

For the first time since the passage of the Kentucky Education Reform Act, the Commonwealth has received federal funds to support our education initiatives. This year, the bulk of those funds, available through the goals 2000 Educate America Act, will be used to support parental involvement and public-engagement projects across the state. Of the $1.4 million available to the Commonwealth this year, nearly $500,000 will be distributed in grants to local school districts for parental involvement and public-engagement projects.

This commitment of funds should indicate to you just how important you are. We need you to become involved; you must be involved if we are to succeed and if our children are to succeed. Make no mistake, we are making progress.

As we all know, the Kentucky Education Reform Act is a major initiative that addresses school finances, school governance, and school curriculum. We are now four years into our reforms, and sometimes we forget where we were before its passage. We cannot forget the extreme inequity that existed in school districts across the Commonwealth. Here in Elliott County in 1989 the total revenue available to schools was $3.9 million. But today, because of the new funding formulas developed through KERA, there is now $6.5 million available to this school district—an increase of nearly 70 percent.

State revenue for Elliott County since that time has increased by nearly 63 percent—from $3 million to $5 million. Not only did state revenue increase significantly, but the local board of education stepped up to the plate as well. Since the passage of KERA, Elliott County has built a new high school. The average teacher's salary has increased 20 percent, from $23,417 to $28,259.

Elliott County has reached the technology standards established by KERA and continues to make extraordinary gains. The 1993–94 KIRIS scores indicate that Elliott County is one of the school districts with the biggest gains and is set to receive awards from the Kentucky Department of Education.

This summer, the school district received grant funds for its first youth services center. So education is improving in Elliott County, just as it is throughout the state. In fact, 80 percent of our public schools in Kentucky improved on tests scored in the past year. That is a positive change. And now, it is my pleasure today to announce another positive change for this school community.

Through a competitive process, Elliott County has received $45,000 in year-end funding to support a new family-resource center that will serve this community. I would like to present this official notification letter from the family resource youth services center branch to Superintendent Eugene Binion. Your efforts to provide support for families and children in this community have not gone unrecognized. You have reason to be proud. I want to thank everyone here for coming. And now it is time to "come and see for yourself."

"COME SEE FOR YOURSELF" SCHOOL VISIT
Southgate / March 2, 1995

WE'RE here today because your support for education is the key to the success of all of our children. Without your involvement as parents, grandparents, business and community leaders, teachers, neighbors, volunteers, we will not reach our educational goals for Kentucky children. Without your support, our children will not experience academic success or attain the basic skills necessary to ensure that they will become productive members of this community.

Because your support for public education cannot be underestimated, I want you to have the opportunity to see for yourselves the progress we are making in our community schools. As public facilities, our schools are always open to you, and I hope that you will never hesitate to come to this campus, to observe a classroom, or stop in to say hello to a student, teacher, or principal. Just stop by the principal's office first!

But I wanted to take this special opportunity to bring together vital members of this community—the bank manager, the veterinarian, your hairdresser, the dry cleaner, and parents, so that we can see for ourselves the progress we are making in our local schools and to challenge you to become more involved. Make no mistake, we are making progress.

As we all know, the Kentucky Education Reform Act is reform that addresses virtually every aspect of how a school operates. We are now four years into our reform effort, and sometimes we forget where we were before its passage. We often forget the extreme inequity that existed in school districts across the Commonwealth.

Here at Southgate Elementary in 1989, the total revenue available to schools was just over $846,000. I'm sure that Superintendent Sandfoss[1] can tell us many stories about the circumstances that existed in this school district at that time. But today, because of the new funding formulas developed through KERA, there is now nearly

$1.3 million available to this school district. That's better than a 50 percent increase. Since the passage of KERA, Southgate Independent schools are in the process of adding four new classrooms and making major renovations needed to be in compliance with the Americans with Disabilities Act. The average teacher's salary has increased 20 percent.

Southgate has reached the technology standards established by KERA and continues to make extraordinary gains. The local school board purchased computers for the classrooms, and they have further enhanced the educational program. Two days a week, the computers are set up in the auditorium for large-group computer use. The 1994–94 KIRIS scores indicate that Southgate Elementary exceeded the thresholds established by the state board and is set to receive awards from the Kentucky Department of Education.

I think you'll see that education is improving in this district, just as it is throughout the state. And the efforts of this school community are continuing to contribute to positive educational changes. Southgate has joined together with Bellevue and Silver Grove to create the Tri-City Family Resource Center. By working together, these districts are able to pool their resources, expand services to families, and help more children. The Family Resource Center provides the children in this district with school nurse services, family intervention services, and some adult training classes.

I would like to commend Superintendent Sandfoss on the great achievements being made here at Southgate. Your efforts to provide support for families and children in this community have not gone unrecognized. You have reason to be proud.

I want to thank everyone here for coming. Now it is time to "come and see for yourself."

---

1. Bernard Sandfoss, superintendent of Southgate Independent School District, Campbell County, Kentucky.

SCOTT COUNTY HIGH SCHOOL GROUND BREAKING
Georgetown / March 6, 1995

LAST Friday, I was at the Toyota Motor Manufacturing Plant, just a few miles from here. We were announcing a new promotional campaign in which Toyota is participating that will benefit tourism in Kentucky. Today, we are breaking ground on a new high school for Scott County, a construction project that would not be possible without Toyota's involvement.

In Toyota, Scott County and Kentucky have the ultimate "corporate citizen," a company that is determined to contribute to the community in which it resides. They have enriched this area, not just by providing jobs, but by helping provide a better way of life. And when this community really needed more space to educate its young people, Toyota stepped up and said, "Let us help." That is the type of company Toyota is, and we appreciate what they've done.

Of course, it's not just a "one-way street." Several years ago, when I was in Japan visiting with officials from Toyota, I had lunch with Dr. Toyoda,[1] and I asked him, "How do your workers in Kentucky compare with the rest of your labor force?" He answered without hesitation, "They are the best."

So Toyota has been good for the people of Scott County, and the people of Scott County have been good for Toyota. It is a perfect match. And it will continue to be a good match because of the young people who will be trained in this building that we break ground for today.

We are educating the workforce of tomorrow, the people who will have to compete with workers throughout the world. And we must train them well to get ready. Having the proper facilities is just one piece of the puzzle. But having a superior educational system is more important. That's why I am so supportive of the Kentucky Education Reform Act. With it, we are laying the groundwork for Kentucky to have the best educational system in America. Yes, it takes time. And yes, some alterations will be made along the way.

But KERA is working. The fact that 95 percent of all Kentucky public schools have improved their test scores in the last two years is proof of that. Students are learning more, and much of the credit for that must go to our teachers. Teachers are working harder, and they're finding new and innovative ways of engaging a student's curiosity. And we owe our teachers a tremendous debt of gratitude.

There's one other person that I want to praise, and that is your superintendent, Dr. Dallas Blankenship.[2] He's done a tremendous job of coming up with a creative and appropriate way to finance this building, just as he has found creative solutions to other problems in the Scott County school system. That's why he is regarded as one of the best in his field.

In a recent newspaper article, Dr. Blankenship is quoted as saying, "I truly think we're going to have the best school system in the state." With his leadership, with Toyota's commitment, and with the hard work by students, teachers, and the people of Scott County, I have no doubt that you will prove him right, and that you will have the best school system in the state.

---

1. Dr. Tatsuro Toyoda (1929–), educated at Tokyo University; Toyota Motor Corp., 1953– ; exec. vice-president of international operations, 1988–92; president, 1992–95. *Who's Who in the World 1995,* 12th ed. (New Providence, N.J., 1994).

2. Dr. Dallas J. Blankenship (1947–), A.B., Marshall University, 1969; M.A., Marshall University, 1971; Ed.D., West Virginia University, 1975; superintendent of Scott County Schools, Georgetown, Kentucky.

MONROE COUNTY SCHOOL VISIT
Tompkinsville / April 10, 1995

I AM surrounded today by champions. We have the Lady Falcons basketball team, which won the state championship in the Class "A" tournament in Richmond, back in February. And we have the Lady Falcons' championship coaching staff: head coach Tony Harlan, assistants Lisa Newton and Dawn Harbison, and athletic director Sam Clark. We have the varsity cheerleading team, winners of the Class "A" state championship, and their sponsors Debbie Wiland and Dana Gillenwater. We have the Monroe County High School marching band, Class A state fair champions, and band directors Ken Holbrook and Terri Collins. We have the Monroe County Academic team, the Class "A" state champions, and their coaches,

Louis Carter and Karen Linkous. We have Machell Hale and Chandra Maxey, the winner and first runner-up of the statewide essay contest on "the war against drugs." From the middle school, we have Kerri Beth Myers, who won the state savings bond poster contest and, along with it, a $1,000 savings bond! Also from the middle school, we have Sara Carter, winner of the statewide essay contest on Americanism. These are amazing accomplishments!

But there are other champions in this audience today. Each one of you is a champion. Maybe you didn't dribble a ball, lead a cheer, play a musical instrument, write an essay, or have the correct answer on the academic team. But each of you studied harder, learned more, and made your schools better. And that is more important than anything else. The numbers show the facts.

The KERA test scores show that every school in Monroe County improved. That means every student learned more, every teacher taught more, and every administrator worked more. KERA is making champions of a lot of Kentucky students. Test scores show that 95 percent of all Kentucky schools improved their test scores in the past two years. And a new study shows Kentucky ranks number seven in the country in the number of computers available for each student. And Kentucky is outpacing the rest of the country in getting ready for the high-tech world of the twenty-first century.

So there are a lot of people throughout the state who are working to provide you with the tools that will help you be a success. It's up to you to take advantage of those tools, because your success here will make you champions in life. As you continue your education, or as you enter the workforce, you will be competing with the best and the brightest from all over the world. And by working hard today, you will win that championship tomorrow. You'll get the top grades, and you'll get the top-paying jobs, because you will be prepared for the future.

Students, when that happens, you need to remember your parents, your teachers, your high-school principal George Wilson, your middle-school principal Larry Moore, your superintendent James Graves, and all the people who have put in the extra effort to help you succeed. They are your champions.[1]

---

1. In a speech on March 13, Jones congratulated the Governor's Cup Award winners at a ceremony in Louisville. He credited KERA for the improvement in Kentucky's educational system, shown by the large increase in students' involvement and success in statewide academic com-

petitions; in 1995, seventeen thousand students from nearly six hundred schools participated. In a speech on April 20, Jones congratulated the members of the State Advisory Panel for Exceptional Children on their work to help the disabled; he noted that Kentucky was ranked seventh in the country in educational technology systems.

FAMILY LITERACY CONFERENCE
Louisville / April 24, 1995

I CAME here today to welcome you and to thank you for doing such an important job. Family literacy programs are very important. They're important to our communities, important to our states, and important to our nation.

They're important because literacy provides the foundation for all education and training, and a highly trained workforce is critical to economic vitality. For example, before we can train people in electronics technology, robotics, or computer programming, they must be literate. Before we train people to assume the responsibility required of today's workforce, where each worker is individually responsible for meeting production goals, delivery dates, and quality standards, they must be literate. Since literacy is the foundation of all knowledge, it can also be considered the foundation of economic vitality—economic vitality for individuals, for families, and for nations.

Permit me to brag a little about Kentucky. Family literacy is a priority in our Commonwealth, and we're very proud that the Pace Program was an idea of Sharon Darling,[1] president of the National Center, who helped develop the concept while working for adult education in Kentucky. Kentucky's Pace Program is a statutory, state-funded initiative and has served as a national model. Kentucky and other states also are working on family-preservation efforts, and literacy is a crucial part of helping families.

Through your family literacy programs, you are providing educational services to both the current and emerging workforce. You're also ensuring that parents have the skills to support their children's educational efforts. This is significant because research has shown that the educational level of parents has a direct relationship to the educational achievements of the child. It also should be noted that family literacy programs help achieve such national "Goals 2000" objectives as school readiness, adult literacy, lifelong learning, and parent participation.[2]

---

1. Sharon Darling, president and founder of National Center for Family Literacy; 1998, Albert Schweitzer Prize for Humanitarianism.

2. On February 10, Jones spoke to the Advisory Council for Adult Education and Literacy in Frankfort about the importance of basic education and technical skills.

ASHLAND OIL TEACHER ACHIEVEMENT CEREMONY

Frankfort / May 8, 1995

I WANT to echo the praise that has already been heaped upon the outstanding teachers we are honoring today. I've said before that I believe our teachers have one of the most important jobs around. They are preparing our next generation of leaders. And it's days such as these that I know our future is in good hands.

Education in Kentucky has made great strides in the past few years. Ninety-five percent of our schools have experienced higher scores in the most rigorous testing conducted in the entire nation. Kentucky currently ranks seventh in the country in the number of computers available for students. And in the upcoming special session we will address ways to put even more money into computer technology in our schools, so Kentucky students will have the tools necessary to compete to be the best in the world.

We've also been able to fully fund, for the first time, local building programs and pupil transportation programs across Kentucky. So there's no doubt, we are moving in the right direction. And it's good to know there are corporate citizens in Kentucky, such as Ashland Inc., who share our dedication to improving the quality of education in the Commonwealth.

For seven years Ashland has presented awards of $2,500 to ten outstanding teachers in Kentucky. Beyond that, Ashland has pledged its continuing support for the education reform efforts that are under way in Kentucky. This company's public stand in support of education is an outstanding example for others to follow.

I want to publicly thank Ashland for its commitment to the students and teachers of Kentucky. Now, to the most important people in this room today, the award recipients, I want you to know that all Kentuckians are very proud of you and what you are doing for our students. As educators you know the importance of a good education. An education is essential in preparing informed citizens, an excellent workforce, and stronger families. That's why you and thousands of other teachers who are just as dedicated are so important to Kentuckians. You are receiving special recognition today. But we all know that the greatest rewards you receive come on a daily basis as you watch the development of the young people whose lives you touch. Keep up the great job you are doing. . . .

KENTUCKY TECH SCHOLARSHIP AWARDS PROGRAM

Frankfort / May 16, 1995

As I look at these outstanding young people who are receiving scholarships here today, I'm reminded that, not too long ago, people thought a technical school was for those who didn't have the ability to succeed in college. Unfortunately, that erroneous concept probably prevented a lot of talented students from pursuing technical careers.

Here's an example, and it's a true story. A man who works as a manager for a large plant in Western Kentucky tells how a high aptitude test [score] indicated he should consider a technical career, perhaps plumbing. He was very excited about the possibility of being a plumber, but his parents opposed the idea, insisting that he attend a traditional four-year university. He honored his parents' wishes, graduated from college with a B.A. degree, and makes a good salary. But this man says that his income doesn't come close to the money earned by the local plumbing contractor. And he's reminded of this every day when he drives past the plumber's $500,000 home. Today that plant manager is a strong supporter of technical education and the Kentucky Tech System, and still wonders if he should have been a plumber.

Actually, it's not too late for that man to study plumbing. There are college graduates now enrolled in the Kentucky Tech System because they finally realized something you scholarship winners already know: that Kentucky Tech provides education and training that lead to good jobs that pay good wages. As a matter of fact, enrollment in some Kentucky Tech schools has recently increased by as much as 50 percent, because Kentuckians are recognizing the value of technical training.

Technical training provides you with a valuable possession that no one can ever take away, a skill. How important are skills? The skills of our forefathers helped build this nation. America's skills have brought our country back from economic depression, protected our democratic form of government during two world wars, and given our citizens the highest standard of living. Skills can provide citizens the highest standard of living. Skills can provide a plumber with a $500,000 house.

It's obvious that, as winners of these scholarships, you know the importance of skills and are proud of your abilities. We're also proud of your skills, but most of all, we're proud of you.

MILTON ACADEMY GRADUATION
Boston, Massachusetts / June 9, 1995

I WANT to thank the Milton Academy[1] for inviting me to deliver this commencement address. More importantly, though, I want to thank Milton for the wonderful opportunities it has given to each of you. I also want to thank Lucy for having the courage to come hear her father give this address. If I had been given the same opportunity at the same age, I probably would have been a no-show. I am certain that today you are feeling a number of emotions; among them, happiness at the prospect of finally graduating; sadness at the prospect of leaving your friends; a little nervousness, and perhaps fear, at the uncertainty of what will happen in the future; and at the same time, excitement and enthusiasm about what could happen in the future.

In the past twelve years of schooling, you have been given a strong foundation on which you now stand, and on which you will build the rest of your life. You will learn to deal with both success and failure. You will learn how to make difficult choices and how to live with the choices you have made. You will decide what you will do with your life and what you will not do. And you will have to decide whether you will change the course of destiny; that is a possibility and must be a conscious decision on your part.

Up to now, you may think you've just learned a lot of useless information. You may think you're like the college student who needed a short, two-hour course to fill out his schedule. The only class that fit was in a subject called wildlife zoology, so he signed up for that class. After the first week, the professor gave the class a test. He passed out a sheet of paper divided into squares. In each square was a carefully drawn picture of some birds' legs. No bodies, no feet, just legs. The test asked students to identify the birds by looking at their legs. The student sat and stared at the test and got more and more angry. Finally, he stomped up to the front of the classroom and threw the test on the professor's desk. "This is the worst test I have ever taken," said the student. "It's totally absurd." The professor looked up and replied, "Young man, you have just flunked this test. What is your name?" The student looked him squarely in the eye, pulled up his pants to show the professor his legs, and said, "You tell me!" Some of the information you have learned has no doubt appeared to be useless. But you will be surprised at the long-term value of the process of learning such information.

Millions of people have come before you in life, have graduated from high school, gone on to college and professional careers, and they have all had basic information and similar preparation as you now have. Maybe not quite as good, but similar. However, I believe that what makes the real difference in a person's life is his or her attitude. People who are optimists, who have a positive attitude, tend to be more successful because they take control of their lives. They refuse to allow themselves to be brought down by negativism or constant pessimism.

In today's world, that is easier said than done. There was a story recently in the newspaper about a poll that had been taken that shows the public is extremely cynical about American institutions. The poll found that only 18 percent of the public believes that honesty and ethical standards in Washington are high. That same poll showed only one in three Americans thinks the CEOs of major corporations are ethical and honest, and only half of Americans think religious leaders have high ethics. Some of this cynicism may be understandable, but where does this rampant mistrust and pessimism come from? Let me offer this idea as one possibility. You wake up in the morning, and you turn on the radio. The news on the radio is all about murders, rapes, robberies, corruption, payoffs, and the like. You can change stations, but you still get the same news. So you turn on the morning television news shows, and you see the same things you've just heard on radio. So you turn off the TV and open the newspaper, and you read the same things you've just heard. On the way to work or school, you hear on talk radio how everything is wrong, how crooked all politicians are, and how people are cheating the system and getting something for free.

Throughout the day, at every opportunity, you are bombarded by the same negative news. And when you go home at night, you face it all again. I'm convinced that a steady diet of negative news day in and day out can greatly distort your perception of life and can leave you depressed and cynical, if you allow it to happen. Yet, do you remember the last time you saw or heard something positive on the news? It happens, but not very often.

There seems to be a prevailing attitude in much of the media that if it is not negative or bizarre it isn't news. This constant dose of negativism is taking its toll on our society. Don't allow this to continue. The news should be reported fairly and honorably. If it is good it should be reported as good news. If it is bad, it should be reported as bad news. The public deserves the truth. It's not very complicated. We must all make this reasonable demand of those who report the news. For all the good that our news media does by serving as "the fourth estate," I believe that is one area where it is failing us right now. I do not believe that "freedom of speech" means a "freedom *from* responsibility."

If you listen to some of the talk-show hosts on radio, you hear them constantly attacking the president of the United States, the first lady, and anyone else who might not agree with them politically. These talk-show hosts badger people into believing that only *they* have the solutions for this country's problems. They have developed an "in your face" kind of mentality that is terribly destructive. They have painted liberals as the enemy of mankind and have twisted the value of a social conscience. Look up the definition of the word "liberal" in the dictionary, and here's what you find: "Liberal: favoring progress and reform. Open-minded, tolerant." Is this supposed to be bad? Is it wrong to favor progress and reform? Is it wrong to be open-minded or tolerant? Of course not.

Certainly we must hold people accountable for their actions. However we must not forget the most basic Sunday school lesson ever taught: "Do unto others as you would have others do unto you."

We must be fair to each other. It really isn't very complicated. Don't let yourself be taken in by those who constantly build themselves up by tearing others down, or by those who promise better times by telling you that *they* have the only answer. Whether you are a conservative or a liberal, or somewhere in between, use the information you have accumulated so far to make your own decisions. Don't fall in the trap of categories.

Make each decision based on your own moral compass and don't be concerned about labels. Shakespeare said "to thine own self be true," and I cannot give better advice. Don't be afraid to ask tough questions and demand answers, and then base your decisions on good information. Then go one step further, use something that you have right now in your lives, something you have going for you that many people do not have, and that is enthusiasm.

Dr. Norman Vincent Peale once said to a group of graduates, "Your enthusiasm will be infectious, stimulating and attractive to others. They will love you for it. They will go for you and with you." Dr. Peale's message was, if you are enthusiastic about your future, and if you can keep this excitement, you can improve your chances of being successful. It's human nature to want to be around people who are enthusiastic and excited about life.

So as you work to maintain a positive attitude, work just as hard to maintain your enthusiasm. Now I don't want to mislead you; it won't always be easy, just as life won't always be easy. You will experience hard times, days when you feel you just can't take any more. You'll feel your positive attitude slipping away and your enthusiasm waning. There will come a time when you want to give up. That is when your faith and your determination will have to keep you going. Dr. Martin Luther King Jr. once said, "The ultimate measure of a man is not where he stands in moments of comfort, but where he stands at times of challenge and controversy."

Remember the title of a book written by Dr. Robert Schuler, "Tough times never last, but tough people do." Show your toughness every day by being *determined* to succeed. This determination will pull you out of bad times and away from failure and will lead you to success. The difference between the impossible and the possible often lies in a person's determination. Let me tell you a story that serves as a classic example of determination; the story of a man who believed in himself; a story about a man who felt a sense of obligation and a duty to serve.

When he was seven years old, his family was forced out of their home, and he had to go to work to help support them. When he was nine, his mother died. At the age of twenty-three, his first business failed. The next year, he ran for the state legislature and lost. Also that year, he lost his job, and tried, but failed, to get into law school. The next year, he borrowed some money from a friend to start another business. By the end of the year, that business went bankrupt, and he would spend the next seventeen years paying off that debt. The year after that, he ran for the state legislature, and this time he won. The next year, he was engaged to be married, but his sweetheart died. Shortly thereafter, he had a total nervous breakdown and was hospitalized for six months. Two years after his recovery, he ran for speaker of the house in his state's legislature and lost. Five years later, he ran for congress and lost. Three years after that, he ran for congress, and this time, he won. But two years later, he lost his re-election bid. So the next year, he tried to get the job of land officer for his state but was rejected. Five years later, he got the bug to run again, and he ran for the U.S. Senate and lost. Two years after that, he sought the vice-presidential nomination of his party at their national convention and lost. Another two years went by; he ran for the senate again and lost. And two years later, he ran for president. And you know what? He won! The man with the remarkable determination was Abraham Lincoln.

And you know what a difference he made in the lives of Americans by holding together the United States during the Civil War. This story shows what can happen when you believe in yourself and never give up. When you take the basic foundation that you've been working on all your lives, and add a positive attitude, enthusiasm, and determination, there is absolutely no limit to what you can accomplish. You *can* make a difference. You *can* change the course of destiny. Rosa Parks refused to go to the back of the bus. Martin Luther King Jr. refused to accept discrimination and at the same time refused to resort to violence. Abe Lincoln refused constant defeat and held this nation together during one of its most trying times.

You can change the course of destiny. But don't be afraid to fail, because there is no disgrace in coming up short. I'd like to read a short clip that was published in the *Wall Street Journal* a few years ago. "You've failed many times, although you may not remember. You fell down the first time you tried to walk. You almost drowned the first time you tried to swim, didn't you? Did you hit the ball the first time you swung a bat? Heavy hitters, the ones who hit the most home runs, also strike out a lot."

R.H. Macy failed seven times before his department store in New York became a success. English novelist John Creasy got 753 rejection slips before he published 564 books. Babe Ruth struck out 1,330 times, but he also hit 714 home runs. Don't worry about failure. Worry about the chances you miss *when you don't even try*. The key to this is *you*. There is nothing that I or anyone else can say that will convince you that you can succeed, or that you can change the world. You have to realize and accept the fact on your own that you can make a difference.

In closing, I'd like to relate to you one final story. A man saw a young girl on a beach throwing something into the ocean. As he approached her, he asked, "Young lady, what are you doing?" She replied, "I'm throwing these starfish back into the water. You see, it's low tide right now, and if I don't throw them back, they'll die from a lack of oxygen." The man smiled and said, "I understand. But there must be thousands of starfish on this beach. You can't possibly throw them all back in time. Also, there are hundreds of beaches all up and down this coast. Can't you see that you can't possibly make a difference?" The young girl bent down, picked up a starfish, and threw it into the ocean. "I made a difference to *that* one, didn't I!" You too can make a difference; no excuses are acceptable. Your family has done their part, Milton has done its part, and now it's up to you. Good luck.

---

1. Milton Academy, Milton, Massachusetts; chartered in 1798 under that state's land-grant policy; preparatory boarding and day school; grades 7–12.

PINE KNOT SCHOOL VISIT
Pine Knot / September 1, 1995

[GREETINGS] . . . Those of you who work or go to school here are very lucky people. . . . We are breaking ground today on what will be a world-class facility. And you're getting this new and expanded school because you deserve it.

The teachers here at Pine Knot and teachers throughout the Commonwealth are working harder than they've ever worked to implement the most ambitious education reform act in this country.

The administrators are looking for new and innovative ways to run schools, and parents are starting to get more involved in the way their schools are being run. The students here and throughout Kentucky are improving their test scores against the most rigorous testing methods in the country. They're getting the kind of education that will allow them to go into the workforce at the end of their schooling and compete with the best workers from throughout the world.

We're making good progress in Kentucky. The teachers, the students, the administrators, and parents are all working harder. And that's why it is up to those of us in Frankfort to ensure that the facilities are the very best they can be. I'm proud to tell you that for the first time since education reform passed, our administration has been able to fully fund the pupil transportation and facilities support portions of KERA. McCreary County was able to receive an extra $710,000 because of what we've been able to do. These are the funds that are helping to build this addition to the Pine Knot Elementary School.

So those of you here at the school have a lot to look forward to in the next few months, as the addition is built. But you'll be able to look back in a few years and say that you were part of something special.

SAFE SCHOOLS MONTH PROCLAMATION SIGNING

Frankfort / October 11, 1995

WE'RE here today to advance the efforts of several organizations and state agencies that are taking the initiative to ensure that Kentucky children are safe and protected in their schools and communities. We know that just as it is difficult for children to learn if they're hungry, they can't learn if they are afraid for their safety. We must recognize that it takes an entire community, including schools, families, businesses, government, law enforcement, all elements of our cities and towns, to collaborate toward workable solutions to the safety issues that impact our children.

Last spring we announced a program coordinated by our Commission on Families and Children designed to bring government agencies, businesses, and organizations together to create a more streamlined, efficient approach for human services at the community level. Mark Guilfoyle, secretary of the [governor's] cabinet, has taken a lead role in this commission, and he is here today to present its efforts.

We must help our families function better; we must eliminate barriers to learning and we must improve child health and child development. We're here today to proclaim October as Safe Schools Month in Kentucky. But more than talking about how important it is for Kentucky's children to be safe, we're going beyond issuing today's proclamation. The Kentucky School Boards Association, in conjunction with the State Department of Education and the National School Safety Center, is launching a program to develop school violence prevention plans through the establishment of safe schools planning teams.

Later this month, school board members, administrators, teachers, police, court officials, and other community leaders will begin the process of creating these teams at intensive workshops scheduled in Lexington and Madisonville. The goal is to have "safe schools planning teams" in place in each community by early next year. Furthermore, the Kentucky School Boards Association has joined forces with the Great Financial Bank of Louisville and, again, the National School Safety Center to provide copies of "Safe Schools: A Handbook for Violence Prevention" free of charge to every public school in the Commonwealth.

ANDERSON COUNTY TECHNOLOGY CENTER DEDICATION
Lawrenceburg / October 26, 1995

DURING the first year of our administration, I participated in the dedication of a new Kentucky Tech facility in Lexington. I told those attending that day that as we approached the twenty-first century, our vision was of a new Kentuckian, a Kentuckian who is healthier, smarter, and happier. Healthier because of health-care reform, smarter because of our emphasis on education and job training, and happier because of economic growth and state government's emphasis on meeting human needs.

There's now a little more than a month remaining in our term, and in reviewing the past four years and the vision discussed at that earlier dedication, we can be proud of what has been accomplished. More Kentuckians now have the opportunity to be protected by health-insurance coverage because of health-care reform. We stayed the course on education reform even though we faced severe financial difficulties in the first two years of the administration. Also, we strengthened the Workforce Development Cabinet by unifying all state job training and employment services under its umbrella.

Kentucky has become one of the national leaders in economic development. There are 200,000 more Kentuckians working today than on the day we took office. In addition, Kentucky ranks among the top ten states nationally in the growth of manufacturing jobs. The number of Kentuckians on welfare has declined by 22 percent, and we've expanded social-service programs so more of our citizens will be able to live satisfying and productive lives.

The Kentucky Tech system has been a major player in helping our vision become a reality. Its record has been outstanding. For example, the placement rate for students who completed Kentucky Tech programs now averages 96 percent; Kentucky companies who employ Kentucky Tech graduates give the students close to perfect scores in technical knowledge, quality, and productivity, rating the former Kentucky Tech students 4.23 of a possible 5.0; Kentucky Tech enrollment has skyrocketed during the past three years.

People are now realizing that most new jobs in the future will *not* require a four-year baccalaureate degree, but *will* require two years of training after high school, exactly the type of training that Kentucky Tech provides. Enrollment at the Northern Kentucky Technology Center increased by 20 percent this year, by 18 percent at Kentucky Tech-Owensboro and by 17 percent at the Kentucky Advanced Technology Center in Bowling Green. We are so impressed and confident in Kentucky Tech's quality that, in 1992, we began a program that guarantees the skills of Kentucky Tech graduates.

If an employer finds that the job skills of a Kentucky Tech graduate fail to meet the standards identified by the diploma, he or she will be retrained at no cost to the company or the individual. Our faith in the quality of Kentucky Tech training was justified because, in the more than three years since the policy was implemented, no graduate has needed additional training under the guarantee agreement.

Kentucky Tech has strong partnerships with business and industry. Last year, it trained more than 43,000 employees of Kentucky companies in customized training programs. This training was provided at the work site as well as at technical schools and was available at night and on weekends. If you need more proof of how important Kentucky Tech is to our state's economy, consider the fact that the managers of several plants new to Kentucky have said that a key reason they chose to locate here was to have access to Kentucky Tech training and assessment services.

We are proud of the Department for Technical Education, the Cabinet for Workforce Development, and their many accomplishments; we are proud of this beautiful, modern technology center that is Kentucky Tech's newest facility; we are proud of the cooperation and partnerships between the citizens of Anderson County and state government that caused this building to be built; and we are proud that the Anderson County Technology Center will make a great state even greater. Thanks to all of you for helping make yesterday's vision today's reality.[1]

---

1. A similar speech was given on November 27 at the dedication of Southeast Tech in Middlesboro.

ECONOMIC DEVELOPMENT

JAMES RIVER CORPORATION ANNOUNCEMENT CEREMONY
Bowling Green / December 18, 1991

IT IS truly a pleasure for me to have this opportunity of sharing in the very special occasion for which we come together. This is a special day for Bowling Green and Warren County, and for the Commonwealth of Kentucky, for today we are announcing a new industry for this community and a new member of Kentucky's corporate family. The James River Corporation, a Fortune 500 company, is going to locate a new manufacturing facility in Bowling Green that may ultimately employ two hundred people. A part of James River's [Paper] Division, the new facility will represent an investment of approximately $32 million, making it the largest new industrial investment to be announced in Kentucky this year.

This new plant will not only be a state-of-the-art facility, but it will be on the cutting edge of new technologies and management practices, making it all the more important as a new industrial-development project. Each new industry or business that is announced in Kentucky is important, but the project we are announcing this morning has a special significance. This new manufacturing facility is important first of all because of the new jobs and the new investment it represents. But also important is the fact that the James River Corporation has been a corporate citizen of Kentucky since 1958, when it began operating a plant in Lexington.

It is always good to have an existing industry expand or build a new plant, because this is not only a testimony to the state's business climate, but is also an expression of confidence in the future of the Commonwealth of Kentucky. Today, more than ever before, I think it is important that we be confident in the future that is before us. We all know that there is a great amount of economic uncertainty throughout our state and nation today, but projects like we are announcing this morning help to allay fears we might have about Kentucky being competitive in attracting new industries and expanding our industrial base, which is the foundation of our state's economy.

I want to thank James River Corporation for choosing to locate its second facility in Kentucky, and I am confident that you will be pleased with the choice of Bowling Green and Warren County as home for your new plant. In welcoming this new facility to Kentucky, I pledge to you the fullest measure of support toward helping you to be a successful and growing part of Kentucky's business community. I can assure you that state government will work with you in every way possible. In fact, this venture will benefit from a combination of programs in place in the Economic Development Cabinet. Specifically, I am referring to the KREDA [Kentucky Rural Economic Development Authority] program, which Lieutenant Governor Patton initiated and which I support.

Additionally, funds from KEDFA [Kentucky Economic Development Finance Authority] and the Bluegrass State Skills Corporation will be utilized with this project. So let me assure you there will be a close partnership between you and all the fine industries doing business in Kentucky, just as we will work in cooperation and harmony with communities like Bowling Green and Warren County. As my administration begins charting the state's economic-development course for the years ahead, I am proud to have a distinguished company like James River Corporation to be the first to announce a major project like we are announcing here this morning. What better way to launch a new administration and a new era of industrial development than through this project.

As many of you may know, the Cabinet for Economic Development has been working on this project with representatives of James River for several months, and I am so pleased that a project of this magnitude has been brought to fruition and that I have been given the opportunity of sharing in the delivery of such good news for this community and for the Commonwealth of Kentucky. As I said throughout the campaign, economic development is going to be a focal point of my administration, and by working closely with community leaders like you have here in Bowling Green and Warren County and with the help of members of the General Assembly like Sen. Nick Kafoglis[1] and Reps. Jody Richards[2] and Billy Ray Smith,[3] I am confident that we can bring an era of unparalleled growth and development to Kentucky.

Together, we can make events like today's announcement a regular happening throughout Kentucky. Let's hope that today's announcement not only marks new growth for James River Corporation and its consumer products division, but also that it signals new and rewarding times for the people of Kentucky.

---

1. Nick Kafoglis (1930–), B.A., Yale University; M.D., University of Pennsylvania; U.S. Air Force, 1957–59; elected to Kentucky house, 1972; re-elected, 1974–76; elected to Kentucky senate, 1987, re-elected, 1991–98; majority caucus chairman, 1993–98; Kentucky Long-Term Policy Research Center Board, 1992–98, chair, 1997; member: American College of Obstetrics and Gynecology, Warren Co. Medical Society, Warren Co. Chamber of Commerce, Russellville-Logan Co. Chamber of Commerce. *Who's What in Kentucky Government, 1997–98* (Frankfort, 1997).

2. Jody Richards (1938–), A.B., Kentucky Wesleyan College; M.A., University of Missouri; attended Indiana University; Army Reserve; Governor's Task Force on Education Steering Committee; Southern Region Education Board; Legislative Advisory Committee; elected to Kentucky house, 1975; re-elected, 1977–2000; Democratic caucus chairman, 1987–97; speaker of the house, 1997–2000; owner, Superior Books. *Who's What in Kentucky Government, 1999–2000* (Frankfort, 1999).

3. Billy Ray Smith (1944–), B.S., Western Kentucky University; elected to Kentucky house, 1982; re-elected, 1984–94; chairman, Banking and Insurance Committee; elected Kentucky commissioner of agriculture, 1995–99; re-elected, 1999–2003; president and director, Kentucky Polled Hereford Association; secretary-treasurer and director, Bowling Green-Warren County Farm Bureau; WKU Agriculture Advisory Board; co-owner/executive vice-president, Pan American Mills, Inc.; farmer and cattle breeder. *Who's What in Kentucky Government, 1999–2000* (Frankfort, 1999).

NEWS CONFERENCE
Frankfort / March 2, 1992

IN MY State of the Commonwealth Address, I spoke of our administration's commitment to working our way out of the recession that is taking a daily toll on the working men and women of Kentucky. Our people are hurting, and they need help; for instance, the number of Kentuckians who receive food stamps and Aid to Families with Dependent Children [AFDC], those who are on Medicaid, and the number of children who receive free or reduced school lunches. In every category the number has grown dramatically over the past year. The number of persons receiving food stamps increased by almost 10 percent, from 480,808 in December 1990, to 525,739 this past December, an increase of 45,000 families.

Parents and children receiving AFDC increased by 25,000 or about 9 percent during the same year. Kentuckians on Medicaid increased by almost 60,000 or about 9 percent during the same year. On the average, 49.1 percent of all Kentucky students eating lunch at school were on free or reduced lunches, up from 46.5 percent the year before, an increase of some 27,000 children who could not make it without this help. The current economic downturn only motivates us more to build for the brightest possible future for Kentucky.

We all recognize how vitally important it is to protect the jobs we already have and to create new good-paying jobs in all parts of our state. Today, we will recommend to the General Assembly two bills which I believe will equip Kentucky to compete with any state in the nation in providing jobs for our people. Our first initiative is the Kentucky Industrial Revitalization Act. This bill creates an authority that will provide incentives for manufacturing companies that are on the verge of closing their facilities and laying off Kentucky workers. These incentives will take two forms, a credit against the company's Kentucky income tax and an assessment on wages equal to 6 percent of the company's total payroll. The combination of the revenue generated by these two incentives can total up to 50 percent of the company's new investment in its facility. To qualify for this assistance, a company must verify to the authority that the shutdown of its facility is imminent. In addition, this information must be verified by an independent third party, and a public hearing will be required.

Final approval of an economic-revitalization agreement authorizing the incentives is contingent upon the approval of a majority of the workers and all local governments affected by the wage assessment. To provide protection to workers whose wages are assessed, they will be permitted to claim an income tax credit of two-thirds of the assessment. In addition, they can claim a credit against their local occupational taxes of one-sixth of the assessment. The bottom line for employees is they will give up income equal to one-sixth of the assessment to help preserve their jobs. Of the 3,174 companies in Kentucky, over 2,000 of them have been in operation over 20 years. A significant investment must be made in these industries to revitalize and keep them growing.

Our second initiative is known as the Kentucky Jobs Development Act. The purpose of this legislation is to create jobs in the service sector. The fastest-growing segment of the nation's economy continues to be in the service-sector arena. Service-sector jobs typically tend to be higher-paying positions and ones which provide the greatest stability over time. Kentucky currently does not have aggressive tools for recruiting corporate or regional offices which fall in the category of service-sector employment.

Sales and marketing functions, telecommunications, data processing, and customer service and distribution centers are all attractive job-producing entities. The Kentucky Jobs Development Act will give our state the tools to create a balanced mix between creating solid manufacturing jobs as well as service-sector jobs. Under this act, service companies that want to locate or expand in Kentucky will have tax credits available to them from the Kentucky Jobs Development Authority. It will be the authority's responsibility to determine that the credits are necessary to create jobs or to keep Kentucky from losing jobs to another state. The company may use the credits to pay up to one-half of its annual rent or lease costs for a maximum of ten years as well as to finance half its relocation and start-up costs.

The credits will come from two sources: up to 5 percent of all wages paid for the project under consideration and the company's corporate tax liability for the project. Companies which qualify for this incentive must create at least twenty-five new jobs for Kentuckians. Both new and existing companies will be eligible. The legislation will stop the brain drain of Kentucky's skilled people leaving home, depriving us of our children and grandchildren and depriving the state of its economic lifeblood. With this legislation, the Commonwealth will be poised on its two hundredth birthday to compete with any state in the nation in the creation and protection of jobs for our people.

SACHS AUTOMOTIVE PLANT DEDICATION
Florence / March 4, 1992

GREETINGS. It is indeed a pleasure for me to be in Florence and Boone County to share in this very special occasion. On behalf of the people of Kentucky, I want to welcome Sachs Automotive of America as our newest corporate citizen and to say how proud we are to now have one of Europe's finest manufacturing firms, a company with 122,000 employees and operations on five continents, to be a part of Kentucky's industrial family.

I am confident that the operation being dedicated here this morning in Florence, Kentucky, will add to the quality name that Sachs Automotive has throughout the world. The association between Sachs Automotive of America, this community, and the Commonwealth of Kentucky will continue to grow in the years to come, and we welcome you as a new Kentucky corporate citizen.

Today is indeed a special day because this new facility represents new jobs for this community, new revenue for our state, and a strengthening of our industrial base. Just as state government made economic-development bonds and training monies available to Sachs Automotive upon coming to Kentucky, we in state government are putting in place new support services for our existing industries.

Just this week, I announced in Frankfort two new measures that will provide Kentucky with vital new programs to fight the recession by attracting more new industrial and service industries. The bills, introduced Monday, also will help existing plants modernize to preserve and expand jobs for Kentuckians at a time when they are needed most. We want all our companies, including Sachs Automotive, which from this day forward is an existing industry, to know that they are an essential part of life in Kentucky and Kentucky's economy and, as such, will be supported accordingly.

While we dedicate a building here this morning, what we are really dedicating is an opportunity for the people who own and manage Sachs Automotive, along with the people who operate the machines and those who in many different ways benefit from the products and the successes of this company. When we invest in new or expanding industries, we are really investing in people whose incomes and livelihoods depend on these industries. Today, I congratulate Sachs Automotive of America upon the official opening of this new facility and pledge to them the fullest measure of support in the years to come. I commend and congratulate the people and leadership of this community for making your community a place where industry wants to locate and be a part.

FRUIT OF THE LOOM ANNOUNCEMENT
Franklin / March 18, 1992

GREETINGS. I regret that I cannot be with you in person this morning, but I am pleased to join my good friends John Holland and Jack Moore, by way of this special hook-up, to formally announce that Fruit of the Loom, Incorporated, is opening a manufacturing facility here in Franklin that will create 250 new jobs in your community. Through efforts of the Cabinet for Economic Development and with the support of your city and county governments, a lease has been negotiated with Fruit of the Loom to take over the former Washington Apparel Cutting Center.

Renewal of this idle manufacturing unit is the result of direct action between state government and one of our major existing industries . . . and underscores the importance of a cooperative relationship between government and private industry. Economic realities tell us that we are going to lose jobs, which we cannot always replace. Today, that fortunately is not the case. This creates 250 new jobs which will replace nearly one-half of those lost when economic circumstances caused the closing of the previous operation.

As we celebrate the new jobs that will be created, we should not overlook what went into making today's announcement possible. First of all, we must recognize that without an outstanding company like Fruit of the Loom, the Economic Development Cabinet would not have had a partner with whom to negotiate a lease of the building. The second crucial element in the negotiating process was having progressive leadership at the local level and the backing and support of your mayor and city council and your judge executive and county fiscal court. These are the key ingredients that go into a successful economic-development undertaking and are the things that brought today's announcement to fruition.

I want to commend Mayor [William] Young, Judge Harper,[1] and members of your city council and fiscal court for working to make things happen in Franklin and Simpson County. I commend each of you for the pride you have in your community and all the things you have done and continue to do to make your community a better place in which to live, to work, and to own and operate business. I also appreciate very much the prominent role which Fruit of the Loom plays in Kentucky's industrial economy and its many contributions to our state.

Fruit of the Loom is our second-largest manufacturing employer, with some 9,800 employees and eight operations in Kentucky. We take our support of industry in Kentucky seriously, and we are serious when it comes to retaining the jobs we now have and in creating new jobs. Lt. Gov. Paul Patton and I are supporting legislation which we believe will place Kentucky on the cutting edge of existing industries' services and in the recruitment of service and technology-intensive businesses and corporate headquarters.

The Kentucky Senate has already passed the Industrial Revitalization Act, which will enable us to help existing industries modernize in order to stay in business and to remain employers of Kentuckians. The Job Development Act has also been approved by the senate, and this act will allow Kentucky to compete for industries and businesses that will complement the strong manufacturing base we have in Kentucky. These are difficult economic times for thousands of Kentuckians and Kentucky businesses.

There are no easy solutions, and we know that the solution to many of our problems must be triggered by forces outside Kentucky. What we are seeking to do is to be innovative in our thinking and in our planning so as to give Kentuckians and Kentucky industries an edge in recovering from the recession and for moving ahead when recovery does occur. The project we are announcing today encompasses the spirit and the components we need within our economic-development efforts here in Kentucky. It is important that we continue to have cooperation between government and private industry like that which exists with Fruit of the Loom and cooperation between state government and local communities like we see here today. If we all work together, Kentucky's economic growth and vitality are assured, job opportunities for all Kentuckians are assured, and a brighter future for our young people is assured.

---

1. Ken Harper, magistrate, 1970–81; Franklin County judge-executive, 1982–98; president of Kentucky Association of Counties, 1989; chairman of

local health board; Kentucky representative on the National Association of Counties; treasurer and vice-chairman of the Barren River Area Development District. Information provided by Harper on April 5, 1998.

FIDELITY INVESTMENTS ANNOUNCEMENT
Covington / April 23, 1992

IT IS always a special occasion when we can come together to announce new growth in our state, and a special joy when this new growth means new jobs for our people. I want to thank Fidelity Investments for choosing to locate in Covington and to welcome this fine company to our state. Over the past few years, Kentucky, and northern Kentucky in particular, has been successful in attracting new industrial jobs and expanding its manufacturing base, and we certainly want to do everything we can to sustain this growth in manufacturing. Where we have not been as successful as I would like for us to be is in non-manufacturing jobs, or white-collar jobs, like those that will be created by Fidelity's new regional headquarters facility here in Covington.

Talks with Fidelity began in the previous administration and were well under way before I took office, so I do not wish to claim credit for this outstanding company's looking to Kentucky for the location of this new regional office facility. I do hope, however, that the strong commitment we have made to business and economic development in general proved a decisive factor in the company's decision.

The recently concluded 1992 session of the Kentucky General Assembly was the most productive ever in terms of economic-development legislation. Seven major economic-development measures were enacted, measures which Lt. Gov. Paul Patton and I believed were needed if Kentucky was to do for business and the people of Kentucky all we need to do in terms of retaining existing jobs, creating new jobs, and helping our communities get into a position where they can compete for new industries. Never before has such a broad range of programs been enacted to meet the needs of our existing industries, to help new industries locate in Kentucky, to help communities build new infrastructures, to help Kentucky's world-famous horse industry, and to work with our coal industry.

These are the programs that will shape Kentucky's future, and it is companies like Fidelity Investments that will help us provide the jobs we want for our people. I want state government to be responsive to the needs of business so that businesses in turn can grow and prosper in Kentucky. I want state government to be responsive to the needs of our local communities. And I want government to be responsive to the needs of our people. But so much of what we want to see accomplished for Kentucky requires a team effort between the public sector and the private sector and between state government and local governments.

The Commonwealth of Kentucky and the city of Covington have joined together to work with Fidelity Investments in bringing this new corporate facility to Kenton County. Only through such a team effort was today's announcement possible. Today, as I welcome Fidelity Investments to Kentucky, I want to also say to you that economic development in our state will continue to be a team effort because only by working together can we make our efforts and our investments mutually rewarding to our communities, to our companies, and to the Commonwealth of Kentucky. . . .

HITACHI AUTOMOTIVE PRODUCTS EXPANSION PROJECT OFFICIAL OPENING
Harrodsburg / May 13, 1992

WHAT a pleasure it is for me, and I am sure for each of you, to be here this morning to join with our friends at Hitachi Automotive Products (USA) to celebrate the official opening of their newest expansion. And how fortunate Kentucky is to have successful companies like Hitachi that continue to grow and expand, and which continue to provide good jobs for the people of Kentucky. Hitachi is more than a good employer; it is also a good corporate citizen, as evidenced by its continuing donations to the community and the encouragement it gives for its employees to be involved in contributing to the community.

Mr. Okumura, I congratulate you this morning upon the official opening of your phase-four expansion, and I also thank you this morning on behalf of all the people of this community and the Commonwealth of Kentucky for all that your company is contributing to Kentucky. I also want to congratulate all of the some five hundred employees of Hitachi for the outstanding job you are doing in helping Hitachi manufacture the quality products that are making this operation so successful. Kentucky's workforce is one of the best in the country, with our value per dollar of production wages being almost 10 percent higher than the national average, and the employees here at Hitachi can take great pride in helping Kentucky to gain that achievement.

The fact that this is a phase-four expansion shows just how successful Hitachi Automotive Products (USA) has been since it was established here in 1985. Hitachi is a major supplier of electronic and electrical components for the automotive industry, having among its customers Ford, General Motors, Nissan, Honda, Isuzu, and Subaru. But Hitachi sells not only domestically, but also exports to Mexico and Japan, which, as I understand, then export to Europe.

Not only has Hitachi added to the international sector within Kentucky's economy, but it is expanding Kentucky's prominence in the world economy through the export of products manufactured here in Harrodsburg, Kentucky. I and Lieutenant Governor Patton and others will be traveling to Japan later this month to visit with the parent companies of Japanese firms having plants located in our state. Among those we will be meeting will be Dr. [Tsutomu] Kanai, the president of Hitachi, Limited, and Mr. Hiro, who is here today. I am looking forward to meeting Dr. Kanai and to telling him personally how much we appreciate having Hitachi Automotive (USA) Inc. in Kentucky and just how proud we are to have Hitachi Automotive as one of Kentucky's best employers and most outstanding corporate citizens.

Today's economy is truly a world economy, and Kentucky needs to take its rightful place in that economy. To do that, we must have companies like Hitachi coming to Kentucky and growing with Kentucky. We must have people like Mr. Okumura come to Kentucky to share our culture and to share his culture with us, because that, too, is a vital part of the world community. So, today I not only congratulate Hitachi Automotive Products upon the opening of this expansion, I also thank the company for being a part of this community and part of Kentucky's business community. May you continue to enjoy much success in the years to come.

QVC KENTUCKY CRAFTS SHOW
June 14, 1992

(GOV.) HELLO, Phyllis.[1] And hello to the thousands of viewers whom we have invited into the beautiful Commonwealth of Kentucky tonight. We are so happy to share Kentucky's natural scenic beauty, our wonderful recreation and vacation opportunities, and our fabulous "Kentucky-crafted" treasures with the rest of the nation. You know, Phyllis, it is particularly fitting that we are on the QVC network this evening, because Kentucky has just celebrated a very special birthday. On June 1 we celebrated our two hundredth birthday as the fifteenth state to enter the union.

(Libby) Hi, Phyllis. Brereton and I want to thank you for all you have done to bring the rich treasure of Kentucky crafts to the rest of America. We remember with great pride when you, as first lady of Kentucky, exposed the world to the wonderful crafts of Kentucky. I can't think of a better person to be national chairperson of the Year of the American Craft. I want to extend a special welcome to our viewers from across America tonight. You are in for a real treat! The craft tradition is alive and well in Kentucky, and you are going to see some breathtakingly beautiful and, I might add, very useful, Kentucky crafts for your home. And how great it is to be on the QVC shopping network! We know everyone will enjoy tonight's show!

(Gov.) That's right, Libby. QVC is providing our viewers with a great opportunity to take their pick of the finest example, of the Kentucky craft tradition. We are certain that you will come to know, as we do, that Kentucky crafts are among the finest anywhere. Many say it is the land, Kentucky's mountains, lakes, forests, and farmlands, which inspire our artisans. We hope that Phyllis George and our wonderful crafts will inspire you to visit us and help celebrate Kentucky's two hundred years of statehood. Kentucky's cultural heritage is more than places and things. It lives in the hearts of our people and in the warm hospitality that we show to our guests. Libby and I invite you to come to Kentucky and share with us this special year, our special places, and the special talent of our people, the crafts of Kentucky!

---

1. Phyllis George Brown (1949–), attended North Texas State and Texas Christian Universities; Miss America, 1971; first lady of Kentucky, 1979–83;

"Candid Camera" regular, 1974; "The NFL Today," 1975–84; "CBS Morning News," 1985; author; former wife of Gov. John Y. Brown Jr.

TOYOTA CAMRY EXPORT MEDIA EVENT
Georgetown / July 24, 1992

TODAY'S ceremony marks another milestone both in Toyota Motor Manufacturing U.S.A.'s Kentucky operations and also in the partnership between Toyota and the Commonwealth of Kentucky. Toyota's decision just a little over seven years ago to come to Kentucky launched the beginning of a new era of industrial growth and development in our state. Not only did Kentucky become home to one of the world's premier automotive manufacturing operations, but Toyota's coming to Kentucky provided a catalyst that helped bring fifty-eight other new automotive-related plants to Kentucky. Toyota and these 58 automotive-related plants represent nearly seventeen thousand new jobs for Kentucky.

Toyota, together with these new automotive facilities and the automotive firms that have operated in Kentucky for a number of years, has made Kentucky a prominent player in what has been termed the nation's new automotive corridor. As important as the new jobs brought to Kentucky are, Toyota's presence in Kentucky reaches far beyond the direct economics associated with a major industry. The bonds of friendship between Kentucky and Japan have been strengthened, and our understanding of each other's culture has been broadened.

As a major industrial investor in Kentucky's business community, Toyota has contributed greatly to the role of foreign industrial investment in Kentucky's economy and has expanded the international focus upon Kentucky as a state where foreign companies are welcomed. More and more people, especially people involved in business, are recognizing the fact that today's economy is a world economy. Here in Kentucky, we know that our industrial economy is to a great extent tied to how successful we are in competing in the world economy. That is why today's event is so important, not only to Toyota, but also to our state.

How exciting it is to know that a Japanese vehicle made in Georgetown, Kentucky, by Kentucky workers, will now be sold in

Japan. What a tribute it is to the management of Toyota Motor Manufacturing U.S.A. and to the some four thousand workers here at Georgetown that their work meets the demanding standards of Japanese car buyers. Last May, when Lieutenant Governor Patton and Gene Strong[1] and I were in Japan and met with the officials of Toyota Motors, Dr. Toyoda[2] talked about how pleased he is with the workforce here at Georgetown, saying they are some of the best workers in the world.

Today's ceremony marking the beginning of export to Japan of vehicles made in Georgetown gives testimony to just what a good job you are doing here in Georgetown, and the fact that our workers turn out quality products. We are not only happy for the added market the export of these automobiles means to Toyota but we appreciate so very much the promotion your marketing efforts in Japan will mean for Kentucky, through the video and posters, and most certainly the Kentucky crafts your dealers will provide as gifts to buyers of the Camry wagon or, as I believe it will be known in Japan, the Scepter.

Congratulations for what you have achieved, and thank you for making Kentucky a part of those achievements.[3]

---

1. Marvin E. "Gene" Strong (1953–), born in Jackson, Kentucky; B.S., Eastern Kentucky University, 1974; director of fiscal affairs, Kentucky State Police, 1976–81; executive vice-president of leasing, The Webb Companies, Lexington, 1981–91; deputy secretary, Kentucky Cabinet for Economic Development and special advisor to governor, 1991–93; secretary, Kentucky Cabinet for Economic Development, 1993–present. Information provided by Strong, April 29, 1998.

2. Dr. Tatsuro Toyoda (1929–), graduate of Tokyo University; Toyota Motor Corporation, 1953– ; executive vice-president of international operations, 1988–92; president, 1992–95. *Who's Who in the World 1995,* 12th ed. (New Providence, N.J., 1994).

3. In a speech on June 29, Jones announced the opening of Technotrim, a company that produces automobile seat covers.

FORD MOTOR ANNOUNCEMENT
Kentucky Truck Plant, Louisville / July 27, 1992

It is a pleasure for me to be here this morning to share in a truly special occasion for one of our finest corporate citizens for Louisville and Jefferson County and for all of Kentucky. Today's groundbreaking ceremony marks another milestone in Ford Motor Company's growth and development in Kentucky and its importance as one of the state's primary industries. State government is pleased to join with Louisville and Jefferson County in a partnership with Ford to support its continued growth and prominence as a good employer and major contributor to our economy. We appreciate so very much the investment that Ford Motor Company is making in its Kentucky truck plant here in Louisville and new job opportunities this expansion will create.

We believe that industrial development works best when it involves a partnership between state and local government and private enterprise, so this morning I am happy to announce that incentives totaling $44.3 million are being offered Ford Motor Company by the Commonwealth of Kentucky and Louisville and Jefferson County. Two of Kentucky's new economic-development programs, the Kentucky Industrial Development Authority and the Jobs Development Act, are being used to assist Ford in financing this $650 million expansion project and the creation of fourteen hundred new jobs. This incentive package represents a commitment on the part of the Commonwealth of Kentucky and Louisville and Jefferson County. As we are telling the nation through our television spots, Kentucky is serious about jobs, and to have jobs, we must be supportive of our existing industries like Ford Motor Company.

But the support of this expansion by state government and city of Louisville and Jefferson County is only part of the commitment making this project possible. The other necessary ingredient is the support of labor and the men and women who make the quality trucks for which Ford is known throughout the world. Without a quality workforce, a company cannot produce quality products, and it is workers like you have here at the Kentucky truck plant that enable Kentucky to have one of the top worker-productivity rankings in the country. Ford Motor Company has been a part of Kentucky's business family since 1912, and today is the second-largest manufacturing employer in Louisville and Jefferson County and the third-largest manufacturing employer in Kentucky.

The investments that Kentucky has made in Ford Motor Company through the years have been returned many times over in the investments Ford continues to make in Kentucky and the jobs it continues to provide Kentuckians. Yes, today is a good day for Louisville and Kentucky. We applaud Ford's partnership with government and Ford's harmonious labor-management teamwork. It exemplifies the way we believe economic development should work and the way we like to do business in Kentucky. Again, we congratulate Ford Motor Company upon this project and its continuing success in Kentucky, and we thank you for being a solid partner in a partnership that is making a difference in the future of the Commonwealth of Kentucky.

ECONOMIC-DEVELOPMENT ROUNDTABLES
Governor's Mansion / December 2, 1992

I AM so pleased that you have taken time from your busy schedules to come to Frankfort and honor us with your presence. Along with welcoming you, I also want to express my appreciation to each of you for your willingness to serve as a member of our economic-development roundtables. Lieutenant Governor Patton and I believe that the regional economic-development roundtables represent an invaluable resource in Kentucky's economic-development efforts. We believe that the roundtables can be excellent forums for the sharing of ideas and information and in addressing the economic-development opportunities in all areas of our state.

You will recall that during my campaign for governor, one of my main commitments was the establishment of regional economic-development offices. I have always believed that for government to be effective, government must not only offer good programs, but it must also be responsive in the delivery of services. I believe that the more localized the delivery of services, the more effective they can become. That is the reason I wanted the Cabinet for Economic Development to have regional offices. In my economic-development platform, I said that we were going to address the specific needs and opportunities in each of the regions in our state. I believe that the best way to do this is through our regional economic-development offices.

I also believe that the best way to solve the problems of a specific region is to work with those who best know those problems. And if we at the state level are to be realistic and confident of the greatest level of success in reaching our objectives, we must work with those who have the best first-hand knowledge of the areas and the regions. That is why your participation in the roundtables is so important. The knowledge and expertise which enable you to perform your individual jobs successfully can enhance the success of our regional offices and the state's overall economic-development efforts.

You are, I know, familiar with the many new economic-development tools that we now have to support our existing industries and to attract new industries to Kentucky. We have the Jobs Development Act to help us bring non-manufacturing, service- and technology-oriented jobs to Kentucky. We have one of the nation's best tools for rural economic development in the Kentucky Rural Economic Development Authority, or KREDA, as we know it.

Tomorrow, Lieutenant Governor Patton will meet with county judges and other interested persons from our coal-producing counties to discuss guidelines for the new Local Government Economic Development Fund that was made possible through legislation that increases the percentage of coal severance tax monies being returned to coal-producing counties. We have many other new and innovative tools, but I mention these to show the new initiatives underway to make the 1990s the most progressive years the state has ever known. If we are successful in retaining and creating new jobs, we will be able to do the many other things we want to do for the people of Kentucky, like health-care reform.

We at the state level are committed to providing the very best possible leadership to moving Kentucky forward. Government, however, is a catalyst. We must work in harmony with local governments and local initiatives. You, the members of our economic-development roundtables, are the key force in those local initiatives. Together, we can bring to all areas of Kentucky the level of development we want for the people of Kentucky.

BRUENING BEARINGS, INC.
Florence / December 8, 1992

SELDOM does a governor get to participate in three ribbon cuttings in one day, and especially for three outstanding facilities like we are celebrating in northern Kentucky today. I can't tell you how thrilled I am to be in northern Kentucky to join with you in celebrating the outstanding growth that is occurring throughout this region of Kentucky. I want to thank John Dannemiller and the people of Bruening, Inc., for choosing Kentucky as the location for this new distribution center. I welcome you to the Commonwealth of Kentucky.

I mentioned this being the third ribbon cutting for us today, because as many of you know, we celebrated earlier in the opening of the new General Cable and International Paper offices and distribution centers. We, of course, appreciate very much the new jobs and new investment each of these facilities mean for Kentucky. But the significance of the new facilities we are spotlighting today reaches far beyond the jobs and investment they represent. They show that the advantages Kentucky offers as a good location for manufacturing operations also make Kentucky a good location for corporate offices and distribution and service centers.

Kentucky is among a small number of states that have been gaining back some of the manufacturing jobs lost in the early eighties. Today, new innovative programs are helping us attract corporate offices, distribution centers, and other non-manufacturing operations. This added diversity means a greater range of job opportunities for Kentuckians and greater stability for our economy. As I welcome Bruening Bearings, Inc., to Kentucky and to this community, I also want to thank this fine company for choosing our state. I want to commend Judge Lucas[1] and Mayor Kalb[2] for making Florence and Boone County a place where industry wants to locate and a community where industry is appreciated. Through your efforts here locally, and with the help of your legislators in Frankfort, Kentucky is moving into a new era of economic growth, education reform, and the enhancement of human services.

That is what we are really celebrating here today, the growth of business and industry, the partnership between the public and private sectors, and the mutual rewards that come to business and the community when we work together toward common goals and objectives. Let me again say welcome and thank you to Bruening

Bearings, Inc. We are proud to have you in Kentucky and look forward to working with you as a new corporate citizen of this community and our Commonwealth.[3]

---

1. Ken Lucas (1933–), B.S., University of Kentucky; M.A., Xavier University; honorary doctorate, Northern Kentucky University; major in U.S. Air Force; Florence city councilman, 1967–74; Boone County commissioner, 1974–82; chairman, Northern Kentucky Chamber of Commerce, 1987–88; Boone County judge-executive, 1992–98; elected Democratic U.S. representative from 4th congressional district, 1998; re-elected, 2000; CIGNA [health care and insurance provider] financial consultant for thirty-one years; chartered financial consultant degree and chartered life underwriter degree; past president and chairman of executive committee, Boone State Bank.

2. Evelyn Kalb (1926–), paralegal certificate, Chase College of Law; board member, Kentucky Women's Commission, 1978–84; delegate to White House Commission on Women in Carter administration; member of Boone County Consolidation Commission; Florence city councilwoman, 1979–91; mayor of Florence, 1991–1998. Information provided by Kalb, March 30, 1998; *Kentucky Post,* January 4, 2001.

3. Similar speeches were given at the openings of Universal Fasteners, Inc., in Lawrenceburg on August 6, General Cable Corporation in Highland Heights on December 8, and International Paper Company in Covington on December 8.

MONTAPLAST ANNOUNCEMENT
Capitol / December 9, 1992

It is with a great deal of pleasure that I join the president of Montaplast, of Morsbach, Germany, to announce that Montaplast plans to open a new manufacturing plant here in Frankfort, Kentucky. The new manufacturing facility will be located in the Frankfort Industrial Park II and is expected to employ up to 120 people within three years. Montaplast is one of the largest European suppliers of automotive plastic parts. The plant here in Frankfort will be the company's first manufacturing operation in the United States.

Montaplast is a fine addition to Kentucky's automotive-parts industry and to the industrial sector of our business community. I am proud, and I know that we all are proud, that Montaplast chose Kentucky for its first U.S. manufacturing operation. I welcome this fine, new industry to Kentucky and pledge the fullest measure of support through the many programs we have for new and expanding industries.

Montaplast becomes the sixty-seventh new manufacturing operation we have announced this year. These new industries represent over six thousand potential new jobs and an investment of more than $264 million. Montaplast also becomes the ninth automotive-parts plant to be announced in Kentucky this year. This demonstrates, I think, the strength and vitality of our automotive-parts industry. I am confident that as long as we continue to attract fine companies like Montaplast, Kentucky's economy will continue to benefit greatly from the manufacturing of automotive parts.

I want to commend Lieutenant Governor Patton and the Cabinet for Economic Development staff for the fine job they did in helping to bring Montaplast to Kentucky. We, of course, cannot attract new jobs and retain existing jobs if we don't have strong leadership at the local level, and I want to commend . . . all those involved with industrial development locally for their efforts in bringing new industry to Frankfort and Franklin County. . . .

SMALL BUSINESS INVESTMENT PROGRAM ANNOUNCEMENT
Louisville / December 11, 1992

WE ARE in Louisville today to announce an innovative, first-of-its-kind partnership between state government and private industry that will create jobs throughout Kentucky. Over the next few weeks, Kentucky will become the first state to use a new federal law permitting investment in a small-business investment company to create jobs in minority businesses and disadvantaged areas of the state. These investment companies, called SBICs [Small Business Investment Companies], are privately managed companies that receive three-to-one matching funds from the federal government in return for providing capital to small business.

Kentucky will take advantage of this matching formula by being the first state to purchase $900,000 of stock in Equal Opportunity Finance, Inc., a subsidiary of Ashland Oil and Kentucky's only minority enterprise SBIC. This investment, coupled with a $100,000 commitment from the Paducah community, is expected to leverage several million dollars in new capital for small business in Kentucky.

During his campaign, President-elect Clinton repeatedly spoke of the need for a "new covenant" between the public and private sectors, the need for making government more entrepreneurial and empowering the individual. In fact, Bill Clinton and Al Gore in their book *Putting People First*[1] proposed that minority investment companies be energized to create new jobs in our communities. Therefore, we are justifiably proud to put Kentucky at the leading edge of economic development through a partnership using both the human and fiscal resources of the state and the private sector. Simply put, this program allows Kentucky to leverage federal dollars to assist small businesses that cannot obtain financing from state and other private sources. With Kentucky being practically last in the nation in the availability of venture capital, we can afford to do no less for our citizens.

In announcing this program I want to commend Lieutenant Governor Patton for his excellent work in economic development and for his hard work on this unique partnership, which is a product of many meetings with Ashland officials, the Paducah community, and his August trip to Washington, where he met with federal officials. I also want to thank Ashland Oil and specifically John Hall for their work on this partnership and for making the resources of its subsidiary available to create new jobs in our state.

---

1. Bill Clinton and Albert Gore, *Putting People First: How We Can All Change America* (Times Books: New York, 1992).

LOUISVILLE AREA CHAMBER OF COMMERCE ANNUAL MEETING
Louisville / January 25, 1993

I APPRECIATE very much the invitation to be here and to have this opportunity to take part in your annual meeting. If anyone had a reason to wonder about the enthusiasm that exists within the Louisville business community, they would only need to witness the attendance here this evening to understand why the greater Louisville area is on the move. I commend each of you for your support and involvement with the Chamber of Commerce, and thank you not only for your leadership in the region, but also your continuing interest in the things we are doing to help all of Kentucky.

Individually and as members of the Chamber of Commerce, you are members of Kentucky's economic-development team and a vital part of the partnership that exists between state government and our local communities and between the public and private sector. I know we use that term an awful lot, but it takes a team effort to accomplish all that needs to be done, and the many outstanding accomplishments over the past year are the result of a team effort.

Louisville and Jefferson County, as the state's largest metropolitan area, play a very special role both in terms of our economy and also in attracting business to the state that only a city of this size can do. State government is proud to be a continuing partner in many of the growth activities here in Jefferson County like the expansions at the Kentucky Fair and Exposition Center and the Waterfront Development, while we appreciate the real rewards of the growth and revitalization taking place today will come in the years that are before us.

Through the leadership of Mayor Abramson[1] and Judge Armstrong,[2] Louisville and Jefferson County are recognized nationally as a progressive community. Kentucky, as you know, continues to receive national recognition for what we are doing in education reform. Our tools for economic development, such as the Kentucky Jobs Development Act, which recently helped to attract two outstanding companies to Louisville, are the envy of economic-development leaders throughout the country.

Kentucky was the first state to take advantage of changes in federal legislation allowing indirect state funds to be invested in a small business investment company (SBIC). State government purchased $900,000 of stock in Equal Opportunity Finance, Incorporated, a subsidiary of Ashland Oil, and Kentucky's only minority SBIC. The state's investment, coupled with a commitment from Paducah banks, will leverage more than $4 million in new investment capital for small and minority Kentucky businesses. I would note that the *Courier-Journal* is an investor in equal opportunity finance.

To further aid entrepreneurs and bring about greater development within the small and minority business community, the Cabinet for Economic Development and the Louisville/Jefferson County office for economic development are implementing a computerized network to link entrepreneurs with potential investors. Known as the investment capital network, the program will make available additional venture capital for start-up and early-stage financing of small and minority businesses.

These are just some of the exciting things state government, in partnership with the local community, is doing to improve the economy and employment opportunities in the greater Louisville area. If Kentucky is to continue to grow and to reach the level of quality of life we want for all our people, we must reform health care in our state. We must have a health-care program that will give every Kentuckian access to vital health-care services. To do this, we must have your support and the support of people all over Kentucky. There will be costs . . . but there will also be savings. The health of our businesses is essential to the economic health of our Commonwealth. But our administration, just as President Clinton's administration has said, is convinced that we cannot unlock the problems of our economy without addressing the rising cost of health care and bringing health-care coverage to so many that have none.

As a businessman and farmer for most of my adult life and having had to make a payroll for about thirty years, I understand and appreciate the challenges small businesses face every day. I also know that about 80 percent of the job growth in any state comes from cultivating existing businesses, and our administration considers that to be of paramount importance. And from my involvement in the health-care community for much of my public life, I also know that the health-care crisis in this nation and our Commonwealth, if unaddressed, will bankrupt us all.

The humanity involved is staggering, with about 500,000 Kentuckians having no health-insurance protection at all, keeping them on the edge of financial disaster with any medical emergency. So we have a dilemma, and your businesses and companies may have concerns that our efforts to reform health care could be harmful to your economic health. I am here to address those concerns because I believe sincerely that we can have comprehensive health-care reform and protect the viability of our small businesses. I do not want to solve one problem and create another. I promise you now that in our reform package we will help those economically sensitive businesses adapt, adjust, and accommodate to our health-care reform efforts, and I am asking you to join our team to see that this happens to the benefit of us all.

With vulnerable businesses, we will have a system of softening the impact on economically sensitive companies with state assistance depending on a number of factors, but those small businesses will not have to shoulder it alone and at the expense of the company's existence. I'd also like to emphasize a point that I feel tends to get lost in the debate over health-care reform and economic development. I strongly feel that health-care reform will become one of our most effective economic-development tools, giving Kentucky a significant advantage over other states in attracting businesses. Just think how much of a benefit it will be for companies which are considering locating in Kentucky to know that their health-care costs will not rise each year above a specific rate.

Our administration has worked with the chambers and others to figure out how best to assist small- and medium-sized businesses who simply won't be able to afford the required coverage. Our initial calculations include $140 million set aside for the first two years to provide subsidies to these vulnerable businesses. Obviously, we can't solve the health-care problem by putting businesses out of business on a wholesale basis. We cannot create an economic-development problem to solve the health-care crisis, and we will do our best to see that they not only survive, but thrive to help our entire Commonwealth. In the very near future we will be coming forth with our completed plan with every "i" dotted and every "t" crossed.

We still plan to have a special session on health-care reform early this year. I ask for your help, your comments, your good-faith efforts to be a part of the solution. For too long we've wrung our hands over this problem and said "it's too big to solve" or "let Washington solve it." That approach has gotten us farther into the hole and with a much greater number of people in desperate need of our help now. I for one don't want to wait for Washington to tell Kentucky how to solve this problem; I want Kentuckians to meet this challenge, and I sincerely want our administration to lead the way. President Clinton has asked me personally to go forward with our effort, and in many ways lead the nation, and lay groundwork that can help him develop a national policy. It is possible that health-care reform can provide coverage to replace the present system of workers' compensation, an important issue with business and industry.

Health-care reform is something we must do, and to get the job done, we will need the support of all Kentuckians, those within the business community and those in all walks of life. Your cooperation and support in this endeavor, which is of such critical importance to so many, is greatly appreciated. And, if I or anyone in my administration can help you, your company, or your community better understand our efforts, just call. Thank you very much again for allowing me to be a part of your annual meeting.

---

1. Jerry E. Abramson (1946–), Indiana University graduate, 1968; Georgetown University School of Law, graduated with honors, 1973; L.L.D., Kentucky Wesleyan College, 1990; partner, Greenebaum, Doll & McDonald, Attorneys, 1973–85; lecturer in law, University of Louisville, 1974–75; member, board of aldermen, Louisville, 1975–79, chairman, Finance Committee, 1975–79; general counsel to Gov. John Y. Brown Jr., 1979–81; mayor, Louisville, 1986–98; vice-chairman, Democratic platform committee, 1992; Democratic National Committee, 1992; president, U.S. Conference of Mayors, 1993–98.

2. David Armstrong (1941–), B.S., Murray State University, 1961; J.D., University of Louisville, 1969; attorney general, Kentucky, 1983–87; county judge-executive, Jefferson County, 1994–98; mayor, Louisville, 1998– .

EARTH SUMMIT STEERING COMMITTEE
Louisville / January 25, 1993

It is my pleasure to welcome you to the Commonwealth of Kentucky for the first meeting of the National Steering Committee for the "From Rio to the Capitals—State Strategies for Sustainable Development" Conference. I want to thank Mayor Abramson for hosting us this afternoon. I know that many of you have come from around the country, and I thank you especially for taking the time to join us. To all of you I express my heartfelt appreciation for agreeing to serve on this committee. Most of you know the details of the conference to date. It will be held in Louisville, May 25–28. It begins

Tuesday afternoon and ends Friday afternoon. The conference is national in scope and will focus on state and local activities that promote sustainable development—the theme of last year's Earth Summit.

We do anticipate international guests and participants. We have learned since the inception of this project that the rest of the world is watching. They want to see how our nation pictures its goals and responsibilities as they relate to economic stability and protection of our planet. Your participation on this committee gives us an opportunity to avail ourselves of your expertise. But we recognize that no group will represent every single point of view. Knowing this, we have invited participants whom we feel will think beyond their own daily needs and aspirations and encompass, in their suggestions and advice, a sense of how their own needs and those of others will be met given the challenges facing our nation.

We also need to make it clear that we have been and will continue to be in contact with people around the country in order to build a balanced and informative program. As a governor in the United States, I know that government cannot proceed without the will of the people. Anyone who has tried to govern at any level knows this. In my tenure, I have constantly been impressed with the nature of our citizens and their willingness to participate in the process when asked. That is why we are working to fashion this conference in such a way that will allow the fullest possible participation by both government officials and citizens. It is our intention that this conference will serve as a forum for state and local leaders to discuss the concurrent needs of job creation and environmental protection.

You might be wondering how the idea for this conference came about. Last summer, before the Earth Summit convened, Dr. Lilyalyce Akers[1] of the United Nations Association of Kentucky brought to my attention the fact that there were no plans for any type of follow-up here in the United States to the Earth Summit. She made the very strong point that, no matter what happened in Rio, there was no avenue for communicating new ideas or initiatives to interested citizens or decision-makers in this country. She suggested, and our administration agreed, that Kentucky should take the lead in the nation by bringing together these interested citizens and decision-makers to determine what the agreements of the Earth Summit mean for our communities, states, and nation.

Since that time, many individuals have been involved in preliminary planning work for the conference. As evidenced by your membership on our national steering committee, our efforts have also extended beyond the boundaries of Kentucky as we seek advice on putting together a balanced, worthwhile conference program. To my way of thinking, Kentucky is the logical site for this conference. We fully recognize that our state can no longer afford to choose between jobs or a clean environment. We must have jobs and a clean environment. That is why we have such a keen interest in defining what sustainable development means for our communities and our state.

As many of you know, sustainable development is a term that has surfaced not only in theoretical literature but in the speeches of President Clinton. It should be a basic tenet of any state or community's plan for the future. But what does it mean? I know that I can agree with the most commonly held (and shortest) definition, "Development that meets the need of current generations without compromising the ability of future generations to meet their needs." I don't think anyone would contest this objective.

The problem lies in the definition of needs and the interpretation of what actions and decisions compromise those needs, now and in the future. While many people followed the planning and agreements which came out of the Earth Summit in Rio de Janeiro, it is clear that most of us in the United States need a better understanding of our role in promoting sustainable development and of what it means to make a commitment to work toward sustainable development. We enhanced communication and education on all levels. Most citizens, business people, and politicians are already asking, "What am I going to be asked to do?" And finally, "How much is it going to cost me?"

Defining what sustainable development will mean for states and localities will be a formidable task. Constant communication among diverse participants will be key to the success of this conference and follow-up activities on the state and local level. At the conference this May, we are inviting representatives from business and industry, civic leaders, state and local officials, non-governmental organizations, educators, professional associations, and citizens to come together to discuss their needs and their particular concerns about the future. We know that in large part the needs and concerns for Paducah, Kentucky, and Casper, Wyoming, will be different. With this in mind, we will highlight successful partnerships that have worked for a broad spectrum of problems and communities.

As members of our National Steering Committee, you will be asked to assist us in finding examples of market-oriented solutions to environmental problems as well as good examples of government programs that promote sustainable development. We want to showcase these successes and provide information on tools that are useful in addressing continual challenges facing communities and governments. We are inviting groups and individuals from across the nation to assist in planning the programs, exhibits, and special events for the conference. Our planning committees have grown to include experts from around the country and, of course, the best the Commonwealth has to offer. We look forward to welcoming the nation to Louisville and Jefferson County next May. . . .

---

1. Dr. Lilyalyce Akers, former sociology professor at the University of Louisville.

FOLLOW-UP CONFERENCE TO EARTH SUMMIT
Governors Only Session / NGA, Washington, D.C. / February 1, 1993

I. ALL governors have already received from you an invitation to the conference. We have also asked them to designate a contact person in their administrations for us; several have responded. The list is on the following page.

II. GENERAL points about the conference:

A. Kentucky is hosting the first national follow-up conference to the Earth Summit. It will be held May 25–28 in Louisville. We decided to undertake this project after it became evident that there were no plans in the United States for nationwide follow-up activities to the Rio de Janeiro meeting. We felt that elected officials, citizens, business leaders, and environmentalists should have an opportunity to come together to discuss what the agreements of the Earth Summit mean for our states and communities.

B. The focus of the conference will be on sustainable development. The conference title is "From Rio to the Capitals—State Strategies for Sustainable Development." As you know, sustainable development has many "definitions." But we recognize that it won't mean the same thing in every state or community. What is important is to help people understand what strategies work when they confront sustainable-development issues back home. We also believe it is imperative for all parties involved in development/environmental decisions to come to the table at the beginning of the process to reach mutually beneficial decisions. Helping people learn how to do this will be the objective of the conference.

C. Governors or their designees will have a very important opportunity to hear from people in their states and regions at the end of the conference about what they have learned. In reports to the governors that will be shared in a general session on Friday of the conference, the conference participants will tell the governors what their views are on strategies that could be incorporated in their state or community decision-making.

D. The NGA [National Governors's Association] is on our National Steering Committee, as are a number of other national entities and concerned individuals. We are involving as many people/groups as possible in the conference planning to ensure a balanced program. And balance is the key to the success of the conference.

E. We have invited and are optimistic that Vice-President Gore will be our major keynote speaker. We are also working with EPA and other federal agencies in an effort to have their input and representation at the conference.

F. We will be sharing additional information directly with them in the coming weeks and hope they can be with us for the conference. Should they have questions, they can contact your chief of staff or Ann James, conference coordinator, who is on the governor's office staff.

CINTAS CORPORATION ANNOUNCEMENT
Hazard / March 26, 1993

THERE is nothing any more enjoyable than being able to come to eastern Kentucky. And it is a double pleasure when I can be here to announce new jobs. I am happy to announce that Cintas Corporation, which already has three operations in Kentucky, is going to open a new manufacturing facility in Hazard. This new plant will initially employ 125 people and employ up to 250 people within the next two to three years. Each new plant expansion or new plant location we announce in Kentucky is special, but the project we are announcing today, and for which we will break ground shortly, is special for several reasons.

First of all, Cintas Corporation, with its operations in Clay City, Mount Vernon, and Owingsville, is one of our fine existing industries. Any time an existing industry expands in Kentucky, it means more than just the new jobs being created, although we are always concerned about new jobs. Whenever an existing industry expands, it shows that a company likes our workforce, our positive business climate, and it displays a vote of confidence in the future of Kentucky.

Second, this new Cintas plant is the first to be located on an industrial site acquired through the use of the new Local Government Economic Development (LGED) program that is funded through the additional coal severance tax monies now being returned to coal-producing counties like Perry. Because of the LGED program, our coal-producing counties, most of which desperately need new job opportunities, have for the first time monies which they can use to acquire industrial sites and do other things necessary to attract new industries. Throughout my campaign for governor, I advocated that more of the coal severance tax be returned to the coal-producing counties. I proposed, and with the support of members of the General Assembly who saw the wisdom of using coal tax revenues to bring other types of economic development to eastern Kentucky, got approved, legislation increasing the amount of the coal severance tax being returned to the respective coal counties. Over the next four years, Perry County can expect to receive an estimated $4.7 million in coal severance tax dollars.

The project we are announcing and beginning here today proves, beyond any doubt, the wisdom of the LGED program. This project demonstrates that earmarking a percentage of coal severance tax dollars for economic development and returning that money to coal-producing counties like Perry can be an effective tool for creating new, non-coal jobs. If we are to help all our communities grow, we must be innovative in doing those things that enhance economic development, like health-care reform that serves the interests of both the employee and the employer. With the health-care reform we have proposed, a company can locate and expand in Kentucky knowing that its health-care costs will not be burdensome.

I want to thank . . . the East Kentucky Corporation for working with Judge/Executive Sherman Neace[1] and others here in Perry County to bring this project to fruition. It is that type of team effort that is making economic development work in Kentucky. I want to welcome this new Cintas Operation to Kentucky, and to thank . . . all the fine people at Cintas for continuing to make Kentucky a vital part of their corporate endeavors. We are proud of our workers and our communities, like Hazard and Perry County, and look forward to seeing Cintas Corporation becoming an even greater part of Kentucky's future.

---

1. Sherman Neace (1941–), born in Hazard, Kentucky; Perry County judge-executive, 1986–98; coal operator, Building and Construction Company; president of Kentucky River Area Development District; chairman of Kentucky Association of Counties.

ECONOMIC DEVELOPMENT PRESS CONFERENCE
Owensboro / April 1, 1993

I AM very pleased to be here today to recognize the kind of effort that is crucial to the future of Kentucky's agriculture industry. Long before I became a public servant in this state I came to realize that agribusiness held the key to any opportunity for agriculture's growth. Only a small percentage of the food that is consumed in this state is processed here. Given our wealth of agricultural commodities, there is tremendous opportunity for growth in this industry. This produce processing project that we are announcing here today represents an important step toward realizing our full agricultural potential. It also represents what can be accomplished through the cooperative efforts of the public and private sectors. This project would not be possible without the commitment of Ellis Estate [national produce company], the Chamber of Commerce, the Economic Development Cabinet, and the farmers who will provide the production necessary to make this feasible. I commend everyone who has supported this endeavor.

Many projects of this nature have been discussed through the state. But unfortunately, few have advanced past the planning states.

More often than not, these plans are shelved due to lack of capital or insufficient interest among producers. The project is moving forward because Ellis Estate made a tremendous investment and received the necessary support from the state, the Chamber of Commerce, and farmers. Ellis Estate has joined with the state government in providing the capital, and more than forty farmers have committed the production necessary to operate this grading and packaging facility. The result is an exciting new opportunity to strengthen the farm economy in this area.

While agriculture remains the backbone of our rural economy, we cannot lose sight of the fact that rural Kentucky is dominated by small family farms that depend on off-farm income. It is estimated that about 70 percent of our farm families have off-farm income. When we create new production and marketing opportunities for farmers, we're also adding jobs that improve our quality of life. I can think of only one other initiative that is as important to the future of our farmers—and that is providing for affordable health care. For more than a year our administration has participated in one of the most important projects ever undertaken by Kentucky's farm community. I'm referring to Ag Project 2000, an initiative that has unified the farm interests of our state toward developing a comprehensive plan to strengthen our agriculture economy. This plan calls for increased farm production, as well as developing the food-processing industry in the state.

A key component of this plan is expanding agribusiness and value-added opportunities. This project in Daviess County exemplifies how we can utilize our resources to create such opportunities. Kentucky is in a favorable position to respond to growth opportunities such as this. We are endowed with a large, varied, and productive resource base that is geographically well located, within a day's drive of half the nation's population. Our strong interstate highway system and water systems make its location extremely favorable to increased marketing of farm products. If Kentucky has the policies and the economic and business climates favorable to future development of the various agriculture sectors, the state can realize its full potential from agriculture.

As Ag Project 2000 moves forward, as our state's new economic-development partnership moves forward, I hope to have many opportunities to recognize initiatives such as this one. The goal of $5 billion in annual farm income by the year 2000 can indeed be attained through the vision, hard work, and spirit of cooperation that we see here today. At this time, I'm pleased to present a check in the amount of $175,000 to go toward the purchase of equipment to be used in the processing facility. These are economic-development bond funds that the cabinet has invested in this project.[1]

---

1. On January 15, Jones made a similar speech, announcing the plant opening of Huish Detergents in Bowling Green; on March 16, he gave a speech in a similar format, announcing the creation of 250 jobs at the Stride Rite Corporation ground-breaking ceremony; on May 28, he made a similar announcement at the plant opening of Chelsea Industries in Cadiz; on August 25, he made a similar announcement, speaking at the plant opening of Nelson Metal Products Corporation in Glasgow; on September 2, he gave a similar speech at the Owensboro Grain Company opening; on October 18, he made a similar announcement, speaking in regard to the opening of Dana Corporation in Elizabethtown.

ECONOMIC DEVELOPMENT PARTNERSHIP
Frankfort / June 11, 1993

I WANT to thank each of our board members for being here this morning and to say also how much I appreciate your taking time to serve as a member of the partnership. I am excited about what is happening in regard to economic development throughout Kentucky and the role that the partnership will play in seeing that Kentucky continues to move forward in a progressive manner. Secretary Gene Strong is providing outstanding leadership in the Cabinet for Economic Development, and the cabinet's staff under Gene's leadership is doing a tremendous job in a professional manner, and they are to be commended.

Since the beginning of this administration, we have announced over 24,600 manufacturing and supportive-industry jobs in Kentucky. During this period we lost some 5,100 jobs due to plant closings, leaving us with a net gain of 19,500 jobs. Of the total number of new jobs announced, 12,600 came from plant expansions, and 11,800 came from new plant locations. Secretary Strong tells me that the number of active projects on which the cabinet is working continues to be high, and among these projects are a number that involve significant investments and job numbers. I mention these things not in a boastful way, rather to let you know that a lot of things are happening, things that are making a difference in the lives of all Kentuckians and in building a strong economic base upon which we build our future. Thanks to the support of the General Assembly, Kentucky has some of the most innovative economic-development tools of any state in the nation, and these programs are allowing us to be competitive in the recruiting of new industries and in the support of our existing industries.

Today, you will take another step toward the development of a strategic plan for economic development in Kentucky, giving Kentucky its first-ever statewide blueprint for economic development. I hope you are as excited about what we are accomplishing as I am and that you share the optimism I have for the future if we all work together and if we are willing to commit ourselves to doing those things we believe to be in the future interest of our state. I regret that my good friend W.T. Young[1] has chosen to resign from the partnership, but I know that W.T. has many demands on his time, just as I am sure that he will remain available for counsel whenever we need to call upon his expertise and guidance. Again, let me say how much I appreciate what you are doing and the opportunity I have, as governor and chairman of the partnership, to work with you.[2]

---

1. William T. Young (1922–), born in Lexington, Kentucky; B.S. in mechanical engineering, University of Kentucky, 1939; major in U.S. Army; founder of W.T. Young Foods, 1946; founder of W.T. Young, Inc., 1958; founder of Overbrook Farm; chairman, Royal Crown Companies, 1966–84; active member of board of Humana, Inc.; chair, Transylvania University board, 1977–2000; chair, Shakertown board; chair, Lexington Opera House Fund board; philanthropist.

2. On February 22, the governor gave a similar speech at the announcement of GTE's reorganization in Lexington; on August 25, he gave a similar speech at a ribbon cutting for Wagner Brake in Scottsville.

GOVERNOR'S CONFERENCE ON SMALL BUSINESS
June 16, 1993

IT'S MY pleasure to join you today to kick off this conference and to tell you what you already know: that small businesses are a major portion of the Kentucky and the national economies. Our administration recognized this fact in our earliest days. Within a month of taking office, we became the first state to use a new federal law to invest indirect state funds in an existing small business investment company. We felt it essential to tap the program and help create jobs in minority businesses and in disadvantaged areas of the Commonwealth. This cooperative, first-of-its-kind, public-private partnership has created new capital for Kentucky small businesses and put us at the leading edge of economic development.

We worked with the SBA [Small Business Administration] and our congressional delegation to forge a successful alliance that got the job done and brought Kentucky its fair share. With this conference, as with that small business investment company, we build with an eye to the future. This conference is about preserving and strengthening our existing small- and medium-business base and the team effort that is required to accomplish that task. We all know that it takes not only the immediate community to support a business effort, but that a partnership with regional, state, and federal entities strengthens our economy's very foundation. The conference we launch today is testimony to that fact.

. . . The organizations and businesses that have worked together to bring you this forum are to be congratulated for giving form to a program that truly offers much for many. On behalf of the Commonwealth of Kentucky, I want to personally thank everyone who has been a part of this effort. And despite what you might see elsewhere, positive things have [occurred] and continue to occur for Kentucky business. In 1992, we announced 14,700 net new manufacturing and support-industry jobs. In 1993, we have announced more than 4,000 similar jobs from new and expanding businesses, representing an investment of nearly $600 million. Our Economic Development Cabinet is actively involved with additional projects that will add to the quantity of new jobs being created and the quality of the job opportunities we want for our young people—the business leaders of tomorrow.

And I encourage you, as you participate in this conference, to keep an eye toward tomorrow and the changes it will bring. Changes always are accompanied by new opportunities which we have to be able to identify and meet. That's why we're here—to sharpen our skills to do just that—individually as well as collectively. Small- and medium-sized businesses make remarkable contributions to our communities and society as a whole. Our leaders in these businesses are known for their innovation, adaptability, and for creating the very jobs that sustain our communities. The rest of this decade is sure to offer new challenges to these skills. The next several days are essential tools in honing what it takes to continually succeed. I welcome all of you and encourage you to reach for all that's possible while you're here.

KENTUCKY COAL COALITION
Frankfort / July 16, 1993

GREETINGS. It's a pleasure to be with you today to celebrate accomplishments in our coal-producing counties of which we can all be proud. For twenty years, members of the Coal County Coalition have worked for a fair shake from Frankfort for your counties. I am honored to be the governor who, with strong support from you and your legislators, launched a new day for the coal regions of Kentucky.

The new local government assistance fund already is pumping millions of additional severance tax dollars into your counties for economic development. And the Coal Marketing and Export Council is hard at work developing ways to ship more coal throughout the nation and throughout the world. The council's Coal Education Committee is working with the Department of Education to develop new lesson plans and classroom materials on coal. These materials will be made available to teachers and students in all Kentucky schools. Another council committee is analyzing the impact of workers' compensation on the competitiveness of Kentucky coal. The council is also working with the Natural Resources and Environmental Protection Cabinet, railroad companies, electric utilities, and coal companies on post-combustion by-product development and disposal. These and other environmental issues being addressed will help Kentucky's lifestyle and employment.

Clean coal technologies research will lead to dramatically reduced sulfur dioxide emissions. I recognize that the people in this room undoubtedly know more about Kentucky's coal industry than I, but I think it is important to remind ourselves just what the coal industry means to Kentucky. The Kentucky coal industry employs about 28,000 persons in mining. About 112,000 jobs in Kentucky exist as the result of coal production. During the last fiscal year, coal paid over $184 million in severance taxes alone. Total revenues resulting from coal production in Kentucky in fiscal year 1992 were an estimated $552 million. Through legislation passed in the 1992 Kentucky General Assembly, the contributions of coal to our producing counties will become even greater than we now know. For many years I have believed that a much greater percentage of the coal severance monies should be returned to the coal-producing counties. During my campaign, I promised the people of all our coal-producing counties that, as your governor, I would work to change the law to allow more coal severance dollars to be returned to the local coal-producing communities. With the help of your legislators, Senate Bill 205 was passed. The new law calls for a 38 percent increase in the amount of coal severance tax monies being returned to your counties by the end of my term. This means that the amount of coal tax monies being returned will have increased to 50 percent, which had been my goal, and what I had talked about during the campaign. This new money, you know, is earmarked for economic-development projects.

The details of the operation of this program will be explained later in the program today. Lt. Gov. Paul Patton, who also served until recently as secretary of economic development, has worked hard on putting together guidelines that will enable communities to use these new development dollars in the most effective manner. Coal, as you see, is not only important for what it means as an industry unto itself, but it is helping to fund projects that will mean opportunities for the people of your counties to create new non-coal jobs.

Under the leadership of the Coal Marketing and Export Council these revenues from coal can continue to increase and foster more expansion and diversification of job opportunities. Industrial development today is highly competitive. We know from recent experience that it is not easy to attract new industries to some of the coal counties which are among those who need more jobs the most. But at the same time, we have new tools, a new spirit, and a new determination. And there have been some successes. We have new initiatives to support and sustain existing industries like our coal industry.

It is through industry that we have jobs for our people. And it is only through jobs and strong employment that we are able to do the many other things we want and need to do. We must have jobs to fund education . . . to fund health care . . . and to provide the human services and infrastructure that enhance quality of life. That is what we are focusing on in state government and that is what we want to work with you to achieve. Together we can do the job. Together we are bringing a new way of life to the coal-producing and coal-impact areas and a better life for all Kentuckians.

KENTON COUNTY ISTEA ANNOUNCEMENT
Covington City Hall / August 20, 1993

I AM pleased to announce a total of eight transportation enhancement projects throughout northern Kentucky totaling over $1 million. These projects have been tentatively approved to receive funding through the Transportation Cabinet's federal aid program. We're here at Covington City Hall this morning to announce that the City of Covington and the Covington Business Council will receive $81,000 to make enhancements to the Pike Street Corridor from I-75/71 East to the CSX Railroad tracks and Willow Run from 15th to 9th Streets. The project will include painting of the railroad overpasses, landscaping, and the creation of a program to help local businesses and property owners in restoration projects. The city of Covington will also receive $54,880 for the placement of sidewalks and berms along West 43rd Street between Winston Avenue (Ky. 16) and Latonia Avenue. The pedestrian corridor will connect two highway projects. The reconstruction of Winston Avenue is now complete, and the construction of a connector road between Latonia Avenue and 43rd Street is scheduled for completion this year. The grants we're announcing today are made possible by the federal Intermodal Surface Transportation Efficiency Act of 1991 (ISTEA), which created the new transportation enhancement program. The new law sets aside 10 percent of Kentucky's annual surface transportation program funds for projects or activities that add community or environmental value to any planned or completed transportation project and which fall into one of ten categories such as historic preservation, landscaping and scenic beautification, or pedestrian or bicycle facilities. Kentucky's share of enhancement funds will average approximately $7 million each year between 1993 and 1997. The enhancement provisions of ISTEA provide an excellent opportunity to assist local communities in their efforts to improve the appearance and character of many historic or culturally significant facilities which have a unique relationship with our transportation network. We are extremely pleased with the response from local groups and with the vast diversity of projects which have been selected. This new funding will provide the means to begin indispensable transportation enhancements. . . .[1]

---

1. Jones announced other Kenton County ISTEA grants on August 20 for the cities of Crestview Hills, Edgewood, and Florence, and the Roebling Gateway Task Force, as well as a grant for the cities of Newport and Cold Spring in Campbell County. On August 23, he announced grants to the cities of Middlesboro and Harlan, the Cumberland Development Corporation, the Lions Club of Jamestown, and the McCreary County Heritage Foundation. On August 25, he announced a grant for Simpson County Historical Properties Trust, Inc., in Franklin. On September 23, he announced grants for the cities of Morehead, Ewing, and Ashland, Mason County, and Bracken County. On October 5, he announced grants for Jefferson County and the cities of Anchorage and Louisville. On October 6, he announced a grant to the city of Frankfort, and on October 7, for the Lexington-Fayette Urban County Government, the Lexington-Frankfort Scenic Corridor, and the Kentucky Department of Highways, as well as grants for Larue County and the city of Hodgenville. On October 9, he announced grants to Jessamine County, the city of Stanford, the Kentucky Department of Parks, and the Garrard County Historical Society. The Kentucky Railway Museum, Inc., and the cities of Hopkinsville, Bedford, and Cadiz received grants three days later. On October 14, he announced a grant for the West Point Fort Duffield Memorial Committee and on November 19, the city of Bellevue.

NORTHERN KENTUCKY PLANT ANNOUNCEMENTS
Drawbridge Inn / September 27, 1993

EACH time that I have come to northern Kentucky to announce a new project, I have said that not only is this one of the fastest-growing areas in Kentucky, but one of the most dynamic business regions in the United States. I also said that we were looking forward to announcing several other new projects and many more new jobs, and this afternoon we have come together to do that. This afternoon we are formally announcing, or recognizing, five plants that are expanding or locating a new facility in the tri-county area. Through this ceremony, we want to recognize these private industries that have invested in this region and which are contributing to the economy of Kentucky through the jobs they are providing and the dollars they have invested in Kentucky. We also want this ceremony to be a salute to the people and the leadership in Boone, Campbell, and Kenton Counties for the job they are doing supporting and creating new economic growth in this region, new jobs and new investments that will continue to improve the lives of the people who live and work in northern Kentucky.

You know, we talk a lot about economic development being a team effort and a partnership between state and local governments and between the public and private sectors. State government can do things that support and stimulate the creation of new jobs, but government must look to private enterprise to create jobs like we are announcing this afternoon. Ultimately, economic development must happen at the local level, and this is why it is so important that we have good leadership and community involvement like you have here in the tri-county area.

With the help of members of the Kentucky General Assembly, Kentucky has some of the most innovative programs in the country to help lower the government-imposed costs of doing business, and many of the new jobs being created in Kentucky are due in great part to the incentive programs we have to complement the other advantages Kentucky offers new and expanding businesses. The theme of the new campaign for the Economic Development Cabinet's industrial marketing program is "Think Kentucky."

We want corporate America to think of Kentucky as a state with a pro-business climate, a productive workforce, a state that welcomes new industries, a state with ongoing programs to assist existing industries, and a state that is a leader in education and health-care reform. Kentucky is serious about jobs: serious about the jobs we now have, and the businesses and industries responsible for those jobs. We are serious about creating new jobs in Kentucky, both those created through plant expansions and new plant locations. Only by creating new jobs, and better jobs, can we give all Kentuckians the opportunity for a brighter future. Since the beginning of my term as governor, we have announced 22,520 (net) new manufacturing and supportive-industry jobs in Kentucky. Of this total, 2,254 have been announced in Boone, Campbell, and Kenton Counties.

This afternoon, we are recognizing five companies, which together are creating 505 additional new jobs, either through a plant expansion or new plant location. In alphabetical order, the companies are CR Services; Dyment, Ltd.; Roosevelt Paper Company; Tastemaker; and United Dairy Farmer.

Representative Callahan[1] will be coming forward to give you a brief overview of the individual projects, but I want to thank each of the new companies for becoming a part of Kentucky's future and to thank the existing industries for expanding their presence in Kentucky.[2]

---

1. James P. "Jim" Callahan (1939–), Thomas More College; city of Southgate councilman, 1978–81; Southgate mayor, 1982–86; elected to Kentucky house, 1986; re-elected, 1988–2000; majority caucus chairman, 1995–2000; human resources manager, Carlisle Enterprises Inc.; board of directors, Boys/Girls Club of Campbell Co.; board of directors, Northern Kentucky Convention and Visitors Bureau; board of directors, Covington Business Council. *Who's What in Kentucky Government, 1999–2000* (Frankfort, 1999).

2. On October 21, Jones gave a similar speech announcing the plant opening of Custom Food Products and made an expansion announcement the same day in Hazel Green, Kentucky, regarding the expansion of Whiting Manufacturing Company; on December 15, he gave a similar speech, announcing the plant opening of Texwood Industries in Mount Sterling; on December 14, at the Jones Plastics luncheon he announced more jobs for Lawrenceburg.

BOONE COUNTY CDBG ANNOUNCEMENT
Burlington / December 20, 1993

I'M PLEASED to be here today to give you an early Christmas present. That present comes in the form of a Community Development Block Grant in the amount of $268,222. This money will help you build the Boone County sewer system project. Thanks to this grant, seventy-one households will soon get modern sewage treatment service. This may not sound glamorous unless you don't have it.

It is critical that we continue to work toward providing these basic services to all citizens of the Commonwealth. I congratulate your leaders here in Burlington and Boone County for their work to bring this project to a reality. It will not only enhance the quality of life for many residents, but it will also foster a feeling of pride and will forge a strong sense of community here in Boone County.

Again, congratulations to you, and Merry Christmas.[1]

---

1. In similar speeches on December 20, Jones also presented CDBG grants to Robertson County for a health center; to Newport for a new facility to house the Boys and Girls Club; and to Prestonville for the Prestonville sewer collection system. Earlier, on December 13, Jones presented a CDBG grant to Ohio County to construct a senior citizens center.

SUSTAINABILITY ROUNDTABLE INFORMATION FORUM
Frankfort / February 14, 1994

IN THE summer of 1992, the Earth Summit in Rio [de Janeiro] brought nations together to discuss sustainable development issues. Last May, the "Rio to the Capitals" conference in Louisville encouraged the states to begin sustainability projects. While some people may have thought of last year's conference as strictly an "environmental conference," you know it was much more than that. It also dealt with such issues as economic development, transportation, and human services. Those of you who were there know that sustainability takes into account not just one of those issues, but all of them and more.

"Rio to the Capitals" was a multi-agency approach to the multifaceted topic of sustainable development. And it was a good example of how we can all work together toward that common goal of sustainability. Your presence here today indicates sustainable development is not just a buzzword in this Commonwealth. It is a process whose time has come. It means cooperative action among individuals, businesses, industry, schools, and government. Here's what's being done so far:

1. The Economic Development Partnership is developing the "Kentucky Strategic Plan for Economic Development," the first effort in the history of the Commonwealth to sustain and develop a long-term economic plan.
2. The Department of Agriculture has a similar planning project called "Agriculture 2000." It looks at how farming must be developed in concert with economic planning, environmental protection, education, and government help.
3. The Transportation Cabinet continues its long-range planning for a highway system that will work well into the next century.
4. And most recently, the Kentucky Long-Term Policy Research Center's "Kentucky Outlook 2000: A Strategy for Kentucky's Third Century" has begun to look at improving the way decisions are made in state government.

Those are just a few examples. They're all very important projects to Kentucky's future. And they will all help make this great Commonwealth even greater. While there is no set method for creating a sustainable development plan for Kentucky, I hope what has been said so far today, and what will still be said, will help you find a way to decide how we move toward sustainable development and how we can turn this talk into action, positive action, for the future of Kentucky.

I want to thank each of you for giving your valuable time to this forum. I also want to thank those state employees who have worked to keep the sustainable development process moving for this Commonwealth. And I wish you every success as you turn talk into action.[1]

---

1. On June 14, the governor gave a similar speech at the Kentucky Issues Conference in Louisville; on June 15, at the Economic Development Partnership Board Meeting in Louisville; on June 16, at the "Rio to the Capitals" reception; on September 6, he gave a related speech at the Financial Institutions reception at the Governor's Mansion in Frankfort; on September 8, he gave a related speech at the White House Conference on Small Business in Louisville; on September 23, at the Council of State Governments Building dedication in Lexington; on November 1, at the Industry Appreciation Luncheon in Madisonville; and on December 19 at the opening of Image Entry/Compunet America in Mount Vernon.

R.J. TOWER CORPORATION ANNOUNCEMENT
Bardstown / March 3, 1994

I AM very happy to join with Mr. Dugald Campbell, president and CEO of the R.J. Tower Corporation, to announce that the R.J. Tower Corporation is locating a new manufacturing plant in Bardstown, Kentucky. We are excited that this new plant will create 350 new jobs in Bardstown and Nelson County. This entire area will benefit from the fact that the company will invest about $26 million in the plant initially, and within two years, that investment will grow to $47 million.

Mr. Campbell, it's appropriate you've chosen historic Bardstown in which to expand your business. Your company also has a long and distinguished history, 120 years in the production of a wide range of iron and steel products. The project we are announcing today is not only an outstanding development for Bardstown and Nelson County, but also a welcome expansion of automotive-parts production in Kentucky. Mr. Campbell, I welcome you to our old Kentucky home, and I thank you for choosing Bardstown. I also want to commend Judge Dean Watts, Mayor Harry Spalding, members of the Bardstown Industrial Development Corporation, and all the fine people of Bardstown and Nelson County for the outstanding job you are doing to bring new jobs to your community.

Economic development requires a team effort, and it takes all of us working together to get the job done. The executive branch needs the support and leadership of legislators like Kenny Rapier[1] to help us create the innovative economic-development tools to attract companies like the R.J. Tower Company to our state and to help our existing industries keep existing jobs and create new ones. I say over and over again as I speak to groups throughout Kentucky, "there is no limit to what we can accomplish if we all work together."

Happy Chandler used to say, "Opinions die, but the record lives forever." And the record will show that we have been working together extremely well. Last year we announced a net 14,591 new manufacturing and supportive-industry jobs in Kentucky. The latest industrial activities scoreboard, published by *Site Selection* magazine, has Kentucky ranked sixth nationally in the number of new facilities and plant expansions announced in 1993. And Kentucky is one of just a handful of states in the U.S. that continues to gain manufacturing jobs. Again, the record speaks for itself. That record also shows that from 1988 through 1992, manufacturing jobs in Kentucky increased by 4.8 percent, while the number of manufacturing jobs in the United States dropped by 6.6 percent.

I am pleased to say that Kentucky's manufacturing today is at its highest level since 1979. And new plant openings in 1994 may well bring the number of manufacturing jobs in Kentucky to an all-time high. The record shows that these new and better jobs have improved per capita income for Kentuckians. For the past six years, Kentucky's percentage increase in per capita income has been greater than the percentage increase in the U.S. In fact, in 1992 Kentucky ranked fourth among all the states in the growth of per capita personal income. That's a pretty good record, isn't it?

And all of this has happened because of the partnership that has been formed between state government, local governments, and private companies like R.J. Tower Corporation. By providing a positive business climate that is conducive to growth and profitability of private enterprise, we are enhancing new and better opportunities for all Kentuckians. So today, we celebrate new opportunities for this company, this community, and the people who make this state so unique. If we can keep this forward progress, one day we will "weep no more" about unemployment in Kentucky.[2]

---

1. Kenny Rapier (1936–), Democrat from Bardstown; B.A., Bellarmine College; self-employed; army; chairman, Building Fund for Nelson County Mentally and Physically Handicapped; director, Bardstown-Nelson County Industrial Development Corp.; former member, Bardstown Independent School Board; elected Kentucky house, 1980, re-elected, 1982–96; Democratic whip, 1985–86. *1996 Kentucky General Assembly Directory.*

2. On April 8, Jones gave a similar speech announcing the creation of 155 new jobs at a welcome ceremony for American Tape Company in Richmond; on June 28, he gave a speech in Bowling Green, thanking Corvette for staying in Kentucky; on July 21, he gave a similar speech, announcing the creation of 150 new jobs for Madisonville at Automotive Industries; and on September 2, he gave a speech at CSX in Raceland regarding their plan to stay in business in Kentucky.

FOREST INDUSTRIES ASSOCIATION
Louisville / March 3, 1994

THIS is an exciting time for the Commonwealth's forest industry and for Kentucky. Now, more than ever, there is a great interest in Kentucky's forests and its forest industries. We have a $1.6 billion forest industry in the Commonwealth with 26,000 jobs as a result. With the decline of western woods, there is a greater demand for eastern hardwoods. So the spotlight is on Kentucky and the quality wood grown in this region. This is good news for the forest industry and for Kentucky's economy. I can proudly say to you today that Kentucky is preparing to meet the demands of this forestry "boom" with the assistance of a qualified and professional staff in the Division of Forestry.

The division has established programs that provide information to landowners on stewardship and forest management. Several programs, such as the forest stewardship program and the stewardship incentive program, offer incentives for better forest management. The Kentucky master logger program is an excellent example of how the Kentucky Forest Industry Association [KFIA}, the Division of Forestry, and other agencies are working together to meet the training needs of loggers in the state. I feel confident we are well prepared to meet this interest in Kentucky's forests. And I want to assure you that, as far as the future is concerned, yes, we can "see the forest for the trees" in Kentucky. We are making plans to increase our efforts in the coming years.

As many of you know, the Division of Forestry requested a number of new forester positions that went unfunded for this biennium—the limit put on state employees prohibited this increase. However, the Natural Resources and Environmental Protection Cabinet has requested and received authority from the legislature to transfer two service foresters from the Department for Surface Mining Reclamation and Enforcement to the Division of Forestry. The first order of business for these employees will be to work with the Economic Development Cabinet to further Kentucky's forest industries and to work with private landowners. Providing adequate assistance to forest landowners and the forest industry is a priority for the cabinet and for this administration. It is the intent of the present budget bill to place between ten and twenty new foresters in the division within the next two years. We know there is a need for this extra professional personnel, and we're trying hard to meet it within our budget constraints.

It is my pleasure to announce that the 19th annual Governor's Conference on the Environment, set for September 29 through October 1, will focus on forestry in Kentucky. Immediately before the conference, I am convening a forest summit to discuss the needs of private landowners, the forest industry, its employees, and forest products manufacturers. I want to bring everyone together to discuss the pressing issues of the industry. I am looking forward to KFIA and interested environmental groups joining with the Division of Forestry and the Natural Resources and Environmental Protection Cabinet to play a large role to make this summit a success for the future of Kentucky's forests and related jobs.

POWELL COUNTY INDUSTRIAL BOARD APPRECIATION BANQUET
Natural Bridge State Park / April 12, 1994

I THINK it is extremely appropriate that you are recognizing your existing industries tonight. We all work hard to attract new companies to Kentucky, and when a new industry moves in, that usually grabs the headlines. But we must also appreciate and take care of the many fine businesses we already have. This banquet here tonight shows that you are doing that on the local level. And I must tell you, our record shows we are doing that on the state level as well. In the first twenty-seven months of our administration, we added 32,000 net new manufacturing jobs in Kentucky. Half of those jobs have come from 171 new industries that have moved into the state.

In Powell County, that includes C-F-C International in Stanton and H.S. Lumber and Red River Hardwoods in Clay City. Just those three new industries here involve nearly 150 new jobs and an investment in Powell County of $4.1 million. But in addition to those new industries that have come into the state, more than one thousand *existing* plants in Kentucky have expanded. And those expansions have resulted in sixteen thousand new jobs. Whether a company adds one new job, or ten, or a hundred, that's extremely good news for the person with a family, who now has money to buy food and clothes and medicine. And that's good news for the community, because more people will have money to spend *in* the community. So, the benefits of even *one* new job affect many more people.

And remember, here in Kentucky, since our administration began, we've been able to add 32,000 new jobs. I'm proud to be able to say . . . Kentucky is one of only a few states in which the number of manufacturing jobs is *increasing. Site Selection* magazine, in its annual scoreboard of industrial activity, ranked Kentucky *sixth* in the entire country in the number of new plants and plant expansions announced in 1993. And this year, we expect manufacturing employment in Kentucky to reach a record level. All this has helped the state's unemployment rate to stay nearly a full percentage point below the national average. And these new jobs are good-paying jobs.

Kentucky ranked fourth in per capita income growth in the United States in the past two years. All of these numbers I've been mentioning illustrate this important fact: in Kentucky, we're working *with* business to provide work for Kentuckians statewide. And here in Powell County, you're working with the industries you have to provide work for a lot of people in this area. The things you have done and are doing here in Powell County exemplify what communities must do to be successful to retain existing jobs and to attract new ones.

You have an industrial authority that is a cooperative effort between city and county governments. And you have invested in industrial sites, which a community must have if it expects to compete for new industries. But you have gone one step further, and tonight is a good example. You are providing what we like to call "service after the sale." Once you have good businesses here, you're determined to keep them happy, and keep them here. And that is the key to your success.

There is another area in which "service after the sale" is needed, and that is in the state parks system. For a long time, we have "sold" tourists on the fact that Kentucky state parks are the crown jewel of this nation's parks system. But they are also jewels in Kentucky's economy. Listen to these numbers: the 15 state parks in Kentucky are responsible for 7,500 jobs in the parks and the surrounding communities. The people who come to our parks spend $290 million *every year*. And the parks generate $30 million in state and local taxes *every year.*

As we all know, the tourism industry in Kentucky is the *third* largest industry in the state, and one of the fastest growing. But look around you, and you can tell, we have let the crown jewel become tarnished. As these wonderful facilities began to show some wear, as pools cracked and roofs leaked, we did not repair them. As a result, our parks are in disrepair. Just as we cannot ignore the needs of existing industry in Kentucky, we cannot ignore the needs of our existing state parks. That is why two years ago, I proposed a $100 million bond issue to rebuild the parks system. This money will prevent further deterioration of our park infrastructure and upgrade the system to ensure it remains competitive for the years ahead.

Over the past two years, our Tourism Cabinet has conducted a comprehensive need analysis of every park in the state to determine exactly what has to be done and where. Here at Natural Bridge, we have identified many critical problems. The three current sewage-treatment plants here are outdated and ineffective. They must be demolished and replaced. There are portions of the lodge foundation that are washed out and must be replaced to prevent further structural damage. The fire alarm and electrical systems badly need modernization, and the plumbing in the lodge has to be replaced. The Natural Bridge State Park has been targeted for more than $5 million in repairs.

1. Improving the campground will cost $325,000;
2. Renovating Hoedown Island will take more than a half million;
3. The price tag on renovating the lodge is right at $800,000;
4. Replacing the pool will cost $2.6 million;
5. And the new sewer plant has a cost of just over a million dollars.

As you can tell, these aren't flashy, sexy projects. They are, however, improvements that are absolutely essential for the future of the park. Without immediate attention, this park could be shut down. And Natural Bridge State Park is too important to this region and to the state to take that risk. We are at a critical crossroads that will dramatically affect the future of the entire parks system. I believe we must act now to save the parks, and I call on you for help. We must find a way to finance our $100 million parks' bond [issue]. And I'm confident that the good men and women in the legislature will work with us to come up with the right way.

Sen. John "Eck" Rose and Rep. Adrian Arnold and Rep. Drew Graham[1] are all good people, and I think you all know they listen to you. I'm asking you to let them know how important it is to renovate this state park and the others in the state. Our parks are an important industry in this state. And we must continue to keep this industry growing strong.[2]

---

1. Adrian Arnold (1932–), of Mount Sterling; attended Morehead State University; elected to Kentucky house, 1973; re-elected, 1975–2000; farmer. *Who's What in Kentucky Government 1999–2000* (Frankfort, 1999). Rep. Drew Graham (1961–), of Winchester; B.S., M.A. from University of Kentucky; elected to house, 1992; re-elected, 1994–98; farmer, businessman. *Who's What in Kentucky Government 1997–98* (Frankfort, 1999).

2. Jones gave a related speech on July 21 to the Kentucky Crushed Stone Association in Frankfort.

FOSROC GRAND OPENING
Georgetown / May 5, 1994

GREETINGS. We are extremely pleased to help you celebrate the grand opening of the Fosroc North American Corporate Center here in Georgetown. The Kentucky Derby is still two days away, but Kentucky's economy is already in the winner's circle, and Fosroc is one of the companies we have to thank for it. You have a slogan here at Fosroc: "The right chemistry for construction and mining." I'd like to borrow part of that phrase for a moment, because it accurately describes what's been going on in Kentucky in the past two years.

In Kentucky, we have the right chemistry for economic growth. The proof is in these numbers: the most recent unemployment statistics show Kentucky's unemployment rate at 5.2 percent. The national jobless rate is 6.8 percent. So Kentucky is a full 1.6 percent better than the national average. And we're continuing to improve. Over the past twenty-eight months, we have announced 33,000 net new manufacturing and supportive-industry jobs in Kentucky, and 4,200 of those jobs have come in the first quarter of this year. At this rate, we may reach a record level of manufacturing employment in Kentucky in 1994.

Now, let's talk about income. Paychecks are getting better. Kentucky now ranks eighth in the country in per capita income growth. Over the past two years, Kentucky's per capita income growth has been 10.9 percent, compared with the national average of 8.6 percent. Our growth rate is better than forty-two other states. So here in Kentucky, we're offering more jobs, and those jobs are paying more. Why is this happening? I believe there are two big reasons.

The first is Kentucky's willingness to invest in its economic future. We are willing to share in the investment that private companies are making in Kentucky. We make it attractive for companies to modernize, to expand, or to build new facilities. We also invest in worker training, whether it is for entry-level jobs or upgrading skills.

The second big reason for Kentucky's economic success is that our investment in our students is beginning to pay off. Usually when we talk about raising capital, we're talking about money. But the Kentucky Education Reform Act is raising the *intellectual* capital of our young people. This past year, nearly four of five schools in Kentucky showed improvements against one of the most rigorous testing programs in the nation. We are helping students increase their traditional knowledge, but we're also teaching them how to improve their thinking and writing skills. That will help them land even better jobs in the future, not just here in Kentucky, but throughout the world.

And as more international companies, such as Burmah Castrol, invest in Kentucky, our workforce will stand ready to compete with the best in the world. All of these things—per capita income, job growth, lower unemployment, and education reform—serve as the right chemistry for economic growth. Thank you again, Fosroc, for making Kentucky your home.

CAGLE'S INC. ANNOUNCEMENT
Franklin / May 20, 1994

Good news always excites me. And the good news we are announcing here today is among the most exciting I've had the pleasure of announcing since I became governor. I stand here today with Douglas Cagle, chairman and C.E.O. of Cagle's Incorporated, to announce that this outstanding company is locating a $30 million chicken broiler complex right here in Franklin, Kentucky. This new operation will create up to sixteen hundred new jobs and will require contracts with up to two hundred chicken growers in the area. In addition to the jobs created by the different units of this complex and the number of people working as chicken growers and producers, this operation will create a new market for grain farmers in this region. That's because nearly five million bushels of grain will be needed each year. The total investment in this project will be about $47 million.

Ladies and gentlemen, this is great news for the city of Franklin, for Simpson County, and for all of Kentucky. Throughout the state, we are creating jobs for Kentuckians. And we're not just bragging . . . that's fact! The latest unemployment figures for the state show that Kentucky's unemployment rate now stands at 4.9 percent. That is the lowest unemployment rate in Kentucky in more than sixteen years, and it compares with a national unemployment rate of 6.2 percent. Since this administration began, we have added 36,680 net new jobs. That includes 7,339 net new manufacturing and related jobs in Kentucky just this year. At this rate, we may well see manufacturing jobs at a record high in Kentucky later this year. And for this, we have to thank Cagle's and many other new and existing businesses in Kentucky.

They have shown the confidence in Kentucky to invest in Kentucky's future. Just think of what sixteen hundred new jobs will do to help lower Simpson County's 7.0 percent unemployment rate! In addition, thanks to Cagle's, this project is opening up new enterprise opportunities for farmers and creating new markets for grain producers. This is the type of economic development that rural Kentucky needs and these are the types of new economic opportunities we want to develop for Kentucky agriculture.

Mr. Cagle, I welcome you on behalf of the Commonwealth of Kentucky and thank you for choosing Franklin, Kentucky, for this new project. I assure you that the excitement and enthusiasm being shown here this afternoon will continue as you move forward into production. We have a great labor force here in Simpson County and throughout Kentucky from which you can hire some of the most productive workers in America. We have progressive farmers in this area who will prove to be efficient chicken growers and producers and progressive grain farmers who can supply you with quality grain.

We have in Kentucky a very strong partnership between state and local governments, which together join in a strong partnership with the private sector. Agriculture has always been a basic part of Kentucky's economy, and projects like Cagle's Incorporated can bring new direction and new opportunities to this important industry. We receive the best of two worlds from projects like this. We gain new manufacturing jobs, while creating new agricultural enterprises and new markets for farm products. Mr. Cagle, thank you again for making this a great day for all of Kentucky. We are proud to have you in Kentucky and proud for Kentucky to be a part of your company's future.

DOUGLAS AUTOTECH CORPORATION
Hopkinsville / June 9, 1994

IT IS a real pleasure to be in Hopkinsville and Christian County this morning to announce an economic-development project that will mean new jobs and new investments for this community. I am happy to join Mr. Jerry Higgins, president and C.E.O. of Douglas Autotech Corporation, in announcing that Douglas Autotech plans to locate a new manufacturing plant here in this facility that will create 140 new jobs. This new operation will represent an investment of about $17 million, and will manufacture automotive steering columns. Mr. Higgins, on behalf of the people of Kentucky, I welcome you to our state and thank you for choosing Kentucky for this new plant. You have chosen a fine community as the location of your new plant, and I can assure you that you will find Hopkinsville and Christian County to be very progressive and very supportive of business and industry.

Douglas Autotech is a subsidiary of Fuji Kiko, Ltd., a Japanese firm. I was scheduled to meet with officials of Fuji Kiko during the economic-development trip to Japan had I been able to go, but as you know, I had to cancel and ask Lt. Gov. Paul Patton to represent me on that trip. Lieutenant Governor Patton and Secretary Gene Strong have told me of the cordial reception they received from all the officials with whom they met and the high esteem Japanese business leaders have for Kentucky and the people of Kentucky. Douglas Autotech becomes the eighty-second Japanese-owned business in Kentucky. The 140 new jobs this plant will create bring to 23,640 the number of announced jobs these Japanese-owned facilities mean for Kentucky. These eighty-two projects represent an investment of more than $4.1 billion. Douglas Autotech is the eighty-seventh automotive-related company to announce in Kentucky during the past ten years, with several of these projects being located right here in Hopkinsville and Christian County. These eighty-seven automotive plants represent over 19,900 new jobs and more than $3.6 billion in new investments and are located in thirty-five different Kentucky counties.

Kentucky's business economy is highly diversified, and I don't want to overlook other industries as I point to how much the automotive industry means to Kentucky. Rather, I mention these facts to show why Kentucky's economy is growing and why our per capita income is growing, and why our manufacturing employment is nearing a record level. We are doing many things right in Kentucky. We are accomplishing good things because of the strong partnership that exists between state government and our local communities like Hopkinsville and Christian County, and between the public and private sectors. I want to share some other good news along those lines: I met again this morning with Rep. Ramsey Morris and Rep. Jim Bruce[1] regarding the Hopkinsville Industrial Park. Ramsey and Jim, by the way, along with Senator Pendleton,[2] wanted to be here today, but unfortunately couldn't join us because of legislative commitments.

After talking with them and with Secretary Gene Strong, I am pleased to announce that we are committed to funding over $100,000 worth of infrastructure improvements at the Hopkinsville Industrial Park through economic-development bonds. Construction should begin as early as next month. I might also mention we are committed to another project here, which will enhance economic development in Christian County and the region. Our budget proposal, currently before the legislature, sets aside $8 million for bonds to fund the Hopkinsville Regional Technichal Training Center. This joint project between our Workforce Development Cabinet and the UK Community College System will provide job training and retraining within this community.

It is important for both the recruitment of new business and the success of existing business. If it is approved by the General Assembly, we hope to open the center in the summer of 1997. The center will serve three hundred to four hundred students. The new Douglas Autotech Plant we are announcing today is a tribute to the leadership and commitment of a lot of people, and a celebration of what we are accomplishing by working together . . .

---

1. James E. Bruce (1927–), B.S., University of Tennessee; Democratic Kentucky state representative, 9th District, 1963– ; re-elected, 1965–2000; chair, Banking/Insurance Committee; farmer. *Who's What in Kentucky Government 1999–2000* (Frankfort, 1999). Ramsey Morris (1940–), elected Kentucky house, 1976, re-elected, 1978–94; chairman, State Government Committee; self-employed businessman, wholesale tobacco/mobile homes; Marine Corps. *1994 Kentucky General Assembly Directory.*

2. Joseph Pendleton (1946–), Hopkinsville Community College; Murray State University; Democratic Kentucky state senator, 3rd district, elected, 1992; re-elected, 1996–2000; senate president pro tem, 1997–99; farmer, farm operations manager, Murray State University. *Who's What in Kentucky Government, 1999–2000* (Frankfort, 1999).

CDBG ANNOUNCEMENT
Richmond / July 8, 1994

I'M PLEASED to be able to bring you not one, but three pieces of good news today. First, I'm happy to announce that the city of Richmond has been awarded a Community Development Block Grant of $1 million. This will allow you to proceed with Phase Three of the Linden Street Project. Specifically, this money will allow you to acquire twenty-four structures and seven vacant lots, relocate eighteen households and a church, and rehabilitate nineteen structures. In addition, sidewalks and curbs will be installed and streets will be paved. This money will go a long way toward improving living conditions for people in the Linden Street area and will greatly improve the neighborhood. So it is with great pleasure that I present to Mayor Ann Durham a check for $1 million.

My next announcement affects our neighbors in Estill County. Estill County has been awarded a Community Development Block Grant of $685,250 that will allow the county to provide water service to several hundred families in the southeastern part of the county. This money will pay for the construction of nearly thirty miles of water lines to serve 242 rural customers in the Barnes Mountain and Wagersville areas. The water will be provided by the Estill County Water District. This new water supply will replace private water supplies which—in some cases—have been contaminated. The block grant money will be combined with a Farmers Home Administration Grant and a loan to make this project possible. So now, I'd like to present this check for $685,250 to Estill County Judge/Executive Dwight Arvin.

And my final announcement today concerns the city of Brodhead in Rockcastle County. We are pleased to announce to you today that a Community Development Block Grant of $300,000 has been awarded for the Brodhead Wastewater Treatment Upgrade and Line Extension Project. This money will allow the city of Brodhead to upgrade its sewer collection and treatment system. Sewer service will be provided for the first time to residents of Cash Street. And service lines will be provided and tap fees waived for people with low and moderate incomes. This will make a tremendous difference for the nearly four hundred households that will be affected. I'd like to present C.B. Owens, who is representing Mayor Billy Bussell, with a check for $300,000.[1]

---

1. In 1994, Jones traveled the Commonwealth announcing CDBG Grants for many counties and communities. On March 24, he presented Cave City with money for a sewer extension project; Powdery with funds for its Hillside Redevelopment Program; Shepherdsville with money for the Salt River Revitalization Project; and Warren County with funds for the Girls Incorporated Activity Center. On March 28, he presented Beattyville with money to acquire property for the Happy Top Affordable Housing Subdivision; Somerset with funds for the Clifty Street Re-Development Project; and Wolfe County with money for its Senior Center Historical Renovation Project. On May 5, Jones presented Owen County a CDBG to renovate the Owen County Courthouse to bring it into compliance with the Americans with Disabilities Act. During July, the governor made a number of trips presenting CDBG Grants: to Middlesboro to rehabilitate the Queensbury Heights area; to Shelbyville to help the Martinsville neighborhood; to La Grange to fund the Redevelopment Project for the Sauer Alley-First Street Area; to Danville for the Third Street Revitalization Project; to Catlettsburg to modify the wastewater treatment plant; to Carter County to install approximately twenty-three miles of distribution waterline; to Morehead to fund the second phase of the West Morehead Project; to Morgan County for water improvements; to Vanceburg to rehabilitate homes and provide water and sewer lines; to Prestonsburg to install storm water drainage pipes and construct catch basins; to Nelson County for improved water services in Nelsonville; to Clinton County to install thirty-seven miles of water lines; to Breathitt County to acquire and renovate the Jefferson Hotel in Jackson for independent living opportunities for very low income mentally and developmentally disabled adults; to Salyersville

to expand its wastewater treatment facility; to Pike County for water improvements; to Kenton County to fund the water expansion project; to Glencoe for housing renovations; to Grant County for the Bullock Pen Water Expansion Project; to McCracken County to fund the Woodlawn Redevelopment Project; to Hardin to improve its water system; to Mayfield for the Kings Drive Redevelopment Project; to Fordsville for the Community Infrastructure Rehabilitation Project; and to Providence for the Green Street Redevelopment Project. On August 19, Jones announced CDBG grants for Bourbon County, Bracken County, and the city of Carlisle for improvements in their water services. In October, he presented CDBG grants to Clay City for the Third Avenue Redevelopment Project and to Paducah for the Martin Luther King Area Housing Initiative Project.

INTERNATIONAL TRADE CONFERENCE
Northern Kentucky / November 2, 1994

I AM happy to have this opportunity to welcome all of you to the sixth annual Kentucky World Trade Conference. In a moment, it will be my pleasure to introduce the keynote speaker of the evening, Kenneth D. Brody, the chairman of the Export-Import Bank of the United States. Before I do that, I want to congratulate everyone who planned this conference. I am really impressed with the qualifications of the people who have come here to share their international trade expertise with Kentucky companies and development officials. I am pleased that business men and women from a number of countries are here to give us their insight. I am grateful that the federal government is showing its support of this conference through the participation of Chairman Brody and the assistant commissioner for commercial operations for the U.S. Customs Service, Samuel H. Banks. In addition, I am honored that the ambassador from Singapore to the United States, the Honorable S.R. Nathan, has come to speak with us. To each of our guests, I say welcome to Kentucky, and be assured that my office is always open to you.

This conference is an excellent way to provide practical information and advice about the "Hot Spots for International Trade" and how to do business in these hot spots. I believe that this theme is especially appropriate, because I believe that Kentucky is a hot spot for international trade. We have unique products recognized throughout the world. These include bourbon, thoroughbred horses, and tobacco. This also includes automobiles, metals, chemicals, electrical equipment, high-tech office equipment, agricultural products, and many other goods and services. Kentucky's workers are becoming recognized by the entire world for the quality of their work. For example, our Georgetown, Kentucky, Toyota plant is now exporting vehicles to Japan. Kentucky's Ford Explorers, heavy trucks, and utility trucks are recognized everywhere for their quality. The Corvette is one of a kind and has devotees throughout the world.

I understand from the U.S. Department of Commerce office that Kentucky in 1993 exported more than $4.2 billion of goods and services to some 150 countries. That's good news, but we want to do more. This Kentucky World Trade Conference is showing the great opportunities for expanding our Commonwealth's international trade. I am particularly impressed with the opportunities that are arising in the so-called big emerging markets (B.E.M.s). Presently, these are China, Indonesia, India, South Korea, Mexico, Argentina, Brazil, South Africa, Poland, and Turkey. These will likely be joined in coming years by others such as Vietnam, Thailand, Venezuela, and Colombia.

It is almost staggering to imagine what has been predicted: that by the year 2000, the United States may be trading more with the big emerging markets than we do with Europe and Japan. This is not to overlook the importance of Europe and Japan. It is simply to illustrate how the fundamentals of world trade are changing and the magnitude of opportunities that are being created. President Clinton has made a major commitment to ensure that U.S. businesses can and will seize the great new opportunities in world trade. His leadership was crucial for congressional approval of NAFTA. He is giving strong leadership on the agreements reached in the general agreement on tariffs and trade. His National Export Strategy is a far-sighted commitment to effectively harness the full resources of the U.S. government to stimulate exports and ensure the ability of U.S. businesses to compete globally.

International trade is vital to Kentucky, as it is to the entire United States. We are undertaking similar initiatives in Kentucky. The Cabinet for Economic Development has developed an excellent international trade office. That office is to extend its services to Kentucky companies which are either entering the export market or expanding their world trade activities. The strategic plan for economic development, which is being developed and implemented by the Economic Development Partnership Board, has three major tactics to achieve the goal of making Kentucky globally competitive. These are:

(A) create a foreign trade and investment office in the Cabinet for Economic Development;
(B) offer seminars for Kentucky firms in doing business overseas; and
(C) encourage and support industry-based consortia for export development.

Teams of leaders in business, economic development, government, research, law, and other fields are working together to ensure that Kentucky continues to be even more competitive in the global market. I applaud the work of the tactic teams, and I look forward to helping achieve the goal of making Kentucky even more competitive globally. I want the label, "Made in Kentucky," to be a label of global quality, because that will reflect well on Kentuckians, the best group of people on this planet. . . .

DELTA RIBBON CUTTING
Covington / December 1, 1994

ON behalf of the people of Kentucky, I wanted to come here today to thank Delta for showing the confidence in Kentucky to expand here. This $375 million expansion shows to me your belief that Kentucky is the right place for you to do business. Doubling the number of gates here from twenty-five to fifty is indicative to me that you believe that Kentucky is on the "grow." And, I believe, the fact that this Delta hub is your third busiest is further proof of that growth. Your growth is good business for you. But it is also good business for northern Kentucky.

Delta's operations here add more than $425 million to the economy. That means jobs, more than 3,700 from Delta alone. And Delta's success is being repeated throughout Kentucky. Here's an example: more than 61,000 more Kentuckians are working right now than at this time last year. In fact, Kentucky's unemployment rate for October, the most recent reporting period, is the lowest October rate in seventeen years. Those jobs and our downsizing of state government by eliminating more than 1,800 full-time jobs has given Kentucky its largest budget surplus in history. So I want to thank Delta and Ron Allen[1] for contributing to Kentucky's bright economic picture. This is further proof that we're all working together to keep Kentucky "Flying High."[2]

---

1. Ron Allen (1942–), B.S., industrial engineering, Georgia Tech, 1964; named Delta Airlines' youngest-ever CEO in 1987.

2. Jones gave a related speech on July 28 to the Kerr Group in Bowling Green regarding their corporate opening.

OPENING OF THE GREEN RIVER CORRECTIONAL COMPLEX
Central City / December 16, 1994

It is good to be in Muhlenberg County, and particularly here in Central City, as we open this new correctional facility. Secretary Paul Isaacs and Commissioner Lewis[1] have both told me that they will have no problem filling these 550 new cells. Corrections is certainly a "growth industry," so there's quite a bit of "job security" for the staff of the Department of Corrections. Crime and crime-related issues have hit the top of the political agenda at the national, state, and local level. That's because crime is no longer just a "big city" problem.

While the overall rate of serious crime in America fell by 3 percent in the first half of 1994, murder rates increased by 14 percent in cities of 50,000 to 100,000 in population. Kentucky is not immune to this increased level of violence. We face many challenges in state government, but none is more important than protecting our people. The citizens of this Commonwealth have a right to expect that action will be taken against those who deal drugs and commit crimes that threaten the order and security of our communities. That's why, as you may know, I included major changes in Kentucky's drug laws in my legislative agenda in 1992. The General Assembly enacted most of our recommendations, and we now have much tougher laws that specifically target drug dealers who prey on juveniles and tougher laws for repeat drug offenders. Earlier this year, our administration proposed a complete crime-control legislative package. Our proposals included increasing the penalty for crimes involving the deadly combination of drugs and guns; criminalizing the possession of any firearm by a convicted felon; penalizing those people who carry firearms into bars and taverns; requiring state officials to give notice to victims when convicts are released; and new penalties for using ammunition called "black talon," whose only purpose is to maim or kill people. These proposals were adopted.

Of course, if you have tougher laws, you have to have a place to put the lawbreakers. And the opening of the Green River Correctional Complex will significantly expand the flexibility of the Department of Corrections in meeting the need for more secure prison beds. This facility will employ 209 full-time staff members and will have an annual operating budget of $8.8 million. While the costs associated with building and operating a prison can be mind-boggling, the economic spinoffs for Muhlenberg County and Central City have been significant. Those economic benefits will increase as the facility becomes a stable source of employment for this region and pumps most of its annual operating budget back into the local economy.

To give you a couple of examples: over 70 percent of the people hired to work at the prison are from Muhlenberg or surrounding counties. And already, a new motel, the Hatfield Inn, has been constructed due to the opening of this facility. Even in the planning stages, this correctional facility has had a positive impact on Muhlenberg County. The Peabody Coal Company donated 175 acres of reclaimed strip-mine land to Central City. The city then purchased an additional twenty-five acres and donated the entire two hundred–acre site to the state. Central City assisted in site preparation and provided all utilities at no cost to the state. The enthusiasm, commitment, and community support has been overwhelming. In addition to being a good neighbor economically, this new facility also will be a responsible neighbor.

The latest security technology has been utilized throughout the grounds. This advanced security system includes a double security perimeter fence with rolls of lethal razor ribbon and a sophisticated electronic-detection system. Of course, the most important security component of any correctional facility is a well-trained staff and a well-managed program. The Green River Correctional Complex will operate on a unit management concept with staff providing direct supervision of inmates at all times. Basic education programs and vocational classes in carpentry, masonry, plumbing, and computer-aided drafting will be available to those inmates who wish to prepare themselves for life after prison. Individual counseling and a variety of self-help groups also will be available. In addition, some of the inmates here will be helping the taxpayers of Kentucky as they help themselves.

There is, within this complex, a 15,000–square-foot furniture plant, operated by correctional industries, which will employ up to sixty inmates. These inmates will manufacture an estimated $500,000 worth of office furniture each year for use by state and local government agencies. Profits from the sale of this office furniture will be turned back to the state to help defray the cost of incarceration. This concept of "inmates paying their own way" will reduce taxpayers' burden in maintaining the operation of this facility.

Not only will the Green River Correctional Complex become a producer of prison-made products, the facility has been and will continue to be a consumer of inmate-made products as well. In fact, the majority of furnishings in the administration area, dorms, dining hall, and visitor areas were made by inmates working in correctional industries. The janitorial supplies and even clothes the inmates wear are supplied by correctional industries. So far, almost $750,000 worth of supplies and furnishings for this new facility have been supplied by our own correctional industries. I think all of these things help in our overall effort to make state government more efficient, to save money wherever possible, and to eliminate waste.

And I'm proud to announce today that we have another example of how we've been able to cut costs. As you are aware, health-care reform has been a major priority for my administration. As a part of this overall effort, Commissioner Lewis and his staff in the Department of Corrections have worked diligently to reduce and control expenditures while providing the level of health care the law requires. In 1992, that cost for medical services was $1,930 per inmate per year. In fiscal year 1993, that decreased for the first time in the department's history, to a cost of $1,638 per inmate per year. And in this year, in fiscal year '94, that cost has gone down again to $1,585 per inmate per year. So we've gone from just over $1,900 a year to just under $1,600 a year in two years!

This represents an astounding 18 percent reduction during a time when the consumer price index for medical services rose nationally by 10.8 percent. During the same period, per-inmate costs for outside physician referral decreased by 15 percent and costs for outside hospitalizations decreased by 36 percent. And now, in a further effort to control what had become an unchecked system of medical care upon demand, this administration is implementing a new policy that will require inmates to pay two dollars for each medical office visit that they request. Only inmates who can afford to pay will be charged this nominal fee. But what's important here is that we're installing some responsibility. This new policy is expected to slow down the sometimes frivolous access to scarce medical resources without regard to financial consequences. This system will force inmates to make the same type of choices you and I make when considering medical treatment. Where it has been tried in other jurisdictions, significant cost savings have resulted.

This new Green River Correctional Complex is symbolic of the progress we have made during the past three years. However, our work is not yet done. So, as the staff of this new prison begins to carry out its mission to provide safe and secure incarceration for those who violate the laws of the Commonwealth, we all will increase our efforts, in this, the final year of our administration, to make the Commonwealth of Kentucky more secure for our citizens. I know we can count on your support. . . .

---

1. Justice Secretary Paul Isaacs and Corrections Commissioner Jack Lewis.

INFORMATION SUPERHIGHWAY ANNOUNCEMENT
Frankfort / December 22, 1994

EIGHTEEN months ago, I directed Pat Mulloy,[1] my finance secretary at the time, to undertake one of the most ambitious tasks of this administration. I asked him to identify and round up a qualified group of state government technology experts for the purpose of developing a request for proposal (RFP) for an information superhighway. This is the electronic equivalent, if you will, of the interstate highway system, with one big difference. I told him there had to be an access ramp for every one of Kentucky's 120 counties and it had to be in place before I left office. I became interested in the concept of a state information backbone through my involvement with the National Governors' Association, where I learned of similar initiatives in Iowa and North Carolina. It became clear to me that if Kentucky was going to lead the nation in areas such as education and health-care reform and continue our success in economic development, we had to rapidly develop a means to bring Kentuckians closer together.

Because our 120 counties are so diverse socially, economically, and geographically, the idea of tying everyone together through technology became more and more appealing. During the 1994 session, the legislature passed HB 900, which gave us the authority to establish this service, and I signed it into law on April 11 of this year. We were able to borrow from the staffs of the Public Service Commission, KET, the Finance and Administration Cabinet, the Department of Information Systems, the Division of Telecommunications, and the University of Kentucky. And on July 12, we collaboratively produced a request for proposals for a Kentucky information highway.

Our objective was not to commit the taxpayers of this state to hundreds of millions of dollars in capital construction costs as some states have done. Instead, we wanted to identify and harness existing systems in state government and public universities that could be used, so that we could utilize our collective purchasing power for the private construction and operation of the network. Today, I am pleased to announce the awarding of a contract to the local exchange carrier telephone group, called LECTG, and LCI International. LECTG is a telecommunications partnership consisting of every local exchange carrier presently operating in Kentucky and LCI International of Dublin, Ohio, also.

When we started this process, we had hoped to be able to stand here today and announce a contract that would create a tremendous information infrastructure for both public and private use without spending any taxpayer money over and above those already appropriated for these kinds of services. We are delighted to report, with the acceptance of this proposal, that not only was our goal realistic, but that because of this contract, Kentucky State Government's data transmission costs will be virtually cut in half in the first year of the contract. And that will save taxpayers $1.1 million a year.

Implementation of this project will also open dozens of cost-saving and service-improvement opportunities for state agencies as envisioned in our recent quality and efficiency study. It will help us achieve the technology goals of the Kentucky Education Reform Act; it will offer enhanced distance-learning possibilities, such as the Kentucky tele-linking network project; and it will improve health-care delivery to rural Kentucky through rapidly emerging tele-medicine applications.

This project also will become an essential tool in our economic-development program, because it will virtually create a level playing field for all 120 counties for the recruitment of high-tech, information-sensitive industries. There are dozens of people who have been involved in this project. And rather than mention everyone's name, I just want to offer a sincere thank you to each and every one of you for your valuable assistance. This may be one of the most progressive steps that the Commonwealth of Kentucky has ever taken. And now, we look forward to working with the contractor toward full implementation. With the availability of this technology, I am today asking the Kentucky Information Resources Management Commission to sponsor a symposium early next year for the purpose of informing and educating state agency heads about this project.

We challenge each agency of state government to explore new ways to take advantage of information-age technologies that can reduce the price of government and further restore taxpayer confidence in our ability to deliver services in more and more cost-effective ways.

---

1. Patrick Mulloy (1953–), born in Louisville; B.A., Vanderbilt University, 1974; J.D., Vanderbilt University School of Law, 1977; secretary of Finance and Administration Cabinet, 1992–94; attorney, Greenebaum Doll & McDonald, 1994–96; president, CEO, and director of Atria Communities, Inc., 1996–present; co-chair, Governor's Commission on Tax Reform.

RURAL EMPOWERMENT ZONE ENTERPRISE COMMUNITIES RECOGNITION CEREMONY
Frankfort / January 17, 1995

HOW wonderful it is to see all of you this morning. I want to thank you for giving me this opportunity to publicly recognize our empowerment zone and enterprise community designees and to thank the many people who made this outstanding achievement possible.

We come together to honor and to pay tribute to the leadership and cooperation that made it possible for Kentucky to receive one of the three rural empowerment zone designations made by the U.S. Department of Agriculture as part of President Bill Clinton's initiative to bring new growth and development to rural America.

We likewise honor and pay tribute to those whose leadership and innovative planning enabled Kentucky to have two enterprise communities designated by the U.S. Department of Housing and Urban Development. I congratulate and commend Jerry Rickett, president of Kentucky Highlands Investment Corporation, and all the people who worked on Kentucky Highlands' proposal to make the counties of Clinton, Jackson, and Wayne a rural empowerment zone. Former Secretary of Agriculture Mike Espy told me that this proposal was one of the best ones submitted. This is a tribute to Clinton County Judge-Executive Charlene King, Jackson County Judge-Executive William Smith, and Wayne County Judge-Executive Hallice Upchurch, who joined with Jerry and his staff in the visioning and planning process that made the Kentucky Highlands proposal a winner.

President Clinton's empowerment zone initiative was designed to be a partnership between the federal government and the rural counties or communities receiving an empowerment zone or enterprise community designation. Its ultimate goal is to give families access to decent housing, good-paying jobs, and basic infrastructures. Empowerment is about helping communities determine their own future. Development cannot occur without adequate funding, but certain things must take place before dollars alone will work. People within the community must see the need for growth and recognize the many components that make economic development happen.

The proposal that won an empowerment zone designation for Clinton, Jackson, and Wayne Counties was developed through grassroots visioning and strategic planning. Empowerment will be brought to the respective counties through the support and encouragement of entrepreneurship involving agriculture, wood products, manufacturing, and tourism. Investments will be made in infrastructure improvements that will enhance economic growth and the quality of life.

Yes, Jerry and all the local government officials and business men and women who developed the zone proposal more than met the key objectives of self-sufficiency and self-support, innovation, partnership, and coordination and the removal of barriers to implementing grassroots initiatives. As we meet here today, it is hard to comprehend just what this all can mean for the people of Clinton, Jackson, and Wayne Counties in the years ahead. . . .

Beyond winning one of the three rural empowerment zones, Kentucky, as you know, won two enterprise community designations. Visioning, innovative planning, and cooperation were the key factors in Kentucky's two winning proposals for enterprise communities. Louisville is known not only as the largest city in Kentucky, but also as a center of innovative programs for the arts, minority business development, and urban renewal. Mayor Jerry Abramson is recognized nationally for his strong leadership and the innovative initiatives he has undertaken to revitalize downtown Louisville and to promote business growth within the urban area.

When we hear the term grass roots, we generally think of a rural or small community, but Mayor Abramson used a grassroots approach in developing Louisville's proposal. It was not a city government project, but a people's project. It is my pleasure to introduce to you, the Honorable Jerry Abramson, mayor of Louisville. Thank you, Mayor Abramson.

McCreary County, Kentucky, a truly rural county, is located adjacent to Scott County, Tennessee, which is also rural. A coalition of progressive and forward-thinking Appalachian communities formed the Scott/McCreary Area Revitalization Team, or "SMART," and developed a proposal that enabled McCreary County and Scott County to be designated as an enterprise community. This vision of SMART is to create a viable, sustainable economy for McCreary and Scott Counties. SMART will carry out its mission by capitalizing on the human, cultural, economic, and natural resources that abound in the region. To Jimmie Greene, judge-executive of McCreary County, I say congratulations for a job well done, and thank you for what this will mean to the people of McCreary County in the years ahead. . . .

We all should be proud that our largest city and four of our most rural counties have been selected to be a part of this new federal development and revitalization initiative. I have only touched upon the highlights of the winning rural empowerment zone proposal and the two winning enterprise community proposals. Time does not permit an in-depth review of all the innovative plans that will unfold in the years ahead—innovative actions that will change the lives of thousands of Kentuckians. So again, thanks to all of you for what you have accomplished on behalf of your communities and the people of the Commonwealth of Kentucky.[1]

---

1. On January 17, Jones made a similar speech at the Rural Empowerment Zone Enterprise Communities Recognition Ceremony; on May 3, he made a similar speech in Frankfort at the Rural Empowerment Zone Memorandum of Agreement Signing.

PORK PRODUCERS ASSOCIATION
Owensboro / January 27, 1995

I WANT to offer my sincere thanks to you for this award tonight. It means a great deal to me because I, too, am a farmer, and I believe farmers should stick together. I believe you know of my commitment to agriculture in this Commonwealth, for many reasons. But primarily because it's the right thing to do.

Agriculture is economically vital to Kentucky. The Commonwealth's agriculture industry is a $3.25 billion business, responsible for a quarter of a million jobs and more than $20 billion in total economic activity. And the bottom line is this: a strong farm economy benefits the entire Commonwealth. That's why we have undertaken steps to ensure that the farm economy continues to grow. Ag Project 2000 pulled together every farm organization in the Commonwealth to find ways to dramatically increase Kentucky's farm income. A comprehensive plan was developed for a $5 billion farm economy by the year 2000. Many of the specific proposals are well underway.

We are continuing to work extremely hard to attract new agribusiness to Kentucky. The poultry plants are the most recent examples of our success in this area. They provide jobs, and they provide more opportunities for farmers to raise more and different kinds of livestock, and to grow more and different kinds of crops. And we will continue to do whatever possible to recruit and to keep agriculture-related businesses in Kentucky.

Farmers can make more if we grow more, raise more, process more, and sell more Kentucky-made products. But we must have enough farmers to keep us moving forward. And that's why something that's going on in Frankfort right now is vitally important to the future of the Kentucky farmers. We must eliminate the inheritance tax to save more family farms. As you know, the legislature is finishing work on my proposal to eliminate the inheritance tax. You told me about this problem while I was running, and I heard about it from one end of the state to the other. Time and time again, a family farm has had to be sold to pay the inheritance tax, and then the family was out of the farming business. When I started this fight, Kentucky had the highest inheritance tax in this country. And when I am finished, Kentucky will have the lowest!

As you know, I also have asked legislators to remove another tax that I believe is unfair, and that is the tax on private pensions. Government workers don't have their pensions taxed in Kentucky, but private pensioners do, and I don't think that's right. Lawmakers have—for the most part—agreed with my plans, and I hope to be signing those tax cuts into law very soon. We've been able to pay for these cuts because we've worked very hard over the last three years to downsize government. We've cut more than sixteen hundred full-time permanent positions through attrition. And we cut the fat and the waste throughout government.

We've also created more than 54,000 net new jobs in this Commonwealth by vigorously going out and attracting new businesses to come in and enticing existing businesses to expand. And those new jobs helped create even more jobs, and the spiral continues upward. In fact, there are 153,000 more Kentuckians working today than on this day three years ago!

I'm also proud to be able to tell you that, despite an increasing population, there are 10 percent fewer people receiving welfare payments than when we took office, and that decline will continue through the last year of our administration. So we've cut jobs in state government, increased jobs in the private sector, and put more Kentuckians to work. That has allowed us to expand our tax base and invest that surplus money into our people. Because, I guarantee you, you can spend your money a lot smarter than government can!

I ask for your continued cooperation and support in our last year. We're not done yet. I have promised to make this the most productive last year of any administration in history. With your help, and with God's blessing, we'll make it happen.

HUDSON FOODS GROUND BREAKING
Sebree / March 8, 1995

IT'S NOT often that we have the opportunity to join with officials of a *Fortune* 500 company and one of America's top food-processing firms to break ground for facilities that will be located in not one, but three Kentucky counties. I understand from James "Red" Hudson that this is an exciting time for Hudson because it will be the first chicken complex Hudson has ever constructed from the ground up. Red, this is also an exciting time for Kentucky—especially for the people of Henderson, McLean, and Webster Counties. We are proud those counties will be home to your new chicken processing complex.

On behalf of the Commonwealth of Kentucky, I want to welcome you. And I want to pledge to you and to all who will become a part of Hudson Foods' new Kentucky operations, our complete support and cooperation. We look forward to helping you be successful here because your success means success for the people of this area, and—in fact—for all of the people of Kentucky.

The thirteen hundred jobs that will be created by this complex helped make 1994 a record year for the number of new manufacturing and supportive industry jobs we announced in Kentucky. In fact, Kentucky ranked ninth in the nation last year in *Site Selection* magazine's annual scoreboard of new manufacturing facilities and expansions announced, and tenth in the number of new manufacturing facilities alone. For the period of 1992–94, Kentucky ranked fourth in the number of new facilities and expansions per one million population. Last year, employment in our manufacturing and processing industries reached an all-time high—more than 305,000.

Kentucky continues to be one of only a handful of states where the number of manufacturing jobs is increasing. The job that our Economic Development Cabinet has done attracting new jobs and keeping existing ones has been nothing short of amazing. Today, there are nearly 162,000 more Kentuckians working than were employed three years ago when we took office. In January 1995, the unemployment rate in Kentucky (5.5 percent) was the lowest January unemployment rate in seventeen years. And throughout 1994, Kentucky's average unemployment rate was well below the national average.

During this past year, Kentucky also enjoyed the tenth-highest per capita personal increase of any state in the nation. Now, that good news is not spread evenly throughout Kentucky, but that's what we're trying to do, and I think we're getting there. We know that unemployment rates around here are higher than Kentucky's average, but new businesses such as Hudson's will make the situation here dramatically better. Good things are happening in Kentucky, and they're not just happening by accident.

Today, we have a strategic plan for economic development in Kentucky. And it has a clear and simple mission: "To create more and higher-quality opportunities for all Kentuckians by building and expanding a sustainable economy." Each time an existing industry expands in Kentucky, and each time an outstanding company like Hudson Foods chooses Kentucky for a new plant location, we are helping to fulfill that mission. So again, I welcome Hudson Foods to Kentucky, and I thank you for choosing to be part of the future we are building for people and businesses alike.

I also want to thank everyone from Henderson, McLean, and Webster Counties who worked on this project, because without your hard work this day and this celebration could not have been possible. Thank all of you and best wishes for the future.

NATIONAL ASSOCIATION OF WOMEN BUSINESS OWNERS LUNCHEON
Lexington / March 21, 1995

YOU don't have to convince me of the fact that "women mean business." I've seen that a lot on the state level since the start of our administration. As you may know, our administration appointed more women and minorities to cabinet-level positions than any administration in history. And in just the first three years of the administration, we appointed more women to state boards and commissions than ever before. I've seen the tremendous accomplishments that the women in our administration have achieved. And I've seen firsthand the knowledge, the will, the intelligence, and the sensitivity that women bring to the table. So you don't have to convince me that women have gotten down to business in the corporate world.

The facts tell the story:

1. Women-owned business is the nation's fastest-growing economic sector;
2. Women currently own approximately one in three businesses in this country; in another five years, women could own as many as half the country's businesses;
3. Women-owned businesses employ more people than the *Fortune* 500 companies, and these companies are highly stable.

I don't need to preach to the choir, and that's not why I came here today. I came here to acknowledge your success and to promise our support for the future. The fact is we need you to keep Kentucky growing strong. Right now, the picture is bright. Last year, we announced a record number of jobs for the Commonwealth. And 162,000 more Kentuckians have jobs than on the day we took office. You are responsible for a good part of our success. And we need for you to keep it going.

I realize that two of the largest obstacles to starting and growing a business are accesses to capital and markets. But I think we have started to address how to overcome those obstacles. When I ran for governor, I told you I wanted to create an environment to give Kentucky women greater opportunities for economic and personal success. And last October, I named a task force to study businesses owned by women in Kentucky. This task force is gathering information on women-owned businesses in the Commonwealth and the opportunities and obstacles that you face. This information will be the foundation on which future programs for the enhancement of women-owned businesses in Kentucky will be based.

Whatever problems there are, whatever barriers there are, we must overcome and eliminate them. We must do this, because the need for jobs in Kentucky will continue to increase. And if women business owners create more jobs, that means more Kentuckians will be paying taxes, and fewer Kentuckians will be on welfare rolls.

Changes are taking place. For example, the number of Small Business Administration loans made to women in Kentucky is on the rise. More contracts with women-owned businesses are being let by the state's Finance and Administration Cabinet and the Transportation Cabinet. The task force, which is just beginning to gather and assemble information, will study financing, marketing, management, and networking. It also has the freedom to explore other areas it sees fit to investigate. I expect great results from this study and the fine group of women and men who have agreed to serve on this task force.

Finally, we are here today to honor sixteen outstanding businesswomen. I know that all of them are exceptional individuals, but I am sure they will agree that they are representative of a much larger group of prominent women in Kentucky who have devoted their talent and efforts to being successful in the business world. It is because of these efforts that I have officially proclaimed this month as "Women-Owned Business Month" in Kentucky. The Commonwealth appreciates you. We need you. And we want you to succeed, because your success ensures the future success of the Commonwealth.

ASIAN TRIP REMARKS
May 1995

[GREETINGS] AS many of you may know, the first Saturday in May each year, we run a very special horse race back home, the Kentucky Derby. This year marked our 121st Derby Day, attended by more than 100,000 fans with the live telecast watched by millions more around the world. Although I've been involved with thoroughbred racing for many years, I've got to share with you *my* excitement at the "internationality" of this year's race—because what happened at Churchill Downs on May 6 epitomizes what's going on these days all across Kentucky.

The Derby was won by Thunder Gulch, a chestnut colt owned by a gentleman named Michael Tabor, who is English but resides in Monaco. The winning jockey, Gary Stevens, flew to Kentucky from over here—where he's been enjoying a successful season of riding in Hong Kong. Also entered in this year's Kentucky Derby was a fine three-year-old English Colt owned by a Saudi; two British-bred horses; a Canadian horse; a beautiful gray colt named Ski Captain, owned by the Shadai Racehorse Company, Ltd., in Japan and ridden by Yutaka Take; and also there were four other mounts ridden by jockeys from Central and South America.

All of this constitutes what can best be described as a microcosm of that global economy which Secretary Strong described a few months ago: Kentucky *has* become a significant entity worldwide, and we're becoming more and more involved and competitive each day, which is why we're here today. *Here's our bottom line*: we're interested in doing business with companies within the Pacific Rim—

because our experience has shown us how innovative and quality-conscious you traditionally are. By "doing business," I mean both by encouraging your domestic companies to select Kentucky for expansion operations "stateside," *and* by encouraging all of you to become more active trading partners of ours. When you choose to do business from within our state, you'll join an impressive list of companies which have already discovered the numerous advantages of being able to put labels on their products that say "Made in Kentucky, USA."

We point to companies such as Toyota Motor Corporation, which began operations in Georgetown, Kentucky, in 1987 by manufacturing Camry Sedans for domestic usage. Now, Toyota in Kentucky has expanded its scope of operations to the point where today, six thousand proud Kentucky workers manufacture Camry—thousands of which are exported—plus the new Avalon sedans—and engines for both. Along the way, Toyota's Kentucky operation has been awarded the prestigious J.D. Power and Associates Gold Plant Award for overall excellence not once, not twice, but three separate times.

That says a lot about our Kentucky workforce, and the heritage of craftsmanship we put into every automobile we make. Companies such as Hitachi, American Air Filtration, Akebono Brake, Clarion, Sumitomo, American Tape Company, and Sammi Sound Technology are all doing business from within our Commonwealth—and are doing very well. Part of the reason they've been so successful has nothing whatsoever to do with P&L's, movement of inventories, or international currency exchanges. Instead, it has everything to do with the human side of things—the dynamics of the people involved. Kentuckians are, by nature, friendly, outgoing folks, eager to make your acquaintance and to make you feel welcome.

And today, all across our state, you'll find alliances and friendship between those of Asian descent, who have been assigned to operations in Kentucky, and our native families. The cross-cultural exchanges are remarkable—and they exist on every level. Some of our public-school teachers come across the Pacific and spend two weeks in your classrooms—and Asian teachers come back to Kentucky and do the same thing. The young people go to school together, play soccer, tennis, and music together—and the families of these kids socialize, cook out, and entertain each other, from one corner of our state to the other. We've learned a bit about sushi and sake, and our visitors have learned about bluegrass and bourbon—and everyone has benefitted enormously from the process.

I mentioned encouraging more trading partnerships between

your country and our Commonwealth, and I'd like to expand that idea for just a moment. That Kentucky workforce I was bragging about a few moments ago creates an amazing array of goods and services which could be readily exported to fulfill needs and demands here in your country. We're already shipping chemicals and food additives, industrial machinery and transportation equipment, tobacco, stone, clay, and glass materials to Japan, Korea, and Hong Kong, and we're keenly interested in increasing our exportation of Kentucky-made items. Secretary Strong, Commissioner Navolio,[1] and I are pretty well versed on the subject of "Made in Kentucky," so we'd welcome your inquiries later this afternoon, or at the reception this evening.

When I became governor, I pledged my administration's energies and resources to helping create a business climate within our state which could encourage the infusion of capital earmarked for economic development. And that capital is being invested by Kentuckians, by companies from all over America, and by companies and institutions from all over the world. We know there's an enormous amount of competition out there, but we're not here to talk about the others. We're here to tell you about Kentucky, where you'll be welcomed not just when you announce your decision to do business in our state, but also when you build your facilities in Kentucky and train your workforce and become a part of the community in which you've located. Kentucky *is* famous for its southern hospitality. I'd like to personally invite each of you to experience it for yourselves. We are the place *with a plan* to help realize your goals.

---

1. Jim Navolio, commissioner of job development in the Economic Development Cabinet during the Jones and Patton administrations.

ECONOMIC DEVELOPMENT PRESS CONFERENCE
Nagoya / Tokyo / May 1995

- It is a pleasure to again visit a beautiful country with so many friendly people.
- This is my second visit to Japan, and I find it to be one of the most enjoyable places in the world to visit and some of the most enjoyable people in the world.
- Kentucky has, for many years, enjoyed a close relationship with the people of Japan.
- We have come to Japan to visit the companies that have plants and facilities in Kentucky.
- We want to thank those companies for choosing to be a part of Kentucky's business community.
- We now have 88 companies with Japanese ownership.
- These 88 companies represent an investment of more than $44.4 billion.
- These 88 plants employ 24,902 people.
- As these numbers show, Japanese-owned businesses are very important to Kentucky's economy.
- We have come to Japan to make a courtesy call on a number of the companies now operating facilities in Kentucky and to thank them for their investments in Kentucky.
- We want them to know that we will be supportive of their plans to expand their Kentucky-based operations.
- We also want to let other Japanese companies know that Kentucky is a great place for them to locate their plants in the United States.
- Kentucky is centrally located, and our workforce is very productive, consistently exceeding the U.S. average for value added per dollar of production wages.
- Kentucky has a positive climate for businesses, and we have incentive programs that will help new and expanding businesses recover certain costs associated with getting the new or expanded business in operation.

EXPORT TRADE

- Japan is Kentucky's second-largest trading partner, exceeded only by our North American neighbor, Canada.

- In 1994, Kentucky firms exported more than $759 million worth of goods to Japan.
- During our visit to Japan, we want to explore opportunities to sell Kentucky products in Japan.
- Like the people of Japan, we in Kentucky are proud of the quality products we produce.
- We want to make those products available to people in Asia and throughout the world.

GLOBAL ECONOMY

- Although Kentucky is an inland state, we recognize that today's economy is a world economy.
- Kentucky's businesses must be prepared to be a part of the global economy.
- We want Kentucky companies to seek a place in world trade.
- We also want Kentucky to be a place where foreign-owned companies, like the fine Japanese companies we have in Kentucky, are welcomed and helped to grow and to be profitable.
- Kentucky is richer economically and culturally because of the relationship we enjoy with the people and businesses of Japan.
- We want both our business and personal relationship to grow.

TALKING POINTS FOR PRESS CONFERENCE
Seoul, South Korea / May 1995

- This is my first visit to Korea and I am enjoying myself very much.
- Everyone I have met has been as friendly as I expected, and your country is as pretty as I had pictured it to be.
- The hospitality has been wonderful, and I and those traveling with me appreciate the warm welcome we have received.
- We are honored to have had the opportunity to meet with President Kim and the other officials who so graciously took time to meet with us.
- The investment seminar we hosted was very successful, and

we appreciate the Korean Trade Promotion Corporation and the Small and Medium Industry Promotion Corporation joining us as co-sponsors.

- We had a threefold purpose in coming to Korea:
  —first, we wanted to see firsthand your dynamic business community;
  —second, we wanted to visit personally with the leaders of business and government who are moving your country forward;
  —third, we wanted to make it known that Kentucky is interested in forming stronger ties with Korea.
- Two outstanding companies, Sammi Sound Technology and STC Corporation, now operate plants in Kentucky.
- We are interested in having more Korean companies consider Kentucky their location in the United States.
- As our promotional materials say, we want them to *"think Kentucky."*
- Kentucky is centrally located, within a day's driving time of 70 percent of the U.S. population.
- Kentucky's workforce is one of the most productive in the country, regularly exceeding national average for productivity.
- Kentucky has a positive business climate with a strong partnership between the public and private sectors.
- Kentucky provides financial incentives that can help businesses recover much of the cost associated with opening a new plant or expanding an existing plant.
- Kentucky is enjoying growth in manufacturing, service, and trade sectors of our economy.
- All three sectors, manufacturing, services, and trade, set new employment records in 1994.
- Kentucky's manufacturing employment is at an all-time high, making Kentucky one of a few states in the United States that is growing in manufacturing employment.
- We would like to have more Korean companies choose Kentucky for their new plant location in the United States.
- Kentucky businesses also want to do business in Korea.
- In 1994, the export of Kentucky products to Korea increased by 37 percent.
- Through our visit to Korea, we want to learn more about market opportunities for Kentucky products.

GLOBAL ECONOMY

- Although Kentucky is an inland state, we recognize that today's economy is a world economy.
- Kentucky's businesses must be prepared to be a part of the global economy.
- We want Kentucky companies to seek a place in world trade.
- We also want Kentucky to be a place where foreign-owned companies, like Sammi Sound Technology and STC Corporation, are welcomed and helped to grow and to be profitable.
- By building a strong relationship with the people and businesses of Korea, Kentucky will be richer economically and culturally.
- We want both our business and personal relationship to grow.

FIDELITY INVESTMENTS GRAND OPENING
Covington / June 13, 1995

THIS has been quite a week for northern Kentucky, and it's only Tuesday! Yesterday, we were in Florence, where Mazak announced an expansion and the creation of more than one hundred new jobs for Kentuckians. Today, we come together to celebrate the dedication of Fidelity Investments' new operations complex. If you look up the word "fidelity" in the dictionary, you'll find that the word means "faithfulness to obligations, duties, or observances." I'm sure Fidelity Investments chose that name because they are faithful to their clients. But in choosing to locate here in Covington, they are also showing a faithfulness to the people of Kentucky. We appreciate that trust, and I can assure you, your employees and the people of Kentucky will also be faithful to you.

In my travels as governor, I have had the opportunity to speak with the heads of many worldwide companies that have business operations in Kentucky. I asked the head of one of those businesses once, "How do the Kentucky workers compare with workers from the rest of the world?" And I was told, "The Kentucky worker is the best." Obviously, as governor, that made me extremely proud. But I think most companies, once they move to Kentucky, come to realize that fact: that the Kentucky worker is the best. Our workers are dedicated, hardworking, and faithful. And I believe you have already come to realize this.

Several years ago, near the beginning of this project, Fidelity Investments projected the creation of five hundred new Kentucky jobs here. However, by the end of this year, this facility is expected to employ more than eighteen hundred people. I believe that Fidelity Investments knows that in Kentucky, we really are working together to make good things happen. That's not just a cliche, that's a fact. Our Economic Development Cabinet, headed first by Lieutenant Governor Patton, and now by Gene Strong, did an exceptional job putting together a package that helped the company choose Covington. Our Transportation Cabinet made sure the proper access roads were in place. And the city of Covington, under the leadership of Covington Mayor Denny Bowman,[1] was able to help with the infrastructure improvements to the site. So you can see that by all of us working together, we have shown Fidelity Investments that Kentucky means business . . .[2]

---

1. Denny Bowman (1949–), elected city commissioner, Covington, 1984–85; vice-mayor, Covington, 1986–87; mayor, Covington, 1988–present; owner of sporting goods store; sales representative; manager of bowling establishment.

2. On March 14, Jones made a related speech to Insteel, Inc., in Campton; on June 12, he made a related speech in Florence at the Mazak Corporation announcement; on September 7, he made a pitch for Toyota's new plant at the Toyota Motor Corporation taping; on October 2, he made a related speech at the Toyota Seat announcement in Flemingsburg; on November 2, he made a related speech in Frankfort at Give a Gift from Kentucky; on November 15, he made a related speech at the Commonwealth Convention Center in Louisville; on November 30, he made a related speech at the Northern Kentucky Convention Center.

LEXMARK ANNOUNCEMENT
Lexington / September 25, 1995

WHAT a difference time can make! Just five short years ago, the future of this facility was extremely uncertain. There were reports that the plant—owned by IBM at the time—might close. People were worried about their jobs. Then, it was acquired by an investment firm that named the company Lexmark International, and an ambitious course was set for the future.

Who would have thought five years ago that we would be standing here today, celebrating news of a major expansion? These things don't "just happen." They are the result of a lot of people working together. First, you have a company committed to maintaining high-tech jobs in a clean, safe, well-maintained workplace. You have a company willing to train its workers and to continue that training to allow workers to move up into even more skilled positions. You have a company willing to pay competitive salaries and provide good benefits. You have a company that President Clinton used as a shining example of how American jobs are *not* on the highway to Mexico, as some NAFTA opponents feared.

In addition to a strong company that is getting stronger, you have magnificent employees. You have people who are committed to making Lexmark work because they are committed to putting out a top-quality product every day. Employees have consistently made such a top-quality product that Lexmark has increased its inkjet market share by 20 to 30 percent a year. You also have a city that is a wonderful place to work and live, a city that's been committed to helping Lexmark succeed. Finally, you have a state economic-development plan that is working wonders. Gene Strong and the Economic Development Cabinet have been able to entice more than 2,100 companies to either move into Kentucky or to expand their existing facilities in the Commonwealth.

It's always big news when a new company moves into Kentucky, but this expansion shows how we've been able to work with existing businesses to allow them to expand. Our efforts have brought nearly 62,000 *net* new jobs for Kentuckians. And success breeds success. The salary paid to those workers turns over several times in the community and enables other companies throughout Kentucky to add workers. And now, there are more than 200,000 more people working in Kentucky today than on the day we took office. Our unemployment rate is 4.7 percent, nearly a full percentage point below the national average. In fact, Kentucky's unemployment rate has been below the national average for forty-two consecutive months.

While we've been creating jobs in the private sector, we've reduced the number of jobs in the public sector. We've downsized state government by eliminating more than eighteen hundred permanent full-time jobs through attrition. We've cut 18.6 percent of the people off the welfare rolls, by working one-on-one with them and helping them find jobs. All of these things working together have allowed us to enjoy the best financial picture Kentucky has enjoyed in modern times.

When we started, we couldn't even pay our income tax refunds on time because the checks would have bounced. Now, we have $200 million in our Budget Reserve Trust Fund, and more than $34 million surplus in the General Fund. That's a surplus of nearly a quarter of a billion dollars! And it's all because of cooperation.

Employees, city and state officials, and business all working together to make good things happen for Kentucky. Lexmark is leaving its mark on Kentucky every day. And it's a mark of quality. Thank you for investing in the Commonwealth. I guarantee you, you're making the right investment.

KENTUCKY WORLD TRADE CONFERENCE DINNER
Louisville / November 3, 1995

I THINK that most of us realize that, even with modern technology, bad news travels faster than good news. So I have some good news that, until tonight, you may not have heard. That good news concerns the Commonwealth of Kentucky. Whether or not you do business in Kentucky, I believe you will be interested in some statistics that prove we are exporting Kentucky worldwide. Tonight, I want to share this good news with you.

Last year, Kentucky exported $5.4 billion worth of goods and services. In the past five years, our exports have grown by more than 12 percent a year, a rate much higher than the national average. We export everything from explorers to explosives; from ball bats to ball bearings; from bricks to brakes; from pool tables to pews; from sausage to saw blades; and from printers to preserves. And the top four destinations for these "made in Kentucky" products are Canada, Japan, France, and Mexico; however, we export to 150 countries worldwide. And our efforts to sell Kentucky to the world have paid tremendous benefits at home.

Foreign trade and investment are responsible for nearly 150,000 jobs in Kentucky, nearly 9 percent of the total employment in the state. Kentucky commodity exports are responsible for $264 million in individual income taxes, $239 million in sales and use taxes, and $40 million in corporate income taxes. All told, more than 15 percent of the Kentucky tax revenues. Kentucky exports have come a long way, but we can, and will, do more. And technology will help us get there.

Kentucky is one of a handful of states that have gotten on the information highway. Last December, we announced that we had signed a contract to get all of Kentucky's 120 counties onto the information highway. Our intent was to level the playing field throughout the state, so that people in small, rural counties could compete for jobs throughout the world with larger, urban counties. And last December, we said that all of our counties would be hooked up and ready to use the information highway in four years. Well, we were wrong. It won't take four years; it will be finished next month.

Now, we have started an informational campaign, aimed at getting Kentuckians to take a ride on the information highway and see just how far it will take them without ever having to leave home. Our Cabinet for Economic Development is one of several cabinets of state government on the Internet. And the cabinet is using technology to recruit business worldwide. Again, we are ahead of the rest of the country, and we must continue to stay there. In our schools, our students are learning how to use the information superhighway, and they are learning quickly. Kentucky ranks among the top ten in the country in the number of computers in the classroom available for our students. This is another area where we are leading the country. We are telling our students that they must stay up to date with technology, because they must be trained to compete for jobs against the best and the brightest, not only from this country, but from the world. And they can get that training right here in Kentucky.

The information highway is taking us all on a global odyssey, and the beauty of it is, we don't have to leave Kentucky to take this fascinating trip. We are competing worldwide, and we are winning worldwide. But we are only as good as our last success. This incredible advanced technology will help us continue to win only if we are able to continue to educate ourselves and our children on all that it has to offer. We are riding to economic prosperity on the information highway, and we're taking Kentuckians on the ride of their lives. All of you can make sure we get the most out of that ride.

COOPER TIRE AND RUBBER
Mount Sterling / November 8, 1995

FOUR years ago, the unemployment rate in Montgomery County was just over 18 percent. And a lot of people had to leave the county to find a good job. And when we campaigned here for governor, we said we'd try to do something about this problem. As we gather here for today's ground breaking, the record will show we *have* done something.

Today, the unemployment rate in Montgomery County is not 18 percent but 5.5 percent, and Cooper Tire is adding several hundred more new jobs here. Cooper Tire is the third and largest automobile-parts facility to locate in this industrial park, which was established the year we took office. Cooper Tire's is the fourth announcement of a new company coming into the Mount Sterling area since January of this year. In 1995, Mount Sterling has had more jobs created by new companies moving in than any other city in Kentucky. And that included Louisville and Lexington. We are excited about Cooper Tire's plans for the next few years. It means that a lot of families here in Montgomery County will get to stay here and not have to commute somewhere else to go to work. They'll be able to spend their paychecks in *this* community. They'll be able to buy food and clothes and medicine and gas for their cars right here. They'll be able to take their families out to dinner or a movie; in short, they'll have a better quality of life.

And their paychecks will turn over several times in Mount Sterling and Montgomery County, so that even more people will be hired, even more people will receive paychecks, and even more people will benefit. This is the type of growth that Kentucky has been enjoying during our administration. We've known that if we are able to bring in new businesses and to encourage our existing businesses to expand, we will be able to get people off the welfare rolls and onto the work rolls. Instead of paying out tax money for welfare, we are receiving money from taxpayers who are proud to be able to contribute to society.

And our record of success speaks for itself. There are some 200,000 more Kentuckians working today than on the day we took office. There are 22 percent fewer people on welfare in Kentucky. And while there are more people working and paying taxes in the private sector, there are fewer people in the public sector. We have downsized government by eliminating approximately two thousand state jobs through attrition. All of these things, taken together, have given us the largest surplus in Kentucky's history. We will pass on to the next administration $300 million.

So the future looks bright in Mount Sterling and Montgomery County, just as it does throughout Kentucky. And we're happy to have played a part in laying the groundwork for that bright future. To Patrick Rooney and everyone at Cooper Tire, thank you for choosing Kentucky. I promise you that you will soon be saying that your Kentucky workers are your company's *best* workers. And I also want to promise you something else. We will not forget you, now that you've chosen Mount Sterling. We like to provide what we call "service after the sale." We want to keep you happy and satisfied, because we want you to continue to grow. Your success will ensure Kentucky's success. And if we continue to work together, there is absolutely no limit to what we can accomplish.

APPALACHIA

APPALACHIAN GOVERNORS' QUORUM
Frankfort / February 4, 1992

KENTUCKY'S Education Reform Program is making significant progress in its second full year of implementation. The budget address that I will deliver to the General Assembly Thursday promises that these advances will continue. The constraints of the national recession will not stop key programs. I regret that I cannot be with you, but the budget address prevents me from accepting in person this $120,000 Appalachian Regional Commission Grant. Kentucky appreciates the ARC's contribution to the uplifting of our mountain people. These funds will be used to reduce the number of drop-outs by giving special math training to at-risk students. Immediate help will be given through existing personnel. Local training in accelerated math teachings will be given in all forty-nine Appalachian counties. Funds also will go to several regional colleges to prepare teachers in accelerated math training. The third part of our math skills improvement involves one of the key aspects of Kentucky's new education reform: more local control by teachers and parents. School-based decision-making councils will award grants of $1,000 to $5,000, to be matched at least 50 percent locally, for a school to improve math skills. These three projects should dovetail to create an ongoing, state-of-the-art program for accelerating math learning.

As at-risk students master math, middle and high school won't seem so alien. The current rate of students dropping out of school will dip dramatically. Kentucky's mandate is to assure every child an equal chance for an excellent education. And, with your help, each child, regardless of ethnic or geographic background, will have math skills. This project is urgent because advancement without math, in our modern world of technology, is impossible. . . .

APPALACHIAN REGIONAL COMMISSION GRANTS
Frankfort / October 23, 1992

I AM very pleased and excited today that so many of you have traveled here to take part in the announcement of more than $5.5 million in grant funds that have been approved by the Appalachian Regional Commission. When the selection process for awarding funds is one that requires choosing one community over another, and they are all quality projects, the decision is never an easy one. However, I feel that every unit of local government that puts forth the effort to apply for funds to improve the quality of life for their citizens is truly a winner.

While there is never really enough money to fund every project we would like to see completed in our Commonwealth, I can assure you that we will continue to work each day that I serve as your governor to send every available dollar back to local communities. I am extremely pleased that many of the projects that we will announce today are designed to enhance the infrastructure in our Commonwealth. These projects create a climate that will enable us to continue our mission of bringing new jobs to Kentucky in an ongoing effort to ensure that every Kentuckian who seeks a job at a liveable wage will be able to find one without uprooting their families.

While thirty-six of the forty-nine counties in the Appalachian region of the Commonwealth are currently categorized as distressed, together we can turn this number around through continued teamwork and perseverance. Together there is no task too great for the citizens of this Commonwealth. I challenge each of you to leave here today with a renewed commitment to improving the quality of life for our children and grandchildren.

TESTIMONY TO HOUSE ECONOMIC DEVELOPMENT SUBCOMMITTEE
Washington, D.C. / June 22, 1993

[GREETINGS] It is a pleasure to appear today before you on behalf of the governors of the thirteen Appalachian states and to speak in support of the Appalachian Regional Commission. As you may know, Governor Doug Wilder of Virginia is our states' co-chairman this year. He sends his apologies for not being able to be here today. This subcommittee has been steadfast in its support of the Appalachian Regional Commission. As governor of Kentucky, in the heart of Appalachia, I know firsthand what your support of this program has meant to our citizens, and I thank you. In fact, Mr. Chairman,[1] as you well know, it is in our two states that the effort to change the face of Appalachia began. You and I have both seen the dramatic impact of ARC programs on the quality of life in much of the region. I personally applaud your aggressive leadership in holding these hearings and in promoting multi-year re-authorization legislation. I also applaud President Clinton. For the first time in thirteen years we have a budget recommendation from the president which contains adequate funding for the Appalachian Regional Commission. Of course, we could effectively spend considerably more money to improve the quality of life and create jobs in Appalachia. But we recognize the fiscal realities, and we are grateful for the president's support of a funding level which is consistent with what the Congress, in its wisdom, has provided us for the past two years.

Let me also say that we pride ourselves on the bipartisan support we have had in Congress over the years, particularly on this committee. . . . There is strong bipartisan support among the governors as well. In 1981, it was the bipartisan leadership of Governors Lamar Alexander of Tennessee and Jay Rockefeller of West Virginia which resulted in all thirteen Appalachian governors, nine Democrats and four Republicans, at that time, standing strong and united against the Reagan administration's effort to abolish the Appalachian Regional Commission. Earlier this year, Mr. Chairman, the thirteen Appalachian governors, now ten Democrats and three Republicans, unanimously reaffirmed their strong support in a resolution recommending continuation of the Appalachian Regional Commission. With your permission, I would like to enter this resolution as part of the record of this hearing. The resolution extols the work of the ARC in helping the thirteen Appalachian states to overcome the isolation of the region by completing more than 2,200 miles of a planned highway network of 3,025 miles; enhance the quality of job training and readiness for employment; expand access to health care; create more than two million new private-sector jobs in the region through investments in physical infrastructure and human development; and put our states on the cutting edge of issues such as job skills and training, rural education reform, technology transfer, export promotion, telecommunications, and manufacturing competitiveness. Because of the ARC, more than 700 vocational and technical education facilities with the capacity to serve over 400,000 students per school year have been created; a network of health-care facilities and personnel has brought primary care within thirty minutes of virtually every resident; 20,000 housing units have been rehabilitated; [and] more than 2,000 water, sewer, waste disposal, and other community-development projects to provide basic services, enhance the quality of life, and attract private-sector jobs have been completed. We are involved in demonstration projects in manufacturing competitiveness, telecommunications, and workforce training, and our highway system is more than two-thirds complete.

The resolution also identifies the unique characteristics of the ARC which have enabled it to deliver on its promises. First, its federal-state-local partnership substantially reduces bureaucratic red tape and insures more responsible and responsive decision-making. Second, the flexibility of its programs allows locally determined needs to be addressed without federally imposed artificial restrictions. Third, its regional approach produces significant economies of scale and helps to focus attention on economically distressed areas, which otherwise could be easily ignored. For such areas it supplements rather than duplicates the work of other government agencies. Fourth, it requires cost sharing by state and local governments in both program and administrative expenditures. This magnifies the impact and insures that scarce federal dollars are spent efficiently. ARC's $2.2 billion in non-highway funding has attracted more than $5.5 billion in other government funds. By working in close partnership with the private sector, ARC has managed in some cases to leverage its spending at a ratio of better than 6 to 1.

But, Mr. Chairman, despite the significant progress we have made, much of Appalachia still lags behind the nation in key indicators such as per capita market income, rates of poverty and unemployment, condition of infrastructure and levels of literacy and access to health care. In 1990, Appalachia's per capita income was

80 percent of the U.S. per capita income. In 1990, 15.2 percent of our people lived in poverty compared with 13.1 percent in the United States. In December 1992, one-fourth of Appalachia's 399 counties had unemployment rates of at least 150 percent of the national average. More than one-third of Appalachia's three hundred non-metropolitan counties are considered economically distressed. During the decade of the 1980s our population grew by approximately one quarter of the rate that the U.S. population grew. Our manufacturing employment has declined by a rate greater than the national average, our regional share of national coal output has fallen, and our regional mining employment has been cut almost in half. To compound the problem, Appalachia receives approximately 15 percent less than the per capita national average in federal expenditures.

We have seen the progress, Mr. Chairman, but we also know how much remains to be done. That is why the governors unanimously and enthusiastically support multi-year authorizing legislation for the Appalachian Regional Commission. We believe that a bill of three to five years in duration at a funding level at least consistent with the current funding level would enable us to continue significant progress toward achieving parity of economic opportunity with the nation. At the same time, we would welcome increased flexibility in the allocation of funds between highway and area development programs. This would enable us to insure that we get the maximum impact from our dollars. Of course, Mr. Chairman, we would be happy to discuss with you any other provisions which you may wish to consider. I want to make one other point. We believe that the flexibility, the responsiveness, the cost effectiveness, and the broad local, state, and national support for the ARC partnership make it a model for how to effectively address concentrations of rural economic distress wherever they may exist. As you can see on this map, the primary concentrations of severe rural economic distress, denoted by the solid red, are in central Appalachia, the lower Mississippi Delta, and along our border with Mexico. We believe that a serious examination of ways in which the ARC programs can be strengthened and its lessons applied to other concentrations of rural economic distress is in order. We would welcome the opportunity to work with the Congress and the administration to accomplish such an examination. . . .

---

1. Robert E. Wise Jr. (1948–), B.A., Duke University, 1970; J.D., Tulane University, 1975; Democrat; West Virginia senate, 1981–83; U.S. House of Representatives, 1983–2000; elected governor of West Virginia in 2000.

APPALACHIAN REGIONAL COMMISSION GRANTS
Ashland / February 25, 1994

As you know, I have long felt that eastern Kentucky has been overlooked, even forgotten. And I promised, when I ran for governor, to do what I could to get eastern Kentucky its fair share. These Appalachian Regional Commission grants serve as another step in the right direction for people in the area. I come to you today to make two separate but very important announcements.

First, I am recommending that the Appalachian Regional Commission provide you with a grant of $375,000 to renovate the Education and Economic Development Center. The center was founded to join several public and private agencies to promote economic development in the five-county region, with particular emphasis on linking education to small business, job training, technology transfer, and telecommunications. The grant money, along with funds from the Area Development District, will allow for the renovation of two floors of the buildings housing the center to make it safer and more accessible. Also, the third floor will be renovated to accommodate the expansion of Morehead State University. It will include a laboratory for skilled nursing and general science, offices for economic-development activities, and classroom space.

The second announcement I'd like to make today concerns the city of Catlettsburg. I am recommending that the ARC provide the city of Catlettsburg with $400,000 to be used for improvements to the sewer system. Among other things, this project will help upgrade the sewer system for Catlettsburg so that it meets current regulations. It will allow for the renovation of eight pump stations. And it will enable the city to install new equipment and repair much of the existing system, so that it will be up to proper standards.

In both cases, I am impressed with the fact that there is so much support for these programs. That shows me how important these projects really are to you. Even with our assistance, your local government leaders have had to go through a tough federal application process to be eligible for this grant. This money will give you a great opportunity. But it's up to you to spend it carefully. Lee Iacocca, the former head of Chrysler, was in a board meeting during the days when Chrysler was very near bankruptcy. He told the board that in order to control costs, he'd cut his salary to one dollar a year. One of the stockholders questioned the wisdom of his decision to cut his salary to a dollar a year. But Iacocca said, "Don't worry. . . . I'll spend it carefully!" I know you'll do the same.[1]

---

1. Also on February 25, Jones announced other ARC grants to the towns of Sandy Hook, Sharpsburg, and Morehead. Jones made similar announcements on March 4 in Frenchburg, Irvine, Stanton, and Richmond; on March 8 in London, Mount Vernon, and Williamsburg; on March 11 in Prestonsburg, Hindman, Booneville, Blaine, and West Liberty; and on March 28 in Stanford.

APPALACHIAN TASK FORCE MEETING
Frankfort / January 17, 1995

I THINK each of you knows how important the Appalachian area of Kentucky really is to me. I've given it special attention since I became governor, because I believe it is essential to be fair to every part of the state, and, quite frankly, that has not always happened in the past. So, the Appalachian Task Force was our way of trying to "unlock the mountains." That's because in the form of the Appalachians, the Commonwealth is blessed with mountains of potential. Mountains of experience. Mountains of expertise. And mountains of pride. If we can provide the proper ways for all of that potential, experience, expertise, and pride to be tapped, we will provide the people of Appalachia with mountains of opportunities. That's why your report today is so important. With this report, we are starting to find the proper ways to unlock the mountains. And for that I am deeply grateful. The Appalachian Regional Commission has been a godsend to Kentucky since it was formed. The ARC is responsible for helping the mountains play catch-up with the rest of the Commonwealth and the rest of the country. There is a great amount of data available on the impact of ARC in the past thirty years. The real story, though, lies in the differences ARC has made in people's lives in the communities throughout Appalachia—clean water, roads, educational opportunities, health care, leadership training, and loans for new businesses. I have asked you to tell those stories to members of Congress, and I appreciate your response to that request. We have a powerful message.

As the states' co-chairman of ARC this year I'll be working with Jesse White, the federal co-chairman, and the governors of the ARC states to present the ARC message to Congress. The ARC will have to justify its existence in the current budget-cutting efforts in Washington. In some respects, this "justification" will be good, because we all need to re-focus from time to time and make sure we are headed in the right direction. We know we cannot depend on Washington to solve all problems. We must work, and work hard, to help ourselves. We can, and we must, determine our own future, because the solutions lie within each of us. The work of this task force clearly illustrates the power of the people. I will take your report under advisement. The members of my cabinet will review these recommendations, and I will respond to you by February 15. . . .

REPORT OF ARC STATES' CO-CHAIRMAN
January 28, 1995

[GREETINGS] There is no question ARC is facing a critical time in the efforts to either significantly reduce or eliminate its funding. It is a time to assess our strengths:

1. ARC's federal/state partnership and regional approach to problem-solving result in a minimum of federal bureaucracy, a maximum of local decision-making, and the most effective use of scarce tax dollars.
2. This partnership allows us to target funds on areas which most need assistance and on programs and projects which more directly address the problems and opportunities of a diverse region.
3. The flexibility of the ARC funds has stimulated other federal, state, and private investments and the growth of the private sector, which drives economic and social development.
4. While Appalachia has not yet reached parity with the rest of the nation in economic and social development, the ARC partnership has enabled the region to close the gap, initiate innovative approaches to solving problems, and bring a new sense of hope and opportunity to millions of Americans.

5. This partnership has potential for application in other programs involving federal resources. It allows the planning and administration of programs to be closer to the people they serve.

There is a great amount of data available on the impact of ARC in the past thirty years. The real story, though, lies in the differences ARC has made in people's lives in the communities throughout Appalachia—clean water, roads, educational opportunities, health care, leadership training, and loans for new businesses. We have a powerful message:

6. [We] are communicating this message with members of Congress, particularly new members and members of key committees, to make them aware of the unique ARC structure, its impact on the region, and the needs which remain.
7. Our local development districts are making sure that members know of the strong grassroots support which exists for the ARC.
8. We are preparing to testify at House authorization hearings next month and at our House Appropriations Subcommittee hearing on February 28.
9. Governors have a direct stake in maintaining this partnership. I urge you to determine the most effective way you can be involved, including using your state's Washington office. It will take a commitment by all of us to make sure the story gets told.

At the same time we are defending ARC, the commission is moving full speed ahead in its mission to Appalachia. The commission is engaged in a comprehensive strategic-planning process to set a regional agenda for the next decade. It will culminate in an ARC Visions Conference in Lexington, Kentucky, in July. . .

The Kentucky Appalachian Task Force recently issued its report, entitled *Communities of Hope*. Copies are before you. You will find throughout this report a determination of the people to work together to make their communities better. I believe we will find this same determination in the regional strategic-planning process which ARC will complete this summer.

Today, there will also be presented three new regional initiatives—export trade, telecommunications, and leadership development. These are issues which have been identified as significant to the future of the region and your discussion of them will be important.

So as we review our past and assess our current status we must continue to plan our work and work our plan for the people of Appalachia. . . .[1]

---

1. Jones announced ARC grants on February 9 for Estill County, Madison County, Montgomery County, and Powell County. On March 14, he announced ARC grants for Lewis County, Morgan County, and Rowan County; on March 15, for Boyd, Floyd, Lawrence, Magoffin, Pike, and Lewis Counties; on March 16, for Breathitt, Harlan, Knott, Letcher, and Perry Counties; on March 17, for Lincoln and Rockcastle Counties; on March 22, for Lee, Laurel, Jackson, and Madison Counties.

HOUSE COMMITTEE ON APPROPRIATIONS TESTIMONY
Washington, D.C. / February 28, 1995

MR. CHAIRMAN [John T. Myers],[1] Ranking Minority Member [Tom] Bevill,[2] Congressman [Hal] Rogers,[3] other distinguished members of the Appropriations Subcommittee on Energy and Water Development. As the states' co-chair of ARC, I am pleased to be with you here today.

I want to begin by thanking the members of this committee for their support of the Appalachian Regional Commission over the years. All of the Appalachian governors are well aware of the crucial role you have played to keep the commission alive under difficult circumstances. All of us, Democrats and Republicans alike, appreciate your support. And most importantly, so do the people of Appalachia. To you, Mr. Chairman, from our neighboring state of Indiana, thank you for recognizing how important it is to our nation that no region of the country be left behind as our economy moves forward. To you, Mr. Bevill, who provided strong support as chairman of this committee for so many years, thank you for ensuring that we could continue to serve the needs of this neglected region of the country. And to you, Mr. Rogers, my fellow Kentuckian, thank you for representing a district which epitomizes the need for this program and for working so hard to ensure its continuation.

All of the Appalachian governors recognize that the challenge before us to continue this vital program is no less daunting than it has been for the past fourteen years. And yet, we all believe it is a challenge we must face and overcome for the good of the people we serve. In this era of scarce resources at all levels of government, we are all seeking ways to streamline so that we can give our taxpayers the absolute most for his or her tax dollar. A spirit of cooperation between the federal government and each state brings efficient government closer to the people. In the ARC, we find the perfect model. It has helped one of the most isolated and poverty-stricken regions of our country overcome the isolation and promote economic development. The ARC has been successful in doing this, not by fully funding any programs, but by providing a portion of the cost and thus leveraging federal, state, and private funds. Forty-nine counties in Kentucky are located within the boundaries of ARC. Thirty-eight of these counties are officially listed as distressed counties [with] high unemployment and low per capita income. There are 150 such counties in the thirteen-state Appalachian Regional Commission boundary. Many statistics have been presented to this committee on the ARC and its effectiveness. The most convincing evidence, however, is to travel through the area and see the differences in people's lives. I always enjoy being in eastern Kentucky, and, as Congressman Rogers knows, the natural beauty and the warmth of the people make it a special place. The mountains, however, present challenges in building roads, installing water and sewers, providing access to health care, and making needed community improvements. All of these things cost significantly more in mountainous terrain, and when you add in the distressed economic factors, you immediately increase the odds against these areas keeping pace with the rest of the country. ARC's role has been to better those odds for Appalachian communities. There is still a lot to do, but you don't have to go far in any direction in eastern Kentucky before seeing the benefits of the ARC program in housing, clean water, roads, health clinics, educational programs, and small businesses which got a chance due to revolving loan funds. These are real differences which people experience in their daily lives.

Last year, I personally went to each community in Kentucky that was receiving ARC money, and I'd like to share with you some of the things I experienced. I went to Blaine Elementary School in Lawrence County, Kentucky, where $430,000 had been approved to help build thirty-one miles of water lines for the area. The principal, who met me at the door, was nearly in tears because she was so excited. The 320 students who went to that school had to drink bottled water because of the presence of radioactive sludge from nearby oil-field pits. Some of them had never, ever, had running water in their homes. And that $430,000 was only a part of the funding. The community also had gotten a Community Development Block Grant of $750,000, a Farmers Home Administration grant of $500,000, a Farmers Home loan of $400,000, plus more than $118,000 in local money and almost $35,000 in in-kind labor. So that $450,000 has been parlayed into a construction project exceeding $2.3 million.

I went to the Hindman Settlement School in Knott County, Kentucky, to take word that the school would be receiving $75,000 to give scholarships and to hire tutors who will help dyslexic children there learn how to read. During my stop, some of the students read to me, to show me how much they had learned so far. And during a six-week summer program, the students there advanced, on the average, a full grade level in math, reading, and comprehension. The $75,000 in ARC money was supplemented by more than $160,000 that came mainly from contracts the school had with surrounding school systems. So the school started with $75,000 and ended with $235,000.

I went to rural Pike County with $381,000 in ARC money that would help that community purchase a modular building to be used as a health clinic and medical equipment for that building. Eighteen thousand people in that county did not have access to primary health care, and to show you how important this clinic was to them, more than 20,000 people signed a petition asking for it. That's 20,000 of the county's total 73,000 population. The 381,000 was a start. The local community contributed $40,000, and income from the program, $392,000, would fund the rest. So again, we started with $381,000 and we ended with more than $813,000.

I went into Whitley County, which does not have a public sewer system, to announce that $450,000 in ARC money would help fund a sewer project for Whitley City, Stearns, and Marshes Siding. Many of the 566 homes that would be affected still had only outdoor facilities. And the treatment plants that had been built to serve two large schools and several public-housing projects did not work properly. The $450,000 in ARC funds will be supplemented with nearly $1 million in Farmers Home loans, a Farmers Home Administration grant of nearly $900,000, a block grant of $750,000, and $74,000 in local money. The total project, with a $450,000 ARC investment, is more than $3.1 million. Perhaps a sewer system is not big news to those of you here today, but the people of McCreary County were simply overjoyed because it will help them improve their own lives.

The Kentucky Highlands Investment Corporation is a grassroots organization which has, over the past several years, received ARC assistance to help finance many new small businesses through equity investments or loans. Right now, it has invested in about forty private companies which employ more than 3,700 people. Of those 3,700 people, 60 percent had been on public assistance before they were hired. If those people did not have jobs today, the cost of providing them public assistance would be about $38 million per year. Instead, these men and women are working and paying $9 million per year in taxes. That's a turnaround for the government of $47 million a year! Similar stories can be told by governors from other ARC states as well.

One reason for this success is because it is not a federal program, but rather a partnership of the federal government and the governors of thirteen Appalachian states. And yet, we recognize that it is important always to be looking at ways to improve ourselves, to reinvent what we do so that we are always operating at the highest possible level of efficiency. The ARC has undertaken such an effort with its strategic-planning process, which will culminate in a major conference in Lexington, Kentucky, in July.

In Kentucky, we undertook this effort over a year ago when I created the Kentucky Appalachian Task Force to review how the program has operated in eastern Kentucky and how it can operate even more effectively. More than five hundred people participated and the result is this report, which we've entitled *Communities of Hope*. In it are Task Force Committee recommendations on, among other things, education, health, economic development, justice, transportation, telecommunications, housing, and governance. It is a people's report, and with the help of the ARC, we will address these recommendations in the coming days and months.

The bottom line, Mr. Chairman, is that my fellow governors and I believe it is crucial for this program to continue. And furthermore, I believe we ought to look beyond the mission of the ARC to explore whether the way we operate, the concept of the federal-state partnership, may be a way to operate other government programs. That is why all thirteen Appalachian governors, recognizing the need for government to operate in the most cost-effective manner possible, remain committed to the continuation of the Appalachian Regional Commission.

---

1. John T. Myers (1927–), B.S., Indiana State University, 1951; elected 1966, served U.S. House of Representatives, 7th congressional district,

Indiana from 1967 to 1997; Republican.

2. Tom Bevill (1921–), B.S., University of Alabama, 1943; L.L.B., 1948; elected to U.S. House of Representatives, 4th congressional district, Alabama, 1966; re-elected, 1968–2000.

3. Harold "Hal" D. Rogers (1937–), B.A., University of Kentucky, 1962; L.L.B., University of Kentucky, 1964; private law practice, Somerset, Kentucky, 1969–80; Republican member of Congress from 5th congressional district, 1981– ; member Appropriations Committee, subcommittees of Commerce and Justice, Energy, and Water Transportation.

MORGAN COUNTY ANNOUNCEMENTS
West Liberty / March 14, 1995

WHEN I ran for governor, I promised to you that I would be fair to all parts of Kentucky. After you hear today's announcements, I hope you'll think I've lived up to that promise. First today, I'd like to announce that Morgan County is receiving a grant from the Appalachian Regional Commission. The grant is for the Blair's Mill water project, which will provide water service for sixty homes in the Blair's Mill area of northern Morgan County. Right now, many of the private water sources that residents in the area rely on are contaminated. Nine miles of new water lines and a forty-thousand-gallon storage tank should alleviate that problem. So, I'd like to present Judge [Sid] Stewart this check for $150,000. That's not the only check I brought for Morgan County. A Community Development Block Grant has been approved for the Morgan County Community and Youth Center. This project will help Morgan County renovate a portion of the old Morgan County Middle School building for use as a community and youth center. So now, I'd like to present to Judge Stewart this check for $430,000. Those are all the checks I brought, but I still have more good news for Morgan County. I'd like to announce that a $500,000 Abandoned Mine Lands water line grant has been awarded to Morgan County. This is for the first phase of a project that will provide water service to six hundred homes, businesses, and churches, plus a new school in the Elk Fork watershed. Two years ago, a study determined there were groundwater contamination problems in the watershed as a result of conditions at an abandoned mine site. The first phase will include design of the project and construction of 7.5 miles of water lines along Kentucky Highway 172 near Crockett, and Kentucky Highway 457, parallel to Williams Creek, Cow Branch, Straight Creek, and Fannins Creek. I understand the new school will be served by this first phase.

There are several road projects in the area that I'd like to tell you about. The first has to do with the Blair's Mill Hill renovation of Kentucky 711. I understand it's one of the worst pieces of road that you can imagine. The Transportation Cabinet is finalizing a study on how to reduce the steep grade, and the cabinet is having a meeting on this project next month to finalize a decision on how best to fix the road. Next is the Cow Branch Road bridge over Elk Williams Creek. This bridge is expected to be replaced this year, which would make it safe for school bus traffic. Next, the Wallen Road bridge. Fifty thousand dollars has been appropriated to replace the bridge on an emergency basis. In addition, the Malone-Jones Creek bridge has been scheduled to be replaced, and $100,000 has been set aside for that. We've also been able to provide the county $50,000 to buy more gravel for various county roads.

I have a couple of other projects for the county that I'd like to call to your attention. I have recently recommended twenty-two city and county agencies for funding from the land and water conservation fund. This program makes grant money available for public outdoor recreation, acquisition, development, and renovation. I have recommended that Morgan County receive a $20,000 grant for the acquisition of a fifteen-acre tract of land for the construction of an athletic field. In addition, the Gateway Area Development District has approved a request by Judge Stewart and has awarded Morgan County $2,164.50 for the Cannel City Park project for a picnic shelter and picnic tables.

So if we were to total up all of these projects, we'd be talking about an investment in Morgan County of more than $5 million. So I'd believe you'd have to say people in West Liberty and Morgan County are getting their fair share! However, we may have saved the best for last. I'm happy to announce that the Continental Metal Specialty Company is planning to locate a plant here in West Liberty that will employ up to 120 people. This is an exciting announcement because it will mean jobs here and also because this is Continental's fourth operation in Kentucky. Continental's headquarters is in Richmond, but it also has plants in Clay City and Stanton. I think that's good proof that Kentucky is a good place to do business. Continental is in good company. In the past year, we were able to announce more than 25,000 net new jobs for Kentucky, thanks to the work of our Economic Development Cabinet. That is a record number of new jobs for one year. And nearly 162,000 more Kentuckians have jobs today than on the day we took office. Our unemployment rate is the lowest it has been in nearly two decades, and Kentucky is showing up on top-ten lists nationally because of its positive business climate. In Kentucky, we are helping businesses succeed. Because when they succeed, so do we. We look forward to the new jobs that this new facility will provide. . . .[1]

---

1. Other ISTEA announcements were made by Jones on February 6 for Nelson, Hardin, Simpson, Green, Hart, Barren, and Warren Counties. On February 8, he announced ISTEA funding for Boone, Campbell, Kenton, and Pendleton Counties; on February 9 for Bourbon, Estill, Fayette, Madison, and Powell Counties; on February 10, for Bullitt, Jefferson, and Shelby Counties; on March 16, for Letcher and Harlan Counties; and on March 17, for Bell, Pulaski, and Wayne Counties.

ARC SATELLITE TOWN MEETING
Lexington / April 27, 1995

As the states' co-chair of the Appalachian Regional Commission, I am pleased to be with you tonight. I want to begin by thanking all of you for your support of the ARC over the years. You are well aware of the work that is being done to keep the commission alive under difficult circumstances. And it is our hope that what we do here tonight will help us chart our future. The challenge before us to continue this vital program is no less daunting than it has been for the past fourteen years. And yet, we all believe it is a challenge we must face and overcome for the good of the people we serve. I think most of us would agree, government has gotten too big and too wasteful. We in Kentucky realized this three years ago, and we have been working to downsize government and to eliminate duplications and waste so that we can give our taxpayers the absolute most for his or her tax dollar. As federal lawmakers look for ways to make the federal government more efficient, they should look no further than the ARC.

Since the infancy of the ARC in the early 1960s, we have been determined to improve the economic-development situation in Appalachia. We've worked to convince lawmakers that statistics cannot tell the story of a child in a remote area of Appalachia, whose opportunities were limited to the hills that surrounded him. Really, the way the ARC is constructed is the perfect model, a "bottoms up" philosophy. The process starts at the local level with an idea designed to improve a community. Then the state gets involved and, finally, the federal government. It takes a spirit of cooperation and a lot of oversight to make sure that the money gets spent in the most efficient way possible. Money from the ARC has helped one of the most isolated and poverty-stricken regions of our country overcome the isolation and promote the creation of jobs. The ARC has been successful in doing this, not by fully funding any programs but by providing a portion of the cost and then leveraging federal, state, and private funds. I want to give you a perspective of the ARC from the state level.

In 1960, per capita income in the Appalachian region of Kentucky was $841, only 44 percent of the U.S. level. Now, it's closer to $13,000, or 65 percent of the U.S. level. We're still behind, but the ARC is helping us to catch up. In 1960, more than 58 percent of our mountain people lived below the federal poverty level, compared with 22 percent in the United States. Now, our poverty rate is around 29 percent. Again, we're starting to catch up. I think that is ARC's role, to help people catch up to the rest of the country in the basics—things like improved roads, clean drinking water, modern medical clinics, adequate housing, vocational schools and libraries, better jobs, flood control, and leadership training. And if you wonder whether the ARC does any good, the most convincing evidence is to travel through the area and see the difference being made in people's lives. I think we have to convince lawmakers of the fact that money spent with the ARC is an investment. Here's an example. The Kentucky Highlands Investment Corporation is a grassroots organization which has over the past several years received ARC assistance to help finance many small businesses through equity investments or loans. It has invested in about forty private companies which employ more than 3,700 people. Of those 3,700 people, 60 percent had been on public assistance before they were hired. If those people did not have jobs today, the cost of providing them public assistance would be about $38 million per year. Instead, these men and women are working and paying $9 million per year in taxes. That's a turnaround for the government of $47 million a year!

One reason for this success is because it is not a federal program, but rather a partnership of the federal government and the governors of thirteen Appalachian states. And yet, we recognize that it is important always to be looking at ways to improve ourselves, to "reinvent" what we do so that we are always operating at the highest possible level of efficiency. The ARC has undertaken such an effort with its strategic-planning process. In Kentucky, we undertook this effort over a year ago when I created the Kentucky Appalachian Task Force to review how the program has operated in eastern Kentucky and how it can operate even more effectively. More than five hundred people participated and the result is a report, entitled *Communities of Hope*. In it are Task Force Committee recommendations on, among other things, education, health, economic development, justice, transportation, telecommunications, housing, and governance. It is a people's report, and with the help of the ARC, we will address these recommendations in the coming days and months.

An Appalachian Institute is being established to bring together higher education, community leaders, and area development leaders to coordinate resources for the region and to implement the task force's recommendations. The bottom line is that my fellow governors and I believe it is crucial for this program to continue. It allows people, and actually forces people, to work together in the manner in which all of government should operate. That's why the thirteen governors in the ARC, Democrats and Republicans alike, are so supportive. The ARC helps people who want to help themselves. It helps build roads and water lines, and it helps build hope. It helps develop jobs, and it helps develop opportunities. It helps train the leaders of tomorrow, so those leaders can go out and make tomorrow better. Kentucky depends on the Appalachian Regional Commission, and we are determined to do whatever we can to not only save it, but help it flourish in the years to come.

AMERICORPS/APPALACHIAN SELF-SUFFICIENCY PROGRAM
Prestonsburg / August 31, 1995

THERE has been a lot of talk recently about our welfare system and about ways to change it. Today, while the talk continues, we are announcing a pilot project that will get underway immediately. This exciting new initiative addresses one of the most important challenges of our time: moving able-bodied welfare recipients into jobs and self-sufficiency.

I have always been a strong proponent of moving all able-bodied individuals into the workforce, but I also realize that several barriers inhibit such movement. While Kentucky has made progress in this area through the Jobs Program, issues such as the lack of child care, transportation, and adequate job skills keep far too many Kentuckians on the welfare rolls. This is a problem which directly or indirectly affects everyone. And, to reach a long-lasting solution, we must involve everyone within the community.

As with all complex problems, to be successful, people must unite and work together. Too often solutions to community problems are mandated in Washington or Frankfort. Our approach for this program has been to set parameters and goals and then let local communities take the initiative and propose their own creative solutions.

Recently the Community Service Commission held a competition to find the local proposal with the greatest potential to move individuals from welfare to self-sufficiency. There was stiff competition from all corners of the state for this new grant. Today I am pleased to announce that the Big Sandy Area Development District's Americorps/Appalachian Self-Sufficiency Program has emerged as the strongest plan and has been selected as our pilot project for this special initiative. The program will serve Floyd, Johnson, Magoffin, Martin, and Pike Counties.

As you have heard from our speakers, there is a tremendous need in this area. I am confident that you have the plan and the people needed to tackle this problem and make a major impact in the community. We believe that this pilot project will serve as a model for the rest of Kentucky and the nation. If this pilot project is successful, this approach could become an integral part of future efforts to reform welfare. It will also provide valuable hands-on experience as we continue to work to find ways to alter the current welfare system. It will help us isolate and focus on the real causes of welfare dependency, and, hopefully, it will be a positive approach to a problem which has long been plagued with negatives.

This program by itself is not meant to represent a comprehensive solution to welfare reform. Such reform must include policy change. It must address health coverage and economic development for depressed areas. But if the effort to move individuals from welfare to work is to have a lasting impact, the entire community must get involved. This program will be a catalyst for community development. It will provide an opportunity for everyone who truly cares to lend a hand.

Currently our society provides increasingly prominent forums for those who want to voice an opinion or, more often, a complaint. As the family structure continues to weaken and reports of violence and crime cause neighbors to become isolated from each other, we must make extraordinary efforts to create opportunities for civic involvement. Our society, quite simply, cannot survive the next century unless people help each other. That is why I am so proud of our Community Service Commission and their stated goal to create an ethic of service among all Kentuckians and why I'm so pleased that the state is able to sponsor this new pilot project.

So it gives me great pleasure to present this check for $281,565.40 to Roger Rectenwald, director of the Big Sandy Area Development District.

ARC MEETING
Frankfort / November 2, 1995

I'M GLAD to be here today for the first meeting of the Kentucky Appalachian Commission. This marks yet another step in our working together for eastern Kentucky. I've had several conversations with a number of you about how best to marshal the human resources of the region to address its needs. Since our conversation in 1993, Governor Breathitt,[1] we've come a long way working together to set the foundation. All of you have given so much already, and it pleases me to see you gathered here today to work collectively to realize the great potential of Appalachian Kentucky while working through the unique and persistent challenges.

In December of 1993, I appointed the members of the Kentucky Appalachian Task Force and charged them with a very important job. They were to recommend ways to maximize funding for Kentucky through ARC, assess programs which serve Appalachia, and prepare a plan for Kentucky Appalachia in the context of planning for the entire state. Their report, *Communities of Hope*, was issued in January of this year. As a result of that report, I took the following actions:

1. An Appalachian development working team was appointed which established an advisory council. This body is composed of the rank and file, if you will. Anybody who wants to participate may do so. Its committees bring together people from across the region to work for solutions.
2. And this body, the Kentucky Appalachian Commission, was formed.

Your job is to work within the region and with leaders outside the region to address the needs of Appalachia. Then, bring those needs to the attention of statewide policymakers. You, the fifteen members of this commission, are to carry on the work of the Kentucky Appalachian Task Force. Without a good foundation, nothing stands for very long. The same goes for development in the Appalachian region. Kentucky's share of non-highway ARC funds in 1995 was $8.6 million, the largest of all the ARC states. The 1995 investment package, which I recommended to ARC, contained thirty-nine projects. Nineteen of these were water and sewer projects totaling approximately $5 million. Twenty-one were a mixture of such basic needs as health care, education, housing, civic development, and business development, which totaled $3.6 million. As the states' co-chair of ARC, I recommended projects from the Co-Chairman's Fund, which included a victims' advocacy program for the Lake Cumberland Area Development District, a pre-employment program for soon-to-be-released prisoners, and some additional funding for the Appalachian Task Force. Other projects have been recommended through the regional initiatives allocation. For instance, the Economic Development Cabinet will focus an export trade development proposal on Appalachia which has the promise of opening markets to products currently produced in eastern Kentucky and providing incentive for developing new products. The proposal includes public/private marketing strategies and financial and technical training. This program will be expanded statewide as soon as possible. Libraries, schools, government, and the private sector will be brought together through Kentucky Information Resource Management. ARC funds will be used to identify communities in need of technical assistance and training to make maximum use of the Kentucky information network. Last week, I announced that this network is three years ahead of schedule. It will be especially valuable to eastern Kentucky.

In every meeting of the Appalachian Task Force, the abilities of citizens to resolve problems was a recurring theme. The need for leadership development for youth, women, and community leaders also was recognized. This is essential if we are to involve everyone. In response to these needs, I have recommended the funding of a "Train-the-Trainers" program, administered through area development districts, so that leadership may be offered to a wider audience; a program for people in public office to hone their skills in effectively leading public meetings; a program for young people in distressed areas that develops positive experiences in leadership and civic involvement; a program for women, especially those new to the workplace; a program in leadership training directed at non-traditional college students.

In 1995, the total ARC dollars directed to Kentucky from the ARC non-highway funds, the LDDs, the Regional Initiative, and the co-chairman's Fund is $9.9 million. Highway funds for Kentucky were $20.8 million. These numbers reflect the reduction of more than a million dollars caused by the rescission of ARC appropriations by Congress. Many, in fact most, people predicted that ARC would not survive Congress in 1995. When I became states' co-chair of ARC in January 1995, I was hailed by some as the last states' co-chair of ARC. We told the ARC story throughout Congress. Its value to the country is evident when we can get people to listen. And we did that. I requested all the governors in ARC states to actively support ARC with their own congressional delegation and to submit written testimony to the congressional committees considering the ARC appropriation. Every governor responded, and remember there are now eight Republican governors in the thirteen ARC states. I made personal phone calls, wrote letters, and appeared before congressional committees. In addition, the local development districts had a strong outpouring of support and Kentucky's ADDs led the efforts. So, today, I can tell you the budget which goes to President Clinton has an appropriation for ARC in the amount of $170 million, $13 million less than the '95 appropriation. Obviously, the battle is not over; ARC will have to defend its existence next year and the year after. But I believe we can all feel a great sense of victory to have survived this budget cycle.

In the *Communities of Hope* report we were asked to help Kentucky's Appalachian citizens realize their dreams for the future. I feel we have conscientiously used ARC funds to help make those dreams come true. Today, I challenge you to carry on the work that is so vital to Kentucky's forty-nine ARC counties. Help provide leadership. Encourage public and private involvement. Make state government aware of the issues affecting eastern Kentucky. Review strategic plans for the area from government agencies. You were asked to serve on this commission because you are leaders and because you are interested in what happens to Kentucky's Appalachian region. I know you will accept this challenge and take your task seriously.

---

1. Edward T. Breathitt Jr. (1924–), B.S., University of Kentucky, 1948; L.L.B., University of Kentucky Law School, 1950; Democrat; state representative, Kentucky, 1952–58; speaker chairman for Kentucky for Stevenson campaign for President, 1952; commissioner of personnel, Kentucky, 1959–63; governor of Kentucky, 1963–67; vice-president, Southern Railway System, 1972– ; attorney; chair of University of Kentucky Board of Trustees, 1991–99.

ENVIRONMENT

USED MOTOR OIL RECYCLING PRESS CONFERENCE
Frankfort / April 16, 1992

AMONG the greatest assets that we have in Kentucky, in addition to the skills and vitality of our people, are our great natural resources and the state's natural beauty. As you know, our effort to win approval of a far-reaching solid waste recycling bill was unsuccessful in the just-concluded session of the General Assembly. I said then, and I repeat today, that it still remains our goal to establish strong recycling programs throughout the state, and that I will use the next two years to explain the need for such programs to the people of Kentucky. I predict that we will pass a significant recycling measure in the next session of the General Assembly.

In the meantime, there are many things that we can do to protect our environment and stop the degradation of our water, land, and air. And that is why we are here today. I want to thank each of you for coming today and taking part in a program that addresses one of the most serious environmental problems we have in our state, that is, improper disposal of used motor oil. Unfortunately, over the years this problem has been caused by well-intended Kentuckians who have not had an environmentally safe alternative to either dumping it on the ground, throwing it in the garbage, or pouring it into the sewer. While it may have seemed harmless in the past, these practices are environmentally devastating, and they must stop.

Thanks to a unique public-private partnership, we now have a statewide system for the safe disposal of used motor oil, and it is my goal to extend service to every Kentuckian. Any Kentuckian can learn more about this program and the location of disposal tanks by calling our new toll-free number, 800–282–0868. The program also will be discussed and promoted in radio, TV, and newspaper ads paid for by the private-sector participants.

I want to commend the Natural Resources and Environmental Protection Cabinet for its role in coordinating this effort, and I want to thank those private-sector participants and, most importantly, our local government counterparts for making this program a reality. Now I'd like to turn the program back to Phil Shepherd, who will recognize the key players from both government and private industry who are making this program possible.

HAZARDOUS WASTE TRAINING CENTER
University of Louisville / August 6, 1992

ON BEHALF of the Commonwealth, I want to welcome all of you, President Swain from the University of Louisville, and Greer Tidwell,[1] the regional administrator of the U.S. Environmental Protection Agency in Atlanta. I am pleased to announce that the University of Louisville has been selected as the hazardous waste training center for the southeastern United States. The center will serve not only Kentucky, but Alabama, Florida, Georgia, Mississippi, North Carolina, Tennessee, and South Carolina.

The proper management of hazardous waste is critical to protecting our environment. We have made tremendous progress in improving this state's capabilities to manage hazardous waste and to protect our environment. Despite the severe budget constraints, with which we are all familiar, we were able to increase the Department for Environmental Protection's budget this past year. The Department for Environmental Protection has seen unprecedented growth in the last three years, and the training center will assist the state in improving its capabilities to protect our environment through better-trained state employees, a better-informed industry, and a general public with a better understanding of hazardous waste issues.

The selection of the University of Louisville is particularly gratifying to this administration because of the process through which it was selected. The eight states in the Southeast decided several years ago that additional, practical, "hands on" training was needed to assure that state hazardous waste inspectors and permit writers were adequately trained. A number of universities in the Southeast applied to be the training center. The selection committee was composed of representatives of each state and the U.S. Environmental Protection Agency. Although they could choose from any of the universities in the Southeast, the University of Louisville was their unanimous choice.

The U.S. Environmental Protection Agency and the eight states will provide funding of almost $200,000 per year to provide ongoing training. The selection of the University of Louisville is a further demonstration of the critical link between the university, and its fine research and training capabilities, the industrial community, and state agencies. The training center will be an important activity at the University of Louisville, which has a key role in carrying out the state's environmental training and research activities. The university is actively involved with the state already, providing technical assistance to industry on pollution prevention opportunities through its nationally acclaimed Kentucky Partners Program.

More recently the university has established the Institute for the Environment and Sustainable Development. The institute will focus the university's resources on environmental issues and play a key role in our environmental protection programs. The cooperative partnership of the university, industrial community, and state will help us achieve our goal of a clean and healthy environment. . . .

---

1. Greer C. Tidwell (1949–), bachelor's and master's degrees in engineering from Vanderbilt University; graduate study at Harvard University as a fellow of the National Institute of Public Affairs; worked for Tennessee Valley Authority in Tennessee and Alabama, 1964–71; chief of the EPA Tennessee-Kentucky Liaison Office, Nashville, 1971–74; president of his own environmental management, planning, and engineering company in Nashville, 1974– ; chair, Tennessee Solid Waste Disposal Control; regional administrator for EPA's Region 4, Atlanta; registered professional engineer.

GOVERNOR'S CONFERENCE ON THE ENVIRONMENT
Lexington / November 12, 1992

IT IS a pleasure to welcome you to the seventeenth annual Governor's Conference on the Environment, a conference which promises to achieve new successes in the number of attendees, in the variety of topics we are coming together to discuss, and in the potential for strategies which we will assemble with a group as talented and concerned as are those of you here today. As we welcome you to this event and as we gather to discuss the many challenges facing us in protecting our environment, all Kentuckians during this bicentennial year should pause to reflect.

Our Commonwealth is celebrating its two hundredth birthday, and we are ever more aware of the wonders and richness of the natural heritage that we call Kentucky. Over the past two hundred years our landscape has changed. Our woodlands are fewer, our rivers and lakes are not as pristine, and our landscape is more populated. But never has this natural heritage been so valuable and so cherished by our citizens. During this bicentennial year, we must reflect on how we, as a state, can preserve the natural areas remaining in the Commonwealth as we work to provide jobs and economic security for our citizenry.

During our opening session today, we will discuss three main areas which come to mind as we reflect on our natural heritage. These are, first, what has this administration put in place to protect our environment? Second, what plans do we have over the next three years of our administration? And finally, what can we as individual Kentuckians do? What opportunities and challenges do we have to make this Commonwealth the greenest state in our great nation?

First, our administration outlined several bold plans with respect to environmental protection. We said we'd eliminate political influence from the Natural Resources and Environmental Protection Cabinet through qualified appointments and through strong and aggressive enforcement of the law. We said we'd increase the public access to the decision-making process in the cabinet and ensure that all Kentuckians had access to the people and the information that affected environmental decisions in their communities. We said we'd work to protect Lake Cumberland and keep jobs and employment in that area. In December of 1991, when we appointed Phillip

Shepherd and Greg Higdon[1] to lead the Natural Resources and Environmental Protection Cabinet, we institutionalized a defining statement in the environmental decision-making process.

These individuals represented the broad spectrum of interests involved in environmental-management concerns, and through their appointment and the exemplary and open manner in which they have made decisions, we have demonstrated that different and sometimes diverse interests can come together, voice their opinions, share their differences, but work toward common goals to make strong decisions for the good of the Commonwealth. Our administration emphasizes that the Commonwealth can have high-quality jobs and a clean environment and that leaders can come together and make this happen.

One key to ensuring this philosophy is a defensible, open enforcement process that acts on cases efficiently and fairly. Our team in natural resources has reorganized the process that we use for hearing enforcement cases to ensure that highly qualified and competent professionals review and decide on cases in an equitable and efficient manner. During the 1992 legislative session, our natural resources team worked to ensure that divergent interests on various legislative proposals came together, that divergent viewpoints were heard, and [we] worked toward consensus solutions in hazardous waste clean-up laws, air-quality legislation, and laws concerning spills and mining.

Our administration has worked to implement the Kentucky Environmental Management plan, as we committed to doing, and to implement the solid waste laws of the 1991 special legislative session. Even before our team of Shepherd and Higdon was brought in, we outlined a consensus-building approach for addressing the problems at Lake Cumberland and came up with a plan that all parties have agreed to. Recognizing that clean water is a fundamental necessity for sustaining both a high quality of life and a growing economy, we have undertaken a major initiative to ensure that our groundwater resources are protected. That effort will be a major topic of discussion at this conference. It will become one of the hallmarks by which we demonstrate that consensus building and public participation will result in better public policy.

During the past two days, almost three hundred people came together to learn more about Geographic Information Systems, called G.I.S., and how we can use this technology to make decisions about our environment. Our administration created, on October 1, a new office of Geographic Information Systems to coordinate this information from across state government and to work with local governments to help their work in environmental planning for water supplies, siting new industries, and other possibilities using G.I.S. Again, this approach features all the state agencies working together, combining resources, and eliminating duplication so that we can better serve Kentucky.

But where are we going from here, now that we've established a consensus-building philosophy and put a team in place to implement the programs? We have already begun to outline plans for ensuring that Kentucky will move toward an economic strategy that ensures environmentally sound economic development. Our Economic Development Cabinet and the Natural Resources Cabinet are working together under the new Economic Development Partnership Act to implement a process whereby citizens define the economic future for their communities. And in Kentucky that future will include clean air and water and landscapes where natural areas and green spaces are protected for future generations.

In addition, we will work with Kentucky's industrial community to ensure that pollution prevention is a vital part of our economic-development strategy. Our focus on recycling market development may require new legislation, and we will work with all the diverse interests, once again, to ensure that our legislation creates markets for recycled products and reduces the waste going to our landfills. Our economic-development strategy will include industries that use recycled products and create jobs with secondary materials. Our strategies will focus on our renewable resources, such as forestry and agriculture products, and develop jobs that add value to the natural resources that we produce in Kentucky.

Our strategies will work to ensure that our special natural areas of Kentucky are preserved and protected and that our tourism industry is bolstered by our programs for protecting natural areas and ensuring clean lakes and fishing streams. Most importantly, though, we challenge all of you here to move Kentucky forward in bringing together environmental protection and economic development for the future of our state and our children. My challenge to each of you here today is this: use this conference and this meeting to determine how, by the twentieth annual Governor's Conference on the Environment, to make Kentucky the nation's leader in integrating environmental protection and economic development. By the fall of 1995, we will have had twenty events such as this in Kentucky, twenty conferences in which people from across Kentucky come together to share ideas, discuss concerns, and learn more about protecting our natural resources.

We all know that environmental protection is not something that only the government can do, or only the industries. Protecting our environment is the responsibility of all Kentuckians, and we in Kentucky have many opportunities to move our state forward. Let's use this opportunity over the next two days to discuss how we can all participate in improving our environment and the economy in Kentucky, working together, as in the theme of the conference.

I challenge each of you to return to your communities and work with your leaders, your mayors, city councils, county commissioners and judges, your schools, businesses, and civic organizations, to participate in an environmentally sound future for your community. Kentucky's new Economic Development Partnership Act gives us this responsibility and this opportunity. Kentucky communities have already put together our solid waste plans. We're working on water plans for our future. Now we have the responsibility to put all this together in a plan for our future that includes both economic development and environmental protection. I challenge you to ensure that our communities and cities realize not only the responsibilities for these plans, but also the opportunities.

During this conference you'll learn more about the new environmental technologies associated with environmental protection. How can our communities create jobs from these industries? How can our towns work with our agriculture community to provide better markets for Kentucky's farmers and their products? During these next three years, we are entering a new era in economic renewal and environmental management in America and in Kentucky. Let's put Kentucky at the forefront by demonstrating these basic, common-sense philosophies that we've put in place, building consensus with all parties at the table, outlining mutual goals for economic development, and working together to achieve those goals.

I look forward to meeting with you again in 1993 and meeting our challenge in 1995, for the twentieth annual Governor's Conference on the Environment.

---

1. Greg Higdon (1947–), B.S., Brescia College; Democrat from Fancy Farm; elected state senate (1st district), 1982; re-elected, 1984–91; chair of Agriculture and Natural Resources Committee, 1987–91; Democratic whip, 1991; director of operations, McCoy and McCoy engineering firm; deputy secretary of Natural Resources under Jones, 1991–95.

GOVERNOR'S CONFERENCE ON THE ENVIRONMENT
Fort Mitchell / October 13, 1993

GOOD morning, and thank you for that kind introduction, Secretary Shepherd. It is a pleasure for me to spend a few minutes with you at the eighteenth annual Governor's Conference on the Environment, a conference with a tradition of promoting discussions on a broad spectrum of concerns by citizens with diverse interests and opinions. Despite our diverse backgrounds and opinions, we gather to bring the Commonwealth closer to the shared goal of making stronger decisions for the good of Kentucky. Our administration, and the Natural Resources and Environmental Protection Cabinet, have a proven record of resolving differences and disputes concerning environmental issues through discussions and consensus building. As we gather at this conference to discuss the many challenges facing us, we can pause to reflect on the accomplishments we have achieved and to identify the issues which wait before us as we strive to protect and preserve our environment.

Our administration has tackled numerous issues that had been languishing in the public arena for years, with no promise of resolution on the horizon. Under the leadership of Phillip Shepherd and Greg Higdon, our Natural Resources Cabinet began the process of analyzing the problem and identifying potential solutions. An issue such as the proposed pipeline from the Jamestown Wastewater Treatment Plant into Lake Cumberland, which had moved from town halls into courtrooms, was resolved when representatives from the interested and affected groups were brought together by us. Likewise, the process for developing groundwater regulations, which began in 1987, is nearing completion because citizens with diverse opinions were brought together to resolve their differences.

Over the past nineteen months, the cabinet has instituted procedures which efficiently and fairly deal with the enforcement of environmental laws. As a farmer, as a businessperson, and as a public servant, a fair deal, or a level playing field, allowed me to achieve the goals I had set for myself. No less is required for the thousands of coal companies, plants, factories, federal agencies, or private citizens who come into contact with the regulatory agencies in the Natural Resources Cabinet. The cabinet has been successful in stepping up enforcement of ownership and control violations at surface-mining sites and has resolved outstanding civil penalties assessed to mining companies. New strategies are in place to improve the enforcement of state environmental regulations, including coordinated compliance inspections with air, water, and waste inspectors.

The cabinet is using teams of program and legal staff to develop legal cases against major violators and is requiring persistent violators to install self-monitoring systems which transmit data to state field offices. There is a renewed emphasis on public participation in the decision-making process regarding issues which affect citizens in their own communities. A key component in this open approach is the office of the ombudsman, a position established in 1992. The ombudsman meets with community leaders and interested citizens to help find solutions to their environmental problems. Once again, the process of involvement and consensus building is at work in the cabinet.

No longer do bureaucrats in an office in Frankfort dictate environmental policy without regard to citizen input. The cabinet has conducted public hearings across the state on environmental issues, and most of the time those hearings were not required by law. One of the most exciting activities the cabinet has been involved in is preserving natural areas and, in some cases, acquiring natural areas. This year, the Kentucky State Nature Preserves Commission and the Department for Fish and Wildlife Resources will begin an intensive campaign to promote the tax check-off refund program for the non-game wildlife/natural areas fund. This fund, unfortunately, has been one of the best-kept secrets in Kentucky state government. This year, these two agencies are making more Kentuckians aware of the fund and how their dollars can be used to acquire natural areas, to preserve endangered plants, and to reintroduce endangered non-game animals to the Commonwealth.

Another exciting land acquisition program involves an old-growth forest in eastern Kentucky. Blanton Forest, a 2,350-acre old-growth forest, is on Pine Mountain in Harlan County. More than 150 years old, the trees in this forest have never been logged, and the forest has been undisturbed by humans since the settlement of Kentucky. Imagine, if you will, how Kentucky must have appeared to Daniel Boone in 1767, when he entered the area on a hunting expedition. Thick forests with hundreds of species of grasses, flowers, and trees greeted the first white visitors to what was to become Kentucky. Today, Blanton Forest is as close as we can come to what Daniel Boone saw so long ago. Actually in two parcels, this is the largest old-growth forest in Kentucky and one of the largest in the United States. The Nature Preserves Commission is negotiating for the purchase of one of the two parcels of land.

But buying such an important tract of land is going to be expensive, and the commission is requesting budget money to fund it. Given the state's budget, it is realistic that private-sector fund raising will be necessary. But once acquired, Blanton Forest will be dedicated as a state nature preserve and given the strongest land protection in the Commonwealth. Once dedicated, the forest can become a place for hiking, a haven for bird watching, and a wonderful natural laboratory for research.

Perhaps the greatest achievement of our administration cannot be measured in terms of acres committed to wetlands, or violations issued at surface-mining permit sites, or regulations drafted to protect the environment. The achievement, in fact, is a belief, a philosophy, a conviction by this administration that the Commonwealth can have high-quality jobs and a clean environment and that we as leaders and citizens of this state can come together and make this happen. Two years ago, at the beginning of our administration, if someone had predicted that Kentucky would be a leader in the concept of sustainable development, that person would have been labeled a dreamer at best, or a fool at worst. But in May of this year, Kentucky state government—not the federal government, not the state of California, not Harvard University, but Kentucky state government—brought together representatives from forty-nine states and several foreign countries to discuss what state and local governments need to do to promote sustainable development. As a follow-up to the 1992 Earth Summit in Rio de Janeiro,[1] our conference brought together more than twelve hundred officials, industry representatives, environmentalists, and interested citizens who want to share our vision for the future.

I believe that future is bright as we put into practice this concept of providing jobs for our citizens today while sustaining our resources for future generations. And speaking of future generations, they were represented at the "Rio to the Capitals" conference by students from across the country who were exposed to the public policy process. Hosting the conference was only the first step as we begin to define what sustainable development will mean for Kentucky and our communities. As we look to the future, we cannot ignore the concept of biodiversity. I will ask this task force to develop a statewide strategy on biodiversity. The executive order has the support of the Environmental Quality Commission, the Cabinet for Natural Resources, the Department of Fish and Wildlife, and many others, and I am excited about the possibilities that will come out of the task force study. Those of us who are closest to the people and to the problems must be willing to set aside preconceived notions and prejudices in order to make the right decision for our state and our communities.

While we undoubtedly have diverse goals and backgrounds, we must look through each other's eyes, employ innovative thinking, and put our ideas into practice. This is a commitment we must make if our children, and all future generations, are to judge us as faithful stewards of our environment and our natural resources. This conference has been another opportunity to build on the progress made at the "Rio to the Capitals" meetings.

"Ecosystems/Econosystems, Jobs, Food and Energy" have been the theme of the eighteenth annual conference, as we examined the resources which affect our daily lives. The past three days provided us with an occasion to look at the jobs to be gained and maintained in the Commonwealth, jobs tied directly to our natural resources, involving agriculture, forestry, and energy.

We have focused attention on how Kentucky farmers can implement sustainable practices in their operations. County extension agents across the state are already working with farmers to develop field operations which reduce groundwater pollution and enable the farmer to have an ample supply of fertilizer on hand when he or she needs it. By using this plan, our farmers are not only reducing groundwater pollution, but are also reducing the need for store-bought chemicals used to fertilize their crops. The Natural Resources Cabinet is continuing to form partnerships with private landowners in the management of forests, a tremendous task when you realize that over 90 percent of the 12.7 million acres of forest land in Kentucky is privately held. And while there is great opportunity for the economic development of our forest industry, this must be coupled with a plan to make our forests sustainable. It will take a partnership between private landowners, corporations, timber cutters, and our Economic Development and Natural Resources Cabinets to create a sustainable forestry program in Kentucky.

I have great hope for this industry, for the jobs which will be created, and for the new partnerships and management programs which will be initiated for the good of the Commonwealth. Our state has been blessed with wonderful forests, now showing their beautiful fall colors, with lush meadowlands supporting an abundance of wildlife, and great rivers and streams which provide drinking water for our people, economic opportunity for our state, and recreational activities for people from all across the country.

1. The 1992 Earth Summit in Rio de Janeiro, Brazil, united countries to adopt sustainable development "as the principle that should guide the world's economic activity." Planned as a major step in defining the future economic and environmental development of the world, it set the stages for many of the following conferences and Summits.

HERITAGE LAND CONSERVATION ACT PRESS CONFERENCE
Frankfort / February 3, 1994

LAST Friday in the House, Rep. Mark Brown[1] introduced a very important piece of legislation. It is House Bill 368, and it seeks to amend the Kentucky Heritage Land Conservation Act. Among other things, it would provide money to buy and maintain land for wildlife management areas, recreation areas, state forests, nature preserves, and wetlands. Libby and I support House Bill 368, because we feel it is important to preserve the natural heritage of this Commonwealth.

As Kentucky enters its third century of statehood, we must continue to protect and preserve the past, as well as to prepare for the future. Quite frankly, we must be better stewards of Kentucky's wealth of natural resources. Benjamin Franklin once said, "When the well is dry, we know the wealth of water." We want to make sure that the wealth of Kentucky's natural heritage never runs dry. Already, we are recognizing rare and endangered plant and animal species that should be protected. We find fewer and fewer natural areas that exemplify the forests and grasslands and abundant wildlife that sustained Native Americans in Kentucky thousands of years ago. Our remaining high-quality streams and rivers need to be protected. And we must save a generous portion of that "rich land beyond the mountains" that enticed settlers through the Cumberland Gap.

The 1990 General Assembly enacted the Kentucky Heritage Land Conservation Act to provide for land acquisitions that would preserve natural areas, as well as provide critical wildlife habitat and outdoor recreation areas. The act also established a board to set priorities for the purchase of available land. Unfortunately, money to buy the land was *not* provided. So the intent of this important act has not yet been realized. Up until now, Kentucky has been doing what it could with very limited general funds, grants, and some private donations. Without consistent funding, we have to struggle to protect our natural heritage.

One example is Blanton Forest in Harlan County. Blanton Forest contains more than two thousand acres on rugged Pine Mountain. It is recognized as the largest tract of old-growth forest in the state. Had funds been available to the Heritage Land Conservation Board, we could have moved quickly to negotiate for its purchase. Yet, more than a year and a half after its discovery, we still have no money to buy it. Thanks to the landowners, we have been given some time to buy Blanton Forest and protect it. Unfortunately, time is not always on our side. We have missed many opportunities to protect similar, unique places all across Kentucky. And once they're gone, like rare paintings and books that are destroyed or defaced, they cannot be recreated.

With this legislation, we can offset these losses in the future. If House Bill 368 passes, land could be purchased on a willing seller/willing buyer basis and managed by the Department of Fish and Wildlife Resources, the Division of Forestry, the Department of Parks, Kentucky State Nature Preserves Commission, and the wild rivers program. Also, money would be available to local governments and colleges and universities to purchase and maintain heritage land. And part of the proceeds (from the environmental fines) would be allocated to the environmental council to develop and implement a sustained statewide educational program to protect the environment and natural resources of the Commonwealth. This legislation will benefit all of us. It will protect land and water for present and future generations.

It will also contribute to the state's economy by providing even more outdoor recreational areas that Kentuckians and our visitors can enjoy. I'd like to take this opportunity to thank Representative Brown[1] and Sen. Ed Ford, who will handle this bill in the senate, for their support of this bill and their willingness to work for its passage during this legislative session. It is just another example of how this administration and the legislature can work together to make strong decisions for the good of Kentucky.

---

1. Mark S. Brown (1951–), attended Western Kentucky University; board of directors, Doe Run Employees Federal Credit Union; Member United Assn. of the Plumbing and Pipefitting Industry, Local 522; Democratic Kentucky state representative, 27th district, 1984–98; pipefitter, mechanical technician.

ARBOR DAY CEREMONY
Frankfort / April 1, 1994

I AM glad to be here today because this event gives me an opportunity to recount a very special moment that occurred earlier in the legislative session. We were in Bath County in late February when a group of students from Bethel Elementary School showed me a banner and asked me to veto House Bill 128. It was a bill that the General Assembly had passed in which the tulip poplar would replace the Kentucky coffee tree as the official state tree.

The students wanted to keep the Kentucky coffee tree as the official state tree, partially out of respect for Joe Creason,[1] the late *Courier-Journal* columnist who is buried in Bath County. Creason has been credited with convincing lawmakers in the mid-1970s to designate the Kentucky coffee tree as the official state tree. Those Bath County students made a convincing argument. So I told them at the time that I wanted them to know they had made a difference, and that because of their commitment to Joe Creason's ideas, I planned to veto the bill. However, when I returned to Frankfort, I discovered that lawmakers were determined to make the change and would override my veto. So I asked some of the students to come to my office in Frankfort to help me make a tough political decision.

And on a day when school was out because of snow, a high-level delegation of students came here to the capitol from Bath County. The contingent included four students, Dustin Thornsburg, Matthew Sorrell, Sheena Stanford, and Chelsea Cline, accompanied by their teacher, Bonnie Bowling, and the boys' grandmother, Irene Thornsburg. And let me tell you, they were tough negotiators! We sat in my office and discussed the problem, and together, we came up with a compromise solution that was acceptable to all sides. I made a commitment to them to let the tulip poplar bill become a law without my signature. And to give the Kentucky coffee tree its due by designating it the Kentucky Heritage Tree at this ceremonial planting today, Arbor Day in Kentucky.

We all can thank the students from Bethel Elementary for making a positive contribution to the people of Kentucky. I would also like to take a moment to pay tribute to the late Joe Creason. He was a wonderful writer and a lifelong Kentuckian who "accentuated the positive" things about this state. In 1974, Creason started campaigning in his newspaper column to have the Kentucky coffee tree designated the *official* state tree, primarily because it was the only tree with the word "Kentucky" as part of its accepted common name. For many years, the tulip poplar had been the *unofficial* state tree. But Creason wanted the Kentucky coffee tree to have the "official" designation, and that's what happened when the legislature passed and then-Gov. Julian Carroll[2] signed the bill into law in 1976.

By the way, there is an interesting relationship between the Kentucky coffee tree and Kentucky's early settlers. Explorers found the tree to be more abundant in Kentucky than in regions to the north. And with commodities scarce in the early days, they used its ground, roasted beans as a substitute for coffee. That's how the tree acquired its name. When the tree was more plentiful, its hard and durable wood was used for tobacco sticks, railroad ties, and posts. Recently, it's been used by woodworkers for gavels, lamps, and carvings. The wood easily lends itself to staining and produces a beautiful finish. So while the tulip poplar has now become the Commonwealth's official state tree, the Kentucky coffee tree also has a rich state heritage. And that's why, in just a moment, I will sign the proclamation to officially designate the Kentucky coffee tree as the Kentucky Heritage Tree. . . .

---

1. Joe Cross Creason (1918–74), educated at the University of Kentucky; became editor of the *Benton Tribune-Democrat* in 1940; *Courier-Journal,* 1940–44; Navy, 1944–46; returned to *Courier-Journal* in 1946, where he was feature writer until 1963, when he began writing "Joe Creason's Kentucky."

2. Julian Morton Carroll (1931–), B.A., University of Kentucky, 1954; J.D., University of Kentucky, 1956; member of Kentucky House of Representatives, 1962–72; lieutenant governor of Kentucky, 1971–74, governor, 1974–79.

GOVERNOR'S CONFERENCE ON THE ENVIRONMENT
Louisville / September 30, 1994

GOOD morning, and thank you, Secretary Shepherd, for that kind introduction. It is a pleasure for me to be with you this morning as we open the nineteenth annual Governor's Conference on the

Environment. This conference has always been an opportunity for open discussion on a broad spectrum of environmental issues by citizens from across the Commonwealth. Our administration and the Natural Resources and Environmental Protection Cabinet continue to work to bring our citizens together to resolve disputes through discussion and consensus building. This cabinet, under the direction of Phillip Shepherd, Greg Higdon, and Karen Armstrong-Cummings,[1] has made great strides in solving problems by reaching out to industry, to environmental groups, and to local citizens.

The Lake Cumberland pipeline and the formation of groundwater regulations are just two examples of how the cabinet has brought citizens and groups with diverse interests and opinions to the table to reach a consensus. Another example is the work of the Biodiversity Task Force. Our state has a hugh diversity of plants, animals, and ecosystems that range from hardwood forests and grasslands to caves and wetlands. At last year's conference, I announced the formation of the Biodiversity Task Force and requested that it submit to me, by October 1995, a written report on the status of biodiversity and specific recommendations for maintenance and conservation of all levels of biodiversity in Kentucky.

Dr. William Martin,[2] commissioner of the Department for Natural Resources, and Tom Bennett,[3] commissioner of the Department of Fish and Wildlife Resources, serve as co-chairs of the task force. Serving with them are university and consulting scientists and representatives from agriculture, industry, environmental groups, education, and government. This thirty-five-member group is assessing the current status of biodiversity in the Commonwealth, looking at what species and ecosystems are in significant decline or are in need of special attention. The task force will also look at how government agencies, universities, and private organizations can actively maintain and conserve biodiversity and how to better educate the public on these issues.

Inter-agency cooperation has never been better. The Division of Forestry and the Department of Fish and Wildlife Resources, for example, are working on a management agreement for land owned by the U.S. Army Corps of Engineers. Also, several state agencies in Kentucky, Tennessee, and Alabama are working together with landowners in a regional partners-in-flight program to address the decline in our native migratory songbirds. Our administration and the cabinet continue to form partnerships with private landowners, with industry, with universities, and with other government agencies to improve the conservation of our natural resources.

As we continue to reduce the size of state government, these partnerships become even more valuable. We very strongly believe that we can have high-quality, good-paying jobs for our citizens and at the same time have a clean environment. As leaders and as citizens we can make that happen, and that is one of the reasons why we are gathered here today. The theme of this year's conference is "Kentucky's Forests: Thinking Beyond Today." Our forest resources are environmentally, socially, and economically important to the Commonwealth. Recognizing there are many divergent opinions concerning how these resources can best benefit the state, I called together about seventy-five citizens to discuss the future of Kentucky's forests. This forest summit served as the kick-off for this year's conference. And tomorrow you will hear about the issues that were discussed, problems that were identified, and potential solutions. We cannot underestimate the value of our forest resources and the need for better management of timber supply, wildlife habitat, watershed protection, and recreation and tourism. That management is key to the development of a sustainable economy for Kentucky.

A number of issues related to the role of forests in economic development, forest protection, and health makes the summit and this conference most timely. Our goal for the forest summit is to discuss these issues and reach common ground that will avoid the divisive debate that's plagued other states addressing forestry issues. One issue of particular concern is the protection of our forests and natural areas. The General Assembly was aware of the importance of protecting the natural features of Kentucky when, earlier this year, it passed House Bill 368 and, for the first time, secured funding for the Heritage Land Conservation Fund. As you recall, I strongly supported this bill and had no hesitation signing it.

The state portion of the unmined minerals tax, environmental penalties, and the sale of environmental license plates will provide the funding for the purchase of natural areas with unique features, areas important to migratory birds, lands which perform important functions, and areas for public use, outdoor recreation, and education. Half of the funds will be shared among the Department of Fish and Wildlife Resources, the Division of Forestry, the Department of Parks, the Kentucky Nature Preserves Commission, and the Wild Rivers System. The other half may be allocated to state or local agencies, colleges or universities, and the Environmental Education Council.

Through the use of these funds to expand our state forests, we will be able to protect biological diversity, provide watershed protection, provide recreational opportunities, conduct ecological research, and develop demonstration areas to illustrate sound forest-management practices. We can also use these funds to acquire and preserve significant and unique natural areas. Most of you have heard of Blanton Forest in Harlan County. The General Assembly has provided $500,000 to purchase this valuable old-growth forest, and efforts are underway to obtain additional money.

The Heritage Land Conservation Fund will now make it possible to preserve places such as Blanton Forest and other unique pieces of our natural heritage. The Heritage Land Conservation Fund is going to need sustained funding, and I am going to share with you how you can help. Starting next year, you can purchase an environmental license plate for each of your vehicles, and by doing so, you will be supporting the acquisition of natural lands. The plate features the Kentucky Warbler sitting on a tulip poplar branch, with the words "Kentucky" and "Nature's Finest." The warbler is one of the songbirds being studied by the partners-in-flight program I mentioned a moment ago, and, as you know, the tulip poplar became our official state tree this year.

Another issue of big concern is forest management. Over 90 percent of the 12.7 million acres of forest land in Kentucky is privately owned, so the Division of Forestry has a tremendous task working with 400,000 landowners. Today, less than 10 percent of our landowners take advantage of the services of the Division of Forestry. This administration has placed a high priority on assisting landowners. The cabinet and General Assembly have taken steps to place more foresters in the field and significantly increase contact with landowners.

Kentucky is already a national leader in forest stewardship programs, and we want to improve our performance. In addition to protecting forests, we also recognize the economic potential of the forest industry in Kentucky and the development of primary and secondary wood products. This development must be coupled with ways to insure that our forests are sustainable; so today, I am announcing the appointments to the Kentucky Forest Products Council and am asking each member who serves to be committed to the development of our wood products industry. I have selected a diverse group of Kentuckians to serve on this council, representing industry, agriculture, tree farmers, and public-interest groups. This council will promote cooperation between industry representatives and landowners, and it will work with industry to set in place landowner assistance and education programs, implementation of best management practices, promote forest stewardship and master logger programs, and forest fire prevention. The goal of this council is to develop a comprehensive strategy with industry and economic development to provide high-quality, good-paying jobs for our citizens and insure these forest resources are also sustained for future generations.

This conference is reaching out to another group of citizens in a special way this year: Kentucky's teachers. Our teachers have been invited this afternoon to participate in an outdoor classroom project, and they'll meet tomorrow in an environmental education forum. And speaking of education, I want to recognize Deputy Secretary Karen Armstrong-Cummings, who earlier this week was given the Individual Achievement Award for Environmental Education by the National Environmental Education Association. Congratulations, Karen, for your outstanding work in this area.

In closing, I want to thank each of you for taking the time to join us as we bring to the forefront public discussion of Kentucky's forests. Please take advantage of every opportunity to participate as we develop strategies for sustainable forest resources for the Commonwealth.

---

1. Karen Armstrong-Cummings (1949–), born in North Carolina; B.A., Mars Hill College, 1972; M.P.A., Kentucky State University, 1985; deputy commissioner, Kentucky Department for Environmental Protection, 1985–87; president, ACI Research, 1989–90; director, division of administrative services, 1992–93; deputy secretary, Kentucky Natural Resources and Environmental Protection Cabinet, 1993–95; Tomorrow Board of Directors, 1996–present; Kentucky Center for Public Issues Board of Directors, 1996–present; Green Mountain Institute for Environmental Democracy Board of Directors, 1996–present; National Campaign for Sustainable Agriculture Steering Committee, 1997; director, Center for Environment at Council of State Governments.

2. William Martin (1938–), born in Bath Springs, Tennessee; B.S., Animal Science, Tennessee Technological University, 1960; M.S., University of Tennessee, 1966; Ph.D., University of Tennessee, 1971; professor of biology; director, division of Department for Natural Resources, Eastern Kentucky University, 1969–present; president, Southern Appalachian Botanical Society, 1985–86; commissioner, Kentucky Department for Natural Resources, 1992–98; senior editor of award-winning, three-volume work, *Biodiversity of the Southeastern United States* (1993); chair, Kentucky Heritage Land Conservation Fund Board, 1994–98; co-chair, Kentucky Biodiversity Task Force, 1994–95.

3. C. Thomas Bennett (1953–), B.S. and M.S., Eastern Kentucky University; deputy secretary of the Governor's Executive Cabinet; deputy secretary of the Kentucky Natural Resources and Environmental Protection Cabinet; commissioner of the Kentucky Department for Surface Mining Reclamation and Enforcement; chief of staff to the Kentucky secretary of transportation; energy conservation and communication business in Louisville; director of Parks and Recreation, Richmond; chairman of the Law Wildlife Agency; president, Southeast Association; secretary-treasurer, International Association of Fish and Wildlife Agencies; commissioner of the Department of Fish and Wildlife Resources.

AMERICORPS EVENT
Lexington Cardinal Valley Elementary School / March 21, 1995

I WANTED to come here today to congratulate the students of Cardinal Valley Elementary School for the work you have done to improve your school environment. You saw that your school could be beautified by planting trees and flowers, and you took action to make it happen. This is the kind of responsible action that we need from all Kentuckians so that our state will continue to be a great place to live. Too often we hear only negative things about our young people. Today you have demonstrated that young people are capable of making important contributions to our communities. I hope that your service project today is just the beginning of your involvement as active Kentucky citizens. I want to thank the "Getting Things Done for Kentucky's Homeless" Americorps program for organizing today's event.

This program is making a difference in the lives of more than two thousand low-income and homeless individuals across Kentucky. In addition, through special projects like the one today, Americorps helps promote the importance of service. In fact, more than six thousand Kentuckians have volunteered to serve alongside the state's two hundred Americorps members. Kentucky has been recognized as a leader in this new Americorps program. This was demonstrated when President Clinton recognized a Kentucky Americorps member during his State of the Union Address in January. In particular, I would like to thank Pam Yazell from the group "Getting Things

Done for Kentucky's Homeless" for your efforts in planning today's event. You have provided an invaluable service by teaching the value of volunteering to these students.

I'd like to close with a story. There was once a terrible storm that washed thousands of starfish onto the shore. A young girl went down to the beach and tried to save the starfish. One by one, she'd pick up a starfish, carry it down to the water's edge, and throw it safely back into the ocean. An old man approached her and said, "Little girl, what are you doing? There are thousands of starfish on this beach. You can't save them all. You can't make a difference." The girl looked at the man, picked up another starfish, and threw it back into the ocean. And as she did, she said to him, "I made a difference to *that* one." Don't let anyone tell you that you can't make a difference. Today, you have shown that we all can, and must, make a difference in our communities.

ENVIRONMENTAL QUALITY COMMISSION AWARDS
Frankfort / April 20, 1995

I AM pleased and honored to join with you today to celebrate the twenty-fifth anniversary of Earth Day. When I came into office, I pledged to the people of Kentucky that our administration would work cooperatively to make the Commonwealth a green state. Protecting, conserving, and improving the quality of our environment has been a top priority of my administration. I am happy to report we continue to make progressive strides in addressing some of our most pressing environmental challenges. While our economy has grown, Kentucky's environmental health has improved:

1. Our waterways are cleaner than they were ten or even two years ago.
2. The level of pollutants in our air continues to decline.
3. The closures of substandard solid waste landfills and their cleanup will remove the ways that some chemicals contaminate our groundwater.
4. And populations of some rare species of wildlife, such as the

bald eagle, the black bear, and the bobcat, are increasing due to the protection of natural habitats.

This is clear evidence that our environmental policies and programs are working. At the same time we have been able to create a record number of jobs for Kentuckians. This is proof that economic development and environmental protection not only can exist together, but can also thrive together. Even so, we still have a long way to go to achieve our vision of a sustainable state. Last session we passed important laws to preserve our natural heritage for future generations. We also enacted measures to cut back on the amount of toxic chemicals released into the environment. And we established a cost share fund to minimize the impact of runoff pollution in our creeks and rivers. Kentucky's commitment to meeting our environmental challenges is increasing every day. Individuals, industries, government agencies, and communities are joining forces to solve environmental problems while, at the same time, preventing new ones. Nowhere is this dedication for a clean environment more exemplified than in the accomplishments of our Earth Day Award winners.

I am heartened by the great efforts that Kentuckians are making to improve the state's environmental health. From the efforts of state trooper Lathram, who plunged into a cold lake last winter to preserve evidence against mussel poachers, to Trigg County Judge-Executive Burlin Moore Jr. and others, who committed themselves to restoration of the Little River, the dedication of Kentuckians to improve our environment is unequaled. I am pleased to commend all your efforts and join with you in celebration of Earth Day. I am confident we will accomplish our vision and make Kentucky an even better place for our children to grow and prosper.

GOVERNOR'S CONFERENCE ON THE ENVIRONMENT

Lexington / October 27, 1995

TODAY marks a watershed time in Kentucky's environmental future, as we celebrate our twentieth annual conference on the environment. As governor of Kentucky, I have had the opportunity to welcome you to four of these conferences, exactly one-fifth of those we've held. At each conference, we've been able to build on the themes which we established at the beginning of this administration—building consensus, developing cooperation, and forming partnerships for a sustainable economic future for Kentucky.

We knew that building consensus was crucial if we were to be able to reach our twin goals of protecting our valuable natural heritage and securing jobs for our citizens. At the 1992 Governor's Conference, we discussed the consensus negotiation process that we used to reach an agreement in the controversy surrounding the protection of Lake Cumberland and the need to continue with industrial operations in that region. I encouraged conference participants to take this type of conflict-resolution process home with them to solve problems in their local communities. And I'm happy to report today that communities across Kentucky have successfully used this model to solve local environmental and land-use problems, from post-mining land-use discussions in Harlan to environmental mediation classes in Bowling Green, Louisville, and elsewhere across the Commonwealth.

In addition, our Natural Resources Cabinet established the environmental mediation program to help speed the resolution of environmental disputes pending before the cabinet. This mediation program now serves as a national model. In 1993, we brought together business and environmental leaders from around the country to build a consensus on the concept of sustainability. More than sixteen hundred participants took part in the "Rio to the Capitals" conference and almost four hundred Kentuckians attended that meeting. Our citizens at that conference told us that Kentucky needed a mechanism for continuing the dialogue between businesses, agricultural leaders, and environmentalists. We listened to those recommendations and with the help of the Kentucky Economic Development Partnership Board, we established the Kentucky Roundtable on Environment and Economy.

Today, the roundtable members include the renowned Kentucky author Wendell Berry[1] and the head of Kentucky's Chamber of Commerce, Ken Oilschlager,[2] among other key leaders. At the roundtable's meeting last month, the members decided to focus their energy on the important issue of Kentucky's forests and the need for sustaining the forests while keeping timber-related jobs here in Kentucky. Because of this type of effort, Kentucky emerged as a leader in the effort to focus attention on the need for business and environmentalists to work together to build jobs while protecting the environment. We've received national awards and international recognition for these efforts.

At the 1993 Governor's Conference, held in northern Kentucky, we learned more about environmental technology from a native Kentuckian, Dr. Darryl Banks,[3] a former Rhodes Scholar who is now with the World Resources Institute. At that conference, we again encouraged the continuing theme of building cooperation and developing partnerships for a sustainable future. Our Economic Development Cabinet and Natural Resources Cabinet began working even more closely to encourage the growth of environmental technology companies in Kentucky. Just yesterday, these agencies held a joint news conference in which we announced that Kentucky was one of eight states receiving a national grant to develop international markets for environmental technology in Asian countries.

Also at the 1993 conference, we announced that we would establish a cooperative venture, the Biodiversity Task Force. This group was made up of business, agriculture, university representatives, public-interest groups, and many others determined to conserve and sustain Kentucky's biodiversity. We are pleased to announce that the task force co-chairs, Dr. Bill Martin and Tom Bennett, have worked diligently to bring this issue to all Kentuckians.

At the 1994 conference, we discussed the legislation that created the Heritage Land Conservation Fund. This law, sponsored by State Representative Mark Brown, again symbolized our efforts to build consensus and cooperation from diverse groups not accustomed to working together. Our administration brought together the coal industry, businesses, agriculture, public-interest groups, and even elementary and high-school students, in support of this law. Money from this fund will help purchase the renowned Blanton Forest in Harlan County, which will now be protected through a public and private donor partnership program. This famous old-growth forest and all Kentucky's forests are under stress from a number of sources. At last year's conference in Louisville, we heard Kentuckian Thomas Clark challenge us to begin to better protect and manage our forests.

As we have worked with citizens and businesses interested in environmental quality, a continuing theme has been the need for more and better environmental education. We have tried to address that, both through this conference and through our agencies. At last year's conference, we invited Kentucky's teachers to attend the meeting, free of charge. And more than two hundred teachers from Paducah to Pikeville came to that conference. This year, we have worked to continue that theme of partnership with educators by sponsoring an environmental career meeting at this conference. Almost six hundred high-school students and their teachers have participated in this activity.

I would also like to recognize the work of the newly created Environmental Education Council and its energetic director, Jane Wilson. With their help and with money from the Heritage Land Conservation Fund, we provided small grants for environmental education to schools across Kentucky.

Forestry, agriculture lands, environmental education, and other issues have been discussed as part of the "Kentucky Outlook 2000 Project," which is releasing a draft report of its findings here at this conference. Through the "Outlook 2000 Project," we have learned that Kentuckians from all walks of life are concerned about the environment and the economy, and they are willing to work together for a sustainable future. More than fifty scientists, engineers, and technical experts from business, schools, governmental agencies, and elsewhere have worked to help us with our process of setting environmental priorities. All of the successes of this administration have come because people throughout this Commonwealth who truly care about business and the environment have worked together, formed partnerships, and developed a consensus for a sustainable future. I would hope that the next administration will build on these themes and will improve on what we have been able to do. . . .

---

1. Wendell E. Berry (1934–), B.A., University of Kentucky, 1956; M.A., University of Kentucky, 1957; teacher at Georgetown College, Kentucky, 1957–58; held fellowship at Stanford University, 1959–60; professor at City College of New York, 1962–64; teacher at the University of Kentucky, 1964–78, 1987–94.

2. Ken Oilschlager (1950–), B.S., University of Mississippi, 1971; graduate of the Institute for Organizational Management and the National Economic Development Institute; committee member, Center for Communities of the Future; president and CEO, Kentucky Chamber of Commerce.

3. R. Darryl Banks, B.A. with honors in chemistry, Coe College, Iowa; Rhodes Scholar, molecular biophysics, D. Phil., Oxford University; Rand Corporation; executive assistant to the assistant administrator for research and development, U.S. Environmental Protection Agency; a Congressional Science Fellow of the American Association for the Advancement of Science; staff scientist in the Office of Technology Assessment of the U.S. Congress; deputy commissioner for the New York State Department of Environmental Conservation; senior fellow, World Resources Institute.

AGRICULTURE

KARDA TASK FORCE MEETING
Frankfort / June 9, 1992

AGRICULTURE has been and continues to be Kentucky's number-one industry. Kentucky farmers generate almost $4 billion in cash receipts from the sale of farm products. There are almost 91,000 farms in the Commonwealth, which covers 56 percent of the total acreage in our state. Kentucky ranks fourth in the number of farms behind Texas, Missouri, and Iowa. We have maintained the ranking in spite of the fact that Kentucky, like other states, has been losing farms every year. Kentucky is truly an agricultural state, but all too often Kentucky's farmers go without the recognition and appreciation they so richly deserve. Never before in history have so many been fed so well by so few for so little. Today, a typical farmer provides enough food for himself and 125 other people.

Some of you may recall that as lieutenant governor I chaired the Commission on the Future of Agriculture in Kentucky. That commission issued a report entitled *Plowshares to Profits: Agriculture Options for Kentucky*. One of the recommendations in that report was for our agricultural community to work together to improve its ability to communicate and to choose its leadership statewide. That recommendation is no less important today than it was when the report was released in May of 1989.

Given the steady decline nationally in the number of farms to the lowest level on record, the present-day economic uncertainty, and the rapidity of technological advances in genetic, biological, computer, and mechanical engineering, it is imperative that all facets of our Commonwealth's agriculture industry work together. Commissioner of Agriculture Ed Logsdon and I are committed to an administration of cooperation and unity for the betterment of Kentucky farmers, agribusinesses, processors, wholesalers, and retailers. Today I am naming Commissioner Logsdon as chairman of the Kentucky Agriculture Resources Development Authority. I am confident that we can provide the leadership necessary to unify the efforts of Kentucky farmers and agricultural groups.

KARDA will receive a major focus from our administration, and we are asking much of its members: to advise state officials on economic-development initiatives to improve the farm economy; to shape long-range planning and provide continuity for agriculture and agribusiness; to work with executive and legislative branches on legislation and programs with specific emphasis on increasing farm income and strengthening rural communities; to develop markets and encourage the "value-added" concept to its full potential; to capitalize on our strengths and evaluate additional opportunities; and to improve the flow of information and technology from the federal and state governments and the university system to agriculture commodity organizations, their members, and the farm community in general.

Some of you may be wondering why I am issuing a new executive order when there was already one in place authorizing this agricultural entity. First, I wanted to emphasize to each of you my belief that cooperation is critical and that agriculture must be unified in its approach to state, regional, national, and international marketing. Second, I wanted to ensure that Kentucky farm marketing advocacy groups are appropriately involved in selecting members to KARDA. I have chosen to give the agricultural commodity organizations, other than those whose representatives serve as ex-officio members, the liberty to elect from their membership the individual they wish to represent their particular commodity. This process will be instituted as staggered terms of the initial appointees expire. We believe staggered terms will help insure continuity.

In addition to representatives of the various Kentucky agriculture commodities, we have attempted to include representatives from the agribusiness community in KARDA's membership. We hope that KARDA will develop ideas and proposals to improve agricultural education, the marketing of Kentucky farm products, efficiency and productivity, environmental protection, farm financing programs, and long-term agricultural strategies. For example, KARDA and the Department of Education could work together to develop a comprehensive agricultural science education curriculum and improve adult agricultural education programs. KARDA should develop a program to coordinate the marketing of Kentucky farm products, explore the feasibility of an information clearinghouse for those products, expand the labeling program, and develop additional farm enterprises. In the areas of farm efficiency and environmental protection, KARDA should encourage the development of new technology and technology transfer to Kentucky farmers, propose long-range sewer and water supply plans, propose comprehensive non-point source pollution control programs, and encourage the development of comprehensive soil-conservation programs. In farm financing, we must explore programs to help first-time farmers and those who want to diversify their businesses, encourage technical assistance to producer cooperatives and farmers markets. And we must develop a long-range plan for Kentucky agriculture which includes working to win passage of the constitutional amendment making the commissioner of agriculture an appointed position. . . .[1]

---

1. Jones gave a similar speech on August 30 at the Agricultural Summit in Louisville.

KENTUCKY FARM BUREAU
Louisville / December 11, 1992

. . . LOOKING ahead, I want to talk a moment about our goals for Kentucky agriculture. During this past year we have worked with the Farm Bureau, Agriculture Commissioner Ed Logsdon, and the various farm groups in the state to build partnerships that will enable us to effectively address agriculture issues.

Kentucky's farm community is working in harmony on a wide variety of projects to enhance the future of this industry. I believe we are well on the way to meeting our objectives. In October, I appointed a special task force that is assessing how our state's policies affect agriculture. President Sprague and Hoppy Henton[1] are representing the Farm Bureau on this task force, which will make recommendations on farmland conservation programs, right-to-farm laws, ag districting, economic-development opportunities, tax policies, and related issues. Libby [Jones] also is a member of this task force.

This project was funded by a grant from the Ashland Oil Foundation. I was pleased to appoint President Sprague to the board of the new economic-development partnership that will direct our state's economic-development policies and programs. You can be sure that agriculture will receive every consideration in efforts to strengthen our economy. Our administration also is involved in the development of an agricultural water quality model of excellence that will enable Kentucky to qualify for a greater share of federal funding for water quality programs. This program should go a long way in helping our farmers use the best management plans to protect water quality in a cost-effective manner.

Libby has worked with Commissioner Logsdon and President Sprague on establishing the new agriculture and the environment in the classroom program. Currently, this involves thirty-one teachers from across the state who are using agriculture as a theme for teaching traditional subjects. More than one hundred teachers have applied to participate; the goal is to have 150 involved by the start of the 1993–94 school year. I believe all of us can be encouraged by the unified effort to develop a plan for agriculture's future in our state.

The Farm Bureau is among more than forty farm organizations that are participating in a special project coordinated by the University of Kentucky to determine how we can expand farm income. It's very encouraging to see all of the farm groups working together on this plan. Our administration had pledged to support this in every way possible. Kentucky is indeed fortunate in that we have a solid agricultural base to build upon. Agriculture is responsible for more than $11 billion in economic activity in the state each year.

One of every four jobs in the state is tied to agriculture, and we are seeing an increase in agribusiness. We are indeed a diverse agricultural state. We have six farm commodities (tobacco, cattle, hogs, corn, soybeans, and dairy) that each account for more than $100 million in cash receipts a year. Our horse industry has nearly $500 million in sales per year. The value of the forages we produce each year is nearly $500 million, and our greenhouse and nursery industry is valued at about $400 million. When you add it all up, Kentucky has an enormous wealth of agricultural resources.

But, as we all know, agriculture's greatest strength is its people. Indeed, the Farm Bureau's strength lies with the grassroots support from thousands of farm families throughout the state. You can be justifiably proud of this rich tradition. You can also be proud to be a part of agriculture, Kentucky's most vital industry. . . .[2]

---

1. Hampton "Hoppy" Henton Jr. (1948–), B.S., agriculture economics, Purdue University; state executive director of U.S. Department of Agriculture Farm Service Agency in Kentucky; state executive director of the Agricultural Stabilization and Conservation Service, 1993– ; served on various state and regional agricultural and economic groups, including the State Board of Agriculture and Bluegrass Tomorrow; established the Kentucky FSA Labor/Management Partnership Council, 1995.

2. The first part of this speech to the Kentucky Farm Bureau dealt with health care; this portion can be found in the section on health-care issues.

AGRICULTURE TASK FORCE WORKSHOP TAPING
Frankfort / March 3, 1993

[GREETINGS] I really regret that I cannot be with you today to discuss ideas for strengthening agriculture in Kentucky. As you probably know, our administration has undertaken a massive and extremely complicated effort to improve our state's health-care system. Kentucky has tremendous need for major reform, and it is urgent that we inform our citizens of the proposal in order to build consensus and enact legislation as soon as possible. If it were not for the urgency of this effort, I would certainly be with you today. But I do welcome this opportunity to speak with you because I feel that what you are doing today will play a very important role in determining how we can build upon a tradition of agricultural excellence.

Kentucky's soil and what it grows and nourishes has been a very important part of the history and economy of the Commonwealth, and that still holds true today. Kentucky's agricultural industry is a $3.2 billion business responsible for nearly a quarter of the jobs and $20 billion in overall economic activity. It is absolutely vital that we do all we can to protect and preserve its unique character and long-term economic viability. Thanks to the support of the Ashland Oil Foundation and the American Farmland Trust, we have formed a special task force to assess and make recommendations on issues, policies, and programs affecting agriculture production. The task force members are uniquely qualified for this project and are dedicated to serving our farm community. I commend them for initiating this consensus briefing process and I commend *you* for participation in this workshop.

Today you will be discussing three issues that form the framework toward building a better future for Kentucky agriculture: (1) conserving our agricultural land base; (2) promoting economic development; and (3) environmental protection. These are issues that must be addressed singularly and yet are unmistakably linked to any future agricultural growth. Any effort to bring new agribusiness to the state hinges on our ability to produce from our farmland and to maintain that growth through environmentally friendly production practices.

Although our farmers have become incredibly productive, the challenges facing them are enormous. The world food supply is expected to double in the next thirty years to meet the anticipated population growth, and yet the natural resource base is becoming more and more limited. Growing population, pressure from development, less arable land, and unrelenting crop pests are but a few of the challenges facing today's farmer. Meanwhile, society appears to be giving agriculture a new mandate for the future: to develop a food and fiber system that continues to be productive and efficient but is also ecologically sound. The farmers' challenge is to maintain or develop production systems that are environmentally sound but economically viable. And make no mistake—profitability has to be the number-one consideration in developing sustainable agricultural practices. If there is no economic viability, the farmer simply cannot survive. You're left with a cleaner environment, but a shortage of the food and fiber that sustain our society. Anyone who understands agriculture knows that the overwhelming majority of farmers are good stewards of their natural resources. To be anything less would only serve to put them out of business, and our farmers are too wise for that. Our challenge is to develop and promote economically viable practices that enable farmers to do an even better job of protecting our soil and water. And we must reach those who need to be doing a better job.

I am especially pleased that this workshop will address ways to promote economic development of agriculture. Long before I became a public servant in this state I came to realize that agribusiness held the key to any opportunity for agricultural growth. Only a small percentage of the food that is consumed in this state is processed here. Given our wealth of agricultural products—we have seven commodities with sales of more than $100 million a year—there is tremendous opportunity for growth in this industry. While agriculture remains the backbone of our rural economy, we cannot lose sight of the fact that rural Kentucky is dominated by small, family farms that depend on off-farm income. Kentucky, in fact, leads the nation in the number of small farms, and it is estimated that about 70 percent of our farm families have off-farm income. When we bring an agricultural processor to this state, we're not only providing a market for the farmers, but we're adding jobs that improve our quality of life.

I can think of only one other initiative that is as important to the future of our farmers—and that is providing for affordable health care. And that's what I'm working on today. Your agenda today truly reflects pressing concerns of our agricultural community, and I look forward to reviewing the proceedings. I appreciate your interest in Kentucky's future and look forward to working with the task force.[1]

---

1. On July 9, Jones gave a similar speech at the Agriculture Task Force Workshop in Frankfort.

AGRICULTURAL SUMMIT
Louisville / November 18, 1993

I AM pleased to be able to take part in the second-annual Kentucky Agricultural Summit. I thank Commissioner Logsdon, the Kentucky Farm Bureau, the Associated Industries of Kentucky, and Mayor Abramson's office for organizing this event. This conference is extremely valuable, because it helps us to determine how we can build upon a tradition of agricultural excellence. Not only does this provide a forum to discuss issues facing our farmers and agribusinesses—issues such as economic development and the environment—but this summit also brings together rural and urban interests. The end result is a better understanding of how a strong farm economy benefits the entire Commonwealth.

I feel very fortunate to be serving as governor during a period when agriculture has pulled together as never before to work for a more prosperous future. The spirit of cooperation is perhaps best shown by the work of AG Project 2000 and the Governor's Agriculture Policy Task Force. For those of you who are not familiar with AG Project 2000, let me simply say that it is a project unprecedented in our agricultural history, and it is unsurpassed in its importance to the future of farming in our state. The reason this project is so unique is that it has engaged virtually every farm organization in the state to find ways to dramatically increase Kentucky's farm income. The hundreds of farm officials involved in AG Project 2000 have developed a comprehensive plan for a $5 billion farm economy by the year 2000. To give you an idea of the enormous amount of work that has been undertaken, and still remains to be done, the comprehensive master plan details more than four hundred recommendations from fourteen farm-commodity groups. All of us realize that this is a huge undertaking, and it's not going to happen overnight. But we all realize that by working together in an organized way, we can put in place the policies and programs necessary to meet our objectives.

To determine how state government could best meet the needs of our agricultural industry, I appointed an agricultural policy task force last year. The seven-member task force developed fifteen policy recommendations from more than 140 ideas that were reviewed over the past year. The task force recommendations fall in line with some of the major issues discussed at this conference. Economic development, conservation of farm land, and the promotion of environmentally sound farming practices clearly are at the top of the industry's agenda. That is evident in the AG Project 2000, the Task Force Report, and what you have discussed during these two days.

It's essential that we pull together because of the real problems that are facing farmers, especially tobacco farmers, today. I do not need to tell you that for the thousands of tobacco farmers in Kentucky, tobacco is not just a job, it is a way of life—it remains the backbone of our agricultural communities. It is our largest cash crop, valued at almost $1 billion in 1992. Nearly one-half billion pounds will be sold in 1993. The threat to this vital link in our culture and economy is only increasing. Imports of foreign tobacco continue to cut into our domestic market. Thanks to Senator Ford's vigorous and visionary leadership on this issue, we now have taken steps to slow this process. If the analysts are correct, however, we still face a tough road for tobacco. Tobacco farmers can look forward to a continuing annual reduction in their quotas for the foreseeable future, and domestic consumption will continue to decline. These tough issues, coupled with President Clinton's proposal to tax tobacco as a source for funding for health-care reform, mandate that we tackle these issues head-on.

I did not come here today with all of the answers to this intractable issue. You and I together must engage in this debate and help craft solutions for our rural communities and families. To use a popular buzzword, we must begin the process of "re-engineering agriculture." We cannot stick our heads in the sand and ignore this debate. No one in the Jones administration is advocating an increase in the tobacco tax. We did not use it as a source of revenue in our health-care reform proposal and do not advocate its use in Washington, D.C. But, if it comes, we must be prepared.

If there is to be a tobacco tax to fund health care, at least 10 percent of the revenues raised through this tax must be "plowed back" into the tobacco states to compensate tobacco farmers for the expected negative impact from the tax and to assist the impacted regions in developing alternative agricultural strategies. Our analysis shows that a 10 percent "plow back" provision based in the administration's 75-cent-per-pack increase [for cigarettes] could return as much as $450 million to Kentucky in the first year. While this funding source could be used to offset losses to farmers, tenant farmers, and communities affected by this tax, it also provides us the opportunity to diversify our agricultural and economic base. Additionally, a portion of these funds from the "plow back" proposal could be used initially to purchase quotas at a fair market price from those farmers who wish to sell them. Farmers not wanting to sell will be advantaged by the fact that quota reductions would be limited due to the buy-out. Additionally, a portion of these revenues could be used to establish retraining, education, and employment programs. These funds can also be used to create investment incentive programs to encourage alternative-crop development, value-added livestock programs, investment in agricultural infrastructure, marketing, and community development.

As I said at the outset, my purpose here is singular—it is not to suggest all the answers to these difficult problems; rather it is to ask you to join with me and engage in a vigorous debate of these issues and help Kentucky lead rather than follow in the ensuing months. Our challenge then is to develop a vision, a fresh look, and to help shape the solutions, rather than be shaped by them. No one knows better than I the significance of farming and tobacco, in particular, to our economy and communities. Our legacy must not be one of rancorous debate but of a unified partnership in re-engineering agriculture and meeting agriculture's needs in the next century.

KENTUCKY AGRICULTURAL COUNCIL
Governor's Mansion / January 10, 1994

I FEEL fortunate to be serving as governor during a period when agriculture has pulled together as never before to work for a more prosperous future. This spirit of cooperation is perhaps best shown by the work of groups such as AG Project 2000, the Governor's Agriculture Policy Task Force, and the hard work of the groups represented here today that were involved in putting together various legislative initiatives for consideration by the 1994 General Assembly. To determine how state government could best meet the needs of our agricultural industry, I appointed an agricultural policy task force last year. The seven-member task force developed fifteen policy recommendations from more than 140 ideas that were reviewed over the past year. The recommendations of the task force are at the heart of "farmland" legislative initiatives that Mrs. Jones and others support, and they serve as a strong indication of my administration's understanding and commitment to the agricultural industry in Kentucky. Economic development, conservation of farm land, and the promotion of environmentally sound farming practices clearly are at the top of the industry's agenda. It is essential that we pull together to support initiatives like these because of the real problems that are facing farmers today.

I would like to focus on the tobacco farmer in particular as an example of just how critical these problems are. I do not need to tell you that for the thousands of tobacco farmers in Kentucky, tobacco is not just a job, it is a way of life—it remains the backbone of our agricultural communities. It is our largest cash crop, valued at almost $1 billion in 1992. Nearly one-half billion pounds have been sold in 1993. The threat to this vital link in our culture and economy is only increasing. Imports of foreign tobacco continue to cut into our domestic market. Thanks to Senator Ford's vigorous leadership on this issue, we now have taken steps to slow this process. Make no mistake, we still face a tough road ahead for tobacco. Tobacco farmers can look forward to a continuing annual reduction in their quotas for the foreseeable future, and domestic consumption will continue to decline. In fact, the news media has reported that post-holiday burley sales are even worse than expected, with as much as 30 to 60 percent of the burley going into surplus pools. The cigarette companies and leaf dealers are simply not buying.

Some have argued that the cigarette companies and leaf dealers are slowing their purchase of burley due to uncertainties imposed on the market as a result of President Clinton's proposed 75-cent-per-pack increase in the federal cigarette tax to help fund national health-care reform. While an increase in the tobacco tax may exacerbate some of the problems currently faced by the industry, it could also provide us a unique opportunity, a once-in-a-lifetime chance to provide real dollars for real solutions to assist an already ailing industry so important to the Commonwealth.

Let me emphasize that no one in the Jones administration is advocating an increase in the tobacco tax. We did not use it as source of revenue in our health-care reform proposal and do not advocate its use in Washington, D.C. But, if it comes, we must be prepared to turn it to our advantage. If there is to be a tobacco tax to fund health care, at least 10 percent of the revenues raised through this tax must be "plowed back" into the tobacco states to compensate tobacco farmers for the expected negative impact from the tax and to assist the impacted regions in developing alternative agricultural strategies. Our analysis shows that a 10 percent "plow back" provision based on the administration's proposed 75-cent-per-pack increase could return as much as $450 million to Kentucky in the first year. While this funding source could be used to offset losses to farmers, tenant farmers, and communities affected by this tax, it also provides us the opportunity to diversify our agricultural and economic base. There are numerous ways in which we could propose that these dollars be spent to "re-engineer" and better position our agricultural communities to face the challenges of the future. For example:

1. Dollars could be used for quota buyout to enhance the situation for the active tobacco grower to offset the need for future quota reductions due to the reduced demand.
2. Dollars could be used for rural-development purposes to encourage alternative-crop usage in impacted agricultural communities.
3. Dollars could be used to fund specific research programs at the state universities to further "re-engineering" efforts.
4. Dollars could be used for grants/loans for on-farm and off-farm investments so tobacco communities can continue to adapt to changing market conditions.

As I said before, my purpose here is not to suggest all the answers to these difficult problems; but rather, it is to ask you to join with me and engage in a vigorous debate of these issues and help Kentucky lead rather than follow in the ensuing months. As you are probably aware, during the president's recent visit to Kentucky to promote NAFTA, I was able to discuss the possibility of the inclusion of the "plow back" plan in his tobacco tax proposal. He indicated his interest and asked me to bring him the details of a plan. I intend to do that at the National Governors' Association Conference, January 30–31. Before I propose any details, I would like to invite each of you and the groups you represent to work with us to prepare such a plan. . . .[1]

---

1. The previous year, on January 10, Jones gave a speech to the Kentucky Agricultural Council in Louisville.

PHILIP MORRIS AG LEADERSHIP DEVELOPMENT PROGRAM
Frankfort / February 9, 1994

I KNOW that this is a very full day for you, but I also know that your experiences during this three-day program will give you a better understanding of how your state government works. When I entered the office of governor, I was fully aware that there aren't many simple solutions to all the problems facing our state. Making changes and improvements can be complicated. Now, more than two years into this administration, I remain aware that there are few easy answers. It's not unlike farming. I am proud of the fact that I am a farmer. But too often, I believe, people like to play up the idea that I only operate a horse farm. I also raise crops and cattle. One of those crops is tobacco. Believe me, I know the problems that farmers in Kentucky face on a daily basis. But I feel fortunate to be governor during a time when agriculture is pulling together as never before to work for a more prosperous future. This spirit of cooperation is perhaps best shown by the work of AG Project 2000 and the Governor's Agricultural Policy Task Force.

If you are not familiar with AG Project 2000, let me explain that it is unprecedented in our agricultural history, and it is unsurpassed in its importance to the future of farming in Kentucky. Virtually every farm organization in the state got together to find ways to dramatically increase Kentucky's farm income. Hundreds of participants developed a plan for a $5 billion farm economy by the year 2000. And a seven-member task force developed fifteen policy recommendations. Economic development, conservation of farmland, and the promotion of environmentally sound farming practices are at the top of that list of recommendations. It is essential that we act together today on tomorrow's farm economy because of very real problems that challenge farmers, especially tobacco growers.

For thousands of people in Kentucky just like you, tobacco farming is not just a job, it's a way of life. Tobacco is the backbone of our agricultural community. It is our largest cash crop. But a rough road lies ahead. Imports of foreign leaf threaten our domestic market. Thanks to Sen. Wendell Ford's vigorous leadership, we have taken steps to slow this process. However, we can still expect continued annual reductions in quotas and a decline in domestic consumption. These challenges, coupled with a proposal to quadruple the tax on cigarettes as a source for funding federal health-care reform, mandate that we tackle the future head-on. I want to stop at this point to be certain that each of you understands my position regarding the tobacco tax. There have been false reports that I support a higher tax on tobacco products. Those reports bear no semblance to reality. I am opposed to the tax. I must, however, take a realistic position regarding the possible passage of such a tax. If there is to be a tobacco tax to fund a federal health-care program, we must fight for at least 10 percent of the tax revenues to be returned to the tobacco states, to compensate tobacco farmers for the expected negative impact of the tax and to assist the impacted regions in developing alternative agriculture strategies. We cannot stick our heads in the sand and ignore the problems facing us. We must begin the process of re-engineering agriculture in Kentucky.

Based on a 75-cent-per-pack tax increase, the return to Kentucky could be as much as $450 million in the first year. Farmers and communities could use part of the money to offset losses. Additionally, a portion of the money could be used to purchase quotas at a fair market value from those growers who want to sell them. Farmers wishing to stay in tobacco would see a lessening of quota reduction due to the buyouts. Revenues also could be used to establish retraining, education, and employment programs. And the plowed-back tax would, perhaps most importantly, help us diversify what we grow. We can either take advantage of the situation and turn it to our benefit, or we can fight what experts tell us is a losing battle. I am for the farmer. I want you to succeed, but our success must be based on reality.

I want to close my remarks with an example of what I am talking about. A few years ago, Wal-Mart announced it was building a new store in a small Wisconsin town. The initial reaction was one of horror. Most local business people went into shock. They could see the ruin of their businesses and the death of their downtown. But cooler heads prevailed. Wal-Mart, after all, could not provide all of the services that some smaller businesses could. So the community organized. The town spruced itself up. And new marketing strategies were developed. Today, that community has a stronger economic base than it had before Wal-Mart opened its doors. It was simply a matter of turning a threat into new opportunity. That's exactly what I'm trying to do for Kentucky's tobacco farmers. Let's join together to make the most of the future. Together, with imagination and a positive attitude, Kentucky agriculture will emerge stronger than ever.

FARM BUREAU KENTUCKY HAM BREAKFAST
Louisville / August 24, 1994

I WANT to talk today, in a personal way, to farmers. I am a tobacco farmer. In fact, I grow more than 150,000 pounds of tobacco a year. You and I both know that a tobacco tax would be very damaging to tobacco farmers. But much of the rest of the country doesn't see it that way. You've probably heard the saying that the only fair tax is the tax that somebody else has to pay. And the senators and representatives in a majority of states—the states that don't grow tobacco—think it's fair to put a bigger tax on tobacco, because their people don't have to depend on tobacco to live. We must work, as Senator Ford has, to keep the tax as low as possible. But if we lose that fight, do you want our congressional delegation to return home empty-handed and say, "Well, I tried . . ." or do you want them to insist that Kentucky farmers get something in return?

We all know the beatings that tobacco is taking on all fronts. And we all know that consumption and allotments continue to go down. At the same time, foreign competition keeps getting stiffer. And my greatest fear is that in five or ten years, we as tobacco farmers will wake up one day, our allotments will be gone, and we'll wonder where our leaders were when we needed help. That's why I have said that if we lose the fight, and the tobacco tax gets increased, we must insist that a portion of that tax gets plowed back into Kentucky's farm economy, to compensate the burley industry, to explore alternative crops and better ways of doing business.

Farmers are trying a lot of things right now to supplement their income, and that's good. For example, this year, a group of farmers in Henry County grew 150 acres of cucumbers to be used for pickles. Some farmers in western Kentucky are growing four hundred acres of tomatoes for major commercial processing. Throughout the state, a variety of vegetables are being grown. But as farmers experiment with growing different crops on larger scale, there is one common need. They must have a market. As you may know, Agriculture Commissioner Ed Logsdon has been working for a long time on a proposal to build a farmers' market in northern Kentucky. I'm not talking about a wide spot in the road where farmers would sell vegetables out of the back of their pickup trucks. I'm talking about a large facility, and agricultural center, located on twenty-two acres of land in Boone County. It would include an area for retail sales, a garden center, and a restaurant. But it also would contain a 60,000-square-foot processing plant, a packing shed and cooler, plus a 7,000-square-foot building for produce wholesalers. The idea is to have a place where farmers can sell their crops and where those crops can be processed and sent throughout the country. This is not a radical idea. You can find similar markets in Knoxville, Nashville, Atlanta, Birmingham, St. Louis, and Raleigh, North Carolina. The one in Asheville, North Carolina, has worked well for sixteen years. You can find them throughout Florida and California. In fact, the three farmers' market operations in Los Angeles take in more than $2.5 billion a year. Here in Kentucky, we think the agricultural marketing center in northern Kentucky could sell $2.5 million worth of produce the first year, and nearly another million dollars in produce could be handled through the packing shed. And that's just in the first year! These farmers' markets are also tourist attractions. In Knoxville, for example, a half-million people came through in that market's first year of operation. And the market under construction in Nashville will include river-taxi rides from Opryland to the farmers' market, so people can come in, look around, and buy. Estimates are, the northern Kentucky project will add more than five hundred jobs to the payroll of more than $6.6 million every year to that area's economy. Plus, the construction of the center itself will add fifty jobs, and a $1 million payroll. Should the northern Kentucky facility operate as expected, similar agricultural marketing centers could be built in other parts of Kentucky.

Again, this won't replace tobacco. The "golden leaf" is and will remain important to Kentucky farmers. But this will give us an opportunity to supplement our tobacco income. The sticking point has been funding. We included $3 million in our surplus expenditure plan to help fund the project, with additional federal and local money making up the difference. However, as you know, the legislature this year decided not to fund this project. I believe that was a mistake, and we must find a way to correct that mistake and get construction started. Over the past two and one-half years we have focused on stabilizing our state finances. We inherited close to a $400 million budget imbalance—like any businessman we cut spending and worked to create more jobs to bring in more revenue. We have eliminated over 1,500 state jobs, and since taking office we have created over 41,400 net new jobs. We have realized savings across state government and built our state savings account from $29 million to $90 million. We already spent $34 million of our savings on education and the state parks, and we still have a surplus of $53 million. All this hard work has changed our state's fiscal health—we are ready and able to make investments for our future. We cannot let this opportunity pass by. We must make needed investments in projects like the farmers' market if we are to insure a strong future for our Commonwealth.

In the months ahead we will continue to attract businesses into this state to stimulate and perpetuate the farming economy. For example, we have been extremely successful over the past few months in attracting several chicken-processing plants to Kentucky. Those plants are investing more than $185 million in Kentucky; then when the processing plants are in full production, they will employ more than forty-two hundred people. The companies also will have contracts with more than eight hundred farmers, who will raise the five million birds needed every week. In addition, the plants will need thirty-four million bushels of grain each year, at a value of approximately $100 million. Folks, that's a lot of chicken feed! And we're not through. As you may know, we're in serious negotiations with another major poultry operation, and we hope to be able to make an announcement soon.

We will continue to go after as many agribusinesses as possible to help our farmers. All of this is essential, if we are to meet the major goal of AG Project 2000, which is to more than double the state's agricultural farm income to $5 billion a year. So as you leave this morning, please remember these three promises I make to you today:

(1) We will continue to fight the tobacco tax.
(2) We will continue to look for new ways for tobacco farmers to supplement their income.
(3) And we will continue to work to attract other agribusinesses to Kentucky that will give farmers other markets for their crops.

HEMP TASK FORCE ANNOUNCEMENT
Frankfort / November 23, 1994

EVERYONE knows how important agriculture is to our economy and how important the family farm is to agriculture and to Kentucky. As farmers ourselves, Libby and I know firsthand the difficulties facing the family farm, and we are committed to doing everything within our abilities to help. Too many times in the history of this Commonwealth, politicians ignored certain problems or purposely bypassed opportunities because they perceived these issues to be too controversial and therefore too politically risky to confront. This administration has never shied away from tackling tough issues in our effort to serve the people of this Commonwealth. We were not elected to deny that problems exist or to refuse to explore potential solutions.

Recently, in my conversations with farmers and agricultural business people I have been asked about the possibility of once again growing a crop that flourished in this state as recently as the 1940s. I have had reports of great success in Europe and advancements in Canada, and I had many questions. But I soon found that no one could supply me with the answers. That is why today I am announcing the formation of a task force to study the agricultural viability of hemp. The members of this task force are agricultural leaders from across the state. They will engage in a fact-finding mission to determine whether it is feasible to grow and process an industrial-use hemp in Kentucky. If there are crops which can legally be grown for a profit in Kentucky which we are currently not growing, then we as public officials have a duty to examine these crops and provide answers for the farmers of Kentucky. When the work of this task force is completed, we will know whether or not Kentucky can grow a drug-free hemp; whether this crop can supply needed agricultural commodities such as fiber and oil; whether there are existing markets for these commodities; whether these commodities can be processed in Kentucky; and whether this industry could be profitable for our farmers. I want to stress from the beginning that I am opposed to the legalization of marijuana. This effort will in no way interfere with our anti-drug, crime prevention, or law enforcement activities.

I am pleased to announce that Billy Joe Miles, of Owensboro, Kentucky, has agreed to serve as chairman of this task force. He is greatly respected in this state as a farmer and a businessman, and he has consistently stayed on the cutting edge of agriculture. I am equally pleased to have the assistance and leadership of Agriculture Commissioner Ed Logsdon; Joe Wright, president of the Burley Tobacco Growers Association; Commissioner Lovitt of the Kentucky State Police; the agriculture deans of our land-grant colleges and universities; and representatives of the Farm Bureau and other agricultural organizations. This task force has the talent, the commitment to agriculture, and the respect of the agriculture community needed to bring this project to completion.

There are politicians and others who may be tempted to purposefully misinterpret our message in order to create a controversy. If that happens, these people will be doing a grave injustice to the people of Kentucky. Right now we don't know if hemp is a viable agricultural crop. When this task force completes its work, we will.

4-H BREAKFAST
Louisville / August 18, 1995

I THINK you'd be hard pressed to find anyone in Kentucky who has not been directly or indirectly affected by 4-H. Just spend some time here in Cloverville during the fair, and you'll see the people who come through this exhibit looking at all the things that are made or grown by 4-H-ers. For years, 4-H has been a major force in the lives of young Kentuckians, and its impact continues. More than 205,000 young people are involved in 4-H in Kentucky today. Thirty-two thousand young people are able to go to some type of camp each year. More than 26,000 volunteer leaders give their time to work with young people on 4-H projects. Each volunteer spends an average of $50 in educational supplies, drives 350 miles, and donates 220 hours a year. Using those averages, it's estimated that the time and money contributed by the 4-H volunteers represents a value of $44 million a year. All of the donated time is the equivalent of more than 2,800 people working full time. These are all impressive numbers, but no one can adequately measure the impact 4-H has in Kentucky.

4-H develops an appreciation for what we have; an appreciation for what we can grow or make; and an appreciation for what we are. 4-H builds leaders, and everyone in this room knows it. I'm here today to show my support and to thank each and every one of you for donating your time to help mold the leaders of tomorrow. You are developing the head, the heart, the hands, and the health of the future of Kentucky, and you are doing a terrific job.

KENTUCKY FARM BUREAU HAM BREAKFAST
Louisville / August 24, 1995

A FARMER has to be an optimist to survive in today's world. For example, a farmer walked into a bank to borrow $50,000. The loan officer talked to him, then said, "We can probably arrange the loan . . . but that's a lot of money. We'll need a statement from you." "Well," said the farmer, "you may quote me as saying that I'm very optimistic." That's what it takes to survive on the farm. Farmers have always had a dose of optimism; but also a dose of realism. We all know how quickly a bumper crop can turn into a total loss due to a bad storm or a drought. But we still persevere. A farmer also has to be an opportunist. A farmer always has to be on the lookout for a better way to do business, a better machine to use in the field, a better crop that will produce a higher yield. A farmer must always look for a better tomorrow.

Farming is critical to Kentucky's economy, and in Kentucky's economy of tomorrow, farming will still be critical. Yet, right now, more than ever, we have to constantly look for new opportunities to help farmers make money. Let me use tobacco as an example. I raise some 200,000 pounds of tobacco, so I don't have to *pretend* to be interested in tobacco. I depend on it, as most of you do, and I'm worried about its future, because tobacco is under attack. Washington is trying to give the Food and Drug Administration the power to regulate tobacco as a drug. I've talked with President Clinton twice about this, and both times, I've told him he's dead wrong to try to have the FDA try to regulate tobacco. I've told him the FDA had much worse problems. They need to do more about getting rid of cocaine and crack and all the terrible drugs that are killing our children. They don't need to be messing with tobacco.

We've got to fight, and with the help of our congressmen, we will win this fight. However, while we all fight to save tobacco and to keep it out of the hands of the FDA, we have to go a step further. Did you know that a farmer gets only four and a half cents from every pack of cigarettes sold? Only four and a half cents out of a dollar sixty to a dollar seventy-five. I think the farmer is getting the short end of the stick. So I have asked President Clinton to consider a plan to get farmers a larger share of the pie. I've asked him to return the ten cents of the existing federal tax on every pack of cigarettes to agriculture. Now I want to make this very clear—I don't want any new taxes; I'm talking about the existing tax. But the farmer is entitled to more of this money to be able to find ways to increase farm income. The president asked me how he could make up the difference if we channeled this money into agriculture. I told him that he could do it the same we've done it in Kentucky: by downsizing government, by eliminating fraud and abuse, and by giving taxpayers the absolute most for their money. President Clinton has promised to look into this proposal.

Tobacco has always been the major cash crop in Kentucky, and it will continue to be, but we have to always be on the lookout for crops that will help us supplement farmers' income. We have to give the farmer a chance to make money, or else we won't have any farmers left. During our administration, we have worked to bring new opportunities to farmers, and we've had some real successes. During our administration, we've announced some 40 new agribusinesses for Kentucky, and we've gotten 173 existing businesses to announce plans to expand. Those new and expanded businesses represent 8,800 new jobs and an investment of some

$600 million in Kentucky, so we've been able to take a strong industry here in the Commonwealth and make it even stronger. According to the U.S. Department of Agriculture, 422,000 Kentucky jobs are agriculture-related. That's 25 percent of all the jobs in the state, one in four, and no state has a higher number of small family farms than Kentucky. Our farms have annual sales of $3.2 billion, and if you calculate the total economic impact from the production of crops and livestock, you come close to $17 billion.

I've enjoyed my time as governor, trying to help family farms survive, and when this administration is over, one of the most important things that will have been done for family farms happened just this past January. That's when we were successful in getting the legislature to eliminate—over a four-year period—the inheritance tax and the tax on private pensions. No longer will family farms have to be sold to pay the taxes. Kentucky will go from having the highest inheritance tax in the country to being tied for the lowest, and, hopefully, that will allow farmers to keep on farming from one generation to the next. As you prepare for the next generation of farming, continue to keep your optimism, keep your realism, and keep looking for opportunities, and don't forget to keep a strong dose of faith handy. There's a sign that I've seen that describes how most farmers operate. The sign says, "Pray to the Lord for a good harvest—but keep on hoeing."

HEALTH, WELFARE, AND PUBLIC SAFETY

CHILDREN FIRST
Louisville / December 16, 1992

ANY way you look at the issue of a sexual attack on a child, you come to the same conclusion: it is a revolting crime that cries out to society for action. If you look simply at the statistics, your reactions range from alarm to shock. Nationally, it is estimated that as many as 2.7 million American adults were sexually assaulted when they were children. Reports of child sexual abuse in Kentucky in the 1992 fiscal year exceeded 5,700. That represents an increase of more than 1,100 cases over the previous year alone. More than 1,100 of those 5,700 incidents of reported child sexual abuse in Kentucky occurred right here in Jefferson County.

But we often hear the saying that numbers don't tell the whole story, and that is truly the case with this issue. That's because every single one of those sexually abused children is a victim, and the other members of their families are victims. They are individuals, people, children, families. Statistics can't cry for help. But molested or raped children can. And without intervention, their cries will go on for the rest of their lives. As somber as this situation is, we're here today in justifiable celebration, celebration of a victory in the making in the lives of these children.

"Children First" is Kentucky's first complete child advocacy center. It's not a ground-breaking concept nationally; there are about one hundred similar centers in thirty-four other states. But "Children First" is a good step in the right direction. This represents the culmination of work that has been going on in this community very quietly for the last several years. Private citizens, mental-health experts, child advocates, social workers, police, and prosecutors have been working diligently to improve their response to child abuse in general and particularly to the sensitive but thorough investigation and treatment of cases of sexual assault on our children.

"Children First" is designed to bring together all the specialists needed to evaluate and treat child victims and their families immediately following the discovery of the abuse. This center represents perhaps the highest possible example of the good that can come from the so-called "Public/Private Partnership." The Department for Social Services has supported this project since last year to the tune of $80,000.

"The Family Place," another outstanding community organization, is using another $435,000 social services grant in conjunction with "Children First" to provide crisis mental-health counseling as soon as an investigation substantiates the allegation of child sexual abuse. The crimes against children unit of the two local police departments, the Jefferson County commonwealth's attorney's office, Seven Counties' Services community mental-health services, all are state and/or community resources that will be pulled together to improve the crisis response to these children's needs. This center will be a tremendous new resource to Social Services Commissioner Peggy Wallace[1] and her child protection workers in the incredibly challenging job that they have to do.

And while I have a moment, I would be remiss if I let this opportunity pass without addressing the whole area of Child Protective Services in this administration. I want the people here today and the people in this community and this state to know that I am acutely aware of the problem facing our state social services agency and the tremendous task posed by our state economy. Even as we grow out of the effects of the national recession, we are still feeling the impact, both in terms of highest numbers of child as well as adult abuse reports and in our administration's tight budget difficulties in addressing that growing need as sufficiently as I and everyone else would like.

Commissioner Wallace has been an effective advocate as to the needs of her workers, here in Jefferson County and across the state. That's why we have spared child protection specialist positions from our budget-related hiring freezes. That's why we included in this year's budget funds for an additional fifty front-line social workers to be hired, trained, and put into this battle as quickly as possible this fiscal year. And that's why I'm so proud that this administration has supported projects like "Children First."

I firmly believe it will prove to be an invaluable asset to our child protection system. And I want to pledge to you all that this administration has not reached the point of saying, "Well, we've done enough on this situation of child abuse. Now let's concentrate on something else." Yes, our priorities do include better health care for all Kentuckians, continuing achievements of education reform, and improving the business attractiveness of Kentucky so that this generation will have the jobs they need to stay at home and to be productive at home.

But we will not be so short-sighted as to fail to recognize that families in trouble, children being neglected or sexually assaulted, spouses being raped and beaten, all represent Kentuckians who may not fully benefit from health-care reform, education reform, or new jobs, if their lives have been shattered by abuse and broken homes. Our commitment to you today is that we are working on behalf of our abused children, just like the people who have made "Children First" a reality. And we will continue that commitment throughout this administration so that Kentucky's children, their families, and the people who care for and protect them know that we're in this fight with them to the finish.[2]

---

1. Peggy Wallace (1943–), commissioner, Cabinet of Human Resources, Dept. of Mental Health/Mental Retardation under Governors Jones and Patton.

2. In an earlier speech on October 28, at the Red Ribbon Rally in Frankfort, Jones spoke about the importance of drug awareness. The following year he spoke at the Red Ribbon Rally in Louisville on October 25; and he talked to students at Buechel Metropolitan School about drug abuse.

CHILD SEX ABUSE
Frankfort / February 22, 1994

CHANCES are, if you asked everybody in this room what is most important to them, most everyone would say, their families. That's where we put our love, our faith, our trust. But when that trust is betrayed, it can ruin lives. That's the tragedy of child sexual abuse.

It so often ruins the life of a child, because it destroys a child's ability to have faith or trust in their family, or any adult for that matter. Child sexual abuse can rob a child of the ability to love.

Earlier today, I signed a proclamation declaring today as Childhood Sexual Abuse Awareness Day. I did that because we as Kentuckians need to know the facts:

1. We need to know that one in five adults in Kentucky admits being sexually abused as a child.
2. We need to know that more than two thousand reports of childhood sexual abuse are substantiated each year.
3. And we need to know that because of childhood sexual abuse, Kentuckians spend as much as $116 million dollars each year for investigations, prosecution, incarceration, treatment for children, and foster care.

The images we see on the walls here today are disturbing. But they do serve a purpose. They show us that we must continue our resolve to do whatever is necessary to fight and eliminate child sexual abuse. We must, for the benefit of the children. And we must do it for all the families of Kentucky. . . .

OAK AND ACORN GROUND BREAKING
Louisville / June 29, 1994

I WANT to echo what has been said so far today about the need for this facility and how unique it will be in bringing together our children with our senior citizens. Since the number of children growing up in poverty is increasing, and the number of senior citizens is increasing, having a facility that eases a critical need in both areas is truly inspiring. I'm confident that both young and old will be enriched because of the experience.

I want to talk a little today about commitment, and how important it is. I tend to think that when you make a promise or a commitment to someone that you absolutely must follow through with that promise or commitment. But that doesn't always happen. I think we all know how committed Elderserve has been in helping our older citizens—in essence, paying them back for all that they have contributed to our community and our state. We also know of the commitment of Louisville Central Community Centers to the young people in the area. And because these two agencies are so committed to making life better, they found a way to work together to help both young and old.

They didn't fight to enlarge or protect their own turf. They cooperated, so that everyone would benefit. They promised to make life better for the people they serve, and they have kept that promise. The end result is a better quality of life for both generations; the children will serve as a stimulant for older people, and the senior citizens will provide a nurturing, caring environment for the children. The state has long been committed to help older and younger members of this Commonwealth, and that's why we have committed $697,500 to help fund this project. The city of Louisville also is honoring its commitment to its people, by investing $250,000. And the Brown Foundation, the Bingham Foundation, the Providian Corporation, the Humana Foundation, Philip Morris, and the Kroger Company are all showing their commitment to the people in this community by making sizeable donations that will make the Oak and Acorn Center become a reality.

All of these groups made a commitment, and today's ground breaking is proof that they are making good on their commitment. However, even though we will begin construction today, there is still more to be done. Although more than $1.3 million has been raised, the Oak and Acorn Center needs more than $400,000. I'm confident there are enough committed people and organizations, perhaps represented in our audience today, who will step forward to fund the rest of this project. . . .[1]

---

1. Jones gave a number of speeches relating to health, welfare, and public safety issues in 1994. On March 29, in a KET Housing Teleconference, he discussed Kentucky's Fair Housing initiatives. On May 14, he participated in the opening of the Family Health Center in Dayton; he emphasized the importance of primary care. On July 6 in Frankfort, he discussed the value of the seat belt law, giving dramatic statistics about the number of people injured while not wearing seat belts. On November 3 in Frankfort, he held a Gun Safety Press Conference, noting the number of children using guns against others, and he encouraged everyone to take responsibility for their guns.

PEOPLE FOR PEOPLE RALLY
Frankfort / April 26, 1995

IT IS very easy to "talk the talk" about welfare reform and federal budget cuts. It is much more difficult to "walk the walk." Cutting the federal budget and reforming the welfare system are popular topics among hardworking, taxpaying citizens. I think we all know that there is some waste in the current welfare system and that some changes are necessary.

But as we work to cut the fat, I want to caution against cutting the muscle and bone. If some budget cutters in Washington get their way, Kentucky stands to lose as much as $890 million over the next five years. That could be devastating to the people who need help the most. I firmly believe it is government's job to help those who are *unable* to help themselves. But it is not government's job to help those who are *unwilling* to help themselves.

It is my hope that as changes are considered in Washington, lawmakers will look to the states for guidance. Here in Kentucky, we have a good story to tell. We've created a record number of new jobs in Kentucky during this administration. There are some 163,000 more people working today than when we first took office. In addition, in the past three years, we have been able to reduce *by ten percent* the number of Kentuckians on welfare. We haven't given people a deadline to be off welfare. We haven't arbitrarily cut them off. We've worked with them to obtain the proper education and training so they could find jobs. And we've helped them get child care so that it becomes profitable for them to work. We've also been cutting waste. According to the federal government, Kentucky has the most efficient food stamp program in the nation.

And we've received more than $11 million in federal bonus money in the last three years because we've worked so hard to eliminate fraud and abuse. In the months to come, you'll hear much more about welfare reform and budget cuts from the politicians in Washington and from the candidates for statewide office here in Kentucky. As you listen to the debate, I want you to know the facts. We've made tremendous progress on reforming the state's welfare system, putting people back to work, and cutting the size of the government bureaucracy right here in Frankfort. And we want Washington to give states the right and the flexibility to continue to make progress.

But no one should forget, we're dealing with people, not statistics. And we must do what's best to help people improve their lives.[1]

---

1. In an earlier speech in Louisville on April 20, Jones spoke at the Governor's Safety and Health Conference. He discussed the importance of providing the necessary state and federal matching funding for safety and health programs.

TREE-PLANTING CEREMONY HONORING OKLAHOMA CITY VICTIMS
Frankfort / May 19, 1995

I'M HONORED to be a part of this ceremony today. It is right that we are establishing this living memorial to the victims of the bombing in Oklahoma City. It also is right that we can show our appreciation to the members of Kentucky's post-trauma response team. Each of them volunteered to share their expertise to help the rescue workers who worked so diligently at the site of the blast.

A month ago we were all shocked and deeply troubled to hear the horrific news out of Oklahoma City. We waited and prayed for miracles as the enormity of the tragedy unfolded, and we prayed for guidance on how to understand how such a thing could be allowed to happen. Now, a month later, we continue to struggle with the healing that such a catastrophe requires. And we continue to think of ways to reach out to our fellow Americans in Oklahoma City to help them return their lives to normal.

Today, we are able to thank two groups of Kentuckians for working to make a difference. First, I want to thank the Oddfellows Capital Lodge for their thoughtfulness in adding this living memorial to the capitol grounds. This tree will stand as a reminder to all of us that our freedom is something to be cherished and that our country remains strong and continues to grow. Also today, we gather to express appreciation to ten members of Kentucky's post-trauma response team who helped emergency workers deal with the emotional aftermath of working at the blast site. The emergency workers saw things that no one should ever have to see, and our trauma team helped many of these workers find ways to deal with their emotions and get their own lives back to normal.

I think it's reassuring to know that these ten people are members of a group of 135 Kentuckians from across the Commonwealth who stand ready to volunteer their skills to help in many different kinds of tragedies. Our Kentucky post-trauma team is unique compared to those in most other states. They are skilled to provide emergency services that directly help disaster victims. But they also can assist in debriefing, as they did in Oklahoma City. This team was created in 1990, and since that time has helped about five thousand survivors and emergency and rescue workers. They are ready to go wherever they're needed whenever officials dealing with emergency situations request assistance. . . .

WELFARE TO SELF-SUFFICIENCY PRESS CONFERENCE
Frankfort / June 30, 1995

THERE has been a lot of talk recently about our welfare system and about ways to change it. Today, while the talk continues, we are announcing a pilot project that will get underway immediately. This exciting new initiative addresses one of the most important challenges of our time, moving able-bodied welfare recipients into jobs and self-sufficiency. I have always been a strong proponent of moving all able-bodied individuals into the workforce, but I also realize that several barriers inhibit such movement.

While Kentucky has made progress in this area through the *Jobs* program, issues such as the lack of child care, transportation, and adequate job skills keep far too many Kentuckians on the welfare rolls. This is a problem which directly or indirectly affects *everyone*. And, to reach a long-lasting solution, we must involve *everyone* within the community. As with all complex problems, to be successful, people must unite and work together. Our new program is called the *Americorps/Welfare to Self-Sufficiency Initiative*. Americorps . . . is the new national service program where individuals perform a year of direct service to help pay for their higher education. Americorps, as implemented by the Kentucky Community Service Commission, has proven its value in Kentucky during the past year. The Americorps model, we believe, is the perfect facilitator for the broad community involvement we want to stimulate.

With at least twenty full-time members, this new Americorps program will be uniquely suited to reach out to civic groups, community agencies, churches, and others to leverage their resources and involve them directly in the program. This effort is being made possible through a partnership between the Community Service Commission and the Department for Social Insurance in the Cabinet for Human Resources. The Department for Social Insurance will make available up to $293,625 for the project through existing state and federal funds.

The commission will hold a competition to select the local organization with the best plan for utilizing the Americorps funds. The request-for-proposal has already been developed and is now available. I would like to encourage all interested agencies, civic groups, and community leaders to apply for this grant. To receive more information, contact the Kentucky Community Service Commission office or call our office here in the capitol. I would like to emphasize that we will be able to implement this pilot project without any new state dollars. I also want to emphasize that this pilot project gives a great deal of flexibility to localities to develop their own approach to meet the needs of their community; it stresses a grassroots solution.

The Community Service Commission will collect the applications and choose the group with the best plan to use these funds. They will be looking for a creative plan with well-defined goals which fits the community and maximizes volunteer participation and other local resources. We anticipate the program will move hundreds of individuals from welfare to work and self-sufficiency, and we will hold it accountable for producing these results. If this pilot project is successful, this approach could become an integral part of future efforts to reform welfare. It will also provide valuable hands-on experience as we continue to work to find ways to alter the current welfare system. It will help us isolate and focus on the real causes of welfare dependency, and, hopefully, it will be a positive approach to a problem which has long been plagued with negatives.

This program by itself is not meant to represent a comprehensive solution to welfare reform. Such reform must include policy change. It must address health coverage and economic development for depressed areas. If the effort to move individuals from welfare to work is to have a lasting impact, the entire community must get involved. This program will be a catalyst for community involvement. It will provide an opportunity for everyone who truly cares to lend a hand. Currently our society provides increasingly prominent forums for those who want to voice an opinion or, more often, a complaint.

As the family structure continues to weaken and reports of violence and crime cause neighbors to become isolated from each other, we must make extraordinary efforts to create opportunities for civic involvement. Our society, quite simply, cannot survive the next century unless people help each other. That is why I am so proud of our community service and their stated goal to create an ethic of service among all Kentuckians, and why I'm so pleased that the state is able to sponsor this new pilot project.

FARM AID PRESS CONFERENCE
Louisville / July 28, 1995

LET me be among the first to thank Willie Nelson[1] and all the people representing Farm Aid for considering Louisville for this event. Willie, you and Farm Aid have done more than just "talk" about helping farmers. You've done it. Raising $12 million over the years has been nothing short of amazing. And farm organizations in Kentucky have benefitted to the tune of $150,000. What's more, you've been able to shine a spotlight on the problems that farmers face. And as a farmer who will be back on the farm in a few months, I appreciate what you've been able to do. On the state level, we've been able to help the farmer by encouraging the development of supplemental crops and agriculture industries. Also this year, we were able to eliminate the inheritance tax in Kentucky, so the family farm can stay in the family from one generation to the next.

But farmers deserve all the help they can get, and that's why we appreciate your coming here. We promise the full support of Dan Ulmer, Harold Workman, and the staff here at the Kentucky Fair and Exposition Center. Please consider this your new Kentucky home.

---

1. Willie Nelson (1933–), country music singer; Farm Aid activist.

VICTIM INFORMATION AND NOTIFICATION EVERYDAY (VINE) NEWS CONFERENCE
Frankfort / September 13, 1995

JUDGE Armstrong, we've been to Jefferson County several times to present checks from state government, but this is the first time I can recall a county government giving a check to the state! Thank you for your generosity, your support, and your commitment to this important project. As the judge has stated, *VINE* has been a phenomenal success in Jefferson County. We have been watching it develop and have been very impressed.

As you may know, the idea of victim notification has been extremely important to this administration. It was part of our crime-control bill which was passed in the 1994 session. Our bill requires the state prison system to notify victims pending the release of offenders. But, there is not a similar requirement for the seventy-nine county jails currently in operation across the Commonwealth. I believe it is fitting that we try to take *VINE*, which has worked on the local level, and expand it to cover the entire Commonwealth. I have instructed the Justice Cabinet to issue a request-for-proposal for bids to implement such a system. And I want to commit to you today that we will include in the next biennial budget, which we are currently preparing, the financial resources necessary to operate this system so that victims from all parts of this Commonwealth will have access to up-to-date information about offender location and release date. This will be an invaluable tool for law enforcement in Kentucky, because it will give state and local police a database of inmates that does not currently exist. But most important, it will allow victims and their families to be alerted if and when the criminal who has terrorized them is being released. It is the right and the fair thing to do.

I am extremely impressed at the level of cooperation between the local and state government on this issue. And with the support of our legislators, this *VINE* program will grow to be an important asset to our crime-control efforts throughout Kentucky. The bottom line is, it will make our people feel safer, because they *will* be safer. And that is our responsibility as a government.[1]

---

1. In a later health, welfare, and safety speech on September 29, Jones

spoke about the importance of breast cancer awareness and the need for screening programs.

GOVERNOR'S HOUSING CONFERENCE
Louisville / October 6, 1995

AS YOU know, in just a little over two months, my term as your governor will come to an end. Since we intend to work non-stop until the last day, we have not had a lot of time to reflect on our successes in the area of affordable housing. However, we can say that we have been able to establish a firm foundation for future growth and development.

Among our accomplishments in the housing arena, for example, you'd have to consider our efforts to bring national attention to the problem of rural homelessness following Kentucky's homeless survey in 1993. This was the first survey of its kind in the nation, and it shockingly documented the portrait of the rural homeless, that of a single woman, approximately twenty-three years old with two children under the age of seven. She is most often a victim of domestic violence and has completed the twelfth grade, but possesses little or no work experience. Every month, her primary source of income consists of a $228 AFDC check and food stamps. This is certainly not the traditional picture of the homeless, that of substance abuse in an urban setting.

Kentucky has been bold enough to tell the nation that this young homeless mother and her children are here now, walking among us, yet typically unrecognizable. We must continue to reach out and help these people. However, because of diminishing federal assistance, this is becoming even more of a challenge. With 42 percent of Kentucky's households classified low or moderate income, we need new and innovative ways to offer near-homeless families the direction they need to become, and remain, self-sufficient. Of the 3,369 families receiving tenant-based certificate and voucher rental assistance from the Kentucky Housing Corporation, the average annual income is $2,118 and more than half are single parents. And there's a serious need for more housing, with more than seventeen thousand families on the waiting list for these 3,369 allocated units.

We need to continue the fight for funds to accommodate the affordable housing needs of our communities. We need to further pursue low-income, multi-family developments. We need to ensure that our elderly citizens and our physically and mentally challenged citizens can remain independent for as long as they choose. Together, we have shared many successes in meeting the housing needs of Kentuckians and have worked hard to improve the quality of life for those we serve. Nearly forty thousand households have become homeowners through the Kentucky Housing Corporation's single-family loans at below-market interest rates. This number has increased in the last four years in part due to Habitat for Humanity. Libby has been particularly active with Habitat, having chaired the '94 Homecoming project in which the Kentucky affiliate built more than one hundred new homes. Also, she worked many hours to convince the former president to make Kentucky the location of the 1997 annual Jimmy Carter work camp, which she will tell you more about.

Those of you gathered here today hold the key to addressing these needs that haunt the hillsides of western Kentucky, the mountains of eastern Kentucky, and the more urban settings in central and northern Kentucky. It is you, Kentucky's affordable housing advocates, whom we turn to, to "make things happen." As this year's conference theme states, we must find "creative housing solutions in a changing environment." Thank you for your dedicated work. . . .

CORRECTIONS, CRIME, AND THE LAW

NEW STATE POLICE COMMISSIONER ANNOUNCEMENT
Frankfort / November 1, 1993

I AM joining [you] to say goodbye to a man who has always held you and your agency in the highest regard. I know that you have come to respect him as a commissioner over the years, and I hope that you realize your place in his heart is also very special. Even though Billy Wellman[1] is leaving this building as commissioner, he will remain the secretary of justice and will continue to oversee the state police as well as corrections, justice training, and other programs under the umbrella of the Justice Cabinet. He will soon be fighting for your interests in the upcoming legislative session as well.

When Billy talked to me about the demands of the state police commissioner, Billy felt one person had been invaluable in helping accomplish the goals of this administration. Today, I am appointing that person, Jerry W. Lovitt, commissioner of the Kentucky State Police. Jerry has been serving as deputy commissioner and director of the Operations Division since January. In his twenty-five years with this organization, he has served in many field positions that qualify him for this top position. Rising from the rank of trooper, to detective, then lieutenant, captain, colonel, and deputy commissioner, Jerry has worked our highways, undercover narcotics, organized crime, post command, and branch command. He is also a professor in police administration at Eastern Kentucky University and has had a distinguished career with the Kentucky National Guard. He's an active member of his community in Jessamine County. . . .[2]

1. Billy Wellman (1933–), Ashland native; served as adjutant general under three governors; secretary of Justice under Governors Brown and Jones.

2. On November 19, Jones gave a similar speech in Wheelwright at the Otter Creek Correctional Facility.

CRIME COMMISSION MEETING
Frankfort / December 7, 1993

THANK you for the opportunity to speak to you today, and on behalf of the citizens of Kentucky, thank you for accepting your commission and volunteering your service to the Commonwealth by being members of the Kentucky Crime Commission. Crime in this country, and in particular violent crime, has reached epidemic proportions. Even though the FBI has just announced that the overall crime rate has dropped since last year, I cannot stress enough that the crime rate is still much too high and is unacceptable. A serious crime occurs in Kentucky every 4.2 minutes. A robbery was committed every 2.8 hours in the Commonwealth during 1991. Rape is committed in Kentucky every 4.5 hours. There has been a 16 percent increase in murders in Kentucky in the first six months of this year compared to the first six months of last year. Last year there were 890 people killed with *handguns* in this country, more than in any other country in the world. Japan was in second place and Sweden was third. There were forty-six people killed in Japan and twenty-one in Sweden. Altogether there were twenty thousand homicides in this country in the last year [for which] we have complete data.

Congress has enacted the Brady Bill[1] which President Clinton signed just last week. That legislation represents an important step in addressing violent crime in America, but it is not a complete solution to our problems in Kentucky. In 1992, the most recent year for which we have complete statistics, 58 percent of the murders in Kentucky were committed with a firearm. Twenty-six percent of all robberies and 17 percent of all aggravated assaults were committed with firearms. Almost 10 percent of all assaults against police officers were committed with a firearm. Firearms valued at over $2 million were stolen in Kentucky last year, the vast majority of which are still in the hands of criminals.

Of particular concern to me are the violent crimes which involve our children. Firearms are now reported in this country to be the *leading* cause of death among children of ages five to fourteen. Kentucky is not immune to this phenomenon. Recent instances of juveniles being involved in criminal activity related to firearms and incidents of children bringing guns into our schools demand our attention. By the year 2000 there will be fifty million more children between the ages of five and seventeen in this country, and we have a duty to them and all the citizens of the Commonwealth to do all we can to make their schools, homes, and streets safer.

I recognize the gravity of the problem with violent crime and firearms that exists in Kentucky. I believe that parents and communities are essential to developing a solution to this problem. I also believe that we as public servants must work with them. I am convinced that we must enact comprehensive legislation to address the problem of violence in our society. I am further convinced that such legislation must include meaningful limits on the use and possession of guns by our youth. As we recommend legislation that will protect the citizens of Kentucky, I ask you to continue to support our efforts. Working together, I know that we can make Kentucky a safer place.[2]

---

1. The Brady Bill, Public Law 103–159, was enacted on November 30, 1993. The Brady Handgun Violence Prevention Act amended the Gun Control Act of 1968. Its main objectives were imposing a waiting period when buying a handgun and requiring background checks on persons buying firearms.

2. On December 17, Jones also gave a speech in Frankfort, presenting checks from confiscated drug money.

KENTUCKY STATE POLICE AWARDS CEREMONY
Frankfort / May 15, 1995

THANK you for allowing me to be part of this awards ceremony. I consider it an honor to be able to recognize certain members of the state police and several citizens of this Commonwealth whose deeds and actions have set them apart. Just being a police officer takes a special kind of person, a person with exceptional courage, determination, and dedication to duty. But these officers we honor today have gone beyond the normal course of duty, and we think it is important to recognize their efforts and pay tribute to them. You might say . . . you were just doing your job, but we're here to say . . . your abilities were challenged and you responded by meeting the challenge and then exceeding the standards. You might say it was "no big deal," but we're here to say your acts of bravery, service, and life-saving are indeed a "big deal." I want you to know that I am proud of you, and all Kentuckians are proud of you, and we deeply appreciate what you do.

Also today four civilians are being honored for their achievements. These are four people who, in some way, assisted the state police, and because of this, they are receiving the highest accolade given to a civilian by the state police, the Meritorious Achievement Award. Three were instrumental in a rescue operation that was, by all accounts, extremely dangerous. The fourth, a retired state police officer, extended his service to the state police beyond his retirement. Each of you gave invaluable assistance, and we owe you our gratitude.

Also today we are announcing the 1994 trooper of the year. The nominees have excelled in their areas of expertise, and while it is difficult to select one officer from so many outstanding candidates, you are all to be commended for your hard work and commitment to protect and serve.

There is one final reason we are gathered here today, and that is to remember that this week is National Law Enforcement Officers Memorial Week. It is a time to remember those police officers who sacrificed their lives in the line of duty. Since 1948, twenty-three Kentucky state troopers have died while serving this agency and this Commonwealth. It is the ultimate price to pay for justice, and their commitment to that end should never be forgotten.

To those of you coming forward today, I say "thank you," not only for serving in the highest traditions of the state police, but for performing above and beyond the call of duty. You've added even more respect to the "thin gray line" in Kentucky. My congratulations to you all.

KENTUCKY STATE POLICE PROMOTION CEREMONY

Frankfort / August 1, 1995

I AM extremely proud of the Kentucky State Police and the officers who dedicate themselves to law enforcement as their chosen profession. The Kentucky State Police has a distinguished heritage and continues to build on its tradition as one of the finest law enforcement agencies in the nation. That tradition is very much in evidence today as twenty-four of our officers are being promoted this morning. Each officer has paid his or her dues and earned the right to advancement. A sergeant from the Academy is also earning a place in state police history today—she will be the first woman to earn the rank of lieutenant within the agency. I am sure she, the other officers, and their families take pride in their accomplishments which we celebrate here today. That pride is a common thread running through the Kentucky State Police, and I congratulate each of you.

Today is particularly special to me because I have the opportunity to announce several plans that will give Kentucky State Police officers some well-deserved financial benefits. First, we are going to increase entry-level salaries 5 percent. Based on a salary survey conducted on twelve out-of-state law enforcement agencies, this raise was needed to bring the state police starting salary in line with other comparable law enforcement agencies. The second plan I want to announce is a merit pay program. Rewards and recognition increase morale and productivity and create a positive cycle in which employer and employee ultimately benefit. The new merit pay program for Kentucky State Police officers is one such program. Commissioner Isaacs[1] and I believe this plan will enhance the effectiveness of the state police officers and provide the encouragement needed to strive for excellence in the workplace. This is an outstanding managerial plan and a model program for other state agencies.

To receive the annual merit pay increase, an officer must meet five specific criteria during a twelve-month evaluation period: first, an officer must attain physical fitness standards that have been established after three years of testing incumbent officers. Second, there can be no more than one vehicle accident assessed against the officer. Third, the officer must not, during the evaluation period, receive disciplinary action resulting in an official written reprimand, reduction in pay or grade, or involuntary suspension from duty without pay. Fourth, the officer must not take more than forty sick hours during the twelve months (excluding absences from injuries incurred in the line of duty, maternity leave, and other serious health circumstances). And fifth, the officer must attain an overall average rating of "above standard" on the quarterly officer inspection reports. Those who meet these standards during the first year will receive 1 percent of their gross annual salary paid in a lump sum.

This program will benefit the agency and each officer through achieving several objectives: it will promote healthy lifestyle choices to improve efficiency and effectiveness on the job. It will reduce the amount of sick time used by Kentucky State Police officers. It will reduce the number of worker compensation claims resulting from injuries received while performing work-related activities. It will reduce the number of assessable state police vehicle accidents and upgrade overall compliance with the agency's vehicle preventive maintenance program, and it will improve morale by recognizing consistent levels of individual performance and discipline.

Kentucky's troopers pay a great service to this Commonwealth. The very nature of an officer's job is stressful and potentially dangerous. Incentives are important. Those who achieve or exceed these standards of excellence should be rewarded. This is why I am so pleased to announce this program. It is a well-defined plan and one that will recognize those officers who meet these standards of excellence.

---

1. Paul Isaacs (1954–), commissioner of corrections under Governor Jones; director of the Administrative Office of the Courts, 1995–99.

KENTUCKY JUVENILE TREATMENT FACILITIES
Frankfort / November 13, 1995

IT IS with great pleasure and satisfaction that I appear here today to sign this consent decree with U.S. Attorney General Janet Reno,[1] Human Resources Secretary Masten Childers, and other federal officials. I am particularly pleased that as my administration draws to a close we are part of a new and important beginning. With this consent decree we are establishing a more structured treatment program in Kentucky's juvenile treatment facilities. It will serve as a solid foundation that we and others can continue to build upon far into the future.

We can talk today about how this decree improves conditions in facilities. Better medical services will be provided; improper isolation practices have been discontinued; but we can also say that we are making important improvements to the way that we are responding to juvenile crime. We will be making better assessments of juveniles on the front end so that they are placed in the programs and facilities best suited to them individually. We are going to make meaningful changes to the mental-health services that these young people receive, and, just as importantly, we will be following up with important aftercare services when they return to their communities. The impact of all of these changes will be to make the juvenile commitment experience work, to turn these kids around, and to reduce the problem of recidivism. I do want to emphasize, however, that the signing of this decree only addresses part of the serious and growing problem of juvenile crime.

The problem must be addressed not only at the stage of correction and treatment but at the level of prevention as well. The complete solution must include persons from a wide spectrum of disciplines and interests: parents, teachers, family members, law enforcement officers, as well as those public officials who deal with juvenile offenders after they have committed crimes. This decree has resulted from an intensive cooperation effort between the United States Justice Department and the Commonwealth of Kentucky. Working together, with a shared vision and common goals, state and federal officials have put in place this one piece of the solution. Our coming together here today and the consent decree itself exemplify what state and federal governments can accomplish when they work cooperatively. Just as the contents of this consent decree are a blueprint for the future, the process that gave rise to the decree might also serve as an example for the future. And lastly, I especially want to thank Attorney General Reno, Secretary Masten Childers, and the Department of Justice attorneys for their contributions to this process and to these important reform efforts that will benefit all Kentuckians.

---

1. Janet Reno (1938–), A.B. in chemistry, Cornell University, 1960; L.L.B., Harvard University, 1963; associate, Brigham & Brigham, 1963–67; partner, Lewis & Reno, 1967–71; staff director, judiciary committee, Florida House

of Representatives, Tallahassee, 1971–72; counselor, Florida Senate Criminal Justice Committee for revision of Florida's Criminal Code, spring 1973; administrative assistant to the state attorney, 11th Judicial Circuit Florida, Miami, 1973–76; appointed state attorney for Dade County, 1978; elected 1978 and on four subsequent occasions; 1978–93; U.S. attorney general, 1993–2001.

STATE GOVERNMENT

COUNCIL OF STATE GOVERNMENTS GROUND BREAKING CEREMONY
Lexington / April 16, 1993

[GREETINGS] THE Commonwealth of Kentucky's support of CSG goes far beyond this organization's arrival to Kentucky in the late [19]60s. Kentucky's elected officials have always been aware of the value of this organization and have used CSG's many services. Throughout the year, our state has been an active participant in the Southern Governors' Association, many CSG conferences designed for elected and appointed officials, and the CSG Executive Committee, of which Sen. Eck Rose is a current member.

CSG is truly a unique organization. And the state of Kentucky is proud to support and participate in this organization's executive and legislative branch activities. As part of Kentucky's support, I am pleased to introduce Sen. John "Eck" Rose and Rep. Joe Clarke, who are here with me on the stage today. . . . Our involvement with CSG is across the board in Frankfort.

I would be remiss in my remarks to you today if I did not mention how proud I am that the Commonwealth was able, through Governor Breathitt and my late father-in-law General Lloyd,[1] to lure CSG to Kentucky. This organization has been, is, and will continue to be a major asset to the state of Kentucky and the Lexington community. Kentucky's state officials believed in this organization when they first approached CSG about moving here from Chicago.

Today we are still committed. As part of our support, the Commonwealth has authorized bond funds for the expansion of the CSG headquarters facilities. We believe that this new facility will enhance the solid services that CSG already provides to us and to the officials of this nation. I think this new building is also symbolic of the role the council and its member states, commonwealths, and territories will play in the future of our country.

State governments today face greater demands and greater challenges than at any time in this nation's history. We need only to read the daily newspapers and watch the evening news to see and appreciate the role that state governments are playing in seeking to find answers to the problems and concerns facing people throughout this country. I am proud that Kentucky is a leader in education reform. I am proud that Kentucky is among the states tackling the issue of [health] care reform.

I and my fellow governors are concerned with protecting our nation's environment and creating jobs for our people. As many of you know, on May 25–28, Kentucky will host a follow-up meeting to last year's Earth Summit in Rio de Janeiro. We expect civic and government leaders and individual citizens to join us in Louisville for this conference, "From Rio to the Capitals: State Strategies for Sustainable Development," which will focus on strategies state and local governments can initiate to meet the concurrent needs of development and environmental protection.

While each state government must at times plan and respond to its own agenda, many of our problems are common ones that can best be met through cooperative efforts such as this conference. I believe it is most appropriate that the Council of State Governments is a member of the National Steering Committee for the conference. Again, on behalf of the Commonwealth of Kentucky, we are proud to be a part of this event and proud to be a part of CSG.

---

1. Arthur Y. Lloyd (1908–86), Ph.D., political science, Vanderbilt University, 1934; professor, Morehead State University, 1931–36; director, Kentucky Department of Welfare, 1936–42; U.S. Army and Army Reserve; commissioner, Kentucky Welfare Department; adjutant general, Kentucky National Guard, 1959–67; lecturer, Eastern Kentucky University, 1973–78; president, Kentucky Historical Society, 1982–84; father of Libby Jones.

WYNONNA JUDD PRESS CONFERENCE
Ashland / July 1, 1993

I'M VERY pleased to be here today to recognize Wynonna Judd[1] as she returns to her hometown of Ashland, Kentucky, for the Summer Motion Picture Festival. I want to commend the Tri-State Fair and Regatta for having the foresight to develop such an event to promote commercial, cultural, and social activities. I understand that this is the sixteenth year of the Summer Motion Picture Festival, and I'm sure this area is well aware of the impact of such an event.

I understand that the crowds for the festival double the population of Ashland. With four nights of concerts and crowds of fifty thousand, that means this festival is responsible for an economic impact of nearly $6 million in this area alone. Total economic impact statewide will be more than $9 million. I want to commend the corporate sponsors who have made free concerts like these, as well as other events at the festival, possible.

I'd also like to recognize the board of directors of the Tri-State Fair and Regatta who have worked so hard to plan the event and the hundreds of volunteers who are making it a success. The people of the tri-state area are talented and committed. That's evident not only in the success of this festival, but also in the abundance of entertainers from this region, Billy Ray Cyrus, Earl Thomas Conley, Kathy Mattea, the late Keith Whitley, Ricky Skaggs, Loretta Lynn, Patty Loveless, Dwight Yoakam, Tom T. Hall, Bobby Bare, and, of course, the Judds.

Later today, Ashland and its visitors will be extremely fortunate to enjoy Wynonna Judd's homecoming concert. But for the people of Ashland it will be especially meaningful because you're welcoming back one of your own. You knew her before she and her mother, Naomi,[2] took the country music world by storm, before she branched out on her own to meet the challenge of a solo career.

I'm not sure what this will mean to someone who's won Grammys and had gold, platinum, and even double platinum records, but tonight I'd like to recognize Wynonna and her mother Naomi as Kentucky Admirals. I hope this is an honor they'll cherish as much as the people of Kentucky cherish them.

---

1. Wynonna Ellen Judd (1964–), Billboard Single of the Year, 1992;

Billboard Best New Country Female, 1992; Academy of Country Music, Top Female Artist, 1994; Kentucky native.

2. Naomi Judd (1946–), native of Ashland, Kentucky; mother of Wynonna and Ashley; singer/songwriter; winner of seven Grammys with daughter Wynonna.

SUPREME COURT APPOINTMENT ANNOUNCEMENT
Frankfort / July 16, 1993

IT IS my great pleasure to announce today the appointment of a highly qualified attorney and excellent person to the state supreme court. It happens to be a historical decision because, not only is she the first woman on the court but she also fills the 7th district seat to which her late husband was elected in 1951.

One of the many reasons Sara Mary Walter Combs[1] will make an outstanding judge is because she had a great influence. Few people will disagree that Bert Combs was one of the best judges ever to represent Kentucky on the state and federal benches. The equality in school funding case he won, with Sara at his side, fostered our ongoing education reform, forever dedicating Kentucky to excellent schools for all our children. But before Sara ever met Bert she was an excellent student in language and the law at the University of Louisville. Because they shared so many humanitarian causes and concerns, their marriage was greatly enriched by common interests.

Foremost, she is her own person with many significant and varied accomplishments. One of the most appealing things about her qualifications is her diversity of experience. She is a widely experienced attorney working in almost every aspect of the law, with special emphasis on domestic relations, criminal law, contracts, probate, and general litigation.

She has also had experience at both the state and federal level in appellate practice. And Sara Combs also brings with her extensive business experience. She has been vice-president and legal counsel for a large corporation in the state's largest city. And she has handled domestic relations, criminal, and small claims cases for hundreds of average, rural Kentuckians. She has argued before mahogany appellate benches of state and United States courts, as well as in humble country courtrooms.

Sara has accomplished all these things and much more in the thirteen years since her admission to the bar. She will bring to the bench both a broad and brilliant mastery of the law and a fresh understanding of the everyday needs and desires of ordinary Kentuckians. It is a high honor for me to present to you, and to all the Commonwealth, Justice Sara Combs, whom I believe is destined to be a great jurist.

---

1. Sara Combs (1948–), B.A., University of Louisville, 1970; M.A., University of Louisville, 1971; J.D., University of Louisville, 1979; appointed to Kentucky Supreme Court 1993; Kentucky Court of Appeals, 1994– ; member: Christian Appalachian Project, Governor's Scholars Program; board member: Kentucky Mountain Laurel Festival, Kentucky Bar Association, Louisville Bar Association, Montgomery County Schools Education Foundation, Thomas D. Clark Foundation.

FINAL MEETING OF GOVERNOR'S COMMISSION ON QUALITY AND EFFICIENCY
Frankfort / October 19, 1993

EXACTLY seven months ago today, we launched a process that will carry Kentucky's government into the twenty-first century. As I said then, we *had* to meet our responsibility to address lagging state revenue and, at the same time, identify ways to improve the delivery of services to the taxpayers at less cost. Kentucky is in a select group of just a few states that have met the challenge of this process. We are the first to conclude the process since Vice President Gore completed his national review to improve our federal government.

Like the vice president's study, our commission has had a unique element that I think we all agree worked to everyone's advantage. This, the most substantial review of state government operations ever undertaken, as Governor Breathitt said, was conducted by a partnership that involved state employees and private citizens *every step of the way*. Our front-line workers spoke loud and clear throughout, and this commission listened carefully.

The results will yield a better workplace for state employees and a better government for Kentucky citizens. While I realize your work won't be finalized until later this afternoon, your acceptance of the work teams' recommendations at General Butler State Park includes saving the state $900 million over the next five years. But beyond the savings, you are recommending a better operation that will provide our most important resource, state government employees, with a more efficient workplace.

You have considered the whole environment in which state employees perform, from personnel management, to technology, to improved communication, to employee training. You took the challenge to look at what we in state government do, how we do it; what works well and what needs to be changed. Now it's up to those of us in government's driver's seat to take your road map and use it to guide Kentucky into the future.

My office can accomplish some things by executive order. But a substantial amount of what you will finalize here today requires legislative action. I'm here to tell you that I'm willing to do my part. I'm willing to work with the General Assembly to ensure that your efforts are not in vain. Like every other state, we're looking at reduced revenues and increasing expenses. And we can no longer rely on a system that was created in the 1950s to meet the needs of the '90s. You know that the buzz phrase "government should operate like a business" ignores the reality that government's mission is to deliver services to those who need them most.

What government has to do is make sure that our customers, the taxpayers, get *the best* possible service for every cent they pay as citizens of this Commonwealth. On behalf of all Kentuckians, I want to thank you for what you've accomplished over the past seven months. It was a short time frame for such a monumental task. It took courage and commitment. Your last order of business in Carrollton was to approve a meeting next year to check on the progress of your recommendations. You met my challenge and so I will meet yours.

And I hope our legislative bodies will do the same. Before I conclude, I'd like to take a moment to once again thank Jim Gray[1] for lending his knowledge and leadership to the commission. I know it has been a long haul and that few others would have made this commitment to such a challenge. . . .

---

1. James P. Gray II (1953–), B.A., Vanderbilt University, 1976; Loeb

Fellowship, Harvard University, 1996–97; executive vice-president of James N. Gray Construction Company, Lexington, 1976–present; executive committee, Kentucky Historical Society, 1999–present; chair, Shakertown Roundtable, 2000– .

QUALITY AND EFFICIENCY FINAL NEWS CONFERENCE

Frankfort / November 23, 1993

[Greetings] I want to take a moment to thank Jim Gray and all of the members of the commission for the dedication, enthusiasm, and energy you have brought to this effort over the past seven months. The energy and quality of work accomplished in this short time frame is extraordinary. The study is not only comprehensive in scope, but significant in the challenges it lays before each of us in state government. I would also like to thank the many others who are here today and across state government for their contribution to the quality and efficiency study.

From the beginning, this effort has been a "bottom up" review of the work we do here. It has been a unique partnership between citizens from the private sector and our most valuable asset, our state employees. This report is evidence that we can accomplish anything if we work together. Its value lies not in the summary of all of the issues confronting us in state government; rather its value is found in the challenges it poses.

A few weeks ago, I attended the final meeting of this commission, when commission members met at the Governor's Mansion to cast the final vote on the report. Dr. Tom Clark, who attended that session, reminded us then of all the reports and studies that have come and gone before us, all too often to be buried in libraries and archives. He bluntly told each of us that this review *must* succeed if Kentucky is to compete successfully in the next century.

Repeatedly throughout our state's history, we have patched together our government organization time and time again. No one knows this better than our own state employees. Budget shortfalls have become a way of life in Kentucky, occurring in nine of the last fourteen years, constantly requiring cuts, budget adjustments, preventing salary increases, and pushing this government time and time again perilously close to fiscal crisis.

Kentucky's government too often has [operated] and continues to operate in a crisis atmosphere that is destroying morale, efficiency, and quality service to our customer, the taxpayers of Kentucky. This report sets out the road map we need to move in a new direction. Its implementation will give us the opportunity to ensure that our employees have the necessary and appropriate tools needed to deliver quality service to the taxpayers of Kentucky.

The implementation of this report will not be easy. It will require a new vision, boundless energy, and significant change in the way we do business in Frankfort. One of the most remarkable things about this report and its preparation is that our own state employees have provided the vision to change this institution. We sent out over forty thousand surveys to our workforce and received approximately thirteen thousand back. A thousand of them had handwritten letters and notes attached asking this administration to lead the forces for change in the work rules.

The longer I work in Frankfort the more I realize that the problem is not the people who work here, it is the politicians who have failed too often to fight the battles necessary to create a system that will appropriately pay, promote, and energize our employees. Make no mistake about it. This report is a beginning. We must continue the energy and focus of the commission, and the commission must continue to hold this government accountable to implement the changes that are appropriate.

My acceptance of this report today should not signify that I have accepted all 270 recommendations. Clearly, we have not. We do, however, accept the challenge this commission sets out. Today we begin the process of turning around the battleship, as Chairman Gray has often expressed. First, this morning I have executed an executive order establishing a career service system task force that will be created to prepare proposed legislation for consideration by the General Assembly and proposed administrative regulation to reform the merit system.

I have directed that several threads run through the work of this task force. First, I have expressly directed that the protection of our workforce from political hirings and firings be enhanced and strengthened in this process. Second, I have directed that the classification and promotion system of our workforce be simplified and clarified. Next, I have directed that this task force have equal representation from merit state employees, management personnel, legislative members, and private-sector personnel.

This task force is directed to make a report and have enabling legislation prepared prior to the next regular session of the General Assembly. In this regard, I support the commission's call for the creation of a Cabinet for Personnel Management. Second, I have directed that a privatization commission be established consisting of six members, one-half from the public sector and one-half from the private sector. This privatization commission will review all current state services and develop guidelines for privatization. This commission is to report to the governor at least every three months regarding the status of its review and recommendations. This commission will become effective April 15, 1994, and will expire on December 31, 1998.

Third, for the first time, I have directed that a strategic executive planning committee be established that will be chaired by the secretary of the Governor's Executive Cabinet. This committee will be directed together with the Governor's Office for Policy and Management to develop strategic plans and performance-based budgeting plans. We can no longer afford a government that is not held accountable or a government that budgets according to funds available, rather than programs needed.

Finally, I am issuing today executive orders institutionalizing the process of consensus forecasting we have initiated; establishing an office of controller to manage all cash-management functions in the government on a consolidated basis; the consolidation of postal services across this government; and the initiation of a request for proposal to continue to downsize both in-state and out-of-state travel services for state agencies.

I am under no illusions that the work required under these executive orders and this report will be easy. It has been written that citizens who would reap the blessings of freedom have to "undergo the fatigue of supporting it." We must have the energy and commitment to see this work through to completion.

Now, let me say a few words about our greatest asset—the people who work in service to the Commonwealth. Two years ago in my first State of the Commonwealth Address, I acknowledged that our state government "have some of the hardest-working, most qualified people I have ever seen." I recognized then and reiterate now that we must find ways in these tight fiscal times to solve our problems without ever wavering our "strong support" for state employees.

In this vein, I want to state today that this government accepts the challenge of commission member Alex Warren to accomplish the goal of downsizing state government through attrition and job re-engineering, as opposed to massive layoffs. The Jones administration will not shrink from reorganizations where needed, and an ongoing, intense examination of the need for every agency in state government will continue.

When the history of this study is written, however, I want it recorded that this administration created a spirit of cooperation and teamwork where personnel system reform could be accomplished and where, in the end, a new classification and compensation system was created that put more workers on the front lines delivering services to customers and less behind middle-management desks.

Recently, it has been written that the tasks that lay before us, whether in the nature of health-care reform, higher education reform, or government reform, may be too monumental, too significant for us to face. I ask all of you in the coming months to join with me in addressing and dealing with these great issues. I have a deep and abiding trust in our capacity to proceed with boldness regarding these initiatives. . . .

SWEARING-IN OF JUDGE GARY PAYNE
Lexington / March 14, 1994

I am very pleased to be a part of this moment. Judge Payne,[1] I have no doubt that you will be fair and just on the circuit court bench, and that your decisions will be sound and without bias. We would be remiss if we did not recognize the man whose retirement created the position you fill today, Judge N. Mitchell Meade.[2] Judge Meade could easily be described as a person who was not afraid to "tell it as he saw it," without mincing words, and I have every confidence that you, too, will have the courage of your convictions to "tell it like it is."

Judge Payne, you are known throughout Fayette County for your legal ability and for your judicial temperament. But you also bring to the bench a history of caring and involvement in your community. Through your work with young people you have become a role model, a model for the type of person we should all strive to be. Now, as the first African American person on the circuit court bench in Fayette County, you again are a role model for young people. You are making history with your appointment here today, and your actions on the bench will speak to the next generation of African Americans who aspire to a career in jurisprudence.

I thank you for taking on that responsibility, and I encourage you to remember that when you seek justice, "Truth is its handmaid, freedom is its child, peace is its companion, safety walks in its steps and victory follows in its train." Good luck, Judge. And may God bless.

---

1. Gary Payne (1954–), B.A., Pepperdine University, 1976; J.D., University of Kentucky, 1978; Fayette County assistant prosecutor, 1984–87; district judge, 1988–94; appointed Fayette County circuit judge, 1994; elected Fayette County circuit judge, 1994– .

2. N. Mitchell Meade (1927–), born in Letcher County; B.S., University of Kentucky; L.L.B., University of Kentucky College of Law; U.S. Army, Korean conflict; assistant U.S. district attorney for the Kentucky Eastern District, 1958–61; general counsel, Kentucky State Bar Association, 1961–62; practicing attorney, 1962–68; probate judge, Fayette County, 1963–68; circuit judge, Fayette Circuit Court, 1968–94; member, Kentucky Judicial Retirement & Removal Commission, 1978–94; vice-chair, E.O. Robinson Mountain Fund; member, Shriners Hospitals for Crippled Children Board of Governors.

LOCAL ISSUES SPEECH
Louisville / June 2, 1994

As LOCAL officials, you are probably accustomed to hearing about all the problems that affect your area. In fact, one of the reasons you are here today is to hear how other people deal with those problems, so that you may discover a common solution. As public officials, you are, no doubt, used to spending a lot of your time dealing with the "negatives." Today, however, I'd like to take this opportunity to bring you some good news about your state.

Kentucky's unemployment rate is currently 4.9 percent, the lowest in nearly two decades! Since we took office, we have added more than 36,600 net new manufacturing and related jobs in Kentucky! For the past two years, Kentucky's per capita income growth is the eighth-fastest in the country! Since our administration started, we have reduced the full-time state government workforce by more than fourteen hundred, and we did so through attrition, not layoffs.

By eliminating these state jobs and maintaining the level of service, we have saved close to $30 million a year in salaries. The latest estimates from our economists show that we will have $30 to $40 million left in our account at the end of our fiscal year June 30.

I tell you this because our state legislators will be in Frankfort starting Monday to pass a state budget. As you know, at the end of the regular session, a budget was passed that did not include any money to revitalize our state parks, many of which need major renovations. A budget was passed that did not allow us to make good investments in the future of our children, investments such as the new UK library in Lexington and the history center in Frankfort. It allowed for virtually no economic-development projects to spur growth in the Commonwealth.

At that time, I said I could not approve a budget that did not adequately take care of the people. I was told I didn't have a choice, because no governor in state history had ever vetoed a budget. As you know, I did veto that budget. Now, I need your help to put it back together so we can make the needed investments all throughout this Commonwealth to guarantee a better future. I want to make this clear: we do not have to raise taxes to do these things! What I have proposed is a surplus spending plan, a program to invest our savings. I am saying to the legislature that if we do *not* have the money, we do *not* spend it.

We will not burden our people with a debt they will not be able to pay. As public servants, I'm sure you know the wisdom of this. But I'm confident you also know that if the economists tell us the money will be there from year to year, we have a moral responsibility to invest it in the most logical way. If you're thinking that we should hold back any surplus money, let me tell you this up front: we have already budgeted the largest surplus account in the history of the state, $100 million. That means if the economy does take a little dip over the next two years, we'll be prepared, and we won't have to cut the budget again, as has been done twelve times in the last fourteen years.

Let me tell you specifically how we intend to invest this money. First, human needs should come first. We are proposing the first $4.4 million be invested in such programs as tuberculosis intervention, cancer screening, immunizations for our young people, and programs to keep out of jail mentally ill people who have not been accused of a crime. Second, we are proposing to invest in our state parks. Our plan is to pay for the most-needed repairs with cash, nearly $23 million, out of this year's surplus funds. We also would pay $2.3 million for bonds to start construction of the new UK library. Already, more than $20 million has been raised privately. In the 1992 General Assembly, we committed ourselves to this project, and we must honor that commitment.

Finally, we will closely watch the budget surplus, and if the economists are correct and tell us that the surplus recurs from year to year, we will purchase bonds to finish the repairs to state parks. Then, we'll invest in bonds for such projects as the expansion of the Commonwealth Convention Center and construction of the U of L football stadium here in Louisville, the Kentucky History Center in Frankfort, the Northern Kentucky Convention Center, and Northern Kentucky Farmers Market, along with several other facilities throughout the state.

. . . In short, a variation of the escalator clause is what we are proposing. If the surplus is not there, or if it's not recurring revenue, we will not spend it. Don't let someone tell you that we don't have the money to make these investments, because that is absolutely not true. At a time when our unemployment and interest rates are down, and our tax base and per capita income growth are up, our economy is going better than in twenty years.

We have a surplus because we got this money the old-fashioned way, we earned it. The proof is strong: we are building a stronger Kentucky, and we're building it from the foundation up. We have a plan to take advantage of our savings to make a better future for all Kentuckians. Over the past few weeks, I've traveled several thousand miles throughout the state, asking people to contact their legislators. Today, I'm asking you to do the same. You know firsthand how vital it is when your constituents contact you and tell you what's important to them. It is just as important for you to contact the men and women who represent you and your communities.

Our legislators are great people and they want to do the right thing. Tell them you support our plan. Tell them to save our state parks. Tell them to invest in the future of our young people by building the UK library and the history center in Frankfort. Tell them to invest in the future of economic development of Kentucky by approving such projects as the Commonwealth Convention Center, the Northern Kentucky Convention Center, and the other projects throughout the state that I have outlined. This time, much more than ever before, you can make the difference.

QUALITY AND EFFICIENCY COMMISSION LUNCHEON
Frankfort / November 29, 1994

. . . THE vision of all of you, whether as commissioners, members of the work teams, or working members of this government every day, as voiced in your report, *A Wake-Up Call for Kentucky*, is as clear a road map to success as we have in this great state. Your wise judgments, your hard work, your character, and your vision have created a living, breathing document that has had an enormous measure of success in its first year. I promise you it will continue to be the gamebook for this administration in its last year. It will be up to all of us to demand its continued implementation as we elect a new governor nearly eleven months from now.

I am under no illusions about the nature of the tasks required of this "wake-up call." The challenge to implement the measures in this document is enormous, fraught with political perils and blocked at many turns by entrenched special interests. We cannot be deterred in our efforts. This report demands that we re-examine and redefine the mission of every agency of this government and demand accountability in the size, scope, and costs of that agency's mission. All of this work must be coupled with our long-term vision for Kentucky. It must be coupled with our commitment to the implementation of the Kentucky Education Reform Act.

In this noisy political season, it will be tempting and too easy to harp and to criticize and to forget the abysmal state of education we knew in this state before the *Rose* decision and the statutory vision enacted in 1990. It must be coupled with our commitment to the implementation of Kentucky's health-care reform legislation. We must not forget that nearly one-half million Kentuckians do not have health insurance, and too many of our people still do not access the system in cost-efficient ways. We must not fail to implement this law wisely and insure that its reforms succeed.

It must be coupled with our implementation of Kentucky's strategic plan for economic development. Our record of job creation in the last three years is unmatched in modern times in this state. *But* if this state is to compete meaningfully, we must *increase* our commitment to workforce training and retraining, build an information-age infrastructure, rebuild our farm economy, and offer jobs for our people in industries that will grow and compete in the next century.

And the paradox of all of this is our commitment to a progressive community—a community committed to educational reform and health-care reform, and long-term sustainable economic development must be accomplished with less money, less taxes, and a smaller government. That is the challenge of the *Wake-Up Call for Kentucky* report.

One admonition that this administration has tried to live by from its inception is that "we walk our talk." We understand that we cannot lower the tax burden on real, working Kentuckians unless we cut the size of the government. Beware of politicians with magic answers and silver bullets. While other politicians and pundits have filled the airwaves and headlines with angry noise about government, you and this administration have tried to channel that frustration into meaningful accomplishments. I know you have spent the morning reviewing the work of the executive and legislative branches of government over the last year as we have wrestled with the recommendations of the *Wake-Up Call for Kentucky*. I know that former Secretary Mulloy[1] has walked through the report in detail and has asked each of you to "grade" the government in its response. I am very proud of this administration's response to the recommendations and welcome the frank discussion of our performance.

In the time remaining, I would like to focus for a few minutes on our fiscal accomplishments, many of which have resulted directly from the vision of this group. When we took office in 1991, this administration was faced with a bleak financial picture. This grim outlook persisted in the face of the largest tax increase in history, which the state passed in 1990. In 1990, the legislature increased the state's taxes by over $1 billion. In spite of that, this administration substantially cut the enacted 1992 budget because of a $155 million shortfall.

From all indications, the fiscal picture would have continued to deteriorate because of the new KERA funding requirements, out-of-control Medicaid costs, and a rapidly increasing state payroll. When we took office in 1991, to call the state payroll bloated was an understatement, approximately 37,000 full-time employees. Imagine that between 1983 and 1991 the state workforce grew from approximately 30,000 to over 36,000, when the state's population in the same time period remained static.

Additionally, during this same period, the state's credit was allowed to decline. The state's budget reserve trust fund or "rainy day account" was allowed to dwindle to a paltry $4 million on a budget of over $3 billion. It was altogether evident that for too long the state's business had been sold to the highest bidder and the taxpayers and their pocketbooks were forgotten. Clearly, we could not continue to do business as usual or the endless cycle of budget cuts and irresponsible spending would only continue. In the short term, we knew we had to make several adjustments when we came into office.

First, while maintaining our commitment to KERA, we adjusted the spending timetables on this important initiative. Second, we suspended automatic pay raises for state employees for fiscal year 1993 and provided 3 percent raises in 1994 for most state employees. Third, we began the process of building up the state's rainy day account to enhance our credit, save money for contingencies, and stop the endless cycle of budget cuts. Today, this administration will leave the Commonwealth a rainy day fund of $100 million, the largest in the state's history. Additionally, Standard and Poor's recently has raised the state's credit rating for the first time in thirty-two years.

In the long term, we made these additional commitments. First, to stop the growth of the state's payroll, we initiated a hiring freeze. We committed ourselves to "downsizing" the workforce by using attrition and re-engineering the jobs we had in state government. We have had remarkable success in this effort. Today we are down over eighteen hundred full-time jobs, an annual savings of at least $40 million. Second, in order to end the historic competition between the legislative and executive branches of government regarding the amount of available revenue to spend, we instituted "consensus forecasting" with the legislative branch. We believe that this partnership has resulted in conservative, responsible projections of the revenue base. Third, we asked you to examine the mission of every agency of this government, question it, critique it, and help us shape and create a smaller, leaner government.

Yes, we have weathered the fiscal storm of the early '90s, but that only means that our opportunities have just begun. We are working across this government to provide more direct customer service and to reduce unneeded layers of bureaucracy. We have established a privatization commission that over the next four years will define and shape the further reduction of this government through privatization. Finally, we hope to announce in the next few weeks the awarding of a contract to the private sector to build an integrated fiber network across this state, in all 120 counties. Kentucky will be one of the very first states in the nation to hold a competitive bidding process for the construction of the information backbone.

I hope that we have met your expectations for the first year's work on this commission's report. You have heard the statistics, some 26 percent of the recommendations are complete, some 44 percent are in progress, and some 30 percent remain to be examined. Two things I know. First, our work has only begun. If we are to educate our children, retrain our adult workforce, and afford all of our citizens quality health care, we must do it with smaller government, one that listens to the taxpayer, and one that in the end requires less taxes and spending. Second, we cannot accomplish this work alone. Each of you understands that, in the end, in a democracy, every citizen "holds office." As a president once said, "Every one of us is in a position of responsibility; and in the final analysis, the kind of government we get depends upon how we fulfill those responsibilities." I thank you for your judgments, hard work, character, and vision, and for fulfilling your responsibility to Kentucky.

---

1. Patrick Mulloy (1953–), B.A., Vanderbilt University, 1974; J.D., Vanderbilt University School of Law, 1977; Kentucky secretary of Finance and Administration Cabinet, 1992–94; attorney, Greenebaum, Doll & McDonald, 1994–96; president, CEO, and director of Atria Communities, Inc., 1996–present; co-chair, Governor's Commission on Tax Reform; member, Governor's Commission on Quality and Efficiency; board of trustees, Kentucky Country Day School; Assisted Living Federation of America Board; American Senior Housing Association Board.

EMPLOYEE SUGGESTION SYSTEM AWARDS CEREMONY
Frankfort / December 12, 1994

I AM delighted to be here today to be able to thank each of this year's Employee Suggestion System award recipients and the Employee Suggestion System council members. What you have done, and what you are doing, goes to the very heart of the administration: making government more efficient. As you know, we have been able to eliminate more than eighteen hundred permanent full-time positions from state government, through attrition. And you have helped make that possible by your willingness to "roll up your sleeves" and take on the extra work. But you have gone one step further: you also have made state government more efficient.

That is obvious by your suggestions, which will save the Commonwealth more than $90,000 alone. I am really pleased that we have this program in state government, to recognize the efforts of those who have taken the initiative to create a workplace that is more efficient and more sensitive to the needs of the people of the Commonwealth. In addition to the $90,000 in savings that I mentioned earlier, I also think it is important to note that many of the suggestions we are recognizing today have resulted in intangible savings, savings that cannot be directly measured in dollars and cents.

These ideas have greatly improved the areas of quality, efficiency, and employee morale; areas that have a significant impact on the workplace. I think we all realize that we must include our workforce, our greatest resource, in decisions that determine the future of government operations and services. We know that employee involvement is the key to ensuring the continuous improvement of state government programs and services. The employee suggestion system demonstrates that empowering employees to be innovative and creative can only enhance the workplace and job performance.

When you treat the people's tax money as if it were your own, you tend to be more careful with it. That is what the people of Kentucky want, and that is what you are doing. I am so proud of you and of all our state government workers for your hard work, and I want you to know that you have my full support. . . .

STATE RECEPTION ROOM DEDICATION
Frankfort / February 7, 1995

AS WE stand here, getting ready to reopen this magnificent room, I cannot help but think of the pride the people of Kentucky have for their state capitol. Those of us who are in this building on a daily basis frequently encounter Kentuckians who have brought their out-of-state visitors here to see this structure. Since its dedication in 1910, it has been recognized as one of the most impressive state capitols in the United States.

It's not hard to justify that pride. It has a classic design, exterior walls of Bedford limestone, and inside, the corridors, nave, and the like are lined with Vermont granite and Georgia marble. We *should* be proud of this building. One room in this building was designed as a special showplace, and that is this state reception room. It was once a part of the governor's office complex when the office was on the second floor.

George A. Lewis detailed the state reception room in his book *Kentucky's New State Capitol,* which was published in 1910. He told of the murals on the walls, the hardwood floor covered with a rich carpet. At the time, the carpet was said to be the largest specially designed rug ever manufactured. Its weight was over one thousand pounds. He told of the hand-carved furniture which was made by foreign-born artisans in this country. Some of them, according to Lewis, were still wearing wooden shoes from their native Germany. This was the most luxurious room in this building and was one of the few formal reception rooms in the country.

Kentucky's past governors received high-ranking dignitaries here. In 1953, Gov. Lawrence Wetherby[1] decided to move the governor's office to the first floor, where it is now. After that, this room went into a period of decline. It became a lunch and break room for state employees. When Beulah Nunn[2] first walked into the state reception room in the late 1960s, it was a mess. The carpet was dirty and even had chewing gum stuck in its beautiful fibers. Some of the furniture was damaged. Other pieces were stored in the capitol's basement. When she saw it, she was appalled and oversaw a limited restoration project for the room. But since then, its condition has declined again.

It was used as a caucus room, a meeting room, a room for news conferences, and even a break room. Folding chairs lined the walls. But now, thanks to Rex Cecil[3] and his staff, this room has been returned to its original magnificence. Rex, to you and to all who worked on the project, I offer my appreciation and the thanks of all Kentuckians. Your focus on the past will enrich our future.

---

1. Lawrence W. Wetherby (1908–94); L.L.B, University of Louisville, 1929; attorney, Jefferson County Juvenile Court, 1933–37, 1942; lieutenant governor of Kentucky, 1947–50; Democratic governor of Kentucky, 1950–55; Kentucky State Senate, Senate president pro tem, 1966–68.

2. Beulah Nunn (1914–95), born Beulah Cornelius Aspley; married Louie Nunn, 1950; first lady, 1967–71; chairwoman of Kentucky Mansion's Preservation Society for twenty-two years; appointed by President Nixon to President's Council on Historic Preservation; mother of state Rep. Stephen Nunn.

3. Rex Cecil (1944–), B.A., University of Kentucky College of Architecture, 1968; director, Office of Historic Properties under Governor Jones, 1992–95; Versailles architect, 1996– .

WORKERS' COMPENSATION NEWS CONFERENCE
Frankfort / May 9, 1995

WE ARE here today to announce that Kentucky state government is teaming up with the attorney general's office and local prosecutors to tackle fraud in the workers' compensation system. National experts tell us that fraud takes up 20 percent of the cost of this country's $100 billion-a-year workers' compensation premiums. While we cannot prove how much fraud there is in the current system, we do know that the cost of workers' compensation is the most frequently voiced complaint of our business community.

And if you look at this chart of workers' compensation claims, you can see that the number of injuries of a graphic nature has stayed relatively constant over the past ten years, but the actual number of claims has risen sharply. I want to make it clear that as we talk about fraud, we are talking about not only the workers, but also fraud involving health-care providers, attorneys, and employers themselves. It is not fair for a few people to cash in at the expense of others, and that's what these people are doing.

To combat this, we are beefing up the fraud unit in the Department of Insurance. The Department of Workers' Claims will add a fraud lead attorney to serve as a clearinghouse to evaluate leads. These agencies will work closely with the attorney general and local prosecutors. Basically, we have taken several fragmented anti-fraud efforts and pulled them together into one fraud-fighting force.

We also have a toll-free number that anyone can call to report suspected cases of workers' compensation fraud. That number is 1–800–554–8601. We will be publicizing this number throughout Kentucky, so that people will know that if they suspect someone is cheating the system, they can call, and we will check it out. We have to reinstill confidence in the workers' compensation system, and we will do that by catching and prosecuting those who are breaking the law. . . .

FISH AND WILDLIFE OFFICERS SWEARING-IN CEREMONY
Frankfort / May 17, 1995

COMMISSIONERS, commission members, colonels, proud parents, friends, and family members, it is an honor and pleasure to be here with you today. These eleven new Fish and Wildlife Law Enforcement officers, nine conservation officers, and two Kentucky water patrol officers represent the first combined graduating class since we moved the Division of Water Patrol into the Department of Fish and Wildlife Resources sixteen months ago.

To the graduates, I say *congratulations*. You have prepared for this day for a long time. Over the past seventeen weeks, you have prepared yourselves intellectually, physically, and mentally for the difficult challenges ahead. When you take your oath of office today, you embark on an important mission, a mission rich in heritage and heavy in responsibility. Your primary responsibility will be to keep our waterways safe and to protect our precious wildlife resources. As peace officers, people will look to you for help, for advice, and for protection. You will be a role model, and it is important that you conduct yourselves in a model way.

You will soon find that you are not simply law enforcement officers. You will be part biologist, part ecologist, part sociologist, part psychologist, part educator, part farmer, and part peacemaker. And people will expect you to be experts in all these areas. But perhaps the most important responsibility that you will have is the responsibility to protect lives. Always remember the dangers inherent in the tasks you are about to undertake. Three Kentucky conservation officers and two Kentucky water patrol officers have given their lives in the line of duty.

In addition to your jobs as protectors, you also will work closely with those who hunt and fish. The contributions that sports men and women have made to nature and wildlife in Kentucky is monumental. Fifty years ago, the deer herd in Kentucky numbered about one thousand. Today it is more than half a million. Only nineteen years ago, Kentucky was home to less than one thousand wild turkeys. Today that number is closer to seventy thousand. These numbers and recent increases in duck and geese populations are proof of the success of habitat preservation and restoration programs funded by our sports men and women.

The habitat restoration programs funded by fishing and hunting license buyers are helping bring back many different forms of wildlife, from otters to bald eagles. Hunters and anglers also play important roles in our state's economy. A U.S. Fish and Wildlife study shows that hunting and fishing generate more than $1.4 million in economic output every year, and they support 22,000 jobs in Kentucky. That's about $164,000 of economic activity generated every hour in Kentucky by hunters and anglers.

Our waterways are a major boost to our tourism economy, a $7.1 billion industry in this state. With 660,000 surface acres of lakes, 18,500 miles of rivers, and more miles of navigable waterways than any other state except Alaska, Kentucky is a prime attraction for boaters. There were 45.4 million boating visits to Kentucky waterways last year. That is about four times the traffic that existed in 1973, the year the Kentucky water patrol was created.

Yet, even with traffic increased fourfold, boating fatalities have fallen dramatically from fifty-four that first year, to a low of nine in 1993 and twelve last year. That is strong proof of the effectiveness of education and enforcement of boating laws by the Kentucky water patrol. In the past year, all conservation officers have received training in water safety enforcement, and all water patrol officers have been trained in traditional fish and wildlife enforcement. That has effectively and efficiently increased the capabilities of each law enforcement division. Kentucky's wildlife and waterways have benefited greatly; so have our people. Officers, again, I salute you. And on behalf of all Kentuckians, welcome to the Kentucky Department of Fish and Wildlife family.

BUDGET SURPLUS NEWS CONFERENCE
Frankfort / July 10, 1995

TODAY we are prepared to announce that the final state government surplus for fiscal year 1995 is $84 million. This, as you know, is the amount of revenue received by the Commonwealth last year in excess of the amount predicted by our consensus forecasting group. It is a pleasure to be able to stand before you today and explain why Kentucky has brought in more money than expected.

Far too many times this state has faced deficits which have forced budget cuts. As you remember, the first two years of our administration we had to delay sending out tax refund checks because they would have bounced. When we took office, the state's financial picture was dismal. I pledged at that time to do everything possible to remedy the situation, restore the vitality to our budget, and safeguard for the future.

Today I am proud to say that we have kept this promise. The next governor will inherit a truly balanced budget. Our aggressive economic-development policies have successfully created thousands of jobs. Unemployment has reached record lows. Personal per capita income continues to increase at a rate greater than the national average. And our economy continues to outperform the predictions of the budget forecasters.

We inherited a budget reserve trust fund, the state savings account, that contained only $23.5 million. Today, it contains $100 million, and we propose to add to this in the upcoming fiscal session. This commitment to our long-term financial security caused the Wall Street bond firms to raise our bond ratings to A+. This truly is a historic time in Kentucky.

Faced with the bleak budget scenario back in late 1991, I challenged each of our cabinet secretaries to cut government waste, control spending, and cut back their payrolls while maintaining a high level of service and taking on new initiatives. This was a tremendous challenge, but they responded magnificently. Instead of increasing in size over the past three and a half years, our government has shrunk by seventeen hundred permanent, full-time employees.

We have cut travel costs, sold state cars, increased efficiency, and saved millions of dollars. As the agencies close out their books for fiscal year 1995, we will tabulate the official general fund lapse, or the amount budgeted for an agency but not spent. This total will be available prior to the special session and should exceed our earlier estimate of $30 million. It could be as much as $50 million.

The road fund, which provides the funding for the Transportation Cabinet, has also grown more than expected. They report a surplus of over $50 million. This is the money that I propose to spend on rural roads, bridges, and guardrails to make our roads safer. We have hundreds of projects already designed that could be built this summer. We purposefully delayed the upcoming special session until the end of July so the fiscal year would be over and we would know exactly how much money we needed to appropriate.

Today we have the first piece of the puzzle. Our general fund surplus is $84 million and our road fund surplus is $50 million. In less than two weeks we will know the final amount of the lapse. That means, on July 31, when the state legislature convenes, we will know exactly how much unobligated money we have. I am proposing that we save some of this money by adding to our budget trust fund, that we invest some of it back into the state through education projects, and that we return some of it to the taxpayers in the form of a tax break. As I travel the state and speak with citizens, they are very supportive of this plan. I hope to persuade more of our state legislators in the weeks ahead.

BENEFITS NEWS CONFERENCE
Frankfort / September 22, 1995

AS YOU know, two of this administration's highest priorities have been to improve health-care coverage in Kentucky and to downsize state government. We have been successful in both areas. We have been able to cut waste throughout state government, and we have eliminated more than eighteen hundred permanent, full-time positions from the payroll. We were able to do this because the existing state employees have rolled up their sleeves and worked harder to give Kentucky taxpayers the absolute most for their tax dollars.

Because of the savings their hard work has realized and because of the implementation of House Bill 250 and the creation of the Health Purchasing Alliance, we are able to announce today that we will increase benefits for state employees and give them more flexibility in establishing their health-care coverage.

Effective January first of 1996, we will triple the life-insurance coverage for all eligible state employees, from the current level of $6,500 to $20,000. This will be the first increase in ten years. In addition, starting January first, state government will begin to provide a fixed-dollar amount for each eligible state employee to spend on his or her health-care coverage. This will allow state workers to design health-care plans to match their own needs, rather than have to adopt the old "one size fits all" approach. Starting January first, Kentucky state government will budget $175.50 per month for each eligible employee to be used for health care. This will give the state worker options he or she has not had in the past.

For instance, this $175.50 will be more than enough for every employee regardless of age or pre-existing condition to purchase an individual plan equal to Kentucky Kare's standard single coverage, as well as an additional dental rider. If an employee chooses a plan with lesser coverage that carries a premium below $175.50, the difference can be used for additional rider coverage such as a dental or vision plan, or it can be placed in a Commonwealth Choice health-care spending account.

Funds placed in a health-care spending account can be used to defray insurance deductibles of other non-covered, eligible health-care expenses. If an employee chooses a plan to cover a spouse, dependent, or family, state government will contribute $175.50 toward the cost of the plan, regardless of the level of coverage that's been chosen. Because of the range of plans now available to state employees, it will be possible for an employee to use his or her $175.50 to cover a major portion of the cost of coverage for a spouse or family.

We believe that these changes significantly improve the benefits and the flexibility available to state employees. Further explanations will be available to all employees with their September 30 paycheck and during the open enrollment period in November. State employees have increased their efficiency and productivity in the past few years. This is one way that we can show our appreciation for improving the way Kentucky state government operates. . . .[1]

---

1. In an earlier news conference in Frankfort on February 7, Jones announced that state government would raise the minimum rates on the salary schedule for all employees who fell in grades 4 through 9 and that all employees in grade 3 would be raised to grade 4. Over 4,700 state employees would receive raises as a result of the new policy—at a cost of approximately $3.8 million.

CHR NEWS CONFERENCE
Frankfort / October 19, 1995

ONE of the top priorities of this administration has been to be a people-oriented administration, to be fair to all Kentuckians, and to correct inadequacies where they occur. Today, we are here to correct another problem. As you may know, the state's family service workers are underpaid and overworked. They work hard day after day under extremely stressful and sometimes dangerous circumstances, and they do not receive the pay, the thanks, and the recognition they deserve.

That is why we are announcing that we will raise the salaries of those workers by 16 percent, up two full salary grades. In addition, we will hire another sixty social workers to help with the caseload. There is a temptation to try to throw lots of money and people at this situation. However, we feel this is the responsible approach—to adequately pay those who have carried the load and to hire a reasonable number of people to join the existing social workers in the field. This way, we can retain more of our existing social workers.

We also can hire enough qualified people in an orderly fashion to ease a critical shortage, then further evaluate the situation to better determine our needs for the future. Quite simply, this is the right and the fair thing to do. These men and women who are currently working need our support. The families in Kentucky who need help deserve the best qualified and most highly trained social workers available. And because of our downsizing of state government and our job-creation efforts, we can afford to do it. . . .

REVENUE SETTLEMENT NEWS CONFERENCE
Frankfort / November 13, 1995

I AM extremely pleased to announce today that the Commonwealth of Kentucky has agreed to the settlement of a class-action lawsuit over the valuation of used motor vehicles for property taxation. Today at 11:00 a.m. in Franklin Circuit Court we anticipate that Judge Graham[1] will sign the agreed-upon settlement and bring this lawsuit to a close. The net result will mean a tax cut of $24 million for Kentuckians who own used motor vehicles.

Under the terms of the settlement, beginning in January, motor vehicles will be valued at the midpoint between retail and trade-in values set by the *NADA Official Used Car Guide*, thus providing a tax cut for all used motor vehicle owners in the Commonwealth. This settlement and the midpoint valuation will cause some revenue loss to the state and local governments. However, the terms of the settlement are in the best interest of both the taxpayer and the Commonwealth because they will give the taxpayers a break without jeopardizing local services that depend on the money generated by this tax.

No refunds for past years will be granted under the terms of the settlement, which is especially good news for the state and for local governments which operate without any surplus and could not afford to pay such a refund. I am very pleased that we were able to resolve this case before leaving office without spending years of the taxpayers' time and money pursuing this lawsuit. I commend Secretary Burse and her staff for handling this in such a professional and efficient manner. I will now turn the podium over to her for her comments.

---

1. William Graham (1949–), 48th circuit judge, 2nd division, Franklin County.

TOURISM AND RECREATION

REMARKS FOR AUDUBON GROUND BREAKING
Henderson / May 16, 1992

I AM honored to be here today to take part in a ceremony that marks an exciting new chapter in the long history of John James Audubon State Park. As we prepare to break ground, it is important that we remind ourselves of the significance of the treasures that we are preserving for future generations in the name of a man who is synonymous with the preservation of nature. Here in Henderson there is housed one of the world's largest and most complete collections of Audubon artifacts, including important works of art, letters, journals, and personal possessions. Much of this collection is on loan through the generosity of Audubon descendants, who have chosen to keep these priceless works here, despite efforts by world-class museums elsewhere to obtain them. For that we are blessed and greatly complimented.

Other parts of the Audubon collection are owned by the state itself, so all Kentuckians have a stake in ensuring the preservation of these artifacts. This museum is unique in the world. This is the only place where an important collection is displayed on the very ground where he once lived and wandered the woods. The works include "The Birds of America" folio, one of only one hundred copies still intact. The museum also boasts the world's largest collection of oil paintings by Audubon and his sons. This museum also houses journals and letters that illuminate the life of this fascinating naturalist and artist.

Each year, scholars come here from throughout the world to learn more about one of Kentucky's most famous residents. A world-class collection deserves a world-class facility, and that is exactly what the renovated museum will be. These valuable artifacts will be displayed in an attractive, accessible setting so that everyone, young and old alike, can enjoy the collection. Moreover, visitors will have the opportunity to get a taste of the abundance of wildlife during Audubon's time as they explore a new nature center.

Not all of the improvements here at Audubon will be as visible as the museum and the new nature center. The park has hired the museum's first professional curator and an arts programming specialist. The new staff will continue and enhance the operation of the museum in the most professional manner.

In summary, Audubon Museum, I am told, is destined to join the ranks of the best small museums in this country. For that, much of the credit goes to the local leadership here, including members of the General Assembly who allocated the funding for this project. And this is only the beginning. Audubon is an excellent example of a facility that became the focus of our best efforts and was upgraded after more than fifty years in operation. And, as most of you know, it is my intent to return our state parks to the pre-eminent position they once held, to become again the "nation's finest park system."

In the legislative session, at my request, the General Assembly authorized a $100 million bond issue to upgrade state parks. I consider this bond issue to have been one of the major achievements of our administration thus far, because it will help ensure that tourism retains its ranking as the state's third-largest industry, for the betterment of Kentucky's economy.

In closing, I want to say that this administration is committed to joining a strong partnership dedicated to preserving Kentucky's history, its arts, its entire cultural heritage. During this, our bicentennial year, there can be no more important mission. So let this ground breaking symbolize the start of not just one project, as important as it is. Let it stand for a new beginning in which leaders in all walks of life in Kentucky work together to preserve what is unique about our state, for the benefit of this generation and generations to come.

KENTUCKY TOURISM COUNCIL
Louisville / October 28, 1992

[GREETINGS] I wanted to be here so that I could tell each and every one of you how important you are to the economy of Kentucky. Imagine Kentucky's economy without the $5.3 billion that this industry generates, without the 132,000 jobs that tourism supports, without the $373 million in state and local tax revenues that are created by tourism spending. These figures all add up to one central idea—tourism is economic development. And in today's changing economy, tourism must move to the forefront as one of the keys to Kentucky's future economic strength. Of course, tourism differs from other industries in depending so heavily on marketing.

The competition for the tourism dollar grows year by year. That's why this administration is so strongly committed to developing strategic approaches to our marketing that are focused, cost effective, and progressive. This afternoon, Secretary Luallen and our advertising agency, Creative Alliance, gave you an overview of the new marketing strategy:

1. You saw a new approach to public-private partnerships.
2. You saw new strategies for niche marketing and the timing of our advertising.
3. You saw a new merchandising program that has promotional as well as revenue-producing value.
4. And you saw our dynamic, new, creative approach.

I have to tell you that I'm really excited about the campaign. I'm especially pleased that this strategy is a platform for new partnerships with some of Kentucky's leading companies. This truly is a win-win situation in a time of tight state dollars. The Commonwealth benefits from enjoying more advertising reach. Our partnership benefits from having a great product to sell: Kentucky.

I want to take this opportunity to publicly thank Toyota Motor Manufacturing Company for the exposure they have given Kentucky by featuring the state in materials in Japan for the new Scepter station wagon. This is a great promotion, and we truly appreciate Toyota's involvement. I also want to thank Ford Motor Company for agreeing to take part in next season's "Explore Kentucky" sweepstakes. This is an exciting program that will showcase both the

Kentucky-made Explorer and Kentucky-made vacations while dramatically extending the reach of our budget.

This campaign was based not only on extensive research, but also on what we've been hearing from you, because we know how important it is to have a campaign that works for the entire tourism industry. I sincerely believe that this campaign is truly "what you've been looking for." As important as marketing is to tourism, there's another critical area that I don't believe has been adequately addressed until now and that is tourism development. The competition is stronger than ever for the tourism dollar. It is vitally important that Kentucky provide adequate facilities for the increased tourism visitation that we seek. Today's traveler is more demanding than ever before. Today's traveler expects to have a variety of choices in top-quality accommodations, attractions, restaurants, and all other facilities.

During this administration, we want to lay the groundwork for long-range tourism development to guarantee that Kentucky offers that variety of choices. We have already demonstrated our administration's commitment in this area. As you know, last winter, I made a commitment to the state park system. Even at a time of a tight state budget, it was a commitment that I felt was absolutely essential to the future well-being of the tourism industry. That commitment is the largest single renovation of the Kentucky state park system in its sixty-year history.

I can't tell you how pleased I was that the General Assembly agreed to my request for a $100 million bond issue for state parks. I saw that years of inadequate maintenance had robbed Kentucky's state park system of its status as the finest in the nation. I knew that we couldn't allow this to continue. Our parks are too important as tourism facilities, too important as catalysts for private tourism development, and too important as valuable community resources.

This is something that has never been done before. No governor has ever looked carefully at our entire state system and said that we could no longer stand by and watch the gradual decline of our parks. I am proud that we have taken this step. Over the past several months, staff in the Department of Parks and the Tourism Cabinet have undertaken a thorough review of the park system's needs. When the special session is called, I will be presenting a list of proposed projects, based on critical priorities.

First and foremost, we want to renovate the state resort park lodges. Our resort parks are the things that set us apart from other park systems. As you all know, all of our park lodges are at least twenty years old, and some are more than forty years old. They desperately need to be renovated and modernized. Our second priority will be infrastructure needs. Sometimes, these are the less visible but vitally important facilities, like a sewer system at Lake Barkley or improvements to the Levi Jackson campground. We have an aging infrastructure throughout our parks, from electrical systems to marinas. Our third priority is the enhancement of our parks through the construction of new park facilities. An example would be a new interpretive center at one of our historic sites or expansion of needed meeting space to address the changing needs of our visitors.

The Department of Parks is ready to go on this massive undertaking as soon as the General Assembly approves the projects. And at the end of our administration, we will have a park system that once again is second to none in the entire nation, in the entire world. Aside from improvements to the park system, I am committed to finding ways to support future tourism-development projects. I will be asking all the state agencies that have an existing or potential role in the development of tourism facilities to come together and look at our statewide tourism needs. We want to review all the state and federal resources that might be used for tourism development. We want to determine the role that state government can take in working with the private sector on proposed projects.

Just as we forged partnerships on the marketing side, we want to forge partnerships on the development side. I pledge to you tonight that during this administration, state government will develop a pro-active approach to serving as a catalyst for tourism development. By doing so, we will be setting the stage for long-term, substantive results in tourism. It is the emphasis on addressing long-term needs that is a hallmark of the administration.

This is certainly true in health-care reform. Our goal is both simple and incredibly complex. It is to see to it that every Kentuckian will have access to affordable, quality health care. This is a goal that no one person, no one organization, can achieve individually. It is a goal that all of us must cooperatively work toward, together. That is why I hope all of you support our efforts to resolve the questions remaining and become part of the solution to the crisis of health care.

Another goal that will yield long-term results is political reform. I'm referring to the constitutional amendments that will be on the ballot next Tuesday. These amendments represent positive, progressive change. They will allow state government to become more effective in working for the benefit of all Kentuckians. I hope you will give these amendments all due consideration.

In closing, I want to congratulate the Kentucky Tourism Council and its entire membership for all of your contributions to the quality of life and the economic vitality of Kentucky. I want you to know that I strongly support this industry. I believe in its future, and I pledge to give you our continuing commitment to do everything we can to help tourism reach its full potential.

NATIONAL TOURISM WEEK KICKOFF
Bullitt County Welcome Center / May 3, 1993

IT'S a real pleasure for me to be here today to kick off Kentucky's celebration of National Tourism Week. All throughout the nation, events like this one are being held to spotlight the enormous economic value of travel and tourism. Today, I'm pleased to announce that the tourism industry is thriving in Kentucky, and we have the numbers to prove it. I want to share with you the results of the 1992 Tourism Economic Impact Study conducted by the Kentucky Department of Travel Development.

This study was the result of a survey of more than six hundred Kentucky travel businesses and interviews with more than nine thousand travelers. During 1992, total tourism spending in Kentucky grew to nearly $5.7 billion. This represents an annual increase of 4.3 percent, after inflation. The study shows that tourism also grew in terms of employment in Kentucky. During 1992, an estimated 154,000 Kentuckians owed their jobs to the spending that tourism attracted. These figures mean that tourism remains the state's third-largest industry in expenditures and its second-largest employer.

I am also pleased to announce that tourism spending created more than $423 million in state and local taxes in 1992. This is an increase of about $30 million when compared to 1991. As governor, I have been a strong supporter of tourism. I have seen tourism grow steadily year by year over the past decade, at a time of great challenges to some of our other prominent industries. As important as tourism is today to the overall economic health of our state, it is an industry that has enormous potential for future growth here in Kentucky. In this administration, we have moved forcefully to help fulfill that enormous potential, to find ways of getting the most impact from our tourism investment. We have forged new partnerships with the private sector to undertake innovative marketing approaches.

For example, we joined with Ford Motor Company, SuperAmerica stores, and Coleman Equipment Company on a sweepstakes contest involving the Ford Explorer, made here in Kentucky. We also cooperated with a promotion that featured Kentucky travel scenes in marketing material supporting the sale of the Kentucky-made Toyota Camry station wagon in Japan. This promotion was undertaken by Toyota at no cost to the state.

With these innovative partnerships, we are doubling the value of our advertising budget. My commitment to tourism can also be seen in improvements to state tourism facilities. Later this year, I will be calling a special session for legislative approval of a $100 million bond issue to finance improvement at state parks. This bond issue will underwrite the most comprehensive renovation of state parks in the park system's sixty-year history.

I want to thank the members of the General Assembly for their support of Kentucky state parks. In approving the bond issue, the legislature demonstrated its commitment to restoring our state parks to the nation's finest park system. I also look forward to later this year holding ribbon-cutting ceremonies at the Kentucky Fair and Exposition Center for the $25 million expansion of the south wing. This addition will give the fairgrounds one million square feet of exhibit space under a roof, making Louisville one of the top-five convention cities in the entire country.

This new state facility here at Shepherdsville also plays an important part in the overall tourism picture. There is a reason that we chose this welcome center for the opening event of Kentucky Tourism Week. We came here because we wanted to show the huge existing and potential tourism impact of motorists. Each year, millions of motorists travel our interstate highways on trips through Kentucky, but these fifty million business and vacation travelers represent an enormous untapped market. We want them to stop here in Kentucky and decide to stay a night or two. So it is critical that we provide as many opportunities as possible to influence these visitors.

That is why this administration, under the leadership of Transportation Secretary Don Kelly,[1] has constructed two new welcome centers, including this wonderful facility here and one in Christian County. This state-of-the-art facility reflects a new standard of design for all future welcome centers. It was built with sensitivity to the requirements of the Americans with Disabilities Act. And, as you can see, its style reflects the rich southern history of Kentucky. This welcome center was built at a cost of $3.7 million in combined federal and state funds. For Kentucky, it is a wise investment in tourism.

Each year, countless thousands of motorists who may have never visited Kentucky before will stop here and will be greeted by friendly travel hosts in this beautiful building. In tourism, we all know that first impressions are lasting impressions. And with such a positive impression of our state, many of these visitors are certain to decide to spend some of their time and money here in Kentucky. Throughout Kentucky, we now have seven attractive welcome centers where staff from the Department of Travel Development provide information to motorists about things to see and do in Kentucky. In addition to the Tourism Economic Impact numbers that we have announced today, we are also unveiling a new marketing tool that we are trying out here in our welcome centers.

It is a state-of-the-art interactive video system that combines the familiar visitor information listings with exciting videos and an advanced mapping system. If you want to know more about Derby, you get far more than a written description. You get to actually see a Derby race by calling up a video. Then, you can see a map that leads you straight to Churchill Downs. As we will show you, this system is designed to engage people, and to give them the information they need to make travel decisions. We will be evaluating this system over the next six months, and we look forward to seeing the results. If it proves to be an effective tool for tourism, we will work to install these in more locations.

I mentioned partnerships a moment ago. I should point out that this video system represents a partnership between the Transportation Cabinet and the Tourism Cabinet. They are sharing in the cost of this demonstration project. As an added feature to this system, the tourism cabinet has worked with the Kentucky Hotel-Motel Association to provide an on-the-spot telephone reservation service at the seven welcome centers. This feature, which is very successful in other states, makes this interactive system even more valuable to visitors.

In closing, I want to say that we're excited about tourism's role in Kentucky's future. This administration is committed to doing everything it can to develop and nurture this vital industry.

---

1. Don C. Kelly (1942–), born Clarksville, Arkansas; B.S., M.S., University of Kentucky; certificate in transportation management, University of Mississippi; Kentucky Department of Highways, 1967–75; state transportation planning engineer, Kentucky Department of Transportation, 1975–80; associate professor of engineering technology, Murray State University, 1980–86; deputy secretary, Kentucky Commerce

Cabinet, 1986–88; vice-president, Schimpeler-Corradino Associates, 1988–91; program manager, University of Kentucky Transportation Center, 1991; Kentucky secretary of transportation, 1991–95; vice-president for transportation systems development, Jordan, Jones & Goulding, 1996– .

FORT BOONESBOROUGH POOL DEDICATION
Boonesborough / August 10, 1993

IT'S an honor for me to be here on such an exciting day for Fort Boonesborough and the entire region. We are here to celebrate the completion of an important project for Fort Boonesborough's future and to announce the start of another. Today, we are dedicating a wonderful new swimming pool. This complex represents the state of the art in design and operation. More importantly, it is a valuable community resource for the residents of Madison and Clark Counties and for the entire central Kentucky area.

We all know that our state parks play a crucial role in the state's third-largest industry, tourism. Visitors to Kentucky state parks account for $250 million in total tourism spending. Our state parks comprise eight of the state's top twenty tourism attractions. Fort Boonesborough is an example of a popular state park. Each year, more than 550,000 people visit here. But today, we are reminded that our state parks are not only magnets for travelers, they are also valuable community residents, just like this beautiful new pool.

This pool has the overwhelming support of the area, as the numbers clearly show. In the first month of operation, an average of 750 people a day have passed through the gates. This pool is tangible proof to the value of strong partnerships between state government, legislators, and civic leaders. Without such a cooperative partnership, this project would not have been possible. Throughout the years, the park system has added new facilities as recreational needs have been identified. This pool illustrates such a demonstrated need. At the same time, for a variety of reasons, maintenance support for the park system has not kept pace with the huge increase in usage.

That's why I appreciate the support of the General Assembly for a $100 million bond issue to renovate the park system. The improvements that this bond issue will underwrite will produce benefits for decades to come. I'm also pleased to announce today a new project that will benefit Fort Boonesborough and will serve as an important new attraction of statewide significance. In recent months, a multiagency committee has been reviewing applications for transportation enhancement grants from an innovative, new federal program known as "Ice-tea" [ISTEA] or the Intermodal Surface Transportation Efficiency Act. This committee was composed of representatives of the cabinets for Transportation, Education, Arts and Humanities, and Tourism, as well as the Department of Local Government.

Late last week, I reviewed the committee's recommendations. I am pleased to announce today that Fort Boonesborough will receive $800,000 in federal funds to develop a Kentucky River Museum on the land adjacent to lock 10 here at Fort Boonesborough. This federal grant must be matched with 20 percent state or local funding. The property will be transferred from the Kentucky River Authority, which is obtaining the land from the federal government. This exciting new museum will be operated by the Department of Parks. The Kentucky Heritage Council, which prepared the application for this project, will work closely with parks in its design and development. This unique museum and its offices will be located in the two houses that served as home of the lockmaster and assistant lockmaster.

Five other outbuildings also will be restored, so that visitors can tour the entire complex. The story of this river and its role in the growth of Kentucky has never been told until now. So I'm very pleased to announce this new project. The Kentucky River Museum will serve as an outstanding educational and tourism resource for Madison and Clark Counties. It will also enhance the area's economic growth by providing jobs as it is developed and operated.

I am pleased to announce today that forty-five applications have been funded through ISTEA for various projects that enhance our transportation system. These grants must be matched with 20 percent state or local funds. These grants total $10.7 million.

You may recall that Kentucky and the town of Perryville became a model in Civil War battlefields through this program. Today, we will add forty-five projects to the list. They include a wide range of projects such as the Historic Preservation Project here at Fort Boonesborough and scenic beautification of pedestrian trails. These grants benefit thirty-five counties in every region of the state.

I am pleased that Kentucky has moved aggressively to take advantage of this project. The improvements that these grants will help underwrite will have a lasting benefit for future generations of Kentuckians. In closing, I want to pledge my continued support for

Fort Boonesborough and the entire state park system. We look forward to working with all of you to ensure a bright future for your Kentucky state parks.

VISIT KENTUCKY USA VIDEO
Frankfort / September 1993

AS GOVERNOR of the great state of Kentucky, it is my pleasure to invite you to our state. Kentucky boasts beautiful bluegrass and handsome horses, relaxing parks and recreational facilities, and vibrant cities filled with exciting entertainment.

Kentucky sits right at the heart of our country's interstate highway network and has its own international airport. Discover the beauty and charm of Kentucky, what you've been looking for![1]

---

1. Jones was also featured in a series of radio ads promoting Kentucky State Parks and Resorts in March, April, August, September, and October 1993.

PARKS BOND ANNOUNCEMENT
General Butler State Park, Carrollton / December 6, 1993

THE Kentucky parks system has long been considered the crown jewel of all the state park systems in this country. But over the years, wear and tear have dulled the luster of this jewel. Today, I'm here to tell you, we plan to bring back the brilliance. I am announcing the details of a $100 million bond issue I have recommended to the General Assembly to renovate and improve the Kentucky parks system. This money will ensure that we retain the finest system in America. But it will also shore up the foundation of Kentucky's third-largest industry, tourism, and the 7,500 jobs that our resort parks alone provide. The seventy-one projects I am recommending to the General Assembly will ensure that this foundation remains strong for years to come.

We've studied the needs of the parks system and the opportunities for improvement for months, and they fall into three categories:

1. renovating park lodges,
2. improving the parks' infrastructure,
3. and enhancing existing parks.

Let me tell you first about improving our lodges. The extensive network of lodges we have in Kentucky is unique in the entire nation. No other state can boast of having fifteen resort parks with lodges. But the fact is, they are getting older, and they simply must be renovated to make sure their quality is such that people keep coming back to enjoy all that they have to offer.

We must also improve our parks' infrastructure, such as the water, sewer, and electrical systems, because of the ever-increasing demands on our park facilities. Finally, by enhancing our more-developed parks through expansion, we see tremendous potential for future growth that will produce even more revenue for the parks system and the communities our parks serve. Quite frankly, we look at a better parks system as an investment in a strong Kentucky economy. We asked Dr. Charles Haywood[1] and the University of Kentucky Center for Business and Economic Research to conduct an economic-impact study of our state parks. What they found was nothing short of amazing. According to the study, our resort parks alone injected more than $294 million into the state's economy last year, while supporting 7,500 jobs. The study also points out that the new construction we are proposing will have a significant impact on local economies. Every $1 million we spend on construction will produce about $2.4 million worth of economic output, $708,000 in earnings and thirty-eight new jobs.

From time to time, Libby and I take a weekend off and go to one of our state parks. We love the way we are treated, and we enjoy all that our parks have to offer. We want all Kentuckians, as well as people from the world over, to experience all the wonderful and varied things that our state parks have to offer. In closing, I want to extend my heartfelt thanks to the Kentucky General Assembly for its continuing support of our Kentucky state parks. Kentuckians are fortunate to be represented by lawmakers who understand the value of our parks. I look forward to working with them as they review and act on our recommendations. I truly believe that this

$100 million bond issue will ensure that our parks system, the nation's finest, retains the pre-eminent position it has earned.

---

1. Charles Haywood (1927–), B.A., Berea College; M.A., Duke University; Ph.D., University of California, Berkeley; dean, College of Business and Economics, University of Kentucky, 1965–75; secretary of development, Kentucky, 1973; professor of economics and finance, University of Kentucky, 1975–93; National City Bank Professor of Finance, 1993–present.

KENTUCKY FAIR AND EXPOSITION CENTER
Louisville / May 16, 1994

I'M PLEASED to be here today to help spotlight one of the shining lights of Kentucky's economy, tourism. I'm especially happy to be joined by a special guest who came here from Washington to take part in our observance of National Tourism Week. We are honored that Greg Farmer, the under-secretary of commerce for travel and tourism, has taken time from his busy schedule to be here today to help us draw attention to the economic strength of Kentucky's tourism industry.

I have two messages to bring to you today. One is that tourism is a growing force in Kentucky's economy. The other is that, with wise investment, tourism can and will do even better. I am pleased to announce today the results of the annual economic impact survey conducted by the Department of Travel Development in the state Tourism Cabinet. These figures come as a pleasant surprise because 1993 was widely viewed as a year of modest growth throughout the nation. So I am especially glad to announce that total tourism spending in Kentucky last year rose to $6.8 billion. This represents an increase of 9.4 percent over 1992's adjusted total. This tourism spending supported some 143,000 jobs for Kentuckians, an increase of 4,000 jobs over the revised 1992 total.

Tourism also continued to be a strong source of state and local tax revenues. In 1993, some $520 million in taxes was generated by travel spending. This includes $443 million in state taxes and $77 million in local taxes. Here in Jefferson County, direct tourism spending amounted to almost $892 million. This is an increase of 10.3 percent over 1992. This spending supported over 21,000 jobs in 1993. When you add it all up, Kentucky tourism showed outstanding success as an economic force in 1993.

And we are confident that tourism will thrive in the future, especially if we take steps now to provide the kind of facilities that can help us remain competitive in the marketplace. A perfect example of what I'm referring to is the Commonwealth Convention Center. I want to be clear on what the convention center expansion means to Kentucky's economy. The expansion means money and jobs. It's important to consider what this wonderful facility and the downtown convention center, both operated by the State Fair Board, mean to our state's economy. These two facilities attract direct spending of nearly $142 million a year. When you add in the indirect benefit, that total comes to $250 million.

In the past few years, we have recognized the enormous economic benefits of the Fair and Exposition Center and the importance of maintaining it as a world-class facility. That is why we made a wise investment in building this wonderful south wing, so that the Fair and Exposition Center now has one million square feet of exhibit space under one roof. This expansion allows the fairgrounds to compete for some of the nation's largest conventions and trade shows. It was an investment that took into account the competitive forces at play in the convention business. Aging facilities simply can't compete on an equal footing with larger, more modern facilities. And because of our investment here, the community and the state are already receiving increased economic benefits. Sixteen years ago, the Commonwealth Convention Center downtown was a fine facility, and it has served us well over the years. But it is time to act to protect our investment, to provide a modern facility that has sufficient space for today's needs, not the needs of the 1970s. After sixteen years, we must either upgrade this facility or say goodbye to tens of millions of dollars in lost convention business. A survey by the Louisville Convention and Visitors Bureau estimates that in the past three years, the convention center lost eighteen conventions representing a total economic impact of $4.5 million. Past experience also can lead us to predict future bookings. It is estimated that there are forty-one conventions considering coming here in the next ten years, but only if the center is expanded. Those conventions represent potential revenue totaling $140 million.

When you add it all up, this expansion will yield additional spending totaling $50 million a year and it will support sixteen hundred new jobs. The improvements to the convention center will require an annual state appropriation of $2.4 million. But the annual return in tax revenues comes to $4 million. Now if *that's* not good business, I don't know what is. This expansion will double the exhibit space of the center, and will add meeting rooms and other facilities. And it will also make the convention center more visually appealing, because the project includes redesign of the existing façade.

In summary, this project is going to yield an outstanding return on investment. And best of all, it's an investment shared by out-of-state visitors who will be paying the room tax that will cover half of the total $50 million project. Mayor Abramson, County Judge-Executive Armstrong, the Downtown Development Corporation, and the Louisville Convention and Visitors Bureau have all been important partners in this effort.

I know many of you here are also excited about the benefits of the other capital construction projects in Jefferson County. We're working hard to make these projects come to pass. The University of Louisville deserves an outstanding facility for an outstanding football team. Fifteen million dollars already has been raised privately. We will work to get the state funding restored for the new stadium; just $666,000 annually will create a $50 million facility. Those of you here who also understand how important the U of L Medical Research Building is to the area's quality of life have an ally in Frankfort. With our proposed budget, that building will be constructed, with a $1.4 million annual appropriation from the state.

Louisville needs a court complex that can meet present-day needs. If my recommendations are approved, that building will soon be serving this community, with a modest contribution of $500,000 from the state. And the Kentucky Center for the Arts is in need of $1 million for seating and lighting improvements. That bit of assistance from us can maintain world-class artists and performers. Now, I need your help and support in bringing these projects to completion. Let your representatives and senators know you support these investments in your community. Help us help you.

NATIONAL TOURISM WEEK LUNCHEON
Louisville / May 16, 1994

I WANT you all to know how happy I am to be taking part in this celebration of Kentucky tourism. I want to thank each of you for your role in supporting Kentucky's economy. The strength of the tourism industry is its people, outstanding professionals such as you, who provide the leadership for the state's third-largest industry. Just a few moments ago, I shared with the news media wonderful news on the impact of Kentucky tourism in 1993.

Those numbers bear repeating now. Tourism during 1993 grew to a $6.8 billion industry. That represents an increase of 9.4 percent over 1992, after adjusting for inflation. Tourism also continued to be a major employer in 1993. Tourism spending supported 143,000 jobs last year. And as you might expect, the impact of tourism on tax revenues also was substantial. In all, $520 million in taxes were generated by tourism expenditures in 1993. This includes $443 million in state taxes and $77 million in local taxes. The message that these numbers carry is clear: tourism is critical to Kentucky's economy.

At a time when other Kentucky industries are facing unprecedented challenges, tourism continues to grow and prosper. As we look at tourism's future, it is important that we commit ourselves to providing the quality facilities and infrastructure that today's demanding business and leisure travelers expect. This beautiful new south wing is an excellent example of the kind of facility that is needed to attract tourism dollars. We were pleased to have completed this expansion so that the Kentucky Fair and Exposition Center could remain one of the nation's outstanding convention facilities.

A few moments ago in our news conference, I also talked about the Commonwealth Convention Center. This is another facility that we need to invest in so that it can reach its potential as a downtown convention [center]. Expanding the convention center will bring in $50 million in new revenue and result in sixteen hundred jobs. If any of you happened to notice the bus parked outside today, you know that I have a job to do Tourism Week. I have to spread the word about the importance of the $100 million parks revitalization project.

From now through Saturday, Secretary Crit Luallen, Parks Commissioner Mark Lovely,[1] my staff, and I will be visiting parks all around Kentucky to talk to the people about our proposed park improvements. These are their state parks, and they have a right to know what we want to do. Many of you here in this room understand how critical our parks are to the overall tourism economy. You know that our parks attract travelers from all over the country and that those visitors spend money throughout our tourism economy. A recent University of Kentucky study shows that spending by resort park visitors totals $176 million. Here's how that spins out into Kentucky businesses. Nearly $142 million of the $176 million goes directly to businesses that are not part of the state parks system. The spending at parks also generates nearly $33 million in taxes. And it translates into 8,200 jobs.

Those figures add urgency to our mission this week. We must invest in our parks, so that we can restore the luster of what was once the finest park system in the nation. I will be traveling to parks from Gilbertsville to Greenup this week to spread the message that our state parks must be saved. I know you share my commitment and concern. And as we make these stops, I would invite you to join us as we highlight the growing economic importance of tourism and the critical need to renovate our state parks. Your presence at the news conferences we'll hold at the parks is important, because it underscores the strong support we have all across Kentucky for the tourism industry. I hope I see all of you again this week, as we hit the road to save our state parks. I congratulate you on the work you do to promote Kentucky, and I thank you for your support.

---

1. Mark Lovely (1933–), Kentucky State Parks commissioner from 1991 to 1996.

HISTORY CENTER NEWS CONFERENCE
Frankfort / May 23, 1994

I'D LIKE to offer my thanks to the Franklin County High School Band for the marvelous music they've been providing. It's appropriate that they and so many other students are here today. That's because this proposed History Center will help further their education and, for that matter, the education of all people in Kentucky. In addition, it will greatly help the economy of this region and this Commonwealth. And any time you can improve education and the economy in Kentucky at the same time, you've really accomplished something.

As you know, I have spent the last week traveling throughout the state, explaining the importance of tourism and our state parks system. And as we rode our bus throughout the state, Tourism Cabinet Secretary Crit Luallen shared some incredible facts with me on just how much Kentucky depends on tourism.

Total tourism spending in Kentucky for last year totaled $6.8 billion, a healthy 9.2 percent increase over 1992. And, as you well know, the economy in this area relies heavily on tourism. Here in Franklin County, tourism and travel added $57.6 million to the local economy last year and accounted for nearly 1,250 jobs.

We are fortunate that so many people come to see the beauty of our state capital, and we're confident that they get their money's worth. But we think it is important to be able to provide more for them to see. And we'd like to attract more visitors. And that's part of why the Kentucky History Center is crucial to the growth and development of tourism in Kentucky.

The Kentucky Historical Society says more than 110,000 people, including 50,000 schoolchildren, come each year to see the Old State Capitol, the Kentucky History Museum, the Kentucky Military History Museum, or to use the research library. And those people spend $4.2 million a year. However, the estimates are that the proposed Kentucky History Center will triple the number of tourists who come through here each year. And instead of spending $4.2 million, they would spend three times that, nearly $12.9 million a year. And all that for a state investment of just over $1.6 million a year over the life of a twenty-year bond issue.

But I think even more important than the economic benefit is the educational benefit that this History Center will have for our young people. Did you know that right now, more than 90 percent of the artifacts that the Kentucky Historical Society has are hidden from public view because there's no place to display them? How can a young person learn about Kentucky's history if 90 percent of that history is packed away?

This Kentucky History Center will provide young people—in fact, all Kentuckians—with a state-of-the-art "hands-on" museum experience. It will triple exhibition and collection space so more artifacts can be collected and displayed. It will provide environmentally safe storage conditions for historical items, so they won't be damaged further by time. And it will upgrade the educational facilities and programs, in keeping with standards set by the

Kentucky Education Reform Act.

Our students have come so far in the early stages of the Kentucky Education Reform Act. Schools are improving against the most rigorous statewide testing system in the nation. Our students are improving their thinking and writing skills. In short, they are doing their part. We must do ours.

This History Center is an investment in the intellectual capital of our students. And it's an investment that we cannot afford to delay. I am asking each of you to talk with your legislators and others throughout the state. Please let them know that this History Center makes sense in economic terms. And it makes sense in educational terms. Help us make the Kentucky History Center become a reality.[1]

---

1. Jones gave related speeches promoting the $100 million bond issue to benefit tourism in Kentucky on May 16 in Henderson; on May 17 in Bardstown, Glasgow, and Gilbertsville; on May 19 in Slade, Hazard, and Prestonsburg; on May 20 in Pineville and Jamestown; and on May 21 in Yatesville and Greenup.

COLUMBUS-BELMONT DEDICATION
Columbus / July 25, 1994

IT'S A real pleasure for me to be here today in Hickman County to take part in this dedication ceremony, because this is an important day in the history of this park, and this park has a remarkable history. Columbus-Belmont is best known as one of Kentucky's most important Civil War sites. It was here that Confederate troops stretched a huge chain across the Mississippi River to keep Union gunboats from moving south. In fact, you've probably seen the anchor and a length of the chain that are on display here at the park. Gen. Ulysses S. Grant fought his first battle of the Civil War in this area.

Columbus-Belmont also is renowned for its natural beauty. This scenic overlook may be the most compelling view in the entire state, and nature lovers from all over come to enjoy it. And, of course, people come here for recreation: hiking, picnics, reunions, miniature golf, the museum, and community activities. Today, we gather to dedicate a new multipurpose building that will enhance recreation and provide outstanding facilities for meetings. The activities building features two conference rooms. The larger room can seat up to two hundred people and is outfitted with a video system, overhead projector, and other amenities. The second conference room can be used for groups of up to fifty people. The entire building complies with all requirements of the Americans with Disabilities Act.

We are especially proud that the design of this building has been integrated into the natural beauty of the site, through the use of wood siding and stone veneer. This building is an investment in the future of Hickman County and of western Kentucky. But our investment in Columbus-Belmont State Park does not end here. This project also includes the installation of four interpretive panels on the park grounds. These signs will tell visitors about the historic significance of Columbus-Belmont. We also will be investing $370,000 through the park's revitalization program to convert the old Civil War hospital building into a new museum.

In closing, I want to thank all of you for being here today. One of our park system's strongest assets is the support from local communities. And you can see that spirit of cooperation here today. Together, we are working to improve Kentucky, and I appreciate your support.

KENTUCKY STATE FAIR OPENING DAY CEREMONIES
Louisville / August 18, 1994

I'M HONORED to be here today to join you in celebrating the best of Kentucky. As we stand here today, I know I can say without fear of contradiction that inside this "Circle of Champions" is located the best state fair in America. And one of the most important reasons for that is the outstanding quality of its staff. I want to take a moment to congratulate Harold Workman and his staff for their hard work throughout the year to produce this wonderful event.

This Kentucky State Fair is many things to many people. First and foremost it is the source of a lot of fun and recreation for the people of Kentucky; it's a chance to see so many of the good things Kentucky has to offer. From Kentucky Kingdom and the Midway, to the exhibits, to the horse shows, to the concerts, there is something for everyone here at the fair.

The Kentucky State Fair also means money for the tourism industry. That's important because our tourism industry means so much to Kentucky. It's an industry that accounted for total spending last year of $6.8 billion. Moreover, the tourism industry supports 143,000 jobs. And the tourism industry provides state and local tax revenues totaling $520 million. There are many reasons why the tourism industry is so strong in Kentucky. One of the most important is the facility right here. The Kentucky Fair and Exposition Center is an outstanding resource for all Kentuckians. And it is getting better all the time.

This administration has maintained a strong commitment to this complex. Just last year, we dedicated Phase II of the south wing expansion. It has been, and will continue to be, a great investment in our tourism economy. Because of the state-of-the-art facilities in the south wing, we have retained many nationally recognized shows that had outgrown the existing facilities. Projects such as the Phase II expansion and the new "Circle of Champions" will help make this state fair an even bigger and better event in the future.

Last year, the Kentucky State Fair set an all-time record for attendance with 677,000 people. We had a single-day record of more than 100,000. This year, with features such as the nationally recognized Native American exhibit, we plan to build on that success. In closing, I want to welcome all of you here from out of state. We hope you will return to Kentucky often. And to my fellow Kentuckians, thank you for supporting your Kentucky State Fair. You are extremely important inside our "Circle of Champions."

TOYOTA SWEEPSTAKES ANNOUNCEMENT
Georgetown / March 3, 1995

I THINK it's fitting that we are here at this wonderful new visitors center to announce an exciting new opportunity to promote Kentucky tourism. It's an innovative program that allows the people of the Commonwealth to get the absolute most for their tax dollars. Early in our administration, the leadership of the Tourism Cabinet developed a strategy to leverage our advertising dollars through partnerships with the private sector. These partnerships have resulted in promotional campaigns that have yielded outstanding exposure for Kentucky as a travel destination.

To understand why we consider this strategy to be so important, you should know that tourism has grown into a $6.8 billion industry in Kentucky. It also supports 143,000 jobs. Those figures make tourism the state's third-largest industry in economic impact and its second-largest employer. By joining with leading Kentucky companies, we have extended our advertising reach to stimulate tourism's continued growth. We believe that this new program, which we are kicking off today, will be every bit as exciting and successful as our previous campaigns.

Today, we mark the beginning of the "Kentucky Thoroughbred Sweepstakes." This campaign brings together Toyota Motor Manufacturing, Long John Silver's Seafood Restaurant, Churchill Downs, and the Commonwealth of Kentucky to promote Kentucky travel through a sweepstakes contest. The grand prize for this contest is a brand-new 1995 Camry just like the one right here and, of course, made right here in Georgetown. The prize package also includes four V.I.P. box seats for this year's Derby. Other prizes that will be awarded include a one-week vacation at a Kentucky state resort park and a one-week camping vacation at a state park with camping equipment provided by Coleman.

This campaign lasts from now through the end of April. The grand prize will be awarded to the lucky winner right here on May 4. At that time, the winner will pick up the keys to a new Camry, take a V.I.P. plant tour, and enjoy the sights here in the area. Then on Saturday, May 6, he or she will enjoy the most exciting two minutes in sports. Toyota is doing far more than simply providing us with an outstanding grand prize. Toyota will promote the campaign in more than $2 million worth of TV advertising over the next six weeks. In addition, one hundred Toyota dealers throughout this region will have contest displays with entry forms in their showrooms. The contest also will be promoted in $500,000 worth of TV advertising by Long John Silver's, and more than two hundred Long John Silver's restaurants will offer entry forms.

For our part, the Kentucky Department of Travel Development has placed ads in popular publications such as *Southern Living* magazine. And the Department of Parks will donate up to three thousand room nights for Toyota dealers as sales incentives during this promotion. In all, the state's participation comes to $200,000 or less, depending on the number of park room nights that are redeemed. By joining with corporate sponsors, the state's investment will be multiplied more than *tenfold*. This is a great return on our investment. Each contest entry will include a postcard to receive our 1995 official *Kentucky Vacation Guide*. We expect to receive more than fifty thousand entries, and we know that many of the contestants will send for the full-color vacation guide. As a result, we will be promoting Kentucky travel to a wide audience of potential visitors just in time for the summer vacation season.

This is an excellent example of how the public sector and private sector can work together for a common purpose. I want to thank Toyota, Long John Silver's, and Churchill Downs for taking part in this campaign. We are proud to join forces with these outstanding corporate citizens, and we look forward to a great campaign that will set the stage for a record-breaking summer travel season.[1]

---

1. Jones gave another tourism promotional speech on May 26 in Tokyo at the Kentucky reception and KFC presentation for corporate citizens. He announced that a toll-free phone number for people to call about Kentucky would be placed in all KFC restaurants in Japan.

WHITE HOUSE CONFERENCE ON TOURISM
Frankfort / June 8, 1995

I WANT to welcome all of you to Frankfort for this important conference. As you know, today signals Kentucky's participation in the first-ever White House conference on travel and tourism. We in Kentucky are excited to be taking part in this process. I want to express to Secretary [Greg] Farmer our heartfelt appreciation for his being here. We are honored to have the nation's ranking tourism official join us for our conference. I want you to know, Secretary Farmer, that we here in Kentucky appreciate the efforts of U.S.T.T.A. [United States Travel and Tourism Administration] in promoting the United States in the world tourism marketplace.

We in Kentucky have made great strides in opening up new markets in Japan, Great Britain, and Germany. In fact, I just returned from Japan, where we announced a new promotion in which KFC-

Japan will display Kentucky travel posters in more than one thousand KFC restaurants in Japan. There is no doubt that U.S.T.T.A. continues to play a critical role in our international marketing efforts. I know I speak for virtually everyone here today in saying that we strongly support U.S.T.T.A. and we urge Congress to continue to fund this important agency.

When President Clinton established a White House conference on travel and tourism and encouraged states to hold preliminary conferences, he sent a very powerful message. That message is: tourism *is* an industry, and it is big business throughout the United States. Here in Kentucky, that message was underscored a few weeks ago when I announced the results of our 1994 Tourism Economic-Impact Report. This report showed that tourism spending in Kentucky soared to $7.1 billion last year, an increase of $300 million over the year before. That means that tourism spending in Kentucky has grown for fourteen straight years. I can't think of another industry that has had such an outstanding record of growth. Tourism has grown to become the state's third-largest industry in value added to the economy.

Our study also showed that tourism now supports nearly 145,000 jobs for Kentuckians, making it the second-largest employer. All this economic activity has a huge impact on our state and local tax revenues. Those revenues, in turn, allow us to carry out our state tourism programs designed to attract more travelers. In fact, the study shows that tourism spending generated state and local taxes totaling $732 million last year. When you add it all up, tourism is a major player in Kentucky's economic-development picture.

During this administration, we have been pleased to carry out a number of initiatives to increase tourism business in Kentucky. On the development side, we were able to obtain funding for the most comprehensive renovation of our state park system in its sixty-plus-year history. We also completed Phase II of the south wing expansion at the Kentucky Fair and Exposition Center. And in marketing, we have carried out an ambitious program of public-private partnerships that has allowed us to leverage available promotional dollars. This initiative has resulted in the highest return on advertising investment ever experienced in the Department of Travel Development.

For every dollar we spent on advertising last year, our economy received $13.82 from travelers who responded to the advertising and subsequently visited Kentucky. But perhaps the most gratifying thing about our efforts to grow here in tourism has been the opportunity to work with all of you. You are the heart and soul of the tourism industry. It is your efforts to promote tourism at the local and regional level that has the most impact on tourism in Kentucky. Your energy, your experience, and your vision have blazed a trail to a bright new future for tourism in Kentucky.

Today, we take another important step on that journey. That's because today we become partners in a national dialogue on the future of tourism. As we examine issues such as the environment, infrastructure, and information technology, we are carrying out a process that is mirrored in virtually every state in the nation. And on October 30 and 31, the collective ideas from all of these state conferences will be presented and discussed at the White House conference. The end result will be a blueprint for growing the national tourism economy.

I can't think of a more exciting, productive undertaking. For my part, I want to express support for this process. I know that the delegates who will be representing Kentucky in Washington will do an outstanding job. And I look forward to learning about the outcome of the White House conference. I want to close by expressing my appreciation to all of you for your support of this administration. We look forward to working with all of you in the coming months. Again, thank you for being here today. And good luck with your conference.

DALE HOLLOW GROUND BREAKING
Dale Hollow Lake / June 14, 1995

I AM pleased to be here today to give you some exciting news about Dale Hollow State Park, news that many of you have waited decades to hear. As you know, a lodge for Dale Hollow State Park has been on the drawing boards for years. Well, the time has now come to get the lodge off the drawing boards and get it built. That's why today, we will break ground for a thirty-room resort lodge complex that will be built right here at Dale Hollow State Park. I can't think of any area of the state that has worked for so long to make a dream come true. This dream dates all the way back to the late 1960s, when the original master plan for Dale Hollow was completed.

The master plan envisioned a resort lodge as part of development of the park. But as you all know, funding was not obtained, and the lodge itself was never built. Then in 1990, the General Assembly approved bonds to build the lodge and the access road, and bonds were actually purchased. However, when the project came in over bid, we went back to the General Assembly in 1994 for more money to develop the lodge as planned. However, the extra money was not appropriated. I just could not accept that as the final outcome. After all, we had sold $6.5 million in bonds to develop the lodge, and we still had that money in the parks budget. We already had spent $300,000 to build the road that you are standing on. And we had already obtained a federal E.D.A. grant for $730,000 to build the infrastructure.

Just as important as our financial investment was the outstanding support of your local leaders in this project. I don't know any two people in the General Assembly who have worked harder for a park project than have Senator Williams[1] and Representative Mullinix.[2] They knew, as I did, that this lodge will be a magnet for economic activity in Clinton and Cumberland Counties and throughout this region. For example, we have economic-impact figures for Greenbo Resort Park, which is about the same size as the new lodge will be here. And based on those numbers, our data show that Dale Hollow will add three and a half million dollars into this economy each and every year.

What a shot in the arm that will be! Clinton and Cumberland Counties will benefit not only from the jobs maintained at the park, but also from the spin-off effect of tourism dollars. The money that travelers will spend will circulate to local laundries, retail stores, gas stations, and other businesses that will benefit from this park. When you add it all up, we estimate that the spending that will be attracted by the lodge will support nearly one hundred new jobs. We already know that on the state level, tourists spend $7.1 billion in Kentucky each year. Tourism supports nearly 145,000 jobs in the state each year, and it generates more than $731 million in state and local taxes.

Improving our tourism facilities in Kentucky just makes good sense, and building this lodge at Dale Hollow just makes good sense. I know that people around here sometimes feel that Frankfort doesn't listen to them. Well, this governor has been listening. I understand your need for this lodge. I share your view that it just didn't make sense to walk away from this investment. And if anyone had any doubt about the wisdom of putting a lodge here on this site, all you have to do is look behind me. You won't find any more beautiful scenery than what you see right back there. So to make this project happen, we went back to the drawing boards, literally.

We redesigned the project to make it work with the money we had available. We came up with a plan for a thirty-room lodge with a 150-seat dining room, as well as a swimming pool. We sent our requests for bids for the redesigned lodge and infrastructure, and they came back in under budget. So, today, we are able to officially break ground. Today, your dream comes true. I want to take this opportunity to express my appreciation to Senator Williams, Representative Mullinix, and all the other local leaders who have served as such strong, unified, bipartisan partners in this project. When I look back over some of this administration's achievements, I have to say that our commitment to the park system stands as one of the most significant.

We recognized the critical nature of our parks to our state's economy, and we recognized that our park system was slowly falling apart. So we made a major commitment to restore our parks to their standing as the nation's finest park system. Thanks to the efforts of Secretary Crit Luallen, Secretary Greg Ginter, Commissioner Mark Lovely, and his entire staff, we planned a massive renovation and succeeded in obtaining legislative support. We are now hard at work laying the groundwork for this $70 million, system-wide renovation. With the construction of Dale Hollow Lodge, we are underscoring our support for an outstanding park system that serves both a source of community pride and community revenue and jobs.

To all of you gathered here today, thank you for helping make this day possible. I look forward to coming back here as a private citizen in the fall of 1996 when this project is completed to see the new lodge complex and to again enjoy this wonderful view.

---

1. David L. Williams (1953–), B.A., University of Kentucky; J.D., University of Louisville; Kentucky house, 1985–86; Kentucky senate (16th district), 1986–present; Constitutional Review Commission, 1987; Republican Caucus chair, 1990; Commonwealth Advisory Committee, Lindsey Wilson College; elected Kentucky state senate president, 2000– ; *Who's What in Kentucky Government, 1999–2000.*

2. Ray Mullinix (1948–), broadcaster; Lindsey Wilson College; Chamber of Commerce; City-County Fair Board; Tourist Association; Kentucky Broadcasters Association; Economic Development Corp.; Republican, elected Kentucky house (53rd district), 1989; re-elected, 1990–94.

PLEASANT RETREAT GROUND BREAKING
Lancaster / August 24, 1995

I AM pleased to join you today to mark the beginning of a new era in the history of Pleasant Retreat, the home of Gov. William Owsley,[1] who so ably served the citizens of Kentucky in not just one but all three branches of government during his life. As we launch this effort to blend the old with the new in Garrard County, I think it's interesting to note that Governor Owsley played a prominent role in a notorious and controversial episode in Kentucky history when old and new clashed bitterly. The "old court/new court" dispute is a great chapter of Kentucky history that took place in the early 1820s, when he made his home here. So much of our history and heritage is fascinating, and this particular period was no exception.

In fact, these years were described as a time when the state found itself in what was called a "moral, political, and financial panic." It seems that the legislature came up with some fancy banking procedures to give some folks relief from their debts during tough economic times. Owsley, who was serving with two others on the court of appeals at that time, deemed the move unconstitutional. Despite their being called "tyrants and kings," pretty nasty stuff in that era, the members of the court held their ground. The legislature, in a move that I believe would be regarded as gutsy even in this day and time, passed a law to do away with this so-called "old court."

But the court declared that law unconstitutional as well. The issue was finally put before Kentucky voters in an election, and the "old court" party defeated the "new court" party by an overwhelming majority in the state house and eventually in the state senate. Owsley continued to serve on the bench until he resigned to go into private practice in 1828. As Kentuckians, we have a fascinating and rich history. Events like this make us pause to recollect some of the accounts that came before. It's this rich heritage that makes restoring homes such as Pleasant Retreat a living symbol of our Commonwealth and our nation when they were new. In times like these, we are reminded just how very much we can accomplish by working together.

Besides the public/private partnership you have forged to restore Pleasant Retreat, we are surrounded today by ongoing efforts to build a prosperous Garrard County for future generations. Business and residential growth are occurring right alongside continuing activity to restore downtown Lancaster and now Pleasant Retreat. I'd like to also take this opportunity to point out something that Governor Owsley and I have in common, yet another link between Kentucky history and present day. When William Owsley ran for governor of Kentucky in 1844, he was elected by the greatest majority of any other gubernatorial candidate up to that time. That's a modern-day record that our administration is proud to hold, and as we look at the closing months of our term, I am ever-mindful of the confidence that Kentuckians placed in me in 1991.

It is that confidence that has allowed us to accomplish so much in the last four years. I'm honored to join you on this special day. And I look forward to the day when Libby and I can visit this grand home and see it restored to its original splendor. By all accounts Governor Owsley is remembered as a popular and dedicated public servant to the citizens of Kentucky. I think he would be very pleased to know that the home where he lived when he contributed so much to our system of government is going to stand for future generations to enjoy.[2]

---

1. William Owsley (1782–1862), elected to the Kentucky house, 1809; appointed to the Kentucky Court of Appeals, 1810; elected to the Kentucky house, 1811; served a second time on the court of appeals, 1813–28; private practice, 1828–31; elected to the Kentucky house, 1831, and to the Kentucky senate, 1832; Kentucky secretary of state, 1834–36; governor of Kentucky, 1844–48. *Kentucky Encyclopedia* (Univ. Press of Kentucky, 1992), 702–3.

2. Jones gave other promotion of tourism speeches on August 17 and 18 at the Kentucky State Fair in Louisville.

STEARNS DEPOT
Stearns / September 1, 1995

I CAME today for a couple of reasons. First, to help break the first board and officially start the renovation of the Stearns Railroad Depot. As you may recall, we came here back in August of 1993 with a check for the McCreary County Heritage Foundation to help renovate the depot, which was built in 1903. The foundation took the $1,275,000 that we brought and added to it, and now we are finally ready to begin the actual construction work.

When we came here back in 1993, I told you we wanted to be fair to Stearns and to McCreary County. I said that, for too long, this part of the state had been forgotten. And I promised that we would do what we could to help McCreary County catch up to the rest of the state. The renovation of this depot will help a great deal. It will help bring more tourists here, and I believe that is critical to the future of this area. I wanted to come back here today to let you know that even in the final months of this administration, we will not forget Stearns or McCreary County.

However, I also came here today for another reason. I've brought more money that will be used to help people in McCreary and nearby counties. I have brought a grant from the Appalachian Regional Commission that is going to the Lake Cumberland Area Development District. This money will support the establishment of a new regional Justice and Victims Advocacy Council. The council will address the problem of domestic violence in a ten-county area that includes McCreary, Adair, Casey, Clinton, Cumberland, Green, Pulaski, Russell, Taylor, and Wayne Counties.

This project is a significant new element in our overall strategy for improving the well-being and quality of life of the citizens of Kentucky's Appalachian region. The council will include judicial judges, prosecutors, public defenders, law-enforcement officers, social service agency members, private employers, and citizens among its members. It will provide professional counseling for crime victims, establish an emergency shelter program, offer a twenty-four-hour toll-free assistance number, and coordinate existing services for victims.

An estimated 250 victims will be served during the council's first year of operation. The grant will support start-up costs for the council. However, when the council is fully operational, it is expected to become self-sufficient through income generated through the fines and forfeiture system. So it is with great pleasure that I present to Bill Parson, the executive director of the Lake Cumberland Area Development District, this check for $100,000.

HISTORY CENTER GROUND BREAKING
Frankfort / September 25, 1995

BEFORE you leave this ceremony today, take a good, long look around you, so you can remember the day. Within three years, you'll be able to come back here with your friends and family. You'll be able to tell them you were here when this mish-mash of concrete and blacktop began its transformation into something truly inspirational, something truly educational, the Kentucky History Center.

Inside the walls that will soon go up, the Kentucky Historical Society, one of the oldest institutions in the state, will continue the mission it accepted in 1836, to protect important pieces of history and to tell the story of all Kentuckians. The Historical Society and all of us who have worked so hard to make the dream of a new center a reality are the trustees of the future. This building will allow us to carry our mission forward, for our children and for generations to come. Above all, this building is an *investment in the future*, in more ways than one.

According to the Kentucky Department of Travel Development, tourists currently spend around $5 million each year in Frankfort and Franklin County. They estimate that once this History Center is open that number could triple to $15 million a year, and more than two hundred new jobs could be created. Experience has taught us that history sells. The heritage of our Commonwealth is one of its strengths, and this center will build and capitalize on that.

But even more than economics is what this center will do for education. The Kentucky History Center will be a *classroom for Kentucky*. When its doors open in 1998, the center will feature state-of-the-art exhibits and "hands-on" activities, the kinds of attractions that make history fun and adventurous. It will be a place for discovery. Each year, thousands of schoolchildren will discover Kentucky's roots in a way that will stimulate them and create a lifelong love for learning. And through television and computer connections, events at the center will be available to virtually every classroom in every county of Kentucky.

Those things we consider the core of our history, those things that are irreplaceable, those things that we hold in trust for our descendants, now will have a proper home. No longer will they languish unseen in a distillery warehouse. No longer will they be endangered daily. No longer will we have to answer harsh questions regarding our commitment to the past. Now we will have a place of which we all can be proud, a place where we can collect those things that are part of our past, as we move into our future.

There are many people to thank for their persistence in this historic endeavor: Gov. Ned Breathitt, Dr. Thomas Clark, and my wife Libby, who has shown time after time her love for her native state. Also, we owe gratitude to the presidents of the Kentucky Historical Society, from Jo Ferguson through Dick Frymire to Tom Riley, as well as the legislators who voted for this project. And we can never forget the people of this Commonwealth who spoke up for Kentucky's past and told policymakers that this was important to them.

It is an exciting time for history in Kentucky. Now, our future is limited only by our imagination. The quality of life for our people will be higher, our tourist industry will be stronger, our historical collecting efforts will be better, and our children's education will be brighter. As Dr. Clark wrote when this center was funded: "This means we will pour some concrete, erect some steel piers, and bring all God's children to see us." It's time to begin.

HORSE TOURISM

REMARKS FOR ABC-TV PRIOR TO TROPHY PRESENTATION
Louisville / May 2, 1992

For two minutes the first Saturday in May every year, the world watches Kentucky at its finest. The Kentucky Derby is a 118–year tradition that transcends borders and nations. Everyone loves and appreciates the power, grace, elegance, and beauty of this phenomenal event, the first jewel in the Triple Crown of racing. We in Kentucky know, however, that this is a part of our heritage, part of our daily lives, and that there is this and much more to our Commonwealth.

It is with great pride that we invite the world to come to Kentucky, and see our uncommon wealth, from the fine arts and River City traditions of Louisville, to the down-home simple beauty of our mountains and hills, to the scenic and historic pastures and horse farms of the Bluegrass. It's a part of us, and we'd like to share it with the world.

DERBY FESTIVAL BOARD LUNCHEON
Frankfort / April 16, 1993

[GREETINGS] Last year was my first year to experience the Derby Festival and Derby weekend as governor, and I've said publicly many times, that truly was among the first duties I actually enjoyed as governor. Derby time brings out the best in all of us, especially those of you who will give hundreds of hours of your time during the next two weeks to make sure that all events go off safely and well. Now, I understand that David Snowden is in charge of the weather, so the pressure's on you, David!

Seriously, I have said many times since last year's Derby that the Kentucky Derby Festival is *the* greatest civic celebration in the *world*. And I believe that. The incredible amount of energy and commitment each of you, as board members and staff, gives to this effort pays off in spades each year in April and May. And you've earned a well-deserved reputation. I know wherever I go and mention the Kentucky Derby Festival, they've heard of you, and this is the part I like the best: Everyone is envious that we have the festival here in Kentucky!

Dan Mangeot, you have done an amazing job in bringing this festival to the pre-eminent position it enjoys today, and I salute you. And I also know that you're the first one to say that you haven't done it all yourself. This board, the staff, and the thousands of volunteers you involve every year make this festival what it is today, the greatest festival celebrating the greatest two minutes in the sports world!

You know last year I broke tradition, or maybe I started a new tradition, by wearing my Pegasus jacket on Derby Day. In fact, it was at this luncheon last year that one of your board members (Mr. D.A. Sachs) came up to me afterward and asked if I would do this so that when I present the trophy on ABC following the race, the rest of the world could observe the resplendent sports coat that we all love to wear this time of year. And I was happy to do it and proud to represent the jacket.

We have several people from the Tourism Cabinet here today, and I know they recognize and appreciate, as I do, what this festival does in terms of boosting Kentucky as a great place to visit. At no other time of the year are the eyes of the world focused on Kentucky as they are around Derby time. And, the Kentucky Derby Festival provides the perfect backdrop of color, excitement, and world-class events to put Kentucky out there as a great place to come and visit. Tourism is important to our economy. It's our second-largest industry and our third-largest employer. And the Kentucky Derby Festival is important to tourism in Kentucky.

I'm very pleased that we will again be broadcasting the Pegasus Parade on TNN on Derby Day so that families all across Kentucky can get a sense of what this celebration is all about. I'm pleased the Commonwealth, through the Tourism Cabinet, is involved with this telecast because this is the time of the year to put our best foot forward and send out the message loud and clear—Kentucky is the greatest place in America for a safe and affordable family vacation. As you know, I'm a big believer in our state parks system, and we're getting ready to invest $100 million to restore them to their rightful place as the best state parks in the nation. So this festival, and tourism, and our state parks, and the way people perceive us as a state and a people are all related, and that's why this time of the year is important to us. But it's also fun. David, I like your theme this year, "All for fun and fun for all." Because we shouldn't ever lose sight of the fact that with all the history, color, and pageantry surrounding the Kentucky Derby, it's also a time to relax and enjoy our state and the many blessings all around us.

So as we all prepare for the marathon of activity that's ahead, let's not lose sight of the real purpose of all this, and that's to have fun and enjoy the celebration and each other. And now, I'd like to tell you about our commemorative poster this year. You unveiled the festival poster in February, and we're unveiling ours for you here today. Many of you may be aware of the "Salute to African-Americans in Horse Racing" exhibit that has been at the Kentucky Derby Museum for over a year now. There is a painting depicted there that caught our attention and has an interesting story. The painting is called "The Undefeated Asteroid," and although the horse featured in the painting is magnificent, it's really the people shown in the painting that caught our attention. (Poster unveiled.)

This painting of the great racehorse Asteroid was done in 1864 by the noted equine artist Edward Troye. In this particular painting, Troye included Asteroid's trainer, jockey, and groom, and their story is the one we want to tell. To the right is the famous African American trainer, Ansel Anderson. Ansel Anderson's story is a fascinating one: a freed slave, Ansel Anderson worked for R.A. Alexander at Woodburn Stud Farm. I'm somewhat familiar with this farm because it is the site of where Libby and I live today, Airdrie Stud. Ansel Anderson, through his work at Woodburn, became a respected trainer and really paved the way for other African Americans in the sport of horse racing. Following Mr. Alexander's death, Ansel Anderson trained for H. Price McGrath, who had a horse called Aristides, the first Kentucky Derby winner.

The man kneeling in the painting is Ed Brown, a well-known jockey at the time who would also go on to become one of the most successful African American trainers in the country—training Derby winner Baden-Baden in 1877 and three other Derby winners before his death in 1906. I'm very proud of this painting because it depicts not only a great race horse, Asteroid, but more importantly, it reminds us of the important role African Americans played in the development of thoroughbred racing in America. It is with pleasure that I present this poster to you today, and I hope you will enjoy it as a memento of Derby '93. Again, it is a pleasure for Libby and me to have you with us today, and let the fun begin![1]

---

1. At the sixtieth annual Kentucky Colonels' Banquet in Louisville on April 30, Jones talked in glowing terms about the Derby breakfast and thanked the Colonels for their continued support.

RUSSIAN DERBY TELECAST TAPING
Frankfort / May 3, 1994

JUST as Kentucky is known for its bluegrass and bluegrass music, another tradition for which our state is known throughout the world is the Kentucky Derby. We are happy to welcome our friends throughout Russia to this telecast of the 120th Kentucky Derby, the greatest two minutes in sports. Thoroughbred horse racing is a very big part of the history and tradition of Kentucky, and we are pleased to share the color and pageantry of the Kentucky Derby with the people of Russia.[1]

---

1. In an earlier horse tourism speech on April 29 in Louisville, Jones discussed the seventy Kentucky Derby festival events; he noted that an estimated 1.5 million people participate in the activities.

KENTUCKY INTERNATIONAL THOROUGHBRED INSTITUTE
Lexington / November 9, 1994

I'VE ALWAYS believed that Kentucky should build on its best, and today, I have the pleasure of announcing a new program that will allow us to do that. I am announcing the formation of "The Kentucky International Thoroughbred Institute," a new international training program that will bring to Kentucky aspiring thoroughbred horsemen and women and racetrack administrators from around the world.

The program will be administered by the Kentucky Thoroughbred Association, and training will be provided through the joint efforts of the University of Kentucky's Maxwell Gluck [Equine Research] Center and the University of Louisville's Department of Equine Administration. The Kentucky International Thoroughbred Institute is scheduled to enroll its first trainees next spring. The trainees will choose between two courses and will spend up to eight months in Kentucky. One course will emphasize hands-on care of race horses and will prepare the trainees to become professional thoroughbred trainers in their native countries. The other course will emphasize the skills of racetrack administration. We expect the first program to include eight to ten trainees, with more trainees to be accepted in future years.

While this program will be open to applicants from throughout the world, the emphasis on the first year will be on enrollees from Southeast Asia, because nowhere in the world is the thoroughbred industry growing faster. And in the next few years, as Hong Kong becomes part of the People's Republic of China, there's a tremendous potential for even more economic development. In fact, we have just received confirmation from the Royal Hong Kong Jockey Club asking us to reserve at least two positions in the first training program for trainees from Hong Kong. There are two people I'd like to acknowledge publicly for their role in making this institute become a reality. Thomas and Howard Liang from Hong Kong, and the owners of the Oaks Farm in Ocala, have been extremely instrumental in developing this program and lending a considerable amount of support. Howard called from Hong Kong yesterday morning. Unfortunately, he and Thomas are unable to be with us today, but they wish to express their thanks for our assistance and are very proud of the program. They are working on behalf of the program in their part of the world.

The enthusiasm about the institute, both worldwide and here at home, has been tremendous. We are especially grateful to Keeneland and Churchill Downs for their support. But what it all boils down to is just good common sense. The Kentucky thoroughbred industry has more to export than race horses and breeding stock. Kentucky is known throughout the world as a center of expertise about all matters related to thoroughbreds. We believe we can strengthen our position as a world leader if we share that expertise, and at the same time we can expand our worldwide market for Kentucky horses. The sales here in Lexington this week and the crowds who followed and wagered at the Breeders Cup last Saturday is further proof that the thoroughbred racing industry is strong. This institute will help us keep it strong into the twenty-first century. . . .

DEMOCRATIC PARTY LEADER AND POLITICS

JEFFERSON-JACKSON DAY DINNER
Frankfort / February 21, 1992

THANK you very much for giving me the great pleasure of speaking tonight to this momentous gathering of Democrats. Jefferson-Jackson Day dinners traditionally give us the opportunity to come together to enjoy our victories and discuss our hopes and objectives for the greatest party in America. My theme tonight is keeping the lines of communications open from the statehouse to local governments.[1] The only way any administration can do this is to keep the lines of communication open between the governor and you, the people, and that is what the Jones administration is all about. We are a party that is too often and somewhat unfairly seen as slow to change, a party of power-plays and backroom deals, of go-along to get along, and of ideas without tough solutions. We must be a party willing to listen and to change, of reforming the system by which we elect our leaders and allowing the many good people we have to run for and obtain office so that their strengths might be brought into play against the field of problems that face our state. We must be a party ready and willing to remove politics from our educational systems, from our university boards of trustees and regents to school boards in the hills and hollows, building a system that is concerned from top to bottom with improving the minds of youngsters all across the state.

Yesterday, I signed into law House Bill 149 restructuring the system to appoint regents and trustees. I believe this proposal will begin removing politics from our campuses. By forming selection committees to make three nominations for every vacancy, it places a safety barrier between the political world and the world of higher education. A governor will no longer be able to handpick the people that populate our college and university leadership on the basis of who contributed to his political campaign. The aim is to bring [into] our institutions of higher learning people of the highest motives and abilities. This is a signal from the top that it is time to run our educational system for the right purpose . . . to train and refine the minds of our young people in a world that has rapidly turned fiercely competitive as we prepare to enter the twenty-first century. We cannot stop there, while we improve the educational climate under the Kentucky Education Reform Act, we must begin to re-examine the structure that often turns the focus from the classroom to the backroom where those in power can too often put their interests ahead of our children's welfare.

It is a time of growing concern and economic difficulty in our state and nation. The time is ripe for reordering our political hierarchy so that it is more responsive to the people that elect it. This effort can bring about a mechanism that puts the reins of our government back into the hands of the voters. Just this past Wednesday we introduced major legislation to begin sweeping campaign reforms. Working together with the legislative leaders, such as Sen. Mike Moloney[2] of Lexington and Sen. Joe Meyer of Covington, we have proposed revamping our election system. Many of you have read about our plan, but for those of you who may not as yet know the full breadth of these proposals, let me outline them. Under our plan, we are calling for succession for future governors and other statewide officials so that they might serve two consecutive terms. Candidates for governor and lieutenant governor would run together as a team. The governor would retain powers while outside the state but in the continental United States. The Supreme Court, at the attorney general's request, could declare a governor disabled. Terms for state legislators would be lengthened to continue the balance of power between an executive branch that is able to succeed itself and the legislature which has become a truly independent and strong forum on leadership. Elections would be held only in even-numbered years, thus saving millions of dollars for our taxpayers. These proposals would abolish elections for the offices of state treasurer, secretary of state, and agriculture commissioner and abolish the offices of superintendent of public instruction and the railroad commission. All of this would streamline our leadership and save the taxpayers of the Commonwealth millions of dollars. Our effort would also limit individual campaign contributions to $500 from the current $4,000 limit. Gubernatorial campaigns that did not agree to limit spending could take contributions no larger than $100, putting a stick along with the carrots of campaign reform. Gubernatorial campaigns that agree to limit total spending to $1.8 million would get two-for-one matching money from the state once they raised $300,000.

There are detractors that say combining all these reforms into one big effort is too big a pill for the public to swallow and that one facet or another will doom the entire effort, but I say it's time to turn from the "it won't work" hand wringing that stymied our state. It is time to roll up our sleeves and stump for campaign reforms that will be a lasting legacy to progressive, honest government in our state. Our legislative leadership has shown again the kind of moral courage that made education reform a reality. There were many people who said education reform was a political impossibility. Now KERA is a working reality, and I say the same effort and concern by everyone in Frankfort for campaign and election reforms, taken to the people, can be accomplished. I am not diminishing the size of our task. It is obvious and formidable. The task of holding our unity and gaining strength and acceptance as a party, to better a state and a nation . . . it will not be done in a day or without considerable sacrifice and compromise. As they say, one fine day does not a summer make. The task of continuing education reform, of removing politics from our schools and colleges, of reforming our system of elections, of finding a solution to our economic woes to help people find good productive jobs; the challenge of finding quality, low-cost health care for everyone is a huge endeavor. Taken together they are a burden that would make Atlas shrug and bring Job to his knees. But, taken one step at a time, building a consensus and working together to find solutions we can at the very least begin to find answers to problems that plague not only our Commonwealth, but our nation. We are in this together. And I say, let the nation look to Kentucky . . . watch us as we work together on these problems. Watch us as we draw from our own ranks and from the great resources of our Commonwealth, from the leadership in Frankfort, to the minds of our universities, and the experience of our business and industries, the kind of effort and knowledge that can and will find the way toward solutions.

I say Andrew Jackson and Thomas Jefferson are alive and well in Kentucky, in the U.S., in our Democratic Party because there is a little Jackson and Jefferson in us all, in a party that has such strengths and diversity, in a state that is both urban and rural, with people that are both rich and poor, educated and less educated, with an economy that mirrors our national dilemma. The problems are here, not in Washington, and it is out here that there are some answers. History teaches us that the founders of our party, Thomas Jefferson and Andrew Jackson, were two very different men. Yet, they continue to represent our party's highly divergent philosophies. They were two very strong men with contrasting views and personalities who helped forge this nation. Jefferson was an educated, polished individual who could write poetry and was an accomplished violinist; Jackson, a rough-hewn backwoodsman, Indian fighter, military man, who lived by his strength and wit. And yet these party symbols are also the lines along which our contentious, cantankerous collective can be fragmented. Will Rogers once said, "I belong to no organized party. I am a Democrat." We are the party of the BMW and the pickup truck, the party of the white collar and the work shirt, the formally educated and the educated by life. Our diversity is both a strength and a weakness that can be exploited by our opponents and ourselves, dividing us into warring camps and allowing our nation and state to continue in economic and political recession.

Some of that division became evident lately in the New Hampshire primary when the Democratic candidates turned more on each other than on an administration that continues to pander to the privileged, ignore the poor, and allow the middle class to fall through the cracks. We cannot allow the Republicans the avenue to our disarray and to their perpetuation. The times cry for new leadership from our nation's capital, and I believe it's time for Washington to listen to us. Too often our elected leaders in Washington lose touch with their constituents, and progress is thwarted by epidemics of Potomac fever which causes politicians' eyes to glaze over and ears to close, unable to see or hear the true condition of our nation, unwilling to listen to the many voices that can help. Many of those voices are here in this room tonight; many of the solutions are out here in the hinterlands if Washington would only listen. Let us begin, calling on the best that is within us, within our reach, and we can, here in Kentucky, start today the process of bringing us together to build the answers for change and healing in our nation tomorrow.

---

1. A similar Jefferson-Jackson speech was given in Florence on March 14, on October 24 in Ashland, and on October 31 in Pulaski County.

2. Michael (Mike) Moloney (1941–), B.S., Xavier University; LL.B., University of Kentucky; Democrat; elected Kentucky senator (district 13), 1971; re-elected, 1975–96. *1996 Who's What in Kentucky Government.*

REMARKS ON BREATHITT ADMINISTRATION
Frankfort / April 4, 1992

WHEN Ned Breathitt was taking Kentucky to a position of national prominence in model government programs, I was just out of college with only a glimmer of a dream of becoming a Kentuckian, but his reputation for progressive policy stretched beyond the borders of Kentucky to my native West Virginia and throughout the nation. He curbed the abuses of strip mining and instituted far-reaching conservation and environmental protection, human rights, education, election finance [reforms], and improvements in general government operations. This litany of Governor Breathitt's accomplishments is remarkable in itself. Even more remarkable is that all this was done twenty-five years ago—before all these key issues had the popular support they enjoy today. In fact, he was so far ahead of his time that those issues he met headlong are still the key issues today. It would seem that, if all the leaders who came after him had been as daring and dedicated as he, Kentucky would have solved many of those problems and moved onto other areas of leadership.

As he prepared to leave office, the young governor of Kentucky received rave editorial reviews here and around the country. Remember also the political climate—this was done when George Wallace and his states' rights views were the rage. Referring to Kentucky's civil rights legislation of the time, the (London) *Times* in England commented that, if there were fifty governors like Breathitt, the argument for states' rights would be moot. There would be no need for a strong central government if all the states would do their job like Kentucky had. It was the same in various fields. Newspapers throughout the state and national opinion leaders like the *Washington Post* joined in the chorus. Besides the tough strip mine and reclamation laws and the civil rights, public accommodations, and employment acts, thinking people everywhere were impressed that Breathitt:

1. created the Council on Higher Education;
2. fully funded a program for teachers' salaries;
3. established the Kentucky Registry of Election Finance;
4. set up the Kentucky Water Resources Authority.

HE also pushed for laws that authorized the Kentucky Commission on Women, a model state purchases program, and a $1 million bond issue which provided $1 billion in highways, parks, vocational schools, and other facilities. If Ned had been a basketball coach, he would have taken us to the Final Four. Speaking of sports, Governor Breathitt insisted that the sports programs at UK be integrated—and they were to a degree before he left office.

In short, Governor Breathitt fought for what was right regardless of whether it was widely popular. He molded public opinion instead of trying to govern by the public opinion polls. In almost every key area, no matter how controversial, he laid a strong foundation on which we are still building. Tonight, I want to pledge to you that my greatest ambition is to live up to the high standards and ethics of public dedication to an equal chance for every Kentuckian that he set. The Breathitt administration will be forever a benchmark in honest progress in government and what is best and brightest about Kentucky.

JEFFERSON-JACKSON DAY DINNER
Jenny Wiley State Park—Prestonsburg / May 9, 1992

THANK you for the honor of speaking to you this evening at this momentous gathering of Democrats in celebration of the birth of our party two hundred years ago. Jefferson-Jackson Day dinners traditionally give us the opportunity to come together to enjoy our victories and discuss our hopes and objectives for the greatest party in America. We are close to our primary election and only months away from our party's national convention and poised on the edge of a victory in the fall campaign. This is an important year for the Democratic Party. This November is a pivotal election that could change the course of events that have stalled and stymied this nation for almost twelve years. I say "could change" the course of events when it should be "must change" the course of events to bring our federal government back to the people in the year of the party of the people, the Democratic Party, founded on the principle of helping those who can least help themselves.

But I see signs of division that have so often rendered our party a victim of its own diversity. Bill Clinton continues to win primary after primary and now stands poised on the edge of our party's nomination. Yet, we hear within our ranks those who have doubts about him and are looking for some "sainted savior." Surely by now his performance in the primaries and his sincere and eloquent efforts to bring this nation together have laid to rest those doubts, but our hopes rest not just in joining together behind our party's presidential nominee. We must be the party willing to listen and willing to seek change. The violence in Los Angeles cannot be justified and certainly cannot be blamed on the Democratic Party as some have tried. Unfortunately, all across America frustrations have built up over more than a decade of not listening to those in need, not just in our cities, but in rural areas such as eastern Kentucky, where we too have too many in need. Cries for help and healing have gone unheard during the Reagan and Bush years in Washington. The Republican Party is, and continues to be, out of touch and unfeeling toward the everyday struggles of common people. We need to unite more than ever before, to ensure a Democratic victory in November, because more than ever before, our country is in need of new direction, and much of that new direction must come from out here, in our homes, cities, counties, and in our state.

After five months, and in spite of severe budgetary limits, our administration has come through its first legislative session with what we feel are some significant gains for our Commonwealth. We have put in place a mechanism designed to remove politics from our higher educational system, from our boards of trustees and regents. We have restructured the method of appointing regents and trustees by forming selection committees to make three nominations for every vacancy. That system places a barrier between the political world and the world of higher education. We feel we are bringing to our institutions of higher learning people of the highest motives and abilities, people concerned about training and refining the minds of young adults in a world that has become fiercely competitive as we prepare for the twenty-first century. Our administration has instituted sweeping campaign reforms that can begin returning faith in our system of electing leaders. We feel these reforms could be a lasting legacy to create honest, progressive government in our state, return government to the people, and allow many good people the ability to seek political office, free of the expensive campaign requirements of the past.

I signed a strict executive branch code of ethics within seconds of taking office, and that code becomes law this summer. This is another effort to set high standards for those people who run your government so that they will be accountable to the people of the

Commonwealth. We are working with the legislature to adopt a similar ethics code for that branch of government. We are restructuring the Cabinet for Economic Development to insulate it from the winds of political change, to ensure continuity in our efforts to bring jobs to a state badly in need of an economic boost, and we have enacted special economic incentives to preserve existing jobs and bring new employment to our Commonwealth. Our Economic Development Cabinet is already beginning to see results from those efforts, with actual plant and company locations in Kentucky attracted by these incentives, and we are in the process of forging what we hope will be a national model health-care reform package for a special legislative session in the fall. Meetings and town forums will begin in the next few weeks to gather information from those who will be affected by this historic effort. We are beginning to make some headway in our efforts to help those who cannot help themselves, and our efforts will continue for the next forty-three months, in our hope of making things better for Kentucky.

But there is much to be done. As they say, one fine day does not a summer make. Our task is obvious and formidable and will not be accomplished without considerable sacrifice and compromise, but taking it one step at a time, building a consensus and working together to find solutions, we can begin to find answers to problems that plague our Commonwealth and our nation. We are in this together, and I say, "Let the nation look to Kentucky and this Democratic Party united, working together on these problems. Watch us as we draw from our own ranks and from the great resources of our Commonwealth, from the leadership in Frankfort, to the minds of our universities, and the experience of our business and industries the kind of effort that can and will find the way toward solutions."

I say Andrew Jackson and Thomas Jefferson are alive and well in Kentucky, in the U.S., and in our Democratic Party because there is a little of Jackson and Jefferson in us all, in a party that finds strength in its diversity. The problems are here, not in Washington, and it is out here that there are answers. History teaches us that the founders of our party, Jefferson and Jackson, were two very different men, yet they continue to represent our party's highly divergent philosophies. They were two very strong men with contrasting views and personalities that helped forge a party and a nation. Jefferson was an educated, polished intellectual who could write poetry and was an accomplished violinist. Jackson was a rough-hewn backwoodsman, Indian fighter, and military man who lived by his strength and wits. In keeping with our party's "creed" and grand traditions, we share Jefferson's belief in individual liberty and responsibility. We endorse Jackson's creed of equal opportunity for all and special privileges for none. We embrace [Franklin D.] Roosevelt's thirst for innovation and [Harry S.] Truman's faith in the uncommon sense of common men and women. We carry on [John F.] Kennedy's call to civic duty and public service, [Lyndon B.] Johnson's passion for social justice, and [Jimmy] Carter's commitment to human rights.

"Where do we stand?" asks our party's creed. We believe the promise of America is equal opportunity. We believe the Democratic Party's fundamental mission is to expand opportunity, not government. We believe in the politics of inclusion. Our party has historically been the means by which aspiring Americans from every background have achieved equal rights and full citizenship. We believe that economic growth is the prerequisite to expanding opportunity for everyone. The free market, regulated in the public interest, is the best engine of general prosperity. We believe the right way to rebuild America's economic security is to invest in the skills and ingenuity of our people and to expand trade. We believe the purpose of social welfare is to bring the poor into the nation's economic mainstream, not maintain them in dependence. We believe in the protection of civil rights and the broad movement of minorities into America's economic and cultural mainstream, not racial, gender, age, or ethnic separatism. We cannot tolerate another decade in which the only civil rights movement is backward. We believe government should respect individual liberty and stay out of our private lives and personal decisions. We believe in the moral and cultural values that most Americans share: liberty of conscience, individual responsibility, tolerance of difference, the imperative of work, the need for faith, and the importance of family. Finally, we believe that American citizenship entails responsibilities as well as rights, and we mean to ask our citizens to give something back to their communities and their country. We believe in an America that is united and healed.[1]

---

1. On May 16, Jones gave a similar speech at the Jefferson-Jackson dinner in Owensboro.

KENTUCKY DEMOCRATIC CONVENTION
Frankfort / June 13, 1992

I JUST wanted to say with this kind of a turnout, "How can the Democratic Party not be successful in Kentucky come November?" Thank you for inviting me here today to participate in what I believe is the most important and most significant gathering of Democrats we will have in this state during our administration. Because we are here today laying the framework for the most successful, the best organized, and the most unified Democratic Party this state has ever seen. United and well organized and with the enthusiasm and leadership you are showing here today, there are no objectives that we cannot achieve together as a party over these next three and a half years. Yes, our work is cut out for us. The great objective facing us is a landslide Democratic victory in November at every level, from our legislative districts, to each of our six congressional districts, to the U.S. Senate, to the White House. We will not rest until we have re-elected Democrat Wendell Ford to the U.S. Senate, Democrat Tom Barlow[1] in the First Congressional District, Democrat Bill Natcher[2] in the Second Congressional District, Democrat Ron Mazzoli[3] in the Third Congressional District, Democrat Floyd Poore[4] in the Fourth Congressional District, Democrat John Doug Hays[5] in the Fifth Congressional District, and Democrat Scotty Baesler[6] in the Sixth Congressional District. And more than this, we will not rest until we elect Bill Clinton as the first Democratic president in the White House in twelve years.

There is nothing more important to a rousing Democratic success in November than the organizational work you are doing here today. You are laying the groundwork for a new, revitalized, unified Democratic Party, which we have not really had in this state for years. I know most of you and have worked with most of you. In fact, many of you went to war for me, and I want you to know I appreciate the work you did. I will never forget it. The team we put together in the campaign gave us a great victory last November. We worked together to send a clear message to all of our great Commonwealth that days of business as usual in Frankfort were over. Our team took the philosophy we shared to the Capitol, and we have already made great strides together in campaign finance reform, in changing the way our university governing boards are selected, in putting the foundation in place to create jobs in every part of our state. But we continue to face challenges, and I know that our team can meet them head-on for the good of our state and our children and grandchildren.

Today I want to touch on three particular areas where I need your help and where Kentucky needs your commitment. We will soon begin gearing up our fall campaign in support of the constitutional amendments which were approved by the General Assembly. As you know, these amendments will strengthen the entire structure of state government by removing outmoded elective offices and will bring Kentucky into the mainstream of modern states by allowing people to decide whether they want to give a governor and the lieutenant governor second terms to complete the work they have begun. We worked hard to get the succession amendment on the ballot, and as I am sure every one of you here knows, I took myself out of this process so this amendment can succeed on its own merit. We need your support of these amendments and your hard work in your neighborhoods back home to make sure they succeed.

Perhaps the greatest single challenge we face in the months ahead is reforming our health-care system. As you know, the task force we established on health care has held public hearings throughout the state, bringing hundreds of people to the table to share their views and concerns, but we still need your help to identify the problems and find the solutions to this very real, very personal problem for our state. I urge each of you to be a part of this process as we immerse ourselves in this very formidable task. Speak up on the subject. Let me and your legislators know how you feel about health-care problems. You may have a solution in mind that no one else has considered, and if we are on the wrong track, let us know how you feel. We need your help because, come November, we plan to call a special session to confront and overcome this challenge. I predict that after November, Kentucky will take a leadership position nationally in ensuring quality, affordable health care to every Kentuckian. That is my goal, and we can reach it by working together.

During my first few months as governor, it has become very clear to me that there is one fundamental obligation that we must meet if we are to effect positive change, and that is restoring the public's confidence in their government. While we have made a good start on reforming our political system, I don't need to tell you how troubling recent events have been for everyone in public service. The effects of this investigation,[7] whatever the outcome of the individual cases, are being felt throughout our state, and unfortunately, they are reinforcing the negative feelings about government that have been simmering for years in the public's mind. This reality makes even greater our responsibility as Democrats, as Kentuckians, to do everything we can to restore faith in the process and the institutions that have been bruised. Our actions must be those that let all Kentuckians know that the vast majority of political activists and elected officials are honest, honorable, hardworking people who really do want to make a positive difference.

I know that we are all committed to reform in this state and that reform is totally consistent with our efforts to build the strongest and most unified Democratic Party we have ever had in Kentucky. I urge you to continue to be active in Democratic organizational work at every level: local, state, and national. It is through this kind of solid organizational work that we can select our best Democratic candidates and elect them to office. We desperately need new leadership both at home and in the White House. I have asked Dr. Stumbo[8] to convene a meeting of every elected Democratic nominee from the legislature and the congressional districts to plan an all-out coordinated campaign that will ensure a Democratic success in November. That meeting is scheduled for 10:00 a.m., June 20, and I hope that all of our Democratic candidates will plan to attend, whether or not you have opposition in November. While this is the first such meeting of this kind, I hope that it will become traditional in future campaigns as we work to rebuild the Democratic Party in this state.

Finally, I am very pleased to report that this afternoon I will submit the name of our very hard-working chairman, Dr. Grady Stumbo, for re-election to another term as chairman of our party. Grady's commitment to honest, progressive government and his interest in the great issues facing this state make him a real force, not only in Kentucky Democratic politics, but in Democratic politics nationally as well. I am very proud of the work he has done in rebuilding our party, and we are at a crucial point where his leadership is more important than ever. I urge you to support his nomination and allow him to continue his great building efforts at this important time in the history of our state and of our party.[9]

---

1. Tom Barlow (1941–), B.A., Haverford College, 1963; U.S. representative, 1st district, Kentucky, 1993–95; unsuccessful congressional candidate, 1st district, Kentucky, 1994, 1998; Paducah businessman.

2. William H. Natcher (1909–94), A.B., Western Kentucky State College; L.L.B., Ohio State University; federal conciliation commissioner, Western District Kentucky, 1936–37; county attorney, Warren County, Kentucky, 1937–49; president, Young Democrats Club Kentucky, 1941–46; common-

wealth's attorney, 8th judicial district, 1951–53; U.S. representative, 2nd district, 1953–94.

3. Romano L. Mazzoli (1932–), B.S., University of Notre Dame, 1954; J.D., University of Louisville, 1960; U.S. Army, 1954–56; delegate, Democratic National Convention, 1968; Kentucky senate, 1968–70; chairman of the Education Committee, Kentucky General Assembly, 1970; U.S. representative, 3rd district, 1971–94.

4. Floyd Poore (1937–), B.S., Georgetown College, 1958; M.D., University of Louisville Medical School; transportation secretary under Gov. Martha Layne Collins, 1983–85; fund-raiser for Gov. Wallace Wilkinson; public liaison for Governor Wilkinson, 1988–90; gubernatorial candidate, 1991; unsuccessful congressional candidate, 4th district, 1992.

5. John Doug Hays (1939–), Kentucky state senator in the 31st district, 1979–83; unsuccessful congressional candidate, 5th district, 1992.

6. Scotty Baesler (1941–), bachelor's degree, University of Kentucky; law degree, University of Kentucky Law School; master's degree, education and human development, George Washington University; administrator for Fayette County Legal Aid, 1967–73; Lexington vice-mayor, 1974–78; Fayette County district judge, 1978–82; Lexington mayor, 1982–92; U.S. representative, 1993–98; unsuccessful candidate for U.S. Senate in 1998 and in 6th congressional district in 2000; tobacco farmer.

7. Jones is referring to BOPTROT. An explanation of this FBI investigation is found in the endnotes for Jones's legislative address on January 13, 1992.

8. W. Grady Stumbo (1945–), A.A., Alice Lloyd College, 1965; B.S., University of Kentucky, 1967; M.D., University of Kentucky, 1971; gubernatorial candidate, 1983, 1987; board member, Eastern Kentucky Job Creation Authority Inc., 1989– ; chairman, Kentucky State Democratic Party, 1991–95.

9. On March 6, Jones spoke to supporters of Sen. Wendell Ford in Louisville; on August 8 in Daviess County, he introduced Ford; on August 28 in Louisville, he introduced Bill Clinton; on October 17, he spoke at the John Doug Hays fund-raiser in Pikeville. On January 26, 1993, Jones spoke at the Asa Rouse (candidate for state senate) fund-raiser in Frankfort; on February 19, 1993, he spoke at a meeting with U.S. Transportation Secretary Federico Peña in Louisville; on May 14, 1993, he introduced Ron Mazzoli at the Wendell Ford Trust dinner in Louisville; on July 17, 1993, he spoke in Frankfort at the Democratic Headquarters Twentieth Anniversary; on September 29, 1993, he spoke in Frankfort at the Century Club's reception for the Rev. Jesse Jackson.

FANCY FARM SPEECH
Fancy Farm / August 1, 1992

GOOD afternoon, Democrats and all others seeking a revitalized Commonwealth and nation. It is my sincere pleasure to address this time-honored traditional gathering at Fancy Farm, the opening of the campaign season in Kentucky. Here in the heat of western Kentucky, we stand poised on the edge of a historic Democratic victory. In just a few short months, Americans will elect change, vitality, new direction, new hope, and new efforts as we, the Democratic Party, pull ourselves together for the task of rebuilding America with a platform of answers, not a policy of destruction, after being torn apart by failed and flawed policies for twelve years under Republican administrations. The Democratic ticket, from Bill Clinton and Al Gore to our Kentucky Democratic congressional candidates, is forged into a united effort for new direction as has not been seen in decades. Our candidates: Tom Barlow in the 1st congressional district, Bill Natcher in the 2nd, Ron Mazzoli in the 3rd, Floyd Poore in the 4th, John Doug Hays in the 5th, and Scotty Baesler in the 6th, form a team that is dedicated to returning to the people the rightful say in how this country is run. For this nation has withstood a dozen years of Republican oppression greater than the fire and heat of a hundred summers, more dry and desolate than can or should be endured; policies that have drained our national energy and left our nation divided and depressed. But now there is more than hope coming from Hope, Arkansas, and Carthage, Tennessee, and from the Big Sandy to the mighty Mississippi, there is unity of purpose and the willingness to work hard to rebuild America.

After months of primary campaigning, our party has a ticket that will bring to our nation the energy and the will to seek solutions, to find answers to the national dilemmas of health care, jobs, education, and the environment. In Kentucky, our Democratic ticket brings the willingness to work with a Democratic president to lift this nation from decades of drifting to a new direction, providing the leadership that will be responsive to the long-ignored cries of our people. "Put the people first" is not just a party slogan, it is a pledge, emblazoned across our platform and the crucible for change. For too long Washington has not responded to growing national frustration, bordering at times on anger, to stop the deterioration, to boost jobs, to invigorate the economy, to give all Americans quality health care at an affordable price, to give our children the best possible education, to clean up our environment, and to restore our economic might at home and abroad. We are the party for change. We are the party seeking answers, not the party of divide and conquer.

In Kentucky, we are working together to send a clear message to all of our great Commonwealth that the days of business as usual in Frankfort are over. We have made great strides in campaign finance reform, in changing the way our university governing boards are selected, and in putting the foundation in place to create jobs in every part of our state. But we continue to face great challenges, and I know that our team can meet them head-on for the good of our state and our children and grandchildren. We are beginning our fall campaign in support of constitutional amendments which were approved by the General Assembly. As you know, these amendments will strengthen the entire structure of state government by removing outmoded elective offices and will bring Kentucky into the mainstream of modern states by allowing the people to decide whether they want to give a governor and lieutenant governor second terms to complete the work they have begun. We worked hard to get the succession amendment on the ballot, and as I am sure every one of you here knows, I took myself out of this process so this amendment can succeed on its own merits. We need your support of these amendments and your hard work in your neighborhoods back home to make sure they succeed and create the necessary atmosphere for change.

Perhaps the greatest challenge we face in the months ahead is reforming our health-care system. As you know, I have offered some suggestions for change. I have made it plain that there is no greater problem facing America and our Commonwealth today, and only bold efforts will keep this problem from bankrupting our nation and state. We also need your help to identify the problems and find the solutions to this very real, very personal problem for our state. Speak up on the subject. Let me and your legislators know how you feel about health-care problems. You may have a solution in mind that no one else has considered, and if you think we are on the wrong track, let us know how you feel. Because, come November, we plan to call a special session to confront and overcome this challenge and provide a solution for our dilemma and a new direction for the nation. I predict that after November Kentucky will take a national leadership position in ensuring quality, affordable health care for every Kentuckian. That is my goal, and we can reach it by working together and through a willingness to make sacrifices for the good of all.

During my first eight months as governor, it has become very clear to me that there is one fundamental obligation that we all must meet if we are to effect positive change: restoring the public's confidence in their government. While we have made a good start on reforming our political system, I don't need to tell you how troubling recent events have been for everyone in public service. The effects of this investigation and the indictments, whatever the outcome of the individual cases, are being felt throughout our state, and unfortunately, they are reinforcing the negative feelings about government that have been simmering for years in the public's mind. This reality makes even greater our responsibility, as Democrats and as Kentuckians, to do everything we can to restore faith in the process and the institutions that have been bruised. Our actions must be those that let all Kentuckians know that the vast majority of political activists and elected officials are honest, honorable, hardworking people who really do want to make a positive difference. I know that we are all committed to reform in this state and that reform is totally consistent with our efforts to build the strongest and most unified Democratic Party we have ever had in Kentucky. It is also responsive to what the people are calling for, and we must rally to their call. Our own party chairman, Dr. Grady Stumbo, has pledged to forge an alliance for responsiveness, an agent for change, and a vehicle for a better tomorrow.

For twelve long years there has been no vision from Washington, and as you have heard me quote before, the Bible says, "Where there is no vision the people perish." George Bush has belittled and reduced this crucial need with arrogance and disdain into what he called "the vision thing." There can be no vision when the Republicans are blind to the needs of our people. There can be no change when the Republicans turn their ears away from the cries of the vast majority who are worse off now than they were twelve years ago. There can be no direction from those who haven't a clue as to how to lead. Bill Clinton, Al Gore, their families, their strength and commitment, and our party stand ready to listen, to lead, to restore, to revitalize, to unify, and to work for the good of all. We have answers; they have rhetoric. We have the willingness to work; they have the need to preserve the status quo which has helped the rich at the expense of the middle income and the poor. We call for unity; they exploit along racial and income lines. We seek change; they mouth the word in desperation. It's time for us to lead; it's time for them to go. We must not fail on our promises of prosperity. The nation needs us, and we must be ready, willing, and able to show results; for history will turn on our greatest endeavor . . . or our legacy will be hollow. We see tomorrow and *our* vision is clear.

INTRODUCTION OF SEN. WENDELL FORD
Daviess County Democratic Picnic / August 8, 1992

WHEN you think of Kentucky and you think of Democrat, you think of the man I am honored to introduce tonight. Kentucky's senior U.S. senator is seeking another term, but more than that, he is seeking to continue his significant contributions to our great Commonwealth and, as a leader in the U.S. Senate, to our great nation. Our Commonwealth and our country need Wendell Ford in the U.S. Senate. Most of us know the history of this man, and all of us recognize his positions of leadership. For some people positions of leadership can mean little more than a title, but for a very few, those positions of leadership come from within, from a special nature and ability to lead. These are the people that stand out in times of trouble and about whom history records their words and deeds. Sen. Wendell Ford is such a leader, and never was there a more crucial time for his presence in the U.S. Senate. Senator Ford puts the people first, returning home nearly every weekend to keep in touch with Kentucky. Whether he's fighting to extend unemployment benefits for laid-off workers or promoting an economic stimulus package, he's always putting the needs of Kentucky's hardworking families first. Sen. Wendell Ford makes sure Kentucky's voice is heard at the highest levels. As majority whip, he is in a position to make sure Kentucky gets her fair share of critical highway dollars and funds to keep our airports equipped with state-of-the-art equipment. Senator Ford has kept motor voter legislation alive because, while the Republicans think it's better to keep people out of the democratic process, we know that the more people participating in a democracy, the better it works. Senator Ford has helped our farmers and tobacco growers more than any other representative through decent prices and innovative ways to improve markets abroad, including an international agricultural trade center right here in Kentucky. He has cut hundreds of millions of dollars in government waste by reforming the mass mailing system and putting the government on a recycled paper diet. Wendell Ford is a true leader. His bottom line is "Kentucky comes first; our hardworking Kentucky families come first." So now and in November, for the kind of representation in Washington that has never lost touch with the people, I give you Sen. Wendell H. Ford.

JOHN DOUG HAYS FUND-RAISER
Pikeville / October 17, 1992

IT IS my pleasure to be here this afternoon with the tried and true of our Democratic Party in Kentucky. Eastern Kentucky Democrats are stalwarts in our party, and I know we can count on all of you as we move forward with the campaign, the constitutional amendments, and health-care reform. We are here this afternoon to rally support for John Doug Hays for Congress. Why should eastern Kentucky elect John Doug Hays? The answer is simple. He best represents this region and its people and cares most about their needs.

For example, health-care reform. The cost of health insurance has tripled since Hal Rogers took office in 1980, and yet, Mr. Rogers voted to cut $25 billion from Medicare, the program upon which so many of our elderly citizens depend for medical assistance. Rogers endorses the George Bush philosophy of health care which would cover only one-fourth of those who are without health insurance and cost the taxpayers billions more than Bill Clinton's plan to cover everyone. John Doug Hays backs Bill Clinton, as I do, and works with President Clinton to solve this national dilemma and works with our administration to bring health-care reform to Kentucky. John Doug Hays, a man of principle and integrity, knows how devastating it can be for those who are without health insurance, and he has seen what happens when catastrophic illness wipes out a family's savings, destroying the lives of those who are ill and the families that care for them. John Doug Hays knows the pain of these people, and he will bring change to Washington.

Congressman Rogers' salary has doubled in his twelve years in Washington to nearly $130,000 a year, and he voted against raising the minimum wage to $4.55 an hour. That shows his commitment to the men and women of Kentucky and their families. The fifth [congressional] district has ten counties where the percentage of children living in poverty is higher than it is in Detroit, Michigan. Yet, Hal Rogers voted against increased funding for the women and infant children's nutrition program, showing the greatest insensitiveness to our most needy and defenseless. Hal Rogers voted against family and medical leave, against a tax cut for the working people of our country, and against increased funding for Head Start, an education program aimed at helping those who have it toughest to get a better beginning in our schools. At the same time, however, Hal Rogers voted for a bill which uses American tax dollars to move our businesses to foreign soil, making it even tougher for those most in need to find work.

This is the legacy of the Reagan-Bush years, completely out of touch with the people of this country, and Hal Rogers is a part of that legacy. John Doug Hays will be a messenger and an advocate for those who have long been ignored and have for so long been in need. John Doug Hays represents compassion and change. It's time to elect those who will turn our country back to its original path of being responsive to the people and away from the twelve years of protecting the special interests of the privileged few. John Doug Hays is a man of the people, and he will not forget who he is, where he is from, nor those who send him to Washington. I ask you to vote for John Doug Hays November 3.

This is the season of change and nowhere is fall more brilliantly demonstrated than in eastern Kentucky. With politics and fall at a peak, I also ask you to "Vote Yes for Change" on the constitutional amendments that will be on our ballot on November 3, and I ask you to campaign for their support. Call on your friends and others to be architects for change and strength. That is why we formed the "Vote Yes for Change" committee, to support government reform. That committee is organizing a statewide, grassroots effort to promote passage of two amendments to the Kentucky constitution. The main elements of Amendment #2 would allow the governor and other state officers to serve two consecutive terms, require the governor and lieutenant governor to run as a team, and reduce the frequency of elections. Amendment #3 would change from elective to appointive the offices of commissioner of agriculture, secretary of state, and treasurer. Some of the lesser offices which no longer have any viable duties would be abolished, streamlining and making our government more efficient and responsive. Through these constitutional changes, we "elect" opportunities for more efficient, effective government that will work for the benefit of all Kentuckians. As the head of our state Chamber of Commerce, Charles Johnson, noted with the formation of the "Vote Yes for Change" committee, "we need not settle for the so-called revolving door system which has plagued the efforts of our gubernatorial leadership to enact and implement long-term and far-reaching solutions to the problems we face." Efforts to move our state forward are hampered by changing administrations every four years. As you know, I intentionally excluded myself from this consideration, so succession could be considered on its own merits and our Commonwealth could benefit from the change. The amendments are an opportunity for historic change, for all of us to shape our constitution for a better tomorrow.

As November 3 approaches, it is hard to remember a presidential campaign of greater importance to our state and nation than the one in which we are now involved. In just a few short weeks, I am confident that Kentuckians and all Americans will elect change, vitality, and new direction as we come together to rebuild America and abandon the policies of division and destruction. This nation has been torn apart by failed and flawed policies for twelve years under Republican administrations. The Democratic ticket, from Bill Clinton and Al Gore to our Kentucky Democratic congressional candidates, is forged into a united effort for new direction as has not been seen in decades. Our candidates form a team that is dedicated to returning to our people our rightful say in how this country is run. Republican policies and failed promises have drained our national energy and left our nation divided and depressed, but now there is more than hope coming from Hope, Arkansas, and Carthage, Tennessee, Bill Clinton and Al Gore, and there is hope coming from all parts of the Commonwealth, from the Big Sandy to the mighty Mississippi. Now there is unity of purpose and the willingness to work hard to rebuild America, not divide and conquer it.

Knowing the importance of Kentucky and other southern states, the Republicans would have us quarrel among ourselves about issues long past, painful dilemmas of twenty and twenty-five years ago. Let us not be diverted. Let us not be used against ourselves. Instead, we must focus on the next two decades and the pressing problems of tomorrow. Our party has a ticket that will bring our nation the energy and will to seek solutions, to find answers to the challenges of health care, jobs, economic revitalization, education, and the environment. In Kentucky, our Democratic ticket brings the willingness to work with a Democratic president to lift this nation from decades of drifting to a new direction, providing leadership that will be responsive to the long-ignored cries of our people. "Put the people first" is not just a pat slogan. It is a pledge emblazoned across our programs. . . .

ASHLAND/BOYD COUNTY JEFFERSON-JACKSON DAY DINNER
Ashland / October 24, 1992

IT IS my pleasure to be here this evening with the tried and true of our Democratic Party in Kentucky. Eastern Kentucky Democrats are stalwarts in our party, and I know we can count on you as we move forward through the final weeks of the campaign, in the effort to adopt our constitutional amendments and to reform health care. The strength of our nation's constitution is its ability to adapt to new directions and changes in our society, but our state constitution is one hundred years old, and its inflexibility keeps our state from being as progressive as it could be. That is why I ask you to "Vote Yes for Change" on the constitutional amendments that will be on our ballot November 3, and I ask you to campaign for their support. Call on your friends and others to be architects for change and strength. That is why we formed the "Vote Yes for Change" committee. That committee is behind a statewide grassroots effort to promote passage of the amendments to the Kentucky constitution. The main elements of Amendment #2 would allow the governor and other state officers to serve two consecutive terms, require the governor and lieutenant governor to run as a team, and reduce the frequency of elections. Amendment #3 would change from elective to appointive the offices of commissioner of agriculture, secretary of state, and treasurer. Some of the lesser offices which no longer have any viable duties would be abolished, streamlining and making our government more efficient and responsive. Through these constitutional changes, we "elect" opportunities for more efficient, effective government that will work for the benefit of all Kentuckians. As the head of our state Chamber of Commerce, Charles Johnson, noted with the formation of the "Vote Yes for Change" committee, "We need not settle for the so-called revolving door system which has plagued the efforts of our gubernatorial leadership to enact and implement long-term and far-reaching solutions to the problems we face." Efforts to move our state forward are hampered by changing administrations every four years. As you know, I intentionally excluded myself from this consideration so succession could be considered on its own merits and our Commonwealth could benefit from the change. The amendments are an opportunity for historic change for all of us to shape our Constitution for a better tomorrow.

As November 3 approaches, it is hard to remember a presidential campaign of greater importance to our state and nation than the one in which we are now involved. In just a few short weeks, I am confident that Kentuckians and all Americans will elect change, vitality, and new direction as we come together to rebuild America and abandon the policies of division and destruction. This nation has been torn apart by failed and flawed policies for twelve years under Republican administrations. The Democratic ticket, from Bill Clinton and Al Gore to our Kentucky Democratic congressional candidates, is forged into a united effort for new direction as has not been seen in decades. Our candidates, Tom Barlow in the 1st congressional district, Bill Natcher in the 2nd, Ron Mazzoli in the 3rd, Floyd Poore in the 4th, John Doug Hays in the 5th, and Scotty Baesler in the 6th, form a team that is dedicated to returning to our people our rightful say in how this country is run. Here in the new 4th Congressional District, Floyd Poore in Congress and our senior statesman, Sen. Wendell Ford, represent this region's best interests, your interests, the interests of the working men and women, not the special interests that for so long have gotten the full attention of the Republican leadership in Washington. Jim Bunning is leading the pack in Washington to take care of those who need it the least and ignoring those who need our help most. Wendell Ford has a proven record of putting Kentucky first and is a recognized leader in the U.S. Senate. He has for years and years been our best ally in Washington. Floyd Poore has shown continuously throughout this campaign that, unlike Jim Bunning, he, Floyd Poore, cares about average, hardworking people. The best interests of this region are best represented by re-electing Wendell Ford and by sending Floyd Poore to Washington to replace one of the staunchest advocates of a failed economic policy and a blatant disregard for helping those who cannot help themselves.

Republican policies have drained our national energy and left our nation divided and depressed. But now, there is more than hope coming from Hope, Arkansas, and Carthage, Tennessee, Bill Clinton and Al Gore, and there is hope coming from all parts of the Commonwealth, from the Big Sandy to the mighty Mississippi. Now there is unity of purpose and the willingness to work hard to rebuild America, not divide and conquer it. Knowing the importance of Kentucky and other southern states, the Republicans would have us quarrel among ourselves about issues long past, painful dilemmas of twenty and twenty-five years ago. Let us not be diverted. Let us not be used against ourselves. Instead, we must focus on the next two decades and the pressing problems of tomorrow. Our party has a ticket that will bring to our nation the energy and will to seek solutions, to find answers to the national challenges of health care, jobs, economic revitalization, education, and the environment. In Kentucky, our Democratic ticket brings the willingness to work with a Democratic president to lift this nation from decades of drifting to a new direction, providing leadership that will be responsive to the long-ignored cries of our people. "Put the people first" is not just a party slogan. It is a pledge, emblazoned across our programs and the crucible for change. For too long, Washington has not responded to a growing national frustration, bordering at times on anger, to stop the deterioration of our country, boost jobs, reinvigorate our economy, give all Americans quality health care at an affordable price, give our children the best possible education, clean up our environment, and restore our economic might at home and abroad.

Perhaps the single greatest challenge we face in the months ahead is reforming our health-care system. As you know, I have offered a program for change. My wife, Libby, is fond of saying you only need two things to be happy, a clean conscience and good health. I can't do much about your conscience, but we certainly can help the citizens of our Commonwealth find good health care. I know, as you do, that there is no greater problem facing America and our Commonwealth, and only bold efforts will keep this problem from bankrupting our nation and our state. Now Kentucky is taking a leadership position, and we will set the pace and direction of health-care reform in this nation, if we act out of conviction, compassion, and courage. There are all sorts of questions and concerns about time, funding, equity, and other matters, but this problem has been festering for decades. Waiting only worsens the condition and diminishes the hopes of Kentuckians who stand defenseless in the face of rising health-care costs. To not act now, to not act with every fiber of our collective strength, is cowardice, and I know you are not afraid to get behind this effort and help lead us to solutions. This is my goal, and we can reach it by working together and by being willing to make sacrifices for the good of all. We will help those who cannot help themselves and not by pressing any undue burden on any one segment of our Commonwealth. We must all carry the load. I also want to emphasize one point that tends to get lost in many discussions about health-care reform. Controlled health-care costs will give Kentucky an economic-development tool unmatched by any other state. When we can assure our existing businesses and prospective employers alike that these costs are controlled in Kentucky, I have no doubt that we will see significant economic growth. Our administration and our party are forging an alliance for responsiveness, for change, for a better tomorrow.

For twelve long years, there has been no vision from Washington, and as you have heard me quote before, the Bible says, "Where there is no vision, the people perish." George Bush has belittled and reduced this crucial need with arrogance and disdain into what he called "the vision thing." There can be no vision when the Republicans are blind to the needs of our people, and the only thing they can see is that they are in trouble, and the only thing they can do is resort to the politics of desperation. There can be no change when the Republicans turn their ears away from the cries of the vast majority who are worse off now than they were twelve years ago. There can be no direction from those who haven't got a clue as to how to lead. Bill Clinton, Al Gore, their families and commitment, our party, and our administration stand ready to listen, to lead, to restore, to revitalize, to reform, to unify, and to work for the good of all. We have answers; they have rhetoric and distraction. We have the willingness to work; they have the need to preserve and protect the status quo which has helped the rich at the expense of the middle income and the poor. We call for unity; they exploit old wounds and divide us along racial and income lines. We seek change; they mouth the word in desperation. It's time for us to lead, and it's time for them to go, and we must not fail in our promises of prosperity, better education, better government, individual and family security, and health-care reform. Our nation and this Commonwealth need us, need our leadership, and we must be willing, ready, and able to show result and make sacrifices. For history will turn on our greatest endeavors, or our legacy will be hollow. *We* see tomorrow, and *our* vision is clear. Thank you.

Vote for the amendments. Vote for democratic change. Vote for Sen. Wendell Ford and for Floyd Poore, and help us bring health-care reform to everyone in our great Commonwealth of Kentucky.

TALKING POINTS FOR PADUCAH RALLY
Paducah / October 30, 1992

YOUR rendition of waking up November 4th was great in the rotunda Wednesday. You might consider doing it again. The politics of division have been business as usual in Washington the past twelve years. The only place George Bush has brought us together has been in the unemployment line. George Bush keeps talking about a rebounding economy while businesses close and more Americans sign up for unemployment. He's a lot like the Peanuts character Lucy who says, "If you can't be right, be wrong as loud as you can." George Bush is a proponent of trickle-down economics. A question: Does anybody feel wet yet? Now the principal proponent of the failed "trickle-down" economic theory, Bush once called it "voodoo economics." One political wag says after twelve years, we're in "deep voodoo." I liked the comment in the rotunda Wednesday about how Bush's view of himself is distorted: "He was born on third base and thinks he hit a triple." George Bush has criticized Bill Clinton as the governor of a small southern state; this from a man who has FOUR *home* states. Bill Clinton is proud of his home state and has worked hard to make it better, while George Bush doesn't know where to call home. George Bush criticizes small southern states and then travels through the South wanting our vote and trying to act like he knows something about rural southern living. George Bush, as Bill Clinton is fond of saying, "wouldn't know 'come here' from 'sick 'em.'" George Bush told Soviet leader Mikhail Gorbachev not to pay any attention to what he might say during the campaign. Then, how are we to believe anything he says? George Bush himself said he'd do anything to get re-elected, and it's becoming obvious in the way he's attacking Bill Clinton. It reminds me of the political cartoon with George Bush dressed up like George Washington standing next to a chopped down cherry tree and saying, "Congress did it." Now George Bush says he wants four more years to help our economy and create jobs when we've lost 35,000 jobs in the private sector alone. If we had the jobs George Bush has sent overseas, the economy might be better, but betting on Bush to create jobs is like buying a new suit from the man who took the shirt right off your back. George Bush has also had a significant impact on farming. The last time anything affected farming in this nation the way George Bush has, it was called the DUST BOWL, and it wiped out thousands of family farms, much the same as has happened under twelve years of Republican administrations. Locusts don't destroy as much farmland as the Republicans have.

JEFFERSON-JACKSON DAY DINNER
Pulaski County / October 31, 1992

IT IS my pleasure to be here this evening with the tried and true of our Democratic Party in Kentucky. Fifth congressional [district] Democrats are stalwarts in our party, and I know we can count on all of you as we move forward through the final days of the campaign and the effort to adopt our constitutional amendments, and I know you'll be there to help with health-care reform. The strength of our nation's constitution is its ability to adapt to new directions and changes in our society, but our state constitution is one hundred years old, and its inflexibility keeps our state from being as progressive as it should be. That is why I ask you to "Vote Yes for Change" in the constitutional amendments that will be on our ballot next Tuesday, and I ask you to campaign for their support. Call on your friends and others to be architects for change and strength. That is why we formed the "Vote Yes for Change" committee. That committee is behind a statewide grassroots effort to promote passage of these amendments. The main elements of amendment #2 would allow the governor and other state officers to serve two consecutive terms, require the governor and lieutenant governor to run as a team, and reduce the frequency of elections. Amendment #3 would change from elective to appointive the offices of commissioner of agriculture, secretary of state, and treasurer. Some of the lesser offices which no longer have any viable duties would be abolished, streamlining and making our government more efficient and responsive. Through these constitutional changes, we "elect" opportunities for more efficient, effective government that will work for the benefit of all Kentuckians. As the head of our state Chamber of Commerce, Charles Johnson, noted with the formation of the "Vote Yes for Change" committee, "We need not settle for the so-called revolving door system which has plagued the efforts of our gubernatorial leadership to enact and implement long-term and far-reaching solutions to the problems we face." Efforts to move our state forward are hampered by changing administrations every four years. As you know, I intentionally excluded myself from this consideration so succession could be considered on its own merits and our Commonwealth could benefit from the change. The amendments are an opportunity for historic change, for all of us to shape our government for a better tomorrow.

As election day approaches, it is hard to remember a presidential campaign of greater importance to our state and nation than the one in which we are now involved. In just a few short days, I am confident that Kentuckians and all Americans will elect change, vitality, and new direction as we come together to rebuild America and abandon the policies of division and destruction. This nation has been torn apart by failed and flawed policies for twelve years under Republican administrations. The Democratic ticket, from Bill Clinton and Al Gore to our Kentucky Democratic congressional candidates, is forged into a united effort for new direction as has not been seen in decades. Our candidates, especially John Doug Hays in the 5th congressional district, form a team that is dedicated to returning to our people our rightful say in how this country is run. Here in the new 5th congressional district, John Doug Hays in Congress and our senior statesman Sen. Wendell Ford, represent this region's best interests, your interests, the interests of the working men and women, not the special interests that for so long have gotten the full attention of the Republican leadership in Washington. Why should the 5th congressional district elect John Doug Hays? The answer is simple. He best represents this region and its people and cares about their needs, for example, health-care reform.

The cost of health insurance has tripled since Hal Rogers took office in 1980, and yet, Mr. Rogers voted to cut $25 billion from Medicare, the program upon which so many of our elderly citizens depend for medical assistance. Rogers endorses the Bush philosophy of health care which would cover only one-fourth of those who are without health insurance and cost the taxpayers billions more than Bill Clinton's plan to cover everyone. John Doug Hays backs Bill Clinton, as I do, and would work with President Clinton to solve this national dilemma and work with our administration to bring health-care reform to Kentucky. John Doug Hays, a man of principle and integrity, knows how devastating it can be for those who are without health insurance, and he has seen what happens when catastrophic illness wipes out a family's savings, destroying the lives of those who are ill and the families that care for them.

John Doug Hays knows the pain of these people, and he would bring change to Washington. Congressman Rogers's salary has doubled in his twelve years in Washington to nearly $130,000 a year, and yet, he voted against raising the minimum wage to $4.55 an hour. That shows his commitment to the men and women of Kentucky and their families. The 5th district has ten counties where the percentage of children living in poverty is higher than it is in Detroit, Michigan, yet Hal Rogers voted against increased funding for the Women and Infant Children's Nutrition Program, showing the greatest of insensitivities to our most needy and defenseless. Hal Rogers voted against family and medical leave, against a tax cut for the working people of our country, and against increased funding for Head Start, an education program aimed at helping those who have it toughest get a better beginning in our schools. At the same time, however, Hal Rogers voted for a bill which uses American tax dollars to move our businesses to foreign soil, making it even tougher for those most in need to find work. This is the legacy of the Reagan-Bush years, completely out of touch with the people of this country, and Hal Rogers is a part of that legacy.

John Doug Hays will be a messenger and an advocate for those who have long been ignored and have for so long been in need. John Doug Hays represents compassion and change. It's time to elect those who will turn our country back to its original path of being responsive to the people and away from twelve years of protecting the special interests of the privileged few. John Doug Hays is a man of the people, and he will not forget who he is, where he is from, nor those who send him to Washington. I ask you to vote for John Doug Hays November third.

Wendell Ford has a proven record of putting Kentucky first and is a recognized leader in the U.S. Senate. He has for years been our best ally in Washington. He cares about average hardworking people.

The best interests of this region are best represented by reelecting Wendell Ford and by sending John Doug Hays to Washington to replace an advocate of a failed economic policy and a blatant disregard for helping those who cannot help themselves. Republican policies and failed promises have drained our national energy and left our nation divided and depressed, but now there is more than hope coming from Hope, Arkansas, and Carthage, Tennessee—Bill Clinton and Al Gore—and there is hope coming from all parts of the Commonwealth, from the Big Sandy to the mighty Mississippi. Now there is unity of purpose and the willingness to work hard to rebuild America, not divide and conquer it.

Knowing the importance of Kentucky and other southern states, the Republicans would have us quarrel among ourselves about issues long past, painful dilemmas of twenty and twenty-five years ago. Let us not be diverted; let us not be used against ourselves. Instead, we must focus on the next two decades and the pressing problems of tomorrow. Our party has a ticket that will bring our nation the energy and the will to seek solutions, to find answers to national challenges of health care, jobs, economic revitalization, education, and the environment. In Kentucky, our Democratic ticket brings the willingness to work with a Democratic president to lift this nation from decades of drifting to a new direction, providing leadership that will be responsive to the long-ignored cries of our people. "Put the people first" is not just a party slogan. It is a pledge, emblazoned across our programs and the crucible for change. For too long, Washington has not responded to a growing national frustration, bordering at times on anger, to stop the deterioration of our country, boost jobs, reinvigorate our economy, give all Americans quality health care at an affordable price, give our children the best possible education, clean up our environment, and restore our economic might at home and abroad.

Perhaps the single greatest challenge we face in the months ahead is reforming our health-care system. As you know, I have offered a program for change. My wife, Libby, is fond of saying you need only two things to be happy, a clean conscience and good health. I can't do much about your conscience, but we certainly can help the citizens of our Commonwealth find good health care. I know, as you do, that there is no greater problem facing America and our Commonwealth, and only bold effort will keep this problem from bankrupting our nation and our state. Now Kentucky is taking a leadership position, and we will set the pace and direction of health-care reform in this nation, if we act out of conviction, compassion, and courage. There are all sorts of questions and concerns about time, funding, equity, and other matters, but this problem has been festering for decades. Waiting only worsens the condition and diminishes the hopes of Kentuckians who stand defenseless in the face of rising health-care costs. To not act now, to not act with every fiber of our collective strength, is cowardice, and I know you are not afraid to get behind this effort and help lead us to solutions. This is my goal, and we can reach it by working together and by being willing to make sacrifices for the good of all. We will help those who cannot help themselves and not by pressing any undue burden on any one section of our Commonwealth. We must all carry the load. I also want to emphasize one point that tends to get lost in many discussions about health-care reform. Controlled health-care costs will give Kentucky an economic-development tool unmatched by any other state. When we can assure our existing businesses and prospective employers alike that these costs are controlled in Kentucky, I have no doubt that we will see significant economic growth. Our administration and our party are forcing an alliance for responsiveness, for change, for a better tomorrow.

For twelve long years, there has been no vision from Washington, and as you have heard me quote before, the Bible says, "Where there is no vision the people perish." George Bush has belittled and reduced this crucial need with arrogance and disdain into what he called "the vision thing." There can be no vision when the Republicans are blind to the needs of our people, and the only thing they can see is that they are in trouble and the only thing they can do is resort to the politics of desperation. There can be no change when the Republicans turn their ears away from the cries of the vast majority who are worse off now than they were twelve years ago. There can be no direction from those who haven't got a clue as to how to lead. Bill Clinton, Al Gore, their families, their strength and commitment, our party, and our administration stand ready to listen, to lead, to restore, to revitalize, to reform, to unify, and to work for the good of all. We have answers; they have rhetoric and distraction. We have the willingness to work; they have the need to preserve the status quo which has helped the rich at the expense of the middle income and the poor. We call for unity; they exploit old wounds and divide us along racial and income lines. We seek change; they mouth the word in desperation. It's time for us to lead, and it's time for them to go, and we must not fail in our promises of prosperity, better education, better government, individual and family security, and health-care reform. Our nation and this Commonwealth need us, need our leadership, and we must be willing, ready, and able to show results and make sacrifices. For history will turn on our greatest endeavors, or our legacy will be hollow. *We* see tomorrow, and *our* vision is clear. Thank you.

Vote for the amendments. Vote for Democratic change. Vote for Sen. Wendell Ford and for John Doug Hays, and help us bring health-care reform to everyone in our great Commonwealth of Kentucky.

REMARKS AND INTRODUCTION OF CONGRESSMAN RON MAZZOLI

Wendell Ford Trust Dinner, Louisville / May 14, 1993

"NOW is the time for all good men (and women) to come to the aid of their country." "Evil triumphs where good men (and women) do nothing." These phrases with the politically correct and rightfully fair additions have been axioms for most of our lives. While for most of us they've become over-worn and even trite, never before have they been more true than they are now. Our nation and state are facing challenges that surpass any which have come before. Now is a test of true leadership and real courage, moral courage, and old words with renewed strength and deeper meaning—*convictions, character, integrity*—have risen to the surface again and are the minimum now expected and rightfully demanded by the electorate. From Bosnia to the national economy, from our leadership in Washington to health-care and education reform in our Commonwealth, our abilities to find solutions are being tested. With health-care reform, there are those that continue to proclaim that our efforts are certain to fail. Other states have tried to solve the health-care dilemma, and all have come up short. We seek to get control of health-care costs and to provide health-care coverage for every single Kentuckian without regard to any pre-existing condition. We are willing to listen to new ideas but cannot compromise away these goals as other states have, bowing to the special interests. It is sometimes better to stand alone for the right reasons than to compromise away all you really believe in. I continue to believe that our legislators, with the right information and full understanding of the dimensions of this crisis, will do the right thing, but we are in a new age. The expectations are even higher, and our people are demanding more. *How* we reach our solutions has become as important as the answers that we find, and public life has, in many cases, become a trial by fire.

This evening's special guest speaker, Bob Kerrey,[1] faced the fires of trial in distant jungles decades ago, rose to the occasion with great sacrifice, and won the nation's highest honor [Medal of Honor]. Other of us in public life face more subtle and insidious trials, but it is in this fire that the real mettle of a person is found. It is in the face of compromise that real courage can be shown. With all of this in mind, it is my distinct honor tonight to introduce

Congressman Ron Mazzoli. Most of us know that for many years Congressman Mazzoli has exemplified integrity. In his recent congressional race, faced with a challenge on a deeply dividing and highly controversial issue, he was publicly pounded by his opposition, and it was showing results in the polls. Where others might have equivocated, or fought fire with fire, or sought a new strategy, Ron Mazzoli stuck to his principles and again won the respect of an electorate that continues to believe in him as a person. This is the kind of leadership our nation expects and is finding more and more as good men and women seek public office to work for the common good. All of us face moments where our beliefs are tested, and how we answer these personal dilemmas tells *everything* about who we really are and what we are made of. It is with great pleasure that I introduce to you the congressman from the third district of Kentucky, the Honorable Ron Mazzoli.

---

1. Robert Kerrey (1943–), M.S., University of Nebraska, 1966; Navy, 1966–69; recipient of Medal of Honor; governor of Nebraska, 1983–87; U.S. Senate, 1988–2001; president, New School University.

DEMOCRATIC HEADQUARTERS TWENTIETH ANNIVERSARY
Frankfort / July 17, 1993

TWENTY years ago when ground was broken for the construction of this building, our nation was a very different place in which to live and work. Here in Kentucky, Sen. Wendell Ford was governor, while in Washington Richard Nixon was in the White House; "Watergate" was in the early stages of revelation; Vietnam was mired down after eight years of bloody warfare in the sweltering jungles, draining the national resolve and dividing us in bitter dispute. The dollar purchased about twice what it does now, and we were all a lot younger. Most of this past twenty years, there has been a Republican in the White House, and the national debt has soared, while our economy has been in rapid decline. Who would have known then that the Soviet empire would collapse and we would be the world's sole superpower, engaged in global *economic* warfare and defending ourselves, our allies, and world interests against the flailings of third-world despots and their terroristic tirades at home and abroad?

In Kentucky we've seen our tax base erode as the national economy and most of our Commonwealth's traditional revenue producers have been in decline. As with most states, our economy has been mostly at the mercy of the whims of Washington under the deficit-spending, budget-busting practices of twenty years of Republican fiscal irresponsibility and congressional confusion. Now, a young Clinton administration is struggling to turn around, in months, what took two decades to severely damage—the strength and ability of this nation. The people voted for "change," and they have given our party another chance at making it happen, making it work, bringing our spending in line with our abilities, and building our economy once again to world dominance in the midst of critical world competition. It's no easy feat, in Washington, or here in Frankfort, to turn things around, and for us it's all the more frustrating as we in Kentucky grapple with enormous problems that Washington has exacerbated, and the economy hamstrings our resources.

But, while money may be in short supply, there is no shortage of leadership, ability, and sheer will in this Commonwealth and nation and in the Democratic Party, as long as we are agents of social and fiscal responsibility. The people have spoken that they want the economy fixed, but they don't want the old ways of tax and spend. The new Democratic Party is a progressive party of ideas and solutions based on time-proven business practices and fiscal reality that can return our economy to a sound base without overly straining the economy of the families in America, but we are foolish to think we can do it all without some pain. We have, unfortunately, inherited a situation where the runaway, reckless approach of the past two decades will require some sacrifice on the part of all, and it will have to happen on our watch. But we in the Democratic Party are ready and willing to meet the challenge, and I feel confident that Kentuckians and Americans alike understand and are willing to make the necessary sacrifices, provided they soundly result in the needed changes.

We are also foolish to think that this can happen overnight, following twenty years of neglect. The observers of the governmental process need to preach patience, while also holding government accountable. It is too easy to make gains focusing on disparity and difficulty than to educate and facilitate the process of change. It is easier to stand by and criticize, antagonize, and instigate than to intelligently join in the effort to solve, but there are many reasons for hope because just as this building has weathered twenty years of our nation adrift, our party has endured many difficulties and divisions and grown stronger and more progressive than ever. But, just as this building is only as strong as each individual brick and how it is bound together by mortar, so is our party only as strong as each individual is bound together for the common good. Here in Kentucky we have launched nationally acclaimed education reforms and are at the forefront of the debate on health-care reforms. We are also re-evaluating government, trying to downsize it, streamline it, and make it more efficient, to use every tax dollar as wisely as possible. Without health-care reforms, this effort will be turned from difficult to near impossible, but we have the resolve, the resources, and the ability to accomplish it all, by remaining united and progressive as a party. We have accomplished a lot and can yet accomplish a lot more.

In just the short span of two years, our administration campaigned for and helped win passage of the gubernatorial succession amendment for future governors, which will forever transform that office and allow progressive government to be nurtured and furthered to the benefit of all Kentuckians. Within seconds of being sworn into office, our administration issued a strict executive branch code of ethics that now is law and guarantees to the people that those who serve are of the highest integrity and honor. We have won the passage of wide-ranging election reform legislation that will alter the state's political structure and reduce the number and costs of Kentucky's elections, and we have established the state's first mechanism of public funding of future campaigns for governor and lieutenant governor, changing forever the structure of campaigning, making it more responsive to the people. Our citizens are demanding responsiveness and responsibility on the part of those who govern and those who seek to govern. Our administration has supported and signed into law a bill changing the system of selecting members of the state's seven university governing boards. This legislation ensures that future appointments will be based on merit, bringing to our educational institutions our best and brightest. We have instituted a procedure for awarding state architectural and engineering contracts that assures to the people of the Commonwealth that the most qualified companies are selected, irrespective of political connections or contributions. And, we have reorganized and strengthened the Cabinet for Economic Development to bring continuity and professionalism to the crucial role of providing jobs for our people, insulating this process and institution from the shifts of political winds and changing administrations.

Perhaps no greater compliment was ever paid our administration than when one of our greatest Democratic governors, Gov. Ned Breathitt, noted that neither he nor Gov. Bert Combs could pass gubernatorial succession, but *we* did. And, he said that any one of our achievements in our first year in office would justify our entire four years in office as a success. This is a great compliment to us all and our efforts on behalf of the Commonwealth, but our greatest accomplishment is yet to come. That is when the legislature and the executive branch together solve the crisis of health care in this state. If we don't get control of the health-care costs, they will bankrupt us all, from governments to individuals, and we cannot get control of health-care costs unless we provide coverage for everyone and stop the cost shifting, where those of us who are insured pay for the more expensive medical care of those who are not insured through increases in our premiums and more expensive care ourselves. This is a fiscal strain that will sap the remaining strength out of our economy and siphon off money from our budget that is so vitally needed for our education and economic development. I feel confident that the party of the people can provide the leadership necessary to solve this dilemma and become an example for the nation.

We cannot and should not wait for Washington to find the solution for us. We do not have the luxury of money or time for such delay, and the people of our Commonwealth who count on us will pay with their very lives and suffering with each day that we wait. Twenty years—two decades of divisiveness and lack of direction at the hands of the other party—five presidents, and five governors later, and what seems like a lifetime of struggle that has served to temper and strengthen our Democratic Party, its will, direction, and our ability to contribute to a brighter future for our Commonwealth and this nation. The people are waiting. We have been called upon to lead this nation and this state through tough times that will demand tough decisions and unpopular sacrifices. "These are the times that try men and women's souls," to paraphrase Thomas Paine, but we are not "sunshine patriots nor summertime soldiers." We must lead. The people expect it, and we must not, we cannot, do anything less.

CENTURY CLUB JESSE JACKSON RECEPTION
Governor's Mansion / September 29, 1993

WE ARE very pleased that Reverend Jackson[1] is with us this evening. Thank you for being here. I believe I speak for all of us when I say that we appreciate the stand you take on the front line of democracy, to uphold the tenets of the democratic process, the very principles upon which this party is based: empowerment, peace, economic justice, social equity, gender equality, and civil rights. You've been called the "conscience of the nation." You've worked very hard to bring people together, across lines of race, class, gender, and belief. Again, we thank you. We applaud your efforts, and we appreciate your being here to help us recognize these wonderful folks who keep our party going through their kind generosity.

---

1. Jesse L. Jackson (1941–), attended University of Illinois, North Carolina A&T State University, and Chicago Theological Seminary; assistant to Dr. Martin Luther King Jr.; president, National Rainbow Coalition, 1986–present; U.S. presidential candidate, 1984 and 1988.

JEFFERSON-JACKSON DAY DINNER
Kentucky Dam Village / June 11, 1994

I'M HERE this evening because I believe that when we all work together as one, we can accomplish many positive things. As you know, we are waiting this weekend to see what comes out of a legislative conference committee on the state budget for the next biennium. I'm hoping that they will see the need to approve a budget that will allow us to make good investments in the future of our children. We need to use our projected state surplus to invest first in human needs, and then in our state parks, to restore them to what they once were: the finest in the nation. After that, if surplus revenue continues to come in as projected, I want an investment in economic- development projects that will pay off for years to come in jobs and extra tax revenue. I encourage you to contact your legislators and encourage them to invest in the future. I don't have any doubt that the majority of the public is behind our plan, and I don't have any doubt that the public wants the legislature to agree with our plans for the future. The public is looking for unity, and we need unity in Frankfort. Democrats need to work together, not against each other. The people elected a Democratic legislature, and the people expect us to work together to get things done. I firmly believe that people are getting tired of the apparent lack of effort to get along. They'll show how tired they are when they go to the polls in November. Democrats are in danger of losing their seats, seats they've held onto for years because of the lack of Democratic unity. We must get back on track.

Speaking of a lack of united effort, allow me to say a few words about the election in the second district. We were shut out by a few days of campaigning by some out-of-towners who fooled the public into believing they would be better off if a Republican gained control of the district. How wrong they are!! The writer P.J. O'Rourke, who considers himself an expert on national politics, tells us, "Republicans are the party that says government doesn't work, and then they get elected and prove it." That's what I see happening in the second district if we don't all get together and work for the party in November. I'm willing to say I didn't do enough to help Joe Prather win the seat in the primary election, and now I'm saying we all have to do as much as we can to preserve the legacy of democracy left to the U.S. by Bill Natcher, when voters go to the polls in the fall.

In the first district, we have an all-around good congressman in Tom Barlow. He has demonstrated his loyalty to the Clinton agenda by remaining loyal to the president, and he has been true to the people by staying firm on issues. Tom Barlow deserves all the support we can give him, especially as he runs against a former Democrat who may get a lot of Democratic support. Let's all work together to help Tom beat Ed Whitfield![1] We also must support the candidates who are toughing it out for a win on the local and state levels. We need to unite behind them; folks like Bob Leeper, Freed Curd, Jimmie Morphew, John Arnold, Fred Reeves, Don Moore, Preacher Nelson, Larry Grayson, and David Boswell.

And while I encourage you all to throw your weight behind these candidates, I would also encourage the young people here tonight to become more involved in your party and public service. Your ideas, your energy, and your talents are all vital to the long-term viability of the Democratic philosophy. We need you to volunteer; we need you to participate; we need you to run for office! Those of us who are older and are already a part of the political process have a responsibility to encourage young people to get involved. And what do we tell them about the Democratic Party? We tell them "we're the party of the people." We believe in the values of the average citizen, not in the power of wealth and the influence it can wield, but in the power of individual rights and collective responsibility.

Finally, I am here tonight to encourage you to seek financial support for the Democratic Party. We're faced with an ironic political reality that is a direct result of our having changed the old ways. In the old days, a lot of people knew they'd get special treatment if they bellied up to the bar and contributed to the party, but those old, bad days are gone, thank goodness, and we're all on a level playing field now. Now we need the help of everyone here who can support the party, not only by supporting our philosophical agenda, but also by promoting the wisdom of those who would carry out that agenda. They cannot do it without financial backing. They cannot run for office and win without money. Let's all do what we can do.

---

1. Ed Whitfield (1943–), B.S. in business, University of Kentucky, 1965; J.D., University of Kentucky, 1969; member Kentucky house, 1974–75; private law practice, 1970–79; legal counsel, Seaboard Systems Railroad, 1979–83; vice-president, CSX Corp., 1983–91; legal counsel to chairman Interstate Commerce Committee, 1991–93; Republican, U.S. representative, district 1, 1994; re-elected, 1996–2000. *1999–2000 Who's What in Kentucky Government.*

FORD FOUNDATION
Louisville / July 8, 1994

SOMEBODY once wrote about politics, "Democrats are the party of government activism, the party that says government can make you smarter, taller, and get chickweed out of your lawn. Republicans are the party that says government doesn't work, and then they get elected and prove it." To me, the difference between Republicans and Democrats is crystal clear. The Republican Party is the party that says we can't, we won't, and we shouldn't. The Democratic Party is the party that says we can, we will, and we must. It was a great Democrat, Hubert Humphrey, who once said, "The moral test of government is how it treats those who are in the dawn of life, the children; those who are in the twilight of life, the aged; and those who are in the shadows of life, the sick, the needy, and the handicapped."

I believe Congressman Ron Mazzoli's record shows he has adhered to this moral test of government, and the House has been blessed to have his morals and integrity standing firm throughout the years. Since 1971, he has served the people of the third congressional district of Kentucky with honesty and grit. Those of us in the Democratic Party are proud that he is a member of our ranks. We know that he is a person who has put the people above everything else. He is a man with heart who has always made it his policy not to be swayed by pressure from others. Instead, he has relied on his strong personal beliefs and values to make final judgments. A reporter asked him what he would like as his epitaph after twenty-seven years as a public servant. Ron replied with the words of Paul from the New Testament, "He fought the good fight. He finished the course. He kept the faith." While this man is a long way from having those words etched in granite, I know they are words he will continue to live by as he carries on his life of service. It has been my great personal pleasure to know and work with this man, who has devoted so many years to the people of Louisville, Kentucky, and this nation, and it's my honor to introduce to you now a great Kentuckian, Congressman Ron Mazzoli.

APPENDIX A

Timeline of Some Important Events of the Brereton C. Jones Administration

1991

November 5—Jones defeats Republican U.S. Representative Larry Hopkins by a 2-to-1 margin in the race for governor.

November 7—Jones announces that he hopes to create "a model program that could help show the nation how to deal with the health-insurance crisis."

November 21—Governor-elect Jones selects Lieutenant-Governor-elect Paul Patton to serve as secretary of the Cabinet for Economic Development.

December 9—Former Governor Ned Breathitt and fifteen heads of newspapers or broadcasting companies sponsor a fund-raising dinner in an effort to help defray Jones's 1987 campaign debts.

December 10—Jones is inaugurated as governor, promising "cooperation over conflict"; he propounds, within sixty seconds of taking office, an ethics code for the executive branch of government.

December 12—Jones, at the request of members of the General Assembly, calls his first (of a record nine) special session to reapportion legislative districts to reflect the results of the 1990 Census.

1992

January 13—Jones gives his first State of the Commonwealth address, pledging to create a new norm of "mutual respect and cooperation" between the legislature and the executive branch.

February 4—Jones endorses long-shot candidate Bill Clinton for president in the Capitol rotunda.

February 6—Jones advocates a slim budget, cutting money allotted for higher education and increasing the amount of money for the public school system. To reward successful horse breeders, he seeks $3.7 million from the General Assembly.

February 19—In cooperation with the senate leadership, Jones advocates campaign reform legislation, which includes gubernatorial succession, spending limits, and partial public funding for gubernatorial campaigns.

March 31—FBI makes public its investigation of unethical behavior in state government. Carried out covertly for eighteen months, the BOPTROT investigation was responsible for the conviction of twenty-one individuals, including fifteen current or former legislators. Jones is told that his executive branch was excluded from the probe.

April 3—Jones angers many legislators by stating that BOPTROT is "going to be a good thing. From time to time I think you have to clean out the system, and I think this is a good cleansing process."

April 14—In the first regular legislative session of the Jones administration, the governor's priority, health care, is postponed. However, the session ends with the passage of campaign-finance reform legislation, including partial public funding of gubernatorial campaigns and a proposed constitutional amendment which will allow governors after Jones to succeed themselves.

April 30—Jones receives the prestigious Keene Daingerfield Award from members of the horse industry.

July 1—Jones's "trustees" bill (passed in April) dissolved and then reconstituted all state university boards and the Council on Higher Education. Former Governor Wilkinson is not selected by Jones for the University of Kentucky Board of Trustees under the new appointment system, nor are most other Wilkinson supporters.

August 7—Jones suffers a bruised kidney and a painful back injury when a state helicopter carrying the governor and five others crashes near the Franklin-Shelby County line. The life-threatening experience, he says, allows him to refocus his energy on health-care reform.

September 9—Jones announces his health-care reform plan, which would provide universal coverage for all citizens of the Commonwealth and would establish a board to rein in the costs of health care.

October 2—Now that $1 million has been raised by Jack Hall (a key advisor and chief campaign fund-raiser) and others to pay off Jones's 1987 campaign debt, Jones declares all such fund-raising complete. Later, on October 16, he appoints Hall as chair of a commission to oversee the removal of underground gas tanks.

November 3—Voters of Kentucky adopt the constitutional amendment permitting governors after Jones and other statewide officials to succeed themselves.

November 12—Speaker of the House Don Blandford is indicted by the FBI in the BOPTROT investigation. Later, Blandford is convicted after resigning his position.

1993

February 1—Promising to stay out of the matter, Jones convenes a special legislative session to deal with legislative ethics.

February 17—The General Assembly passes a legislative ethics code—one of the toughest laws in the nation—which is signed by the governor.

March 1—Jones announces his second health-care reform plan, insisting on universal coverage for all Kentuckians.

March 12—Jones makes a $52 million state budget cut to keep Kentucky fiscally solvent. Later, he postpones delivery of tax refunds in an effort to balance the budget.

May 10—Jones convenes a special legislative session on comprehensive health-care reform.

May 21—Leaders of the General Assembly threaten to leave the special session due to Jones's unwillingness to compromise on reforms.

May 25—Representatives from forty-nine states and several foreign countries come to Louisville—"Rio to the Capitals"—at the governor's invitation to discuss continuing the initiatives of the 1992 "Earth Summit" in Rio de Janeiro, with special emphasis on sustainable development. Vice-President Al Gore delivers the keynote address and praises Kentucky for hosting the event.

May 27—The special session on health care ends in disappointment for the governor. However, legislation has been passed that establishes the Health-Care Data Commission and enacts a health-care provider tax to prevent the loss of $600 million in federal Medicaid funding. At the adjournment, legislative leaders agree to work with Governor Jones to develop a new bill that would address Jones's goals of universal coverage and cost containment.

July 16—The first female appointee to the Kentucky Supreme Court, Sara Combs (the widow of Gov. Bert T. Combs), is named by Jones.

August 1—Jones introduces a plan to cut state spending by $347 million due to revenue deficits.

September 22—Jones states that additional taxing of cigarettes is an acceptable method to fund national health-care reform, thereby angering many tobacco farmers.

November—Jones signs a series of Executive Orders—to establish a commission to modernize state government personnel practices; to adopt the first state government–wide strategic-planning procedures; to set up a privatization commission; to institute centralized money management; and to design improved methods for forecasting state revenue.

December 4—Jones opens his office to the public-at-large with his first monthly "Open Door After Four."

December 6—Jones recommends enhancing and restoring state park facilities through a $100 million bond issue.

1994

January—After an enormous amount of snow hits the Commonwealth, Jones declares a state of emergency and closes down the interstate highways.

February 1—Jones accepts the American Medical Association's most prestigious honor for government service to advance the public health, the Dr. Nathan Davis Award.

February 10—Jones creates the African-American Heritage Commission to promote statewide awareness of African American culture in Kentucky.

April 1—On the last day of the 1994 regular legislative session, Jones uses Kentucky Educational Television's airwaves to promote his health-care bill and his budget. He says that lobbyists influenced some legislative leaders to oppose him.

April 2—Jones kills the health-care reform legislation, and, hours later, the cabinet secretary states that his administration now advocates it. The following day, Jones alters his position but changes back to supporting the legislation several days later.

April 13—In vetoing the budget for the first time in Kentucky's history, Jones criticizes legislators for "cut[ting] out every single project and every single dollar for parks revitalization, no matter how meritorious, how urgently needed, or how basic."

April 15—With Jones's backing, health-care legislation is passed by the legislature. It includes insurance reforms but excludes universal coverage. Jones signs the health-care bill into law.

May—Jones conducts statewide bus tour to "Save Our State Parks," and calls on lawmakers to fund a parks revitalization package.

June 6—The General Assembly begins a special session on a revised budget plan.

June 22—Jones signs the new budget passed by the special legislative session. It includes $70 million for parks renovation, but excludes many of the governor's other priorities, including most of his construction projects.

July—Jones is appointed to the executive committee of the National Governors' Association and as states' co-chair of the Appalachian Regional Commission.

July 29—A December deadline is established by Jones for Lexington to begin constructing a cultural center or return $8.5 million to the Commonwealth.

August—Jones creates $100 million "rainy day" account—the largest budget reserve trust fund ever established for the state.

November 8—In congressional and state legislative elections, Republicans increase their numbers of elected officials in Kentucky and across the nation. The leadership of both parties call for tax cuts. Jones announces he will call a special session in January 1995 to fund three economic-development projects and to cut taxes.

November 16—Jack Hall is appointed to chair the Kentucky Health-Policy Board.

November 23—Jones announces the Hemp Task Force to study the agricultural viability of hemp.

December 1—Jones announces a $375 million Delta Airlines expansion at the Greater Cincinnati/Northern Kentucky International Airport in Boone County.

1995

January 27—The end of the special legislative session is marked with the passage of three of Jones's priority construction projects (the Kentucky History Center in Frankfort, the Northern Kentucky Convention Center in Covington, and the expansion of the Commonwealth Convention Center in Louisville) and cuts in income taxes on private pensions and inheritance taxes.

May 9—Jones announces a new initiative to combat fraud in the state workers' compensation system.

May 22—In an effort to reclaim state money given for a cultural center, Jones sues the city of Lexington.

June 12—The Kentucky Bluegrass Chapter of the National Forum for Black Administrators honors Jones for the progress his administration has made in appointing minorities to cabinet positions and to seats on state boards and commissions.

July 10—Jones announces an $84 million budget surplus.

July 31—A special session called by Jones begins. Jones persuades legislators to place $100 million in Kentucky's "rainy day" account and spend $50 million more on rural roads. Lawmakers adjust a redistricting plan that has been struck down by the courts as unconstitutional.

August 4—Jones says the new redistricting plan remains unconstitutional and vetoes the bill.

August 26—Jones participates in the 75th Anniversary of Women's Suffrage celebration at the Kentucky State Fair in Louisville.

September 4—Jones re-injures his back when thrown from a horse on his farm.

September 25—Ground is broken for the Kentucky History Center in Frankfort.

October 11—Jones announces federal approval of an amendment to Kentucky's statewide health-care demonstration program. The modified program would allow the state to implement a managed-care program for its Medicaid population. The Health-Care Partnerships formed as a result of the waiver should save Kentucky over $170 million at full implementation.

November 13—Jones, alongside U.S. Attorney General Janet Reno, signs a consent decree with the U.S. Department of Justice that specifies reforms for Kentucky's juvenile treatment facilities.

November 21—Criticizing rulings by the U.S. Supreme Court, Jones, at a pre-Thanksgiving luncheon for state employees, advocates the posting of the Ten Commandments in public schools.

December 11—On his last day in office, Jones commutes the sentences of nine women convicted of killing or trying to kill their abusers. Jones's action makes the women eligible for early release from prison, which the state parole board grants on January 4, 1996.

APPENDIX B
Calendar of Governor Jones's Speeches

Note: Asterisks denote speeches included in this volume.

INAUGURAL ADDRESS, Frankfort, December 10, 1991*

JAMES RIVER CORPORATION ANNOUNCEMENT CEREMONY, Bowling Green, December 18, 1991*

WHAS-TV, December 31, 1991

STATE OF THE COMMONWEALTH ADDRESS, Frankfort, January 13, 1992*

KENTUCKY LEAGUE OF CITIES, Frankfort, January 14, 1992

UNIVERSITY OF KENTUCKY COLDSTREAM VIDEO, Frankfort, January 14, 1992

APPALACHIAN GOVERNORS' QUORUM, Frankfort, February 4, 1992*

EXECUTIVE BUDGET MESSAGE TO THE GENERAL ASSEMBLY, Frankfort, February 6, 1992*

BOY SCOUTS LUNCHEON, Louisville, February 18, 1992

TALKING POINTS, Frankfort, February 19, 1992

JEFFERSON-JACKSON DAY, Frankfort, February 21, 1992*

HARLAN PLANT ANNOUNCEMENT, Harlan, February 27, 1992

KSBA, Louisville, February 28, 1992

NATIONAL GUARD, Drawbridge Inn, February 29, 1992

ARTICLE FOR AREA DEVELOPMENT MAGAZINE, Frankfort, March 1, 1992

ECONOMIC DEVELOPMENT NEWS CONFERENCE, Frankfort, March 2, 1992*

ARTICLE FOR KENTUCKY INDUSTRIAL DEVELOPMENT COUNCIL NEWSLETTER, Frankfort, March 4, 1992

SACHS AUTOMOTIVE PLANT DEDICATION, Florence, March 4, 1992*

KENTUCKY TEMPERANCE LEAGUE, Frankfort, March 4, 1992

BICENTENNIAL COMMISSION NEWS CONFERENCE, Frankfort, March 6, 1992

WENDELL H. FORD SUPPORTERS, Louisville, March 6, 1992

CHAMPIONS PROGRAM PARTICIPANTS, Frankfort, March 9, 1992

HOUSE BILL 157 AND HOUSE BILL 239 SIGNING, Frankfort, March 10, 1992*

NEWS CONFERENCE ON HEALTH CARE, Frankfort, March 11, 1992*

PRESS CONFERENCE, Frankfort, March 13, 1992

JEFFERSON-JACKSON DAY, Florence, March 14, 1992

KENTUCKY CHAMBER OF COMMERCE, March 16, 1992

FRUIT OF THE LOOM ANNOUNCEMENT, Franklin, March 18, 1992*

STATEMENT ABOUT CAMPAIGN FINANCE BILL AND GUBERNATORIAL SUCCESSION AMENDMENT, Frankfort, March 20, 1992*

PRESENTATION TO AFL-CIO DELEGATION, Frankfort, March 23, 1992

WAR MEMORIAL SERVICE, Frankfort, March 23, 1992

HEALTH CARE TASK FORCE AND COMMISSION, Frankfort, March 26, 1992*

TALKING POINTS/NEWS CONFERENCE, Frankfort, March 27, 1992

HEALTH CARE REFORM TOWN FORUM VIDEO SCRIPT, Frankfort, April 1992*

PROMOTION OF KERA, Frankfort, April 1, 1992

REMARKS ON BREATHITT ADMINISTRATION, Frankfort, April 4, 1992*

AMERICANS WITH DISABILITIES PRESS CONFERENCE WITH SENATE BILL 210 SIGNING, Frankfort, April 8, 1992*

TOAST TO HUNGARIAN AMBASSADOR, Frankfort, April 10, 1992

HOUSE BILL 28 SIGNING, Frankfort, April 13, 1992*

USED MOTOR OIL RECYCLING PRESS CONFERENCE, Frankfort, April 16, 1992*

KENTUCKY BROADCASTERS ASSOCIATION, Frankfort, April 20, 1992

KENTUCKY HARVEST HEADQUARTERS DEDICATION, Louisville, April 20, 1992

FIDELITY INVESTMENTS ANNOUNCEMENT, Covington, April 23, 1992*

PARTNERSHIP FOR KENTUCKY SCHOOL REFORM LUNCHEON, Frankfort, April 23, 1992*

EAST KENTUCKY LEADERSHIP CONFERENCE, Ashland, April 25, 1992

ACCEPTANCE OF KEENE DAINGERFIELD AWARD, Louisville, April 30, 1992

MAKERS MARK BRUNCH, Louisville, May 1, 1992

REMARKS FOR ABC-TV PRIOR TO TROPHY PRESENTATION, Louisville, May 2, 1992*

KENTUCKY DERBY TOAST TO WINNERS, Louisville, May 2, 1992

SMALL BUSINESS APPRECIATION LUNCHEON, Drawbridge Inn, May 8, 1992

UNIVERSITY OF KENTUCKY CENTER FOR EXCELLENCE FOR RURAL HEALTH CARE, Hazard, May 9, 1992

JEFFERSON-JACKSON DAY DINNER, Prestonsburg, May 9, 1992*

PRESS CONFERENCE / WATERFRONT DEVELOPMENT, Louisville, May 12, 1992

HITACHI AUTOMOTIVE PRODUCTS EXPANSION PROJECT OFFICIAL OPENING, Harrodsburg, May 13, 1992*

VIDEO SCRIPT FOUNDATION FOR THE TRI-STATE COMMUNITY, Ashland, May 16, 1992

REMARKS FOR AUDUBON GROUND BREAKING, Henderson, May 16, 1992*

JEFFERSON-JACKSON DAY DINNER, Owensboro, May 16, 1992

CUMBERLAND COLLEGE, Cumberland College, May 18, 1992

FOCUS LOUISVILLE, Louisville, May 19, 1992

DONNELLY CORPORATION ANNOUNCEMENT, Mt. Sterling, May 19, 1992

NEWS CONFERENCE BLUEGRASS STATE GAMES, Frankfort, May 20, 1992

INTERNATIONAL PAPER ANNOUNCEMENT, Bowling Green, May 21, 1992

JUDY CLABES TRIBUTE, Drawbridge Inn, May 21, 1992

NATIONAL FEDERATION OF DEMOCRATIC WOMEN'S CLUBS, Frankfort, May 22, 1992

JAPAN TRIP RECEPTION, Imperial Hotel—Tokyo, May 28, 1992

WEST KENTUCKY AREA LABOR MANAGEMENT COMMITTEE, Frankfort, June 1, 1992

KENTUCKY BICENTENNIAL STATEHOOD LUNCHEON, Frankfort, June 1, 1992

KENTUCKY BICENTENNIAL STAMP DEDICATION CEREMONY, Frankfort, June 1, 1992

KENTUCKY BICENTENNIAL STATEHOOD CELEBRATION, Frankfort, June 1, 1992

BIG YANK PRESS CONFERENCE MOREHEAD PLANT, Morehead, June 3, 1992

BOYS STATE CONVENTION, Morehead, June 4, 1992

SPECIAL OLYMPICS KICKOFF, Lexington, June 5, 1992

PERRYVILLE BATTLEFIELD PRESERVATION, Perryville, June 5, 1992

SHELBY'S RIDE RE-ENACTMENT, Lexington, June 6, 1992

TOAST TO DEPUTY SECRETARY OF THE INTERIOR—FRANK BRACKEN, Frankfort, June 6, 1992

KARDA TASK FORCE MEETING, Frankfort, June 9, 1992*

LOCAL ISSUES CONFERENCE, Louisville, June 9, 1992

SENATE FINANCE COMMITTEE, Washington, D.C., June 10, 1992

HEALTH CARE ACCESS FOUNDATION ANNOUNCEMENT, Frankfort, June 11, 1992

KENTUCKY DEMOCRATIC CONVENTION, Frankfort, June 13, 1992*

QVC KENTUCKY CRAFTS SHOW, Frankfort, June 14, 1992*

KENTUCKY STATE POLICE, Frankfort, June 29, 1992

TECHNOTRIM ANNOUNCEMENT, Glasgow, June 29, 1992

PRINCETON KIWANIS CLUB, Princeton, July 1, 1992

ONE-MILLIONTH CORVETTE CELEBRATION, Bowling Green, July 2, 1992

DRAKESBORO CDBG ANNOUNCEMENT, Drakesboro, July 7, 1992

GUTHRIE CDBG ANNOUNCEMENT, Guthrie, July 7, 1992

PEMBROKE CDBG ANNOUNCEMENT, Pembroke, July 7, 1992

PRINCETON CDBG ANNOUNCEMENT, Princeton, July 7, 1992

SEBREE CDBG ANNOUNCEMENT, Sebree, July 7, 1992

HARDINSBURG CDBG ANNOUNCEMENT, Hardinsburg, July 7, 1992

WINCHESTER CDBG ANNOUNCEMENT, Winchester, July 8, 1992

SHELBYVILLE CDBG ANNOUNCEMENT, Shelbyville, July 8, 1992

GEORGETOWN CDBG ANNOUNCEMENT, Georgetown, July 8, 1992

MAYSLICK CDBG ANNOUNCEMENT, Mayslick, July 8, 1992

RICHMOND CDBG ANNOUNCEMENT, Richmond, July 8, 1992

MT. STERLING CDBG ANNOUNCEMENT, Mt. Sterling, July 8, 1992

KENTUCKY COMMISSION ON HEALTH-CARE REFORM, Frankfort, July 10, 1992*

AMERICAN LEGION CONVENTION, Paducah, July 11, 1992

GOVERNOR'S SCHOLARS PROGRAM, Louisville, July 18, 1992

BLUEGRASS STATE GAMES OPENING CEREMONY, Lexington, July 24, 1992

LEXINGTON-FRANKFORT SCENIC CORRIDOR PICNIC, Frankfort, July 24, 1992

KENTUCKY FAMILY REUNION SPONSORS RECEPTION, Lexington, Kentucky Horse Park, July 24, 1992

KENTUCKY HOUSING CORPORATION ANNIVERSARY CEREMONY, Frankfort, July 24, 1992

TOYOTA TAPING, Frankfort, July 24, 1992

TOYOTA CAMRY EXPORT MEDIA EVENT, Georgetown, July 24, 1992*

KENTUCKY HOUSING CORPORATION POSTER CONTEST WINNERS, July 24, 1992

FORD MOTOR ANNOUNCEMENT, Louisville, July 27, 1992*

FANCY FARM SPEECH, Fancy Farm, August 1, 1992*

HAZARDOUS WASTE TRAINING CENTER, University of Louisville, August 6, 1992*

UNIVERSAL FASTENERS RIBBON CUTTING, Lawrenceburg, August 6, 1992

ASSOCIATION OF U.S. ARMY, Ft. Knox, August 7, 1992

JOE PRATHER HIGHWAY DEDICATION, Vine Grove, August 7, 1992

DEDICATION OF HARDIN COUNTY MUSEUM OF KENTUCKY HISTORY AND ART, Vine Grove, August 7, 1992

INTRODUCTION OF SEN. WENDELL FORD, Daviess County, August 8, 1992

NATIONAL HOME BUILDERS, Lexington, August 21, 1992

STEDMANTOWN LANE GROUND BREAKING, Frankfort, August 28, 1992

INTRODUCTION OF BILL CLINTON, Louisville, August 28, 1992

6TH ANNUAL EEOC, Louisville, August 29, 1992

AGRICULTURAL SUMMIT, Louisville, August 30, 1992

KENTUCKY STATE AFL-CIO BIENNIAL CONVENTION, Louisville, October 5, 1992

CONSTITUTIONAL AMENDMENTS TALKING POINTS, Frankfort, October 6, 1992

HEALTH CARE ACCESS FOUNDATION, Frankfort, October 13, 1992

ECONOMIC DEVELOPMENT PARTNERSHIP BOARD, Frankfort, October 13, 1992

GOVERNOR'S CONFERENCE ON OLDER KENTUCKIANS, Frankfort, October 14, 1992

HIGHER EDUCATION STUDENT RALLY, Frankfort, October 14, 1992

KEIDANDREN LUNCHEON, Frankfort, October 14, 1992

EDITORIAL WRITERS CONVENTION, Lexington, October 15, 1992

CHEF AMERICA ANNOUNCEMENT GROUND BREAKING, Mt. Sterling, October 16, 1992

KENTUCKY PRIMARY CARE ASSOCIATION, Lexington, October 16, 1992*

KENTUCKY ECONOMIC ASSOCIATION, Lexington, October 16, 1992

TALKING POINTS/NEWS CONFERENCE, Frankfort, October 16, 1992

JOHN DOUG HAYS FUND-RAISER, Pikeville, October 17, 1992*

MT. STERLING DAYS, Mt. Sterling, October 17, 1992

ADA AWARDS LUNCHEON, Frankfort, October 21, 1992

ELIZABETHTOWN/HARDIN COUNTY CHAMBER OF COMMERCE, Elizabethtown, October 22, 1992

REMARKS ON APPALACHIAN REGIONAL COMMISSION GRANTS, Frankfort, October 23, 1992*

JEFFERSON-JACKSON DAY, Ashland, October 24, 1992

UK MEDICAL CENTER PRESS ANNOUNCEMENT, Lexington, October 26, 1992

COAL MARKETING AND EXPORT COUNCIL PRESS CONFERENCE, October 27, 1992

WHEELWRIGHT JOBS ANNOUNCEMENT, Wheelwright, October 27, 1992

KENTUCKY TOURISM COUNCIL, Louisville, October 28, 1992*

RED RIBBON RALLY, Frankfort, October 28, 1992

TALKING POINTS FOR PADUCAH RALLY, Paducah, October 30, 1992*

JEFFERSON-JACKSON DAY, Pulaski County, October 31, 1992

HEALTH CARE ACCESS FOUNDATION ANNOUNCEMENT, Frankfort, November 5, 1992

PENTECOSTAL CHILDREN'S HOME, Barbourville, November 6, 1992

AGRIBUSINESS/GOVERNOR'S SCHOLARS PROGRAM, Frankfort, November 9, 1992

ONE MILLION DOLLAR SHOOTOUT ANNOUNCEMENT, Frankfort, November 10, 1992

KENTUCKY TECH-CENTRAL CAMPUS DEDICATION, Lexington, November 12, 1992

INTERAGENCY COMMISSION ON EDUCATIONAL AND JOB TRAINING COORDINATION, Frankfort, November 12, 1992

GOVERNOR'S CONFERENCE ON THE ENVIRONMENT, Lexington, November 12, 1992*

KENTUCKY CHAMBER OF COMMERCE, Louisville, November 13, 1992

KENTUCKY ASSOCIATION OF SCHOOL SUPERINTENDENTS, Louisville, November 30, 1992*

KERA EVALUATION BOARD ANNOUNCEMENT, Louisville, November 30, 1992*

KENTUCKY PEOPLE WITH AIDS SERVICE ADDRESS, Louisville, December 1, 1992*

ECONOMIC DEVELOPMENT ROUNDTABLES, Frankfort, December 2, 1992*

KET ADA VIDEO SCRIPT, Frankfort, December 3, 1992

CHRISTMAS TREE LIGHTING, Frankfort, December 7, 1992

BRUENING BEARINGS, INC., Florence, December 8, 1992*

GENERAL CABLE CORPORATION, Highland Heights, December 8, 1992

INTERNATIONAL PAPER CO., Covington, December 8, 1992

MONTAPLAST ANNOUNCEMENT, Frankfort, December 9, 1992*

KENTUCKY FARM BUREAU, Louisville, December 11, 1992*

HARLAN COUNTY COAL PRODUCERS, Pineville, December 11, 1992

SMALL BUSINESS INVESTMENT PROGRAM ANNOUNCEMENT, Louisville, December 11, 1992*

FINANCIAL INSTITUTIONS ACCREDITATION, Frankfort, December 14, 1992

ASSOCIATION OF OLDER KENTUCKIANS, Frankfort, December 14, 1992

EMPLOYEE SUGGESTION SYSTEM AWARDS PRESENTATION, Frankfort, December 14, 1992

CHILDREN FIRST, Louisville, December 16, 1992*

KENTUCKY CANCER REGISTRY, Frankfort, December 17, 1992

KENNEDY SCHOOL OF GOVERNMENT, Frankfort, December 18, 1992

JOE PRATHER RECEPTION, Frankfort, December 18, 1992

KATS/KENTUCKY DISABILITIES COALITION, Frankfort, January 6, 1993

EARTH SUMMIT PRESS CONFERENCE, Louisville, January 6, 1993

PRAYER BREAKFAST, Frankfort, January 7, 1993

KERA EVALUATION BOARD, Frankfort, January 8, 1993

TEMPLE ADATH ISRAEL, Louisville, January 10, 1993

KENTUCKY AGRICULTURAL COUNCIL, January 10, 1993

MARTIN LUTHER KING JR. COMMEMORATION, Frankfort, January 14, 1993

LEADERSHIP LEXINGTON, Frankfort, January 14, 1993

HUISH DETERGENTS ANNOUNCEMENT, Bowling Green, January 15, 1993

KENTUCKY PRESS ASSOCIATION, Louisville, January 22, 1993

HOME BUILDERS ASSOCIATION OF LEXINGTON, Lexington, January 22, 1993

KENTUCKY PRESS ASSOCIATION WINTER CONVENTION, Lexington, January 22, 1993

LOUISVILLE AREA CHAMBER OF COMMERCE ANNUAL MEETING, Louisville, January 25, 1993*

EARTH SUMMIT STEERING COMMITTEE, Louisville, January 25, 1993*

GEORGETOWN BYPASS RIBBON CUTTING, Georgetown, January 26, 1993

ASA ROUSE FUND-RAISER CANDIDATE FOR STATE SENATE, Frankfort, January 26, 1993

OUTSTANDING KENTUCKIAN AWARD, Frankfort, January 27, 1993

SOCIETY OF PROFESSIONAL JOURNALISTS, Frankfort, January 27, 1993

BLUEGRASS BOY SCOUT COUNCIL, Lexington, January 29, 1993

INTRODUCTION OF TERRI REYNOLDS, NATIONAL GOVERNORS ASSOCIATION HUMAN RESOURCES COMMITTEE MEETING, Frankfort, January 31, 1993

KENTUCKY STATE PARKS RADIO ADS, Frankfort, February 1, 1993

REMARKS ON FOLLOW-UP CONFERENCE TO EARTH SUMMIT, Washington, D.C., February 1, 1993*

MILITARY AFFAIRS COMMISSION, Frankfort, February 4, 1993

TALKING POINTS—MEETING WITH GE UNION MEMBERS, Louisville, February 7, 1993

CHAMBER OF COMMERCE, Frankfort, February 11, 1993*

TEACHER APPRECIATION MONTH CEREMONY SECOND ST. SCHOOL, Frankfort, February 17, 1993

GOVERNOR'S AWARDS IN THE ARTS, Owensboro, February 19, 1993

MEETING WITH SECRETARY PENA, Louisville, February 19, 1993

GTE ANNOUNCEMENT, Lexington, February 22, 1993

BOY SCOUT LUNCHEON, Louisville, February 24, 1993

NATIONAL GUARD ASSOCIATION, Louisville, February 27, 1993

KENTUCKY STATE PARKS RADIO ADS, Frankfort, March 1, 1993

KENTUCKY HEALTH CARE REFORM COMMISSION, Frankfort, March 1, 1993*

AG TASK FORCE WORKSHOP TAPING, Frankfort, March 3, 1993*

OP-ED PIECE ON HEALTH CARE, Frankfort, March 5, 1993

LOUISVILLE CHAMBER OF COMMERCE / ALLIANT HEALTH CARE SYSTEMS, Louisville, March 10, 1993

STRIDE RITE CORPORATION GROUND BREAKING CEREMONY, Louisville, March 16, 1993

HENDERSON CHAMBER OF COMMERCE, Henderson, March 26, 1993*

PADUCAH LIONS / ROTARY / KIWANIS, Paducah, March 17, 1993

GOVERNOR'S COMMISSION ON QUALITY AND EFFICIENCY MEETING AND PRESS CONFERENCE, Frankfort, March 19, 1993

2ND STREET RECONSTRUCTION PROJECT PADUCAH, Paducah, March 17, 1993

6TH ANNUAL CELEBRATION OF SERVICE CENTER FOR WOMEN AND FAMILIES, Louisville, March 24, 1993

CHR EMPLOYEES, Frankfort, March 26, 1993

CINTAS CORPORATION ANNOUNCEMENT, Hazard, March 26, 1993*

AFL-CIO HEALTH CARE FORUM, Frankfort, March 26, 1993

NATIONAL ASSOCIATION OF WOMEN BUSINESS OWNERS' LUNCHEON, Frankfort, March 30, 1993

KEA DELEGATE ASSEMBLY, Louisville, March 31, 1993

CARDINAL HILL TELETHON PUBLIC SERVICE ANNOUNCEMENT, Frankfort, April 1, 1993

ECONOMIC DEVELOPMENT PRESS CONFERENCE, Frankfort, April 1, 1993*

BILLBOARD SCRIPT—PEGASUS PARADE, Frankfort, April 1, 1993

GRANT COUNTY CHAMBER OF COMMERCE, Williamstown, April 2, 1993*

KENTUCKY CHAMBER OF COMMERCE EXECUTIVES, Eastern Kentucky University, April 8, 1993

KENTUCKY ASSOCIATION OF TRANSPORTATION ENGINEERS, Lexington, April 10, 1993*

SALES AND MARKETING EXECS, Louisville, April 12, 1993

PROJECT ESTEEM RALLY, Frankfort/Kentucky State, April 14, 1993

GOVERNOR'S SAFETY AND HEALTH CONFERENCE AND EXPOSITION, Louisville, April 15, 1993

DERBY FESTIVAL BOARD LUNCHEON, Frankfort, April 16, 1993*

COUNCIL OF STATE GOVERNMENTS GROUND BREAKING CEREMONY, Lexington, April 16, 1993*

ORGAN/TISSUE DONATION WEEK, Frankfort, April 20, 1993

HEALTH CARE TALKING POINTS, Frankfort, April 23, 1993

60TH ANNUAL COLONELS BANQUET, Louisville, April 30, 1993

DONALD INGWERSON TRIBUTE VIDEO SCRIPT, Frankfort, May 1, 1993

KENTUCKY STATE PARKS RADIO AD, Frankfort, May 1, 1993

NATIONAL TOURISM WEEK KICKOFF, Bullitt County, May 3, 1993*

ASSOCIATION OF OLDER KENTUCKIANS LUNCHEON, Frankfort, May 4, 1993*

GREATER LEXINGTON MINISTERIAL FELLOWSHIP LUNCHEON, Lexington, May 5, 1993*

KENTUCKY CHAMBER OF COMMERCE BOARD MEETING, Lexington, May 6, 1993*

STUDENT EXCHANGE PROGRAM, Frankfort, May 8, 1993

TIM FREUDENBERG PARK DEDICATION—OLDENBERG BREWERY, Ft. Mitchell, May 8, 1993

ADDRESS TO JOINT SESSION OF GENERAL ASSEMBLY, Frankfort, May 10, 1993*

KENTUCKY CABLE TELEVISION ASSOCIATION ANNUAL CONVENTION, Lexington, May 11, 1993*

FRANKFORT ROTARY CLUB, Frankfort, May 12, 1993

PEW CHARITABLE TRUSTS, Frankfort, May 13, 1993

NATIONAL FEDERATION OF INDEPENDENT BUSINESS GOLDEN ANNIVERSARY, Frankfort, May 13, 1993

INTRODUCTION OF RON MAZZOLI, WENDELL FORD TRUST DINNER, Louisville, May 14, 1993

LEXINGTON CHAMBER OF COMMERCE, Lexington, May 17, 1993

KENTUCKY MEDICAL ASSOCIATION LEGISLATIVE SEMINAR, Lexington, May 19, 1993*

NEWS CONFERENCE ON ROBERT WOOD JOHNSON FOUNDATION GRANT, Frankfort, May 20, 1993

POPE HOUSE DEDICATION, Lexington, May 21, 1993

HUNT-MORGAN HOUSE CIVIL WAR DEDICATION, Lexington, May 21, 1993

KERA EVALUATION CONFERENCE, Lexington, May 24, 1993*

INTRODUCTION OF VICE PRESIDENT AL GORE, SUSTAINABLE DEVELOPMENT CONFERENCE, Louisville, May 25, 1993

INTRODUCTION OF CHIEF OREN LYON, SUSTAINABLE DEVELOPMENT CONFERENCE, Louisville, May 25, 1993

INTRODUCTION OF DAVID BUZZELLI, SUSTAINABLE DEVELOPMENT CONFERENCE, Louisville, May 25, 1993

INTRODUCTION OF BARBARA BRAMBLE, SUSTAINABLE DEVELOPMENT CONFERENCE, Louisville, May 25, 1993

SUSTAINABLE DEVELOPMENT CONFERENCE, Louisville, May 25, 1993

INTRODUCTION OF SUSAN FALLOWS TIERNEY, STRATEGIES FOR SUSTAINABLE DEVELOPMENT, Louisville, May 25, 1993

CHELSEA INDUSTRIES ANNOUNCEMENT, Cadiz, May 28, 1993

MOUNTAIN LAUREL FESTIVAL CORONATION CEREMONY, Pine Mountain, May 29, 1993

BOYS STATE, Morehead, June 9, 1993

KENTUCKY ACADEMY OF FAMILY PHYSICIANS, Louisville, June 10, 1993

ECONOMIC DEVELOPMENT PARTNERSHIP, Frankfort, June 11, 1993*

HOPE CENTER DEDICATION, Lexington, June 14, 1993

UK SANDERS-BROWN CENTER FOR AGING MCCOWAN TRUST ANNOUNCEMENT, Lexington, June 15, 1993

GOVERNOR'S CONFERENCE ON SMALL BUSINESS, Frankfort, June 16, 1993*

TESTIMONY TO THE HOUSE ECONOMIC DEVELOPMENT SUBCOMMITTEE, Washington, D.C., June 22, 1993*

KENTUCKY HEALTH CARE ACCESS FOUNDATION BOARD MEETING, Lexington, June 24, 1993*

RON CYRUS ROAST, Lexington, June 26, 1993

NATURAL RESOURCES / ENVIRONMENTAL PROTECTION OUTSTANDING EMPLOYEE LUNCHEON, Frankfort, June 30, 1993

WYNONNA JUDD PRESS CONFERENCE, Ashland, July 1, 1993*

GRIFFEN INDUSTRIES DEDICATION OF AMPHITHEATER FALMOUTH, Falmouth, July 3, 1993

CHANDLER FOUNDATION DINNER, Lexington, July 9, 1993

AG TASK FORCE WORKSHOP (TAPING), Frankfort, July 9, 1993

VFW SOUTHERN CONFERENCE, Louisville, July 10, 1993

AMERICAN LEGION, Owensboro, July 10, 1993

PRICHARD COMMITTEE ANNUAL MEETING, Shakertown, July 12, 1993*

SEVEN COUNTIES SERVICES, Louisville, July 14, 1993*

DR. THOMAS D. CLARK RECEPTION, Frankfort, July 14, 1993

LEADERSHIP KENTUCKY, Frankfort, July 15, 1993

KENTUCKY COAL COALITION, Frankfort, July 16, 1993*

SUPREME COURT APPOINTMENT ANNOUNCEMENT, Frankfort, July 16, 1993*

DEMOCRATIC HEADQUARTERS TWENTIETH ANNIVERSARY, Frankfort, July 17, 1993

BLUEGRASS STATE GAMES OPENING CEREMONIES, Lexington, July 23, 1993

BLUEGRASS STATE GAMES GOVERNOR'S PACESETTERS HEALTH FESTIVAL, Lexington, July 23, 1993

SEVEN COUNTIES SERVICES, Louisville, July 24, 1993

FRANKFORT CDBG ANNOUNCEMENT, Frankfort, July 26, 1993

CITIZENS NATIONAL FAIR SCHOLARSHIP AWARD, Pt. Pleasant, W.Va., July 29, 1993

FORT BOONESBOROUGH POOL DEDICATION, Boonesborough, August 10, 1993*

PRESS CONFERENCE BUDGET REDUCTION, Frankfort, August 11, 1993

UNIVERSITY OF KENTUCKY/UNIVERSITY OF LOUISVILLE MEDICAL SCHOOL RECEPTION, Frankfort, August 11, 1993

JUNIOR LEAGUE COALITION OF 100 BLACK WOMEN, Louisville, August 20, 1993

KENTON COUNTY ISTEA ANNOUNCEMENT, Covington, August 20, 1993*

KENTON COUNTY ISTEA ANNOUNCEMENT, Roebling Gateway Park, August 20, 1993

KENTON COUNTY ISTEA ANNOUNCEMENT, Florence, August 20, 1993

KENTON COUNTY ISTEA ANNOUNCEMENT, Thomas More College, August 20, 1993

CAMPBELL COUNTY ISTEA ANNOUNCEMENT, Taylor Park, August 20, 1993

STEARNS ISTEA ANNOUNCEMENT, Stearns, August 23, 1993

SIMPSON COUNTY ISTEA ANNOUNCEMENT, Franklin, August 25, 1993

NELSON METAL PRODUCTS CORPORATION, Glasgow, August 25, 1993

WAGNER BRAKE NEW FACILITY, Scottsville, August 25, 1993

I LOVE TO READ PROMO CHANNEL 25 WEHT, Frankfort, September 1, 1993

KENTUCKY STATE PARKS RADIO ADS, Frankfort, September 1, 1993

VISIT KENTUCKY USA VIDEO, Frankfort, September 1, 1993*

FRANKFORT CDBG ANNOUNCEMENT, Frankfort, September 1, 1993

OWENSBORO GRAIN CO., Owensboro, September 2, 1993

HENRY TOLL FELLOWSHIP PROGRAM COUNCIL OF STATE GOVERNMENTS, Frankfort, September 2, 1993

NATIONAL BAPTIST CONVENTION, Louisville, September 7, 1993

TOGETHER WE CARE, Frankfort, September 10, 1993

HIGHER EDUCATION REVIEW COMMISSION, Frankfort, September 21, 1993*

MOREHEAD ISTEA ANNOUNCEMENT, Morehead, September 23, 1993

NORTHERN KENTUCKY, September 27, 1993

NORTHERN KENTUCKY PLANT ANNOUNCEMENTS, Drawbridge Inn, September 27, 1993*

WELCOME TO U.S. SECRETARY OF HEALTH AND HUMAN SERVICES DONNA SHALALA, Louisville, September 27, 1993*

ASSOCIATION FOR OLDER KENTUCKIANS, Lexington, September 28, 1993

CENTURY CLUB JESSE JACKSON RECEPTION, Frankfort, September 29, 1993*

DEMOCRATIC WOMEN'S CLUB, Frankfort, October 1, 1993*

KENTUCKY STATE PARKS RADIO AD, Frankfort, October 1, 1993

KENTUCKY TECH VIDEO, Frankfort, October 1, 1993

BREAST CANCER AWARENESS MONTH RALLY, Frankfort, October 4, 1993*

LOUISVILLE ISTEA ANNOUNCEMENTS, Louisville, October 5, 1993

UNIVERSITY PARK GROUND BREAKING, Louisville, October 5, 1993

PHYSICIAN ASSISTANTS, Frankfort, October 6, 1993

FRANKFORT ISTEA ANNOUNCEMENTS, Frankfort, October 6, 1993

LEXINGTON ISTEA ANNOUNCEMENTS, Lexington, October 7, 1993

LARUE COUNTY ISTEA ANNOUNCEMENTS, Larue County, October 7, 1993

PEW CHARITABLE TRUSTS, Lexington, October 8, 1993

CAMP NELSON CEMETERY ISTEA ANNOUNCEMENTS, Camp Nelson Cemetery, October 9, 1993

CHRISTIAN COUNTY ISTEA ANNOUNCEMENTS, Christian County, October 12, 1993

TRIGG COUNTY ISTEA ANNOUNCEMENTS, Trigg County, October 12, 1993

TRIMBLE COUNTY ISTEA ANNOUNCEMENTS, Trimble County, October 12, 1993

NELSON COUNTY ISTEA ANNOUNCEMENTS, Nelson County, October 12, 1993

TRUS JOIST MACMILLAN, Hazard, October 12, 1993

TRUS JOIST MACMILLAN, Winchester, October 12, 1993

BREATHITT COUNTY ROAD ANNOUNCEMENT, Jackson, October 12, 1993

GOVERNOR'S CONFERENCE ON THE ENVIRONMENT, Ft. Mitchell, October 13, 1993*

FORT DUFFIELD ISTEA ANNOUNCEMENT, Ft. Duffield, October 14, 1993

SOUTHERN BAPTIST SEMINARY PRESIDENTIAL INDUCTION, Louisville, October 14, 1993

INTRODUCTION OF U.S. SECRETARY OF EDUCATION RILEY, Lexington, October 15, 1993

ASSOCIATED PRESS EDITORS, Lexington, October 15, 1993

HEALTH CARE ACCESS FOUNDATION RETREAT, Jamestown, October 16, 1993

DANA CORPORATION, Elizabethtown, October 18, 1993

FORD TRUCK PLANT, Louisville, October 18, 1993

FINAL MEETING OF GOVERNOR'S COMMISSION ON QUALITY AND EFFICIENCY, Frankfort, October 19, 1993*

SOUTH WING DEDICATION FAIR AND EXPOSITION CENTER, Louisville, October 20, 1993

KENTUCKY HISTORY CENTER PRESS CONFERENCE, Frankfort, October 20, 1993

CUSTOM FOOD PRODUCTS INC. (NEW PLANT), Owensville, October 21, 1993

WHITING MANUFACTURING CO., Hazel Green, October 21, 1993

RED RIBBON RALLY BUECHEL HIGH SCHOOL, Louisville, October 25, 1993

QUALITY AND EFFICIENCY EXECUTIVE ORDERS, Frankfort, November 1, 1993

NEW STATE POLICE COMMISSIONER ANNOUNCEMENT, Frankfort, November 1, 1993*

KETS DEMONSTRATION, Shelbyville, November 1, 1993

BELLARMINE COLLEGE, Louisville, November 2, 1993

VETERANS DAY, Frankfort, November 11, 1993

FRANKFORT CHAMBER OF COMMERCE, Frankfort, November 17, 1993

KENTUCKY ASSOCIATION OF COUNTIES, Louisville, November 18, 1993

MILLION DOLLAR SHOOTOUT CENTRAL HIGH SCHOOL, Louisville, November 18, 1993

AGRICULTURAL SUMMIT, Louisville, November 18, 1993*

KENTUCKY ASSOCIATION OF OLDER PERSONS, Louisville, November 18, 1993

RND DESIGN, INC., Martin, November 19, 1993

BELLEVUE ISTEA ANNOUNCEMENT, Bellevue, November 19, 1993

OTTER CREEK CORRECTIONAL CENTER, Wheelwright, November 19, 1993

SANCTUARY DEDICATION ST. STEPHEN BAPTIST CHURCH, Louisville, November 21, 1993

MORTENSON BROADCASTING CO. TWENTIETH BIRTHDAY, Lexington, November 22, 1993

QUALITY AND EFFICIENCY FINAL NEWS CONFERENCE, Frankfort, November 23, 1993*

LUCILLE LITTLE ENDOWMENT KENTUCKY HORSE FARM, Lexington, November 23, 1993

MILKEN AWARDS, Lexington, December 2, 1993

PARKS BOND ANNOUNCEMENT, Carrollton, December 6, 1993*

CRIME COMMISSION MEETING, Frankfort, December 7, 1993*

BOBBY MEADOWS AWARD, Frankfort, December 7, 1993

KENTUCKY CAREER MANAGERS GRADUATION PROGRAM, Frankfort, December 9, 1993

KENTUCKY WOMEN'S LEADERSHIP NETWORK, Frankfort, December 10, 1993

OHIO COUNTY CDBG ANNOUNCEMENT, Hartford, December 13, 1993

NATCHER BRIDGE DEDICATION, Owensboro, December 13, 1993

JONES PLASTICS LUNCHEON, Lawrenceburg, December 14, 1993

TEXWOOD INDUSTRIES, Mt. Sterling, December 15, 1993

PRESENTATION OF CHECKS FROM CONFISCATED DRUG MONEY, Frankfort, December 17, 1993

BOONE COUNTY CDBG ANNOUNCEMENT, Burlington, December 20, 1993*

ROBERTSON COUNTY CDBG ANNOUNCEMENT, Mt. Olivet, December 20, 1993

NEWPORT CDBG ANNOUNCEMENT, Newport, December 20, 1993

PRESTONVILLE CDBG ANNOUNCEMENT, Carrollton, December 20, 1993

DR. PHILLIP SHARP RECEPTION, Frankfort, January 7, 1994

KENTUCKY AGRICULTURAL COUNCIL, Frankfort, January 10, 1994*

COAL COUNTY JUDGE/EXECUTIVES, Frankfort, January 13, 1994

PRAYER BREAKFAST, Frankfort, January 13, 1994

LEADERSHIP BLUEGRASS, Frankfort, January 13, 1994*

MARTIN LUTHER KING CEREMONY, Frankfort, January 13, 1994

KENTUCKY EDUCATIONAL TELEVISION ADDRESS STATEWIDE, Frankfort, January 18, 1994

STATE OF THE COMMONWEALTH AND BUDGET ADDRESS, Frankfort, January 24, 1994*

PAUL SEMONIN KICK-OFF, Frankfort, January 25, 1994

KENTUCKY SOCIETY OF ASSOCIATION EXECUTIVES, Frankfort, January 26, 1994

HOUSE BILL 443 SIGNING, Frankfort, February 1, 1994*

LEAGUE OF WOMEN VOTERS, Frankfort, February 2, 1994*

HERITAGE LAND CONSERVATION ACT PRESS CONFERENCE, Frankfort, February 3, 1994*

BOY SCOUTS, Lexington, February 4, 1994

LEGISLATION SEMINAR KENTUCKY RETAIL FEDERATION, Frankfort, February 8, 1994

NEWS CONFERENCE WITH MARSHALL LONG, Frankfort, February 8, 1994

PHILIP MORRIS AG LEADERSHIP DEVELOPMENT PROGRAM, Frankfort, February 9, 1994*

AFRICAN-AMERICAN HERITAGE COMMISSION, Frankfort, February 10, 1994

STATE OF THE REVENUE CABINET, Frankfort, February 14, 1994

SUSTAINABILITY ROUNDTABLE INFORMATION FORUM, Frankfort, February 14, 1994*

COMMUNITY SERVICE COMMISSION, Frankfort, February 14, 1994*

LEADERSHIP MURRAY, Murray, February 16, 1994

CHILD SEX ABUSE, Frankfort, February 22, 1994*

HOUSE BILL 238 SIGNING, Frankfort, February 22, 1994*

INTRODUCTION OF ANGELA FUNKE, CHILD ADVOCATE, Frankfort, February 22, 1994

REMARKS ON APPALACHIAN REGIONAL COMMISSION GRANTS, Morehead, February 25, 1994*

SHARPSBURG ARC GRANT ANNOUNCEMENT, Sharpsburg, February 25, 1994

SANDY HOOK ARC GRANT ANNOUNCEMENT, Sandy Hook, February 25, 1994

ASHLAND ARC GRANT ANNOUNCEMENT, Ashland, February 25, 1994

PSA CARDINAL HILL TELETHON, Frankfort, March 1, 1994

TALKING POINTS FROM CITY PARTNERSHIPS, Louisville, March 3, 1994

RJ TOWER CORPORATION ANNOUNCEMENT, Bardstown, March 3, 1994*

FOREST INDUSTRIES ASSOCIATION, Louisville, March 3, 1994*

NATIONAL CONFERENCE OF CHRISTIANS AND JEWS, Lexington, March 3, 1994

FRENCHBURG ARC GRANT ANNOUNCEMENT, Frenchburg, March 4, 1994

IRVINE ARC GRANT ANNOUNCEMENT, Irvine, March 4, 1994

RICHMOND ARC GRANT ANNOUNCEMENT, Richmond, March 4, 1994

STANTON ARC GRANT ANNOUNCEMENT, Stanton, March 4, 1994

KENTUCKIANA ASSOCIATION OF PHYSICIANS FROM INDIA, Louisville, March 5, 1994

HOUSE BILL 359 SIGNING, Frankfort, March 7, 1994*

SALATO WILDLIFE CENTER GROUND BREAKING, Frankfort, March 7, 1994

WILLIAMSBURG ARC GRANT ANNOUNCEMENT, Williamsburg, March 8, 1994

LONDON ARC GRANT ANNOUNCEMENT, London, March 8, 1994

MT. VERNON ARC GRANT ANNOUNCEMENT, Mt. Vernon, March 8, 1994

HEALTH MOTHERS ETC. PROCLAMATION SIGNING, Frankfort, March 9, 1994

BOY SCOUT LUNCHEON, Louisville, March 9, 1994

HOUSE BILL 215 SIGNING, Frankfort, March 9, 1994*

HINDMAN ARC GRANT ANNOUNCEMENT, Hindman, March 11, 1994

BLAINE ARC GRANT ANNOUNCEMENT, Blaine, March 11, 1994

WEST LIBERTY ARC GRANT ANNOUNCEMENT, West Liberty, March 11, 1994

BOONEVILLE ARC GRANT ANNOUNCEMENT, Booneville, March 11, 1994

PRESTONSBURG ARC GRANT ANNOUNCEMENT, Prestonsburg, March 11, 1994

SWEARING-IN OF JUDGE PAYNE, Lexington, March 14, 1994*

LABOR RALLY TALKING POINTS, Frankfort, March 15, 1994

FORD CEREMONY TO HONOR CHARLIE JOHNSON, Louisville, March 18, 1994

CAVE CITY CDBG ANNOUNCEMENT, Cave City, March 24, 1994

BOWLING GREEN CDBG ANNOUNCEMENT, Bowling Green, March 24, 1994

SHEPHERDSVILLE CDBG ANNOUNCEMENT, Shepherdsville, March 24, 1994

POWDERLY CDBG ANNOUNCEMENT, Powderly, March 24, 1994

SOMERSET CDBG ANNOUNCEMENT, Somerset, March 28, 1994

CAMPTON CGBG ANNOUNCEMENT, Campton, March 28, 1994

STANFORD ARC GRANT ANNOUNCEMENT, Stanford, March 28, 1994

BEATTYVILLE CDBG ANNOUNCEMENT, Beattyville, March 28, 1994

KENTUCKY EDUCATIONAL TELEVISION HOUSING TELECONFERENCE, Lexington, March 29, 1994

HOUSE BILL 368 SIGNING, Frankfort, March 30, 1994*

ARBOR DAY CEREMONY, Frankfort, April 1, 1994*

KENTUCKY EDUCATIONAL TELEVISION ADDRESS, Frankfort, April 1, 1994*

AMERICAN TAPE COMPANY, Richmond, April 8, 1994

POWELL COUNTY INDUSTRIAL BOARD APPRECIATION BANQUET, Natural Bridge State Park, April 12, 1994*

HOUSE BILL 250 SIGNING, Frankfort, April 15, 1994*

ROTARY TOAST TO WILSON WYATT, Louisville, April 21, 1994

WORKERS' MEMORIAL DAY, Frankfort, April 28, 1994

"THEY'RE OFF" LUNCHEON, Louisville, April 29, 1994

RUSSIAN DERBY TELECAST TAPING, Louisville, May 3, 1994*

OWENTON CDBG ANNOUNCEMENT, Owenton, May 5, 1994

FOSROC GRAND OPENING, Georgetown, May 5, 1994*

KENTUCKY COLONELS BANQUET, Louisville, May 6, 1994

TEACHER ACHIEVEMENT AWARDS, Frankfort, May 12, 1994

ARMED FORCES DAY SPEECH, Louisville, May 13, 1994

DAYTON FAMILY HEALTH CENTER, Dayton, May 14, 1994

AUDUBON, Henderson, May 16, 1994

KENTUCKY FAIR AND EXPOSITION CENTER, Louisville, May 16, 1994*

NATIONAL TOURISM WEEK, Louisville, May 16, 1994*

BARREN RIVER LAKE, Glasgow, May 17, 1994

KENTUCKY DAM VILLAGE, Gilbertsville, May 17, 1994

MY OLD KENTUCKY HOME, Bardstown, May 17, 1994

LAKE BARKLEY, Cadiz, May 17, 1994

NORTHERN KENTUCKY CONVENTION CENTER, Covington, May 18, 1994

JENNY WILEY, Prestonsburg, May 19, 1994

BUCKHORN LAKE, Hazard, May 19, 1994

NATURAL BRIDGE, Slade, May 19, 1994

CAGLE'S INC. ANNOUNCEMENT, Franklin, May 20, 1994*

LAKE CUMBERLAND, Jamestown, May 20, 1994

PINE MOUNTAIN, Pineville, May 20, 1994

DEMOLAY ANNIVERSARY SPEECH EL HASA SHRINE TEMPLE, Ashland, May 21, 1994

GREENBO LAKE, Greenup, May 21, 1994

YATESVILLE LAKE, Yatesville, May 21, 1994

BLUEGRASS STATE GAMES NEWS CONFERENCE, Frankfort, May 23, 1994

HISTORY CENTER NEWS CONFERENCE, Frankfort, May 23, 1994*

UNIVERSITY OF KENTUCKY KING LIBRARY NEWS CONFERENCE, Frankfort, May 23, 1994*

MOUNTAIN LAUREL FESTIVAL CORONATION CEREMONY, Pineville, May 28, 1994

MOUNTAIN LAUREL FESTIVAL LUNCHEON, Pineville, May 28, 1994

LOCAL ISSUES SPEECH, Louisville, June 2, 1994*

NEWS CONFERENCE APPOINTMENT OF WALT TURNER, Frankfort, June 6, 1994

BOYS STATE, Morehead, June 8, 1994

DOUGLAS AUTOTECH CORPORATION, Hopkinsville, June 9, 1994*

JEFFERSON-JACKSON DAY DINNER, Kentucky Dam Village, June 11, 1994*

KENTUCKY ISSUES CONFERENCE, Louisville, June 14, 1994

ECONOMIC DEVELOPMENT PARTNERSHIP BOARD MEETING, Louisville, June 15, 1994

RIO TO THE CAPITALS RECEPTION, Frankfort, June 16, 1994

BOSOMWORTH DINNER, Lexington, June 18, 1994

VETO MESSAGE HOUSE BILL 2, Frankfort, June 22, 1994

CORVETTE PLANT, Bowling Green, June 28, 1994

CONFERENCE FOR ITINERANT EVANGELISTS, Louisville, June 28, 1994

OAK AND ACORN GROUND BREAKING, Louisville, June 29, 1994*

VETERANS WAR MEMORIAL DEDICATION, Manchester, July 5, 1994

MIDDLESBORO CDBG ANNOUNCEMENT, Middlesboro, July 5, 1994

SEAT BELT CAMPAIGN, Frankfort, July 6, 1994

FORD FOUNDATION, Louisville, July 8, 1994

RICHMOND CDBG ANNOUNCEMENT, Richmond, July 8, 1994*

DANVILLE CDBG ANNOUNCEMENT, Danville, July 8, 1994

LA GRANGE CDBG ANNOUNCEMENT, La Grange, July 8, 1994

SHELBYVILLE CDBG ANNOUNCEMENT, Shelbyville, July 8, 1994

VANCEBURG CDBG ANNOUNCEMENT, Vanceburg, July 11, 1994

WEST LIBERTY CDBG ANNOUNCEMENT, West Liberty, July 11, 1994

MOREHEAD CDBG ANNOUNCEMENT, Morehead, July 11, 1994

CARTER COUNTY CDBG ANNOUNCEMENT, Carter County, July 11, 1994

CATLETTSBURG CDBG ANNOUNCEMENT, Catlettsburg, July 11, 1994

PIKEVILLE CDBG ANNOUNCEMENT, Pikeville, July 12, 1994

SALYERSVILLE CDBG ANNOUNCEMENT, Salyersville, July 12, 1994

JACKSON CDBG ANNOUNCEMENT, Jackson, July 12, 1994

ALBANY CDBG ANNOUNCEMENT, Albany, July 12, 1994

NELSONVILLE CDBG ANNOUNCEMENT, Nelsonville, July 12, 1994

PRESTONSBURG CDBG ANNOUNCEMENT, Prestonsburg, July 12, 1994

EASTER SEALS RECEPTION, Frankfort, July 13, 1994

WILLIAMSTOWN CDBG ANNOUNCEMENT, Williamstown, July 14, 1994

GLENCOE CDBG ANNOUNCEMENT, Glencoe, July 14, 1994

INDEPENDENCE CDBG ANNOUNCEMENT, Independence, July 14, 1994

LATONIA UNDERPASS RIBBON CUTTING, Covington, July 14, 1994

HEALTH CARE NEWS CONFERENCE, Frankfort, July 15, 1994*

LEADERSHIP KENTUCKY, Frankfort, July 15, 1994

KENTUCKY CRUSHED STONE ASSOCIATION, Frankfort, July 21, 1994

AUTOMOTIVE INDUSTRIES INC., Madisonville, July 21, 1994

KENTUCKY WOMEN'S LEADERSHIP NETWORK, Frankfort, July 22, 1994

COLUMBUS-BELMONT DEDICATION, Columbus, July 25, 1994*

MAYFIELD CDBG ANNOUNCEMENT, Mayfield, July 25, 1994

WICKLIFFE CDBG ANNOUNCEMENT, Wickliffe, July 25, 1994

HARDIN CDBG ANNOUNCEMENT, Hardin, July 25, 1994

PADUCAH CDBG ANNOUNCEMENT, Paducah, July 25, 1994

ADA AWARENESS DAY, Frankfort, July 26, 1994

SOUTHERN CHRISTIAN YOUTH CONVENTION, Frankfort, July 26, 1994

KERR GROUP INC. GROUND BREAKING, Bowling Green, July 28, 1994

PROVIDENCE CDBG ANNOUNCEMENT, Providence, July 28, 1994

FORDSVILLE CDBG ANNOUNCEMENT, Fordsville, July 28, 1994

GOVERNOR'S SCHOLARS CLOSING BANQUET, Danville, July 28, 1994

AMERICORPS GRANTS STUDENT SERVICE CONSORTIUM, Richmond, August 15, 1994

AMERICORPS GRANTS MOREHEAD STATE UNIVERSITY CORPS, Morehead, August 15, 1994

AMERICORPS GRANTS "AGENCIES AND COMMUNITIES MERGING EFFECTIVELY," Louisville, August 15, 1994

AMERICORPS GRANTS "SERVICE LEARNING IMPACTING CHILDREN'S EDUCATION," Franklin, August 15, 1994

GENERAL ASSOCIATION OF KENTUCKY BAPTISTS, Lexington, August 16, 1994

AMERICORPS GRANTS FRANKFORT AND NORTHERN KENTUCKY, Frankfort, August 16, 1994

EAST KENTUCKY CORPORATION BANQUET, Lexington, August 17, 1994

KENTUCKY STATE FAIR OPENING DAY CEREMONIES, Louisville, August 18, 1994*

CARLISLE CDBG ANNOUNCEMENT, Carlisle, August 19, 1994

BRACKEN COUNTY CDBG ANNOUNCEMENT, Bracken County, August 19, 1994

PARIS CDBG ANNOUNCEMENT, Paris, August 19, 1994

PRIZE PRESENTATION, Louisville, August 20, 1994

STARS SCHOOL GRANT PRESS CONFERENCE, Frankfort, August 24, 1994*

FARM BUREAU KENTUCKY HAM BREAKFAST, Louisville, August 25, 1994*

FIRST YEAR MEDICAL STUDENTS RECEPTION, Frankfort, August 30, 1994

CSX ANNOUNCEMENT, Raceland, September 2, 1994

FINANCIAL INSTITUTIONS RECEPTION, Frankfort, September 6, 1994

BRACC NEWS CONFERENCE, Louisville, September 7, 1994

COMMONWEALTH NEWS CONFERENCE, Frankfort, September 8, 1994*

WHITE HOUSE CONFERENCE ON SMALL BUSINESS, Louisville, September 8, 1994

TOBA AWARDS DINNER, Lexington, September 9, 1994

SCHOOL-TO-WORK CONFERENCE, Louisville, September 20, 1994*

COUNCIL OF STATE GOVERNMENTS BUILDING DEDICATION, Lexington, September 23, 1994

GOVERNOR'S CONFERENCE ON THE ENVIRONMENT, Louisville, September 30, 1994*

INDUSTRY APPRECIATION LUNCHEON, Madisonville, November 1, 1994

INTERNATIONAL TRADE CONFERENCE, Northern Kentucky, November 2, 1994*

GUN SAFETY PRESS CONFERENCE, Frankfort, November 3, 1994

KENTUCKY INTERNATIONAL THOROUGHBRED INSTITUTE, Lexington, November 9, 1994*

DISABILITIES AWARD LUNCHEON, Frankfort, November 9, 1994

HEILIG-MEYERS OPENING IN WEST VIRGINIA, Pt. Pleasant, W.Va., November 15, 1994

LITANY OF PRAISE AND THANKSGIVING, Louisville, November 22, 1994

HEMP TASK FORCE ANNOUNCEMENT, Frankfort, November 23, 1994*

WORKFORCE PARTNERSHIP COUNCIL, Frankfort, November 28, 1994*

QUALITY AND EFFICIENCY COMMISSION LUNCHEON, Frankfort, November 29, 1994*

DELTA RIBBON CUTTING, Covington, December 1, 1994*

BIBLE READING, Frankfort, December 1, 1994

CHRISTMAS TREE LIGHTING, Frankfort, December 5, 1994

"COME SEE FOR YOURSELF" SCHOOL VISIT, Sandy Hook, December 6, 1994*

BICENTENNIAL MONUMENT DEDICATION, Frankfort, December 7, 1994

BLUEGRASS STATE GAMES TAPING, Frankfort, December 9, 1994

EMPLOYEE SUGGESTION SYSTEM AWARDS CEREMONY, Frankfort, December 12, 1994*

OPENING OF THE GREEN RIVER CORRECTIONAL COMPLEX, Central City, December 16, 1994*

MURRAY DEDICATION/APPRECIATION DAY, Murray, December 16, 1994

IMAGE ENTRY/COMPUNET AMERICA RIBBON CUTTING, Mt. Vernon, December 19, 1994

UNIVERSITY OF LOUISVILLE STADIUM ANNOUNCEMENT, Louisville, December 20, 1994

SMALL RURAL HOSPITALS, Frankfort, December 21, 1994

INFORMATION SUPERHIGHWAY ANNOUNCEMENT, Frankfort, December 22, 1994*

PREVAILING WAGE NEWS CONFERENCE, Frankfort, January 4, 1995

INTRODUCTION OF BOB RUSSELL, PRAYER BREAKFAST, Frankfort, January 11, 1995

PRAYER BREAKFAST, Frankfort, January 11, 1995

MARTIN LUTHER KING JR. CEREMONY, Frankfort, January 12, 1995

STATE OF THE COMMONWEALTH ADDRESS, Frankfort, January 17, 1995*

RURAL EMPOWERMENT ZONE ENTERPRISE COMMUNITIES RECOGNITION CEREMONY, Frankfort, January 17, 1995*

APPALACHIAN TASK FORCE MEETING, Frankfort, January 17, 1995*

MIDWAY CHAMBER OF COMMERCE, Midway, January 26, 1995

PORK PRODUCERS ASSOCIATION, Owensboro, January 27, 1995*

SPECIAL SESSION BILL SIGNING, Frankfort, January 27, 1995*

REPORT OF ARC STATES' CO-CHAIRMAN, January 28, 1995*

ROTARY SPEECH, Louisville, February 2, 1995

BOY SCOUTS LUNCHEON, Lexington, February 3, 1995

NEW HAVEN ISTEA ENHANCEMENT ANNOUNCEMENT, New Haven, February 6, 1995

WEST POINT ISTEA ENHANCEMENT ANNOUNCEMENT, West Point, February 6, 1995

ELIZABETHTOWN ISTEA ENHANCEMENT ANNOUNCEMENT, Elizabethtown, February 6, 1995

SIMPSON COUNTY ISTEA ENHANCEMENT ANNOUNCEMENT, Simpson County, February 6, 1995

GREEN COUNTY ISTEA ENHANCEMENT ANNOUNCEMENT, Green County, February 6, 1995

HORSE CAVE ISTEA ENHANCEMENT ANNOUNCEMENT, Horse Cave, February 6, 1995

CAVE CITY ISTEA ENHANCEMENT ANNOUNCEMENT, Cave City, February 6, 1995

GLASGOW ISTEA ENHANCEMENT ANNOUNCEMENT, Glasgow, February 6, 1995

BOWLING GREEN ISTEA ENHANCEMENT ANNOUNCEMENT, Bowling Green, February 6, 1995

STATE EMPLOYEE WAGES NEWS CONFERENCE, Frankfort, February 7, 1995

State Reception Room Dedication, Frankfort, February 7, 1995*

Boone County ISTEA Enhancement Announcement, Boone County, February 8, 1995

Newport ISTEA Enhancement Announcement, Newport, February 8, 1995

Covington ISTEA Enhancement Announcement, Covington, February 8, 1995

Falmouth ISTEA Enhancement Announcement, Falmouth, February 8, 1995

Paris ISTEA Enhancement Announcement, Paris, February 9, 1995

Estill County ISTEA Enhancement Announcement, Estill County, February 9, 1995

Estill County ARC Grant Announcement, Estill County, February 9, 1995

Fayette County ISTEA Enhancement Announcement, Fayette County, February 9, 1995

Madison County ISTEA Enhancement Announcement, Madison County, February 9, 1995

Madison County ARC Grant Announcement, Madison County, February 9, 1995

Powell County ISTEA Enhancement Announcement, Powell County, February 9, 1995

Powell County ARC Grant Announcements, Powell County, February 9, 1995

Montgomery County ARC Grant Announcement, Montgomery County, February 9, 1995

Bullitt County ISTEA Enhancement Announcements, Bullitt County, February 10, 1995

Jefferson County ISTEA Enhancement Announcement, Jefferson County, February 10, 1995

Shelbyville ISTEA Enhancement Announcement, Shelbyville, February 10, 1995

Advisory Council for Adult Education and Literacy, Frankfort, February 10, 1995

Military Affairs Commission, Frankfort, February 14, 1995

DEPARTMENT OF INSURANCE NAIC ACCREDITATION, Frankfort, February 14, 1995

MARCH OF DIMES PUBLIC SERVICE ANNOUNCEMENT, Frankfort, February 15, 1995

HOUSE COMMITTEE ON APPROPRIATIONS TESTIMONY, Washington, D.C., February 28, 1995*

TAPED MESSAGE FOR CRUSADE FOR CHILDREN, March 1, 1995

"COME AND SEE FOR YOURSELF" SCHOOL VISIT, Southgate, March 2, 1995*

NATIONAL CONFERENCE OF CHRISTIANS AND JEWS, Lexington, March 2, 1995

TOYOTA SWEEPSTAKES ANNOUNCEMENT, Georgetown, March 3, 1995*

PROCLAMATION WLEX-TV 40TH ANNIVERSARY, March 6, 1995

SCOTT COUNTY HIGH SCHOOL GROUND BREAKING, Georgetown, March 6, 1995*

HUDSON FOODS GROUND BREAKING, Sebree, March 8, 1995*

KENTUCKY DAR, Lexington, March 8, 1995

GOVERNOR'S CUP AWARDS, Louisville, March 13, 1995

WEST LIBERTY ARC GRANT ANNOUNCEMENT, West Liberty, March 14, 1995

INSTEEL INC. ANNOUNCEMENT, Campton, March 14, 1995

LEWIS COUNTY ARC GRANT, Lewis County, March 14, 1995

MORGAN COUNTY ANNOUNCEMENTS, Morgan County, March 14, 1995*

ROWAN COUNTY ARC GRANT ANNOUNCEMENTS, Rowan County, March 14, 1995

FLOYD COUNTY ARC GRANT ANNOUNCEMENT, Floyd County, March 15, 1995

LAWRENCE COUNTY ARC GRANT ANNOUNCEMENT, Lawrence County, March 15, 1995

MAGOFFIN COUNTY ARC GRANT ANNOUNCEMENT, Magoffin County, March 15, 1995

PIKE COUNTY ARC GRANT ANNOUNCEMENTS, Pike County, March 15, 1995

LEWIS COUNTY ARC GRANT ANNOUNCEMENT, Lewis County, March 15, 1995

BOYD COUNTY ARC GRANT ANNOUNCEMENT, Boyd County, March 15, 1995

HARLAN COUNTY ARC GRANT ANNOUNCEMENTS, Harlan County, March 16, 1995

HARLAN COUNTY/HARLAN ARC GRANT ANNOUNCEMENT, Harlan County/Harlan, March 16, 1995

HARLAN COUNTY/HARLAN ISTEA ENHANCEMENT ANNOUNCEMENT, Harlan County/Harlan, March 16, 1995

KNOTT COUNTY ARC GRANT ANNOUNCEMENT, Knott County, March 16, 1995

KNOTT COUNTY/HINDMAN ARC GRANT ANNOUNCEMENT, Knott County/Hindman, March 16, 1995

LETCHER COUNTY ARC GRANT ANNOUNCEMENTS, Letcher County, March 16, 1995

WHITESBURG/LETCHER COUNTY ISTEA ENHANCEMENT ANNOUNCEMENT, Whitesburg/Letcher County, March 16, 1995

PERRY COUNTY ARC GRANT ANNOUNCEMENT, Perry County, March 16, 1995

PERRY COUNTY/HAZARD ARC GRANT ANNOUNCEMENT, Perry County/Hazard, March 16, 1995

BREATHITT COUNTY ARC GRANT ANNOUNCEMENT, Breathitt County, March 16, 1995

BREATHITT COUNTY/JACKSON ARC GRANT ANNOUNCEMENT, Breathitt County/Jackson, March 16, 1995

ROCKCASTLE COUNTY/MT. VERNON ARC GRANT ANNOUNCEMENT, Rockcastle County/Mt. Vernon, March 17, 1995

NANCY/PULASKI AND WAYNE COUNTY ISTEA ENHANCEMENT ANNOUNCEMENT, Nancy/Pulaski and Wayne County, March 17, 1995

BELL COUNTY/MIDDLESBORO ISTEA ENHANCEMENT ANNOUNCEMENT, Bell County/Middlesboro, March 17, 1995

LINCOLN COUNTY/STANFORD ARC GRANT ANNOUNCEMENT, Lincoln County/Stanford, March 17, 1995

NATIONAL ASSOCIATION OF WOMEN BUSINESS OWNERS LUNCHEON, Lexington, March 21, 1995*

AMERICORPS EVENT, Lexington, March 21, 1995*

LEE COUNTY ARC GRANT ANNOUNCEMENT, Lee County, March 22, 1995

LAUREL COUNTY ARC GRANT ANNOUNCEMENTS, Laurel County, March 22, 1995

JACKSON COUNTY ARC GRANT ANNOUNCEMENT, Jackson County, March 22, 1995

MADISON COUNTY ARC GRANT ANNOUNCEMENT, Madison County, March 22, 1995

NATURE LICENSE PLATE NEWS CONFERENCE, Frankfort, March 31, 1995

MONROE COUNTY SCHOOL VISIT, Tompkinsville, April 10, 1995*

AMERICAN PUBLIC WORKS ADMINISTRATION AWARD PRESENTATION, Frankfort, April 11, 1995

WATTERSON EXPRESSWAY DEDICATION, Louisville, April 11, 1995

COMMISSION ON FAMILIES AND CHILDREN, Versailles, April 12, 1995

OMICRON DELTA KAPPA, Lexington, April 13, 1995

KENTUCKY ORGAN DONORS AFFILIATES PROCLAMATION SIGNING, Frankfort, April 14, 1995

HITACHI 10-YEAR ANNIVERSARY, Harrodsburg, April 17, 1995

KENTUCKY DERBY FESTIVAL LUNCHEON, Frankfort, April 18, 1995

HISTORIC FARMS BOOK PRESENTATION, Frankfort, April 18, 1995

MARY BINGHAM ROAST, Louisville, April 18, 1995

MEDICAID PRESS CONFERENCE, Frankfort, April 19, 1995

ENVIRONMENTAL QUALITY COMMISSION AWARDS, Frankfort, April 20, 1995*

GOVERNOR'S SAFETY AND HEALTH CONFERENCE, Louisville, April 20, 1995

STATE ADVISORY PANEL FOR EXCEPTIONAL CHILDREN, Louisville, April 20, 1995

"THEY'RE OFF" LUNCHEON, Louisville, April 21, 1995

FAMILY LITERACY CONFERENCE, Louisville, April 24, 1995*

POET LAUREATE NEWS CONFERENCE, Frankfort, April 25, 1995

PEOPLE FOR PEOPLE RALLY, Frankfort, April 26, 1995*

ARC SATELLITE TOWN MEETING, Lexington, April 27, 1995*

ECONOMIC DEVELOPMENT PRESS CONFERENCE IN JAPAN, Nagoya, Japan, May 1995*

TALKING POINTS FOR ECONOMIC DEVELOPMENT PRESS CONFERENCE IN SEOUL, Seoul, Korea, May 1995*

ASIAN TRIP REMARKS, Tokyo, Japan, May 1995*

RURAL EMPOWERMENT ZONE MEMORANDUM OF AGREEMENT SIGNING, Frankfort, May 3, 1995

ASHLAND OIL TEACHER ACHIEVEMENT CEREMONY, Frankfort, May 8, 1995*

V-E Day Ceremony, Frankfort, May 8, 1995

Workers' Compensation News Conference, Frankfort, May 9, 1995*

Bluegrass State Games Press Conference, Frankfort, May 9, 1995

Kentucky State Police Awards Ceremony, Frankfort, May 15, 1995*

Kentucky Tech Scholarship Awards Program, Frankfort, May 16, 1995*

Mercer County Health Department Announcement, Harrodsburg, May 16, 1995

American Travel Writers Dinner, Frankfort, May 17, 1995

Fish and Wildlife Officers Swearing-In Ceremony, Frankfort, May 17, 1995*

Tree Planting Ceremony honoring Oklahoma City Victims, Frankfort, May 19, 1995*

Kentucky Reception/KFC Presentation Tokyo, Tokyo, Japan, May 26, 1995

Education Technology Videotaping, Frankfort, June 1, 1995

Boys State, Morehead, June 7, 1995

White House Conference on Tourism, Frankfort, June 8, 1995*

Milton Academy Graduation, Boston, Mass., June 9, 1995*

Black Public Administrators Luncheon, Frankfort, June 12, 1995

Mazak Corporation Announcement, Florence, June 12, 1995

Fidelity Investments Grand Opening, Covington, June 13, 1995*

Girls State, Cumberland College, June 14, 1995

Dale Hollow Ground Breaking, Dale Hollow Lake, June 14, 1995*

1995 Emergency Management Workshop, Frankfort, June 22, 1995

Disabled American Veterans, Frankfort, June 23, 1995

Cultural Economics Initiative Grant Announcement, Frankfort, June 26, 1995

Dual Sensory Impairment Proclamation, Frankfort, June 27, 1995

Quartet Convention Announcement, Kentucky Fair and Expo Center, Louisville, June 28, 1995

Welfare to Self-Sufficiency Press Conference, Frankfort, June 30, 1995*

Check Presentation, Woodford Memorial Hospital, Versailles, June 30, 1995

MIDWAY 4TH CELEBRATION, Midway, July 4, 1995

REDEDICATION CEREMONY, BARKLEY CONVENTION CENTER AND AIRPORT, Lake Barkley State Park, July 6, 1995

BUDGET SURPLUS NEWS CONFERENCE, Frankfort, July 10, 1995*

EQUITANA USA PRESS CONFERENCE, Louisville, July 12, 1995

A.B. CHANDLER FOUNDATION DINNER, Lexington, July 14, 1995

KENTUCKY HEALTH PURCHASING ALLIANCE PRESS CONFERENCE, Lexington, July 17, 1995*

UNIVERSITY OF LOUISVILLE CHECK PRESENTATION, University of Louisville, July 20, 1995

NAACP DINNER, Frankfort, July 22, 1995

UNIVERSITY OF KENTUCKY CHECK PRESENTATION, Lexington, July 24, 1995

FARM AID PRESS CONFERENCE, Louisville, July 28, 1995*

BLUEGRASS STATE GAMES PACESETTERS, Frankfort, July 28, 1995

KENTUCKY STATE POLICE PROMOTION CEREMONY, Frankfort, August 1, 1995

AMERICORPS GRANT ANNOUNCEMENT, Lexington, August 9, 1995

MINORITY MANAGEMENT TRAINING NEWS CONFERENCE, Frankfort, August 16, 1995

STATE FAIR OPENING CEREMONIES, Louisville, August 17, 1995

4-H BREAKFAST, Louisville, August 18, 1995*

COMMON GROUND EXHIBIT KENTUCKY STATE FAIR, Louisville, August 18, 1995

GIRLS INC. SPEECH, Bowling Green, August 21, 1995

AMERICORPS GRANT ANNOUNCEMENT, Hopkinsville, August 21, 1995

BUTLER COUNTY CHECK PRESENTATION, Morgantown, August 22, 1995

RADIO ANNOUNCEMENT, Frankfort, August 23, 1995

KENTUCKY FARM BUREAU HAM BREAKFAST, Louisville, August 24, 1995*

PLEASANT RETREAT GROUND BREAKING, Lancaster, August 24, 1995*

CAMP NELSON/US 27 GROUND BREAKING, Camp Nelson, August 24, 1995

REHABILITATION CONFERENCE, Lexington, August 24, 1995

WOMEN'S RIGHT TO VOTE, KENTUCKY FAIR, Louisville, August 26, 1995

CLARK/COOPER BUILDING NAMING, Frankfort, August 30, 1995

AMERICORPS/APPALACHIAN SELF-SUFFICIENCY PROGRAM, Prestonsburg, August 31, 1995*

REMARKS ON STEARNS DEPOT, Stearns, September 1, 1995*

PINE KNOT SCHOOL VISIT, Pine Knot, September 1, 1995

TOYOTA MOTOR CORPORATION TAPING, Frankfort, September 7, 1995

VICTIM INFORMATION AND NOTIFICATION EVERYDAY (VINE) NEWS CONFERENCE, Frankfort, September 13, 1995*

JOE PRATHER HIGHWAY DEDICATION, Radcliff, September 18, 1995

INVESTORS' SEMINAR, Frankfort, September 20, 1995

BENEFITS NEWS CONFERENCE, Frankfort, September 22, 1995*

BELLEVUE VETERANS DINNER, Bellevue, September 23, 1995

LEXMARK ANNOUNCEMENT, Lexington, September 25, 1995*

HISTORY CENTER GROUND BREAKING, Frankfort, September 25, 1995*

SHUMAKER INAUGURATION, Louisville, September 28, 1995

BREAST CANCER AWARENESS PROCLAMATION SIGNING, Frankfort, September 29, 1995

AMERICORPS LAUNCH, Frankfort, September 29, 1995

MT. WASHINGTON BYPASS, Mt. Washington, October 2, 1995

TOYO SEAT ANNOUNCEMENT FLEMINGSBURG, Flemingsburg, October 2, 1995

ALZHEIMER'S REPORT PRESENTATION, Frankfort, October 3, 1995

GOVERNOR'S HOUSING CONFERENCE, Louisville, October 6, 1995*

CAMPBELLSVILLE BYPASS, Campbellsville, October 9, 1995

LARUE COUNTY "COME SEE FOR YOURSELF," Hodgenville, October 10, 1995

SAFE SCHOOLS MONTH PROCLAMATION SIGNING, Frankfort, October 11, 1995*

TRAVEL AND TOURISM AWARDS, Louisville, October 12, 1995

KENTUCKY INFORMATION HIGHWAY, Frankfort, October 15, 1995

CLAY CITY CDBG ANNOUNCEMENT, Clay City, October 18, 1995

CABINET OF HUMAN RESOURCES NEWS CONFERENCE, Frankfort, October 19, 1995*

KENTUCKY HOSPITAL ASSOCIATION, Frankfort, October 26, 1995*

ANDERSON COUNTY TECHNOLOGY CENTER DEDICATION, Lawrenceburg, October 26, 1995*

RESPONSE TO BIODIVERSITY TASK FORCE REPORT, Lexington, October 27, 1995

GOVERNOR'S CONFERENCE ON THE ENVIRONMENT, Lexington, October 27, 1995*

GOVERNOR'S CONFERENCE ON THE ENVIRONMENT—SHEPHERD AWARD, Lexington, October 27, 1995

MCCRACKEN COUNTY CDBG ANNOUNCEMENT, Paducah, October 30, 1995

PADUCAH CDBG ANNOUNCEMENT, Paducah, October 30, 1995

ARC MEETING, Frankfort, November 2, 1995*

GIVE A GIFT FROM KENTUCKY, Frankfort, November 2, 1995

KENTUCKY WORLD TRADE CONFERENCE DINNER, Louisville, November 3, 1995*

AMERICAN RACING EQUIPMENT, Warsaw, November 3, 1995

UNITED NATIONS ASSOCIATION 50TH ANNIVERSARY, Frankfort, November 4, 1995

WAL-MART DEDICATION, London, November 7, 1995

COOPER TIRE AND RUBBER, Mt. Sterling, November 8, 1995*

KENTUCKY JUVENILE TREATMENT FACILITIES, Frankfort, November 13, 1995*

REVENUE SETTLEMENT NEWS CONFERENCE, Frankfort, November 13, 1995*

COMMONWEALTH CONVENTION CENTER ANNOUNCEMENT, Louisville, November 15, 1995

BARREN COUNTY HEALTH DEPARTMENT ANNOUNCEMENT, Glasgow, November 21, 1995

HAPPY CHANDLER SCULPTURE DEDICATION, Frankfort, November 22, 1995

JENKINS HIGHWAY ANNOUNCEMENT, Jenkins, November 27, 1995

US 25E—PINEVILLE, Pineville, November 27, 1995

SOUTHEAST TECH DEDICATION, Middlesboro, November 27, 1995

US 27 WIDENING—SOMERSET, Somerset, November 28, 1995

DISTINGUISHED SERVICE MEDALLIONS, Frankfort, November 29, 1995

GOVERNOR'S SERVICE MEDALLION AWARDS DINNER, Frankfort, November 29, 1995

NORTHERN KENTUCKY CONVENTION CENTER, Covington, November 30, 1995

CENTRAL BRIDGE DEDICATION, Newport, November 30, 1995

INDEX